CAREER OPPORTUNITIES IN WRITING

Allan Taylor
James Robert Parish

Foreword by
Brad Schreiber

Checkmark Books®
An imprint of Infobase Publishing

To the memory of

Lois Dwight Cole (1902–1979)
book editor extraordinaire and prolific author

and

Turney Allan Taylor (1897–1968)
journalist, editor, and author

Career Opportunities in Writing

Copyright © 2006 by Allan Taylor and James Robert Parish

Checkmark Books
An imprint of Infobase Publishing
132 West 31st Street
New York NY 10001

Library of Congress Cataloging-in-Publication Data
Taylor, Allan.
    Career opportunities in writing / Allan Taylor, James Robert Parish; foreword by Brad Schreiber.
        p. cm.
    Includes bibliographical references and index.
    ISBN 0-8160-5988-8 (hc : alk. paper)—ISBN 0-8160-5989-6 (pb : alk. paper)
    1. Authorship—Vocational guidance. I. Parish, James Robert. II. Title.
    PN151.T38 2006
    808′.02′023—dc22   2005007206

Checkmark Books are available at special discounts when purchased in bulk quantities for businesses, associations, institutions, or sales promotions. Please call our Special Sales Department in New York at (212) 967-8800 or (800) 322-8755.

You can find Facts On File on the World Wide Web at http://www.factsonfile.com

Cover design by Nora Wertz

Printed in the United States of America

VB Hermitage 10   9   8   7   6   5   4   3   2   1

This book is printed on acid-free paper.

CONTENTS

MEDIA

Internet

Magazines

Newspapers, News Services, and News Syndicates

Radio

Television

SCHOLASTIC, ACADEMIC, AND NONPROFIT INSTITUTIONS

APPENDIXES

FOREWORD

I believe you become a writer in stages. There is the first time you write something that impresses someone other than yourself, and you think, "That proves it. I really am good!" (If it is from either of your parents, you must ignore it, whether it is positive or negative.) There is also, significantly, the first time you sell your work and receive a check for it. And there is the first time you support yourself as a writer.

The first time someone acknowledged my work, it was my fifth-grade teacher, who read aloud a poem I wrote. No one knew who I was because I had just transferred to the school, and when Mister Ault stated the author's name at the very end, the boy across from me leaned over and asked me, in a whisper, "Who's Brad Schreiber?"

Writers generally work alone, but one cannot overemphasize the importance of leaving behind your rich, interior life and connecting with others, in order to develop your career.

For example, I met Mike Tunison—who gave me my own entertainment and politics column, *Development Hell,* when he was editor of the Los Angeles weekly newspaper *Entertainment Today*—at a movie screening. I met Chris Vogler—the author of *The Writer's Journey,* who made me vice president of his literary consulting company—when we were both attending the second wedding of his ex-wife. These people, and numerous others, have helped shape who I am as a writer and a human being.

Writers become working writers not because they literally cannot do anything else or are better writers than anyone else. They simply cannot stand the idea of doing anything else. Writers of all kinds share the conditions of our pursuit: we strive for acceptance, look for sympathy in rejection, hope to find intelligent, measured criticism, and face the sometimes exhausting task of revision.

It is no surprise that many talented people sell their writing but do not subsist on it. Those who choose writing—or have it choose them—have to be either exceedingly fortunate to succeed in their preferred genre or crafty enough to consider making a living writing something else while pursuing their specialized craft.

I am one of those people who have had to reconfigure the specifics of my career path in order to survive. I have done almost every form of writing there is, sometimes because I wanted to explore that field, sometimes because an opportunity presented itself to me, and sometimes because I needed to be doing some kind of writing or suffer the feeling I was wasting my life and my abilities.

I have been published or produced in the fields of books, articles, essays, television, radio, stage, advertising (for print, radio, television, and film), marketing, children's poetry, speeches, lectures, narration for a fashion show, dialogue for costumed characters at parties, and voice-overs for telephone lines. I once had to generate three minutes of insults each week for a national phone line called "Dial-an-Insult," read aloud by some comedian known as the "Insulting Sultan."

This seemingly psychotic eclecticism is not originally what I had in mind for my writing career. But the writer who is adaptable and willing to learn a new technique has a distinct advantage over the writer who, say, only wants to write in the style of medieval Romanian poetry for a living. Adaptability led me to that very lucrative job of writing and producing voice-overs for a television station. It provided travel writing assignments and free trips all over North America.

The good news is there are more opportunities for writers than ever before. In the United States this past year, 175,000 books, a new record, were published. There are new technologies aiding those who do not go the way of traditional publishing, such as Publishing on Demand (POD) or via e-books downloaded from the Internet. The cost of self-publishing has dropped dizzyingly. The field of technical writing has become a major destination for those who earn a living writing. People are paid to "blog," to create Internet Web logs on a variety of topics.

The writers of manuals, advertising, mar-comm (marketing-communications), scholarly texts, greeting cards, or any other literary endeavor that cannot be deemed "sexy" or "brooding" can console themselves with the knowledge that they write for a living and, regardless of their particular discipline, it is creative and challenging work.

Even writing that is very systematic and formulaic involves our talent, prompts us to engage our minds, our vocabularies. Regardless of the nature of the literary task, we must do it well and competently. We must find pride in that work and remind ourselves that, after all, we are not washing dishes at one in the morning in a bustling restaurant.

I was that dishwasher when I was 16. When I look at the modest but respectable living I make now as a writer (as well as consultant, teacher, and lecturer), I feel utterly blessed. I didn't feel blessed when I was the tax librarian or house painter or assistant to a stockbroker. I didn't feel I was honoring anything close to my true calling when I was a Fuller Brush salesman.

Every job teaches you skills. Some skills will serve you throughout your life. Some will only be helpful if you plan to spend the rest of your days repairing belt sanders. But the role of writer is one that teaches you communication skills useful in every aspect of your life.

The profession of writing is not an easy one, even if you find the act effortless. It requires a great and abiding love, one that will see you through the lean and frustrating times that may befall you. It requires a belief in yourself, a cyclical rejuvenation of your spirit, a willingness to say to yourself, often, "That's their opinion. Their rejection doesn't define me. I *define me.*"

You must love this special act of creation. It is special, even to those people who do not know how to do it. Whether you are a copy editor or dreaming up plotlines for that wacky, animated television series *Arnie, the Arthritic Antelope,* you have a talent that is fairly unique in this world.

It is an ability that can be encouraged, perhaps, by careful teaching or consultation, but cannot be purely taught. By repetition, almost anyone can learn how to restock the candy bars in the vending machine. Can the same be said for writing prose that snaps or rhymes that climb, for writing words that move one to laughter or tears, or convey a phenomenal amount of information clearly in few words?

In addition, please remember this, as you explore your future with words: the writing job you obtain and then leave, possibly in disgust, may still be an important learning experience for you. Yes, you learn what you do not want to do. But there is something more.

One of the worst writing jobs I ever had was at a "trailer boutique," an ad agency for motion picture trailers, television, and radio spots. The work hours were abominably long, my boss had no personality, and I had to perform video editing, and even deliver tapes in the unrelenting Los Angeles sun in a car with no air conditioning.

But that boss also taught me the fundamentals of writing voice-over narration, how every syllable matters, how the flow of words should have a certain rhythm. He urged me to choose words that were colorful, suggestive, and onomatopoetic.

And I did get one phrase into a movie trailer: "The motion picture comedy that defies the forces of gravity, sanity and good taste."

Don't be afraid to try new literary genres or to attempt more than one. Writing is one of the few occupations in life in which having multiple personalities is not a liability but an asset.

— Brad Schreiber, Los Angeles

BRAD SCHREIBER's latest book is *What Are You Laughing At? How to Write Funny Screenplays, Stories and More.* He is vice president of Storytech Literary Consulting, administers the international Mona Schreiber Prize for Humorous Fiction and Nonfiction, and is online at http://www.brashcyber.com.

INDUSTRY OUTLOOK

Rumor has it that you want to be a writer. Or perhaps you are a writer already but just want to try some other kind of writing.

You may have a desire to participate in the business of a busy newsroom, keeping your ear tuned to a police scanner for potential news. Or you may want to speak indirectly to voters, via speeches and addresses you pen for a political figure, telling the constituents why a certain bill should be passed, or reasons to wage a war, or to vote for your boss.

You may wish to tout the virtues and usefulness of consumer goods, or prepare studies of consumer behavior and buying options in today's atmosphere of high-tech communication. Or you want to write a screenplay (which someone else will probably rewrite and yet other persons will alter again), looking forward to that moment when an actor mouths words on the big screen that owe their origins to your creativity.

Or possibly your writing will appear in print or, by using a pay-on-demand system, will appear on the screen of someone else's computer in your neighborhood or even in a distant part of the world.

Whatever writing you want to undertake, can afford the time and energy to accomplish, or have the talent to achieve, a wide variety of jobs for such writing are always present. You can probably make a decent living as a writer, but, unless you write that best-selling novel or nonfiction work, or that Oscar-winning screenplay, do not expect wealth to come your way easily or soon. More important, the more comfortable you are with computers, economics, health care, or technical subjects, the better you will do because of the continuing expansion of scientific and technical information and the need to communicate it in easily comprehended text to others. During the next 10 years or more, job prospects for writers and communicators should continue to grow in all those fields and industries that service the public economy. Writing opportunities on environmental-related issues, health, international trade, leisure, and travel should all expand at a continuous rate.

The Information Technology Revolution

Since the initial edition of this book was published in 1983, the writing fields covered here have been revolutionized by computer technology and the widespread use of personal computers and wireless phones, as well as by the enhanced ability to transmit information almost immediately by e-mail and fax, and by the virtual explosion of the electronic and information possibilities of the ever more sophisticated Internet. It is now possible to research nearly any subject you are writing about at home, even if you prefer to work at odd hours of the day or night or on the weekend, and then transmit the completed piece to your publisher with a click of a mouse or even a voice command. Also, with the use of a laptop computer and other portable equipment, writers and editors can work from home or on the road.

Long-established, conventional forms of the printed word—books, magazines, and newspapers—are working hard to keep apace of this new technology, assessing how it hurts their usual methods of dispersion of information, and how they can utilize it for their own benefit. These efforts have spawned specialized magazines and computerized databases aimed at specific audiences, such as financial investors, health care professionals, or other small but sophisticated audiences. In addition, small publishing houses, through the use of economical desktop publishing, now can produce titles for a targeted, small segment of the reading public.

Today, the price of printing information on paper no longer is a limit to companies seeking to communicate with their public (and potential buyers of their products or services). Nowadays, workers no longer must be bound to a central geographic location if they are equipped with a computer, a cellular phone, a modem, and a fax.

In the past two decades, the quantity of computer databases has multiplied exponentially. During that same time, the number of consumer magazines has greatly increased and thousands of small publishing companies (including one-person operations known as self-publishing) have sprung up all over the United States and around the globe.

In the last 20 years public relations has become even more prevalent throughout society. Although the public relations industry traditionally suffers in poor economic times, the need for professional public relations services to polish and promote images (of individuals, companies, services, and objects) has been recognized by most companies and institutions and is expected to continue to grow.

There also has been a significant upswing in the demand for people with skills to perform computer-aided research. These include information managers, librarians, and researchers. Many newspapers (and magazines) have become information brokers on the side, selling (or just making available) their archives of news articles, columns, features, and photos to electronic databases and providing research services for a fee.

The Internet has become an indispensable research tool for writers and communicators of all kinds, whether they work in an office or toil at home. Virtually every single job covered in this book now requires use of the personal computer, e-mail, and the Internet. Surveys done by *Publishers Weekly* over the years have found that more than 98 percent of respondents within the book publishing industry had access to the Internet and used it for more than 10 hours per week (and this time allotment is continually increasing).

The Internet has also dissolved the traditional boundaries between various types of media. Work created for one medium (say a newspaper) is easily transferred into another (say a news computer database). Some old-time professionals among the media may yearn for the days when manuscripts were typed on typewriters and edited with pencils. However, any writer who has written or edited a lengthy (or not-so-lengthy) manuscript on a computer appreciates the tremendous ease and saving of time accomplished when making extensive revisions to a text on the computer. Search-and-replace techniques become a godsend for making last-minute adjustments to style or content, as well as finding terms or words used in the text that need to be defined in either text or a glossary. It is also wonderful to be able to e-mail or fax a finished job to a client rather than having to send hard copy.

Writing Jobs for the Twenty-first Century

The U.S. Department of Labor's Bureau of Labor Statistics estimates that there were about 319,000 employed writers and editors in the United States in 2002, and more than one-third of these were self-employed. The bureau further estimates that this number will increase to more than 385,400 by the year 2010, an increase of 21 percent. And this does not include desktop publishers who are expected to increase in number from 38,000 in 2000 to 63,600 in 2010, an increase of nearly 67 percent! In addition, for public relations specialists, managers, and writers, there were 210,600 employed in 2000, and that number is expected to jump to 289,800 by 2010, an increase of 36 percent. These figures indicate an excellent employment outlook for the writing and editing field as a whole!

In 2002, more than one-half of the jobs for writers and editors were salaried positions in the information sector, which includes book, directory, newspaper, and periodical publishers; radio and television broadcasting; software publishers; motion picture and sound recording industries; Internet service providers, Web search portals, and data processing services; and Internet publishing and broadcasting. Significant numbers of writers and editors also worked in advertising, public relations, and related services, and on journals and newsletters published by business and non-profit organizations, such as professional associations, labor unions, and religious organizations. Others worked in computer systems design and related services, public and private educational institutions, and government agencies. In addition, there is a growing number of writers working exclusively (or partially) on the Internet.

Many technical writers work for computer software firms, or manufacturers of aircraft, chemicals, computers and other electronic equipment, and pharmaceuticals.

Jobs with major book publishers, magazines, broadcasting companies, advertising agencies and public relations firms, and the federal government are concentrated in New York, Boston, Philadelphia, Chicago, Los Angeles, San Francisco, and Washington, D.C. Jobs with newspapers and business, religious, technical, and trade union magazines or journals are scattered widely throughout the country. Technical writers are employed everywhere as well, but the largest concentrations are found in the Northeast, Texas, and California.

Thousands of other writers and editors work on a freelance basis, earning some, or all, of their income from their articles, books, editing or indexing work, and, less commonly, movie and television scripts. Many freelancers support themselves primarily with income from other sources, but just as many find it possible to attain a comfortable living status by working hard as a full-time freelancer. Most freelancers work at home where they control when, where, and how they work. Others do freelance work in offices as on-site consultants. As consultants, they generally receive no paid vacation, health insurance, or other benefits, particularly if they work fewer than 21 hours per week. However, they have more freedom over their scheduled work hours than regular full-time employees.

(Interestingly, as Bob Perlongo noted in his book *The Write Book: An Illustrated Treasury of Tips, Tactics and Tirades* [Art Direction Book Company, 2004] the term "free lance" was invented by the English novelist Sir Walter Scott to refer to itinerary mercenary soldiers who sold their warrior abilities to the highest bidder. Initially, such soldiers were known as "free companions," but, as they usually traveled with their own lances as weapons, Scott dubbed them "free lancers.")

The Internet: Still a Very Hot Field for Writers

Within the burgeoning job scene for writers in the new millennium the profession of communicator/information manager is one of the hottest career tracks. As it is still a relatively new field, job descriptions and titles can vary widely: different job sources refer to such positions as content manager, Web site developer, Web site writer or editor, or Webmaster. Some people who write for the Internet work for a single corporation and continually update and expand its Web site. These employees may have completely different job titles and many other unrelated job responsibilities. Other people work as freelancers, or are employed by consulting or advertising firms that specialize solely in Web site development.

U.S. News & World Report selected Web site developer as one of the top 20 hot career paths in its 1999 annual guide to best jobs for the future. Indeed, Web site posts are still the hot work opportunities for writers. The average annual salary for a chief copywriter working on the Web was $48,400 in 1998. In comparison, in 2004, a median yearly salary for a Web designer (comparable job) in New York was $67,875, whereas, say in Des Moines, Iowa, the same job's median annual salary was $57,200. For content manager the average annual salary in 1998 was $63,200. Again, in comparison in 2004, a median yearly salary for a content engineer (comparable position) in New York is $79,182 and $66,730 per annum in Des Moines. Other studies have indicated that salaries related to employment on Web sites are increasing because these skills are so much in demand. The 2004 edition of *Writer's Market Online* (Writer's Digest Books, 2003) states that freelance Web page writing pays an average of $75 to a high of $120 per hour.

Writers, designers, and editors who develop Web sites must make sure that the information is presented clearly but interestingly (often aided by visual and audio data), and that it scans well to the eye on the screen (which is so very different from the printed page). The use of hyperlinks on each page of the Web site makes it easy to access each (cross-reference) page no matter where the viewer is currently browsing on the site.

E-zines (electronic magazines) offer writers new potential for their creative talents. E-zines on every conceivable topic exist on the Internet, and many of them feature the writings of new authors. A few books and online resources will aid in discovering these online magazines: *Writer's Online Marketplace: How and Where to Get Published Online,* by Debbie Ridpath Ohi (Writer's Digest Books, 2001); *Online Market for Writers: How to Make Money by Selling Your Writing on the Internet,* by Anthony and Paul Tedesco (Owl Books, 2000); WritersMarket.com (http://www.writersmarket.com); and The Writers' Place (http://www.awoc.com). Another way to locate online magazines are directories and electronic newsstands, including Etext Archives (http://www.etext.org), Gebbie Press (http://www.gebbieinc.com), or Zinos (http://www.zinos.com), the last of which is a digest of some of the top e-zines on the Web. Also, the excellent articles on online writing in the 2005 edition of *Writer's Market Online* contain much solid advice for writers looking to utilize this new medium as an outlet for their work.

Job-Hunting: Getting That First Industry Break

Formerly it was a reality that if you had a flair for grammar and spelling and could type 60 words per minute, you could obtain an entry-level post as an editorial assistant or administrative assistant with most publishers. This situation is no longer true. Job applicants to publishers (as well as to other print media, public relations firms, advertising companies, and related industries) should be thoroughly at home with computer methodologies and software programs, as well as utilizing the Internet. Beyond knowing about the various word processing programs (such as Microsoft Word), a familiarity of spreadsheet software, such as Excel or Lotus Approach, or production software, such as Quark, are distinct advantages for any applicant in today's job marketplace.

To win that first entry-level position, several approaches can be of real assistance in the process. For example, working on a college newspaper or other publication, or at radio or television stations, is good experience and will look great on your résumé. Internships during college are also extremely helpful in any aspect of broadcasting, communications, or publishing. Not only are they good learning experiences for your career, there may also arise the chance that you might be offered permanent employment by the organization for which you are working as an intern. Then too, many of the people you meet while an intern can be substantial networking sources in later years for elevating your work position within the industry.

For useful information about using the Internet as a job-hunting tool for any writing (or other) field, look at Richard Nelson Bolles's *Job Hunting on the Internet* (Ten Speed, 2001) or other similar books on the same topic, such as Pat Criscito's *e-Resumes: A Guide to Successful Online Job Hunting* (Barrons, 2004), Margaret Riley Dike's *Guide to Internet Job Searching 2004–2005* (McGraw-Hill, 2004), and Rachel Gordon's *Best Career and Education Web Sites: A Quick Guide to Online Job Search, 4th edition* (JIST Works, 2003). Also, consult the Appendix, *Useful Web Sites for Writers,* at the back of this book.

Factors Affecting Salaries

Many of the salary ranges in this book are quite wide, but this reflects today's actual job market. Here are several key factors that affect where, within a broad salary range, a given job may fall:

1. *Where you are based.* As Richard Bolles points out in his book, *Job Hunting on the Internet,* location is just as essential in job-hunting as it is in real estate (or in many other facets of life). As shown in the above sample of annual salaries of Web site jobs, that of a Web content engineer in New York was $79,182 as opposed to a comparable job in Des Moines, Iowa, where the salary was $66,730. Other examples abound on such salary Web sites as that of the *Wall Street Journal* (http://www.careers.wsj.com) or Salary.com (http://www.salary.com/). Also *American Salaries and Wages Survey* by Helen S. Fisher (Gale Group,

1999) offers a highly detailed look at how salaries for comparable work vary from location to location.

However, before you decide to move to the city with the highest salary (usually New York City), take into account the far higher cost of living there as well. What would cost $100 in New York would be $68.80 in Detroit, Michigan. Another possibility is doing freelance work for a client in a higher-paying city. This way your location does not have to match your employer's. However, you have to remember that you will be selling yourself and your services to a new client with all the attendant problems that entails.

2. *Length of experience in the field.* A worker who has years of experience in a particular job or field of endeavor naturally earns more than one who has just been hired out of school, or who is coming to the field for the first time. Employers tend to seek specific sets of skills, most of which are learned on the job rather than in the classroom. Here again is where having had an internship during school might help.

3. *Size of company.* Generally, the larger the company, the higher the pay.

4. *Level of formal education.* Study after study has repeatedly demonstrated that education pays, and that the earnings gap between those with a college degree and those without one is widening in the United States. The Census Bureau determined that college graduates earned an average of $40,478 a year in 1997. This was 76 percent more than the $22,895 yearly average earned by high school graduates that year. In 1975, the gap was only 57 percent.

In some rare cases—through connections, luck, and/or talent—it is sometimes possible to get a job without the educational background recommended for it in this book. However, your pay level may be affected by the lack of a degree, or your promotion to the next level may be stalled. On the other hand, as *Money* magazine reported in 1998, while getting a graduate degree does increase salary in most technical fields by 18 percent to 28 percent at first, the difference shrinks to only 5 percent after four years of employment in a given field. Thus, in many cases, experience on the job is considered more important by employers.

6. *Gender and race.* Unfortunately, statistics confirm that Caucasian males still earn more than women and minorities in many of the jobs described in this book. This is partly because there are more white men in top managerial positions, and partly because men are still sometimes paid more for doing the same job as women. *Publishers Weekly,* in its 2002 Salary Survey (by Jim Milliot), found that men continued to out-earn women in publishing in 2001, with men earning an average of $112,399 and women taking home $75,464. As stated,

the difference in pay was found to be partially due to males having five more years' experience than women and because men in publishing tend to be found more in management positions, while women gravitate toward editorial jobs. Nonetheless, both these factors are gradually changing. It is now easier for women to compete equally with men at high-tech (and many professional) jobs than at jobs requiring a lot of upper body strength. A majority of associate, bachelor's, and master's degrees are now earned by women. Women are earning pride of place in many businesses, including the television industry where in 1972 only 0.5 percent of news director positions were held by women and, by the year 2004, a third or more of all television news directors are women.

Progress is slower for minorities. However, the American workforce is becoming more and more ethnically diverse, which, in turn, will affect the communications industry as the years go on.

General Trends

Previously, traditional positions offered enough on-the-job comforts that people were not readily willing to leave their positions. Today, benefits packages are less generous (except for the highest-paying jobs), and long-term job security is seldom guaranteed in most industries, making it far easier for people to decide to leave their present position for jobs elsewhere. In fact, in some areas of the communications industry, people typically get bigger raises if they move to another job (in a bigger market) than if they stay in one position for too long.

The Bureau of Labor Statistics classifies most jobs in this book as belonging to the service sector of the economy. Although wages have increased in that sector, as in the overall U.S. economy since the early 1980s, that increase is somewhat deceptive. For example, the average hourly wage in the service sector in June 1999 was $13.23, but when measured in constant (1982) dollars, that amounts to only $7.88. Despite the booming economy of the late 1990s, many employers began to lay off permanent full-time staff and hire freelancers instead in a growing movement to save personnel costs and benefits. That trend continues today.

At the same time, there has been a continuing demand for workers with technical skills on the computer. Those who do not have the technical abilities that will be required to do well in the 21st century will be left behind. However, all studies point to the fact that the skill level of the American workforce is increasing and will continue to do so. Most working- and middle-class Americans—especially the younger generation—are learning what it will take to prosper financially in the years ahead and are preparing for the ever-growing job requirements.

One trend in book publishing that was noted in 1998—of publishing houses downsizing and reducing their editorial staffs, often as the result of mergers and acquisitions—still remains true. During the 1990s the number of editors working in New York City declined by approximately 16 percent. Yet simultaneously, more books were being published. These trends continue today, with only about a dozen major book publishers in existence, mostly based in New York City, that publish the largest amount of popular, or "trade" books. Outside of New York City, there are still a significant number of book publishers, some of them imprints of New York houses and some of them completely independent. Many of them will remain independent despite their expansion and growth, and some will combine with the larger houses, due as much to the advantage of consolidating their book distribution efforts with those of a larger publishing house with more clout as any other reason.

One of the fears for everyone in the book trade was how the Internet was going to affect the overall publishing business. It seems today that the new technologies have had an impact, but not necessarily an adverse one. As Jeff Herman states in his article, *The State of Book Publishing: Today and Tomorrow* (found in his *Guide to Book Publishers, Editors & Literary Agents* [Writer Books, 2003]), the "new technologies don't and won't matter, because it's all about delivery and production systems. It has nothing to do with the evolution of the creative process or the measure of America's appetite for reading books."

Competition remains still in the more glamorous fields of author, playwright, and screenwriter. Advances continue to be relatively high for celebrity books or trendy self-help books by well-known (and best-selling) authorities, but in most other cases, publishers still play it safe with modest advances, particularly in the arena of nonfiction. Because much of present-day book publishing is owned by multinational, multibillion-dollar conglomerates that have priorities other than the mere publication of books, pressure continues on book editors to make profitable choices if their careers are to prosper. Not all editors are so single-minded and still do their best to acquire meaningful books that also make commercial sense. Yet many large publishers are increasingly reluctant to subsidize new authors to nourish a backlist. These "midlist authors" still find it difficult to get their next book published at any of the larger book publishing firms. The one positive effect of this increased corporate ownership of the bulk of the book industry is that publishers are learning to take better advantage of start-of-the-art marketing techniques and technologies and are beginning to have more capital with which to do it.

To counter this trend among large publishers, every year small presses, old and new, publish books that large publishers would not even consider, and some of these books even go on to become best sellers. In addition, university presses put out important (and sales-worthy) books that would never have been published in a rigidly commercial environment, although that line is blurring more and more as campus firms reach out to attract the trade audience.

Yet another tendency in the last several years has been the emergence of book superstores that can create very appealing environments that draw in more public traffic than conventional old-style bookstores ever did. Many people shopping in the super malls of America are taking their time to look through these well-stocked bookstores, where they can browse, sit and read, or purchase a steaming mug of coffee at an in-house café, chat with friends, and even use their laptop computers. In such a pleasing and comfortable environment they are more likely to spend their dollars buying books, magazines, music CDs, and even artwork. In addition, the increased shelf space in these enormous stores provides a marketplace for books on specialized topics that before would not have seen the light of day in most bookstores. The downside of these new stores is the continual closing of independent bookstores that just cannot compete with these chains (though some are adjusting by concentrating on special reader-interest areas). This situation has been exacerbated by the explosion of markets in which books can be purchased, including those online (another new trend) from such outlets as http://www.amazon.com and http://www.barnesandnoble.com.

Another different course today is the expansion of self-publishing. Today, anyone with a computer and some relatively inexpensive software can virtually self-publish his or her own book in cyberspace. Online self-publishing can save the author the trouble and expense of printing and storing thousands of copies to be sold at some future date. The problem for a cyberspace publisher is how to get enough people to know about the book and then motivate them to purchase it. Any author into self-publishing also has to become a businessperson and marketing maven in order to succeed. The answer is usually a well-linked Web site designed to inform and sell, along with frequent and self-generated publicity designed to promote the books and lead people to the Web site, a toll-free number, or both. Nonetheless, the distribution process is tough, to which any book publisher can attest.

Salaries still tend to remain low at many small newspapers. Editors at business-to-business magazines are apt to be paid less than those at consumer magazines. Some editors have expressed concern over the years because they felt they were expected to take on new responsibilities, such as managing Web sites and advertorials (advertising sections prepared by the magazine), without just compensation. Other editors seemed to enjoy the new challenges involved in these new responsibilities.

Median annual entry-level pay remains lower in television and radio broadcasting than in print journalism, mostly due to the higher competition for these positions.

Opportunities continue to be good for freelancers, especially those who offer multiple services. Freelancers in writing and communications specialties still do not make tremendous amounts of money, but they enjoy a freedom and flexibility in their lifestyles. Freelance income and workloads are often irregular—"feast or famine"—and the uncertainty of work and pay means that freelancers have to have good sales skills, perseverance, self-discipline, organization, and sound financial management. In addition, they have to invest in office equipment and bear the cost of running an office and a business.

Freelancers today need to have a good deal of sophisticated equipment in addition to the basics of desk and chair, telephone, and relevant reference books. Now they need a fast computer with sufficient memory, a large disk drive, a fast-speed printer, a fax/modem, reliable access to the Internet, and, perhaps, subscribe to needed online fee-based research sites. Depending upon the nature of their work, they may also require extra items such as scanners and photocopiers. Unfortunately, it is a fact of life that electronic equipment goes obsolete dismayingly fast, which means frequent upgrades are necessary (unlike a refrigerator that may last as long as 15 years). Freelancers' equipment also has to be compatible with their clients' devices so that data transferred by disk will be readable on both systems. All of this means that present-day freelancers have a considerably higher overhead than previously.

Most freelancers remain versatile and do not count on any single market or type of work, as market needs can shift rapidly, and contacts can be lost. Having several years of experience as a full-time staff member of a business can provide a good background for a freelancer.

Today, more than 75 percent of the Editorial Freelancers Association members are women (a situation paralleled in the American Society of Indexers association made up mostly of freelance or consultant indexers). More than half of them say they would never take a full-time permanent job even if one was offered. More than half of the membership says they tended to be overloaded with work some months and far too idle in others. One in five say they have an appropriate amount of work each month, while one in 10 mention they are swamped each month. Almost one in six state that they need more work every month.

Although salaries may not be high in most writing or communication jobs (except those of senior positions), they are above average. As is usually the case, the smaller the company, the lower the pay scale. In some parts of the country, some entry-level jobs may pay as little as $13,000 a year. However, average annual salaries for experienced communications professionals are generally in the $35,000 to $60,000 range. Women continue to experience pay gaps in most fields, especially at the senior level. Salaries tend to be more equal in journalism, where women and men make roughly the same in entry-level jobs, and in higher-level jobs when a pay gap develops it tends to remain smaller than in other sectors.

Whether you find your career destiny in a cramped, busy newspaper office in a large metropolis, in the ivy-covered halls of a distinguished educational institution, in the bustle on a television or film studio set, or in the conformist boardrooms of corporate America, chances are that you will find yourself in the company of creative, interesting people who influence the way other people think and feel.

The persuasive art of advertising, the lucid and concise presentation of news, the business of image creation, the satisfying cadence of a poem or a song lyric, and the excitement of a well-written and produced television program or film *all* depend for their success on the adroit manipulation of words.

Whatever type of writing you find yourself doing—now or in the future—you have a wonderful opportunity to savor utilizing using your own creative talents and imagination to produce work that informs, sells, entertains, and, even, perhaps, alters our world.

ACKNOWLEDGMENTS

We would like to thank the following individuals and organizations for their assistance with this project: Lisa Bastian (Bastian Public Relations), Marilyn Bergman (American Society of Composers, Authors & Publishers), Leslie W. Boyer (American Amateur Press Association), Stephen Cole, Ernest Cunningham, Michael Dougherty, Alex Gildzen, Kim Kennedy (American Federation of Government Employees), Frederick Levy, Jennifer H. McGill (Association of Education in Journalism & Mass Communication), Robert Makinson (The Songwriters and Lyricists Club), Stephen Mooser (Society of Children's Book Writers & Illustrators), Andy Ostroy (American List Council), Paul Raeburn (National Association of Science Writers), Brad Schreiber, Nat Segaloff, Lisa Valladares (American List Council), Tom Waldman (Federal Reserve Bank), and Steven Whitney. We also are grateful to the reference librarians at Beverly Hills Public Library for aiding our research for this book.

With special thanks to our literary agent Stuart Bernstein and to our editor James Chambers at Facts On File for their unfailing help in preparing this volume.

HOW TO USE THIS BOOK

Purpose

Career Opportunities in Writing presents one of the most inclusive directories of writing jobs available in a single volume. It does *not* concentrate on a single field of writing, but covers 90 writing and writing-related professions detailed in eight major fields. Jobs are not merely summarized in a few paragraphs but are explained in detail, including duties, alternate titles, salary ranges, employment and advancement prospects (with a career ladder), prerequisites (including education, experience and skills requirements), organizations to join, and helpful tips for entering the job arena under discussion. It is intended to assist both aspiring writers who are targeting entry-level positions as well as experienced writers who are looking to make career changes within the profession.

Generally the jobs detailed in this volume are available to individuals with appropriate education credentials (typically a bachelor's degree) and with zero to five years or so of experience. These are principally entry- and middle-level posts, those that are available to the largest number of candidates.

Sources of Information

Research for this book includes the authors' own experiences, interviews with professionals in assorted fields, and facts, reports, surveys, and other data obtained from job data banks, professional associations, trade unions/guilds, the federal government, and educational institutions.

The job descriptions provided are based on representative samples of actual job posts. In general, writing jobs are broad in their responsibilities, and they can vary greatly from one employer to another. In many instances, a writing position is what the employee makes of it. Positions at small firms often tend to be broader in range than those at large, structured companies and organizations. The descriptions in this book detail some of the wide ranges of duties and responsibilities for various types of jobs.

Organization of Material

This book has nine parts: eight cover different fields and industries that employ many writers; the final section consists of appendixes listing educational institutions; major trade periodicals, newsletters, and other publications; professional, industry, and trade associations, guilds, and unions; useful Web sites for writers; as well as a glossary of terms for writers, a bibliography of additional sources, and an index. While most of the jobs listed are based entirely on writing and editing skills, a few are writing-related; that is, in addition to substantial writing and editing skills, the positions require additional skills or education. Some of the jobs that fall in this latter category are sales-oriented posts, research positions, and jobs requiring academic, foreign-language, legal, and/or technical training. The introduction provides an overview of job opportunities for writers today, as well as a detailing of employment trends for the next decade or so.

The ever-expanding Internet has created an explosion of information that has revolutionized writers' jobs in every medium and specialty. It is crucial for anyone in the writing/information fields to be very familiar with using a computer and navigating the Internet (including the utilization of e-mail, news/user groups, and chat groups). As increasingly more data is transmitted electronically, the ability to conduct research using computers and distributing information to specialized audiences via the Internet will become increasingly important to writers. Advances in technology have also made it possible for freelancers to provide a far more sophisticated range of services. Increasingly sophisticated computer software (such as desktop publishing programs and indexing programs) have created new avenues of employment for the individual writer or person working for a small firm or organization.

Explanation of Job Descriptions

Each job description follows a basic format and is complete unto itself; the reader does not have to consult another section of this book to obtain a full picture of a particular post. Therefore, readers may note some repetition from job to job within a particular industry.

Jobs are listed by their predominant title, followed by a Career Profile, which summarizes main duties, alternate titles, salary ranges, employment prospects, advancement prospects, and prerequisites of education, experience, and special skills. A Career Ladder diagram depicts a typical career path, including the positions below and above each job. If a job is entry level, school or other related posts are listed as preceding it.

The Position Description is an extended narrative that describes typical job duties and responsibilities, working hours and conditions, the frequency of overtime and travel wherever pertinent, and optional duties that may or may not be part of an individual job.

Salaries explain income ranges and the factors, such as individual skills, size of the employer firm, or geographic location, that often affect how much a particular position may pay annually. Salary ranges are based on yearly averages, and readers may find positions in the job market that pay less or more than the amounts cited in this volume.

Readers will find especially useful the sections on Employment Prospects and Advancement Prospects. Some jobs may sound terrific or seem to be extremely exciting, but, in reality, they also may be extremely difficult to obtain. Others may prove to be employment dead ends, with advancement difficult or impossible. These are certainly important factors to weigh in any job search.

The Education section describes academic requirements for assorted jobs. In most instances, writers who have earned undergraduate degrees in liberal arts or communications will qualify, but some jobs require additional educational backgrounds. Graduate degrees are not often essential but are increasingly advantageous for many positions. At the opposite end of the spectrum, some writing jobs demand only high school diplomas.

In addition to schooling, many jobs require prior experience. The Experience/Skills section details what background is key or helpful in competing for a job. Previous experience may not be required for many entry-level posts, but candidates who have had some kind of related experience—even on collegiate, volunteer, internship, or community levels—often have considerable competitive advantages. In addition, this section points out the skills and qualities employers seek, including personal attributes that enhance one's prospects for success in particular fields.

Most communicators—a generic terms that includes writers, editors, and others in various communications positions—do not belong to a union. Those who are unionized work in organized fields such as print and broadcast journalism, film and television entertainment, schools, and government. Even in those areas, unionization is not uniform throughout. Many do, however, belong to one or more professional associations where they meet others who have similar jobs, exchange information and ideas, as well as network. The Unions and Associations section lists the major associations of interest to professionals in a particular field, as well as the most likely unions/guilds, if any, that would represent them in wage and benefits negotiations. Please note that the associations listed for each job are only a small sampling of the possible organizations to which people in that field might belong. Readers are encouraged to browse through Appendix III to look for organizations that interest them, and to contact those groups to obtain more information about membership eligibility and benefits obtained from joining. (Keep in mind that, on occasion, an organization's title—for example, Local 2110 of the United Auto Workers—may not immediately indicate its relevance to a particular job field. However, a visit to the Web sites listed in Appendix IV or those listed with the organization in Appendix III will clarify the matter.) The Tips for Entry sec-

tion, which ends each job description, provides a list of practical suggestions for breaking into a given work field.

Appendixes

Appendix I, "Educational Institutions," lists college, universities, and educational institutions, in every state and the District of Columbia, that offer undergraduate degrees in major areas of communications—broadcasting, advertising, public relations, education, technical and specialized journalism, newspaper/magazine journalism, as well as courses in publishing. The listing *does not* include every institution that offers courses or degrees in communications, nor, generally, institutions that offer graduate degrees in communications (since such an educational prerequisite is not that prevalent a requirement in communication jobs). The list also does *not* include two-year colleges, since most jobs demand or give preference to degree-holders from four-year institutions. The listings provide each institution's address, telephone number, fax number, e-mail address, and Web site, as well as the major programs, specialties, and courses of particular interest to writers.

Appendix II, "Further Reading," offers a useful resource list of magazines, books, and e-zines that beginner-to-experienced writers in various fields of communication will find of interest. These are organized by field or industry.

Appendix III, "Unions and Associations," lists major organizations for writers, editors, and those in the writing-related fields included within this book. For each entry, the address, telephone number, fax number, e-mail, and Web site are provided. There is a separate list of unions, and the listings of associations is organized by field or industry.

Appendix IV, "Useful Web Sites for Writers," provides a wide range of Internet resources in many categories that are useful to writers in a wide assortment of work areas.

The Glossary of Terms for Writers contains an assortment of useful terminology involved in a wide spectrum of professions/industries in which writers are involved.

The Bibliography contains sources utilized in researching this book to gain information on job descriptions, salary ranges, job prospects, and other pertinent data. In those instances where online sources are cited, you may wish to check the particular Web site to determine whether new updates on the topic are now available.

The Index provides a quick source for locating particular job titles (including cross-references to alternate job names), organizations cited in the text (but not the appendixes), and other relevant information appearing in the text of this volume.

Last, please keep in mind that the Internet is in a constant state of flux and Web sites sometimes change their Web address or, on occasion, cease to exist. If a URL listed in this book—all of which were verified at the time of writing this volume—does not link you to the desired Web site, do a search engine query using the name of the Web site to locate its new home.

ADVERTISING

ACCOUNT EXECUTIVE

CAREER PROFILE

Duties: Direct all advertising activities on client accounts; maintain favorable relationships and contacts with current and potential client accounts

Alternate Title(s): None

Salary Range: $50,000 to $80,000 or more

Employment Prospects: Fair

Advancement Prospects: Fair

Prerequisites:

Education or Training—Undergraduate degree in advertising, business, communication, journalism, or liberal arts

Experience—At least one to three years of experience as trainee or assistant Account Executive

Special Skills and Personality Traits—Good communication and leadership skills; knowledge of graphics, marketing techniques, and media

CAREER LADDER

```
┌─────────────────────────────┐
│    Accounts Manager or       │
│    Accounts Supervisor       │
└─────────────────────────────┘

┌─────────────────────────────┐
│      Account Executive       │
└─────────────────────────────┘

┌─────────────────────────────┐
│  Assistant Account Executive or │
│           Trainee            │
└─────────────────────────────┘
```

Position Description

While most Account Executives function within advertising agencies, some work for firms in their advertising or sales departments. The Account Executive oversees the link between the agency (or the department) and the client and may be in charge of advertising for one or more clients (usually one large and several small ones). The Account Executive plans the nature of the advertising being produced, relaying the client's campaign requirements and philosophy to the agency's creative and media departments. The Account Executive reviews all the creative work before its presentation to the client. Thus, maintaining good communication and interaction with the client is a prerequisite of this position.

Account Executives must be highly motivated, handle stress well, be flexible and decisive. They must have a comprehensive knowledge of all agency operations, as well as understand the clients' businesses, marketing strategies, and competition. They need to judge whether or not the ad copy created and campaign proposed are correct for the client. They must understand market analysis procedures and appreciate the potentials of all media outlets, in order to plan successful advertising campaigns. When these strate-

gies are fully developed, it is the Account Executive who presents them to the client.

Account Executives report to an account supervisor or an account manager, who, in turn, reports to a director or a vice president of account services. In small agencies, the Account Executive may fulfill all functions that, in a larger firm, might be delegated to assistants and clerical staff.

In addition, Account Executives may take part in the campaign and make presentations to persuade new clients to be handled by the firm.

Salaries

Account Executive annual salaries range from a low of $50,000 to a high of $80,000 or more. According to the May 2004 report from Salary.com, the median expected salary for a typical Account Executive in the United States is $57,466, though this figure may be higher in the larger urban centers such as New York. This base pay can be enhanced by bonuses and benefits, bringing the mean average total cash compensation to $76,859, with a high of $116,887 or more. This survey also indicated that pay scales can be affected by employer size and geographic location, the employee's years of experience, and the type and quality of the employee's education.

However, the stagnating economy of the last several years has limited bonus amounts (and pay raises generally) throughout the advertising industry.

Employment Prospects

The U.S. Department of Labor's Bureau of Labor Statistics has projected a 19 percent growth of employment in the advertising industry. New jobs will be created as the economy expands, generating more products and services that need to be advertised and promoted. Nonetheless, layoffs are common in the advertising industry when client accounts are lost, major clients cut budgets, or agencies merge (as happened during the 1990s).

Advancement Prospects

Successful Account Executives can advance rapidly in responsibility and recompense. The top executives in most advertising firms have risen through the ranks of Account Executives. Notwithstanding, competition is fierce and job security is minimal.

Education and Training

Most Account Executives (in either large or small firms) have undergraduate degrees in advertising, business, journalism, or liberal arts. While advanced degrees are not required, further graduate work and/or certification in business or economics will work to the executive's advantage.

Experience, Skills, and Personality Traits

Most Account Executives have worked as assistant account executives, or trainees, before being given full responsibility for clients' accounts. Some may have been journalists previously or involved in advertising sales in some capacity.

Account Executives must comprehend all facets of an advertising campaign, from the judging and editing of ad copy to the purchasing of media space and time. Above all, due to their highly visible position, they must have excellent social skills and demonstrate both sales ability and leadership.

Unions and Associations

Associations include the American Advertising Federation, the American Association of Advertising Agencies, the American Marketing Association, as well as the Advertising Women of New York and the Association for Women in Communications. Some Account Executives may also belong to one or more of the various direct marketing associations. For students there is the Association of Marketing Students.

Tips for Entry

1. Read trade publications such as *Ad Age, Deca Dimensions* (the membership magazine for the Association of Marketing Students), *Promo Magazine,* and others to learn of new trends, marketing opportunities, and job prospects.
2. Contact organizations such as the American Marketing Association (http://www.marketingpower.com), or the American Advertising Federation (http://www.aaf.org) to gain industry insights including trends, technology, and salary ranges.
3. Build a portfolio of sample ad campaigns to show your skills and diversity.
4. Target agencies that you would like to work for and find examples of their current campaigns to see if you are in sync with their advertising approaches and techniques, and if appropriate, submit applications.

ASSISTANT ACCOUNT EXECUTIVE

CAREER PROFILE

Duties: Assist in researching and preparing materials for advertising agencies' accounts

Alternate Title(s): None

Salary Range: $25,000 to $50,000

Employment Prospects: Fair

Advancement Prospects: Good

Prerequisites:

Education or Training—Undergraduate degree in advertising, journalism, or marketing

Experience—None

Special Skills and Personality Traits—Understanding of advertising and marketing; organizational talents and leadership

CAREER LADDER

```
┌─────────────────────────────────┐
│       Account Executive         │
└─────────────────────────────────┘

┌─────────────────────────────────┐
│   Assistant Account Executive   │
└─────────────────────────────────┘

┌─────────────────────────────────┐
│    Trainee or College Student   │
└─────────────────────────────────┘
```

Position Description

An Assistant Account Executive is typically an entry-level position, although in some agencies this post may have been preceded by a trainee period in a clerical or secretarial position.

Assistant Account Executives learn the advertising business from working at basic and routine tasks for the account service department. They may be assigned to one or more account executives or to an entire department of the firm. In this apprentice process they learn how best to respond to a client's needs, how to coordinate the creative and production work on an account, how to obtain and verify information regarding the client company and its products, and how to strategize campaigns and perform market analyses.

Duties encompass assisting in the preparation of reports and proposals, including both writing and graphic responsibilities, as well as undertaking basic research for client proposals and advertising campaigns. The routine tasks of keying, proofreading, and general errands may also lead to participation in meetings with clients or in the presentations of proposed campaigns.

Assistant Account Executives take on the burden of the groundwork on projects, but receive little to no official credit. While work hours are regular, overtime is not uncommon, frequently on short notice when deadlines loom.

Salaries

A 2004 report on "Careers in Marketing" from the Marketing Research Association found that beginning annual salaries for Assistant Account Executives range between $25,000 and $30,000. A survey by Vault, Inc. on advertising salaries finds that entry-level employees usually get promoted sometime between eight and 18 months after being hired, and with the promotion come salary increases. Gaining experience also gains salary boosts. In addition this survey notes that salary increases can be as much as 50 percent, depending upon the agency.

However, within the last two to three years, as the economy has stagnated, salary increases (along with bonuses) have become rarer. Beginning-level employees with less experience are more likely to start with low salaries, which becomes a concern, especially if they are based in large urban centers like New York where the cost of living consumes low pay fast. Frequently, changing jobs to another agency (or an advertising department of a corporation) will provide the sought-after salary increase.

Employment Prospects

Competition is fierce, as there are many more candidates for advertising positions than there are posts available. Starting at the bottom and working up the ladder is a necessity. The good news is that employment in the industry is projected to grow 19 percent over the 2002 to 2012 period, compared with 16 percent for all industries combined.

Advancement Prospects

Working hard and acquiring experience adds to the likelihood of being promoted to the position of account executive. Frequently such advancement occurs through staff turnover, which is high in the advertising field.

Education and Training

Assistant Account Executive positions usually require a bachelor's degree in advertising, marketing, or liberal arts. At some agencies, a master's degree in business administration may also be required. As the work is oriented toward both marketing and sales, an educational background in business and economics is helpful. An advertising-related internship during college years is an additional boost toward employment, and foreign-language skills are another advantage. Many large advertising agencies are establishing offices around the world, opening the possibility that, with experience, work on global campaigns is a possibility.

Experience, Skills, and Personality Traits

Often Assistant Account Executives begin their advertising careers as trainees, little more than clerical or secretarial assistants. Others come directly from college or from an entry-level position in a related field, such as journalism, public relations, or sales.

People skills and communication abilities are paramount. A clear writing facility, good organization, creativity, the ability to sell a concept, and persistence are important attributes.

Unions and Associations

Major associations for advertising professionals include the American Advertising Federation, the American Association of Advertising Agencies, and the American Marketing Association. Others include the Advertising Club of America, Advertising Women of New York, and the Association for Women in Communications.

Tips for Entry

1. Read trade publications, such as *Advertising Age* and *Adweek,* to learn of new trends in advertising and marketing, what an advertising agency does, as well as potential job prospects.

2. Look into internship programs available at many advertising firms.

3. Contact organizations such as the American Marketing Association (http://www.marketingpower.com) to learn about the latest trends, pay scales, and job openings within the industry. As a student join the Association of Marketing Students (http://www.deca.org) to obtain their membership magazine, *Deca Dimensions.*

4. Request interviews with local ad agencies to learn of job opportunities in their firms and to gain a better understanding of the potential career path within the profession. Use the *Standard Directory of Advertising Agencies,* available at most libraries, for specific information about firms, and their key people and policies, available at most libraries.

5. Create a good résumé, assemble a portfolio of your work, and prepare sample ad copy for a campaign to show your initiative, writing skills, and marketing creativity, to be used in your interviews with companies you have targeted.

ASSISTANT COPYWRITER

CAREER PROFILE

Duties: Assists in development and writing of advertising copy; clerical tasks

Alternate Title(s): Junior Copywriter

Salary Range: $25,000 to $39,000

Employment Prospects: Fair

Advancement Prospects: Good

Prerequisites:

Education or Training—Undergraduate degree in advertising, English, journalism, or marketing

Experience—None

Special Skills—Creativity; command of English

CAREER LADDER

```
┌─────────────────────────────────┐
│           Copywriter            │
└─────────────────────────────────┘

┌─────────────────────────────────┐
│       Assistant Copywriter      │
└─────────────────────────────────┘

┌─────────────────────────────────┐
│    Trainee or College Student   │
└─────────────────────────────────┘
```

Position Description

This is an entry-level position, either in an advertising agency or in an advertising or marketing department of a firm. An Assistant Copywriter often comes directly from college or may be employed as an intern while still enrolled in college, undertaking a classroom internship or working during the summer.

The position entails assisting copywriters in editing and proofreading advertising copy, and may include limited work on specific creative projects in developing material for merchandising and sales promotion. Routine work would include researching clients, products, services, or a particular industry for information that will be used to build an advertising campaign. Proofreading copy, trafficking copy between departments, and running errands are also common.

When Assistant Copywriters are assigned creative projects of their own, they function directly under the supervision of a copywriter, a senior copywriter, or copy supervisor who, in the process, may provide career counseling or training. Ample opportunities to learn other facets of the advertising business will most likely follow, even being assigned to generate ideas for products and writing dialogue for media presentations.

Salaries

According to Salary Wizard's basic report on 2004 salaries for beginning copywriters, the national median annual salary was $34,684, with a low of $28,999 and a high of $39,316. They also indicated that salary compensation is greatly affected by geographic area, the size of the firm, as well as the employee's credentials and background.

Employment Prospects

During the 1990s employment slowed and competition increased for entry-level copywriting positions. Then, as stagnation hit the entire economy, many agencies did minimal hiring, instead relying on freelance workers. However, as the economy recovered thereafter, the hiring environment, in turn, improved. The U.S. Department of Labor's, Bureau of Labor Statistics projects an employment increase of 10.7 percent for copywriters for the next eight years.

Advancement Prospects

Once employed, advancement opportunities for an Assistant Copywriter can be solid for those with talent and drive. Innovative, trend-breaking ideas will be both welcomed and well rewarded with commensurate salary, bonuses, and other allied benefits.

Education and Training

The minimum requirement is an undergraduate degree in business, communications, journalism, or liberal arts. Courses in writing and/or creative writing are essential. Additional course work in advertising or marketing is a plus. Advanced degrees are not especially beneficial for the creative side of the advertising business.

Experience, Skills, and Personality Traits

Writing experience of any kind is a highly useful background. Work on school publications or community projects, or for agencies or the media on a part-time basis is preferable. Journalism is a possible career entry point for advertising copywriting.

A solid command of English and a talent for persuasion are prerequisites for success. The ability to write for various media is a bonus.

Unions and Associations

Associations available to advertising professionals are the American Advertising Federation, the American Association of Advertising Agencies, the American Marketing Association, and the Association for Women in Communications. The Writers Guild of America, a union, includes copywriters who also write scripts for film and television.

Tips for Entry

1. Read trade publications such as *Advertising Age* and *AdWeek* to learn of new trends, job prospects, and anything else you can learn about the advertising business.

2. Contact organizations such as the American Marketing Association (http://www.marketingpower.com) to understand the latest trends, pay scales, and job openings within the industry. As a student, join the Association of Marketing Students (http://www.deca.org) to get their membership magazine, *Deca Dimensions*.

3. Make use of the *Standard Directory of Advertising Agencies*, available at most libraries, to begin targeting your prospects by getting the names and titles of key people, the size of agencies and their accounts, and then request an interview with local advertising agencies.

4. Develop your own strategy to communicate your own unique qualities. One way would be to prepare sample ad copy for a campaign to show your initiative, marketing creativity, and writing skills. Frequently ad agencies will ask prospective copywriters to work up a project sheet. This will entail choosing a current ad campaign that they are doing and creating similar and then different advertising for that product. Another type of project sheet they may give you will ask you to invent a product and work up a complete advertising campaign to launch the product.

COPYWRITER

CAREER PROFILE

Duties: Develop ideas; write ads and scripts for the media, sales campaigns, and direct marketing

Alternate Title(s): Technical Writer

Salary Range: $35,000 to $70,000 or more

Employment Prospects: Fair

Advancement Prospects: Fair

Prerequisites:

Education or Training—Undergraduate degree in advertising, art, business, communications, or liberal arts

Experience—Background as a journalist or other professional writing experience is helpful.

Special Skills and Personality Traits—Command of English language, creativity, imagination

CAREER LADDER

```
┌─────────────────────────────────┐
│        Copy Supervisor          │
└─────────────────────────────────┘

┌─────────────────────────────────┐
│          Copywriter             │
└─────────────────────────────────┘

┌─────────────────────────────────┐
│ Assistant Copywriter, Journalist, or │
│        College Student          │
└─────────────────────────────────┘
```

Position Description

The primary job of a Copywriter is to compose the text of ads for television, radio, and other media, as well as provide promotional material for sales campaigns and/or direct marketing campaigns.

Most Copywriters work within the structure of advertising agencies, while some work for in-house advertising, marketing, or promotion departments of companies and corporations. These jobs are often very demanding with a lot of pressure, as overtime beyond the regular weekday working hours is frequently required to meet deadlines.

In large advertising agencies, Copywriters usually report to a senior Copywriter or copy executive, who, in turn, reports to an advertising or creative director. In smaller firms, Copywriters may report directly to the advertising or creative director.

It is key to remember that the creation of an advertising campaign is a group effort. Frequent consultation with the account service or marketing staff is necessary to develop the overall strategy or theme to achieve the client's goals. In many instances, a range of media will be involved in the final campaign: communication media (television and radio), direct mail and e-mail, outdoor advertising (billboards), print, transit ads, or specialties, such as giveaways advertising the client's name, product, or service.

In small agencies, one Copywriter may be responsible for all the media copy for a given client, whereas in a large operation, that responsibility may be divided among several Copywriters, each of whom specializes in a particular kind of media. Television and radio scripts for ads must include instructions for voice-overs and any special effects. Above all, copy and scripts must communicate data in such a way as to persuade people to buy the client's products, services, or ideas.

Additionally, Copywriters may be required to research information for the ads being developed, edit and rewrite copy as necessary, and be responsible for the production of all collateral ad material for the campaign.

Salaries

Employees in creative departments of advertising agencies can expect higher salaries than those in other departments. *Advertising Age* reported in 2003 that the average salary of Copywriters depended a great deal on the amount of experience they had. Those with two to four years of experience had a mean average annual salary of $41,426 (that is, $40,680 base pay plus a $746 bonus). Those with four to six years of experience had a mean average of $55,188 ($54,304 base pay plus a $885 bonus). Those with six to eight years of experience had a mean average of $65,967 ($64,041 plus a $1,196 bonus). The high average salary for those with two to four years of experience was $46,284, while that of a Copywriter with four to six years of experience was $60,453, and that of those with six to eight years of experience was $75,574.

Employment Prospects

Employment in advertising in the 1990s became extremely competitive due to the merging and consolidation of many agencies. Then, as the economy as a whole suffered stagnation, many agencies suffered reduced profitability, depressed job levels, frozen salaries, shelved bonuses, and minimal hiring. According to the annual salary survey made by *Advertising Age,* 56 percent of agencies gave no bonuses during 2003, and 25 percent withheld all raises. Nonetheless, *Advertising Age* reported that agencies were bullish about revenue gains in 2004. The hiring environment, however, will take some time to improve, trailing by several months any revenue gains. But with these gains, in some cases estimated to be as much as 10 percent in growth, new hirings will follow. The U.S. Department of Labor's Bureau of Labor Statistics projects an employment increase of 10.7 percent for Copywriters for the next eight years.

Advancement Prospects

Advertising remains a highly competitive field. However, individuals with initiative, fresh ideas, and talent are assured of advancement and commensurate salary rewards. Good Copywriters are given increased responsibilities, including supervisory positions and more consequential accounts.

Advertising is a career with a great deal of turnover, with resultant tremendous opportunities both within a company and by repositioning to another agency or firm.

Education and Training

The minimum requirement is an undergraduate degree in advertising, art, business, communications, or liberal arts. Advanced degrees are of less value. Education should include courses in creative writing or, even, copywriting itself.

Experience, Skills, and Personality Traits

Writing experience beyond that undertaken as part of the college education is recommended, such as working on school, community, or Internet newspapers/journals. Extracurricular part-time work in advertising or advertising-related jobs would be helpful. Journalistic experience also is recommended.

A Copywriter must have an excellent command of the English language, including contemporary vocabulary, and must be able to visualize ideas. Knowledge of printing production including typography, basic design, and layout is necessary, and proficiency in desktop publishing tools is recommended. Being a team player and exhibiting project management skills are other necessary attributes. Above all, a Copywriter must be imaginative, self-motivated, and willing to experiment with novel and/or unusual uses of language and presentation of ideas.

Unions and Associations

The American Advertising Federation and the American Marketing Association are the primary associations of interest for Copywriters. There are also more specialized groups, such as Advertising Women of New York, the Association for Women in Communications, and the American Association of Advertising Agencies. Some Copywriters also are members of the Writers Guild of America, which is a union for film, radio, and television scriptwriters.

Tips for Entry

1. Read trade publications such as *Advertising Age* and *Adweek* to learn of new trends, and job prospects.
2. Contact organizations such as the American Marketing Association (http://www.marketingpower. com) or the American Advertising Federation (http://www.aaf. org) to understand the latest trends, pay scales, and job openings within the industry. As a student, join the Association of Marketing Students (http://www. deca.org) to obtain their membership magazine *Deca Dimensions.*
3. Make use of the *Standard Directory of Advertising Agencies,* available at most libraries, to target your prospects by getting the names and titles of key people, the size of the agencies you are looking at, and their accounts. Find examples of their current campaigns to see if you are in sync with their advertising approaches and techniques.
4. Keep your résumé constantly updated with examples of your work showing your initiative, writing skills, and marketing creativity.

ARTS AND ENTERTAINMENT

BOOKS

AUTHOR

CAREER PROFILE

Duties: Research and write nonfiction or fiction books or articles

Alternate Title(s): Writer, Novelist

Salary Range: $0 to unlimited

Employment Prospects: Fair to Good

Advancement Prospects: Fair to Good

Prerequisites:

Education or Training—None required: undergraduate or advanced degrees in specialized fields desirable for nonfiction authors; writing courses recommended

Experience—Work as a journalist or professional writer helpful

Special Skills and Personality Traits—Creativity, good writing skills, organizational skills (especially useful in nonfiction writing), perseverance, self-motivation

CAREER LADDER

```
┌─────────────────────────────────────────┐
│   Established Author or Seasoned Author  │
└─────────────────────────────────────────┘

┌─────────────────────────────────────────┐
│                 Author                   │
└─────────────────────────────────────────┘

┌─────────────────────────────────────────┐
│              Novice Author               │
└─────────────────────────────────────────┘
```

Position Description

Most writers work hard, expending long hours researching, writing, editing, and rewriting their work. Much of the time, their writing is done on speculation, that is, they do not receive payment until they have completed their project and submitted it for approval. Even then, rejections are as frequent as acceptances.

Most professional Authors are writers of nonfiction books and articles, which, generally, pay more than fiction (unless one is a best-selling fiction Author). Nonfiction books, frequently on commission from an editor or publisher, include academic textbooks, books on technical subjects, encyclopedias, and topical books (such as health or self-improvement).

The author's life is a solitary one requiring great self-discipline and self-motivation. Authors have to treat their work like any other position, and deadlines have to be met. Their advantage over many other types of employment, however, is that they are able to choose their hours of work and, frequently, can work from home. Writers usually gauge their output in either hours per day, words written, or pages completed. They devote a substantial amount of time to searching for ideas by reading, researching, and observation.

Established Authors seldom complete manuscripts (or even begin writing them) before seeking a sale. They make a sale based on a written proposal, consisting of an introductory argument for their idea, an outline of the proposed book (or article), a list of recently published competing works in the field, and oftentimes a sample chapter. Sometimes the publisher will demand a partial manuscript, which is usually three or four chapters, a synopsis, and an outline. Beginning writers, however, are frequently required to complete their manuscript before a publisher will entertain their work at all.

Many Authors find it advantageous to have a literary agent handle their material. The agent sends the manuscript, the article, or the proposal to publishers. Agents negotiate contracts, collect payments on behalf of the writer, and often mediate in any problems that occur in the process of getting the book published. Agents also find work for their client writers, as they are aware of individual editors' particular interests.

Work on a manuscript is not completed when the book (or article) is accepted for publication. Revisions must be done and page proofs read and approved. Then, also, writers frequently spend their own time and money helping publishers publicize and promote their book through media interviews and networking on the Internet.

Prolific Authors may work on more than one project at a time, or may be researching for one at the same time as writing another. In essence, they operate their own small firms and, thus, must keep records of all tax-deductible expenses. In addition, Authors may find they need to supplement their sporadic book income with freelance writing or part- or full-time jobs, as well as lecturing at writers' conferences, or at colleges or universities.

Salaries

Authors can earn yearly anywhere from nothing (if they cannot sell their work) to $100,000 or far more. Because many Authors write on a part-time basis, statistics on their earnings is nearly impossible to determine. For salaried writers and Authors, median annual earnings for 2003 were $42,790 (an hourly wage of $20.56), with a low of $21,320 and a high of $85,140.

Beginning novelists can earn advances (payment of agreed-upon money before the submission of the manuscript to the publisher) from $500 to $10,000 or more, but the majority of published written material never earns enough royalties (which are typically percentages of the retail price) beyond this initial advance.

Genre novels, such as mysteries, science fiction, horror, romances, and westerns, are steady moneymakers. Nonfiction books, especially if they concern hot topics of the moment, can bring high advances and earn royalties spread over a longer window of time. However, most books—especially those with information that becomes quickly dated—go out of print within a year of publication. Scientific and technical Authors generally earn more money than most other nonfiction Authors.

Employment Prospects

A good many of the books or articles submitted for publication are rejected. It is not uncommon for Authors to wait months, or even years, to sell their books, even with the help of an agent.

Once published, it frequently is difficult for an author to get a second manuscript accepted by the same publisher if there were only moderate sales on the initial one. It is sometimes necessary to find another publisher for the next manuscript. Some Authors prefer to have different publishers for their differing types of work (possibly, one publisher for fiction work, another for nonfiction work), or even to use pen names to distinguish between different types of writing (for example, juvenile and adult markets) or different series of books (say, detective series featuring a different main character).

Advancement Prospects

Upon being published, an author's chances of getting other writings into print increase significantly. If an author's work continues to be published, the cumulative effect greatly helps prospects for new writing projects with the same publisher or other publishers.

Education and Training

For nonfiction, an undergraduate degree is useful. If the writer is positioned as an expert in a specialized field, an advanced degree in that specialty usually is necessary. Fic-

tion writers rely more on their own creativity and ingenuity than any particular form of education, though an undergraduate degree is useful for a broader viewpoint.

Experience, Skills, and Personality Traits

Any kind of writing experience, such as a school newspaper or magazine, a creative writing class, or a media internship, is good training.

Authors have to be very imaginative and self-disciplined and have to spend a great deal of time alone. They will be forced to persevere both in perfecting their craft and handling rejection. Writers cannot afford to be discouraged but press onward and believe in what they are doing.

Unions and Associations

Major national writers' associations include the Association of Authors and Publishers, the American Society of Journalists and Authors, the Author's Guild, the Authors League of America, the National Writers Association, the National Writers Guild, and the PEN American Center. Other organizations represent a wide range of specialized interests. Major women's groups include the International Women's Writing Guild and the National League of American PEN Women. The Writers Guild of America is a union representing radio, television, and film scriptwriters (and any authors who write in these genres as well).

Tips for Entry

1. Read book reviews in trade and consumer publications to learn what qualities and techniques in a book are admired or frowned upon.
2. Study trade and consumer publications (or go online to such sites as the Writer's Market at http://www.writersmarket.com) to learn what categories of books, or topics for articles, are popular in the current marketplace and what else is happening in publishing.
3. Familiarize yourself with styling and formatting guidelines for submission of manuscripts and articles. Check with the *Chicago Manual of Style* for style and either the *Writer's Guide,* or *Writers Marketplace* for information on specific publishers and publications to which you may submit your material.
4. Attend local writers' seminars or access writer's chat rooms or free information sites (such as Dan Poynter's Para Publishing at http://parapub.com) on the Internet to learn tips on the industry and to get feedback on your writing.
5. Check online at Web sites of favorite contemporary Authors (as well as articles by writers in such published guides as the Writer's Guide, or the Writer's Marketplace) to see if they provide biographical background describing how they broke into the writing field and/or their tips for becoming successful in the field.

GHOSTWRITER/COLLABORATOR

CAREER PROFILE

Duties: Work with author to write, rewrite, and edit/proof-read books and articles

Alternate Title(s): None

Salary Range: If the Author receives no credit, $5,000 to $70,000 per project, plus expenses. For an "as told to" project (working with a well-known public person): advance plus 50 percent of royalties, typically $10,000 to $30,000. If a self-publishing project, $30 to $95 an hour, or $115 to $185 per book page. Research time expended is an additional fee.

Employment Prospects: Fair

Advancement Prospects: Fair

Prerequisites:

Education or Training—High school diploma or undergraduate degree in communications, English, journalism, or liberal arts; writing courses a plus

Experience—Background as an author, journalist, or freelance writer helpful

Special Skills and Personality Traits—Excellent editing, organization. and research skills; ability to replicate another writer's style

CAREER LADDER

```
┌─────────────────────────────────────────┐
│    Seasoned Ghostwriter/Collaborator     │
└─────────────────────────────────────────┘

┌─────────────────────────────────────────┐
│   Established Ghostwriter/Collaborator   │
└─────────────────────────────────────────┘

┌─────────────────────────────────────────┐
│     Novice Ghostwriter/Collaborator      │
└─────────────────────────────────────────┘
```

Position Description

While hardly exciting or glamorous, ghostwriting can be quite lucrative. Many books and articles by well-known personalities are in actuality written, rewritten, and/or edited by professional writers who receive little or no credit. The celebrity or expert provides the raw material—sometimes just the basic idea or even just the assignment topic—and the writer constructs a publishable work.

While Ghostwriters' work may differ from project to project, they may do all or part of the researching, interviewing, writing, and editing. In other cases, they may only provide the first draft. Sometimes Ghostwriters are hired to rewrite or edit manuscripts or articles. In order to become the mirror or voice of the subject, a Ghostwriter must do thorough research to be familiar with the subject's manner of expression and level of knowledge on the given subject.

Most ghostwriting is in the nonfiction category, such as articles or papers prepared for businesspeople, politicians, professionals, or academic and scientific individuals who wish to gain recognition and standing through authorship. Many luminaries hire Ghostwriters to write their celebrity autobiographies, just as many experts may require a Ghostwriter to write their textbook or nonfiction book. In addition, some well-known novelists have Ghostwriters fashion parts of their novel for them from their story idea.

Sometime Ghostwriters may be acknowledged in an introduction to a book, or receive credit on the cover and title page using the phrase "with" or "as told to." However, many Ghostwriters prefer to remain anonymous, or are required to do so by their contracts. While invisible to the reading public, these writers gain recognition within the publishing industry by their record of accomplishment in the field.

Collaboration is a more noticeable type of ghostwriting which often involves working in tandem with another writer or celebrity. Collaborators usually share in the tasks of research, revising, and writing.

Ghostwriting or collaborating is an excellent method for writers to get their own works published once their reputation is established. Similarly, it is a way to establish a reputation to pursue other freelance work, such as editing. Some Ghostwriters/Collaborators, however, do no other kind of writing.

Salaries

Pay will differ according to the scope of the project, the fame of the celebrity or expert involved, and the experience of the writer. Higher earnings will come if the book is published under the name of the celebrity or expert. Business articles for trade publications can earn from $500 to $5,000 if published under someone else's byline.

For books, the variables include whether the author is self-publishing or not, and whether the Ghostwriter/Collaborator receives an acknowledgement in the form of an "as told to" line or not. If the latter, the Ghostwriter/Collaborator's fee usually include a portion of the advance and up to 50 percent of the royalties. If the book is self-published, the hourly rate fee varies from $25 low to $55 mid-range to $85 high (with payment by book page from a low of $125 per hour to a high of $175 per hour.

If a Ghostwriter/Collaborator is not receiving any form of public credit, the charged fee may vary from $5,000 to $50,000, depending upon the type of project, and the fee is usually paid in installments throughout the writing of the project.

Employment Prospects

The continued popularity of celebrity books, along with the escalating number of specialized and trade publications that require specific expertise, helps to guarantee opportunities for Ghostwriters and Collaborators. The majority of these writers live near large urban centers with publishing and entertainment industries as well as specialized researching facilities.

Advancement Prospects

Upon successfully working with an author, either as a Ghostwriter or a Collaborator, the chances of securing further such work increases significantly. As a Ghostwriter or Collaborator becomes known within the publishing world from continued achievements with other authors, the cumulative effect greatly helps prospects for new work with the same or other clients.

Education and Training

While there are no minimum education requirements, specialized knowledge and degrees in business, professional, or technical fields are necessary for Collaborators working in

those fields, and are extremely helpful for Ghostwriters writing on such topics.

Experience, Skills, and Personality Traits

Most Ghostwriters and Collaborators are experienced freelance business and magazine article writers, or journalists, or authors. It often is difficult getting published and, thus, many writers break into publishing by ghosting or collaborating with an established author or recognized authority in a field and using their new credentials to help sell their own projects.

Good researching, interviewing, writing, editing, and interpersonal skills are paramount. Even more important Ghostwriters and Collaborators must be able to replicate another author's writing style and level of knowledge on the given topic.

Unions and Associations

Major national writers' associations include the American Society of Journalists and Authors, the Association of Authors and Publishers, the Author's Guild, the Authors League of America, the National Writers Association, the National Writers Guild, and the PEN American Center. Other organizations represent a wide range of specialized interests. Major women's groups include the International Women's Writing Guild and the National League of American PEN Women. The Writers Guild of America is a union representing radio, television, and film scriptwriters (and any authors who write in these genres as well).

Tips for Entry

1. Visit the Web sites of the above-mentioned writers' groups to learn industry guidelines.
2. Read a selection of books or articles in the field(s) in which you feel most knowledgeable to determine if you would be comfortable with, and able to write about, the topic in the style of the authors you are studying as examples.
3. Learn more about ghostwriting and collaborating on the Internet. To generate a list of relevant Web sites, enter the keywords *ghostwriting or book collaborator* in any search engine. These hits will provide examples of how established Ghostwriters and Collaborators promote their services and the scope of typical credentials in the field(s).
4. Establish your own Web site to promote your services. Create a brochure/flyer to send to book publishers alerting them of your availability. Take classified ads in pertinent industry magazines to publicize your services.
5. Network at local/regional writers' seminars and online chat groups.

POET

CAREER PROFILE

Duties: Create various forms of verse and poems for books and magazines

Alternate Title(s): None

Salary Range: Up to $3 a line, and sometimes more

Employment Prospects: Poor to Fair

Advancement Prospects: Poor to Fair

Prerequisites:

  Education or Training—Undergraduate degree in English or liberal arts; if writing for self-expression to be published or self-published, no requirements

  Experience—Background in creative writing helpful

  Special Skills and Personality Traits—Thorough knowledge of English language and grammar; understanding of discipline of poetry

CAREER LADDER

```
┌─────────────────────────────┐
│       Seasoned Poet         │
└─────────────────────────────┘

┌─────────────────────────────┐
│           Poet              │
└─────────────────────────────┘

┌─────────────────────────────┐
│       Amateur Poet          │
└─────────────────────────────┘
```

Position Description

Poetry is a creative form of writing that uses a heightened language and rhythm to express emotions, concepts, and visual images in an intensively imaginative way. There are three fundamental types of poetry: dramatic, which is action-oriented; lyric, which details personal emotions and also includes verses for songs; and narrative, which tells a story. Each of these categories has several specific forms. For example, free verse has no meter or rhythm, necessarily, but permits the Poet to create lines of any given length. On the other hand, haiku poems are structured with a rigid three-line format, with five, seven, and five syllables per line respectively.

Many persons write poetry as a leisure pursuit. Professional Poets publish their works in academic, literary, and some consumer magazines. Infrequently, poems are published in book form, either in anthologies or in collections of a single Poet. Beginning Poets may find their debut publication in book form to be in what is known as a *chapbook,* a smaller collection of poems of a single author put together in booklet form averaging 24 to 50 pages in length and, usually, in a digest form (5$^1/_2$ by 8$^1/_2$ inches) rather than a traditional book size. While chapbooks do not generally attract reviews or qualify for poetry prizes,

they provide an excellent venue for a Poet to begin establishing a reputation as a published writer. Another popular avenue of circulating one's poetry is through a personal Web site or through specialized Internet sites (e.g., http://www.poetry.com, http://www.poems.com), some of the latter sponsoring poetry contests. Some Poets have established Internet blogs, which are designed with lists of links to other Poets and contain information about where to publish poetry online.

Some Poets write traditional, humorous, and inspirational verse for greeting-card publishers, while others write lyrics for songs and plays.

The vast majority of today's Poets earn their income as instructors of creative writing, English, freelance writing, literature, or poetry. Very few individuals are able to make a living from just publishing their poetry.

Salaries

While relatively few Poets earn very much for their output, the large growth of literary and academic magazines in the United States has expanded the market for poetry. While some of these periodicals (and some publishers) still pay only in free copies (usually two or more) rather than money, many more now offer payment for publication. Payments vary from $1.50 to $3 per line, from $5 to $75 per page, or from $5 to $150 per poem.

Books of poems sell only marginally, usually only a few hundred copies, and advances are negligible, at best several hundred dollars. Small poetry collections known as chapbooks have a presently small—but growing—market. Many Poets publish in periodicals (though the competition for publication is intense), or they self-publish in hard copy or on the Internet. Most publishers (books and periodicals) revert the copyright to the Poet upon publication.

There are also many poetry contests available, usually with an entry fee, and, again, the competition is fierce for the monetary awards involved. There is also assistance available in the form of fellowships or grants.

Employment Prospects

Selling poetry is a difficult task. The markets include academic and literary magazines, some general-interest magazines and newspapers, as well as Web sites. The book publishers to investigate are usually small presses or those that specialize in poetry. Then, there is always self-publishing both in hard copy and/or in electronic format.

Advancement Prospects

By being published (even if but a single poem at a time in journals, collections, or on Web sites), a poet's chances of getting other poetry into print increase significantly. If a Poet continues to be published successfully in periodicals (or achieves sales success in a self-publishing format), the cumulative effect greatly enhances the possibilities that a full volume may be published devoted to the poet's work. From there, a career (either part time or full time) as a Poet becomes feasible.

Education and Training

Most professional and successful Poets have extensive backgrounds in creative writing, English, literature, and poetry. An undergraduate degree in English or liberal arts is excellent preparation and typically necessary for understanding the range of poetry formats. Graduate degrees, preferably a Ph.D., are required for college-level teaching positions.

Experience, Skills, and Personality Traits

Many Poets join writing groups and reading groups to read their work aloud for critiques and the sharing of ideas, as well as publishing their poetry on the Internet or sharing it with members of specialized online chat groups. Obviously, command of the English language (a good vocabulary and good grammar skills) is essential. An immersion in poetry of all kinds will help in developing skills.

In the marketing of their written work, Poets need to study the available markets and learn the requisite methods of submission of poetry for publication. To get published usually takes a great deal of patience and persistence.

Unions and Associations

Associations for Poets include the Academy of American Poets; Associated Writing Programs; the Authors Guild; National Writers Association; National Writers Union; PEN American Center; and the Poetry Society of America. The National Federation of State Poetry Societies can supply information on state poetry organizations. There are also associations, such as Poets & Writers, Inc., which publish both directories of their members or others in their field and newsletters and/or monthly magazines. They frequently also sponsor contests and workshops.

Tips for Entry

1. Consult the *Poet's Market* publication as well as specialized poetry magazines for guidelines for submission and to note the range of poetry formats and subject matter they currently publish.
2. Expand your knowledge of past and contemporary poetry by visiting Academy of American Poets (http://www.poets.org), Library of Congress Poetry 180 (http://www.loc.gov/poetry/180), and Poetry Archives (http://www.emule.com/poetry).
3. Besides submitting poetry to hard copy and online publications and contests, consider setting up your own webpage to publish your poetry and allow for reader feedback. This could create a portfolio of credentials to pave the way for future publication in magazines, newspapers, books, and Internet sites.
4. Join a chat group to gain feedback on your poetry and to network with others interested in this field. Do a search at http://groups.yahoo.com.

COMMERCIAL ARTS

CATALOG COPYWRITER

CAREER PROFILE

Duties: Write copy for catalogs for businesses and nonprofit institutions

Alternate Title(s): None

Salary Range: $25,000 to $50,000

Employment Prospects: Fair

Advancement Prospects: Fair

Prerequisites:

Education or Training—Undergraduate degree in advertising, art, business, communications, or liberal arts; degree in marketing is recommended

Experience—Background as a journalist or other professional writing experience helpful

Special Skills and Personality Traits—Creativity, command of English language, imagination

CAREER LADDER

```
┌─────────────────────────────┐
│   Copy Supervisor or        │
│   Promotion Manager         │
└─────────────────────────────┘

┌─────────────────────────────┐
│   Catalog Copywriter        │
└─────────────────────────────┘

┌─────────────────────────────┐
│  Administrative Assistant or │
│  College Student            │
└─────────────────────────────┘
```

Position Description

Catalog Copywriters write the text of catalogs for businesses and stores, and other profit and nonprofit institutions, such as art galleries, auction houses, foundations, museums, and other similar institutions.

Many Catalog Copywriters are freelance writers hired for this specific position. Others are employed by the in-house public relations department of businesses or nonprofit institutions. Their jobs are quite demanding, as their copy will determine the success of the catalog for which it is being written, and the promotional, sales, or information campaigns, if any, that are using these catalogs. While working hours are the usual weekday hours, overtime will be necessary when deadlines have to be met.

Catalog Copywriters must work closely with the catalog's overall designers. These copywriters have to be imaginative and able to create a mood with their words as they describe the items in the catalog. This copy, generally, must be informative, but not heavily detailed. Each item in the catalog usually contains only three or four lines for description, so the catalog copy must be well-organized, succinct, and clear, while it appeals to the potential buyer or user. Its format and content are typically preset by the copywriter's supervisor; however, research may be a part of the catalog copywriter's job.

Catalog Copywriters usually report to a copy supervisor, an advertising manager, a promotion manager, or a sales manager. They must work with graphic artists who are designing the layout of the catalog, and work within the limitations set for its format. Strict deadlines usually mean long working hours. While it is not a high-pressure post, it can become one as deadlines become imminent.

Salaries

Most Catalog Copywriters earn around $28,000, although salaries can range from $25,000 to $50,000, depending upon experience, responsibilities, and employer. For freelance Catalog Copywriters, generally, hourly wages range from $20 to $50, with a variety of flat rates attached to different types of catalogs. The Copywriters' Council of America, a marketer of freelance copywriting talent, charges $200 to $750 per page in a catalog, or a brochure.

Employment Prospects

Although catalog copywriting jobs may not appear as attractive as some editorial jobs, catalogs are an integral part of the promotional and informational efforts of many businesses and institutions, and Catalog Copywriters are a critical resource in creating these important communications, making prospects for this job position very competitive.

Advancement Prospects

Skilled copywriters, generally, can advance to managerial positions in advertising, promotion, or sales. The immediate career promotion for Catalog Copywriters is that of a copy supervisor.

Education and Training

An undergraduate degree in advertising or communications is preferable for all copywriting positions. A degree in liberal arts would be helpful, as well as a bachelor's degree in marketing. In addition, for specific types of catalogs, further degrees in art or business may be necessary. Most Catalog Copywriters have a well-rounded educational background, which allows them to write copy on all kinds of topics.

Experience, Skills, and Personality Traits

A background in advertising or promotion should be supplemented with extensive writing experience. An enthusiasm for the products that a copywriter is describing will come across well in the final copy used.

A Catalog Copywriter must have an excellent command of language and superior organizational skills. Likewise a firm knowledge of production, including typography and layout, is necessary for this position. Specific background, such as in art, business, or finance, may be required for individual catalog projects.

Unions and Associations

Major professional organizations of interest for copywriters include the American Advertising Federation, the American Marketing Association, the American Society of Magazine Editors, and the Copywriter's Council of America. There are also more specialized groups, such as the Advertising Club of America, or the Association for Women in Communications.

Tips for Entry

1. Study catalogs you receive in the mail or see online to determine if this aspect of writing appeals to you.
2. Contact local advertising or business groups to network with people already in the field who can provide tips on the pros and cons of this field and, perhaps, suggest, entry-level positions opening up in the area.
3. Write sample catalog copy for actual or fictional products to create a portfolio to present to potential employers.

GREETING CARD/GIFT IDEA WRITER

CAREER PROFILE

Duties: Write verse and sentiments for greeting cards; prepare copy for sale of novelty items

Alternate Title(s): None

Salary Range: $25 to more than $300 per sentiment or slogan, depending on size of the firm and whether artwork is included

Employment Prospects: Fair to good

Advancement Prospects: Fair to good

Prerequisites:

Education or Training—Undergraduate degree in English or liberal arts

Experience—Background in creative writing necessary

Special Skills and Personality Traits—Appreciation of what draws a sender to a card or novelty item; capacity to be clever, fresh, original, and innovative, while being both sincere and succinct in expression

CAREER LADDER

```
┌─────────────────────────────────┐
│  High-Profile Greeting Card Writer │
└─────────────────────────────────┘

┌─────────────────────────────────┐
│  Experienced Greeting Card Writer  │
└─────────────────────────────────┘

┌─────────────────────────────────┐
│    Novice Greeting Card Writer     │
└─────────────────────────────────┘
```

Position Description

Greeting Card Writers compose poetry and writings suitable for publication on a broad range of greeting cards. Some utilize traditional or inspirational feelings in prose, or humorous verse, either rhymed or rhymeless, and often witty sayings or amusing phrases. Gift Ideas Writers provide humorous slogans for novelties, such as banners, buttons, magnets, or stickers.

According to Sandra Miller-Louden, a veteran Greeting Card Writer, teacher, and author, the "greeting card market is one of the most profitable and high-paying markets for writers." Miller-Louden notes that "greeting card writing is unique in that it is an interactive genre. The Greeting Card Writer is that anonymous third voice between two other people, the card sender and the card recipient."

A successful greeting card will attract the buyer/sender by its universal sentiment, but makes the sender think of the person who will be receiving it. The successful slogan will be original, possibly provocative or irreverent, but always heartfelt and frequently funny.

While larger greeting card companies have their own staff, many of them still buy freelance ideas for cards. According to the Greeting Cards Association, today there are cards for every kind of relationship, for every occasion, for every ethnic group, every age group, every gender, and every special interest group. According to the association, more than 90 percent of American households purchase at least one card a year, and the average participating American household purchases 35 separate cards per year.

Of all the greeting cards purchased, roughly half are geared for holidays, with Christmas being the favorite season by far. Next come Valentine's Day, Mother's Day, Easter, and Father's Day.

Some greeting card companies that draw on freelance writers require illustrations to be submitted along with the copy, while others prefer to use their own illustrations. Even then, suggestions on artwork may be welcomed.

When the Greeting Card Association was founded in 1941, there were only 100 greeting card publishers with approximately $43 million in sales. Today, the industry generates more than $7.5 billion in retail sales divided among more than 2,000 greeting card publishers, indicating strong growth of the industry. While much of that $7.5 billion profit is spent on artwork, paper, and printing, there are still excellent employment opportunities in the industry.

A growing share of the market for greeting cards is being held by electronic greeting cards available either free or from membership Web sites. Individuals can choose pictures with or without words, sometimes accompanied by animation and sound, and then write a personal message. The card is sent electronically, just like e-mail.

Salaries

The greeting card industry is growing more competitive. Some companies like to receive a résumé of past experience and a business card along with the card ideas. Others prefer card ideas to be submitted on index cards. Nearly all require that self-addressed stamped envelopes (SASEs) be included. Freelancers should contact the greeting card company first to determine their submission policies.

Most companies pay per idea, while a few pay per line. Almost none pay any kind of royalty. The range of pay is anywhere between $3 per line of poetry to $15 to $250 per verse.

Some companies have their own writing staffs and do not accept any freelance work. Most Greeting Card Writers, if not employed full time by a greeting-card company, work at other kinds of freelance writing, or have other types of work altogether.

Employment Prospects

Competition is fairly stiff for full-time employment, and those with the most experience have the best chance. However, it is a lucrative market for freelance writers, as well as a good training ground for learning to write succinctly. The most important step is studying the market, as well as studying the specific guidelines for each company before making a submission.

Advancement Prospects

When a writer's card writing is accepted and used by a company, chances of getting other work from that firm or other organizations increase significantly. If a writer's work continues to be utilized within the industry, the cumulative effect greatly helps prospects for a full career as a Greeting Card Writer.

Education and Training

If freelancers have a great idea, most companies are not concerned with their educational background. They are, however, interested in the writer's experience. Most freelancers of greeting cards have undergraduate degrees in communications, creative writing, journalism, or liberal arts. Some companies request a résumé, along with a listing of experience.

Experience, Skills, and Personality Traits

Excellent command of the English language is essential. Creativity, imagination, and originality in finding new avenues to express a well-known sentiment are important. A tremendous sense of humor and abundance of ideas are exceedingly useful.

Unions and Associations

The Greeting Card Association is the primary organization for Greeting Card Writers, and provides an industry market list for artists and writers.

Tips for Entry

1. Study greeting cards at local stores to appreciate the range of creativity and vocabulary essential for preparing effective copy.
2. Create sample cards for assorted occasions to submit to a potential employer.
3. Attend local or regional gift shows to network within the profession for possible (freelance) work.
4. Consult the Greeting Card Association (http://www.greetingcard.org) for a membership list to seek potential full-time or freelance work.
5. Learn more about electronic greeting cards on the Internet. To generate a list of relevant Web sites, enter the keywords *greeting cards* on any search engine. These sites are excellent venues to contact for breaking into the field.

JINGLE WRITER

Duties: Writes lyrics for commercial advertising vehicles

Alternate Title(s): None

Salary Range: $100 to $8,000 or more per jingle package

Employment Prospects: Fair

Advancement Prospects: Poor to Fair

Prerequisites:

Education or Training—An undergraduate degree in English, music, writing, or other liberal or fine arts field is preferred

Experience—Some writing skill desirable; for the music side, no experience required

Special Skills and Personality Traits—Ability to write words that are catchy and easy to sing to; knack of molding a singing verse around a commercial idea or motto; ability to take directions; business and public-relations skills; self-discipline

```
┌─────────────────────────────┐
│   High-Profile Jingle Writer │
└─────────────────────────────┘

┌─────────────────────────────┐
│   Experienced Jingle Writer  │
└─────────────────────────────┘

┌─────────────────────────────┐
│     Novice Jingle Writer     │
└─────────────────────────────┘
```

Position Description

Jingle Writers are songwriters or lyricists who specialize in writing for radio, television, and Internet commercials. They may also compose the music for the jingle, or they may utilize a musical collaborator. Fitting words to music is not an acquired skill but essentially a natural talent. The prime responsibility of Jingle Writers is to represent their client's thoughts musically as directed and not crowd too many ideas into the client's message. Often the client decides the length of the jingle, the specific lines that have to be worked into the verse, as well as the deadline for the material.

A jingle can be contained in a broadcast advertisement as a short, spoken verse, alternating with background music, or the entire commercial can consist of an ear-catching song, the words of which provide all the needed information about the product or service. Usually, a combination of these two approaches is used.

For jingle writing, the critical thing is to be sure that the verse highlights the name of the product or service. The ability to write (and compose) quickly is the prerequisite for a successful Jingle Writer.

Most Jingle Writers work for music production houses or recording studios, and some for advertising agencies, which may have an in-house music department with a staff of songwriters, lyric creators (Jingle Writers), and producers. Other Jingle Writers are freelancers. While jingle writing may be considered less important than actual songwriting, jingle verse is heard instantly by millions on television, radio, and the Internet, and many have appealing tunes accompanying them.

Many Jingle Writers are songwriters (lyricists) and/or musicians as well, with many songwriters starting out as Jingle Writers. Their clients may include video-game makers or movie music supervisors, as well as producers of advertising commercials.

Salaries

Freelance Jingle Writers usually sell their work as a complete package—words and music together. Either they compose both parts, or they have a partner who provides the music. Jingle packages can sell for anywhere from $1,000 to $20,000 or more, depending upon the employer.

The fees paid to a writer for preparing a radio or television jingle can range from minimum compensation to well over $250,000, depending upon the type of advertising campaign envisioned (i.e., national, local, test), the budget set for the music, and whether the writer is an independent free-lance consultant, a member of a jingle production company, or an employee of the advertising agency responsible for the campaign. Jingle production companies offer a wider range of services and expertise, so the amount of money paid to them by the advertising agency will be much greater than that paid to an individual Jingle Writer. Also, higher fees are guaranteed if the writer/composer has a hit song that the agency wants to use, or if the Jingle Writer is a successful recording artist who wants to create and perform music for advertisements.

Employment Prospects

Breaking into the field of jingle writing is difficult, but not impossible. Competition is stiff for both full-time employment (in a jingle production company or advertising agency) and freelancing. Yet there are always fresh opportunities for talented people. A freelancer who submits jingle material on speculation should send a tape-recorded sample either to an advertising agency or to a jingle production house that supplies agencies with new material. Obviously, an established Jingle Writer will find jobs more easily than beginners, but any writer will find it difficult to market a jingle without a familiarity with the agency's philosophy, or the firm's workings, style, and procedures. Submissions should consist of about six jingles of 30 to 60 seconds in length, and jingles should follow each other with only a brief fade-out between them. Agency requirements can be obtained from the *Songwriter's Market* book, published annually. Most agencies (and production companies) lease usage rights from the Jingle Writer/composer. Problems of an independent freelance Jingle Writer/composer include keeping up with the music industry's never-ending stream of new equipment, and the increasing use of synthesizers and computers to replace musicians.

Advancement Prospects

The acceptance of a freelance jingle writer's work increases the possibilities of getting more such assignments. For full-time Jingle Writers, the more experience they have the better, and the easier it will be to find good positions in other firms when changing employers.

Education and Training

There are no academic requirements for work as a Jingle Writer, but prior courses in creative writing and music are helpful. Undergraduate degrees in English, music, or other liberal or fine arts are typical in this field. A thorough knowledge of musical theory and a familiarity with both old standards and new current pop music is important. It is noteworthy that in 2003 there was even a course given at Nazareth College in Rochester, New York, in jingle writing.

Experience, Skills, and Personality Traits

Nothing succeeds as well as experience, but the challenge is to get it. Spending time in a music or recording studio as an observer will provide a grounding in how the system works.

Jingle writers often start with copy provided by the advertising agency, the client, or the jingle production company, so the need for flexibility is paramount. Also, the ability to work quickly—providing almost immediate turnaround—is a big plus in winning more jobs after the first one. Business and public relations skills, self-composure, tactfulness, self-discipline, and versatility are all qualities of a successful Jingle Writer.

Unions and Associations

Most lyricists, Jingle Writers, and musicians join one of the performing-rights organizations—American Society of Composers, Authors, and Publishers (ASCAP); Broadcast Music Inc. (BMI); and SESAC Inc. and/or specific guilds. The Songwriters Guild of America and the Dramatists Guild of America are open to lyricists and Jingle Writers. Guild membership entitles members to have contract review, health insurance, participation in seminars and workshops, as well as networking. Membership in a recognized performing-rights organization helps to guarantee a valid distribution of royalties. Other groups include the Advertising Club of America, the Council of Writers Organizations, the National Association of Composers, the Songwriters & Lyricists Club, and Songwriters Resources and Services.

Tips for Entry

1. Study jingles you hear on radio, television, and the Internet. With repeated listening you can break down the ingredients of the work and better judge its merits in effectively getting its message across to listeners.
2. Prepare sample jingles of existing or fictitious products and services to create a portfolio of audio and written samples.
3. Learn more about the world of jingle writing on the Internet. To generate a list of relevant Web sites, enter the keywords *jingle writer* in any search engine. These hits will provide examples of how established Jingle Writers promote their services and the scope of typical credentials in the field.
4. To explore opportunities in this field, investigate such guides as *Songwriter's Market.*

FILM, THEATER, AND SONG

LYRICIST

CAREER PROFILE

Duties: Write lyrics for musical compositions used in films, musicals, songs, and television

Alternate Title(s): Songwriter

Salary Range: $0 to unlimited

Employment Prospects: Fair

Advancement Prospects: Fair

Prerequisites:

Education or Training—An undergraduate degree in fine arts, humanities, liberal arts, or music is beneficial; knowledge of counterpoint, harmony, music theory, and standard and popular song is crucial

Experience—No experience required

Special Skills and Personality Traits—Ability to write "singable" lyrics; creativity and imagination; business and public-relations skills; a good feel for current popular music trends; self-discipline; versatility

CAREER LADDER

```
┌─────────────────────────────┐
│     Seasoned Lyricist       │
└─────────────────────────────┘

┌─────────────────────────────┐
│    Experienced Lyricist     │
└─────────────────────────────┘

┌─────────────────────────────┐
│      Novice Lyricist        │
└─────────────────────────────┘
```

Position Description

A Lyricist must fit words to music, but must also relate a story in fewer words than an actual narrative would take. The story should not be complicated and it should have a definite point of view. One of the most essential common denominators of a good song, says producer John Ryan, is "simplicity." Fitting words to music is not a science or a learned skill—it is a talent. Yet, talent alone is not enough. It is a craft (like tapestry weaving or woodworking), and, as such, needs to be learned (for instance, what is a true rhyme, or how to scan verse).

Lyricists often are also the composers of the song's music as well, or they may create lyrics for a previously written piece of music, or they may collaborate with a musician on new material. Many Lyricists (especially when writing for musicals, films, or television) actually write the lyrics first and then the music is composed to fit the words.

As a writer, not a musician, Lyricists still must understand the difference between a poem and a song. They need a sense of the phrasing, meter, and mood of music even if they cannot write the melody. In addition, they need to look for what is called a "hook," that is, something that makes the lyric memorable and holds it all together. If writing to music already created, the Lyricist needs to find the strongest notes of the music to hang that hook in order to create an unforgettable song. Thus, the song lyric is a very restricted and structured art form.

Staff Lyricists or songwriters are employed by videogame makers, music publishers, movie companies, record producers, and stage producers, and write exclusively for their employer. On the other hand, songwriters may be hired by, or collaborate with, composer/musicians. Lyricists may also write for specialty markets, such as children's songs, Christian, Christmas, folk/Americana, or Latin songs, and so forth. They also may work on assignment, tailoring songs (and lyrics) for a specific vocal artist.

The lifestyle of Lyricists is hardly "normal" in the sense of keeping regular employment hours. They can count on nighttime and weekend work, have little or no job security, and seldom become famous. However, songwriting can be an extremely lucrative profession.

Salaries

Lyricists can sell songs for one-time flat fees, or on a royalty basis. The usual advance against royalties is $5,000 to $7,500. Fees for songwriters employed by film producers to write new material for a motion picture will depend on the nature of the production, the stature and previous success of the writer(s), the music budget, and the power of the agent involved. Fees can range from below $1,000 to over $100,000 for a song before royalties. For existing songs used in a film, fees can range between $15,000 and $60,000. Staff Lyricists receive a weekly salary, which may be treated as an advance on future royalty earnings.

Freelance Lyricists generate income by selling the rights to use one or more of their songs, usually done through a publisher. Lyricists' contracts with publishers are either for a single song or an exclusive right to their work.

A song's profits are split between the Lyricist and the publisher. According to the Songwriters Guild of America, a good minimum contract with a music publisher should pay the songwriter 50 percent of the gross receipts earned from mechanical reproduction (royalties from the sale of records and CDs, sheet music, or tapes), electronic transcriptions, performances, and synchronization. As Jeffrey and Todd Brabec point out in their book *Music, Money, and Success: The Insider's Guide to Making Money in the Music Industry,* effective January 1, 2004, the compulsory mechanical royalty rate has been increased to 8.5 cents per composition and $1.65 per minute. For example, if an album with a song is licensed at the contractual rate, the publisher and writer (or writers) of the composition would receive a combined 8.5 cents for each album sold during the years 2004 and 2005. The total royalties would be paid to the music publisher, who would then pay the songwriter(s) a share of these royalties dependent upon the terms of their songwriter agreement (usually 50 percent).

Three performing-rights organizations—American Society of Composers, Authors, and Publishers (ASCAP); Broadcast Music Inc. (BMI); and SESAC Inc.—monitor the performances of all members' music and handle payment of royalties. ASCAP uses a formula based on the number of performances within each media group (concert, film, radio, television, and so forth), and weights the performance by various factors to equalize possibility of performances not accounted for. This yields "credits," which are then multiplied by a standard figure. ASCAP then distributes the royalties to member songwriters (and/or Lyricists) based on the fee negotiated in their contract. Both BMI, the largest performing-arts organization in America, and SESAC operate similarly.

If the Lyricist is not the composer, the 50 percent share will be divided between the two songwriting partners. Successful songwriters can earn more than $500,000 a year, and some earn more than $1 million.

Employment Prospects

Freelance Lyricists and songwriters may be contracted to write "work-for-hire" lyrics that are owned and copyrighted by the employer. Songwriters may also work on their own, or under a part-time contract with various companies.

Competition for staff Lyricist positions is very tough. Breaking into the field as a freelancer is difficult, but there are opportunities for talented people. And the need for Lyricists is only increasing.

Advancement Prospects

Success in writing lyrics, whether on staff or freelance, greatly enhances chances of getting other work. The more experience a Lyricist or songwriter has, the more accomplished the lyrics will become and the greater will be the possibilities of a flourishing and prosperous career.

Education and Training

There are really no educational prerequisites for work as a Lyricist, but a background in music and/or writing is definitely needed. Undergraduate degrees in English, music, or other liberal arts or fine arts are normal.

Experience, Skills, and Personality Traits

Successful writing of song lyrics depends on the success of earlier efforts, and the trick is to get the first set of lyrics accepted. Familiarity with the film, recording, song publishing, and theater industries will help achieve that success. Spending time in a music or recording studio as an observer will give good insight into the operation of the system.

Skills for Lyricists and songwriters must include the ability to write clearly, to work accommodatingly with the music's composer, and the willingness to compromise.

Unions and Associations

Most Lyricists and songwriters join one of the performing-rights organizations—ASCAP, BMI, or SESAC—and/or other guilds. Membership in a performing-rights organization helps to guarantee a valid distribution of royalties, and an accurate tally of performances of any given work. Also, the U.S. Copyright Office can search its records and prepare a report upon request.

The primary association for Lyricists and songwriters is the Songwriters Guild of America. Guild membership entitles members to review contracts, health insurance, and participation in seminars and workshops. Other songwriters associations include the Guild of International Songwriters and Composers, the Nashville Songwriters Association International, and the National Academy of Songwriters, among others.

Tips for Entry

1. Study hit songs to break down their components and determine what ingredients successful songs have in common.
2. Expand your knowledge on a wide variety of contemporary topics so you have the ability to write lyrics on many subjects; reading books on the art of songwriting should be part of your education.

3. As with other forms of writing, daily practice in penning lyrics is the best way to hone your skills.

4. Working with a collaborator can provide useful feedback and encouragement, as can participating in lyric-writing workshops and seminars. A great resource on the Internet is the Songwriters Resource Network at http://www.songwritersresourcenetwork.com/page15.html.

5. Keep abreast of changing trends and participants in the various facets of the industry by reading trade publications (for instance, *Songwriter* magazine) and annual guides (for example, *Songwriter's Market*).

6. Prepare a portfolio of song lyrics in different genres, themes, and styles. When making a demo of your song, use a CD (compact disc) or a CD-R (recordable compact disc) to record your work to make it easier to submit to potential employers.

PLAYWRIGHT

CAREER PROFILE

Duties: Write dramatic and/or comedic scripts for public performance

Alternate Title(s): Dramatist

Salary Range: Highly variable, ranging from a percentage of the gross receipts of a performance, to a modest performance fee and royalties with a percentage of the receipts, to $1,000 or more per performance plus royalties and a percentage of the receipts

Employment Prospects: Fair

Advancement Prospects: Fair

Prerequisites:

Education or Training—Undergraduate degree in communications, creative writing, drama, English, or other liberal arts or fine arts subject; advanced courses (or degrees) in drama and writing helpful

Experience—None necessary to start; acting experience may be necessary

Special Skills and Personality Traits—Exceptional command of English; outstanding writing skills, particularly in dialogue; self-motivation; capacity to accept rejection before attaining success

CAREER LADDER

```
+-----------------------------+
|    Seasoned Playwright       |
+-----------------------------+

+-----------------------------+
|    Experienced Playwright    |
+-----------------------------+

+-----------------------------+
|     Novice Playwright        |
+-----------------------------+
```

Position Description

Unlike movies and television, where the words are often less important than the visual images, plays are words put together to examine characters. They are structures of character and dialogue. The goal of a Playwright is to establish a bond between the spectator and the stage, engaging the audience in the play's action and evoking empathy from the playgoer. The main tool of the Playwright is dialogue. Good stage dialogue is tricky to write. It must sound realistic, but not resemble the way in which real-life people speak. It must remain interesting, and furnish the audience with all the background information needed to understand the characters' motivations.

Like working on a novel, writing a play is a lonely labor of love. Playwrights usually create plays in their spare time, receiving income from some other source. As drama is a live medium, the Playwright must aim to make his work performable. Through ongoing study of playwriting and practical dramatic experience (for example, working with a local theater group), the beginning Playwright can learn how to write dialogue, how to structure scenes, and how to develop character through dialogue.

The written word is respected in the theater by the producer, cast, and director to a greater degree than in screenwriting or scriptwriting, in which it can be reworked without the author's permission. When the Playwright has found a theater or group that is interested in producing the play, his or her work is covered by a contract and no changes can be made without the author's approval. Once the play is finished, the Playwright needs to market it, get a reading of the play (local neighborhood theaters or drama departments of nearby schools and universities are a good place to start), get it produced, possibly published, and get an agent. Yet, even with an agent, a Playwright still has to network, establishing ties with directors, other Playwrights, producers, publishers, state art agencies, theaters, and so forth, to get his or her work noticed and performed.

If the work is a radio play, the Playwright must be familiar with narration, music, and sound effects.

Salaries

For playwriting, payment is not so much a salary as a payment for the finished work. Regional theater groups may offer a Playwright a flat $400 to $10,000 for a play, or negotiate a variety of payment schedules. Some theaters will pay a weekly sum set against a percentage of the box office, others pay per performance, sometimes setting one payment for the first performance and then a different one for each performance thereafter. Some theaters will offer only a percentage of the ticket receipts as well as travel and living expenses for the Playwright. Theaters often will negotiate a royalty payment, or offer a flat rate instead. Many of them will accept only agented submissions. Obviously, payment amounts depend upon the size of the theater and the previous success of the Playwright.

Publishers of plays generally offer 10 percent in royalties (some offer less), or will negotiate an outright purchase of the play from the Playwright.

Employment Prospects

Playwrights do not apply for jobs in the same manner as other writers or editors. Upon completing his or her play, the Playwright's job is mainly to market his or her play. As noted, there are established methods of getting a play read, performed, produced, and published. Drama departments usually are receptive to readings of plays by fledgling Playwrights, and community and regional theaters are always looking for new works. For a Playwright's first production, small and regional theaters are the best bet. Writing for play contests sometimes results in both a prize payment and a production. Again, there are procedures to be followed in the marketing of plays, most of which are outlined in any writer's market guide.

Advancement Prospects

Making a career of playwriting is enhanced, of course, by the success of the first play or the first several offerings. Advancement to a full career is based on luck, skill, and determination. There is also the possibility of moving from plays to television or films. There has always been a special cachet in Hollywood for successful Playwrights.

Education and Training

While an undergraduate degree in creative writing, drama, English, or other liberal or fine arts field is desirable, there are no specific educational requirements for a Playwright. Course work in acting and writing is advantageous. A general education provides a wider background upon which a Playwright can draw.

Experience, Skills, and Personality Traits

It is hard to gauge what and how much experience a Playwright needs. A number of authorities feel that only work in the theater itself, acting or backstage, will give the Playwright a sense of how actors transmit words to an audience and what works and what does not. Others need only the proof that a Playwright can write plays. Obviously, an excellent command of the English language is essential, as is the ability to write convincing dialogue. One winning play does not a career make, but it helps, and it gains attention for the Playwright in the follow-up effort.

Unions and Associations

There is no union for stage dramatists, unlike Playwrights who write for radio who join the Writers Guild of America—the union for television, motion picture, and radio writers. However, most stage Playwrights join the Dramatists Guild of America above all, to protect their rights to the play, to stay informed on standard business practices in the theater world, and to learn who or what organization is seeking scripts. Guild membership also offers help in emergencies, access to health insurance, subscriptions to Guild publications, and participation in Guild symposia and workshops. The Dramatists Guild is part of the Authors League of America. Playwrights may also want to join the National Writers Union, or the Playwrights' Center. For women, there is the International Women's Writing Guild.

Tips for Entry

1. Read plays, attend productions, and study theater critiques to learn what makes a successful play in today's climate.
2. Join an amateur dramatic group to learn all aspects of the theater, including the business end. Such participation can provide contacts within the local theater community with a view toward production of your play.
3. Stage informal readings of your current work in progress to gain useful feedback.
4. Submit your play for consideration by local/regional theater groups and playwriting contests, which will also help in the ongoing industry networking process.

SCRIPTWRITER/SCREENWRITER

CAREER PROFILE

Duties: Write scripts and/or screenplays for film, television, and radio

Alternate Title(s): None

Salary Range: $8,000 to $100,000 or more

Employment Prospects: Poor to Fair

Advancement Prospects: Poor to Fair

Prerequisites:

Education or Training—Undergraduate degree in communications, creative writing, English, or fine arts

Experience—Any media writing is helpful

Special Skills and Personality Traits—Imagination; production knowledge; writing ability

CAREER LADDER

```
┌─────────────────────────────────────────┐
│   Seasoned Scriptwriter/Screenwriter     │
└─────────────────────────────────────────┘

┌─────────────────────────────────────────┐
│   Experienced Scriptwriter/Screenwriter  │
└─────────────────────────────────────────┘

┌─────────────────────────────────────────┐
│    Novice Scriptwriter/Screenwriter      │
└─────────────────────────────────────────┘
```

Position Description

Scriptwriters may write for motion pictures, television, play production, or business videos. If a Scriptwriter writes exclusively for motion pictures, that person is a Screenwriter. The main difference between Scriptwriters/Screenwriters and playwrights is that playwrights tell stories verbally and Screenwriters tell stories visually. Or, as one authority puts it, "Film deals with events while [plays] look at the consequences of events." Therefore, film places less reliance on voice than the more verbal play.

A successful Scriptwriter/Screenwriter must be both a talented writer and a savvy businessperson. However, the marketing side must always be subordinate to the writing side. Writing for the entertainment industries, particularly film and television, can be both glamorous and lucrative. It is also highly unpredictable, demanding, and extremely competitive. (The Writers Guild of America registers some 30,000 new screenplays, treatments, and related material each year, whereas Hollywood studios produce only about 100 to 200 feature films annually.) Many scripts and screenplays that are commissioned never get produced, or get changed by so many writers that the original writer may not recognize the finished product, and may not even be credited in the final production.

In the heyday of the studio system in Hollywood, most Scriptwriters/Screenwriters worked under contract to a studio. Today, most Scriptwriters/Screenwriters work freelance on a project-by-project basis, or under short contracts, as for television, where a standard short contract for comedy series, variety programs, or soap operas lasts 13 weeks.

Usually producers will only consider an entire script or screenplay, unless the Scriptwriter/Screenwriter has a proven track record, whereupon the work can be commissioned or optioned on the basis of less—a "treatment," or "story," which is really an outline. According to Guild rules, writers are paid for all work, even outlines and the polishing of another's work. Beginners, however, usually have to work on speculation, that is, they are paid only on accepted work. They may meet with production executives to discuss ideas, a process called "pitching," or "spitballing." Such sessions can lead to being assigned to do a treatment. When writing a script for a given television show, it is important to understand how the characters speak, think, and interact, and write believable dialogue for characters that already exist. There is more freedom in writing an original movie screenplay (since it has an original story line and characters), but it still has to have believable dialogue, realistic characters, and a plausible plot.

Most Scriptwriters and Screenwriters employ agents to help them find work and negotiate contracts. It is also important to register the finished script or screenplay with the Writers Guild of America, the professional guild of Scriptwriters/Screenwriters. This is a service available to nonmembers (for a fee), and the registration of the script establishes the date on which the script was completed and gives it protection. The Guild also registers series formats, story lines, and step outlines; it has guidelines for screenplay and teleplay manuscript formats for nonmembers.

Scriptwriters and Screenwriters usually work on projects in stages and may not ever see the finished product. Some projects never get beyond the treatment stage; others are killed after the first draft. Often writers are called in to polish another writer's work. Payment for work commissioned is negotiated for each step. As the successful selling of scripts or screenplays is a full-time marketing job, it is difficult to write and sell them without living in Los Angeles, though some writers are based in New York City. The day-to-day contact and proximity to producers and studios are vital to that success.

Salaries

The earnings of Scriptwriters and Screenwriters vary enormously. Some never get paid anything. Others, if successful, can make a comfortable living even if they never get anything produced beyond their first success, while others sell lots of scripts even if their first one failed.

The first step is to sell an option (the right to buy the script within a given time period) to use the script, which generally pays the writer 10 percent of the total fee. If the script progresses to actual production, the writer gets the other 90 percent of the fee. Generally, after 18 months, most options end, freeing the Scriptwriter/Screenwriter to obtain another option on the work elsewhere. Some writers earn a living just selling options, never getting a script into production. According to the 2004 *Writer's Market,* options on feature films can range from a low of $1,500 to a high of $50,000, with the possibility of even higher fees up to $400,000.

Scriptwriters and Screenwriters may also receive credit on the final film or television script (also known as the teleplay). Because so many scripts are rewritten, receiving credit depends upon how much rewriting occurred and the industry clout of the writers involved.

Income also varies according to the medium (television, film, or radio), the length and type of script, and the other services that the writer provides, such as treatments, narrations, rewrites, and polishing. Additionally, income will vary if the writer is under contract to a network or studio to write scripts.

According to Guild figures from 1999, an original screenplay (including treatment) can pay from $43,952 to $82,444, whereas a nonoriginal screenplay (including treatment) brings anywhere from $29,536 to $60,456. Payments for a story (original or nonoriginal) and treatment may vary from $17,310 to $32,980. The 2004 *Writer's Market* survey indicates that an original screenplay (including treatment) brings anywhere from a low of $48,738 to a high of $91,495, with the median average being $70,117. This survey states further that business film scripts (training and information) can command a fee from $1,500 to $3,500 per project, whereas educational/training film scripts can get from $1,500 to $6,000 per project. These projects are sometimes paid per hour or by the running time (minutes) of the film.

Employment Prospects

As indicated previously, breaking into the film or television business is very difficult. An agent in Los Angeles is almost obligatory for most film and television work. Steady work is uncertain and extremely competitive. In this freelance field, there are no affirmative-action policies. Opportunities depend on talent, perseverance, contacts, and, above all, luck.

Advancement Prospects

When a Scriptwriter/Screenwriter gets established by having one or more scripts accepted for production, the writer's chances of getting more work increase significantly. Establishing a career as a Scriptwriter/Screenwriter is hard work and a large dosage of luck, with many disappointments on the way, but as the scripts get turned into vehicles filmed or aired, the cumulative effect greatly enhances the possibilities of a successful career.

Education and Training

A broad education, with undergraduate degrees in communications, English, or fine arts, is the major requirement. Some writers have degrees in advertising or marketing and have job experience in that field before turning to scriptwriting.

Experience, Skills, and Personality Traits

While someone with modest prior writing experience might write usable scripts or screenplays, the more experienced writers have a better chance. Experience can come from working in a print or broadcasting medium. Generally, such background counts less than talent, creativity, and the ability to write believable dialogue. Quality Scriptwriters and Screenwriters must have a good appreciation of how real people converse and understand the visual aspects of their craft, that is, how all this plays out on the screen.

Unions and Associations

Writers who work under contract for film studios and television networks must join the Writers Guild of America (WGA). Salaried writers for radio and television also have to be members. They may also belong to such organizations as the American Federation of Television and Radio Artists, or the National Association of Broadcast Employees and Technicians—Communications Workers of America. Scriptwriters and Screenwriters may also belong to assorted specialized writing groups.

Tips for Entry

1. There is no better way to understand the craft of screenwriting than to examine classic films and television productions from the past and present to find their common threads of excellence.

2. Participating in writers' groups will give you immediate feedback from your peers on the quality and uniqueness of your scripts and screenplays.

3. Studying one or more of the several available books on how to break into film/television/radio and/or attending seminars on the subject can provide practical guidelines for networking within the industry.

4. Reading industry trade papers will give you insight into changing trends in topics and formats for new scripts and screenplays and provides useful keys to what is in vogue.

5. Enter script-/screenwriting competitions, which are a good way to attract industry attention from agents and producers.

6. Attending industry functions and making new contacts through industry-oriented Web sites for new talent (e.g., http://www.ifilm.com) can provide helpful entrées into the business.

BOOK PUBLISHING

ADMINISTRATIVE ASSISTANT

CAREER PROFILE

Duties: Assist publicity, promotion, production, or advertising managers with everyday tasks and basic writing assignments

Alternate Title(s): Advertising Assistant, Executive Assistant, Marketing Assistant, Production Assistant, Promotion Assistant, Publicity Assistant

Salary Range: $15,000 to $30,000

Employment Prospects: Poor to fair

Advancement Prospects: Poor to fair

Prerequisites:

Education or Training—Undergraduate degree in advertising, communications, liberal arts, or marketing

Experience—Background in advertising, media, public relations, or publishing helpful

Special Skills and Personality Traits—Clerical skills; organizational skills; good writing abilities

CAREER LADDER

```
┌─────────────────────────────────────┐
│  Advertising Specialist, Marketing   │
│  Specialist, Promotion Specialist, or│
│       Publicity Specialist           │
└─────────────────────────────────────┘

┌─────────────────────────────────────┐
│      Administrative Assistant        │
└─────────────────────────────────────┘

┌─────────────────────────────────────┐
│          College Student             │
└─────────────────────────────────────┘
```

Position Description

Administrative Assistant is a basic position in most publishing companies or departments. Most of the functions are routine clerical and secretarial tasks, although they might encompass different or greater responsibilities. What the job offers is to provide the beginner with a first-rate background and training in the publishing trade: how books are produced, marketed, and publicized. With the expertise come expanded responsibilities, which can lead to more interesting work, such as actual contact with prominent authors.

Administrative Assistants may be based in one department and then restricted to tasks relating to particular functions, such as advertising, production, or publicity. On the other hand, they may be shared among several departments and, thus, have broader, more varied tasks.

However, duties common to all departments include answering the telephone, placing calls, running errands, word processing on a computer, and other general office duties. Administrative Assistants also maintain mailing lists, updating them regularly; handle correspondence, including writing letters for their supervisor to sign; preparing press and sales kits; and arranging materials for meetings and conferences. They also maintain records, such as sales figures, and distribute review copies and press releases.

Writing duties might include departmental reports; press kit material; promotional or advertising copy; and sales catalog copy, which would detail the history and expertise of the firm's authors and the results the publisher anticipates getting from its advertising, promotion, and publicity.

Administrative Assistants often act as links between departments; help organize sales conferences and promotional events; work with film and television contacts concerning movie or television tie-ins; and assist in the booking of author tours and speaking engagements. With a lot of the publishing industry moving into online publishing and Web site development, there are new openings for Administrative Assistants to explore.

Administrative Assistants work long hours and have endless deadline pressures. They must be adaptable to sudden changes. All of this is part of the learning experience.

Salaries

Administrative Assistant salaries differ from department to department, as well as being reflective of the size of the publishing firm and its geographic location. Average starting salaries in the editorial and art departments range from $23,000 to $26,000, whereas the advertising and publicity departments have an average pay of about $27,000. Some beginning salaries may be as low as $15,000.

Employment Prospects

The availability of entry-level positions for job applicants is only fair. The Bureau of Labor Statistics predicts that generally administrative support positions, including clerical, will increase by about 9 percent through the year 2006. This low figure is due partly to the increased use of automation techniques in the office and partly to the increased use of freelance personnel.

Advancement Prospects

Administrative Assistants seldom have opportunities to advance in publicity, due to the limited number of managerial positions available in any given firm. Some assistants may find better possibilities in advertising or sales promotion departments. One other way of achieving advancement is a lateral move to other publishing fields, such as magazines, the news media, or business corporations.

Nonetheless, some assistants may find they can move to a position as editorial assistant, and then on to other higher editorial posts, but these jumps are never easy.

Education and Training

An undergraduate degree in communications, journalism (preferable), or liberal arts gives a candidate a good background for publicity work. Media courses are preferable to those dealing with publishing, and familiarity with advertising and public relations is a definite plus.

Experience, Skills, and Personality Traits

Most Administrative Assistant positions, being entry level, require no specific experience. However, candidates who have had college internships or summer jobs, or have worked on school publications have a definite advantage. In some smaller publishing firms, the position of Administrative Assistant is more advanced with greater responsibilities. For these positions, a year or two of previous work at another publishing company may be required.

Unions and Associations

Administrative Assistants may belong to the International Association of Administrative Professionals (IAAP). Another organization important for entry-level employees is the Young to Publishing Group of the Association of American Publishers. Other organizations are the Association of Women in Communications, the Public Relations Society of America, the Publicists Guild of America, the Publishers' Ad Club, or the Publishers' Publicity Association.

Tips for Entry

1. Experience in publishing can be gained by working for a school newspaper, or by performing an internship with a publishing company.
2. Keep abreast of current genre trends and market conditions in publishing through reading industry journals and newsletters (often available in both hard copy and electronic versions).
3. Many publishers advertise new entry-level positions at their Web sites or in such industry journals as *Publishers Weekly*.
4. Attend book fairs and conventions in your area to network with publishers and express interest in being considered for an entry-level position.

COPY EDITOR

Duties: Edit manuscripts for consistency, grammar, punctuation, style, and typographical errors

Alternate Title(s): None

Salary Range: $23,000 to $45,000 or more

Employment Prospects: Fair

Advancement Prospects: Fair

Prerequisites:

Education or Training—Undergraduate degree in communications, English, or liberal arts preferred

Experience—Background as editorial or production assistant preferred

Special Skills and Personality Traits—Detailed knowledge of grammar and style; close attention to detail; production knowledge

```
┌──────────────────────────────────────┐
│  Production Editor or Managing Editor │
└──────────────────────────────────────┘

┌──────────────────────────────────────┐
│              Copy Editor             │
└──────────────────────────────────────┘

┌──────────────────────────────────────┐
│        Editorial Assistant,          │
│      Production Assistant, or        │
│          College Student             │
└──────────────────────────────────────┘
```

Position Description

When a book manuscript has been accepted for publication, edited, and revised to the demands of both editor(s) and author(s), it is handed over to a Copy Editor for final editing, and proofreading. This final step before printing ensures accuracy and quality in the end product.

The Copy Editor's job is to correct errors in grammar, spelling, usage, and style. The actual checking for typographical and mechanical errors, formerly done by a proofreader, most frequently is done by a Copy Editor, though freelance proofreaders may still be used at any stage in the process.

Most of the Copy Editor's labor is meticulous in its detail. The manuscript (including any appendixes or glossaries, bibliographies, and indexes) must be perused, and errors in grammar, punctuation, and spelling corrected. Each publishing firm has its own internal or "house" style for such things as abbreviations, capitalization, titles, and how words, phrases, typographical elements, and other items are to be used, or not used. Copy Editors must make certain that the manuscript matches the house style.

Copy Editors must check for any inconsistencies, in either fact or logic. This time-consuming process may not prove feasible due to publication deadlines. Copy Editors check with a wide variety of reference works, may confer with editors on grammatical or style problems, and may even be required to contact authors for verification or clarification.

Copy Editors do not change the substance of the manuscript (though, in some publishing firms they may be allowed to tighten up wordy phrasing and smooth awkward transitions), or alter the author's style or means of expression. That job of revisions or rewrites is the prerequisite of the authors and their line editors—assistant, associate, or senior editors.

The thoroughness of Copy Editors is only abridged by production schedules, which must be adhered to, in particular as it involves preset scheduling with printer(s) and binder(s). In the final stages of production, Copy Editors may be called upon to proofread typeset page proofs for typographical errors and to check that all typesetting instructions have been followed. They may also proofread any mechanicals and layouts, such as artwork, charts, and photo captions.

Copy Editors usually report to a production editor or a managing editor, and, in turn, may supervise production assistants and freelance Copy Editors and/or proofreaders. They are the basic link between the editorial and production functions of a publishing firm. Their work is tedious, requiring great patience and scrupulous attention to detail, as errors preferably should be caught early in the production process.

In addition, today's Copy Editors should be thoroughly conversant with computer technology, as most publishers now edit manuscripts on computer and transmit them electronically from one department to another, as well as outside to the author and the typesetter.

Salaries

The median annual salary in 2002 for Copy Editors was approximately $41,000, with the range going from a low of $24,000 to a high of $56,000. For those firms still using full-time proofreaders, in addition to full-time Copy Editors, the median annual salary of such proofreaders in 2002 was $24,300, with the range extending from a low of $15,700 to a high of $39,300. Copy Editors working for smaller publishers earned salaries at the lower end, and men tended to make more than women did. (In a smaller publishing house many of the copyediting and proofreading tasks may be undertaken by one of the line editors.)

Employment Prospects

Most publishers have Copy Editors as salaried positions. Many Copy Editors start out as editorial or production assistants. Much of the task of simple proofreading is being taken up by computerized proofreading/grammar checks when the text is first created by the writer, and by Copy Editors, or line editors, at the final stages.

While New York City is still the hub of American book publishing, much publishing is done elsewhere on the East Coast (Boston; Philadelphia; Washington, D.C.), in Chicago, and on the West Coast (particularly Los Angeles and San Francisco). In addition, small publishers may be found throughout the country, and, of course, there are the university presses (though employment prospects there may be somewhat limited, except in the larger presses).

Book publishing today has changed a great deal from what it was like in the mid to late 20th century. Mergers and acquisitions have brought about downsizing everywhere. Some tasks that used to be accomplished in-house are now done by freelancers to save overhead and benefit costs. As a result, some Copy Editors and most, if not all, proofreaders now are freelancers.

Advancement Prospects

The usual advancement potentials for a Copy Editor are to progress up the ladder on the production side of the publishing business, to a production or managing editor. Nonetheless, it is still possible to make a switch to the editorial side, if the Copy Editor's editorial skills are outstanding and the circumstances are right.

Education and Training

It is preferable for Copy Editors to have an undergraduate degree (though, in some cases, three years of college may be sufficient). Areas of study may include communications, general liberal arts, and publishing. Additional training in editing skills and production methodologies is valuable.

Experience, Skills, and Personality Traits

A Copy Editor, usually, should have a background in production. Work as a production assistant or even on the college newspaper or the yearbook is a plus.

While Copy Editors have to be familiar with the production process and with typesetting symbols and terminology, they also must be excellent spellers and be familiar with the rules of grammar and style. As their work is extremely detailed, a high degree of patience is required. In addition, an understanding of computer techniques and systems is becoming just as important.

Unions and Associations

Industry associations include the Association for Women in Communications, the Association of American Publishers (AAP), Black Americans in Publishing, the Women's National Book Association, and the Young to Publishing Group of AAP. Copy Editors who freelance on the side, or who are full-time freelancers, may belong to the Editorial Freelancers Association. Copy Editors often join a wide range of groups or associations related to writing and book publishing.

Tips for Entry

1. Enroll in a copyediting/proofreading course at a local learning center. An internship with a local publishing company is also an excellent way to get practical experience.
2. Learn more about Copy Editors on the Internet. To generate a list of relevant Web sites, enter the keywords *copy editor* in any search engine. These hits will provide examples of how established freelance Copy Editors and proofreaders promote their services and the scope of typical credentials in the field.
3. Volunteer with individuals and small firms to do freelance copyediting/proofreading to gain experience and credentials.
4. In job searching, keep in mind that there are places other than newspapers and publishing companies that have jobs in copyediting, or production editing (that is, copyediting and layout work), such as nonprofit organizations, or large companies (with newsletters). Such jobs will allow you to build a résumé of work to move upward to newspaper or book-publishing firms.

COPYWRITER

CAREER PROFILE

Duties: Write copy for advertising, promotion, and direct-mail bookselling campaigns; create flap copy and press releases

Alternate Title(s): None

Salary Range: $18,000 to $32,500

Employment Prospects: Fair

Advancement Prospects: Fair

Prerequisites:

Education or Training—Undergraduate degree in advertising, communications, or liberal arts

Experience—Background in advertising or marketing; any writing experience helpful

Special Skills and Personality Traits—Sales and graphic-arts familiarity; writing ability

CAREER LADDER

```
┌─────────────────────────────────────┐
│  Promotion Manager, Advertising      │
│  Manager, or Sales Manager           │
└─────────────────────────────────────┘

┌─────────────────────────────────────┐
│  Copywriter                          │
└─────────────────────────────────────┘

┌─────────────────────────────────────┐
│  Administrative Assistant            │
└─────────────────────────────────────┘
```

Position Description

Copywriters produce much of the promotional materials that help sell books both to the buying public and to booksellers, as well as to wholesalers and the media. Usually they work under the direction of the advertising manager, or the sales or promotion managers. The informational materials they produce are copy for book catalogs, print ads, Internet ads, and scripts for radio commercials and the occasional television ad. In addition, they may write promotional data about the book, such as discounts information, special displays that will be available, and specific advertising and publicity campaigns, and the book's author(s) for the sales force. They may also develop posters, flyers, and displays for use in bookstores.

In some of the larger publishing firms, Copywriters may also take on some of the editorial functions of junior editors, that is, creating press releases for the media and book reviewers, putting together the components for press kits, or even writing jacket copy, which is a brief synopsis of the book and biographical material about the author.

Copywriters must synchronize all their work with the advertising and promotion personnel, as well as editors. They may undertake needed research for their project, or they may designate this to administrative assistants. They frequently work with graphic artists in designing and laying out the ads, brochures, and catalogs. They have to be both imaginative and succinct in their writing to fit the requirements of whatever material they are creating and the space available for it. Some Copywriters may even specialize in direct mail promotions for their firm's new releases.

Salaries

Average salaries for Copywriters run in the low to mid-20s but may range from a low of $18,000 to a high of $32,500, depending upon their industry experience and the type and size of their employer. Generally, Copywriter positions in publishing pay less than those in advertising agencies or businesses. However, if a Copywriter advances into managerial positions, the resultant salary range most likely will be higher than for most editorial posts.

Employment Prospects

While copywriting jobs are not as prestigious as editorial jobs in publishing, they may be easier to come by, as there is an ever-increasing need for effective book promotion and marketing.

Advancement Prospects

Skilled Copywriters can often advance to managerial levels in the advertising, promotion, or sales departments, which, in turn, can lead to higher managerial positions within the business end of publishing.

Education and Training

An undergraduate degree in advertising or communications is almost obligatory for copywriting jobs. Nonetheless, a degree in liberal arts may also be acceptable.

Experience, Skills, and Personality Traits

An advertising or sales-promotion background is usually necessary for this type of work. Some Copywriters have worked in advertising agencies, which others may have started as entry-level assistants at a publishing house.

Copywriters must be able to write clear and persuasive sales copy. They should also have a general knowledge of graphic arts, layout, and production. They should be detail-oriented and well organized.

Unions and Associations

Major professional associations for Copywriters include the Advertising Club of America, the American Advertising Federation, the American Association of Advertising Agen-cies, the Association for Women in Communications, the Copywriter's Council of America, and the Direct Marketing Association.

Tips for Entry

1. Study book jacket copy, direct marketing promotions you receive at home, ads for new book releases in newspapers and magazines, and promotional copy at publishers' Web sites.
2. Learn more about copywriting on the Internet. To generate a list of relevant Web sites, enter the keywords *book copywriter* in any search engine. These hits will provide examples of how established freelance book Copywriters promote their services and the scope of typical credentials in the field.
3. If you have no (book) copywriting experience, create your own sample ads for existing or fictitious books to use as samples.
4. Explore job openings in industry trade publications (such as *Publishers Weekly*), network at local/regional book fairs and conventions, and explore work opportunities at publishers' Web sites.

EDITORIAL POSITIONS

CAREER PROFILE

Duties: Senior/Executive Editor: acquire and develop top books and authors; plan and execute editorial policies. Managing Editor: supervise the entire production of a title after acquisition; develop and oversee production schedules. Editor: develop concepts for books; recommend acquisition of books; negotiate contracts and work with authors. Associate Editors: screen, edit, and rewrite manuscripts; manage projects and recommend acquisitions. Assistant Editors: screen, edit and acquire manuscripts; monitor production. Editorial Assistant/Trainee/Secretary: provide clerical, secretarial, and minor editorial duties.

Alternate Title(s): Acquisitions Editor or Project Editor, Developmental Editor, Editorial Assistant/Trainee

Salary Range: Senior/Executive Editor: $70,000 to $105,000 or more; all other Editors: $28,000 to $80,000 or more

Employment Prospects: Poor to fair

Advancement Prospects: Fair to good

Prerequisites:

Education or Training—All positions: undergraduate degree in communications, English, history, humanities, or liberal arts, with courses in publishing and book production

Experience—Senior Editor: three to five years as Editor; Managing Editor: three to five years as Editor or work in production department; Editor: work as an Editorial Assistant, an Assistant or Associate Editor; Associate Editor: one to two years of editorial experience; Assistant Editor: work as an Editorial Assistant or Trainee; Editorial Assistant: no experience necessary

Special Skills and Personality Traits—Senior/Executive Editor: negotiating, supervisory, business, decision-making abilities; other Editors: ability to work under pressure and work well with others, creativity, organizational skills, and familiarity with the entire publishing process

CAREER LADDER

```
┌─────────────────────────────────────┐
│ Editorial Director or Editor in Chief │
└─────────────────────────────────────┘

┌─────────────────────────────────────┐
│ Senior/Executive Editor or Editor    │
└─────────────────────────────────────┘

┌─────────────────────────────────────┐
│ Associate Editor                     │
└─────────────────────────────────────┘

┌─────────────────────────────────────┐
│ Assistant Editor                     │
└─────────────────────────────────────┘

┌─────────────────────────────────────┐
│ Editorial Assistant, Editorial Trainee, │
│ Secretary, or College Student        │
└─────────────────────────────────────┘
```

Position Description

Senior/Executive Editors are deeply involved in the marketing and business aspects of publishing and help in the development of the long-range plans for the publishing firm, which include acquisition and publishing schedules, as well as budgetary analyses and sales projections. They have responsibility for all facets of book projects and are in charge of acquisitions. (Acquisition involves deciding what manuscripts should be purchased and overseeing contract negotiations.) Subsidiary rights sales to foreign publishers, magazines, paperback publication, and film or television rights are usually handled by a Senior/Executive Editor. They usually work under the direction of Editorial Directors or Editors in Chief, and they frequently make presentations at editorial and sales meetings, important sales conferences, and major industry conventions.

Managing Editors are responsible for the entire production of books after acquisition. They develop the workflow from manuscript to finished product, working closely with senior editorial management and the production department to ensure that the finished book meets the projected expectations. They develop the production schedules, hire and oversee the work and schedules of any freelancers (such as copy editors, proofreaders, or typesetters), review all material for the jacket and front matter, oversee the transfer of author corrections, and ready the author-reviewed manuscripts for typesetting.

Mid-level Editors read manuscripts and proposals made by authors and agents and make the presentations at editorial meetings to recommend acquisitions, as well as negotiate the terms on books that are approved. They may generate book ideas and work with authors and agents to develop them into full-blown proposals. Thereafter they participate in the editing and production processes, as well as coordinate with the art, marketing, production, and publicity departments to meet assigned deadlines. In large publishing firms, an Editor may do the first major edit and ask the author for necessary alterations, after which the manuscript is given to line and copy Editors to check for consistency, grammar, and style. In small firms, all these functions may be handled by the Editor. In addition, Editors liaise with agents on ideas and potential book projects, work closely with authors, and supervise Associate and/or Assistant Editors in the process. They also may devote some time to reading unsolicited manuscripts. At a large publishing firm, an Editor may be responsible for dozens of books a year.

Associate Editors usually concentrate on the screening, acquisition, and editing of manuscripts, which includes examining unsolicited manuscripts and evaluating editorial recommendations for acquisition. They must understand the needs of the publisher for which they work as well as present conditions in the book marketplace. They may edit manuscripts and work with authors on revisions or rewrites, and they may supervise the work of copy editors and proofreaders. They usually work under the supervision of Senior/Executive Editors or Editorial Directors, and regularly attend the in-house editorial meetings that discuss potential books. They also may have contact with agents, supervise special book projects or series, or help in the planning of publicity and promotion.

Assistant Editors are one step above Editorial Assistants, having learned the editorial process of screening manuscripts, and, eventually, editing those chosen. They are responsible for shepherding book projects from manuscript to finished book, coordinating the editing, proofreading, and production processes. They may help plan deadline and production schedules and may even propose publicity and promotion ideas. They also may be involved in recommending manuscripts for acquisition, but the actual contract negotiations are usually undertaken by more experienced Editors. They generally report to Associate Editors or Senior/Executive Editors, depending upon the size of the publishing firm.

Most entry-level positions are either Editorial Assistants or Trainees, or Secretaries. Their responsibilities usually encompass office tasks, such as receptionist duties, filing, word processing (including keying in book contracts), the initial handling and directing to editors of newly received manuscripts, and running errands. Editorial Assistants may also monitor production schedules and draft cost estimates for editors, be responsible for copyright applications, route expense requisitions, invoices, and other bills, act as liaisons with authors, and handle phone duties and general correspondence.

Salaries

According to the 2003 annual salary survey conducted by *Publishers Weekly*, the average salary for Senior/Executive Editors ranges from $73,083 to $107,717, and the average salary for Managing Editors ranges from $52,520 to $84,250. Salary ranges for mid-level Editors extended from $41,000 to $61,087, and Editorial Assistants have salary ranges from $28,378 to $30,400. The variations in these salaries are dependent upon the revenues and the size of the publishing firm. Furthermore, *Publishers Weekly* found that average salary increases rose by 3 percent to 5.1 percent for 61 percent of the publishing workforce, in comparison with the previous year's 4.9 percent overall. For most of the industry, the largest pay increases occurred for those who switched jobs or were promoted, with the average increase coming in at 16 percent.

Employment Prospects

The position of Senior/Executive Editor is very competitive, particularly because this job requires years of publishing experience. Changing firms is often the only means of obtaining a job at this level. Managing Editors also fall into this category.

Many mid-level editorial positions have been lost in the last several years, mainly due to acquisitions, (international) mergers, and sluggish sales across the industry, but also from bad judgment leading to large amounts of debt at given firms. The best opportunities for mid-level Editors still may be with smaller presses and whatever is left of the independent presses that used to flourish. In such cases, lower pay is compensated by greater opportunity.

Turnover in publishing is very high. Low and middle positions, such as Associate Editor and Assistant Editor, have the best chance at advancement, as most promotion is done within a publishing firm. However, chances for promotion from within have lessened, as *Publishers Weekly* found out in its 2004 salary survey of 2003 industry trends, in which

40 percent of respondents who were in a new job said that they had changed jobs within the industry, while 20 percent said they had been laid off from their previous publishing position. Of new hires, 16 percent said they joined publishing from outside the industry, and 12 percent said they got their first job in the industry just after graduating from college.

Advancement Prospects

Advancing from Senior/Executive Editor to Editorial Director or Editor in Chief is very difficult, as many of the higher positions are filled from outside the publishing firm, rather than from within. Turnover in this position is significantly less than lower editorial posts, partly due to the value of the Senior Editor's greater experience in the publishing field. Advancement for Senior/Executive Editors often is achieved by changing employers.

Advancing from Editor to Senior/Executive Editor has similar difficulties, for much the same reasons. The competition for editorial positions above that of Associate Editor is considerably keener. These posts are frequently filled by outside candidates, rather than inside ones. However, Assistant Editors probably have a good chance of being promoted in-house, due to the higher turnover of mid-level Editor positions (as they, in turn, look for promotion by changing firms). Likewise, promotion from a secretarial or Assistant/Trainee position is very likely, due again to the higher volatility of turnover.

Education and Training

Senior/Executive Editors, Managing Editors, mid-level Editors, and Associate Editors must have an undergraduate degree in communications, English, history, humanities, or liberal arts. Courses in book publishing, some of which might be taken at a summer publishing institute, are helpful background for any editorial position.

Managing Editors should have some educational background in book production. For mid-level Editors, some marketing education might prove fortuitous.

Experience, Skills, and Personality Traits

Senior/Executive Editors must have three to five years' experience in editing, and some large publishers may require more than that. Also, a background at more than one publisher is helpful. Senior/Executive Editors must be knowledgeable about publishing contracts and how to negotiate them. They must understand the business and financial side of publishing, be adept at budget planning, and be experienced supervisors.

Managing Editors must have three to five years of experience in editing or in a book production supervisory position. Again, a background at more than one publisher would be helpful. They must be totally conversant with book production methods, procedures, and scheduling, and have experience in layout and design.

An Editor should have had experience as an Associate or Assistant Editor, or an Editorial Assistant, or all of them, depending upon the requirements of the publishing firm. They must be able to work smoothly with a wide variety of people and temperaments, and be well organized. They have to be able to supervise, delegate work, and withstand a lot of pressure. They should be knowledgeable and creative in anticipating trends in both the industry and the book-buying public.

Associate Editors usually have one or two years' experience in a lower editorial position, even working as Editors of magazines or newspapers. They should have strong, instinctive editing skills and a good business sense about a book's commercial qualities. Good supervisory skills and good oral presentation aptitude is essential.

Many Assistant Editor positions require experience as an Editorial Assistant or Trainee, or even as an Editor in another field. Sometimes, however, they may be entry-level positions right out of college. Assistant Editors must have good editorial and grammatical abilities, and they must understand fully the editorial process. Excellent oral presentation skills are a plus.

Most Editorial Assistant/Trainees and Secretaries come to publishing directly from college, or from some allied field. Their enthusiasm for working within the publishing industry is characteristic, and they usually learn and train as they work, leading to fairly easy promotion within the firm.

Unions and Associations

Editors of all kinds may belong to such professional associations as the American Book Producers Association, the Association for Women in Communications, the Society for Scholarly Publishing, or the Women's National Book Association. They may belong to associations of specialty publishing, such as the American Agricultural Editors Association, the Association of Educational Publishers, or the Society of American Business Editors and Writers. They may also belong to a wide variety of groups related to writing or other authors' organizations or even Local 2110 of the United Auto Workers.

Tips for Entry

1. For those intending a career path in book editing, consider an entry-level post of Secretary or Administrative Assistant/Trainee as a viable means of getting a foothold within the industry.
2. Network at local/regional book fairs and conventions to make industry contacts.
3. Reading industry journals and newsletters will keep you abreast of trends within publishing and information about which firms are expanding their staffs.
4. Explore the Web sites of publishers of interest as they often post job openings (with needed qualifications for applicants).

ELECTRONIC PUBLISHING PRODUCT EDITOR/MANAGER

CAREER PROFILE

Duties: Oversee the development of an electronic version of a book to a finished product; choose marketing and promotional strategies

Alternate Title(s): Varied

Salary Range: $35,000 to $50,000 or more

Employment Prospects: Good

Advancement Prospects: Fair

Prerequisites:

Education or Training—Undergraduate degree in communications, English, history, or liberal arts; a master's degree in library science, with training in computer-aided research not required, but a plus

Experience—Several years' background as a promotional assistant, project coordinator, and assistant product manager within electronic publishing; experience in library work or using computer databases in a business environment also helpful

Special Skills and Personality Traits—Awareness of the uses of computer databases; ability to discern books appropriate for electronic publishing; knowledge of what information the users of computer databases want, and how to package it

CAREER LADDER

```
┌─────────────────────────────────────┐
│  Marketing Director or Sales Director │
└─────────────────────────────────────┘

┌─────────────────────────────────────┐
│       Product Editor/Manager         │
└─────────────────────────────────────┘

┌─────────────────────────────────────┐
│  Assistant Production Manager or     │
│        Promotion Assistant           │
└─────────────────────────────────────┘
```

Position Description

Electronic publishing entails producing computerized online versions of books, magazines, and other works usually found in printed form. Books and magazines are converted into electronic products primarily to get around the limitations of print. Electronic versions can be updated continuously, and they are not limited to a specific number of pages. Databases of information can be expanded beyond the usual constrictions of a printed format and will not be outdated, while it typically takes at least a year to get a book into print. In addition, a computer user can take information from a book or magazine directly without having to retype it.

Many textbooks are now published with accompanying CD-ROM disks, since computers with CD-ROM drives are now so common in both homes and schools. In addition, dic-

tionaries, directories, and encyclopedias lend themselves well to the electronic format. Special visual effects and video clips are easy to download from the computer file and greatly help in the learning process. Sometimes an outside packager is utilized to create such discs, and an increasing number of publishers are providing their electronic material on the Internet.

Information in an electronic form can be personalized in format for the customer, merged with information from other sources, or integrated into a software program that allows the end user to arrange the information as needed.

Some books, such as guides to computer programs, naturally lend themselves to the electronic format. Other electronic products include full-text or partial-text databases of magazines, journals, or books, complete with reference citations that allow a user to access the full article cited in the text. Other uses for electronic product formats include business that have databases with information about their companies and their business activities, financial wire services with current stock quotes and other up-to-date financial information, and fax and telephone information services.

Most jobs involved with electronic publishing resemble traditional publishing jobs but, in addition, necessitate a thorough knowledge of their targeted online customers, as well as a complete familiarity with various database programs and their construction. The position of Electronic Publishing Product Editor and/or Manager is really an amalgam of editorial and promotional positions in traditional publishing. The Product Editor/Manager is responsible for guiding an electronic product from idea to the final product and the marketing of it. The Product Editor/Manager must ensure that the final electronic product integrates writing and visuals (and sound) well together and that permissions have been granted for the use of video clips or visual features added to the final product.

Then, the Product Editor/Manager must decide on the most appropriate marketing strategy for the product. While familiarity with traditional book promotion is necessary, an imaginative approach to electronic promotion is key. Much of the work in developing and promoting the electronic product may be aided by specific promotional assistants who, in turn, may employ market research to develop product design and to identify specific customer needs and adopt products to fit those requirements.

Salaries
Salaries will differ according to the size of the publisher and the size of the electronic program instituted by that publisher. Typically, they fall within the $45,000 to $85,000 range. For promotional assistants in the electronic department, salaries will range from the mid $20,000s to $34,000.

Employment Prospects
Depending upon the applicant's background, jobs in electronic publishing may be easier to get than those in traditional publishing, thanks to the downturn in recent years in book sales. Many people employed in the nontechnical side of electronic publishing come from more traditional publishing, and that experience is directly applicable to this new medium.

One problem with this latest form of publishing is the lack of a reasonable compensation structure for writers in the new medium. This new methodology is obviously different from that of traditional publishing in that, while more writing is required in the electronic form, the word count cost is a significantly less important expense for the publisher (with typesetting costs no longer required).

Advancement Prospects
Advancement to unit manager, or department manager, is possible. Alternatively, making a shift to a more conventional marketing managerial position, such as marketing director or sales director, is also possible. For promotional assistants, the next step to becoming an assistant product manager is being a project coordinator within the electronic division, or, instead, making a move to another promotional job within the publishing firm.

Education and Training
An undergraduate degree in advertising, communications, English, journalism, liberal arts, or marketing is usually required. Most important, a formal knowledge of computer systems, applicable software, and computer-aided research is a must.

The first step toward a position as Product Editor or Product Manager is holding the position of promotion assistant. For this entry-level position, a communications or liberal arts degree should suffice. Formal computer education may not be necessary in all cases, but it would be advisable.

Experience, Skills, and Personality Traits
Several years of experience as an assistant product manager, or in another promotional position within electronic publishing, are generally required of all Product Editors/Managers. Experience in copywriting, marketing, market research, publicity, and sales may be a necessity.

While the promotional assistant position may be entry level, a thorough familiarity with computer databases and software is expected, and a background in book promotion provides an edge in getting the position. An ability to communicate technical information clearly in everyday language is essential.

Unions and Associations
Major organizations of interest for electronic publishing personnel are the Advertising Club of New York, the American Advertising Federation, the American Marketing Association, and the Association for Women in Communications. The trade association for electronic publishing is the Software and Information Industry Association. In addition, the Association of American Publishers has a division devoted to electronic publishing.

Tips for Entry
1. Enroll in classes on electronic publishing.
2. Learn more about electronic publishing on the Internet. To generate a list of relevant Web sites, enter the keywords *electronic publishing* in any search engine.
3. Keep up to speed on industry changes through industry magazines such as *Electronic Publishing* (http://ep.pennnet.com).
4. Search for entry-level positions in the field within industry publications and on such job boards as http://monster.com or at individual publishers' Web sites.

PROMOTION MANAGER

CAREER PROFILE

Duties: Oversee promotional activities to bolster book sales

Alternate Title(s): Sales Promotion Manager

Salary Range: $45,000 to $70,000 or more

Employment Prospects: Poor

Advancement Prospects: Poor

Prerequisites:

Education or Training—Undergraduate degree in advertising or marketing desirable

Experience—Two to five years in copywriting, marketing, or promotion positions

Special Skills and Personality Traits—Copywriting capability; knack for selling; marketing expertise; supervisory prowess

CAREER LADDER

```
┌─────────────────────────────────────────┐
│  Director of Marketing or Sales Director │
└─────────────────────────────────────────┘

┌─────────────────────────────────────────┐
│            Promotion Manager             │
└─────────────────────────────────────────┘

┌─────────────────────────────────────────┐
│   Copywriter, Publicity Assistant, or    │
│               Researcher                 │
└─────────────────────────────────────────┘
```

Position Description

Along with advertising, publicity, and direct-sales efforts, promotion plays an important part in the marketing of books once they are published. Promotional efforts can be seen in the floor displays found in bookstores. These displays may include special wall posters, buttons, bookmarks available at cash registers, shelf tags, special table displays, and other eye-catching promotional material.

Additional promotional products may include direct-mail and e-mail brochures with order blanks, exhibits devised for industry conventions, and tie-in products, such as caps with inscriptions, emblazoned T-shirts, key rings, tote bags, and other similar items that can be given away to the public. In addition to products to be used, promotion efforts may include direct mail and telemarketing strategies, television and radio advertising, inserts in newspapers, Internet advertisements or Web sites, and special events.

Working with advertising, editorial, and sales staffs, Promotion Managers develop and coordinate promotion strategies. These plans will contain schedules, deadlines, and budgets. Managers then usually delegate much of the work to assistants, copywriters, and researchers, after which they approve the final products. If items have to be obtained from outside the publishing firm, they supervise their purchase and distribution. Another important function of Promotion Managers is to review the effectiveness of the material produced in the department, as well as managing the costs.

To a certain extent, Promotion Managers may have a say in determining whether a manuscript is purchased by the publisher. If they determine that a potential book is not promotable, in other words, that it would not attract a sufficiently large or diverse audience, the book may be rejected. For these reasons, Promotion Managers frequently participate in editorial meetings to assist in the buying decisions.

As a rule Promotion Managers report to directors or vice presidents of marketing or sales. If a publishing firm uses outside advertising agencies, the Promotion Manager will work closely with them on the advertising campaign. They may also supervise freelance copywriters if required. In some cases, the Promotion Manager may supervise publicity efforts, control the writing of jacket copy, and collaborate on the preparation of sales catalogs.

Salaries

According to the *Publisher's Weekly* 2004 annual salary survey, compiled by Jim Milliot, the salary ranges for Promotion Managers in 2003 ranged from $48,525 to $72,838, depending upon the size and the revenues of the publishing firm.

Employment Prospects

Not all publishing companies have a separate post for Promotion Manager. Such duties may fall to an advertising manager. This may be especially true for small publishers.

While employment of advertising, marketing, promotions, public relations, and sales managers is expected to grow faster than the average for most occupations through 2012, as per the 2004–2005 U.S. Department of Labor Bureau of Labor Statistics *Occupational Outlook Handbook,* the general drop in sales of books may adversely affect employment growth in the publishing industry.

Advancement Prospects

To move upward to director or vice president of marketing or sales, Promotion Managers will face severe competition from their peers in the advertising or sales departments. For this reason, a background in sales provides a definite edge.

Education and Training

An undergraduate degree in advertising or marketing is desirable for promotion work. Some employers may prefer a degree in business administration with an emphasis on marketing. Undergraduate degrees in communications, journalism, liberal arts, or social sciences may also be acceptable.

Experience, Skills, and Personality Traits

At least two years' experience in copywriting, market research, publicity, or sales is considered the very minimum requirement for a Promotion Manager. Five years of such experience is even better.

Promotion Managers should be mindful of advertising and marketing techniques, and their copywriting skills should be exemplary. Managerial skills should include budget making and long-range planning, as well as the hiring, training, and supervising of staff. They need to be able to communicate persuasively, both orally and in writing, and they should be creative, highly motivated, and resistant to stress.

Unions and Associations

Major associations for Promotion Managers include the American Advertising Federation, the American Marketing Association, and the Business and Professional Advertising Association. Others include the Advertising Club of America, Advertising Women of New York, and the Association for Women in Communications.

Tips for Entry

1. To be prepared for career advancement opportunities, take in-house or continuing education (sales) management training courses. Many of these are available at local colleges and universities, frequently sponsored by marketing and related associations.
2. Attend seminars provided by publishers or at conferences of professional societies on changing trends and technologies in the publishing industry.
3. Keep alert to desired job openings at publishing houses by checking the firms' individual Web sites, professional associations' Internet job boards, and industry publications.

PUBLICITY MANAGER

CAREER PROFILE

Duties: Develop publicity for authors and books; organize author tours and arrange for book reviews

Alternate Title(s): Publicist

Salary Range: $40,000 to $90,000 or more

Employment Prospects: Fair

Advancement Prospects: Poor

Prerequisites:

Education or Training—Undergraduate degree in communications, English, journalism, or liberal arts

Experience—Background as journalist or publicity assistant essential

Special Skills and Personality Traits—Excellent organizational and writing skills; sales orientation

CAREER LADDER

```
Director of Publicity
```

```
Publicity Manager
```

```
Publicity Assistant
```

Position Description

Publicity Managers represent their publishing firms to the media and work especially hard to get positive press coverage for their authors and books. Theirs is one of the most visible jobs within the industry.

The majority of books receive only minimal publicity, but a few are targeted, usually from the moment of their sale to the publishing firm, as ones to receive singular effort, due mostly to either the fame of the author or the potential salability of the book. The amount of publicity may fluctuate, from a mailing of review copies with press releases to a major advertising push in support of sales. This campaign can include author tours, as well as extensive advertising and sales promotion.

Publicity planning begins well before the book is printed for distribution to stores, or wholesalers. Publicity Managers coordinate their schedules with advertising, editorial, promotion, and sales departments. Budgets and deadlines are set for materials needed, mailings, travel, and other expenses.

For serious campaigns, the Publicity Manager works in tandem with the author in developing press-kit material, such as the author's background and photograph, notable news coverage that the author may have received recently, personal reviewer contacts, and questions for reviewers to ask. Clips of early reviews as well as initial and later press releases are utilized throughout the publicity campaign.

Review copies and press releases are dispatched to book reviewers, magazines, newspapers, and key Web sites and online newsletters in advance of publication. Publicity Managers are responsible for maintaining up-to-date lists of reviewers, as well as contacts with media outlets. For example, a cookbook needs to go to a different kind of reviewer than, say, a detective novel. Usually, Publicity Managers also maintain clipping files on all authors and their books.

Besides reviews, Publicity Managers focus on generating feature stories or news items in the media. They send out press releases and arrange for author interviews, in not only the print media, but also radio, television, and online/live chat sites. They set up speaking engagements, and book signings at bookstores, libraries, malls, and other places. For author tours, the preparations may be made by the Publicity Manager or delegated to staff or freelance assistants. Based on the campaign's budget, it must be determined what sites to include in the tour and which media to contact for interviews. Thereafter, schedules are established and arrangements made for transportation, accommodations, and travel advances for authors. Tours tend to be complex, with many details to coordinate, and many frustrating last-minute changes with which to deal.

Publicity Managers may be entirely in charge of a publisher's publicity operation, or, in the larger firms, they may report to a director of publicity. The Publicity Manager usually also supervises assistants who handle the routine jobs of publicity.

Salaries

Annual salaries for Publicity Managers range from $40,000 to $90,000 or more, dependent upon the extent of their responsibilities and the size and income of the publishing firm. According to the *Publishers Weekly's* 2004 annual salary survey for the year 2003, average yearly salaries for a publishing firm making more than $1 million would be $43,188, and a firm with revenue in excess of $100 million may pay a Publicity Manager up $83,500 yearly, whereas a firm with revenue in excess of $500 million may reward its Publicity Manager with a salary of $89,500.

Employment Prospects

There is much competition for such an attractive position as Publicity Manager, so this particular job market is tight. Also, this post tends to be one of the first to be hit in bad economic times. Many openings for this type of position are never advertised. The best way to move into such a post is to start as a publicity assistant, hoping to move up within the publishing company and/or make industry contacts for a possible lateral job move within the industry.

Advancement Prospects

Opportunities for advancement are narrow. In addition, in many publishing firms, Publicity Manager is the top position, supervised by a director or vice president of sales and/or advertising. In others, particularly larger houses, the highest position is director of publicity. Advancement is more likely by changing employers, rather than promotion within the company.

Education and Training

An undergraduate degree in communications, journalism, or marketing is preferred for publicity positions in publishing. Sometimes, degrees in business administration, liberal arts, or social science may be acceptable.

Experience, Skills, and Personality Traits

Three to five years of experience as a publicity assistant or journalist for a newspaper or a magazine is usually required for the position of Publicity Manager. Managers should understand thoroughly all aspects of the media and be mindful of what constitutes good publicity material. They must have excellent news-writing skills, and be accommodating, outgoing, and personable in their relations with the media. Their power of persuasion must be exceptional.

Unions and Associations

The main professional associations for Publicity Managers include the Association for Women in Communications and the Public Relations Society of America. They may also belong to a wide variety of groups related to advertising, promotion, publishing, and sales, or even Local 2110 of the United Auto Workers.

Tips for Entry

1. Continuously expand and update your database of media contacts through e-mail and personal contact to prepare for the full responsibilities of a Publicity Manager.
2. Constantly network to establish good relations with press outlets.
3. Participate in industry seminars to expand your depth of knowledge of the obligations associated with the position of Publicity Manager, and to maintain contacts with publicity people in the industry.
4. Take additional course work or attend seminars on sales techniques to broaden your knowledge of this side of the publishing industry.

BUSINESS COMMUNICATIONS AND PUBLIC RELATIONS

COMMUNICATIONS COORDINATOR

Duties: Coordinate internal and external communications and activities with the public, media and community groups

Alternate Title(s): Communications Specialist, Public Relations Specialist

Salary Range: $25,000 to $50,000 or more

Employment Prospects: Good

Advancement Prospects: Good

Prerequisites:

Education or Training—Undergraduate degree in communications, English, journalism, liberal arts, marketing, or public relations

Experience—Background in journalism and/or public relations required

Special Skills and Personality Traits—Exceptionally strong writing skills; organizational, supervisory, and administrative abilities; creativity

```
┌─────────────────────────────────┐
│   Public Relations Manager or   │
│   Director of Development        │
└─────────────────────────────────┘

┌─────────────────────────────────┐
│   Communications Coordinator     │
└─────────────────────────────────┘

┌─────────────────────────────────┐
│   Internal Publications Editor or│
│   Journalist                     │
└─────────────────────────────────┘
```

Position Description

The position of Communications Coordinator is usually utilized in businesses that have several communications professionals reporting to a manager or a director. The coordinator typically has authority to make decisions and to supervise such lower-level employees as public relations or publicity assistants.

The Communications Coordinator's wide scope of duties deals primarily with the written word. They include controlling internal communications, external communications, and maintaining good relations with both the community and the media. The specifics of those responsibilities depend upon the individual company, its size, structure, and revenue.

Internal communications frequently is the primary function of the coordinator, with responsibilities for writing, editing, or supervising the writing and editing of all internal publications, such as newsletters, employee informational brochures on benefits and programs, company magazines and notices, and the company Web site. In addition, a coordinator may be required to assist the personnel department in staff recruitment and employee feedback programs.

External communications often include company financial statements, reports and mailings to stockholders and the public, and all informational material for the media. This material usually includes press kits, releases and advisories, newsletters, development brochures, and exhibits.

Maintaining good community relations might encompass coordinating a speakers' bureau, representing the firm on public or allied industry and trade committees, and working with the in-house public relations and/or advertising departments in providing information to the public and answering questions about the company's services and products. In so doing, the Communications Coordinator helps both these departments shape and refine the public image of the organization. In larger firms, all interaction with the public may be the responsibility of a public information officer.

Salaries

This position seldom is an entry-level job. Based on prior writing and business experience, as well as the specific job requirements for the particular firm (and its geographic location), salaries can range from $25,000 to $50,000 a year or more.

Employment Prospects

Employment of public relations specialists is expected to increase faster than that of most other occupations through

2012, according to the U.S. Department of Labor. While the best options for Communication Coordinators remain in private business and industry (in particular with large firms that have established public relations departments), positions are also available in academic institutions as well as in departments of local, state, and national government.

Advancement Prospects

A successful Communications Coordinator has a good opportunity to advance to a higher managerial level within the public relations department, or a higher supervisory position within the communications department.

Education and Training

Most public relations specialists have earned undergraduate degrees in communications, English, journalism, liberal arts, marketing, or public relations. A further degree in business or economics is a plus, and may ease advancement possibilities.

Experience, Skills, and Personality Traits

A background in public relations is advisable for Communications Coordinators, though experience in journalism may be acceptable.

Creativity and extremely strong writing and verbal skills are necessary, as is the ability to handle many tasks or projects at once with little supervision. Organizational and supervisory skills are additional requirements for this position, as are good computer skills. A demonstrated success in media and public relations planning is an added bonus.

Unions and Associations

Major associations for Communications Coordinators include the American Marketing Association, the Association for Women in Communications, the International Association of Business Communicators, and, above all, the Public Relations Society of America.

Tips for Entry

1. Enhance editorial and writing skills by attending writing and publishing seminars.
2. Increase business and commercial skills and knowledge by attending business symposiums, professional society gatherings, and other career enhancement groups.
3. Get involved with local commerce groups to observe how other businesses promote themselves.
4. Join with local community groups in their activities to establish contacts and to discover how your business can relate to their concerns.

EXTERNAL PUBLICATIONS EDITOR

CAREER PROFILE

Duties: Write articles, informational brochures, letters, news releases, PowerPoint slides and other scripts, and speeches for an out-of-house audience, institution, governmental department or agency, or other organization

Alternate Title(s): Communications Associate, Communications Specialist, Information Representative, Public Information Officer

Salary Range: $25,000 to $45,000 or more

Employment Prospects: Good

Advancement Prospects: Good

Prerequisites:

Education or Training—Undergraduate degree in communications, English, journalism, liberal arts, or public relations

Experience—Background in journalism and reporting useful

Special Skills and Personality Traits—Persuasive writing skills, in particular news writing; strong organizational and analytic skills

CAREER LADDER

```
┌─────────────────────────────────┐
│  Communications Coordinator or  │
│   Public Relations Manager      │
└─────────────────────────────────┘

┌─────────────────────────────────┐
│  External Publications Editor   │
└─────────────────────────────────┘

┌─────────────────────────────────┐
│ Public Relations Assistant, Journalist, │
│        or News Editor           │
└─────────────────────────────────┘
```

Position Description

An External Publications Editor's main function is to advance, through the written word, the interests of an employer with the public, the media, and/or special interest groups. In smaller firms, this job may be combined with other duties, leading to a more generalized job description.

The External Publications Editor is accountable for educating and providing information about a company, institution, or governmental organization to the outside world (including the general public, the news media, any special-interest groups, and stockholders). The position consists of writing and publishing brochures, feature articles for business and trade publications, news releases for the media, and slide scripts and speeches for business meetings and professional trade group conferences.

These communications might cover appointments of new company executives, how ongoing products or services are useful for the public or the community, or announcements of new products or services. Feature articles are usually written for industry, professional, or trade publications. For example, a restaurant chain news release may describe new services, new food preparations, or new entertainment, or pricing specials that would attract a larger customer base. Alternatively, a hotel newsletter may detail hotel services, tourist sightseeing programs, entertainment venues, and discount programs that would attract guests to the hotel. On the other hand, a government pamphlet may inform the public about particular government programs on financial aid, education, health matters, and other topics.

External Publications Editors may also produce informational material, such as booklets or pamphlets that answer questions raised by stockholders or that set forth the history of the firm and its products or services. In addition, an External Publications Editor might write articles for publications internal to the company, or write letters concerning community relations with the company for the signature of top executives. External Publications Editors may also work for educational institutions as well as governmental departments and agencies.

Salaries

An External Publications Editor with experience in journalism or public relations, and with good writing skills, may expect to earn anywhere from $25,000 to $45,000 a year. Depending upon years of experience and the level of the job within the company hierarchy, the salary may go as high as $50,000 or more. It should be noted that the mean average salary for communication specialists, in general, is $30,474, according to a 2002 National Association of Colleges and Employers (NACE) salary survey.

Employment Prospects

Employment of communications or public relations specialists is expected to increase faster than that of most other occupations through 2012, according to the U.S. Department of Labor. As most successful companies, professional organizations, and educational institutions have the need for publication programs, the position of an External Publications Editor is in demand. However, the profession is always susceptible to cutbacks during economic downturns or recessions.

Advancement Prospects

External Publications Editors are in a good position to advance to managerial jobs, usually within the public relations departments. As they often work directly with upper management, they have a visible presence within the company, institution, or agency, which, if they are successful, helps them move higher through the ranks.

Education and Training

An undergraduate degree in communications, English, journalism, liberal arts, or public relations is an absolute necessity for the position of External Publications Editor. Increasingly, degrees in communications or journalism are becoming preferable for most public relations positions. In addition, degrees in business or finance can add cachet to the editor's experience.

Experience, Skills, and Personality Traits

A communications degree and a journalism background are the best preparation for this type of public relations job, with its heavy dependence upon writing skills. An External Publications Editor must be able to write many different types of materials and for a varying audience.

Besides the excellent writing and editing skills, External Publications Editors must understand the mechanisms and needs of every kind of news media. They need to be able to conduct research and gather information, judge the visual and editorial quality and appropriateness of material for publication, and be both highly creative and well organized. Besides these skills, experience in graphics or graphic design, and the principles, practices, and techniques of producing camera-ready copy and artwork are all valuable abilities for an External Publications Editor.

Unions and Associations

Major professional associations include the American Society of Business Publications Editors, the Association for Women in Communications, the Council of Communication Management, the International Association of Business Communicators, the Public Relations Society of America, and the Society of American Business Editors and Writers.

Tips for Entry

1. To become familiar with the specifics of the type of business in which you work, read industry journals and newsletters to keep abreast of trends, new products, and other firms within the industry.
2. Network at industry trade shows, advertising forums, and local and national professional association meetings to make industry contacts.
3. Continually network to establish and maintain good relations with all types of media.
4. Enhance your writing skills by attending writing seminars and by networking with other writers via the Internet and/or chat rooms.
5. Consider further graduate education in public relations or communications, business, or finance to help in the advancement of your career as an External Publications Editor.

GOVERNMENT AFFAIRS SPECIALIST

Duties: Keep abreast of current public-affairs issues and governmental policies of pertinence to the employer; produce position papers for management; supervise the firm's political action committee

Alternate Title(s): Public Affairs Specialist

Salary Range: $30,000 to $60,000 or more

Employment Prospects: Good

Advancement Prospects: Good

Prerequisites:

Education or Training—Undergraduate degree in communications, history, journalism, liberal arts, political science, or public relations; a graduate degree would be useful

Experience—Background in journalism, politics, or public relations required

Special Skills and Personality Traits—Excellent analytical aptitude skills; solid organizational skills, persuasive speaking, and writing proficiencies; thorough understanding of political processes

```
┌─────────────────────────────────────┐
│   Public Relations Director or       │
│   Government Affairs Manager          │
└─────────────────────────────────────┘

┌─────────────────────────────────────┐
│   Government Affairs Specialist       │
└─────────────────────────────────────┘

┌─────────────────────────────────────┐
│   Communications Specialist or        │
│   Public Relations Assistant          │
└─────────────────────────────────────┘
```

Position Description

The Government Affairs Specialist plays a vital part in the well-being and success of many large companies and corporations, primarily by checking carefully the activities of local, state, and federal government bodies and agencies on matters of concern to a company's business and operations. In some firms, the position may be part of the public relations department where specific duties are detailed, or else the post may be the company's sole governmental and political guardian.

Government Affairs Specialists may also work for educational institutions, health institutions, law firms, lobbying firms, nonprofit organizations, and professional consulting companies.

Government Affairs Specialists must monitor such items as consumer rights regulations and legislation, labor regulations and bargaining trends, tax legislation, and other allied governmental or political matters. They keep management alerted and aware of pending issues that have a potential immediate impact upon the organization or a longer-term consequence. Notification to management usually takes the form of position papers, or detailed reports, which summarize the consequences of proposed legislation, regulations, or legal procedures that will affect the company's operation.

These specialists also may serve as the organization's spokesperson, in particular when the media requests information on the firm's position on issues (such as tax increases or decreases, regulations concerning hiring of minorities, or other such matters) of local and national concern. Occasionally, Government Affairs Specialists might testify on behalf of their employers at government hearings; they may also lobby for their company with lawmakers, regulatory agencies, and other government agency employees. In addition, they must be prepared to represent their employer in meetings with trade, industry, and professional organizations.

A Government Affairs Specialist may also oversee an organization's political action committee (PAC). This is the arm of the company that is permitted by law to contribute to political campaigns. One of the duties in such overseeing usually involves providing reports or profiles on candidates for office, both locally and nationally, with assessments on which ones might best be supported by the company. Another facet of this job is the writing of letters and preparing of newsletters for the use of other PAC members to keep them apprised of pending issues, as well as preparing responses to queries from governmental agencies requesting information relevant to the company's concerns in order to help them shape legislation or regulations.

The preparation of speeches or testimony of management on any number of issues for either local, state, or federal government bodies is a further extension of this job's duties.

Salaries

As this position involves much responsibility and requires considerable background experience, it is *not* an entry-level job. Annual salaries may range from the low $30,000s to the high $60,000s or above, depending upon the candidate's experience and expertise, the magnitude of the job requirements, and the size of the company or institution.

Employment Prospects

A Government Affairs Specialist is an essential post in a company's roster of employees because of the increasing number of governmental agencies and the resultant regulations, both on a local and national level. These agencies and their regulations must be scrutinized (as they are usually continuously changing and becoming more complex) for the effect they may have on the policies and practices of the institution in which they are employed, as well as its economic well-being.

Employment prospects are good for the qualified individual. The U.S. Bureau of Labor Statistics projects that the employment of public relations individuals, one of which is the Government Affairs Specialist, will increase rapidly throughout the next five years or more.

Advancement Prospects

The position of Government Affairs Specialist is a decidedly visible one within the hierarchy of an institution as this individual works closely with the highest levels of management. This can only enhance advancement potential, either within the company or with other firms.

Education and Training

An undergraduate degree in communications, government and public policy, journalism, liberal arts, or public relations is absolutely necessary for this position. An advanced degree or continuing education in public affairs is also beneficial. Experience with local community organizations as a volunteer may add expertise on a variety of issues.

Experience, Skills, and Personality Traits

Experience as a political journalist or a legislative or judicial aide at the state or federal level is an ideal background for a Government Affairs Specialist. This is a position that requires more experience rather than less. A knowledge of the legislative process and the methods utilized by the press, coalition groups, and grassroots organizations in their association's operations is essential. Additional background in public relations is a plus, and computer skills, at least at an intermediate level, are required.

Government Affairs Specialists must be able to analyze complex public issues and information, parse out the politics involved in these issues, and be able to explain them clearly and accurately to top management. They must be able to process a lot of information and systematize it in a coherent manner. They should be able to prioritize among projects, as well as conduct research and evaluate information. Above all, they should be extremely well organized, outgoing and personable, persuasive and effective in their speech and manner. They must be comfortable at making speeches and interacting in a public arena.

Unions and Associations

Major professional associations include the Association for Women in Communications, the International Association of Business Communicators, and the Public Relations Society of America. Other potentially useful groups include the American Society of Information Science and the National Association of Government Communicators, as well as other organizations dealing with governmental policies and procedures.

Tips for Entry

1. Take specific courses in public affairs and government to gain background for this position.
2. To acquire governmental expertise, work in the office of a local, state, or federal legislator, to gain perspective on and experience in the legislative process, as well as begin building a contact base for the future.
3. Take advanced courses in oral and written communication to enhance your skills.
4. Gain experience in journalism and/or public relations by working on school newspapers and any local political campaigns.

INTERNAL PUBLICATIONS EDITOR

CAREER PROFILE

Duties: Write, edit, and generate employee magazine, newsletter, and other internal publications

Alternate Title(s): Communications Specialist, Publications Editor

Salary Range: $25,000 to $50,000 or more

Employment Prospects: Good

Advancement Prospects: Good

Prerequisites:

Education or Training—Undergraduate degree in communications, English, journalism, liberal arts, or public relations

Experience—Prior work as a news reporter or news editor helpful

Special Skills and Personality Traits—Excellent writing and editing abilities; knowledge of photography and graphic design; organizational skills; self-motivation and creativity

CAREER LADDER

```
┌─────────────────────────────────┐
│   Editorial Services Manager     │
└─────────────────────────────────┘

┌─────────────────────────────────┐
│  Internal Publications Editor    │
└─────────────────────────────────┘

┌─────────────────────────────────┐
│   Journalist, News Editor,       │
│ Public Relations Assistant, or   │
│        College Student           │
└─────────────────────────────────┘
```

Position Description

Most firms produce a company newsletter or magazine for than employees. Top management view such a publication as a pipeline of information to its staff and a means to enhance goodwill toward and between employees, and to boost company morale. Such a publication may be a two-sided sheet of paper, a slickly produced, multicolored magazine, or an e-mail communication. In other cases, these publications may be produced by management as a weekly newssheet or as a monthly or quarterly magazine. If the latter, it may be supplemented by a weekly or monthly newssheet or e-mail newsletter.

The duties of an Internal Publications Editor include formulating, writing, editing, and designing the internal publications. In addition to the editorial decision-making process, the choice of photography and graphics the layout, and the general production fall under the editor's jurisdiction. By using their range of creativity, most editors can individualize these publications.

Usually, Internal Publications Editors work under the supervision of a communications coordinator, a publications director, or a manager of editorial services. Editors must plan, conceptualize, research, and design issues in advance, and then submit outlines of each issue for managerial review

and approval. Thereafter they arrange for whatever material is to be included, such as interviews, illustrations, or any guest articles.

An editor may produce the publication alone or may utilize freelancers to assist. Depending upon the company's size, the editor may even have an assistant or a full-fledged staff. Editors must be able to spec type (that is, decide on font styles and point sizes to be used in the publication), design page layouts, or work with graphic artists. They should know how to operate personal computer hardware, software, and peripherals. In addition, they need to interface with printing shops. Above all, it is important that the editor be attuned to meeting deadlines and remaining within publication budget limits.

Content of internal publications may depend on the nature and purpose of the magazine or newsletter. Articles may include profiles of departments or employees, newly hired personnel or announcements of promotions, messages from senior management, information on community projects of interest to employees and the company, and any other newsworthy features.

Additionally, an Internal Publications Editor occasionally may prepare press releases or speeches, or produce slide or digital picture shows and films for in-house use.

Salaries

An entry-level Internal Publications Editor can expect to be paid between $25,000 and $37,000 annually. Those applicants with some publications experience may receive between $35,000 and $50,000 or higher. These salary rates depend upon the scope of his/her responsibilities and the size of the company or institution.

Employment Prospects

The position of Internal Publications Editor is one of the most widespread of public relations jobs. Thus, it is probably the easiest way to break into a public relations department. However, it is also one of the highest in turnover. The Bureau of Labor Statistics projects that employment of public relations specialists will increase by 36 percent from 2000 to 2010.

Advancement Prospects

An employee newsletter or other publication is a fine venue to demonstrate the individual editor's creativity, skills, and managerial possibilities. It is a highly visible position, and prospects for advancement to higher-level positions are good.

Education and Training

The absolute minimum requirement is an undergraduate degree in communications, English, journalism, or public relations.

Experience, Skills, and Personality Traits

In some cases, an Internal Publications Editor position is an entry-level one, and can be filled by recent college graduates. In other instances where the firm's publication program is more extensive, several years of experience as a news reporter, writer, editor, or public relations specialist may be required.

Excellent editing, proofreading, and writing skills, coupled with good interpersonal skills and leadership qualities, are vital for any publication editing position. Editors must have a good sense of the newsworthiness of information, and must have superior organizational skills. They need to be able to conduct research and gather information, as well as have a familiarity with graphic arts and print production. They must be able both to work well with others and to take direction themselves. Corporate interests are paramount, and an Internal Publications Editor must follow management direction in designing the internal publications and maintain established publications budgets. They may also need to know the principles, practices, and techniques of Internet publishing.

Unions and Associations

Major professional associations include the American Society of Business Publications Editors, the Association for Women in Communications, the Council of Communication Management, the International Association of Business Communicators, the Public Relations Society of America, and the Society of American Business Editors and Writers.

Tips for Entry

1. Take additional courses in writing and public relations to enhance your basic skills.
2. Work as a public relations assistant to gain experience and establish a résumé of your work.
3. Take commercial art courses, concentrating on layout and design.
4. Do a summer internship with an advertising or public relations firm to gain knowledge of this type of work.
5. Work at a local printing shop to understand the mechanisms of the printing trade.

PUBLIC INFORMATION OFFICER

CAREER PROFILE

Duties: Conduct media relations for a company, organization, or institution; compose and distribute news releases; place articles in news media

Alternate Title(s): Public Relations Manager, Public Affairs Specialist

Salary Range: $30,000 to $60,000 or more

Employment Prospects: Good

Advancement Prospects: Good

Prerequisites:

Education or Training—Undergraduate degree in communications, English, liberal arts, journalism, or public relations

Experience—News writing, wire service journalism, or previous communication experience essential

Special Skills and Personality Traits—Excellent writing skills, in particular, in journalism; organizational ability; good interpersonal skills

CAREER LADDER

```
┌─────────────────────────────────┐
│  Director of Communications or  │
│   Director of Public Relations  │
└─────────────────────────────────┘

┌─────────────────────────────────┐
│    Public Information Officer    │
└─────────────────────────────────┘

┌─────────────────────────────────┐
│    Communications Coordinator    │
└─────────────────────────────────┘
```

Position Description

Public Information Officers provide and coordinate information for the public and the media about the company or organization they represent. They direct, administer, monitor, and evaluate the company's program of public information for appropriateness in representing the firm or organization. They prepare and generate press releases, commendations, resolutions, reports, newsletters, brochures, and other written material and information for public consumption, as well as other publications regarding the company's products and/or services. They generate positive news pieces about the company or organization, placing them in newspapers, on the Internet, in other publications deemed appropriate, and on television and radio. They keep management updated on pertinent issues that relate to the company and that might result from media exposure. They prepare management's responses to probable questions from the media on matters concerning the policies and practices of the organization or company.

The single most important task of the Public Information Officer is to sustain ongoing and effective relations with all the media, establishing a sense of trust with its members. Trust is crucial in getting across a message or projecting an image to the public. They must be capable of responding immediately—or within a set period—to any and all questions from the press. They also tutor company executives on effective methods for handling media interviews.

Public Information Officers must keep up-to-date on all news developments that might affect their employers in order to act quickly and effectively to shield management from unfavorable publicity, or to capitalize on positive exposure. Depending upon the circumstances, they may be responsible for providing top management with daily news clips (or Internet printouts) and analyses.

In addition, they may coordinate special events relating to the public relations of their employer. They may plan, organize, and arrange meetings on-site for dissemination of information to the public and the media. They may also be involved in the establishment and maintenance of the look and content of the company's Web site to maximize its marketing impact, as well as update and ensure the accuracy of the information. In many cases, the Public Information Officer may also write speeches and create the scripts for slide or digital photographic shows concerning the company, or produce other promotional literature.

Most officers supervise a staff of one or more assistants, although in smaller companies they may have only secretarial help. Depending upon the size and complexity of the company, this position may be a mid-level one or a top position at the firm.

Salaries

Salaries may vary according to the size of the company and the complexity of the responsibilities of the individual Public Information Officer, and that person's place in the hierarchy of the management of the company. Average annual salaries are in the $30,000 range, but nearly half of the professionals in this position have yearly salaries of $45,000 or more. The U.S. Bureau of Labor Statistics estimates that the median annual earnings for salaried public relations specialists were $41,700 in 2002, with a range from $31,300 to $56,180 encompassing the profession and the highest paid 10 percent of the professionals earning more than $75,100.

Employment Prospects

The importance of Public Information Officers has become increasingly apparent to top management in both business and government agencies in recent years. This is especially due to the aggressive nature of the (inter)national news media. The Bureau of Labor Statistics estimates that the employment of public relations specialists is anticipated to increase faster than the average of all other occupations through 2012. This will be especially true for private industry. However, jobs in education will be more limited due to cutbacks in funding from both state and national governments.

Advancement Prospects

The position of Public Information Officer is a highly visible one to the public and the media, and, thus, a frontline position within any company or organization. With success, the odds are extremely good for promotion to higher-level, more responsible management posts.

Education and Training

Most Public Information Officers have an undergraduate degree in communications, English, journalism, marketing, public relations, or a closely related field. Some have undergraduate degrees in business, economics, or political science.

Experience, Skills, and Personality Traits

For this position, previous experience working in writing/editing for a print or broadcast media operation is crucial, as well as in other public relations positions. Some employers may require three or more years of experience.

Public Information Officers must have a strong sense for news, as well as excellent writing and editing talents. Their interpersonal skills must be excellent, and they must be able to mix well with a wide variety of individuals. Above all, they have to be well organized and capable of meeting deadlines.

Unions and Associations

Major professional associations include the American Business Communication Association, the Association for Women in Communications, the Council of Communication Management, the International Association of Business Communicators, and the Public Relations Society of America.

Tips for Entry

1. Join professional associations in this field and participate in their range of activities.
2. Gain as much journalism experience as possible, both in college and in summer intern programs.
3. Advance your understanding of Web sites by participating in out-of-school courses in Web design and production, and by communicating with other professionals in such places as online chat rooms.
4. Be active in local community groups to learn to interact effectively with a wide assortment of people on a large range of issues.
5. Take public speaking and creative writing courses.

PUBLIC RELATIONS ACCOUNT EXECUTIVE

CAREER PROFILE

Duties: Carry out public relations functions for clients and advise them on their public relations activities

Alternate Title(s): Public Relations Consultant

Salary Range: $30,000 to $65,000 or more

Employment Prospects: Good

Advancement Prospects: Good

Prerequisites:

Education or Training—Undergraduate degree in communications, English, journalism, liberal arts, or public relations

Experience—Three to five years' experience in public relations or journalism, or in advertising as an account executive

Special Skills and Personality Traits—Good written and verbal communication skills; solid analytical and computer skills; leadership ability and outgoing personality with excellent organizational talents

CAREER LADDER

```
┌─────────────────────────────────┐
│        Account Manager          │
└─────────────────────────────────┘

┌─────────────────────────────────┐
│        Account Executive         │
└─────────────────────────────────┘

┌─────────────────────────────────┐
│  Assistant Account Executive,    │
│  Public Relations Specialist,    │
│  Journalist, or News Editor      │
└─────────────────────────────────┘
```

Position Description

Many public relations professionals work for agencies or consulting firms. These firms operate much like advertising agencies: they plan, manage, and deliver public relations services for clients, creating publicity campaigns and approaches that will establish and maintain goodwill and understanding between their clients and their publics (which may be customers, suppliers, government, or investors). In addition, they advise their clients on public relations matters, for all of which they charge fees or commissions. Some of their clients may be too small to have their own public relations staff, while other larger ones may have a staff, but prefer to use agencies to handle projects that would be too big or too time-consuming for their own staff to manage. Most of this work is achieved by a proactive and close interface with all types of media, including television, radio, and the press.

The account executive is the crucial link between the agency and the client. The individual must produce consistent top-line media coverage for the client, as well as oversee the day-to-day tactical aspects of the customer's programs. The executive usually reports to an accounts supervisor or a sen-

ior consultant within the firm, updating senior management on both client and team project activity. Beginners typically are called assistant account executives and are regularly assigned to routine tasks in order to learn the business.

Specific duties of the Public Relations Account Executive depend upon the types of services requested by the client. They may include preparing (or supervising the assembling of) press kits and press releases, managing press conferences on behalf of the client, arranging media interviews and business tours for client executives, positioning positive news and feature pieces in the media, supervising arrangements for promotional lunches or dinners, preparing material to be utilized in trade shows, conducting opinion polls, and studying market research and media coverage. The account executive is usually responsible for weekly or biweekly client meetings and conference calls, and must develop monthly reports detailing team member activity on the client's behalf.

Advisory duties for the client may encompass planning of publicity campaigns, establishing a public relations department or program to be incorporated into the client's firm, and establishing a lobbying program for the client. In all these activities, Public Relations Account Executives need to coordinate their work with the client's advertising and marketing activities. Throughout this process, it is useful to maintain an ongoing awareness of public relations work being done for other clients of the firm to ascertain where a cross-fertilization of ideas and solutions can be helpful on the public relations project at hand.

Many agencies or consulting firms specialize in certain areas, such as entertainment, education, or government regulations.

Salaries

According to the U.S. Bureau of Labor Statistics, salaried public relations specialists working full time received a median annual salary of $41,710 in 2002. The middle 50 percent earned between $31,300 and $56,180, and the top 10 percent earned more than $75,100. According to a joint survey conducted by the International Association of Business Communicators and the Public Relations Society of America, the median annual salary for a public relations specialist was $66,800 in 2002.

Salaries will vary widely according to the size of the firm or agency, its location in the country, and its particular area(s) of specialty. For example, according to salary surveys made by Salary.com during 2004, public relations specialists who also supervise a support staff have an annual salary range of $62,492 to $79,548 in New York City, as opposed to a national average salary range of $53,412 to $67,990.

Employment Prospects

Employment prospects are best in larger cities where media communication centers are based and most of the trade and business associations have their main offices. Cities such as New York, Chicago, Los Angeles, and Washington, D.C., have many public relations firms to support diverse clientele.

The field of public relations consulting is expected to remain quite competitive, as the number of applicants will most likely grow faster than the estimated job availability. According to the Bureau of Labor Statistics, the employment of public relations specialists will increase by nearly 25 percent from the years 1998 to 2008. The awareness of the need for public relations, both in business and in government, can only escalate and thus help feed the future job market for these positions. Only an economic slowdown, which might result in corporate downsizing, could affect this job growth. Some of this corporate scaling back will have a good outcome for outside public relations firms. It is estimated that employment in those firms should grow as businesses decide to hire out-of-house contractors to provide the public relations services they need, rather than maintain full-time internal staffs.

Advancement Prospects

A successful Public Relations Account Executive is in an excellent position for advancement, either within the agency or by moving to a corporation, professional association, or governmental body. Some Public Relations Account Executives become self-employed consultants.

Education and Training

An undergraduate degree in business management, communications, journalism, or public relations is the customary requirement. A degree in English or liberal arts may be acceptable if accompanied by some hands-on experience in public relations. For consulting, a graduate degree in business or finance is advantageous.

Experience, Skills, and Personality Traits

Most Public Relations Account Executives have backgrounds in public relations work, or experience in the news media as journalists or news editors. Talents must include good interpersonal skills, the capacity to persuade others, excellent writing/editing skills, creativity, and self-motivation. Supervisory skills may be required for larger firms, as executives will be expected to oversee a public relations staff.

Unions and Associations

Major professional associations include the Association for Women in Communications, the Council of Communication Management, the International Association of Business Communicators, and, most importantly, the Public Relations Society of America.

Tips for Entry

1. Consider starting out in journalism, to gain valuable writing and editing experience and knowledge of news values, interaction with the public, and contacts within the media—all excellent preparation for a Public Relations Account Executive position.
2. Join local community organizations to scout potential clients and gain valuable contacts.
3. Increase and expand interest in new technology, in particular the expanding potentials of the Internet.

PUBLIC RELATIONS ASSISTANT

CAREER PROFILE

Duties: Assist editors, the public relations manager, the publications director, and others with public relations activities

Alternate Title(s): Editorial Assistant, Publicity Assistant

Salary Range: $18,000 to $30,000 or more

Employment Prospects: Good

Advancement Prospects: Good

Prerequisites:

Education or Training—Undergraduate degree in communications, English, journalism, liberal arts, or public relations

Experience—School journalism experience is helpful, as well as participation in an internship program in public relations

Special Skills and Personality Traits—Good writing and editing skills; knowledge of graphics and design; ability to work as part of a team and good interpersonal skills; analytic, computer, and secretarial skills

CAREER LADDER

```
┌─────────────────────────────────────┐
│        Publications Editor          │
│ or Public Relations Account Executive│
└─────────────────────────────────────┘

┌─────────────────────────────────────┐
│      Public Relations Assistant     │
└─────────────────────────────────────┘

┌─────────────────────────────────────┐
│     Journalist or College Student   │
└─────────────────────────────────────┘
```

Position Description

The function of the public relations practitioner is to present positively the organization's image to its various targets, which could include business clients, the general public, the investment community, or lawmakers and government institutions.

The public relations job may take many forms in different organizations (such as public information, investor relations, public affairs, corporate communications, marketing or product publicity, employee relations, and customer service or customer relations), and the Public Relations Assistant will be exposed to (nearly) all of these areas. Common to all public relations activities is communication. Well-planned and effectively executed communications to target audiences is increasingly essential to the success (and sometimes the very existence) of organizations. Public relations can be critical to the success or failure of an organization or a cause.

The job of Public Relations Assistant is an entry-level one, and can be found in all aspects of modern society, including business and industry, education, government, health care, and nonprofit associations. Many of the duties are menial and supportive of mid-level management, such as word processing, filing, running errands, and fielding telephone calls.

Most Public Relations Assistants assist on specific public-relation campaigns under the supervision of an account executive. For example, they may write brief pieces for internal newsletters or the company magazine (known commonly as the "house" organ), or they may contribute to other employer communiqués within the firm. They may also help in developing mailing and/or e-mail lists for news releases, even write some simple news releases for approval by their supervisor, assemble press kits, and prepare press packets. They may also lend a hand to arrange speaking engagements, assist in the company's public relations activities with the community at large and with fund-raising drives, help update internal company data about the executives, and assist internal publication editors in their production work.

Salaries

Due to the growing importance of public relations as a field of endeavor, public relations professionals tend to be paid well. The average entry-level annual salary in public relations for a person with an undergraduate degree is somewhere between $18,000 and $22,000. Those applicants with additional education or experience (such as membership in the Public Relations Student Society of America) might qualify for a higher starting salary.

A public relations account executive in a freelance consulting firm can earn between $35,000 and $38,000 yearly, as will a person of comparable responsibility who is employed by a company's in-house public relations department. A public relations director for a small to medium-sized company may earn $35,000 to $40,000 or above, while this range in a larger company may extend from $40,000 to $60,000. Seasoned public relations executives may have salaries ranging from $75,000 to $150,000, depending upon the size of the company, its location, the amount of public relations activities undertaken, and other factors. Such persons may carry the title of vice president.

In one study done by the Puget Sound (Washington) Chapter of the Public Relations Student Society of America, it was found that annual salaries for entry-level positions in agencies ran from $18,000 to $24,000, whereas entry-level posts at private companies typically paid between $24,000 and $32,000 in the Puget Sound region. The report noted that entry-level positions at nonprofit organizations typically paid between $17,000 and $21,000, whereas the same entry position with government agencies earned between $22,000 and $28,000.

Employment Prospects

According to the Bureau of Labor Statistics, public relations will be one of the fastest-growing industries through 2012. It is expected to increase faster than the average for all occupations. According to another bureau study, the number of people in public relations is estimated as 98,000, with more than half of those being women.

However, competition will remain keen for entry-level public relations jobs as the number of qualified applicants still exceeds the number of current job openings. The high-profile nature of the work and good advancement prospects attract many people to this profession. Opportunities should be best for college graduates who combine a degree in advertising, journalism, public relations, or another communications-related field with a public relations internship (many companies offer them) or other related work experience. Since many of the senior executive public relations professionals started out as journalists, this is an excellent stepping-stone to a career in public relations. The experience gained in writing, personal contact with the public from working on newspapers, general or trade magazines, and the broadcasting media is important background for public relations.

Sometimes work in specialized fields, such as education, engineering, finance, medicine, or public administration, can provide worthwhile experience for a specific public relations position in any of those industries.

Advancement Prospects

Public Relations Assistants who perform well in the tasks given them can expect good opportunities for promotion. Exposure to a large assortment of public relations activities can be useful in narrowing specific career goals.

Education and Training

Entry-level jobs generally necessitate a college degree in advertising, communications, journalism, liberal arts, or public relations. In addition, many companies offer internship programs of formal training for qualified students. (Many times, firms will give college credits for work accomplished.) The most valuable internships are ones in which assignments include writing, layout, and editing for internal/external publications, preparing promotional material, brochures, news releases, and feature presentations. In addition, aiding the researching and writing of reports, helping to organize special events, and assisting in fund-raising activities provides valuable hands-on experience and a distinct edge when applying for a full-time public relations position.

Journalism-school graduates may become even more qualified for specialized public relations jobs by working in journalism at first. Assignments that might use their background effectively include Public Relations Assistant positions at newspapers; at magazines, where the planning of press and trade parties may be a part of the assistant's duties; at television stations; in advertising agencies that frequently offer public relations services to their clients; in the federal and state government, where researching and forecasting public reaction to policies may be an essential element of the job; or at nonprofit institutions, where lobbying activities on behalf of the institution may be needed, along with the usual public relations functions.

Experience, Skills, and Personality Traits

Where prior experience in journalism or advertising was important for employment in public relations firms, now many undergraduates with journalism degrees go directly into public relations. While only minimal experience may be required, the field is becoming increasingly competitive. Internships with public relations departments or firms and/or college newspaper/magazine experience are advantageous, giving the candidate for an entry-level position a better chance at employment. In addition, membership in the Public Relations Student Society of America may be worthwhile.

Public relations professionals should be creative, have an outgoing personality (as contact with the public plays a major role in their employment), and be able to motivate and persuade others. They should have excellent writing and editing talents and good analytic skills, understand the mechanism and needs of the media, and be knowledgeable about graphic design/layout. By now, computer skills are a prerequisite.

Unions and Associations

Major professional associations include the Association for Women in Communications, the International Association of Business Communicators, and, especially, the Public Relations Society of America.

Tips for Entry

1. While in college, apply for an internship program to gain hands-on experience in public relations.
2. Take courses in journalism (to understand news values), public speaking (to enhance presentation methods), and writing (to learn to outline ideas clearly and concisely).
3. Join the Public Relations Student Society of America (http://www.prssa.org) to meet with professional public relations practitioners, and to initiate establishing valuable industry contacts.

SPEECHWRITER

CAREER PROFILE

Duties: Prepares and/or writes speeches, briefings and other documents for corporate executives on a variety of topics and for all types of audiences

Alternate Title(s): Management Communications Specialist

Salary Range: $30,000 to $80,000

Employment Prospects: Good

Advancement Prospects: Good

Prerequisites:

Education or Training—Undergraduate degree in business, communications, English, journalism, or liberal arts

Experience—Background in journalism or public relations required

Special Skills and Personality Traits—Creativity; excellent research and organizational skills; persuasive presentation skills; superior writing ability

CAREER LADDER

```
┌─────────────────────────────┐
│   Director of Management     │
│       Communications         │
└─────────────────────────────┘

┌─────────────────────────────┐
│        Speechwriter          │
└─────────────────────────────┘

┌─────────────────────────────┐
│ Public Information Officer or│
│     Publications Editor      │
└─────────────────────────────┘
```

Position Description

Speechwriting jobs are usually staff positions within larger corporations (which have structured communication departments) and in companies where key executives must make frequent public appearances. Speechwriters are accountable for researching and preparing speeches for upper management on a wide range of topics for diverse audiences. For example, a business executive may address a luncheon of Wall Street analysts one day and, in the next week, a community fund-raising organization.

Some executives may like to work closely with the Speechwriters on developing both the content and character of the speech to be given, while others will rely entirely upon the Speechwriter to research and write the address. Before beginning the first draft, the Speechwriter usually meets with the executive and/or his or her assistant to get information on the audience to which it will be delivered, as well as its main topic, general content, and length. Also, the Speechwriter will need to know whether anyone from the company has addressed this specific audience before, when, and on what topic(s). Other elements that the Speechwriter needs to know are who else will be on the dais with the company executive, whether the speeches will be before or after a meal, whether or not questions will be permitted from the audience, and whether the event will be tracked by the media.

Sometimes, a previously delivered speech may provide the basis for the new one. However, usually the Speechwriter must write the address anew, undertaking as many drafts and revisions as necessary to satisfy the executive. Obviously, there may be satisfaction in the accomplishment, but there will be little to no public credit given.

In addition, Speechwriters may be responsible for editorials, press releases, or articles written (for industry or business publications) to go under the byline of company executives. Slide scripts and DVD presentations may also be a part of a scriptwriter's tasks.

Salaries

Speechwriters are paid according to their experience and talent. A beginning Speechwriter may earn about $30,000 yearly and experience can bring salaries up to $80,000 or more. According to salary studies done by Salary.com, the national median salary for an experienced business Speechwriter during 2004 was $60,350 (with a range from $53,150 to $67,900). It should be noted that the same salary study indicated that in New York City, the median was $70,600, based on a range from $62,180 to $79,400.

It is entirely possible for experienced freelance Speechwriters to earn $150,000 or more a year, as they can pick and choose the projects and the companies for which they will work.

Employment Prospects

Speechwriters are always in demand. However, this profession is renowned for its high turnover and its intense pressures. Speechwriters are known either to burn out easily, or to move from company to company to vary their work. The best job opportunities are in private industry and business, as opposed to health care or educational institutions.

Advancement Prospects

The post of Speechwriter has great visibility within a firm. Success provides a good prospect for both higher earnings and for advancement to higher management positions.

Education and Training

An undergraduate degree in communications, English, journalism, or liberal arts is mandatory. Some Speechwriters have additional undergraduate or graduate degrees in business, economics, or political science. For specific industries, such as aerospace, technical communications, and engineering firms, other degrees in the area of that business may be required.

Experience, Skills, and Personality Traits

Speechwriters may have a highly varied background. Many start out in some type of journalism, while others may come from the arena of public relations. Most speechwriting positions demand at least two to four years of experience in the field, or in a related area.

Speechwriters must have an aptitude at writing the spoken word, which is very different from the writing of printed prose. They should be able to imitate the speech patterns, style, and frame of reference of the executive for whom they are writing the address. In addition, they need to have substantial researching abilities, and an abundance of patience/tact in dealing with the extensive rewrites constantly required of them.

Unions and Associations

Major professional associations include the Association for Women in Communications, the Association of Writers and Writing Programs, the International Association of Business Communicators, and the Public Relations Society of America.

Tips for Entry

1. Take every opportunity to write speeches for yourself and fellow students throughout your college career.
2. Extend your reading to stay abreast of news and trends that relate to your (potential) employer.
3. Consider working with a freelance speechwriting firm to gain experience and make industry contacts.
4. Check the Internet for speech and writing courses, seminars, and workshops.
5. Study great speeches of the past for pointers on their success.
6. Knowing your audience is crucial to successful speechwriting, so research social trends, behavior patterns, and concerns in advance.

TECHNICAL COMMUNICATOR

CAREER PROFILE

Duties: Write and/or edit technical materials for both technical and general audiences

Alternate Title(s): Technical Writer, Technical Editor

Salary Range: $40,000 to $90,000 or more

Employment Prospects: Excellent

Advancement Prospects: Fair

Prerequisites:

Education or Training—Undergraduate degree in business administration, computer science, engineering, English, journalism, science, or technical communication

Experience—Previous work as a writer or in some position in a technical or scientific field is helpful

Special Skills and Personality Traits—Facility at writing technical information clearly; aptitude to work with engineers, scientists, and technicians; understanding of the field of endeavor being explained

CAREER LADDER

```
┌─────────────────────────────────────┐
│  Technical Communications Manager or │
│         Publications Manager         │
└─────────────────────────────────────┘

┌─────────────────────────────────────┐
│                                     │
│       Technical Communicator        │
│                                     │
└─────────────────────────────────────┘

┌─────────────────────────────────────┐
│                                     │
│        Writer or Technician         │
│                                     │
└─────────────────────────────────────┘
```

Position Description

Technical Communicators write and edit a wide variety of information of a technical nature and present or transmit it to an assortment of target audiences. They may be technical writers and editors, graphic designers and technical illustrators, information developers, Web and Intranet page designers, or other multimedia artists. Technical Communicators work in almost every industry, from banks to business to manufacturing, from aviation to computer technology to medicine, from education to government departments and the military. Technical information may be found in various formats, such as user and repair manuals, sales materials aimed at engineers and technicians, specifications sheets, inserts for pharmaceutical products, online help systems, policy and procedure documents, speeches for industry conferences and meetings, scripts for slide-presentations and films, Web-based information, computer and other training manuals.

Technical Communicators work closely with engineers and other technical staff in developing products. They must translate the language of engineers and technical staff into words that the marketing/sales staff can understand and use to market the product, as well as make the text understandable to the general public. Their duties may include writing software manuals explaining how a product works, including programming, operation, maintenance, and troubleshooting. They often work with graphic artists in developing professional-looking graphics, audiovisual aids, and sales materials for customers, as well as oversee galleys, proofs, and mechanicals of these materials. They may supervise other writers, assistants, and freelancers.

Technical Communicators frequently have prior experience in journalism or business communications. They may work in some technical field and find they like and are good at writing procedures or reports. Having such a specialty (that is, working within the pharmaceutical or cosmetics industry, or being in the military) may lead to a technical communication position. However, the disadvantage of specializing is that it limits employment options.

The typical member of the Society for Technical Communication, the leading professional organization with more than 20,000 members worldwide, will have at least seven years' experience as a communicator. The majority of them are writers or editors and reside in major metropolitan areas.

Salaries

According to the 2003 salary survey conducted by the Society for Technical Communication, the mean average annual salary of entry-level technical writers/editors in the United

States was $43,260. For mid-level, nonsupervisory writers/editors, the mean salary was $54,510, whereas mid-level supervisory personnel had a mean salary of $60,510. For senior levels, mean salaries ranged from $66,590 to $72,340. The overall mean salary for all technical writers/editors was $61,670, which is approximately a 130 percent increase in median-range salary since 1999.

Technical Communicators with Ph.D. degrees earned an average of $68,030 yearly, as opposed to $65,660 for those with a master's degree and $60,120 for those with a bachelor's degree. Communicators who lived on the West Coast (California, Oregon, or Washington) earned a mean average of $70,000, as opposed to those who lived in New York or the New England area who were paid an average of $66,850, or those who lived in the upper Midwest (Michigan, Wisconsin, the Dakotas, Montana) who earned $52,000 annually.

The same study found that Technical Communicators with six to 10 years of experience earned $60,710 as an average, whereas those with two to five years' experience received $53,540. Men's mean yearly salary tended to be nearly $3,000 higher than women's.

A separate 2001 study by Abbott, Langer & Associates, published on their Web site at http://www.abbott-langer.com, found that the median national salary for technical writers was $45,510.

Employment Prospects

The need for technical writers is expected to increase steadily because of the constant expansion of scientific and technical fields, in particular computer technology, and the continuous call for individuals who can communicate and explain such material to the lay and user public. The U.S. Bureau of Labor Statistics' *Occupation Outlook Handbook* (2004–2005 edition) predicts that during the next several years, the most job opportunities for writers will be in the field of technical writer or writers with specialized training. While many people are drawn to writing and editing jobs, technical writers and editors have better opportunities for employment because of the still relatively limited number of people who can handle technical material and explain it clearly for both technical and nontechnical audiences.

Advancement Prospects

About 19 percent of the members of the Society for Technical Communication have managerial responsibilities. A majority of technical writers and editors surveyed by the society indicated that they valued adequate salary, creative opportunity, job satisfaction and security, and professional development more than advancement into managerial positions. Nonetheless, elevation to higher managerial positions for technical writers and editors do exist and depend, as so often is the case, on performance.

Education and Training

A 2002 survey of Society for Technical Communication members detailed that 90 percent of its members had graduated from a four-year college. Of these, 32 percent had an English degree, whereas 22 percent had majored in technical communication. Business administration claimed 10 percent, while computer science, general science, and engineering each claimed 9 percent, and those with journalism degrees constituted 7 percent of the total.

Most technical writers are hired for their communication skills, and they acquire specialized information on the job. However, advanced degrees in computer science, economics, engineering, graphic arts, mathematics, or science can be helpful when combined with excellent writing ability, and, in some cases, may even be required for specialized technical writing.

Experience, Skills, and Personality Traits

Some technical writers start in low-level assistant capacities (or job trainee positions) within a technical information department and learn about the technology involved before assuming writing positions. Others may transfer to the field of writing from their existing posts as engineers or scientists.

Technical Communicators must be outstanding writers. They must collect, refine and organize technical data, and then explain it clearly, concretely, and correctly in everyday language. Another valuable characteristic is curiosity, as it is far easier to explain to others how something works when you know how it actually works yourself. Expert computer skills are a prerequisite, and some jobs may also demand a specific technical background or degree. Paying close attention to detail, creativity, organization, planning abilities, and self-discipline are important job qualities for a proficient Technical Communicator.

Unions and Associations

The Society for Technical Communication is the primary professional association. Technical Communicators also may belong to general writing associations, such as the Council for Advancement of Science Writing and the Information Technology Association, or particular groups in their areas of expertise, such as the American Medical Writers Association and the National Association of Science Writers.

Tips for Entry

1. Take as many writing courses as possible to improve your proficiency in writing clearly and concisely.
2. Sign up for graphics classes, as this will be a skill you need in technical communication.
3. Familiarize yourself with Web technology, computerized publishing systems, and the powerful standard of Extensible Markup Language (XML) to aid you in setting up technical communication systems.
4. If you have particular skills acquired from another career, consider how they can be used to enhance your value as a technical writer.

FEDERAL, STATE, AND MUNICIPAL GOVERNMENTS

EDITORIAL ASSISTANT

CAREER PROFILE

Duties: Edit and oversee production of printed material, and perform needed clerical duties

Alternate Title(s): Editorial Clerk

Salary Range: $21,000 to $49,000

Employment Prospects: Fair

Advancement Prospects: Good

Prerequisites:

Education or Training—High-school diploma minimum

Experience—General office, clerical, and/or editorial support work required

Special Skills and Personality Traits—Knowledge of editorial methods, grammar, and production procedures; good keyboarding skills

CAREER LADDER

```
┌─────────────────────────────────────┐
│  Supervisory Editorial Associate     │
└─────────────────────────────────────┘

┌─────────────────────────────────────┐
│       Editorial Assistant            │
└─────────────────────────────────────┘

┌─────────────────────────────────────┐
│   High School or College Student     │
└─────────────────────────────────────┘
```

Position Description

Editorial Assistants (or editorial clerks) undertake a wide range of clerical and editorial support work. Their principal duty, however, is to prepare manuscripts for publication and to verify information within the copy. Basic duties include proofreading final copy and page proofs against the original manuscript before the finishing printing process. In addition, they will specify formats, type fonts to be used, and style according to established style manuals; edit for basic grammatical accuracy and clarity of structure; and verify references, footnotes, photo captions, and any tabular material used.

Individual duties will fluctuate according to the specific federal agency and grade level of the post. Some Editorial Assistants work in groups under the direction of a supervisory editorial associate. Others work directly for writers, editors, or subject matter specialists within the agency. Regardless of the work setting, the duties usually remain the same. Most editing jobs deal first and foremost with accuracy and grammar, though Editorial Assistants may be expected to recommend changes and reorganization of the material for a more effective presentation.

Editorial Assistants prepare the layout of the material to be printed, including placement of any graphics (tables or illustrations) used, as well as give specific typesetting and printing instructions. More experienced Editorial Assistants may actually write material, in addition to substantive edit-ing tasks comparable to those expected of writers and higher level editors.

Usually, special knowledge of subject matter is unnecessary, except in some case of highly specialized or technical subjects. However, a thorough knowledge of grammatical rules and production procedures is necessary.

Editorial Assistants usually operate under tight deadlines, high pressure, and many last-minute changes and rushes. Accuracy is of the highest priority. In addition, Editorial Assistants must be equipped to handle a high volume of work on their own, must be able to follow detailed instructions, and be familiar with and properly interpret policies and regulations.

Salaries

Editorial Assistant positions are usually one of the few in the federal, state, or municipal governments in which women may be more prevalent than men, and may earn more than men. Overall, salaries can range from $21,000 to $49,000, depending upon the agency or department and upon the experience of the Editorial Assistant. For the federal government, most of these positions fall within the GS4 to GS9 level (GS stands for General Schedule, the pay system governing the salary rates of the majority of federal workers.)

Jobs within the federal government are managed by the U.S. Office of Personnel Management (OPM), which has an informative Web site at http://www.opm.gov. Another Web site, http://www.opm.gov/fedclass, provides more detailed information about the OPM's federal job classification system, as well as the several pay systems governing the salary rates of federal civilian employees. Information on obtaining a position with the federal government can be obtained at http://www.usajobs.opm.gov, the official Web site of the OPM

Jobs in state or municipal governments are not dissimilar to those found in the federal government. Information can be obtained from the personnel management offices at the state or local level.

Employment Prospects

Federal jobs are highly competitive, as are those in many state and local governments. Growth in new job positions can be slow and very much subject to budget cutbacks, the financial well-being of government agencies or departments, and the growing use of private contractors. About one in five federal employees work in the Washington, D.C., metropolitan area, while the remainder work in cities and towns across the United States.

Advancement Prospects

Advancement by grade (GS) level will bring additional responsibilities and greater pay. Editorial Assistants may also be able to move up to writer or editor positions, or even transfer to other positions in communications.

Education and Training

A high-school diploma is the minimum education requirement for Editorial Assistant positions. Depending upon the needs or policies of individual government departments or agencies, further education (two to four years) and/or specific job experience may be required.

Experience, Skills, and Personality Traits

Two to five years of editorial support background is usually mandated, but a college education may be substituted for experience in order to be eligible for an editorial position. Editorial support experience includes responsibilities for editing for grammar, editorial production, fact-checking, proofreading, researching, and reviewing and screening of manuscript material.

Because of the intense concentration upon the detail of their work, Editorial Assistants must be dependable, highly accurate to a fault, meticulous, and well organized. The work also requires a high degree of patience, and a strong aptitude for exacting work.

Unions and Associations

Major unions and associations that represent federal, state, and municipal white-collar employees are the American Federation of Government Employees; the American Federation of State, County and Municipal Employees; Federally Employed Women; the National Association of Government Communicators; the National Association of Government Employees; and the National Federation of Federal Employees. Editorial Assistants often participate in a range of related professional associations outside of government.

Tips for Entry

1. For information on obtaining a position with the federal government, contact the Office of Personnel Management (OPM) either by telephone (703-724-1850, or 800-877-8339) or by accessing their Web site: http://www.usajobs.opm.gov, or, instead, check out http://jobsearch.about.com/library/weekly/aa102002b.htm, for information on how to apply for federal jobs.
2. To search for potential jobs in the federal government, access such Web sites as http://www.fedworld.gov or the OPM URL cited above.
3. For state, county, and municipal governments, consult local telephone directories or look them up on the Internet.
4. Gain editorial experience by working on high-school or college publications or taking an internship with a local publishing company.

FIELD RESEARCHER

CAREER PROFILE

Duties: By observing and questioning the general populace, collect data and information on governmental, political, scientific, and social matters

Alternate Title(s): Pollster

Salary Range: $17,000 to $60,000+

Employment Prospects: Fair

Advancement Prospects: Poor

Prerequisites:

Education or Training—College degree preferred; advanced degree most likely will be required for some types of research

Experience—One to two years, or more, of interviewing and research study experience

Special Skills and Personality Traits—Familiarity with data collection and statistical analysis; computer and writing proficiency; patience, perseverance, and good interpersonal skills

CAREER LADDER

```
┌─────────────────────────────────────┐
│     Senior Research Associate        │
└─────────────────────────────────────┘

┌─────────────────────────────────────┐
│         Field Researcher             │
└─────────────────────────────────────┘

┌─────────────────────────────────────┐
│  Research Assistant or College Student │
└─────────────────────────────────────┘
```

Position Description

Field Researchers investigate scientific and social phenomena through a meticulous process of collecting (frequently through observation), organizing, and processing data for written studies. In both cases, scientific investigation and social (or ethnographic) research, the research process follows a logical procession of interlocking steps. This includes examining relevant literature, selecting the appropriate area of investigation, and consulting with management and/or advisers to help frame the specific process of data analysis and collection. Next comes entering the field (for social research, this means establishing relationships with the people being studied, and for scientific research, applying scientific methodology to the specific investigation). In the collection of data the researcher must gather extensive field notes on what he/she hears, sees, experiences, and thinks is vital to reconstruct the specifics of setting and interaction. (This applies to both social and scientific types of investigations.)

In the process of ethnographic research in the field, the Field Researcher will do an extensive interviewing process of individuals or individuals in groups, known as focus groups. This step involves setting the theme of the investiga-

tion, to help clarify the thrust of the interviews, and designing the process of the research. After conducting the interview, a written transcription is prepared. After analyzing the text a determination is made of its relevance to the current study. (Each new batch of data processed helps to verify the validity of material already gathered.)

In both scientific and social research the taking of field notes can become extremely extensive, so much so that it may become difficult to determine what is really going on and what is the crux of the information accumulated. Thus it is important to have a focus, a vital question, or a central problem to return to continuously as the data collection process continues. It is vital to write about what has been collected in these field notes as soon as possible so as to capture—while fresh—the event, the time period, or the data in its actual context. Collecting field notes systematically and carefully over the time of the study will help point to patterns or themes that can be supported by the data collected.

Field Researchers can be found in nearly every government agency, encompassing every area of governmental activity, from agriculture, business, and the economy

(Departments of Agriculture, Commerce, and Treasury), defense (Department of Defense, with its assorted agencies, and Homeland Security), environment (Departments of the Interior and Energy, and the Environmental Protection Agency), human endeavors (Departments of Education, Health and Human Services, Housing and Urban Development, Labor, and Veteran Affairs), to law and foreign affairs and development (Departments of Justice and State). For information on such posts in the federal, state, or municipal government, search the Internet for federal, state, or municipal government jobs to access numerous Web sites devoted to them. For procedures on making application for government jobs, examine the Web site devoted to applying for federal jobs at http://jobsearch.about.com/library/weekly/aa102002b.htm.

Salaries

Beginning annual salaries for Field Researchers fluctuate extensively depending upon the type of research and the expertise of the candidate. Federal, state, and municipal pay scales will also vary widely depending upon the depth of experience and education needed, with yearly pay ranging from as low as $17,000 for a beginning research assistant to $60,000 or more (sometimes as much as $100,000) for experienced scientific and professional Field Researchers with several years of experience.

Jobs within the federal government are managed by the U.S. Office of Personnel Management (OPM), which has an informative Web site at http://www.opm.gov. Another Web site, http://www.opm.gov/fedclass, gives more detailed information about the OPM's federal job classification system. Each state and county, and local municipalities has its own Web site devoted to job information and hiring policies.

Employment Prospects

As research is the bedrock of all policy decision-making, employment for Field Researchers seldom lags. However, governmental job openings, either at the federal, state, or local level, are frequently dependent upon budgetary concerns, which, in turn, are reliant on the health of the economy. Vacancies also occur as researchers transfer or retire from governmental departments and agencies.

Advancement Prospects

Chances of advancement to supervisory levels are limited, as there tends to be a small number of openings that are available each year. However, moving into a senior position as a Field Researcher, with its high job grade classification and increased supervisory responsibilities, is a likely step. Other advancements may be possible by moving to related communications jobs within government agencies.

Education and Training

Most research positions require extensive education beyond a bachelor's degree in communications, English, or liberal arts. Field Researchers have to be able to conduct reliable research, with extensive interviewing or scientific inquiry, as well as heavy analysis of the collected data. Expertise in the relevant subject area is a basic requirement of any Field Researcher.

Experience, Skills, and Personality Traits

While a background in journalism or communications would be helpful, it is important not to confuse field research with journalism. While similar techniques (such as researching and interviewing) are employed in both, the relationship to data separates social scientists and physical scientists from journalists. Sociologists and scientists employ field research to understand social or physical life more generally, whereas journalists focus on reporting.

Field Researchers need to be dedicated, highly organized, imaginative, inquisitive, and thorough. They need excellent interviewing techniques if the research is in the field of social sciences; they must be expert in the application of scientific methods to their research for work on scientific endeavors.

Unions and Associations

The American Federation of Government Employees; the American Federation of State, County and Municipal Employees; Federally Employed Women; the National Association of Government Communicators; the National Association of Government Employees; and the National Federation of Federal Employees are the primary unions and associations for governmental researchers. Field Researchers may also belong to various related professional writing or scientific professional associations outside of the federal, state, county, or municipal government.

Tips for Entry

1. For information on obtaining a position with the federal government, contact the Office of Personnel Management (OPM) either by telephone (703-724-1850, or 800-877-8339), or by accessing their Web site: http://www.usajobs.opm.gov. You can also enter the keywords *federal government jobs* in an Internet search engine to access numerous Web sites devoted to this subject.
2. For information on the steps to take in applying for federal jobs, access the Web site http://jobsearch.about.com/library/weekly/aa102002b.htm.
3. To search for potential jobs, or specific research positions in the federal government, consult such Web sites as http://www.fedworld.gov or the OPM site cited above.
4. For state, county, and municipal governments, check local telephone directories.

POLITICAL SPEECHWRITER

CAREER PROFILE

Duties: Research, draft, and edit speeches for political figures or party organizations

Alternate Title(s): Special Assistant for Communications

Salary Range: $25,000 to $100,000+

Employment Prospects: Fair

Advancement Prospects: Fair

Prerequisites:

    Education or Training—College degree in communications, history, journalism, or liberal arts; some jobs may require a law degree or some other advanced degree

    Experience—Varies widely; can include backgrounds in journalism, law, legislative research, political campaigning, public policy, or public relations

    Special Skills and Personality Traits—Must understand the subject matter and substance of the proposed speech and for what target audience it is intended; must know where to find necessary information; must understand the personality of the speaker and be equipped to imitate the style of this person; must be able to cope under considerable and unrelenting pressure

CAREER LADDER

```
┌─────────────────────────────────────┐
│     Director of Communications       │
└─────────────────────────────────────┘

┌─────────────────────────────────────┐
│            Speechwriter              │
└─────────────────────────────────────┘

┌─────────────────────────────────────┐
│    Public Information Officer,       │
│ Press Secretary, or Legislative Director │
└─────────────────────────────────────┘
```

Position Description

Political Speechwriters utilize the agenda of a governing administration, individual politician, or a candidate for office to create an effective tool to communicate with the public. They translate (or simplify) complex political issues and policies and formulate speeches for politicians or government workers to convey those issues and policies to the public. Most commonly, they work on political campaigns.

Political Speechwriters usually are people interested in politics who have had interaction with political life. Often they are taken on for their particular subject expertise and frequently write speeches on topics related to their expertise. In some instances, Political Speechwriters may share the workload on a particular speech according to topic, whereas, at other times, the division of labor can be as broad as foreign and domestic policy and issues.

In smaller offices (such as in local or county government, or in smaller-staffed political offices) the speechwriting duties may be handled by a press secretary or a legislative

director. The work is often extremely high pressure and may occur at any time. Many times speeches have to be prepared in reaction to breaking news events, and data must be gathered quickly and efficiently. The Political Speechwriter has to be flexible and able to think on his or her feet, adapting to last-minute changes in current events, which, in turn, affect policy positions of the politician delivering the speech.

Speeches often have to be geared for a wide range of audiences, and on a wide spectrum of topics. The Political Speechwriter needs to know whether questions from the media and the audience will be allowed, and prepare for necessary responses, as well as being aware of how long the speech should be, and the topic and general content that the politician/governmental individual wishes to cover.

On political campaigns, speechwriters may have to be moved from their regular staff job to one devoted to the campaign, as campaign speechwriters by law must be paid from campaign funds instead of being kept on staff payroll.

Some Political Speechwriters prefer to work on a freelance basis (usually after five to 10 years of experience in speechwriting for individuals or bodies), and some of these writers have their own companies and are hired on a job-by-job basis (or for a single campaign).

Salaries

Being in such a demanding and visible post, knowledgeable and talented Political Speechwriters can earn annually $100,000 or more. Those with little experience who are hired to work for a low-profile legislator or a government committee may initially make only $25,000. In some instances, others may find that their speechwriting tasks are just a part of a number of public relations duties within an office.

For freelance Political Speechwriters, the informal consensus is that minimum charge for a speech is $3,000 (based on 30 hours minimum work on the speech at a $100-per-hour fee), and outside fees of $4,000 to $5,000 are not excessive.

Employment Prospects

The need for Political Speechwriters is always expanding as more professional speechwriting is being used by both politicians and businesspeople. With elections every two and four years (and special elections in between), talented Political Speechwriters are always in demand.

Political offices, committees, and agencies at all levels of government are always hiring speechwriters. It is estimated that, on an average, a principal Political Speechwriter who spends more than half of his or her time on speeches will create 30 or more speeches a year, with some very busy writers claiming anywhere from 75 to 100 speeches annually (which often includes recycling of some past efforts). As an average most speeches take up to 30 hours to prepare, so a speech every two weeks or so on top of other work is a pretty hefty workload.

Advancement Prospects

As Political Speechwriters come from all kinds of backgrounds, they may move on to all different types of careers from speechwriting. Some move into private-sector speechwriting, drafting speeches for company executives and even helping in determining speech making strategies to put forward to achieve corporate objectives. Others may become newspaper columnists, political consultants, or writers of fiction or nonfiction.

For those speechwriters who stay within the public sector, many move from their previous less-visible jobs to those of higher-profile political figures or to departments or agencies. They may become press secretaries or legislative directors.

Education and Training

An undergraduate degree in communications, English, journalism, or liberal arts is essential. An educational back-

ground in history or English literature might also be useful, although being curious and conducting continual research may make up for any educational lacks. An advanced degree in government, journalism, law, political science, or public policy may become an important plus.

Experience, Skills, and Personality Traits

A broad range of backgrounds can be found among Political Speechwriters, with journalism being a common one. Other good preparation for this field is experience in campaigning, legislative research, public policy, or public relations.

The success of a Political Speechwriter must lie in his/her communication skills, so a strong English and communications background is essential. Speechwriters should have an ear for the spoken word (as opposed to the written word), and an insight into the person giving the speech and ability to replicate the speaker's style. Political Speechwriters need to be quick learners, absorbing technical and complex terms and trends as they occur. They need to have strong research skills, a capacity to work under pressure, and forbearance about constant revisions.

Unions and Associations

Major professional associations of interest for Political Speechwriters include the American Society of Journalists and Authors; the International Association of Business Communicators; the International Platform Association; the National Speakers Association; the Public Relations Society of America; and Toastmasters International. In addition, some Political Speechwriters may belong to unions for federal employees.

Tips for Entry

1. For information on obtaining a position with the federal government, contact the Office of Personnel Management (OPM) either by telephone (703-724-1850, or 800-877-8339) or by accessing their Web site: http://www.usajobs.opm.gov, or, instead, check out http://jobsearch.about.com/library/weekly/aa102002b.htm for information on how to apply for federal jobs.
2. To search for potential jobs in the federal government, access such Web sites as http://www.fedworld.gov or the OPM Web site cited above.
3. For state, county, and municipal governments, check local telephone directories and/or the Internet.
4. To test one's abilities as a Political Speechwriter, try writing speeches for student office campaigns.
5. Take speechwriting courses in addition to your regular curriculum. Gain journalistic experience by working on school publications.

PRESS SECRETARY

CAREER PROFILE

Duties: Arrange press conferences and respond to press inquiries; compose press releases; ghostwrite speeches, newspaper columns, letters to constituents, and other materials for legislators; write and produce material for radio, television, and Internet release; remain current with news developments and attempt to anticipate their impact

Alternate Title(s): Public Affairs Specialist

Salary Range: $25,000 to $95,000+

Employment Prospects: Fair

Advancement Prospects: Good

Prerequisites:

   Education or Training—College bachelor's degree minimum

   Experience—Years working in news industry (print, radio, or television); familiarity with media in the legislator's or political figure's home state, or with U.S. congressional environment

   Special Skills and Personality Traits—Excellent organizational skills; ability to anticipate which issues and breaking news events will prompt questions from the media; ability to replicate employer's writing and speaking styles

CAREER LADDER

```
┌─────────────────────────────────────┐
│ Government Affairs Specialist with   │
│ Private Industry or Advanced Position│
│         at Federal Agency            │
└─────────────────────────────────────┘

┌─────────────────────────────────────┐
│          Press Secretary             │
└─────────────────────────────────────┘

┌─────────────────────────────────────┐
│             Journalist               │
└─────────────────────────────────────┘
```

Position Description

A Press Secretary is a senior adviser, usually to a politician or legislative body, who supplies advice on how to deal with the media and, by using news management techniques, helps her or his employer maintain a positive public image and avoid negative media coverage. They usually perform a wide assortment of duties, depending on how much emphasis their employer places on media visibility and also whether they work for an individual or a legislative committee.

Some politicians do not like (or have the time) to write, and rely heavily on their Press Secretaries and/or political speechwriters to write speeches, letters, newspaper columns and magazine articles, and any other needed written material as well as press releases. While press releases are relatively straightforward and written like news items, other materials may require the Press Secretary to know fully how the employer thinks and speaks to be able to write appropriately.

A Press Secretary also has to monitor all news (magazines, newspapers, radio and television shows, and wire services) and anticipate how events may affect an employer's policies, public stances, and statements. Responses to expected questions from the media need to be researched and prepared.

Some Press Secretaries may also act as chief of staff or administrative assistant, making personnel decisions, or even influencing a politician's legislative agenda. They are often spokesperson, cheerleader, and media strategist rolled into one. While most Press Secretaries confine most of their activities to Washington, D.C., state capitals, or local municipal offices, almost all of them visit their employer's home district (be it state, county, or city) from time to time. It is important for Press Secretaries to maintain an active, positive profile with media on the national, state, and local level, who will be reading the press releases and most likely calling with questions. For Press Secretaries working on an election campaign for their employer, their extensive knowledge of, and interaction with, the media is an extremely crucial part of their post.

In addition, Press Secretaries must devote themselves to obtaining positive publicity for their employer's causes, pet projects, or bills (if a legislator) that he or she may be sponsoring. Press Secretaries may also produce short radio or television programs in which questions are asked of their employers, and the result released to radio and television stations. They may also arrange Internet chat group sessions for the same political purpose of introducing their employers to potential voters.

Workdays can be very long. During times of heavy political activity, or when a particular issue of concern to their employer comes to the fore, days of 12 to 14 hours are not unheard of. As in the news business, events often dictate the workload.

Salaries

Salaries diverge widely depending upon the priorities of the employer. Each legislator (national or state) receives a budget for his or her office staff to spend as they want. The same is true of local political figures, such as mayors.

A high-profile politician may hire a Press Secretary with impressive credentials and experience for a higher salary and cut back on staff in other areas. Some highly paid Press Secretaries also serve as chief of staff or administrative assistant, overseeing the office staff and responsible for personnel matters, including hiring and firing. Legislative committees and subcommittees also employ Press Secretaries, and also have a budget for such hiring.

Salaries for public affairs positions within government agencies range from about $19,000 to $70,000. The average Press Secretary to a congressperson makes about $43,500. The average salary for a Press Secretary to a senator is about $61,500.

Employment Prospects

Prospects for a position as Press Secretary are probably best in Washington, D.C., where openings tend to be plentiful, either due to the defeat of incumbents at the polls or because seasoned Press Secretaries leave for other positions (mostly within the business community). It has become increasingly important for politicians to control their agendas (particularly as government has become so much more complex but also transparent via the media, and when information spreads so much more quickly). Press Secretaries who can speak quickly and authoritatively for their employers have become a political necessity for a successful legislator.

However, competition is stiff, and most legislators prefer to hire people who are well acquainted with the media in their home state rather than those versed in the machinations of official Washington power politics.

Related positions in public affairs jobs in the federal agencies account for the highest number of communications-related jobs in the federal government (and this is also true of state governments), and many Press Secretaries come from this pool of qualified applicants.

Advancement Prospects

The wide range of jobs related to public affairs within the federal government (and within state and local governments) makes for good advancement prospects. Press Secretaries can become chiefs of staff or administrative assistants, taking jobs with higher-profile legislators or ones with whom they find themselves to be more compatible, or find related positions with legislative committees of federal/state agencies.

Most Press Secretaries work in a legislature for a particular politician for a few years and then move on to a less-pressured and more stable position, with either a government agency or a firm in the private sector.

Education and Training

It is almost a requirement for Press Secretaries to have undergraduate degrees in either communications, journalism, English, or liberal arts. Actual on-the-job experience in a legislative community also can provide excellent training, as does hands-on participation in the news industry.

Experience, Skills, and Personality Traits

Generally a background in one of the news media or general public relations is necessary, although there is no specific guideline for, or unifying characteristic of, Press Secretaries. A familiarity with news organizations in a legislator's home state, or state district (for state legislators) is extremely useful.

Creativity, intelligence, and the ability to analyze information quickly and to communicate it clearly are also key elements in the success of Press Secretaries. Above all, they must be thorough, accurate, and represent the views of their employer. For these reasons alone, a Press Secretary is a lot more than just a public relations position.

Unions and Associations

Each political party has its own professional organization of public affairs specialists and Press Secretaries in Washington, D.C., and in many state capitals. In addition, Press Secretaries may belong to the Association for Women in Communications, or the Public Relations Society of America.

Some may also belong to the American Federation of Government Employees; the American Federation of State, County and Municipal Employees; Federally Employed Women; the National Federation of Federal Employees; the National Association of Government Communicators; the

National Association of Government Employees; and the National Federation of Federal Employees. Many Press Secretaries find it advantageous to belong to the National Press Club.

Tips for Entry

1. For information on obtaining a position with the federal government, contact the Office of Personnel Management (OPM) either by telephone (703-724-1850, or 800-877-8339) or by accessing their Web site: http://www.usajobs.opm.gov, or, instead, check out http://jobsearch.about.com/library/weekly/aa102002b.htm for information on how to apply for federal jobs.

2. To search for potential jobs in the federal government, access such Web sites as http://www.fedworld.gov or the OPM URL cited above.

3. For state, county and municipal governments, check local telephone directories and the Internet.

4. Gain experience with news organizations or summer internships with local legislative or political organizations.

5. To understand what a political campaign is really all about, join as a volunteer for a local or national election and witness how professional Press Secretaries handle the media responsibilities of such a campaign.

TECHNICAL WRITER AND EDITOR

CAREER PROFILE

Duties: Write and edit technical manuals, specifications, and publications for federal or state agencies

Alternate Title(s): Specifications Writer or Editor; Technical Manuals Writer or Editor; Technical Publications Writer or Editor

Salary Range: $21,500 to $100,000+

Employment Prospects: Poor

Advancement Prospects: Fair

Prerequisites:

　Education or Training—Undergraduate college degree required; an advanced degree in a specific subject area may be required as well

　Experience—Two to six years' writing experience in technical areas, or degree with courses in computer science, engineering, or science

　Special Skills and Personality Traits—Excellent writing and editing skills; good organizational skills and self-motivation; an understanding of and ability to explain technical subjects

CAREER LADDER

```
┌─────────────────────────────┐
│  Supervisory Technical Writer │
│          or Editor            │
└─────────────────────────────┘

┌─────────────────────────────┐
│   Technical Writer or Editor  │
└─────────────────────────────┘

┌─────────────────────────────┐
│   Other Technical Writing or  │
│  Editing Job or College Student │
└─────────────────────────────┘
```

Position Description

Technical Writers and Editors in the federal, state, and local governments fall into three general categories: those who work on manuals, those who write and edit publications, and those who devise and edit specifications.

Both technical manual and specifications positions are found in federal, state, and local governmental activities that are involved in programs of applied scientific research, communications systems, equipment, and devices. In addition, in federal governmental activities, some programs are devoted to the development of weapons. Job duties include writing, editing, and circulating basic instruction materials, maintenance and operation instructions, design information, and training guides. Equipment specifications are commonly used for purchasing and inventory control.

Technical publications Writers and Editors are involved in government activities that manage programs of research, investigations, and/or operations in the natural and social sciences, engineering, law, medicine, and other such disciplines. They are responsible for distributing findings and information to the general public as well as to the administrative and scientific communities. Their work involves the preparation of articles, papers, reports, summaries, and digests based on interviews, research reports, and their own reading.

Many government agencies combine technical writing and editing assignments in one position. Some editors may be assigned to groups or committees, and be responsible for assembling individual reports by members of these groups or committees into a single cohesive document reflecting the total viewpoint(s) of the group.

Most technical writing and editing jobs require considerable knowledge of a particular subject or field of knowledge. Those Technical Writers and Editors who have educational backgrounds or specializations in communications, journalism, or English usually have had the benefit of additional training or education in specific technical subjects.

Nearly three-fourths of the Technical Writers and Editors employed by the federal government work for the Department of Defense, writing manuals and specifications on weapons and instruments for military personnel. The

Departments of Agriculture, Health and Human Services, Interior, and the new Homeland Security, as well as the National Aeronautics and Space Administration, employ many Technical Writers and Editors. At the state and local level, Technical Writers and Editors are employed by both the administrative and legislative branches of government.

Salaries

Government salaries diverge widely, depending on the complexity of the writing and editing job, the geographic area, and other factors. Some governmental technical writing and editing jobs pay in the low $20,000s, whereas others may pay $100,000 or more.

Jobs within the federal government are managed by the U.S. Office of Personnel Management (OPM), which has an informative Web site at http://www.opm.gov. Another Web site, http://www.opm.gov/fedclass, gives more detailed information about the OPM's federal job classification system. States, counties, and local municipalities have their own Web sites for job information and hiring policies.

Employment Prospects

Governmental job openings—whether at the federal, state, or local level—are frequently dependent upon budgetary concerns, which, in turn, are reliant on the health of the economy. Nonetheless, there is a constant need for Technical Writers and Editors for governmental departments and agencies, and vacancies due to retirements or job transfers are always occurring.

Advancement Prospects

Opportunities for advancement to supervisory levels are very limited, as there are only a small number of such openings that become available each year. Rising in job grade classification, however, brings increased responsibilities with attendant rise in salary. Other advancements may be possible by moving to related communication jobs.

Education and Training

Candidates for the job of Technical Writer and Editor should have undergraduate degrees, preferably in science. Those with nonscientific degrees must have had studies in computer science, engineering, or science. Those with graduate degrees in a science have an advantage.

Experience, Skills, and Personality Traits

Actual job experience is not really necessary for an entry-level position as a technical writer, but a year or more of technical writing and editing may qualify a candidate for a higher level beginning position and salary.

Technical Writers and Editors must be able to understand complex scientific and technological subjects and be geared to write clearly and concisely about them. They are often required to communicate to different audiences, such as explicating the same subject to a sophisticated professional or scientific group, and then to a more general audience with little of the background of the first faction. Their job necessitates accuracy and great attention to detail. Besides writing and editing abilities, many of these job positions may also require production and supervisory skills.

Unions and Associations

Primary unions and associations for governmental Technical Writers and Editors include the American Federation of Government Employees; the American Federation of State, County and Municipal Employees; Federally Employed Women; National Association of Government Communicators; National Association of Government Employees; and National Federation of Federal Employees. They may also belong to the Society for Technical Communication (the umbrella organization for technical writers), as well as to related writing or scientific professional associations.

Tips for Entry

1. For information on obtaining a position with the federal government, contact the Office of Personnel Management (OPM) either by telephone (703-724-1850, or 800-877-8339) or by accessing their Web site: http://www.usajobs.opm.gov, or, instead, check out http://jobsearch.about.com/library/weekly/aa102002b.htm for information on how to apply for federal jobs.
2. To search for potential jobs in the federal government, access such Web sites as http://www.fedworld.gov or the OPM Web site cited above.
3. For state, county, and municipal governments, check local telephone directories and the Internet.
4. In preparing for a career as a Technical Writer and Editor, read books about technological topics that are both complex and hard to grasp in order to learn how these technical texts are formatted. Choose books on scientific or technical subjects with which you are unfamiliar in order to learn about the latest discoveries in these fields.
5. Critique a technical or computer manual as to whether its table of contents accurately reflects the key ideas of the text, as well as how effectively the author has explained the subject.
6. Check out any specifications manuals you can find (there are many available online) to understand the methods used to explain effectively the technical instructions.

WRITER AND EDITOR

CAREER PROFILE

Duties: Write and edit articles, news releases, publications, and scripts

Alternate Title(s): None

Salary Range: $21,000 to $75,000+

Employment Prospects: Fair

Advancement Prospects: Good

Prerequisites:

Education or Training—High-school diploma minimum; college degree preferred

Experience—Two to six years' experience writing and/or editing required for most positions

Special Skills and Personality Traits—Excellent writing and editing skills; originality; initiative

CAREER LADDER

| Supervisory Writer and Editor |

| Writer and Editor |

| Editorial Assistant or High School or College Student |

Position Description

Governmental Writers and Editors disseminate information for several purposes: to report research undertaken and investigations carried on by federal agencies; to explain laws and regulations, as well as changes to them; and to make public reports on the activities and plans of agencies and departments of the federal, state, county, and municipal governments. The means of communication include articles, brochures, pamphlets, press releases, speeches, and radio, television and film scripts.

Some writing and editing positions may not require substantial subject-matter knowledge on the part of the writers or editors. However, all positions require the ability to adapt information to a particular audience, format, or style. Most positions do not involve formulating the philosophy or policy behind the content of the information.

Writers collect information through library research, extensive reading, and interviewing subject specialists, policy officers, and others. They turn their manuscripts over to editors who review, edit, or rewrite as required in consultation with the writers. In larger governmental entities Editors may supervise editorial assistants or clerks who are assigned to do routine checking and editing.

Most positions are either wholly writing or editing, but, in some cases (in particular in smaller governmental entities) the two functions are combined into one. These employees are usually called writer-editors. Writers and Editors may specialize in a type of media, working predominantly in print, radio, film, or television.

The scope and responsibilities of a given Writer or Editor depends upon the governmental grade level of the job. At lower grade levels, assignments are very specific, and detailed instructions per scope and content must be followed exactly. There is extremely limited opportunity for creativity. At higher levels, the Writer or Editor has a greater opportunity to take initiative and influence the scope and content of the assignment.

Salaries

Salaries for government Writers and Editors depend on the job grade and years of experience. Most Writers and Editors fall between the pay scales of GS5 and GS12 or GS13, with pay ranging from $23,400 to $79,600 at the top. The highest-paying positions may require two or more years of experience.

Jobs within the federal government are managed by the U.S. Office of Personnel Management (OPM), which has an informative Web site at http://www.opm.gov. Another Web site, http://www.opm.gov/fedclass, gives more detailed information about the OPM's federal job classification system. Each state, county, and local municipalities have their own Web sites for job information and hiring policies.

Employment Prospects

Opportunities for government writing and editing jobs are only fair, due to budgetary concerns and lack of much expansion in the publication programs. The best opportunities for starting are most likely to be found at the local or county levels of government.

Advancement Prospects

Writers and Editors have a good chance of advancing to higher (and more responsible) grade level positions or to supervisory jobs. Lateral transfer to other communication jobs within governmental areas is also common.

Education and Training

The minimum requirement is a high-school diploma. College undergraduate degrees in communications, English, or journalism may be preferred for many of the higher grade level positions. College degrees may, in some cases, be an adequate substitute for job experience in meeting minimum hiring qualifications.

Experience, Skills, and Personality Traits

Applicants without college degrees must be experienced in administrative, professional, technical, or other work that requires the ability to analyze information and present it in clear and concise written form. Specialized experience in writing or editing material for a particular medium (such as television) may also be required.

Basic skills include researching, analyzing, and organizing information; excellent writing skills and knowledge of correct grammar; editing ability; self-motivation; and the ability to work independently and, at times, under the pressure of deadlines.

Unions and Associations

The American Federation of Government Employees; the American Federation of State, County and Municipal Employees; Federally Employed Women; National Association of Government Communicators; National Association of Government Employees; and National Federation of Federal Employees are the primary unions and associations for governmental Writers and Editors. Writers and Editors may also belong to various related professional writing and editorial organizations outside of the government.

Tips for Entry

1. For information on obtaining a position with the federal government, contact the Office of Personnel Management (OPM) either by telephone (703-724-1850, or 800-877-8339) or by accessing their Web site: http://www.usajobs.opm.gov, or, instead, check out the Web site, http://jobsearch.about.com/library/weekly/aa102002b.htm, for information on how to apply for federal jobs.
2. To search for potential jobs in the federal government, access such Web sites as http://www.fedworld.gov or the OPM Web site cited above.
3. For state, county, and municipal governments, check local telephone directories.
4. Take as many writing courses as possible and gain experience in writing for high-school or college publications while getting your degree.
5. Study government pamphlets, style manuals, and other government publications (available in local or college libraries) to become familiar with style requirements of such writing.

FREELANCE SERVICES AND SELF-PUBLISHING

BOOK AND RECORD REVIEWER

CAREER PROFILE

Duties: Write book reviews or record reviews for newsletters, newspapers, periodicals, Web sites, and other media outlets

Alternate Title(s): Columnist

Salary Range: Small or no fee (except a byline and copy of book or record) at Web sites and small newspapers and periodicals; $25 to $400 at larger publications; $20 to $500 or more for magazines

Employment Prospects: For fee: poor; for byline and free book or record: fair

Advancement Prospects: Poor to Fair

Prerequisites:

Education or Training—Undergraduate degree in communications, English, liberal arts, or in area of specific expertise; graduate degree may be necessary in some cases

Experience—For publication and fees in newspapers and periodicals, recognition as an expert in the specific area (whether books or recordings) or in literature may be required; knowledge of similar books or recordings, older or current, helpful

Special Skills and Personality Traits—Criticism skills; good writing ability; researching skills

CAREER LADDER

```
┌─────────────────────────────┐
│   Professional Reviewer     │
└─────────────────────────────┘

┌─────────────────────────────┐
│   Experienced Reviewer      │
└─────────────────────────────┘

┌─────────────────────────────┐
│     Novice Reviewer         │
└─────────────────────────────┘
```

Position Description

A Reviewer is a person who writes evaluations in a professional manner to assist readers and listeners in choosing books or recordings, by providing summaries of the book's contents or contents of the recordings, and opinions as to the merit or flaws of the works. Reviews may be for print/electronic publications or for presentation on radio/television.

Reviewing books or recordings can provide a small, but frequently steady, supplemental source of income for freelance authors, musicians, and writers. However, many review outlets do not offer any fee compensation for reviews, only free copies of what is being reviewed.

Most newspapers, consumer and trade periodicals, as well as some industry newsletters, carry review columns for books and/or recordings in each issue, and many of these rely upon freelancers to supply the critiques. The columns themselves may be produced on a regular basis by freelance writers or editors who, in turn, will assign reviews to freelancers. Since the majority of publications are aimed at specialized markets, these evaluations require specific subject background on the part of Reviewers. A small number of publications are geared entirely to the book industry, or specific listening audiences. Some writers will work regularly (or often) for these publications, while others write occasional reviews upon invitation by the publication. All of these specifics apply as well to electronic publications and most other media presentations on radio or television.

Unless the writer has the responsibility of developing a book (or recordings) review column, generating the material to be used in the review, a publication will ask a writer to review a specific book or recording. The writer is given the book (or recording) with instructions on how the review is to appear and a deadline.

There are several kinds of reviews. A short descriptive review will give the reader the title, author, publisher (or, in the case of a recording, the composer, piece or song, and performers), price (usually not given in the case of a recording), and a few sentences about the content (or plot, if fiction, without giving away the ending), without expressing an evaluation. Then there are short reviews with all the above pertinent information, as well as an evaluation of the book/recording. A lengthier review may include how the book or recording relates to the reviewer's own experience or background, as well as the reviewer's opinion and recommendation. Evaluations of fiction may include a critique of the author's characterizations, plot, and pace, while evaluations of nonfiction works may critique an author's technical skill or historical accuracy. Evaluations of recordings may critique musicianship, presentation, and audience appeal.

Reviews may run from 150 to 400 words for shorter reviews, or 1,000 to 2,000 words for lengthier ones and, for the latter, may include extensive comparisons with the author's previous works (or similar works by other authors), or other recordings of the same work (or song).

Salaries

Many writers are paid small fees for individual reviews—$10 to $30 is typical. In some cases, a free book or recording and a byline are the sole compensation. Large and influential consumer publications may provide a fee of up to $500 or more for essay and critique reviews, but they rely primarily upon well-known writers, musicians, and prestigious experts.

Employment Prospects

Many book/recording reviews are assigned based on the reputation, expertise, and even name recognition of the Reviewer. The best prospects for regular work as a Reviewer usually lie in local markets, and through establishing one's credentials with a publication by first writing articles for them. Aspiring Reviewers can submit queries to publications with a letter outlining their experience and their expertise. This letter might also include sample review clips for the publications' consideration. While opportunities abound on the Web for potential reviewing, they seldom come with any payment attached. Nonetheless, there are many Web sites that can be tapped for application for reviewing. Reviewing for radio or television requires credentials and experience in those media.

Advancement Prospects

Becoming established by having reviews published in journals, newspapers, or online, increases significantly the chances for a Reviewer to have other work put into circulation. If a Reviewer's work continues to be published and a reputation established, the cumulative effect greatly enhances the possibility of winning regular review assignments.

Education and Training

No specific education is demanded of a Reviewer. However, most Reviewers have an undergraduate degree in communications, English, liberal arts, or other subject (such as music, for Record Reviewers).

For the most specialized and lengthier essay and critique reviewing, publications may prefer graduate degrees as a part of the Reviewer's academic background.

Experience, Skills, and Personality Traits

Nonfiction Book Reviewers should be especially knowledgeable of the subject of the book. For fiction, Reviewers should be familiar with the genre to better judge the effectiveness of the author's work. They should know about issues of interest to readers who might be attracted to the book under review. For recordings reviews, the same applies, as a substantial portion of such critiques contain comparisons to other performers' work or to other musical works by the composer or other musicians.

A Reviewer should have good written communication and analyzing skills and, above all, be objective and fair, even in a negative evaluation.

Unions and Associations

There are no associations specifically for Book Reviewers. However, there are several organizations devoted to specific types of reviewing. A membership in the Reviewers International Organization will provide a member with an entry listing as a Reviewer within the organization's published general listings for authors and publications.

Those Reviewers who are writers may belong to one or more national writers' organizations, such as the American Society of Journalists and Authors, the Authors Guild, the National Writers Union, the PEN American Center, or other groups devoted to specific genres of writing. For Recordings Reviewers, there are also numerous musical organizations to explore.

Tips for Entry

1. Read reviews in publications and newspapers and on Web sites, or listen to presentations on radio or television to understand both style and character of reviews.
2. A search on the Internet, using the words *book reviewer or recording reviewer* may be a good place to start looking for potential outlets for your reviews.
3. Check with a local newspaper to determine whether the staff could use a Book or Record Reviewer.
4. Call radio shows or local cable television shows to see if you can become a guest Reviewer.

BOOK PACKAGER

Duties: Create finished books for publishers

Alternate Title(s): Book producer

Salary Range: $0 to Unlimited

Employment Prospects: Poor to Fair

Advancement Prospects: Fair

Prerequisites:

    Education or Training—Undergraduate degree in communications, English, humanities, liberal arts; marketing and publishing courses helpful

    Experience—Previous work as author and/or editor necessary, with solid background in researching useful

    Special Skills and Personality Traits—Ability to gauge marketing possibilities; creativity; good researching skills; innovativeness; knowledge of marketing and finance procedures; production skills; sales knack

```
┌─────────────────────────────────┐
│     Seasoned Book Packager      │
└─────────────────────────────────┘

┌─────────────────────────────────┐
│     Established Book Packager   │
└─────────────────────────────────┘

┌─────────────────────────────────┐
│     Beginner Book Packager      │
└─────────────────────────────────┘
```

Position Description

Book Packagers, often known as book producers, are brokers who contract with freelancers and others to bring together a book or series of books and get it ready as a turnkey operation for a publisher. They provide all the services necessary for publication (editing, formatting, designing) except, usually, printing and binding, sales, and fulfillment. Some Packagers, however, also provide those additional services. By offering package deals to publishers, Book Packagers save publishers money and staff time. Book Packagers work with authors, agents, editors, designers, photographers, illustrators, typesetters, and printers. While most Book Packagers are not involved personally in book manufacturing, they may assist publishers in marketing plans.

Most publishers pay Packagers a percentage of the book's retail price and the number of copies ordered from the printer. The usual percentage is 20 percent. Thus, if a book sells to the public for $30, the Packager gets a fee of $6 per book, and, in order to make a profit, must keep its production costs under $6 per individual volume. Any budgeting errors along the way can mean the difference between profit and loss.

Sometimes, Packagers develop their own ideas for a book or a series of books. They write a proposal, which would include a summary of the book's contents (or that of the series), sample material, market potential, and, if necessary, production specifications (number of pages per book, trim size, type of paper, and so forth). They then sell that idea to a publisher, negotiate a price (usually always adding in a profit margin), and deliver to that publisher completed, edited books. The Packager hires (usually freelance) writers, artists, book designers, typesetters, copyeditors, proofreaders, and others, so that the publisher will have little or no work to do on the production of the book. Most publishers, of course, maintain enough project control under their contract with the Packager to be assured of a finished product in the time schedule allotted and scope/quality agreed upon.

On one hand, a Packager may be approached by an author or an agent about a book concept or actual product, and the author would pay a flat fee (usually a per-page price) or a royalty. The Packager then becomes the editor and possible graphic designer for the work and takes the responsibility of selling it to a publisher. On the other hand, a publisher may approach the Packager with a concept for a new work or series, and the Packager takes on the writing, editing, and production of the project. The Packager regularly consults with the editor of the publishing firm, and, depending upon the negotiated contract, the publisher's editor may have a significant voice in how the book is finally produced.

Packagers devise the production schedules and coordinate personnel and activities. Many Packagers retain rights to their book properties, which they sell piecemeal, or in various forms, to publishers, periodicals, on the Internet, and other outlets. Selling these rights is a time-consuming process and requires a thorough knowledge of the publishing industry, as well as the potentials of the electronic marketplace. Packagers must be astutely oriented to the marketplace, only developing books that are likely to sell.

Most Book Packagers have extensive backgrounds as either authors or editors. They retain many contacts in the publishing world, as well as develop new ones. Many Packagers specialize in one type of book, such as heavily illustrated coffee-table products or serial fiction. As an example of the latter, the series of books on the Bobbsey Twins, the Nancy Drew mysteries, and the Hardy Boys mysteries, all were developed by The Stratemeyer Syndicate, and the latter two are still produced by a Book Packager.

While packaging can provide the rewards of self-publishing without the distribution headaches, it can be difficult to get started in this field, particularly against the competition of already established Packagers. In addition, vagaries in the cash flow from slow-paying publishers can strain a budget.

Salaries

Earnings depend on the type of books being produced, the kind of end product provided (finished books fetch more money, but they cost more to produce), and the number of books sold. Profit margins depend upon the individual negotiations and the expertise of the Packager in keeping costs under control. The profit from any one entry may be merely a few thousand dollars, or, if a big seller, may expand to hundreds of thousands of dollars over time.

Packagers have a heavy startup investment. Typically, in a contract with a publisher the Packager gets paid in thirds (one-third on signing, one-third on delivery, and one-third on publication), or in halves (half on signing and half on delivery). Payments from publishers may be delayed, but work must be done on the book (with freelancers to be paid), and suppliers and authors need to get their payment in a timely fashion per their agreements with the Packager. Finally, if Packagers work out of an office, they must factor in rent and other office overhead expenses.

Employment Prospects

While it is difficult to begin operation as a Book Packager without personal contacts in the publishing world, it is not impossible. Though they can work anywhere, Packagers are overwhelmingly concentrated in or near New York City, where they have easy close contact with major publishers.

Most Book Packagers are relatively small firms, with only a few full-time employees. Nearly all the work is outsourced to freelance professionals, many of whom work out of their own home. To work as a full-time freelance author (or editor, or other professional) for a Book Packager, a candidate should approach them just as they would a more conventional publisher. As most Book Packagers work on various projects for assorted clients, candidates should stress their diverse abilities and attainments.

Advancement Prospects

As the work of an aspiring freelance author (or editor, or other professional) for a Book Packager gets accepted and used more than once by that firm, the likelihood increases of obtaining additional work on a full-time basis with that or other companies.

Education and Training

Most Book Packagers have an undergraduate degree in communications, English, humanities, liberal arts, or in some allied field. They also may have had further education in advertising, business administration, marketing, promotion, and publishing.

Experience, Skills, and Personality Traits

It is essential that Book Packagers have worked as authors or editors to understand the full process of a book, from creative idea to proposal to manuscript to the published work. The Packager functions almost as a publisher, and total familiarity with the publishing world and the book marketplace is absolutely necessary. Skill in making convincing proposals, both written and verbal, is also essential. Finally, Packagers must be able to control cash flow, freelancers, staff, and suppliers. They must be equipped to juggle project deadlines, yet meet each one as per the negotiated contracts.

Unions and Associations

The American Book Producers Association is the primary organization for Book Packagers. Many individual Packagers may also belong to the Association of American Publishers, or various writers' organizations.

Tips for Entry

1. Expand your writing and editing skills to gain familiarity with production processes.
2. Take extra courses in advertising, book manufacturing, business administration, and marketing/promotion.
3. Consider internships with established Book Packagers. Several of them offer programs for students who have majors such as English or journalism, or a writing-intensive liberal arts major, such as history.

CONTRIBUTING EDITOR

CAREER PROFILE

Duties: Propose and write articles for periodicals

Alternate Title(s): Contributing Writer, Correspondent

Salary Range: $1,000 to $50,000 or more

Employment Prospects: Poor

Advancement Prospects: Fair

Prerequisites:

Education or Training—Undergraduate degree in communications, English, or writing; graduate degree may be preferred/required for specialized writing topics

Experience—Extensive published credits and comprehensive knowledge of subject areas; reputation in the field is a plus

Special Skills and Personality Traits—Reliability; superior writing and research skills; solid self-discipline

CAREER LADDER

```
┌─────────────────────────────────────┐
│   Seasoned Contributing Editor       │
└─────────────────────────────────────┘

┌─────────────────────────────────────┐
│   Experienced Contributing Editor    │
└─────────────────────────────────────┘

┌─────────────────────────────────────┐
│    Novice Contributing Editor        │
└─────────────────────────────────────┘
```

Position Description

Contributing Editors are freelance professionals employed by periodicals and other publications to write an article for every issue, or a certain number of pieces annually. They seldom are part of the periodical's in-house staff. Pay is set by article or an annual payment for articles delivered and by the complexity of the subject matter covered.

Contributing Editors typically have considerable experience as writers. They must have a recognized expertise and a reputation for reliability, in order to be asked by periodicals to write regularly for them as Contributing Editors. Some established authors or celebrity writers may be invited by a periodical to submit articles in order to attract a readership for the publication. Then too, small periodicals may use Contributing Editors to minimize their need for staff writers, especially if the subjects covered refer to areas far away geographically, or remote from the usual material found within the publication.

Contributing Editors may be put on retainer to cover specific subjects or areas of interest, or they may be roving commentators who suggest their own topics and, then, are given their assignment by an editor at the publication. Duties may extend from writing articles, reviews, columns, or editorial commentary to attending staff meetings to supervising other writers, both staff and freelance.

As a rule the job of a Contributing Editor is usually only one of various revenue sources for freelance writers/editors.

Salaries

Earnings are based on the nature and size of the publication for which a Contributing Editor works, the tasks required of the position, and the Contributing Editor's credentials, experience, and reputation. Contributing Editors can earn less than $1,000 a year or up to $50,000 a year or more at prominent publications. Celebrity writers, of course, can earn even more.

Employment Prospects

Published credits of a solid nature and an excellent reputation as a writer who can meet deadlines are usually necessary for a potential Contributing Editor to be hired by a major periodical. A writer may move up into this position after a year or so of writing regularly on a single topic or group of topics, or for a specific periodical. However, it is the small periodical, much in need of dependable, freelance Contributing Editors/writers that may provide the best chance for writers in the early stages of their career to realize their ambition of becoming a regular Contributing Editor.

Advancement Prospects

As the work of an aspiring Contributing Editor for a periodical or other publication gets accepted and used more than once, the chances of getting additional work on a full-time basis with that or other firms increases significantly. Once established as an experienced Contributing Editor, the freelance writer has the potential of expanding his/her work into other areas and with other publications.

Education and Training

Most writers have an undergraduate degree in communications, English, humanities, liberal arts, or social sciences. For specialized subjects graduate degrees may be required, particularly for technical or scientific articles.

Experience, Skills, and Personality Traits

Potential Contributing Editors usually have to demonstrate their expertise over a period of years before becoming an actual Contributing Editor to one or more periodicals. They must be creative, dependable, excellent writers, knowledgeable about their subject areas, and very self-disciplined.

Unions and Associations

Contributing Editors often belong to organizations for writers and editors, such as the American Society of Journalists and Authors, the Association for Women in Communications, the Editorial Freelancers Association, or the Society for Technical Communication. They may also belong to trade or professional associations related to the area of their expertise and the topics they cover for publication.

Tips for Entry

1. As a student, look into internships that involve writing to gain both experience and additional elements for your résumé of writing.
2. According to your likes and desires, decide upon areas of expertise on which you want to capitalize by writing for periodicals that cover those areas.
3. Upon deciding on that area (or areas) in which you want to be a specialist, search for outlets in those areas for your writing, whether it be periodicals, or electronic publishing.
4. In applying for a position as Contributing Editor, decide what writings you have done that are most representative of your abilities, to be included with your application.

COPY EDITOR

CAREER PROFILE	CAREER LADDER

Duties: Edit manuscripts and copy for books, periodicals, trade and industry publications, and corporate communications and publications

Alternate Title(s): None

Salary Range: $15 to $75 per hour for trade books (fiction and nonfiction), periodicals, and newspapers; $20 to $80+ per hour for substantive editing of book content; $25 to $70 for general trade and professional journal editing; $17 to $75 per hour for scholarly, scientific, and technical books; $20 to $40 per hour for computer software books; $25 to $50 for Web site editing; $30 to $35 per hour for advertising; $15 to $30 per hour for nonprofit organizations; $15 to $50 per hour for business copyediting

Employment Prospects: Fair to good

Advancement Prospects: Fair to good

Prerequisites:

Education or Training—Undergraduate degree in communications, English, or other field; graduate degree may be required for scientific and technical subjects, or, at least, work experience within these areas

Experience—Any background in communications helpful, as well as prior work as an editor, editorial assistant, production assistant, or writer

Special Skills and Personality Traits—Excellent command of grammar, spelling and style; careful eye for detail; knowledge of subject areas either helpful or may be required

---

```
Seasoned Copy Editor
```

```
Experienced Copy Editor
```

```
Novice Copy Editor
```

Position Description

Freelance Copy Editors edit a highly varied assortment of material for consistency and clarity of thought, correct spelling, grammar, punctuation, style, and word usage. They work within the house style guidelines provided by the employer. In some cases as per request by the employer, the Copy Editor will briefly critique the manuscript and provide a content sheet of that critique to guide the employer in any further self-editing. Copy Editors improve awkwardly phrased sentences, check cross-references, and flag errors or inconsistencies in content, dates, numbers, and other contextual items for the employer to double-check. Their work requires them to be completely familiar with standard style manuals, such as *The Chicago Manual of Style* and the Modern Language Association guidelines, as well as the numerous standard reference works, which they will consult continuously.

Copy Editors are hired to examine book manuscripts (which might include appendixes, indexes, and bibliographies as well as the text), newsletters, periodical articles, and copy for advertisements, in-house communications, manuals, press kits, and similar publications. They work primarily from manuscripts or typeset galleys or proofs and mark corrections directly on the pages. Increasingly, Copy Editors may work with electronic text online, using programs to edit online.

Salaries

Freelance copyediting fees are usually based on an hourly rate. Freelancers usually set their own rate according to the type of job, but usually conform to going rates established by the publishing industry or the employer. The average rate for books, journals, manuals, periodicals, and Web pages ranges from about $15 to $70 per hour. Copy Editors in the fields of advertising, business communications, or public relations may command up to $100 an hour or more. In some circumstances, flat rates for the copyediting job may be preferable to both Copy Editor and employer.

Employment Prospects

Prospects for freelance Copy Editors are consistently good, in particular, as has been noted by the Editorial Freelancers Association, because there is a very real shortage of competent freelance Copy Editors. Hiring freelance editors is a boon for employers who then can limit staff costs by contracting work outside the company. A good and successful freelance Copy Editor can build an ongoing relationship with his or her clients for steady work.

Some freelance Copy Editors prefer to work within the embrace of a copyediting service that has many clients, and needs to keep many freelancers available for the variety of projects contracted to them.

Advancement Prospects

As the work of an aspiring freelance Copy Editor gets accepted by author or publisher and one's résumé expands with more jobs completed, the likelihood improves of establishing a reputation as a seasoned professional Copy Editor. A steady income and burgeoning career is almost guaranteed, but, as a freelancer, it is always important to remember that ongoing self-marketing is a critical component of the continuance of that career.

Education and Training

Copy Editors should have an undergraduate degree in communications or English. Advanced degrees may be necessary if the Copy Editor wishes to specialize in scientific or technical fields.

Experience, Skills, and Personality Traits

Previous employment as a Copy Editor, editor, proofreader, or writer may be desirable on a résumé for potential employers. Scientific or technical backgrounds may be required for specialized work.

Copy Editors must be skilled in the basics of editing, grammar, punctuation, spelling, and style. They must be good at detail work, patient, meticulous, and knowledgeable about manuscript coding for production and printing conventions. They have to be quick to grasp content and to spot errors, inconsistencies, and weaknesses in the text. They must utilize good judgment and not impose their own beliefs on the writing but respect the author's ideas and style. Diplomacy with authors and editors is a given, and Copy Editors frequently have to work under a great deal of pressure in meeting deadlines.

Unions and Associations

The primary association for freelance Copy Editors is the Editorial Freelancers Association. Also there is the American Copy Editors Society. Those who are writers may belong to a variety of writers' organizations, such as the American Society of Journalists and Authors, the Association of Authors and Publishers, the Association for Women in Communications, the National Writers Association, and the National Writers Union.

Tips for Entry

1. As a student, a stint on the college newspaper or journal may be a good place to start in learning the copyediting trade.
2. Look into an internship within either a publishing firm or with an editing company that hires freelancers. Many of these companies can be found easily in an Internet search.
3. Be sure that all your correspondence with potential employers is grammatically correct and contains no spelling errors.
4. Take care with the details of your résumé, as they are a mirror of your capabilities as a potential Copy Editor.
5. Establish your own Web site to promote your services; create a brochure/flyer to send to book publishers alerting them of your availability.

DESKTOP PUBLISHER

CAREER PROFILE

Duties: Produce brochures, magazines, newsletters, reports, and other small publications

Alternate Title(s): Design Engineer, Electronic Publisher, Graphic Designer

Salary Range: $20,000 to $60,000 or more

Employment Prospects: Fair to good

Advancement Prospects: Fair

Prerequisites:

Education or Training—Undergraduate degree in art, graphic design, English, journalism, or mass communications

Experience—Previous work as editor, writer, or in publications production is essential

Special Skills and Personality Traits—Good editing and writing skills; knowledge of desktop publishing software; management and organization skills; resourcefulness in meeting deadlines; sales ability

CAREER LADDER

```
┌─────────────────────────────────────┐
│     Seasoned Desktop Publisher       │
└─────────────────────────────────────┘

┌─────────────────────────────────────┐
│    Experienced Desktop Publisher     │
└─────────────────────────────────────┘

┌─────────────────────────────────────┐
│      Novice Desktop Publisher        │
└─────────────────────────────────────┘
```

Position Description

Desktop publishing specialists use personal computer software to format and combine text, numerical data, photographs, charts, and other visual graphic elements to produce readable, clear, and attractive publication materials (known as publication masters). Depending upon the nature of the particular project, Desktop Publishers may write and edit text, create graphics, convert photographs and drawings into digital images, design page layouts, typeset and do color separation, and translate electronic information onto film or other forms for printing.

The Desktop Publisher works with authors, businesses, associations, agencies, and other organizations to prepare publications. Materials produced by Desktop Publishers may include advertisements, books, brochures, business cards, calendars, forms, instructional manuals, magazines, newsletters and newspapers, slides, and tickets. Desktop publishing is rapidly replacing the prepress work done before by compositors, typesetters, and page layout personnel.

Since the introduction in the 1980s of software that integrated text and graphics, dozens of desktop publishing software programs are now available. As so much material

today is published on the Internet, Desktop Publishers increasingly are responsible for making the publication master "Web ready" and need to know about electronic-publishing technologies that convert documents from print to electronic format.

Freelance Desktop Publishers work with a staff editor or communications manager who provides the specifications for the material's content, design, length, and size. The Desktop Publisher may be given the copy (in printed or electronic form), or may have to generate it in accordance with specifications. The copy is edited, and the pages are formatted on-screen to accommodate graphics and design specifications. Simple documents, such as newsletters, can be printed in quantity using a high-quality printer to produce proofs, which are then mounted on mechanicals and sent to the printer.

Innovations in computer software and printing technology, including digital color page-makeup systems, electronic page-layout systems, and off-press color-proofing systems, have expanded desktop publishing into actual graphic design. Desktop Publishers can use scanners to capture photographs, images, or art as digital data to be incorporated directly into the electronic page layouts. On the other hand, this data can be manipulated further by computer software to correct mistakes or compensate for imperfections in the original images. The final digital files are used to produce printing plates. (While desktop publishing involves the mechanics of producing books, business cards, newsletters, and packaging, graphic design sometimes becomes part of the process.) Although a new field, Web design is becoming an increasingly important part of the desktop publishing process.

Desktop Publishers can be multifunctional—copy editor, designer, editor, typesetter, writer—or they can supervise others who perform some or all of these tasks. All facets of production must be coordinated to ensure that deadlines are met. In the process Desktop Publishers must frequently consult with clients, first to understand their requirements, then to present quotations for work contracts and discuss design concepts, and, finally, to review progress and discuss any problems.

Some Desktop Publishers may specialize in simple office documents, or in the more graphically complex, multicolored materials and publications. Many Desktop Publishers who work within this more elaborate production environment prefer to call themselves design engineers. Some may produce their own newsletters, and most freelance Desktop Publishers (or design engineers) have a Web site devoted to their services.

Salaries

Freelance Desktop Publishers set individual fees per job, usually by calculating a day rate and estimating the time that the assignment will require. Miscellaneous expenses are factored into the final rate. The U.S. Bureau of Labor Statistics states that, in 2002, the median annual earnings of Desktop Publishers were $31,620, with a low of nearly $19,000 to a high of $52,500 or more. It has been further estimated by business writer Mark Landsbaum that average annual income ranges for Desktop Publishers were between $30,000 and $70,000, with some earning more than $100,000 a year and charging up to $250 an hour for their services. The usual hourly rate ranges from $15 to $50. Freelance Desktop Publishers tended to earn less (average of $30,600 in all industries) than those with added graphic design credentials (average of $34,570 in all industries).

It is important to remember that a substantial investment in state-of-the-art equipment and software is necessary to make an effective start in desktop publishing. Besides a personal computer with sufficient memory to handle the wide demands of desktop publishing programs, one needs a word processing program, and a high-speed (laser) printer for just the basics. If extensive graphic work is contemplated, one also needs a scanner, a color printer, and more complicated software to produce any multicolored and complex material desired. Information about equipment and software can be found in such publications as *Desktop Publishers Journal* (http://www.dtpjournal.com) or at the Web sites of individual manufacturers.

Employment Prospects

Job prospects for freelance Desktop Publishers are fair to good, or better. According to the U.S. Bureau of Labor Statistics, Desktop Publishers totaled about 35,000 in 2002, and it estimated that by 2012 that number would climb to 45,200. Among both salaried and freelance Desktop Publishers, two out of three of them worked in book, newspaper, periodical, or directory publishing or printing and its related support activities, while the rest worked in a wide variety of other industries.

Although the numbers of individuals seeking graphic design and desktop publishing work will most likely exceed openings available, there is constant labor force turnover within companies that make way for new hirings. Due to the cost-cutting profitability for a company to print its own newsletters and other reports, the need for experienced Desktop Publishers will continue to grow. Among persons without experience, those with computer backgrounds or who have completed postsecondary programs in desktop publishing or graphic design have the best chance of employment, either as a freelance consultant or as a full-time hire.

The best Desktop Publisher opportunities are at advertising and public relations firms, commercial printers and newspapers, corporations of all sizes, professional associations, and trade organizations. The higher earnings tend to be centered in the printing business and related support activities.

Advancement Prospects

As the work of an aspiring Desktop Publisher gets accepted and utilized on a continuous basis, the chances are better of becoming established as a professional Desktop Publisher working for many clients.

Education and Training

An undergraduate degree in art, English, graphic design, journalism, or mass communications is desirable. While some Desktop Publishers may have no background in design, such training, either on-the-job or vocational, may become useful.

Experience, Skills, and Personality Traits

Computer skills, manual dexterity, and creativity are the three most essential skills that a Desktop Publisher must have. Previous experience as a writer or editor and a thorough knowledge of production procedures and printing technologies are key. While most desktop publishing programs do not require graphics design skill, a knowledge of layout and basic design is helpful to start. If graphic design is the goal, then a visualization sense (how something will look after it is modified or moved and rearranged) and visual color discrimination ability become necessary.

Desktop Publishers must be extremely well organized to create the whole out of a myriad of pieces. Personal interaction skills also are essential, as they must work with a wide variety of people during the process. Above all, patience, good sales skills (to be able to sell themselves), and the ability to work under pressure are important requirements.

Unions and Associations

Desktop Publishers may belong to such communications organizations such as the American Society of Journalists and Authors, the Editorial Freelancers Association, the International Association of Business Communicators, and the Public Relations Society of America. Some who work in the printing and graphics design industries are represented by the Graphic Communications International Union.

Tips for Entry

1. In considering a career as a Desktop Publisher or a graphic designer, study job descriptions and educational requirements for the types of jobs that interest you to determine if more formal or informal education is necessary for entry-level positions.

2. Look into extension programs and private vocational schools for specific programs in desktop publishing, graphic communication, and electronic publishing.

3. Practice by producing brochures or newsletters for local church, school, or community-based organizations on a volunteer basis.

4. Update yourself on new software developments by taking workshops, learning new software programs on your own, and keeping abreast of changing industry technology.

5. Develop a portfolio that demonstrates your communication skills, knowledge, and creativity; establish and use your own Web site to promote your services.

FACT CHECKER

CAREER PROFILE

Duties: Check the accuracy of manuscripts or other material prior to publication

Alternate Title(s): Researcher

Salary Range: $15 to $75 per hour

Employment Prospects: Fair

Advancement Prospects: Fair

Prerequisites:

Education or Training—Undergraduate degree in journalism, mass communications, or other field; knowledge of language other than English helpful

Experience—None required, but previous work as editor, researcher, or writer helpful

Special Skills and Personality Traits—Extreme careful attention to details; knowledge of how best to use library and reference works

CAREER LADDER

```
┌─────────────────────────────┐
│    Seasoned Fact Checker    │
└─────────────────────────────┘

┌─────────────────────────────┐
│   Experienced Fact Checker  │
└─────────────────────────────┘

┌─────────────────────────────┐
│     Novice Fact Checker     │
└─────────────────────────────┘
```

Position Description

Publishers of books, periodicals, and reports tend to rely heavily upon the accuracy of their authors, but most publishers have Fact Checkers double-check for errors. The depth of fact checking can vary from just verifications of dates and spellings of names, titles, and places to verifying every detail. Thus, a Fact Checker helps to guard the reputation of a publisher and its writers.

Fact Checkers usually work from a copy of the manuscript and frequently have access to the author's original notes, interview tapes, and other original material. They must make heavy use of libraries and the Internet to locate needed research material. For example, if an author states that a certain event occurred on a particular date and in a certain place, a Fact Checker must verify all three elements by using such sources as an encyclopedia or specialized biographical dictionaries. Sometimes the checking of a seemingly simple fact can become complicated. In checking birth dates, care must be taken when conflicting records are discovered, as some of the dates available may have been utilized for reasons of vanity.

Depending on the employer's policies, Fact Checkers will call persons interviewed in the article, report, or book to confirm the accuracy of their quotes and statements, as well as research topics to ascertain whether the statements or claims in the manuscript can be validated. They may query the author to find out the sources of certain facts. All their findings must be reported back to the editor.

Fact checking requires a lot of tact and can be extremely tedious. It also carries a great deal of responsibility. Most freelance Fact Checkers also are consultant researchers and analysts.

Salaries

Freelance Fact Checkers typically earn anywhere from $15 (for people starting out in this field) to $75 (for experienced freelancers) per hour. Starting annual salaries for full-time in-house Fact Checkers start at about $30,000. Some freelancers may work for a flat fee, depending upon the type of project or employer, or negotiate to be placed on retainer by specific employers.

Employment Prospects

Fact checking is done extensively at book and magazine publishers, newspapers, and radio and television stations. Having a disciplined, experienced, and unbiased Fact Checker can save these companies money by avoiding libel lawsuits over incorrect information, let alone maintain their reputation in their respective marketplaces. However, some publishers view fact checking as an expendable cost, relying on their authors' statements (and provided source notes) that information in their manuscripts is accurate. Nonetheless, fact checking is pursued rigorously at many prestigious publishing organizations, such as *The New Yorker* magazine and *Reader's Digest*. Both publications have Fact Checkers on staff (or use freelance Fact Checkers as a supplemental group) who involve themselves completely in every article the publications would like to publish. In these cases, allegations, names, organizations, statistics, titles, and written quotations come under scrutiny. Other publishers may check only selected manuscripts. Freelance Fact Checkers are often used as a cost-saving alternative to developing on-staff personnel. Sometimes freelance copy editors are required to do minimal fact checking as well.

Advancement Prospects

As the work of an aspiring Fact Checker gets accepted and used more frequently by publishers and other media outlets, the chances of gaining work on a full-time basis with these organizations increases significantly.

Education and Training

While there are no specific educational requirements for Fact Checkers, an undergraduate degree in communications, English, or journalism is desirable. Also, knowledge of languages other than English, particularly French, German, Italian, or Spanish, is helpful, as is a broad intellectual curiosity. For specialized publications, graduate degrees in the specific subjects of these publications, may be necessary.

Experience, Skills, and Personality Traits

Prior experience as a copy editor, editor, librarian, proofreader, researcher, specialist in a professional field, or writer is advantageous.

Fact Checkers have to be zealous in their search for confirmation of data and completely unwilling to let any inconsistencies go by unchecked. Their intense attention to detail is an absolute must. While dedicated to catching errors, they must also be tactful, polite, and sensitive when dealing with sources and authors. This job requires a lot of general knowledge, an organized mind, and an ability to conduct quick and precise research. Many Fact Checkers specialize in certain subjects, and many publishers and publications ask their Fact Checkers to develop specialties related to their subject areas.

Unions and Associations

There is no specific professional association for Fact Checkers, but freelancers who offer this service usually provide other communications services, and may qualify for membership in the Editorial Freelancers Association. Depending upon what other services they might offer, other professional associations might include the American Library Association, the American Society for Information Science, the American Society of Journalists and Authors, the Reference and User Services Association, the Society for Technical Communications, or the Special Libraries Association.

Tips for Entry

1. Contact the offices of local publications to inquire if they have any openings for a Fact Checker.
2. If you have training in a specific field, say, as a medical technician, check with the professional journals to which you subscribe for any openings as a Fact Checker.
3. Add another foreign language to your résumé, such as Russian or Spanish.
4. Consider internship programs with newspapers or periodicals while in college to gain experience within that field, and ask to practice fact checking while in the program.
5. Consider working within a library (or even an internship where possible) to become familiar with potential reference works and research studies. Similarly, explore the Internet for useful reference/research portals.

FREELANCE WRITER

CAREER PROFILE

Duties: Write nonfiction articles for businesses and magazines; write publicity, promotion, and advertising copy

Alternate Title(s): Writer

Salary Range: $20 to $200+ per hour; $100 to $3,000+ per average-length magazine article (between 1,000 to 2,000 words); $50 to $1,500 per feature article in daily newspaper; $23 to $150 per hour for business writing; $40 to $150 per hour for annual reports for a business; various flat fees for projects

Employment Prospects: Good to excellent

Advancement Prospects: Good

Prerequisites:

Education or Training—No minimum education required; an undergraduate degree in communications, journalism, or liberal arts is preferred

Experience—No specific experience required, but background in journalism is useful

Special Skills and Personality Traits—Solid writing skills, ambition, imagination, organization, persistence, self-motivation, and self-promotion

CAREER LADDER

```
┌─────────────────────────────┐
│  Seasoned Freelance Writer  │
└─────────────────────────────┘

┌─────────────────────────────┐
│ Experienced Freelance Writer│
└─────────────────────────────┘

┌─────────────────────────────┐
│   Novice Freelance Writer   │
└─────────────────────────────┘
```

Position Description

Freelance writing is an unpredictable and very competitive way of making a living, but the rewards can be substantial for those who succeed. Such rewards, besides the increasing income from one's successful writings, can include the satisfaction of bylines and credits, recognition within the field, and the fact that you are (generally) writing about things you love and are being paid for it.

Many Freelance Writers begin their career while holding down full- or part-time employment elsewhere. Most Freelance Writers send out queries or manuscripts to publication editors. As an alternative work option they may write brochures, slide show scripts, or promotional pieces for businesses. Eventually, as they build up their business, there will come a time when it becomes economically feasible to begin freelancing full time.

Acquiring work with general-interest publications is tough going, and many rejection slips may occur before a sale is made. A freelancer who has written an article then needs to find the type of publications that might be interested in the work. Then a query letter (usually one page or so, giving a brief summary of the main theme of the article, its anticipated length, the benefits the publication's readers might gain from reading the article, and when it can be delivered) is sent to a named editor at a publication. Another method is to write articles for mass audiences, hoping to understand their needs and tastes, and submitting it to various publications. A new way of breaking into a marketplace in which editors tend to look for experienced writers is to utilize a virtual publishing community Web site. This is a Web site that accepts articles or other work from authors and sells them to various publications, paying the author a modest fee. It is one way to get started and to build both credentials and a reputation as a published writer.

Consumer-type magazines (for example, culinary, entertainment, ethnic/minority, health, in-flight airline journals, men's, political, religious, romance, school/career, teen's, travel, women's) tend to pay the best. The downside is that the competition is stiff as this is where most Freelance Writers focus their start. Trade journals (aimed at specific careers) pay highly variable amounts. However, if a writer's expertise corresponds to a particular trade, acceptance for publication becomes easier. In these instances, the writer's research may be more important than the eloquence of his/her writing. Literary magazines generally pay low fees. However, there is prestige in writing for this specialized marketplace, and may add greatly to the impression made on publishers when the writer, later, seeks to sell his/her fiction or poetry. Finally, there are e-zines, which, simply, are magazines on the Internet. Articles for them tend to run longer than those in print, but the pay is nonexistent (only a byline given), or negligible. This trend may be changing as some of the more popular e-zines are tending to pay better than before. The other positive aspect is that topics are generally unlimited.

Many Freelance Writers choose to rely on business writing for a regular income, as it pays much better than most periodicals. Business writing might include film/slide show scripts, internal newsletters and magazines, text for the company's Web site, press and publicity material, speeches, and trade stories. Experienced business freelancers may even be kept on a retainer, which is a flat monthly fee in exchange for a stated amount (or hours) of work, say, on an internal magazine. Many advertising and public relations firms also use freelancers extensively.

Other freelancers find constant work by contributing to textbooks, encyclopedias, and other reference books. Such work is usually "work for hire," in that the writer is assigned specific work to be accomplished and receives a flat fee from the publisher in exchange for all rights to the work. In these cases, no royalties will be paid. Some freelancers find they can gain work as freelance editors as well.

Freelance Writers must be highly motivated, well-organized, and quite self-disciplined to function effectively on their own. Most put in long hours, and the work comes in sporadically, with resultant deadlines often overlapping one other. Writers often have more than one project at the same time, all in various stages of development. Freelancers must constantly be seeking fresh assignments, as the time it takes to sell an idea for an article may be lengthy. Freelancers need to be methodical about their finances, keeping their business and tax records in good shape.

Salaries

A Freelance Writer's income depends upon the type of projects, the writer's abilities and persistence, and, to a lesser extent, the writer's location. Accessibility to major businesses, magazines, and publishing offices in major cities used to make the job of selling one's writings that much easier. However, today, with the proliferation of e-mail and fax capabilities, the importance of geographic location has lessened.

Many successful Freelance Writers can earn $20,000 to $30,000 a year or more. Some of them who work for business corporations and industries can earn $40,000 and up. Pay for trade and consumer (general-interest) magazine articles can range from $50 to $3,000 per project, while newspaper feature articles can command from $50 to $1,500 per project.

Freelance Writers working for corporate clients usually charge by the hour or by the day. Rates will vary according to the type of job and the turnover required. Typical day rates range from $160 to $1,100, and hourly rates range from $23 to $150. Flat rates for such items as brochures and fliers, newsletters, press releases, and other such publications may range from $100 to $1,000.

One word of caution: many magazines pay Freelance Writers upon publication of the written work, rather than at the point when they accept the article for publication. Many publications work on tight budgets and prefer time for the publication to earn money from its advertisements and sales. The downside for the writer is that the article might never make it to publication, even if it was accepted, especially if the article is extremely topical or there is a changeover in the publication's management. At that time, of course, no payment will be forthcoming. This is why both the National Writer's Union and the American Society of Journalists and Authors urge writers to negotiate contracts that include payment upon acceptance of the article, not publication. In case an article is killed, writers are urged to look into kill fees (a percentage of their original payment per contract).

Employment Prospects

Most of the trade and consumer periodicals, as well as businesses and associations, rely upon Freelance Writers. However, competition is extremely stiff, particularly for the more prestigious publications or businesses. For writers starting out, it is best to try small publications or local businesses to gain experience and build the credentials needed to penetrate the larger markets.

Advancement Prospects

Despite the competition, once the work of an aspiring Freelance Writer gets accepted and he/she is used more than once by a client, the likelihood of receiving additional work on a full-time basis with that client or other clients increases significantly. However, it is not unusual for a Freelance Writer to take several years to become an established writer with an ongoing clientele and a steady income.

Education and Training

Most Freelance Writers have an undergraduate degree in communications, English, journalism, or liberal arts. For some specialized publications certain educational or work credentials are necessary. Generally, however, a publications editor will be looking for good writing, creativity, and imagination first and degrees secondarily.

Experience, Skills, and Personality Traits

Many Freelance Writers start off with no practical experience other than some writing courses, or writing jobs during college. Others turn to freelancing after years as editors, journalists, or public-relations writers, while others may position themselves as a Freelance Writer as a career change from a business or trade.

To become successful, freelancers must be good writers and be punctual in meeting deadlines. They need to be persistent in the selling of themselves and their work, and not be discouraged by the rejections that inevitably will come. Freelance Writers have to be highly organized in both their finances and in their pursuit of every opportunity to market themselves and their writings.

Unions and Associations

Major national associations include the American Society of Journalists and Authors, Associated Business Writers of America, the Authors Guild, International Women's Writing Guild, National Writers Association, and the Public Relations Society of America. The Writers Guild of America is a union that represents primarily scriptwriters for film, radio, and television, whereas the National Writers Union represents writers and authors.

Tips for Entry

1. Take as many writing courses as possible, and gain experience in writing for college publications while getting your degree.
2. Check out the Internet for guidance from established Freelance Writers. Also check the various writers' guide books and publications for direction within this field.
3. Study magazines, newspapers, and other nonfiction works to determine what successful contemporary writers are doing and how they structured their pieces.
4. Check out such Web pages as that of Worldwide Freelance Writer (http://www.worldwidefreelance.com) and Gallanis Freelance Writing Solutions (http://www.geocities.com/peter_gallanis) for their extensive lists of resources, associations, and actual markets for writers.
5. Remember to ask for a contract for the work you will be doing. It protects both parties.

INDEXER

CAREER PROFILE

Duties: Create indexes to books, databases, journals, maps, newspapers, periodicals, and software manuals

Alternate Title(s): None

Salary Range: $15 to $110+ per hour; $2.35 to $8 per page, with an average of $3.50 per page; 40 cents to $1.25 per line of index; or a flat fee of $200 to $1,000+ per book, depending upon length and difficulty

Employment Prospects: Fair to good

Advancement Prospects: Fair to good

Prerequisites:

Education or Training—Undergraduate degree in English, humanities, liberal arts, or social sciences; graduate degree in library science or in a scientific or technical field may be required

Experience—Background in research or library science is helpful

Special Skills and Personality Traits—Ability to analyze text objectively and accurately and make topical connections in a text; accuracy, command of English and grammar, consistency, attention to detail, a logical and orderly mind, organizational skills, perception and predictive abilities, good reading skills, wide general knowledge

CAREER LADDER

```
┌─────────────────────────────┐
│     Seasoned Indexer        │
└─────────────────────────────┘

┌─────────────────────────────┐
│    Experienced Indexer      │
└─────────────────────────────┘

┌─────────────────────────────┐
│      Novice Indexer         │
└─────────────────────────────┘
```

Position Description

The British Standards Institution defines an index as "a systematic guide to the location of words, concepts or other items in books, periodicals or other publications. [It] consists of a series of entries appearing, not in the order in which they appear in the publication, but in some other order (e.g., alphabetical) chosen to enable the user to find them quickly, together with references to show where each item is located." Thus, an index is a road map that leads readers to a logical sequence of information designed to guide them as clearly and easily as possible in their search within a given published product. A good index should be accurate and concise, with cogent headings and adequate cross-referencing.

The Indexer creates this alphabetical and systematic list of references to terms and concepts in the text from a detailed text analysis. The index guides the reader in a direct manner to data found within the document, and helps the reader discover new information. A good index also shows readers how a particular topic is related to other topics within the document. Without indexes, it would be difficult, if not impossible, to access vast amounts of information available in published nonfiction works.

There is a common misconception that indexing is clerical work and can be done without experience. On the contrary, indexes are complex constructions that require skill and training to produce. The value of an index is in its organization. A good index must discriminate between information on a subject and only a passing mention of that topic. It needs to indicate relationships between concepts and subjects, even if they are scattered by the author's arrangement of the text.

Indexes are usually compiled by professional Indexers, most of them freelancers, who are familiar with different forms of indexes and all the international style standards. Rules and practices are in constant flux, and the professional Indexer must stay abreast of them. Many Indexers have experience in, or actually have been employed by, libraries or publishers, businesses, or database providers.

Prior to working on an index, an Indexer must establish the scope of the job. The length and depth of the index is determined by the number of pages (allotted by the publisher or author), the number of columns per page, the type size and format, and the style rules to be followed. Ideally, the size of the index should be between 2 percent and 5 percent of the text's length. Large reference works, such as encyclopedias, require the most complex indexes, with up to 100,000 entries or more. A short and simple index, however, may have only 1,000 entries. Many indexes require a complex referencing to subject material in the text, along with names and terms used by the author.

Once the job requirements are known, the Indexer must carefully read the entire text before compiling the entries. If the topic of the text is unfamiliar to an indexer, checking with a local library to look at indexes of books with similar subjects will be helpful. (One can often search within a book at Amazon.com and other such Web sites to study a published index.) The Indexer may use computer software programs designed for Indexers, or keep track by marking the text and by keeping alphabetical lists manually in some manner. Many changes may occur during the process as the Indexer gets new ideas for referencing the information. In the final edit, the Indexer checks all the terms created to ensure that they lead the reader to the right information, and that the length of the index is within stated limits.

While indexing, the Indexer can provide another valuable service to the author and the publisher by spotting errors or inconsistencies in the writing and typographical errors.

The average book index is compiled in one to four weeks, but large indexes may require months. Indexers often work under pressure, as indexes are usually undertaken near the end of the publishing cycle just before the manuscript is sent to a printer, and, by this stage of the production, deadlines become critical.

Most professional Indexers now compile their indexes electronically using indexing software programs. This is particularly necessary, as most publishers now prefer the index to be submitted on disk or transferred electronically to them.

In addition to indexing, some professional freelance Indexers may provide other services, such as abstract writing, editing, proofreading, researching, and Web and database updating.

Salaries

Earnings depend on the type of indexing, the expertise of the Indexer, and the subject matter involved. Technical and scientific works often pay more than consumer projects. Freelance fees are negotiated according to the project, the employer's pay scale, and the Indexer's fee structure. Indexers may be paid per line in the index, or by the manuscript page indexed, by the hour, or by a project fee. The average consumer book brings a $300 to $900 fee. Some Indexers work on retainer, so their employer has priority on their services. While rights to indexes usually are retained by the employer, reversion of these rights (and the resultant additional monies for reprints, and foreign translations) to the Indexer has been approved by the courts (but must be negotiated with the employer).

Employment Prospects

The developing realization on the part of authors and publishers that readers increasingly do not want to wade through texts in search of facts has escalated the need for professional Indexers. While some publishers still forgo an index as an unnecessary expense, book reviewers usually note whether an index is present and what its quality is. As people get used to the speed of accessing information via their use of the Internet, they find indexes aid in their search. In addition, corporations, databases, newspapers, and periodicals need indexes to keep track of their collections. Finally, many libraries will no longer buy nonfiction books without indexes.

Advancement Prospects

As the work of an aspiring Indexer gets accepted and the Indexer's services are used more than once by one or more clients, the chances are better of getting additional work on a full-time basis. Once an Indexer's reputation is established (and a personal Web site listing one's résumé of jobs accomplished helps to promote that reputation), the possibilities of a full-time career as a professional and seasoned freelance Indexer can become a reality.

Education and Training

In addition to an undergraduate degree, many Indexers have graduate degrees in library science. Some also have advanced degrees in scientific or technical fields that allow them to specialize in those types of books.

Most schools of library and information science offer courses in indexing, and many offer one-day seminars or extended indexing workshops. Extension programs at some universities, likewise, include courses in indexing that are open to people not enrolled in regular courses in the university. Private companies may even offer occasional indexing seminars. In addition, the American Society of Indexers offer listings of various resources for indexers, including courses and workshops, online discussion groups, online reference sources, conferences and trade shows, and other information useful to Indexers. All these listings can be found at their Web site: http://www.asindexing.org.

Experience, Skills, and Personality Traits

A background in information management and library science is helpful to freelancers looking to make a career of indexing. Indexing is precise work and should be undertaken only after some training.

Indexers have a wide variety of skills to offer. They must have an orderly mind and a passion for accuracy. They must be careful readers and able to grasp the material quickly. They need to keep in mind how a reader would look for a specific piece of information, but also be sensitive to an author's terminology. While indexes must be logical, readers may not be. In addition, Indexers have to keep up with the latest rules, practices, and standards concerning index formats and grammatical style. Above all, Indexers must be good at observing patterns, at organizing information, at being detailed and accurate, and working under pressure.

Unions and Associations

The only organization in the United States devoted entirely to the advancement of indexing is the American Society of Indexers, or ASI. It is affiliated with like organizations in Australia, Canada, and the United Kingdom. Membership is open to anyone interested in the field, and it has local chapters throughout the United States.

Indexers who provide other freelance services may belong to the Editorial Freelancers Association or any number of societies for authors, editors, public relations officers, or technical writers and editors.

Tips for Entry

1. The best way to learn indexing is to index. Take a favorite nonfiction book and create an index for it. Then compare it to the one already in the book to see how another person would index the same material.
2. Study indexing guides and textbooks, publishers' style guides, and check out indexing standards as set by the National Information Standards Organization (and offered in more abbreviated form by the American Society of Indexers). In addition, study what *The Chicago Manual of Style* has to say about indexing and indexes.
3. Learn more about indexing on the Internet. To generate a list of relevant Web sites, enter the keywords *indexing or indexer* in any search engine. These hits will provide examples of how established, experienced Indexers promote their services and the scope of typical credentials in he field.
4. Contact the American Society of Indexers (ASI) for information about their organization and any local branch in your area. ASI can be reached at http://www.asindexing.org.
5. Contact a library or organization in your area and offer to write an index for any of their material. Once it is completed and printed in whatever format, you have a printed index to add to your résumé.
6. Establish your own Web site to promote your services; create a brochure/flyer to send to book publishers alerting them of your availability; take classified ads in pertinent industry publications to publicize your services.

MANUSCRIPT EVALUATOR

CAREER PROFILE

Duties: Evaluate and critique articles, book proposals, manuscripts, and other documents

Alternate Title(s): Book Reader

Salary Range: $1 to $3.50 per page; $50 to $250+ per outline (or book proposal), $150 to $200 for first 20,000 words, $300 to $500 for up to 100,000 words; $12 to $45 per hour for trade books

Employment Prospects: Fair

Advancement Prospects: Limited

Prerequisites:

Education or Training—Undergraduate degree in communications, English, journalism, or liberal arts

Experience—Background and/or previous employment as editor or writer

Special Skills and Personality Traits—Computer and word-processing skills; detail-oriented; excellent writing ability; good grammar, spelling, and style skills

CAREER LADDER

```
┌─────────────────────────────────┐
│  Seasoned Manuscript Evaluator  │
└─────────────────────────────────┘

┌─────────────────────────────────┐
│  Experienced Manuscript Evaluator │
└─────────────────────────────────┘

┌─────────────────────────────────┐
│  Beginner Manuscript Evaluator  │
└─────────────────────────────────┘
```

Position Description

Manuscript evaluation/critiquing, whether by an individual or by a freelance service firm, is performed on manuscripts, articles, or documents that have not yet been accepted for publication. The author is looking for some expert opinion as to the publishing possibilities of his or her work. This work may be a piece of fiction, a nonfiction manuscript or article, or a technical text.

Evaluations may be done in two steps, the first, a preliminary one, stating, after a thorough study of the work, whether the manuscript (or document) is publishable in its current form. If it is not publishable, it has to be determined whether it is unpublishable altogether, or whether, by additional work, either by the client or by a professional editor, it can be brought into line with standard agents' and publishers' criteria. If it demands more work, this preliminary evaluation will describe the scope of work needed and will give a cost estimate if the client chooses to use the freelancer (or service firm) to undertake the work.

A more comprehensive evaluation/critique would be the next optional step for a client. The manuscript would be read once again much as an agent or a publisher would. An analysis of the manuscript's strengths and weaknesses, along with recommendations on how to capitalize on the former and correct the latter. The report also would evaluate whether the author's goals in the writing are realistic in terms of its intended publisher or audience.

A manuscript critique/evaluation does not encompass actual editing or revising, but may include general suggestions on how to go about such tasks. Most freelancers (or firms) who do such evaluations also provide full editorial services.

Many freelance service firms also evaluate book proposals. The proposal package typically consists of a cover letter, an author biography or résumé, an overview of the manuscript, an outline of the chapters, potential marketing possibilities, and one or more sample chapters. A writer may have begun such a proposal package, and, in so doing, finds a need for its professional evaluation. As with the manuscript evaluation process, most freelance service firms will offer to do a critique, a rewriting of the proposal package, or a completely new package. Most proposal packages are no more than 75 pages.

Salaries

Freelance manuscript evaluation fees may be based on an hourly rate, a per page rate, or a project flat fee. As freelancers set their own rates for various types of jobs, so, likewise, the rates will vary depending upon the type of manuscript (or article, or document) being assessed. A median average rate of $20 to $30 per hour, or $2 per page, is likely. For flat rates, the fees would range from $150 to $500 or more, depending upon the length and complexity of the work being appraised.

It would be unlikely that an individual freelancer doing only book evaluations would be assured of a full year's income, but a freelance service firm, with many freelance evaluators available to it, may make a sizable yearly income.

Employment Prospects

Freelancers have a poor to fair chance of frequent or steady work as a Manuscript Evaluator, with better possibilities when linked with a freelance editorial service firm. The availability of such work will depend greatly on the marketing skills (particularly on the Internet) of those offering such a service. The popularity of this service is attested to by the number of Internet Web sites of publication and freelance writing firms that offer to evaluate manuscripts.

Advancement Prospects

When the work of a Manuscript Evaluator is accepted by clients (either authors or publishers), the chances improve significantly of getting additional work on a full-time basis with that or other clients. As the experience and reputation of a Manuscript Evaluator gains momentum, the cumulative effect of successful evaluations/critiques greatly bolsters the prospects of expanding the Manuscript Evaluator's list of satisfied clients and the opportunity for positive referral and good recommendation.

Education and Training

Manuscript Evaluators should have the same type of undergraduate degree as most copy editors, usually in communi-cations, English, or journalism. Advanced degrees are unnecessary, unless the specific text being evaluated is of a scientific or technical nature.

Experience, Skills, and Personality Traits

Previous experience as either an editor or a writer is desirable. A Manuscript Evaluator has to be meticulous in attention to the detail of the manuscript (or book proposal, article, or document), but also able to view the work in the greater context of publication possibility. An evaluation/critique must deal with the particulars of the author's grammar, spelling, and style, as well as how the work reads as a whole and how an agent or an editor might view it.

Doing such appraisals also requires a great deal of tact on the part of the evaluator in making suggestions to the author on how to improve or rewrite the work. The thoroughness and consideration of the evaluator will help determine whether the author will consider relying upon the evaluator (or the evaluator's firm) for any needed editorial work on the manuscript.

Unions and Associations

The only applicable national association for freelance evaluators would be the Editorial Freelancers Association. Those who also are writers may belong to an assortment of writers' organizations, such as the American Society of Journalists and Authors, and the National Writer's Union.

Tips for Entry

1. Take writing courses while in college and work on whatever school publications you can.
2. Gain editorial experience working as in intern with a publishing firm.
3. Read book reviews (in both consumer and trade publications) to gain insight into how other book reader professionals appraise published writings.
4. Write your own critiques of both fiction and nonfiction and compare them with published book reviews/critiques of the same works.

PROOFREADER

Duties: Check typeset manuscript galleys, page proofs, mechanicals, and blue lines for errors prior to final printing

Alternate Title(s): None

Salary Range: $10 to $55 per hour for books and periodicals; $15 to $55 per hour for business publications

Employment Prospects: Fair to good

Advancement Prospects: Fair to good

Prerequisites:

Education or Training—Undergraduate degree in communications, English, or humanities; graduate degree may be required for scientific and technical subjects, or, at least, work within these areas

Experience—Any background in communications or editing helpful, or work as an editor, editorial assistant, or writer

Special Skills and Personality Traits—Excellent command of grammar, spelling, punctuation, and style; careful eye for detail; knowledge of subject areas either helpful or may be required

> Seasoned Proofreader

> Established Proofreader

> Beginner Proofreader

Position Description

A Proofreader provides the final check for errors before copy of whatever kind (for example, advertisements, annual reports, books, brochures, and periodicals) are sent to the printer. Being the last check before publication entails a tremendous amount of responsibility

Proofreaders may come into the process at any time of production: at the page proof (or galley) stage; when copy and art are pasted onto boards, known as mechanicals (though this is less frequent as so many publications are now produced using sophisticated desktop publishing software); or when a dummy of the final product is produced (printed typically in blue ink, hence, the name "blue lines"). Proofreaders check the typeset copy against the corrected manuscript or corrected page proofs to make sure that all changes marked were executed. They also look for any typographical errors, any unevenness in the print lines, or any other typesetting imperfections. Beyond the text, Proofreaders must make sure that photo captions, tables, and any other illustrations are correct, and that all the artwork is in

its proper place. Even at this late stage in the production cycle, Proofreaders may find inconsistencies or actual errors, which they must bring immediately to the attention of the editor.

Salaries

Freelance Proofreaders usually charge an hourly fee that will vary according to the industry and the type of material being proofed. Book publishers usually pay from about $10 to $30 an hour. Corporations and advertising and public relations agencies typically pay up to $50 or more an hour depending upon the complexity of the project and the amount of proofreading that needs to be done. If the proofreading is just part of the overall editing procedure offered by the freelancer, the work may be billed at much higher rates, particularly if being done for a corporation rather than a publishing firm. Again, as with copyediting fees, Proofreaders may offer a flat rate for the job at hand, which may range from $200 to more than $500 for the project depending on the size and complexity of the assignment.

Employment Prospects

Prospects for freelance Proofreaders are consistently good, especially in business and industry, where a lot of the communication work (internal and external) is contracted out. In many cases, freelance Proofreaders also provide copyediting services. Some freelancers prefer to work within the embrace of a proofreading or copyediting service that has many clients and needs to keep many freelancer Proofreaders available for the variety of projects contracted to them.

Advancement Prospects

As the work of an aspiring freelance Proofreader gets accepted by author or publisher and the proofreader's résumé expands with more jobs completed, the chances are better of establishing a reputation as a professional Proofreader. A steady income and escalating career is almost guaranteed, but, as a freelancer, it is always important to remember that self-marketing is a critical component of the continuance of that career.

Education and Training

Proofreaders should have an undergraduate degree in communications, English, or a related field. Again, scholarly, scientific, or technical employers may require a graduate degree in the field.

Experience, Skills, and Personality Traits

Proofreaders need to have a thorough background and understanding of punctuation, rules of grammar, and style. They must be meticulous readers and scrupulous in their concentration on details. As they frequently work directly with typesetters and printers, they need to be well versed in production and printing procedures.

Proofreading can be extremely tedious, and, to a degree, largely clerical in nature. Patience and great care needs to be taken in order to avoid missing potential errors or inconsistencies.

Unions and Associations

The primary association for freelance Proofreaders is the Editorial Freelancers Association. Those who also are writers may belong to a variety of writers' organizations, such as the American Society of Journalists and Authors, the Association of Authors and Publishers, the Association for Women in Communications, the National Writers Association, and the National Writers Union.

Tips for Entry

1. As a student, a stint on the college newspaper or journal may be a good place to start learning the mechanics of proofreading.
2. Look into an internship within either a publishing firm, or with an editing/proofreading company that hires freelancers. Many of these companies can be found easily in an Internet search.
3. Be sure that all your correspondence with companies for which you are applying for whatever position is grammatically correct, carries the right punctuation, and everything is spelled correctly.
4. Take care with the details of your résumé, as they are a mirror of your capabilities as a potential Proofreader.
5. Establish your own Web site to promote your services; create a brochure/flyer to send to book publishers alerting them of your availability.

SELF-PUBLISHER

CAREER PROFILE

Duties: Independently write and publish books, monographs, periodicals, and other documents

Alternate Title(s): Independent Publisher, e-Book Publisher

Salary Range: $0 to an unlimited amount

Employment Prospects: Fair

Advancement Prospects: Fair

Prerequisites:

Education or Training—Undergraduate degree in communications or English; courses in business, desktop publishing, and finance helpful

Experience—Background as editor and writer useful; familiarity with book production essential; sales experience and financial skillfulness desirable; knowledge of electronic publishing methods often essential

Special Skills and Personality Traits—Ability to sense trends and market opportunities; financial planning and superior record keeping; innovativeness and willingness to take risks; organization; good marketing skills; self-promotion

CAREER LADDER

```
┌─────────────────────────────────┐
│   High-Profile Self-Publisher   │
└─────────────────────────────────┘

┌─────────────────────────────────┐
│    Established Self-Publisher    │
└─────────────────────────────────┘

┌─────────────────────────────────┐
│      Novice Self-Publisher       │
└─────────────────────────────────┘
```

Position Description

Self-Publishers are authors who choose to avoid the traditional publishing firms and publish their work themselves. They may never have had a book published before, or may have had a book published by a vanity press (which charges a fee to print the book), or may have had an unsatisfactory experience with one or more of their books being published in the traditional way or seek more control over the book's appearance.

Self-publishing became realistic with the introduction of the personal computer and desktop publishing software. Now, for a moderate investment, writers can purchase the equipment and the programs necessary to produce manuscript copy, galleys, and page mechanicals ready for processing at a printing plant. At the same time, with the consolidation of publishing firms into large publishing entities, there has been an explosion of small presses (many of which may have begun as self-publishing operations themselves) and self-publishing firms. The availability of this production process to individual authors has furthered the growth of self-publishing. The expansion of the Internet and printing-on-demand technology has made self-publishing an even more viable option for writers.

Self-publishing requires solid business planning and organization, as the Self-Publisher bears all the expenses of producing and marketing the book. An author has to budget every step carefully. Prior to writing the manuscript, the Self-Publisher must determine the book's market potential and how it is to be distributed. Production costs must be estimated and a marketing plan be in place.

After the book is written, typeset, proofread, corrected, and paginated, mechanicals are made for the printing firm. The Self-Publisher should be familiar with production shop operations and able to work with printing shop personnel. A cover must be designed, as well as any interior artwork (which may require hiring a graphic artist). Whatever illustrations are utilized in the text must be collected and commissioned so the artist can position them within the text, as well as execute any additional design layout. The Self-Publisher must be familiar with design layout to work effectively with the artist. Any legal questions about the text must be resolved with an attorney's help.

Once the book is printed, the Self-Publisher must have distribution channels to sell the copies. These will include book and specialty stores (if appropriate), wholesalers, catalogs, direct mail, and online promotion. Orders are placed, prices and terms negotiated, books delivered, and monies collected. In addition, publicity (including advertisements) and reviews must be solicited. Most of these activities are time-consuming, making the Self-Publisher as much a business manager as a writer. It is at the distribution step that so many Self-Publishers stumble.

Nonetheless, success can be energizing. Profits can lead to more books, with lessons learned from initial self-publishing ventures. Once sales are forthcoming, the distribution process becomes easier. The advantages are that self-published authors control the full process and receive all the proceeds of the sale of their books instead of awaiting royalties. They can set their own retail prices to ensure their costs are covered, even with the hefty discounts that wholesalers demand, yet remain competitive in the particular marketplace. In addition, Self-Publishers control their copyrights, but have the burden of any copyright infringement, libel, or other legal challenges related to their published text.

Some self-published writers prefer to utilize a self-publishing firm (sometimes known as an on-demand book publisher). These companies can help in the editing and proofreading phase, contract the design work (or do it themselves in consultation with the author), do the printing and binding, take over the promotion, marketing, distribution and fulfillment processes (all done for a fee and, possibly, a royalty percentage). However, it removes tremendous responsibilities from the Self-Publisher.

A new wrinkle in this process is the increased use of personal computers to produce electronic books (known as e-Books). Electronic publishing entails producing computerized online versions of books, magazines, and other works usually found in printed form. This allows for continuous updating and avoids being limited—by costs—to a specific number of pages. Once finalized, they are ready to be ordered online and instantaneously delivered electronically to a book buyer's own computer or reading device. Thus, both self-published authors and readers save money with no shipping and no taxes and remain competitive with books sold through traditional means. The material sold can be limited to legitimate purchasers by encoding the content to be read by only one authorized reading device, that of the buyer. There are self-publishing firms that now also offer the handling and online distribution of e-books for the author. It is estimated that more than 100 million books have been made available over the Internet to date.

Salaries

A successful self-published book is one that, at the least, earns enough income to cover production costs. Profits can range from hundreds of dollars to several thousand dollars, depending upon the profit margin per copy and the number of copies sold. Some successful self-published books have made hundreds of thousands of dollars in profits over time.

Minimum press runs usually are 1,000 or more copies. Depending upon costs, the Self-Publisher must invest up front an average of $8,000 to $14,000 or more for a typical book (not heavily illustrated). Making a profit may require several months or years. Success depends upon a careful up-front consideration of the risks and the potential market and distribution channels to be used.

Additional income can be generated from the sale of subsidiary rights, such as audiotapes/CDs, condensations, film/television production, foreign sales, or serializations.

The most successful self-published books tend to be self-help and inspirational guides, or subjects aimed at specialty markets (and distributed as such), rather than fiction or poetry. However, e-books may be changing that market configuration.

Employment Prospects

Self-Publishers have multiplied since affordable desktop computer systems arrived in the early 1980s. Successful marketing depends upon trends and perceived needs of the book-buying public. It is always possible to begin self-publishing on a part-time basis while continuing to work at a full-time job. However, the demands of self-publishing will soon interfere drastically with an author's time schedules. Some Self-Publishers take their success a step further and establish a small press, which publishes several titles a year, including the works of others. Thousands of small presses operate in the United States alone.

Advancement Prospects

As the work of an aspiring Self-Publisher gets marketed successfully (by whatever means), and sales increase, the cumulative effect of this escalating enterprise greatly increases the prospects for more published material by the author becoming successful moneymakers as well.

Education and Training

Most Self-Publishers are writers first and have undergraduate degrees in communications, English, humanities, or liberal arts. It is recommended that additional courses in business, finance, and marketing be taken prior to launching a self-publishing enterprise.

Experience, Skills, and Personality Traits

Successful Self-Publishers must be good writers and innovative businesspeople. They must be unafraid to take risks after carefully gauging their marketplace. Editing and design skills are advantageous if Self-Publishers do all the work themselves. Regardless, Self-Publishers must have a working knowledge of production and printing requirements and procedures. Financial, sales, and promotion skills are necessary. Advance planning can be the determining factor in success.

Unions and Associations

Self-Publishers may belong to the Publishers Marketing Association, a national nonprofit cooperative. There are now also associations devoted to self-publishing: the American Self-Publisher Association and the Self-Publishing and Independent Publishing Trade Association. Self-Publishers also may belong to regional small-press associations, local business organizations and writers' groups, such as the American Society of Journalists and Authors, the Authors Guild, and the National Writers Union.

Tips for Entry

1. Research the marketplace for competition in the type of book that you plan to self-publish.
2. To help in formulating a marketing/business plan, study books on the topics.
3. In promoting your book consider radio and cable access television stations, which are always looking for articulate guests who are experts in a subject or who write books with contemporary themes.
4. Consider outlets other than bookstores in which to sell your work, such as sports books in a sporting goods store, or such online sites as Amazon.com and Barnesandnoble.com.
5. Capitalize on reviews of your book, in promotional material to be both mailed and e-mailed (particularly effective if your self-published book is an e-book).

STRINGER

CAREER PROFILE

Duties: Provide ongoing flow of copy to newspapers and/or periodicals, and other media outlets

Alternate Title(s): Contributing Editor, Contributing Writer, Correspondent

Salary Range: Newspapers: $10 to $40 per piece, $1 per column inch, sometimes mileage compensation; magazines: 20 cents to $1 per word based on circulation

Employment Prospects: Fair

Advancement Prospects: Limited

Prerequisites:

Education or Training—Undergraduate degree in communications, English, journalism, or liberal arts; in some cases, at least a high school diploma

Experience—Background as a journalist preferred

Special Skills and Personality Traits—Ability to work independently and meet deadlines; excellent writing skills; nose for news

CAREER LADDER

```
┌─────────────────────────────┐
│      Seasoned Stringer       │
└─────────────────────────────┘

┌─────────────────────────────┐
│     Experienced Stringer     │
└─────────────────────────────┘

┌─────────────────────────────┐
│       Novice Stringer        │
└─────────────────────────────┘
```

Position Description

Most newspapers and magazines cover news from a broad geographic area but are unable financially to maintain writing staff at all the various locations. As an alternative, they rely on writers based in the area to monitor local news of interest to the publication and to provide timely, frequent stories, or material for stories. These writers are usually referred to as Stringers, or correspondents. They are part-time contributors and mostly work freelance, often for more than one publication. Some magazines pay freelance writers to provide copy (stories) on specialized topics for regular columns and departments of the publication. These writers are sometimes called contributing writers or contributing editors.

Stringers function as reporters with assignments to be researched, written, and submitted to the newspaper or magazine. They must keep current with local affairs and news and let their editors know of special events and potential ideas for in-depth pieces, known as feature articles. They may report on local government activities and school-board meetings, conferences, conventions, and exhibits. They may be assigned to do initial research and set up interviews, as well as provide material, for a staff writer.

Deadlines depend upon the publication's frequency. A newspaper Stringer may be expected to attend, say, a local meeting and then dictate the story over the telephone. Some may transmit it via e-mail or a fax machine, and others may only be required to send it in by regular mail. Stringers may submit a certain number of stories a week or a month, or just report as needed. Assignments are usually given by managing editors, or other editors of departments if it is a national publication. Some editors prefer a Stringer to provide news and feature ideas, others not. Most editors using Stringers count on their copy to help fill in publication space or to handle breaking stories and to meet immediate deadlines. Stringers may work as reporters or writers for other noncompeting publications, or they may be full-time freelancers. Stringers may get bylines for their feature articles, or not, depending upon the publication's policy.

Salaries

Most Stringers are not paid very well, but the income can be steady, and it is a job that often leads to other more lucrative writing assignments or positions. Major national news magazines offer either hourly rates, about $10 to $35 plus expenses, or daily rates of $150 to $250 plus expenses. Some will pay weekly, up to $900 plus expenses. Newspapers will pay per piece submitted, from $10 to $40 and a median average of $25. For a full story newspapers may pay from $150 to $300, with a median being $225. Some Stringers may be put on monthly retainers, with fees of $50 to $500 and up, depending upon the publication and the work involved.

Employment Prospects

Today's newspapers are competing with other media, such as television and the Internet, for readers and advertising dollars and are financially hurting in many cases. However, the need for national coverage of events, people, and issues keeps the need for Stringers for both newspapers and national magazines alive. Publications that cover broad areas, such as newspapers and weekly news magazines, are the best place for Stringers to find freelance employment. Another possibility is becoming a Stringer for an online publication on the Internet.

Advancement Prospects

As the work of an aspiring Stringer is accepted and utilized by newspaper or other media outlets, the chances improve for additional work on a full-time basis with one or more of those media organizations.

Education and Training

Most Stringers, like other journalists and writers, have undergraduate degrees in communications, English, journalism, or liberal arts. Those Stringers who specialize in sub-

jects, such as computers or other scientific and technical areas, may have advanced degrees.

Experience, Skills, and Personality Traits

Stringers are invariably established (or soon-to-be established) writers. While some may be employed by other (noncompetitive) publications, most are freelance. Established Stringers will have several years' journalism experience. They must be accurate, dependable, observant, and self-motivated.

Unions and Associations

Major national associations include the American Society of Journalists and Authors, the National Writers Union, and the Society of Professional Journalists. In addition, they may belong to any number of other groups for journalists.

Tips for Entry

1. If you have never written for a newspaper or magazine, a course in journalism would be advised.
2. Before you search out work as a Stringer with a newspaper or a magazine, have some specific ideas about articles you would like to write.
3. Become familiar with the newspaper or magazine and check the editorials to get an idea about the editor you will be approaching for a job as a Stringer. In addition, determine areas of news that the magazine or newspaper is not covering at all, or not covering well.
4. When writing articles try to write about what you know best or, at least, are interested in.

SYNDICATED COLUMNIST

CAREER PROFILE

Duties: Write, self-edit, and deliver columns to client newspapers; prepare sales material; sell columns

Alternate Title(s): None

Salary Range: $4 to $35 per piece for weeklies; $10 to $25 per week for dailies; based on circulation

Employment Prospects: Poor

Advancement Prospects: Poor

Prerequisites:

Education or Training—Most columnists have undergraduate degrees; need for expertise in a given subject may require graduate degree

Experience—Background as journalist or writer necessary; knowledge of specific subject is essential

Special Skills and Personality Traits—Excellent writing and editing talents; conciseness of expression; perseverance; sales and entrepreneurial ability; self-discipline

CAREER LADDER

```
┌─────────────────────────────────────┐
│    Seasoned Syndicated Columnist     │
└─────────────────────────────────────┘

┌─────────────────────────────────────┐
│   Experienced Syndicated Columnist   │
└─────────────────────────────────────┘

┌─────────────────────────────────────┐
│     Novice Syndicated Columnist      │
└─────────────────────────────────────┘
```

Position Description

Every newspaper publishes columns on all sorts of topics, such as feature articles on specific subjects or issues, news analyses, self-help advice, and special interest items. Columns are written daily, weekly, monthly, or bimonthly, and are focused on one particular topic. Some of these columns are written by newspaper staff, but the majority are purchased by the newspaper through syndication.

Writers and journalists who have ideas for columns can try to market them to syndicates (organizations that sell clients' columns to newspapers and newspaper chains) or market them directly to newspapers as self-syndicators.

The multiplicity of columns published in newspapers might make it seem an easy task to become syndicated, gain fame, and become wealthy. The reality is that syndication is a difficult route to take and a highly competitive one. Few Syndicated Columnists become either rich or famous.

A columnist must be able to offer something new and unique, or be able to write about a subject better than other already established columnists. The idea for a column must be sufficiently strong to generate material at least once or twice a week for an extended period, usually four to 10 months or more. Most columns are short, usually anywhere between 500 and 1,000 words. They must be tightly written but also be both informative and appealing. Developing a relationship with readers should be of paramount importance to a columnist.

There are more than 100 syndicates (but only five major ones), and they handle all kinds of columns. A prospective columnist who wants to link with a syndicate should submit at least six sample columns, along with a description of qualifications, an analysis of the column's potential audience, and its potential appeal to readers. The advantage of utilizing a syndicate agency is that they will undertake all the business work (marketing, selling, and handling the financial work), and they have the contacts that an individual fledgling columnist does not possess. The main disadvantage is that the syndicate will take a hefty chunk of the profits (anywhere from 40 percent to 60 percent) as payment for its services.

In addition to columns, syndicates also purchase single articles, called "one-shots," that have a general appeal for readers and can be sold to newspapers for a one-time use. Typically, a one-shot article might be about a prominent personality, or a topic/issue of significant current interest. The author is usually paid a fee of about 20 to 50 cents a word, and sells the article outright.

Self-syndication is a lot harder, more costly and very time-consuming, as the writer must do all the marketing and promotion, sales, setting contracts, invoicing, and other follow-up activity. However, the writer retains all the profits and control. Sample columns and pitch letters need to be sent directly to newspaper editors (usually the managing editor), with follow-up telephone calls. Many newspapers have to be contacted just to get a few dozen orders. The self-Syndicated Columnist becomes solely responsible for writing, editing, and delivering the copy to all clients at set deadlines, and for billing them. Self-syndication can easily become a full-time task. Some prospective columnists prefer to do self-syndication at first in hopes that a syndicate will pick them up after initial success is achieved.

Salaries

Most columns sold by self-promoted columnists command from $4 to $35 or higher per piece to each client. Rates depend upon the popularity of the column and its writer, as well as the publication's circulation. *Writer's Market* estimates in 2004 that fees for local columns can run from as low as $10 to a high of $175 (these usually from syndicated agency sales). A few well-established columnists, such as Jack Anderson, Jimmy Breslin, Art Buchwald, Larry King, Ann Landers, Bill Safire, Liz Smith, and others, earn from $100,000 to $200,000 yearly. A self-Syndicated Columnist who is published, say, in 60 to 70 newspapers and charges an average of $8 per piece can earn about $30,000 a year. Most columnists, however, earn less than that annually.

Employment Prospects

Syndicates and newspapers receive far more proposals for columns than they can possibly handle. Writers need the credentials of having worked as a journalist. If they can identify new and developing trends in popular interest and are knowledgeable about what they write, they may have a good chance of being picked up by a newspaper or a syndicate. Self-syndication, with its long hours and intensive work, is a way to get established. The best place to start is in local news markets or with the many small national daily and weekly newspapers. Other avenues to investigate are Web sites, e-zines, or online versions of print magazines, all of which are beginning to look for original material on a recurring basis.

Advancement Prospects

Despite the intensive competition, if the beginner Syndicated Columnist can offer something innovative, or distinctive, or write about a subject better than established columnists and maintains that excellence more than just a few times, the chance are better of being syndicated on a regular basis. If self-syndication is attempted and succeeds (and there is a great deal of work involved in that process), its success will generate the potential of a full-time career.

Education and Training

There is little concern about education of a columnist unless it is necessary to establish the columnist's authority on a particular subject or issue. However, an undergraduate degree in communications or journalism is helpful.

Experience, Skills, and Personality Traits

Most columnists are already established writers or journalists for several years before selling a column. Regardless of previous experience, a columnist must have excellent writing talents and have a distinct point of view. They must be able to research and develop fresh, succinctly written material on a regular schedule. Self-syndicators also must have (or develop) a flair for sales and promotion, and have good financial and organizational abilities.

Unions and Associations

There are no associations specifically for Syndicated Columnists. However, as most columnists are journalists or writers as well, major national associations would include the American Society of Journalists and Authors, the National Writers Union, and the Society of Professional Journalists. In addition, they may belong to any number of other groups for journalists.

Tips for Entry

1. Look for work on student publications, such as the student newspaper, any campus magazines, or the yearbook, and amass a collection of clips, which are samples of your published work, preferably with your byline on them. Also investigate summer internships with a local newspaper to gain practical journalistic experience and gain contacts.
2. Establish a track record as a journalist at a newspaper that runs your work regularly. Local, county, and state newspapers are the best bet, especially giveaway papers.
3. Create a blog (an online "diary" or webpage) of your own column to develop a following and to show how many visits ("hits") you have weekly to your site to get credentials.
4. Getting the approval of your present newspaper employer, market your column to other newspapers. The best way is to fax, or e-mail as an attachment, copies of your column with a cover note to the managing editor.
5. Remember to build a base of loyal fans for you and your column by keeping them always in mind as you write. In addition, be careful on your contracts to understand the difference between "work for hire" (rights given to the publication) and "freelancer contract" (where you retain the rights).

TECHNICAL EDITOR

CAREER PROFILE

Duties: Supervise preparation of technical information material; coordinate artwork, and supervise production

Alternate Title(s): Instructional Materials Editor, Publications Editor, Technical Communications Editor, Technical Information Editor

Salary Range: $25 to $100 per hour; $200 to $1,000 per day

Employment Prospects: Good

Advancement Prospects: Good

Prerequisites:

Education or Training—Undergraduate degree in communications, computer science, engineering, journalism, science, or technical communications

Experience—Several years of experience as a technical writer

Special Skills and Personality Traits—Ability to translate technical material into common understandable terms; copyediting skills; sense of layout and graphics; supervisory ability

CAREER LADDER

```
┌─────────────────────────────┐
│   Senior Technical Editor   │
└─────────────────────────────┘

┌─────────────────────────────┐
│      Technical Editor       │
└─────────────────────────────┘

┌─────────────────────────────┐
│   Novice Technical Editor   │
└─────────────────────────────┘
```

Position Description

Technical Editors are responsible for the content, accuracy (in most cases, except the most highly scientific or technical), and production of a wide range of technical information material. Many Technical Editors freelance for scientific and technical journals and book publishers. Others work for such fields as banking and finance, business, computer hardware and software companies, health professions, law, Web site development for any business or other activity, or the federal government. They produce advertising and promotion copy, books, films and other multimedia materials, instruction manuals, news releases, and sales and promotion literature, including speeches. Technical Editors' primary job is to ensure that documents are suitable for their target audience. Thus, technical editing is essentially a quality control job.

Technical Editors work with technical writers and edit their output. In some cases, they assist writers in the development of the material, particularly concerning its logical order and structure. They advise authors on the use of graphics, the wording of headings, figure and table captions, and glossary and index entries. They will review, edit, and rewrite all technical copy as necessary, but always in consultation and cooperation with the authors. They may assist with translations, mostly to ensure that technical concepts are expressed idiomatically in English. They may supervise editorial assistants and graphic artists assigned to the project. Often they are required to produce a final camera-ready copy (or the electronic equivalent), interact with print shops or Web site developers, and approve the final page proofs (or electronic equivalent).

Technical Editors should have backgrounds in the specific areas of their work. They need to be familiar with the subject being presented and be acquainted with the technical (or scientific) terminology employed to describe it. Many begin their careers as engineers, scientists, or other technical professionals before becoming Technical Editors. As Technical Editors, they must judge the effectiveness of the material based on its informational content and whether it is presented in an accurate, clear, concise, and complete way. For this reason, a Technical Editor is the reader's representative.

Salaries

Freelance Technical Editors generally are paid between $25 and $100 an hour (with the median income being $51 an hour), with the pay scale dependent on their expertise and the type of assignment. According to the Society for Technical Communication in their 2003 Technical Communicator Salary Survey, the mean salary for Technical Editors and writers in the United States rose from $59,700 in 2002 to $61,730 in 2003, a gain of 3.4 percent.

Employment Prospects

The demand for Technical Editors is expected to be strong through 2012. Developments and discoveries in law, science, and technology create a demand for people to interpret the data for a more general audience, which is the province of the technical writer and the Technical Editor. Major growth areas include computer manufacturing and software development, electronics, health professions, and pharmaceutical manufacturing. Rapid growth and change in high-tech and electronics industries result in a greater need for user's guides, instruction manuals, and training materials.

Advancement Prospects

As the editorial work of an aspiring Technical Editor results in successful publications, chances improve for more editorial jobs within the editor's field of expertise. Experience and work will help greatly in the prospects for continuous freelance work within that field with one or more publications.

Education and Training

While there are no set requirements for technical editing or writing, most Technical Editors have at least an undergraduate degree in computer science, engineering, English, journalism, or science. A common educational background would be an undergraduate degree in engineering or science, and graduate degrees in English or journalism. A degree in almost any field is acceptable, along with a good technical background and excellent writing abilities.

Experience, Skills, and Personality Traits

A professional background as a computer programmer, engineer, scientist, or technician is helpful for technical editing. Many Technical Editors have had several years' experience as technical writers.

Technical Editors need the facility to edit (and write) technical documents for different audiences (such as internal, external, administrative, and end users and readers) and to use varying delivery mechanisms (such as Internet and print). They must be able to organize and design sophisticated and informative documents, and to be creative and flexible. They require strong project and time management skills, must be able to manage multiple projects with changing priorities and varying deadlines, and are always mindful of production schedules and budgets. They must be able to work effectively with writers (especially in the way they convey editorial suggestions to them) and others of the publishing team.

Unions and Associations

The Society for Technical Communications is the key professional association for technical writers and editors. The American Medical Writers Association, the Council for the Advancement of Science Writing, the Editorial Freelancers Association, and the National Association of Science Writers are four of several other organizations to which Technical Editors often belong.

Tips for Entry

1. Add writing and/or editing courses to your curriculum, regardless of the scientific or technical subject area in which you are getting your degree.
2. Gain experience as a technical writer for several years before offering your services as a Technical Editor.
3. Experience in graphic design and Web page design would be useful.
4. Any foreign language study in addition to your technical training might come in handy.
5. Computer skills are essential. Take additional courses or technical training to add to your résumé.

TECHNICAL WRITER

CAREER PROFILE

Duties: Interpret scientific and technical information for both technical and nontechnical audiences; research and write on a broad range of matters

Alternate Title(s): Communications Specialist, Industrial Writer, Information Designer, Instructional Materials Developer, Policy and Procedure Writer, Web Editor

Salary Range: $40 to $110 per hour, depending upon the complexity of the subject and the employer

Employment Prospects: Good to Excellent

Advancement Prospects: Good to Excellent

Prerequisites:

Education or Training—Undergraduate degree in computer science, engineering, journalism, technical communications, or science

Experience—Previous work as engineer, scientist, technician, or writer useful

Special Skills and Personality Traits—Curiosity and imagination; good writing and layout skills; comprehension of difficult scientific and/or technical topics

CAREER LADDER

```
┌─────────────────────────────┐
│   Senior Technical Writer   │
└─────────────────────────────┘

┌─────────────────────────────┐
│      Technical Writer       │
└─────────────────────────────┘

┌─────────────────────────────┐
│   Novice Technical Writer   │
└─────────────────────────────┘
```

Position Description

Technical writing is an exceedingly specialized type of writing that combines engineering, scientific, or technical backgrounds with an ability to organize and write. Technical Writers utilize their particular knowledge to put intricate scientific or technical information into clear language. Their end-user audience might be consumers, or it might be engineers, line workers, plant executives, production managers, or scientists.

Technical writing encompasses a large assortment of tasks. In this field one creates brochures, catalogs, equipment specifications, and instruction manuals for machinery assembly and operation, multimedia presentations, online documentation and help systems, operating and maintenance manuals, parts lists, product instructions, project proposals, reference manuals, sales promotion materials, technical reports, training manuals, and webpages. Technical Writers prepare reports on scientific research, draft articles for technical publications, compose papers and speeches for engineers and scientists, and even write news releases and corporate annual reports. They also put together—or oversee the preparation of—charts, diagrams, illustrations, and photographs to be utilized in publications.

Technical Writers work directly with engineers, scientists, or technicians, and study blueprints, diagrams, journals, studies, and technical documents to understand the product or procedure before writing about it. In addition, they must analyze the needs of the target audience to best fashion the material for them.

Once they become thoroughly familiar with their subject and collect adequate data, Technical Writers prepare a draft for review by technical professionals, such as computer programmers, engineers, or scientists, as well as project leaders. Usually a technical editor oversees any modifications and makes the final determination regarding artwork and production.

Technical Writers can be found in such industries as aircraft, chemical, and pharmaceutical manufacturing; computer manufacturing and software development; and medical research laboratories and hospitals. They may work for the federal government, or academic institutions, advertising and public relations agencies, or technical publishing firms. Technical Writers often specialize in a specific industry. Within their chosen specialty, many Technical Writers will concentrate on particular topics. As an example, Technical Writers in the computer business might focus on online tutorials, software documentation, or user manuals.

Potential Technical Writers must acquire experience in their area of expertise. They may be research assistants or trainees in a technical information department who develop technical communication skills. Those individuals who display these writing abilities will move into technical writing, starting by doing research and then working on first drafts under the guidance of experienced Technical Writers. Some Technical Writers may transfer from jobs as engineers, scientists, or technicians. Some may be professional writers who learn about technology as they research and write.

Salaries

Freelance Technical Writers are usually paid an hourly rate. Freelance Technical Writers surveyed for the 2003 Technical Communicator Salary Survey indicated that they earned an average of more than $50 an hour (in a range from $20 to $75 per hour). As reported by the *Writer's Market 2004* salary survey, Technical Writers had a mean average hourly salary of $66, with a low of $40 and a high of $110, depending upon the writer's credentials/background, the project's particulars, and the type of employer.

According to the 2004 report of the U.S. Department of Labor, Bureau of Labor Statistics, median annual earnings for salaried Technical Writers were $50,580 in 2002, with the range moving from $39,100 to more than $80,900. The Society for Technical Communication states that the median annual salary for entry-level Technical Writers was $41,000 in 2002.

Employment Prospects

The Society for Technical Communication reports that the number of freelancers and consultants has been increasing steadily since 1985, and will continue in the coming years. The Bureau of Labor Statistics states that opportunities for Technical Writers are the best of any writing profession, because of the increasing demand for writers with expertise in specialty areas and, due to the continuing expansion of scientific and technical information, the growing need to interpret and communicate technical information for a general audience. This expanding need is further widened by the growth of the Internet audience and the explosion of Web sites. One of the challenges facing Technical Writers is just keeping up with the wealth of tools and technologies available to them.

Advancement Prospects

The more the work of an aspiring freelance Technical Writer is accepted and published (either in print or electronic formats), the better the chances of steady professional writing assignments within the particular field of expertise of the Technical Writer. The successful publication of such work will help to secure the growing reputation of the Technical Writer and assure further publication.

Education and Training

Most Technical Writers have undergraduate degrees in communications, engineering, journalism, science, or technical writing. Many also have advanced degrees in specific scientific or technical areas. Many employers will demand a strong background of technical knowledge and expertise, combined with writing talents. Computer skills are also essential, and experience in mechanical drawing and graphic arts is useful.

Experience, Skills, and Personality Traits

While many employers prefer Technical Writers to have some background working in jobs related to the subject at hand, Technical Writers do not necessarily have to be technical people. One important aspect of technical writing is the ability to view the material from the perspective of a typical user, and be able to explain instructions clearly and simply. They need to exhibit strong organizational skills.

Technical Writers must be able to listen to what other people are saying and ask appropriate questions. They need to know how to find information and identify what is essential, structure and classify multiple pieces of data, and then reorganize it for users. They should be creative and curious, have a broad range of knowledge, and be self-motivated and persevering in order to successfully sift through great quantities of detail and then organize the information. They need to be able to work well with others within the group and with scientific and technical personnel. A working knowledge of one or more publishing computer programs (such as FrameMaker, MS Word, and Pagemaker) is helpful. If the technical writing involves Web design, then experience with Web design programs (such as Front Page or HomeSite) is useful. (The HTML Writer's Guild, http://www.hwg.org, is a great place to learn about Web design.)

Unions and Associations

The Society for Technical Communication represents Technical Writers and editors, as well as educators, engineers, scientists, and technicians. Other pertinent professional groups that Technical Writers might join include the American Medical Writers Association, the Construction Writers Association, the Council for Advancement of Science Writing, the Information Technology Association, the International Science Writers Association, the National Association of Science Writers, and the National Writers Association.

Tips for Entry

1. In preparing for a career as a Technical Writer, read several books about topics that are both complex and hard to grasp to learn how these technical texts are formatted. Choose books on subjects with which you are unfamiliar to learn about the latest discoveries in these fields.

2. Critique one of your at-hand technical or computer manuals to see whether its table of contents summarizes the key ideas adequately, how easy the book is to read, and whether the illustrations further one's understanding. Prepare a list of elements you would change about the book.

3. Go to a trade show and pick up at least three to five white papers (which present a concise overview of a specific product). Analyze their presentation and keep them as examples to use in the future. In addition, examine how companies present themselves.

4. Prepare a portfolio of your technical writing samples to utilize in interviews.

5. Work on your social skills, as you will need them in your daily interactions as a technical writer.

6. Join the Society for Technical Communication (http://www.stc.org) to ask questions of other professionals, check on available classes, job openings, and other benefits.

MEDIA

INTERNET

COLUMNIST

CAREER PROFILE

Duties: Write daily, weekly, or occasional column to be posted at one or more Web sites

Alternate Title(s): None

Salary Range: $25,000 to $250,000+

Employment Prospects: Fair

Advancement Prospects: Poor

Prerequisites:

Education or Training—Undergraduate degree in communications, English, journalism, or liberal arts; advanced degrees required for specialized subjects

Experience—Background as journalist; specialist in a particular field of public interest

Special Skills and Personality Traits—Creativity; good writing ability; imagination

CAREER LADDER

```
┌─────────────────────────────┐
│      Managing Editor        │
└─────────────────────────────┘

┌─────────────────────────────┐
│         Columnist           │
└─────────────────────────────┘

┌─────────────────────────────┐
│         Reporter            │
└─────────────────────────────┘
```

Position Description

The Internet has presented a wide variety of fresh and exciting opportunities and challenges for news organizations, both newspapers and magazines. Nearly every newspaper and most trade and specialty magazines now have their own dedicated Web sites, posting news items, feature stories, commentary for users, and, frequently, downloadable multimedia materials such as video and audio clips. (In addition, many of these sources supply e-mail newsletters to interested recipients.) Much of this information is offered free, or at moderate cost, to Internet users. Many television and radio show hosts also have their own weekly Internet columns. Industry, trade, and business journals have, likewise, found that many of their readers want a daily dose of news from their industry and do not wish to wait for a printed version to be available. This dramatic change in the way news information gets distributed has, in turn, opened up a wide range of new opportunities for journalists and writers.

The position of Columnist has always been considered a prestigious one, and the job is achieving additional stature with the multiplicity of Internet columns on all type of information, not just news. Internet Columnists can be found covering every aspect of American life, and in a wide variety of subject areas. For example, the Village Voice Web site (http://www.villagevoice.com), one of many Web sites dealing with jobs and salaries—utilizes research experts as Internet columnists who are designated to give regular and timely information on specific job markets to be posted on the job-scene Web site.

Many Internet Columnists write for both online and print publications, and may write for more than one publication. Some are strictly freelance journalists, while others are considered staff members of the publication, even when they write for other outlets as well. Many Columnists have been or are a part of the industry about which they write, and some of them are syndicated so that their columns will appear in a variety of publications.

Salaries

Starting salaries for established Internet Columnists may be as low as $20,000, but most Columnists earn anywhere from $40,000 to $100,000 or more annually. When a Columnist gains an audience and a celebrity status, this yearly salary range may expand to $250,000 or more. While some Columnists may be represented by the Newspaper Guild, most Internet Columnists are not and, thus, not subject to the caps of negotiated salary ranges.

Employment Prospects

Most newly hired Internet Columnists for major Web sites need an established track record as journalists (or, at least, a high visibility within their field of expertise). The best way to obtain an Internet Columnist position with a recognized online outlet is to use a journalist's position (whether with a newspaper, magazine, or on television, radio, or online) to build a readership on the Internet and, thus, gain a reputation and a ready-made audience.

Advancement Prospects

Most Internet Columnists have no desire to change their prestige position for any managerial positions on the Web sites on which their material appears. The majority of Internet Columnists are journalists, authors, or authorities in their chosen fields and, often, have positions in the industry that they cover in their columns. Some, however, may aspire to editorial positions as a further enhancement of their present status.

Education and Training

Like their fellow journalists, Columnists usually have an undergraduate degree in communications, English, journalism, or liberal arts. Columnists who specialize in specific areas, such as business, health, law, or technology will most likely need to have the appropriate educational degree and credentials to support their writing as an expert. They also must be constantly on top of events, changes, and advances within their particular fields of expertise.

Experience, Skills, and Personality Traits

Nearly all Columnists are first and foremost experienced journalists. Some have been (or still are) freelance writers specializing in one or more subjects and have become regular or syndicated Columnists for Web organizations devoted to their subject area(s). All are experienced writers who specialize in in-depth coverage of their areas of expertise.

Columnists have to be highly creative, writing concisely, but also engagingly, on a regular basis. They have to be very deadline-conscious, as they may have to handle on a weekly basis several closing dates for articles. Columnists who cover human-interest subjects must be excellent storytellers, whereas Columnists who focus on technological issues have to be both technically accurate and have the ability to explain clearly their subject area to lay readers. For news and political Columnists, such writers must possess good analytical skills and well-honed news instincts.

Unions and Associations

Some Internet Columnists are members of the Newspaper Guild union, though most of them are not. Professional associations for Columnists include the American Society of Journalists and Authors; Association for Women in Communications; Investigative Reporters and Editors; the National Association of Black Journalists; the National Association of Hispanic Journalists; the National Federation of Press Women; and the Society of Professional Journalists.

Tips for Entry

1. All the journalistic experience that can be gained during college can be helpful, whether on the campus newspaper or in internships.
2. While working on a college newspaper, try your hand at writing a column and checking thereafter with its readers to gauge their reaction to your writing and the subjects you choose to cover.
3. Read popular newspaper, magazine, and Internet columnists daily to understand their writing style and what the elements of the column are that make them so popular in their forums.
4. Deciding on a specialty aligned with your interests (such as sports, food, healthcare, politics, or technology) may help in focusing your journalistic reporting and catching the attention of editors who may be looking for Columnists to write for the Internet versions of their publication.
5. Keep up-to-date with developments and changes within your fields of expertise to keep your columns current for readers.
6. Develop your own Web site in order to practice and display your own columns and articles as a prelude to getting a paid position with an established Web site as a Columnist.

CRITIC

CAREER PROFILE

Duties: Review artistic performances, books, exhibits, and recordings; write columns

Alternate Title(s): Reviewer

Salary Range: $18,000 to $60,000+

Employment Prospects: Fair

Advancement Prospects: Poor

Prerequisites:

    Education or Training—Undergraduate degree in communications, English, journalism, or liberal arts; specialization in a particular field may require an advanced degree or further course work

    Experience—Background as a journalist and thorough knowledge of the area being reviewed

    Special Skills and Personality Traits—Excellent writing ability; thorough knowledge of subject matter

CAREER LADDER

```
┌─────────────────────────────┐
│   Columnist or Web Editor   │
└─────────────────────────────┘

┌─────────────────────────────┐
│            Critic           │
└─────────────────────────────┘

┌─────────────────────────────┐
│    Journalist or Reporter   │
└─────────────────────────────┘
```

Position Description

Internet Critics are journalists who analyze, evaluate, interpret, and judge literary or artistic works. They have a great deal of influence with the public and can affect the success of artists, authors, books, dance and/or musical productions, plays, and recordings. The Critic can also stimulate a public (online) discussion about the subjects being reviewed and help that discussion by putting the works under consideration in their historical, political, or social contexts.

Critics may review anything connected with their areas of specialty, even to interviewing artists, celebrities, and performers. They may be quite specialized in what they do: music critics do not often review films or plays, art critics may review books about art as well as art exhibitions, and so forth.

Critics are expected to be well informed about their subjects and be current with all the trends and news concerning their subject areas. (To keep current may require such reviewers to do extensive reading and researching in their areas of expertise.) They should maintain a certain objectivity toward their subjects, even when expressing positive or negative opinions. Like columnists, Critics develop audiences who, in turn, trust and act upon their views and opinions.

There are several types of Internet Critics. Some professionals are on the staff of newspapers and/or magazines and their printed critical columns appearing in these publications are also made available online on their publications' Web sites. Some work directly for an online service for which they are paid. Then there those individuals who volunteer their critiques to such outlets as the Internet Movie Database (http://www.imdb.com) or Amazon.com (http://www.amazon.com) and their critiques are available at the service's Web site. Others have created their own dedicated Web site on which they post their reviews, their commentary, newsletters, and other material related to their areas of special interest. Some of the well-established sites also provide chat rooms where online participants can interact with these critics and other viewers. Other Critics are artists, musicians, or writers (paid or unpaid) whose criticism is made available on Web sites devoted to one area of the arts or another, such as the Rotten Tomatoes Web site (http://www.rottentomatoes.com), managed by IGN Entertainment and devoted to the film industry, which also collects reviews from standard publications. Other such Web sites, in this case for the music industry, are AllMusic.com (http://www.allmusic.com), MusicCritic.com (http://www.music-critic.com), and Musicfolio.com (http://www.musicfolio.com).

Internet Critics, unlike their counterparts in the print media, are usually not restricted in the length or breadth of their commentaries due to the unlimited size available on Web sites. Many of these Web sites offer extensive critical comments on the industry they are covering. (On more ambitious Web sites such online reviews often may be accompanied by downloadable slide shows and audio/video clips.)

Salaries

Professional Internet Critics earn roughly the same as, or, in some cases, more than parallel print journalists, roughly $18,000 to $60,000 yearly. High annual salaries depend much upon the Critic's credentials and experience, the popularity of their critical columns, and the budgets of the Web sites upon which material appears.

Employment Prospects

Many Internet Critics start out as reporters or writers and expand their interest in criticism to a full-time paying position by doing occasional reviews for their publication or its Web site. Getting a staff writer position for the lifestyle or arts-and-entertainment sections of a newspaper, or doing comparable work for magazines is one of the best ways to initiate such a career. Once Critics become established and well-known, the possibilities of making their work available on the Internet are greatly increased, and even of setting up their own Web site of critical commentary.

Advancement Prospects

Like print, television, and radio columnists, most Internet Critics would prefer to remain Critics and not necessarily do other types of news work. With the potentials of the ever-expanding and increasingly sophisticated Internet outlet at their fingertips, Internet Critics may prefer to expand their work on this medium only. If their work is initially only available on a general Web site devoted to their area of interest, they may want to develop their own Web site for their commentary work. This could expand their readership and lead to other money-making opportunities in their field. They may also take on weekly or monthly regular column work for one or more media venues or they may decide to expand into the management side of the Web site that has featured their work.

Education and Training

Critics are expected to have a thorough background in their subject area(s), as well as a basic undergraduate education in communications, English, journalism, or liberal arts. Advanced degrees or additional course work in their areas of expertise may bolster the Critic's credentials.

Experience, Skills, and Personality Traits

Critics must be fully familiar with their specialization to write knowing and balanced reviews. This means they need to devote time to reading extensively and studying their field(s) continuously to keep abreast of trends, events, personalities, and changes within their subject specialties. They should be expert in interviewing artists and celebrities and be attuned to meeting deadlines. They need to be responsive to their audiences in order to further enhance their commentary.

Unions and Associations

General professional associations for Critics include the American Theatre Critics Association, the Dance Critics Association, the Music Critics Association of North America, and the Society of Professional Journalists. For Internet film Critics there is the Internet Movie Critics Association and the Online Film Critics Society.

Tips for Entry

1. Gain as much journalistic experience as possible during college, such as writing for campus publications or in internship programs.
2. Try your hand at reviewing while working on your college newspaper (or when you get a summer internship with a local newspaper).
3. Undertake posting your written commentaries on established Internet Web sites of criticism dealing with the arts in order to gain experience in writing for this medium, as well as making potential contacts with both other critics and the general Web audience.
4. Hone your expertise in your chosen field of interest by further course work and lots of reading, all of which can only enhance your reviewing skills.
5. Check out Internet chat rooms and Web sites for contacts also interested in criticism and any possible leads for jobs with established Web sites of criticism.

EDITORIAL WRITER

CAREER PROFILE

Duties: Research and write editorial comments on issues and topics of reader interest to stimulate or mold public opinion in accordance with viewpoints and policies of an Internet publication

Alternate Title(s): Editorial Page Editor

Salary Range: $22,000 to $125,000+

Employment Prospects: Fair

Advancement Prospects: Poor

Prerequisites:

Education or Training—Undergraduate degree in communications, English, journalism, or liberal arts; advanced degree may be helpful

Experience—Background as editor and/or journalist

Special Skills and Personality Traits—Outstanding and clear writing; logical; objective; persuasive; thorough as to accuracy and detail

CAREER LADDER

```
┌─────────────────────────────────────┐
│   Senior Editor or Managing Editor   │
└─────────────────────────────────────┘

┌─────────────────────────────────────┐
│           Editorial Writer           │
└─────────────────────────────────────┘

┌─────────────────────────────────────┐
│      News Editor or Journalist       │
└─────────────────────────────────────┘
```

Position Description

Internet Editorial Writers deal in their work with the issues generated by, or behind, current events rather than the actual news of these events. They are usually responsible for the contents of the editorial pages of the online newspaper or magazine for which they work. Editorials usually reflect the opinion of the publication and represent both the quality and character of that entity. Commonly, editorial pieces are submitted and discussed (often through an exchange of e-mails) with senior editorial staff for necessary approval. In contrast, there may also be editorial pieces, sometimes written by staff members and sometimes by others, which do not necessarily express views that are endorsed by the publication. Such "outside" pieces are not subject to editing but are usually checked by staff Editorial Writers for grammar and punctuation (if not style).

Internet Editorial Writers examine issues that come to the fore from the events that surround them, research those issues, and decide upon a position for the publication. Some editorials may be timely, reacting to breaking news, while others may be on more general topics of interest and result in late "think" pieces. In their research methods, online Editorial Writers are similar to reporters,

in that they call sources, consult library clippings and assorted online news sources, as well as talk with journalists directly involved in the coverage of the events involved.

Because their online audience can be so broad-based, Internet Editorial Writers have to be fully informed about local, national, and international news. They have to be comprehensive, objective, and accurate in their editorial appraisals. All sides of any issues need to be carefully weighed before arriving at an editorial position for the Internet publication, as the influence of such Web-based editorial opinion can be immense.

On Web sites of newspapers and magazines, editorial comments (either given in full or in excepts) are frequently available along with the news events items. In addition, there are both commercial and noncommercial Web sites devoted to the compilation of editorial commentary on issues from a wide variety of sources from around the country. In their choice of material to be collected and made available by them to their subscribers, these venues usually indicate their particular political or social bent. They may even have Editorial Writers write specific editorial commentary just for their Web site.

Salaries

The Newspaper Guild often bargains for print newspaper Editorial Writers on salary matters, but it may depend upon how the management of the publication views its Editorial Writers (that is, as general staff or as management). In some cases, there may be a differential that gives Editorial Writers a higher salary than other journal personnel, especially if the Editorial Writer is experienced and well known. With magazine Editorial Writers (and those who write exclusively for one or more Web sites), again, it greatly depends upon the view of the management as to whether the Newspaper Guild (which also represents magazine writers) has any part to play in salary decisions.

Generally, annual salaries for Editorial Writers may range from $22,000 to $125,000 or higher. The higher salaries are dependent upon the size of the circulation of the publication, the experience and celebrity of the Editorial Writer, and the budgetary flexibility of the Web site.

Employment Prospects

Years of experience are necessary to season a journalist before attaining a position as a print Editorial Writer. These journalists must demonstrate their reporting and analytical abilities before receiving promotions. In some cases, editorial experience as a newsroom editor or a managing editor for a publication is also required. The same would apply to those Editorial Writers who write additionally (or exclusively) for Internet Web sites.

Advancement Prospects

While some advancement opportunities exist for Internet Editorial Writers to rise within the publication's editorial board staff structure, most senior management at most of these businesses are selected from editors who run the daily print or online operations. Besides, many Editorial Writers would prefer to remain as members of the editorial staff rather than go back to either reporting itself or being a part of the management of the reporting staff.

Education and Training

Internet Editorial Writers must have an undergraduate degree in communications, English, journalism, or liberal arts. Graduate degrees (or extensive course work) in specific subjects (such as business, law, medicine, or technology) are helpful in cementing the careers of Editorial Writers and provide them with a professional status for their editorial opinions.

Experience, Skills, and Personality Traits

Most Editorial Writers who work on Internet publications will have had years of experience as print or online journalists and, in some cases, even as newsroom or associate editors. Before gaining the position of Editorial Writer, they will have had to demonstrate their ability to write balanced, clear, and concise news analyses and exhibit accurate reporting of news stories. They must show good news judgment, objectivity, and accomplished editorial skills.

Editorial Writers have to be equipped to do thorough research, as well as extensive reading, to be continuously aware of public opinion and public trends. They must be well organized and able to work under constant deadlines (daily, weekly, or monthly).

Unions and Associations

Associations useful for Editorial Writers include the American Society of Journalists and Authors; the American Society of Magazine Editors; the American Society of Newspaper Editors; the Association for Women in Communications; the National Association of Black Journalists; the National Association of Hispanic Journalists; the National Conference of Editorial Writers; the National Federation of Press Women; and the Society of Professional Journalists.

Tips for Entry

1. All the journalistic experience that can be gained during college (or after) would be of help in gaining a beginning position with a print or online publication. Writing and editing experience on campus print and online publications is preferable.

2. After gaining experience as a journalist with a publication, get acquainted with its editorial style by writing pieces for the Op-Ed page (if a newspaper) or the supplemental editorial pages (if a magazine). This also is a useful way to make an impression with the editorial staff of the publication.

3. Study the publication's editorial page over a period of time to familiarize yourself with the editorial stance of the publication.

4. Become familiar with standard reference and potential research studies, and explore the Internet for useful reference/research portals and Web sites.

5. Be willing to volunteer essays or articles as freebies to be posted on professional Web sites in order to lead up to becoming a paid worker on the site, or develop your own Web site to post your editorial commentaries to gain attention from the professional Web sites.

FEATURE WRITER

CAREER PROFILE

Duties: Collect and report information for feature stories for the Internet on specific or a wide variety of topics

Alternate Title(s): Feature Reporter; Columnist; Journalist

Salary Range: $19,000 to $90,000+

Employment Prospects: Fair

Advancement Prospects: Poor

Prerequisites:

Education or Training—Undergraduate degree in communications, English, journalism, or liberal arts; graduate degree or advanced courses in specialty areas as required

Experience—Several years of experience as a reporter or other journalistic positions

Special Skills and Personality Traits—Ability to research and write in-depth feature stories; curiosity; excellent writing skills; good interviewing and interpersonal skills; persistence; self-discipline

CAREER LADDER

```
┌─────────────────────────────┐
│    Web Managing Editor      │
└─────────────────────────────┘

┌─────────────────────────────┐
│      Feature Writer         │
└─────────────────────────────┘

┌─────────────────────────────┐
│        Reporter             │
└─────────────────────────────┘
```

Position Description

With the exciting opportunities and challenges that the Internet presents, most newspapers, as well as most trade and specialty magazines, now have their own dedicated Web sites, which post news items, commentary, and feature stories for users. Much of this information is offered without charge, or at only moderate cost, to Internet users. This dramatic change in the way information and analysis is distributed has, in turn, opened up many new opportunities for journalists and writers.

Consumer monthly publications tend to place less emphasis on news as breaking information, to be disseminated quickly, than on extensively researched feature articles that delve into the stories behind breaking news and examine long-term trends and implications. These feature stories cover their subjects in much greater depth than most daily (or weekly) reporting and include more sources and background research. In addition, there are trade publishers that cover specific industries, relating business news of the field they serve. They, in turn, feature extensive articles on specific aspects of the trade that would be of interest to their special audiences. Such thorough analysis and coverage is ideally suited for the Internet, which is without the length limitations of print media. Journalists adept at research and skilled in writing "thought" pieces are ideally suited to be Feature Writers on Internet outlets.

An online Feature Writer may spend up to six weeks on any one piece (as opposed to the daily or weekly deadlines of reporters and many columnists). They usually are assigned an article subject by the publication's editor, and they need to keep that person fully appraised of developments in the writing of the article and, particularly, if any problems have occurred. In writing the feature article, the Feature Writer needs to monitor current news events for anything that may affect the story, as well as fully research all important news sources for information pertaining to the article the publication is preparing. In addition, they have to maintain good relations with their sources as these individuals can help Feature Writers find the real story behind the topic they are investigating.

Salaries

Online Feature Writers' salaries will vary according to the size and nature of the publication for which they write.

Annual salaries at some of the smaller publications may be as low as $19,000, whereas at larger operations the yearly salaries may well be more than $100,000. Those publications (and their Web sites) that cover specific industries require online Feature Writers to have extensive knowledge of, or background in, that industry, and will offer correspondingly higher salaries for such qualified journalists. The usual Feature Writer, however, can expect an annual salary range between $20,000 and $40,000.

Employment Prospects

Online Feature Writer is not an entry-level position. It is a job earned only by solid experience in the field. Often writers on the Internet looking for such a position offer to write articles or essays for free to gain recognition and then move up the scale to being a fully paid writer on a professional Web site. (Sometimes this may lead candidates to establishing their own Web site to write feature stories about subjects of particular interest to them.) The competition for the position of Feature Writer on an Internet outlet is stiff, more so for the larger national publications' Web sites than for those of trade magazines for various industries where there is much more frequent turnover.

Advancement Prospects

Advancement prospects are generally poor, as with print publications there are fewer openings for Feature Writers than for general assignment reporters. Journalists working for smaller consumer periodicals or industry publications can move to larger national or industry magazines with their more elaborate Web sites and better pay scales. Some Feature Writers may also move into editorial positions on their magazine, or move on to other online publications in such capacities.

Education and Training

The usual undergraduate degree preferred by publication editors is one in communications, English, or journalism, though a similar degree in liberal arts may be acceptable. With industry trade publications, online Feature Writers will likely need to have an additional degree in the subject area of the publication, such a master's degree in business administration for a publication concerned with financial matters. The closer the degree to the magazine's subject area, the better the chance of a position as an online Feature Writer. Nonetheless, most editors of these types of publications will usually prefer solid writing skills first, and technical education second.

Experience, Skills, and Personality Traits

Online Feature Writers are expected to be well-qualified journalists, though the degree of experience required may vary according to the size and the subject matter of the publication. Good journalistic instincts and abilities are essential, as well as a thorough knowledge of how to research and organize information on any given subject.

Online Feature Writers, like other types of reporters, need to be extremely detail-oriented. They must have good interviewing skills and a determination to follow their story through to its logical conclusion, checking the facts and opinions that they will use, and to meet their required deadlines.

Unions and Associations

Professional associations for online Feature Writers include the American Society of Journalists and Authors; Investigative Reporters and Editors; and the Society of Professional Journalists. In addition, there are many professional associations that online Feature Writers for industry publications would find useful, such as the Associated Business Writers of America or the Association for Business Communication for the business or financial industries. There are also numerous professional associations that represent the news industry, as well as online Feature Writers of different racial and ethnic backgrounds.

Tips for Entry

1. Get as much journalistic experience as you can during college, whether on the campus newspaper or other publications, or in internships.
2. Look for internship programs with local newspapers or magazines to add practical journalistic experience to your college course work.
3. Read feature articles in popular newspapers and magazines to grasp their writing style and how feature articles cover their subjects.
4. Deciding on a specialty aligned with your interests (such as sports, food, health care, politics, or technology) may help in focusing your journalistic reporting and catching the attention of editors who may be looking for online Feature Writers for the Internet version of their publication.
5. Practice your interviewing skills as much as you can during your college years and any internship programs in which you enroll. These skills will be critical to you as an online Feature Writer.
6. Practice developing sources of information during your journalistic efforts in college or in internship programs. They will be your livelihood as an online Feature Writer.

ONLINE REPORTER

CAREER PROFILE

Duties: Collect and report information for news and feature stories on a wide range of topics or about a specific area of expertise

Alternate Title(s): Journalist

Salary Range: $17,000 to $80,000+

Employment Prospects: Fair to Good

Advancement Prospects: Fair

Prerequisites:

    Education or Training—Undergraduate degree in communications, English, journalism, or liberal arts; if reporting on a specific area of expertise, graduate degree or advanced courses in the area of specialization is often required

    Experience—Having worked within a journalistic environment during college and/or an internship for a small daily or weekly newspaper or magazine; for specialist reporting, usually one to two years professional journalistic experience along with some journalistic work indicating an expertise in the chosen specialization

    Special Skills and Personality Traits—Aggressiveness; good interpersonal and interviewing skills; persistence; self-discipline; solid organizational abilities and research habits; for specialty reporting, a talent for researching and writing longer in-depth stories

CAREER LADDER

```
┌─────────────────────────────────┐
│   Online Feature Writer or      │
│    Web Managing Editor          │
└─────────────────────────────────┘

┌─────────────────────────────────┐
│        Online Reporter          │
└─────────────────────────────────┘

┌─────────────────────────────────┐
│   Reporter or College Student   │
└─────────────────────────────────┘
```

Position Description

In detailing their story, reporters interview sources and research records to assemble, collect, and report information for a story, as well as enumerate potential implications of the facts as reported. Reporters who handle general assignments may cover a wide variety of stories at the discretion of an assignment editor. Reporter specialists, on the other hand, usually deal with a single area of expertise. Both types of reporting are to be found on news Web sites (including those developed by specific journalistic publications, and those independent of the print media), but generally the online style of reporting tends to emphasize brevity. In all other essentials of reporting methodology, reporting done for the electronic media is no different than that of the print media.

Reporters on general assignment have to work within tight deadlines, complete their work and then move on quickly to the next assignment, regardless of its subject, which may be completely different from the one just finished. In addition, they may be asked to report on topics last covered by their publication (or their independent Web site) by someone else. In such cases, they will need to become completely familiar with all related material, and all other stories related to the topic, as well as follow any major breaking stories that may pertain to their subject.

Unlike general assignment reporters who focus on one story at a time, reporter specialists typically work on several stories at the same time and have extended deadlines for such. Also unlike general assignment reporters, special reporters frequently are required to have a graduate degree in their field, or have taken additional course work. For example, reporters who cover computer technology might be obliged to have a graduate degree in computer science, as well as stay current with any developments in this field and cultivate potential sources of information. Much of their reporting will be in greater depth on the subject than any such work by a general assignment reporter.

As indicated, news Web sites vary considerably. Some are official Internet bases for newspapers or magazines. Others are independent online magazines or news Web sites (such as the American Reporter, an online newspaper run by a group of international journalists covering a wide range of issues and articles from all over the world). Other Web sites are devoted to specific industries, such as BizWiz (http://www.bizwiz.com) with its The Internet Reporter, a network devoted to business matters, technology, and information. Online Reporters may work directly for the specific Web site, or their reporting may be made available on the Web site, though it had been assembled for another journalistic medium.

Salaries

According to the U.S. Department of Labor's Bureau of Labor Statistics, as reported in their Occupational Outlook Handbook in March of 2004, annual salaries for Reporters in 2002 throughout the United States ranged from a low of $17,000 to a high of $69,500, but within large urban centers, like New York City, the salaries tended to be higher. Even within these guidelines, the yearly salaries of Online Reporters will vary according to the size and type of online publication or other type of Web site for which they work.

Employment Prospects

While employment of reporters is expected to grow more slowly than the average for most other occupations through the year 2012, according to the Bureau of Labor Statistics' *Occupational Outlook Handbook,* the expanding growth of the Internet and abundance of Web sites devoted to news helps to ensure job opportunities for those seeking to establish a career as an Online Reporter. Other reporters may make the transfer from newspaper or magazine general assignment reporting to online reporting.

For beginners, getting a foot in the door at an online publication might be made easier by applying for some other editorial option, such as freelance editing or copyediting, before moving into a full-time position as an Online Reporter for that publication.

Advancement Prospects

Advancement prospects are only fair, as editorial positions within online publications and other types of Web sites are smaller in number than those in print media, and the competition is stiff. However, an Online Reporter may move on to become a feature writer for the online publication

Education and Training

Most publications (print or electronic media) require from any reporter an undergraduate degree in communications, English, journalism, or liberal arts. The usual educational path to being a reporter is a bachelor's degree in journalism. Some publications, on the other hand, would prefer a more well-rounded education, rather than just the practical instruction offered by programs within the usual journalism curriculum.

Specialist reporters frequently are required to have advanced degrees in the subjects related to their area of expertise. In some cases, advanced courses in these subjects may be considered sufficient.

Experience, Skills, and Personality Traits

As with any reporting position, constructive writing experience on a school paper or in an internship program is of tremendous importance. It is essential that reporters be detail-oriented, good listeners, and have a keen curiosity and acute observational skills. They require solid researching skills, a good memory, a nose for news, persistence in tracking stories, and personal initiative.

Online Reporters also need to be proficient on the Internet, extremely knowledgeable about the type of information available on the Net and how to locate it, and have the initiative to network through e-mail, chat groups, and news/user groups.

Unions and Associations

The Newspaper Guild is the primary union for print journalists (including those who also do online reporting). For other Online Reporters there are such professional associations as the American Society of Journalists and Authors; Investigative Reporters and Editors; and the Society of Professional Journalists. In addition, there are various professional associations that represent Reporters in a wide variety of specialties or from different racial or ethnic backgrounds.

Tips for Entry

1. Get as much journalistic experience as you can during college—on campus publications or in internship programs—as preparation for your reporting career.
2. Become proficient on the Internet, and look at examples of online writing styles to get a sense of what is expected. Study the differences between print writing and online writing.
3. Consider expanding your Internet skills by building your own Web site to learn firsthand about the online medium, and on which you can post your own reporting articles.

MAGAZINES

ASSOCIATE EDITOR

CAREER PROFILE

Duties: Assign, read, and edit articles submitted for publication; write articles, columns, and copy as required; handle production

Alternate Title(s): Assistant Editor

Salary Range: $25,000 to $60,000+

Employment Prospects: Fair

Advancement Prospects: Fair

Prerequisites:

Education or Training—Undergraduate degree in communications, journalism, or liberal arts; advanced or specialized degrees for business, scientific, or technical publications

Experience—At entry level, none; for others, background as an Associate Editor, editorial assistant, or journalist on a smaller publication needed

Special Skills and Personality Traits—Excellent editing and writing skills; good graphics sense; organization and production skills

CAREER LADDER

```
┌─────────────────────────────────┐
│    Editor or Senior Editor      │
└─────────────────────────────────┘

┌─────────────────────────────────┐
│       Associate Editor          │
└─────────────────────────────────┘

┌─────────────────────────────────┐
│ Editorial Assistant, Journalist,│
│   Writer, or College Student    │
└─────────────────────────────────┘
```

Position Description

Depending upon the size of the magazine, Associate Editors may have a variety of responsibilities. As an example, on a small trade publication an Associate Editor might be the actual second in command below an editor, or a senior editor. At a larger operation, an Associate Editor may function under the supervision of a senior editor but be assigned to a particular department of the magazine.

Associate Editors allocate articles to freelance writers, as well as review unsolicited pieces that may have been initially screened by editorial assistants. In some cases, the Associate Editor may be responsible for the entire screening process. They also edit manuscripts as well as write headlines, cutlines, and other required copy. They are also responsible for assigning photographic coverage of articles being written, and/or deciding on art illustrations to accompany such pieces. They direct editorial assistants in needed research or fact-checking or are responsible for those duties themselves (which is particularly the case with small publications).

Associate Editors take part in regular editorial meetings at which ideas for features and design are suggested and content for future issues is planned. On larger publications,

they may be assigned responsibility to generate articles on specific topics or subject areas, which they, in turn, assign to writers (staff or freelance).

In many cases, Associate Editors will also be responsible for the production function of proofreading galleys. Finally, they will represent the publication at professional meetings and functions and attend and/or participate in seminars, trade association conventions, and workshops, in order to stay up-to-date on industry needs, techniques, and evolving technologies.

Salaries

The Newspaper Guild, which negotiates the salaries and contracts of unionized magazines, reported that the top average annual salary for Associate Editors in 2003 was $61,100. Generally, Associate Editors earn less than this, somewhere between $25,000 and $40,000.

Employment Prospects

The most useful opening work opportunities are on small or special-interest magazines. As job security in such positions is low, these posts are usually looked upon as stepping-stones to similar positions on larger or more specialized publications. Many trade publications do not require much experience or education in the industry they serve, since the necessary background information is usually gleaned on the job.

Advancement Prospects

An Associate Editor's work provides the necessary skills and background for higher editorial positions. There is a great deal of movement from one publication to another, especially in the larger urban areas, such as New York City, which have a disproportional share of publications compared to much of the rest of the country. Another career move from experience as an Associate Editor in the magazine field is to move directly into book publishing.

Education and Training

Associate Editors are obliged to have an undergraduate degree in communications, journalism, or liberal arts. Additional course work in publishing and production, as well as advanced degrees in communications, provide a highly competitive edge to one's résumé. For business, medical, scientific, and technical publications, advanced degrees in appropriate specialized fields is often necessary.

Experience, Skills, and Personality Traits

Prior experience as an editorial assistant, journalist, or writer is essential for most Associate Editor positions. Sometimes, particularly for small or local publications, an entry position may be available. As required background for an Associate Editor on a large magazine, work as an Associate Editor on a small magazine may be mandatory.

Associate Editors must have excellent writing and editing skills and thoroughly understand the production process. They should be well-organized and deadline conscious. Also, they must be adept at managing and directing others, both staff members and freelance personnel.

Unions and Associations

The Newspaper Guild represents employees of some major news and feature magazines, but, usually, both large and small magazine editors are nonunion. Their primary professional association is the American Society of Magazine Editors. In addition, many editors join other publishing trade associations and are auxiliary members of various writer's groups. The Association for Women in Communications is open to both women and men involved in all media.

Tips for Entry

1. All the journalistic experience that can be gained during college would be useful in gaining entry into a magazine position.
2. Start in an editorial post at a small and local magazine (or Internet publication) to gain hands-on experience.
3. Take courses in printing and production processes, as this knowledge is a necessary component of the skills of an Associate Editor.
4. Many publications have their own Web sites, with hiring information available.
5. Check the print and online job listings found in such publications as *Editor and Publisher* (http://www.editorandpublisher.com), the Sunday editions of national newspapers such as the *New York Times,* or the *Los Angeles Times,* or the various online job-listing Web sites.

COPY EDITOR/PROOFREADER

CAREER PROFILE

Duties: Oversee the editing and proofreading of all copy for grammar and style; prepare copy for production; check facts

Alternate Title(s): Assistant Managing Editor; Copy Chief; Production Assistant

Salary Range: $20,000 to $50,000+

Employment Prospects: Fair

Advancement Prospects: Fair

Prerequisites:

Education or Training—An undergraduate degree in communications, English, journalism, or liberal arts is the minimum requirement, and advanced course work or knowledge of specialized fields may be required for some scientific or technical publications

Experience—None necessary for most entry-level jobs; otherwise experience as an editorial assistant or an assistant to a professor is useful

Special Skills and Personality Traits—Excellent command of English, grammar, punctuation, and spelling; good organizational skills; patience and close attention to detail

CAREER LADDER

```
┌─────────────────────────────────────┐
│  Associate Editor, Assistant Editor, │
│       Reporter, or Researcher        │
└─────────────────────────────────────┘

┌─────────────────────────────────────┐
│       Copy Editor/Proofreader        │
└─────────────────────────────────────┘

┌─────────────────────────────────────┐
│ Editorial Assistant or College Student│
└─────────────────────────────────────┘
```

Position Description

Copy Editors/Proofreaders advance each article through successive steps of checking for accuracy and suitability, readying it for typesetting and, finally, printing. They need to check each article for grammar, punctuation, and spelling, as well as whether the writing fits the style of the publication, and they may be responsible for fact-checking it as well. On smaller publications, the Copy Editor/Proofreader will handle fact research, working directly with the writer and editors.

Copy Editors/Proofreaders must have an excellent working knowledge of magazine production and layout. If a story or article is too long or too short, the Copy Editor/Proofreader is most likely the individual responsible for cutting or lengthening it, either in consultation with the original writer or alone if the pressure of production deadlines interferes.

Copy Editors/Proofreaders typically prepare the headlines, captions and "decks" (the large quotes which highlight a page of copy). They must check vigorously for typographical errors, misspellings, and inaccurate grammar in the original article/story manuscript, as well as proofread the various stages of proofs for error that may have either slipped by in the initial process or have been initiated by the typesetter. Other production duties may include working with the layout or managing editor to select placement of articles, the use and placement of photos and other artwork, and finalizing the page layouts before printing. In addition, Copy Editors/Proofreaders may spend time with manuscript editors at typesetters' or printers' shops, and substitute for the managing editors when necessary.

Large publications frequently have several Copy Editors/Proofreaders for the various sections of the publication, usually supervised by a managing editor. For small publications, however, there usually is only one Copy Editor/Proofreader for the entire publication. Successful Copy Editors/Proofreaders have a reputation as unruffled personalities and for their meticulous attention to detail.

Salaries

Most small trade publications start Copy Editors/Proofreaders at about $20,000 annually, while larger consumer publications may start Copy Editors/Proofreaders at about $25,000 to $30,000 yearly. A good Copy Editor/Proofreader with experience can generally earn about $45,000 to $50,000 per year.

Employment Prospects

Competition for this position is strong and there is a lot of turnover in the field. Some Copy Editors/Proofreaders work on a part-time basis for more than one publication, or work as freelancers.

Advancement Prospects

Advancement potential for Copy Editors/Proofreaders is fair. An experienced Copy Editor/Proofreader can move up to an associate or assistant editor, or even managing editor or senior editor. Knowledge and experience in magazine production is always extremely helpful for higher editorial positions, and a Copy Editor/Proofreader generally acquires this background in the performance of his or her job.

Education and Training

As with all magazine-writing jobs, an undergraduate degree in communications, English, journalism, or liberal arts, is an absolute requirement. Additional course work and/or seminars and internships in polishing grammar and writing skills is also a plus. Advanced studies for specialized publications can give the Copy Editor/Proofreader a familiarity with the technical concepts and language connected to a particular field serviced by the publication.

Experience, Skills, and Personality Traits

While a background in journalism or writing is useful, the most important skill of a Copy Editor/Proofreader is a thorough command of English grammar, punctuation, and style. Copyediting/proofreading experience with any general-interest publication is recommended, and is easily transferable to any other general-interest magazine. Secretarial and organization skills gained along the way are also helpful.

A Copyeditor/Proofreader must be able to communicate easily and courteously with people no matter what the provocation, as many writers can be prickly about criticisms of their sloppy grammar, incorrect or questionable information, and terrible spelling. In addition, a Copyeditor/Proofreader must have tremendous patience to be able to attend to the endless details of the work.

Unions and Associations

There are no unions for magazine editorial personnel. Professional organizations available for Copy Editors/Proofreaders include the American Copy Editors Society, the American Society of Journalists and Authors, and the American Society of Magazine Editors, as well as numerous writers' and journalists' trade groups.

Tips for Entry

1. As a student, a stint on the college newspaper may be a good place to start to learn about copyediting and proofreading.
2. Join a copyediting/proofreading course at a local learning center. In addition, an internship with a local magazine or newspaper is also an excellent method of getting practical experience.
3. Learn more about copyediting and proofreading on the Internet. To generate a list of relevant Web sites, enter the keywords *copy editor* and/or *proofreader* in any search engine.
4. Volunteer with individuals or small firms to do freelance copyediting and proofreading to gain experience and to build a résumé of work to move upward to magazine publications.
5. Job search through the various online job-posting Web sites that specialize in the media, or the classified listings in the Sunday sections of national newspapers.

CRITIC

CAREER PROFILE

Duties: Review artistic performances, exhibits, books, and recordings; write columns on regular basis for magazines

Alternate Title(s): Reviewer

Salary Range: $19,800 to $66,000+

Employment Prospects: Poor

Advancement Prospects: Poor

Prerequisites:

Education or Training—Undergraduate degree in communications, English, journalism, or liberal arts; specialization in a particular field (such as art, film literature, or music) may require further course work or an advanced degree

Experience—Background as a journalist and an expertise in the subject area being reviewed

Special Skills and Personality Traits—Excellent writing ability; thorough knowledge of subject area being reviewed

CAREER LADDER

```
┌─────────────────────────────────────┐
│   Section Editor or Senior Editor    │
└─────────────────────────────────────┘

┌─────────────────────────────────────┐
│               Critic                 │
└─────────────────────────────────────┘

┌─────────────────────────────────────┐
│             Journalist               │
└─────────────────────────────────────┘
```

Position Description

A Critic is a professional writer who analyzes, evaluates, interprets, and judges literary or artistic works. Critics can greatly influence the reading or viewing public and can greatly impact the success or failure of artists, books, films, musical and/or dance productions, and plays. Good reviews can help to ensure financial success, and bad reviews can keep audiences away from films or plays, as well as adversely affect the sales of books, recordings, or even artwork. Critics can also stimulate public discussion of the works being critiqued, helping that dialogue by putting the subjects under consideration into their historical, social, or political contexts in their columns. By motivating readers into becoming involved in the critical process, Critics help to enrich public perception of art forms of all kinds.

Critics often work evenings and weekends, covering art gallery openings, concerts, operas, dance productions, films, nightclub acts, and plays. Or, as book Critics, their time may be devoted to a great deal of topical research, as well as reading. Thus, Critics may review anything connected with the arts and entertainment fields. Their columns may appear in each issue of the magazine for which they work, or may appear only on a irregular basis depending upon their contract with the publisher of the magazine.

Critics are assumed to be knowledgeable about their areas of expertise and are expected to keep current with all trends and news in their subject area(s). Outside their column of criticism, Critics may be called upon to interview artists, celebrities, and performers for special editions of their column. Regardless of their subject area, Critics must do extensive reading in and studying of their areas of expertise. Critics are expected to maintain an objectivity toward their subject areas, and exhibit good judgment in their criticism. Similarly to regular columnists, magazine Critics often develop an audience who trust and act upon the Critics' views and opinions as expressed in their magazine column.

Besides writing their regular (or irregular) review columns, magazine Critics often write articles about celebrities (interviews or in-depth studies), or about trends or other aspects of the arts and entertainment fields.

Salaries

Critics may have slightly higher salaries than their journalism peers, or approximately $19,800 to $66,000 annually or higher. High-end salaries depend to a great extent upon the Critic's credentials (gained through years of writing columns of criticism), as well as the size and market of the magazine for which they work. Large national magazines usually have on their staffs well-established Critics who have built a reputation for themselves by their writings and have attracted a loyal audience for their views.

Employment Prospects

Many Critics start out as journalists of one kind or another, usually with a particular interest in the arts, entertainment, fashion, or food industries. Sometimes they initiate their move into a full-time position as a magazine Critic when they fill in for an indisposed staff Critic, or help out the established Critic on the magazine workforce by reviewing performances, or subjects that the staff member cannot (or prefers not to) cover.

Once a Critic is established and has become well known, he or she can change magazine employers, but the competition is stiff, as the job market tends to be rather small (only so many Critics can be utilized by any one publication). Some magazine Critics may also make a name for themselves with public appearances on radio or television and by having a column on a Web site.

Advancement Prospects

Like columnists, most Critics prefer to remain in their position as Critic and not take part in other newsgathering work. Advancement occurs typically by changing magazines to further both career and salary. Some Critics may become members of the editorial staff of the magazine as an upward step in their journalism career. Other Critics working for national magazines may want to join the staff of specialized magazines in their field as a further enhancement of their career.

Education and Training

Critics are expected to have a basic undergraduate education in communications, English, journalism, or liberal arts, as well as a comprehensive background in the subject area(s) covered by their critiques. This background may require specialized or advanced degrees to guarantee the Critic's credentials.

Experience, Skills, and Personality Traits

Critics must be thoroughly familiar with their specialization to write fair and objective reviews. They need to read extensively and research their field often to be informed of all stated opinions and ongoing trends of thought about their subject matter.

They should be adept at interviewing artists, celebrities, and practitioners in their topic area, and be able to write concisely to meet the deadlines and word limitations set by their magazine's distribution schedule. One advantage a magazine Critic has over those on newspaper staffs, radio, or television is that their deadline schedules typically are not as hectic and that they can pick and choose what they review rather than covering most every possibility.

Unions and Associations

Professional associations for Critics include the American Theatre Critics Association, the Dance Critics Association, the Music Critics Association of North America, the National Association of Black Journalists, the National Federation of Press Women, the National Society of Film Critics, the New York Film Critics Circle, and the Society of Professional Journalists.

Tips for Entry

1. All the journalistic experience that can be gained on campus (preferably including writing experience while working on college publications) or after college is valuable in securing a beginning position with a magazine.
2. Try reviewing while working in other capacities on college publications, or during an internship program with a newspaper or other publication.
3. Develop your expertise in fields of your interest by further course work and lots of reading.
4. Study criticism by well-established Critics to evaluate their work and to help establish your own critical faculties and style.
5. Establish your own Web site on which you can post (and practice writing) your own criticism and commentaries, useful in your job searching for a full-time professional Critic position and in attracting the attention of potential magazine employers.

EDITOR

CAREER PROFILE

Duties: Supervise magazine preparation and set editorial policy; manage staff; rewrite and edit

Alternate Title(s): Editor in Chief; Editorial Director; Editorial Manager; Publications Editor

Salary Range: $50,000 to $100,000+

Employment Prospects: Poor

Advancement Prospects: Poor

Prerequisites:

Education or Training—Undergraduate degree in communications, journalism, English, or liberal arts; advanced degrees helpful and specialized degrees needed for scientific and technical publications

Experience—Background as Editor, journalist, or writer essential; three to five years' experience as senior Editor or associate Editor preferred

Special Skills and Personality Traits—Superior grammar and editing knowledge; highly self-motivated and organized; good administrative ability; intellectual curiosity

CAREER LADDER

```
┌─────────────────────────────────┐
│          Publisher              │
└─────────────────────────────────┘

┌─────────────────────────────────┐
│           Editor                │
└─────────────────────────────────┘

┌─────────────────────────────────┐
│  Senior Editor, Associate Editor,│
│     or Assistant Editor         │
└─────────────────────────────────┘
```

Position Description

The Editor has complete responsibility for the editorial content and production of a magazine, as well as the publication's editorial policy. The Editor reports directly to the publisher; in some cases, the Editor may be the publisher.

The totality of responsibilities will depend on the size of the publication. On a small magazine, the Editor may perform many of the day-to-day editorial functions and production tasks. At a larger operation, the Editor delegates those tasks and, instead, concentrates on broad administrative duties and overseeing the editorial personnel. Some Editors may be in charge of groups of publications under a common ownership

The typical Editor's day is divided among editorial, production, and administrative duties. Editorial responsibilities will include assigning photo coverage for articles/stories, editing and rewriting manuscripts, making assignments to the staff and freelance writers, and planning future issues of the publication. Editors supervise the activities of all subordinate editors, as well as monitor carefully all work-in-progress against stated deadlines. In addition, Editors are

responsible for final approval of all articles, copy, and other material to be included in the issue of the publication.

Production functions include working with the layout editor on placement of articles and advertising, use of photos and other artwork, plus all final approval of page layouts. On small publications, the Editor may have full responsibility for production, which may entail proofreading duties and interfacing with typesetters and printers.

Administrative duties include answering readers' letters, hiring and firing staff members, negotiating freelance contracts, planning and managing budgets, writing reports, and other typical managerial tasks.

In addition, Editors are expected to attend trade conventions as representatives of their publication(s) and employer, and participate in promotional and publicity activities related to their publication. They may also write and sign bylined columns and editorials in their publications.

Salaries

Editors of consumer magazines tend to be paid more than those of business (trade) or scientific/technical publications.

According to *Folio's* 2004 editorial salary survey, the annual salaries of Editors can range from a low of $35,000 to a high of $185,000, with the mean average yearly salaries extending from a low of $59,200 to a high of $107,000. Of those queried for this survey, 69 percent expected to receive a bonus, the average of which was anticipated to be $12,285. These amounts varied according to the Editor's age, how long the Editor has worked in such a position, and how long the Editor has worked at the specific publication. Other factors were how many magazines and employees the Editor supervised, how frequently their magazine(s) were published, how many pages they produced annually, and the circulation of their magazine(s).

Employment Prospects

While the market is competitive and characterized by moderate to high turnover, the 2004 *Folio* survey found that the average length of time that Editors worked at their present company was 11 to 12 years, with an average of six to seven years in their present position. Nonetheless, the best opportunities still remain at trade and scientific/technical publications, especially those serving growth industries, such as computer, health, or management.

Advancement Prospects

An Editor (frequently called editor-in-chief, or editorial director) is the highest post in many magazines, reporting directly to the publisher (who traditionally comes from the advertising and marketing side of the business). Since the Editor is the top position, advancement can only be made by moving on to bigger or more prestigious publications. Such advancement opportunities are slow to materialize, as the higher editorial positions are seldom vacated.

Education and Training

Similar to most editing and writing jobs, there is little agreement by industry experts on what would be the preferred major for an Editor. Many have undergraduate degrees in communications or journalism, which others have degrees in history, liberal arts, philosophy, or the social sciences. For trade publications, business, economics, engineering, medical, or scientific degrees may be necessary.

Experience, Skills, and Personality Traits

The amount of experience required to be an Editor depends on the publication and its publisher. Three to five years or more is the average requirement for many of these jobs, while 10 years or more may be necessary for certain trade publications. Previous experience may include work as an assistant news editor, copy editor, journalist, or section editor; work in book publishing as a junior editor or editor; or work on magazine staffs in lower editorial positions.

Editors should possess solid project management talents, as well as excellent written and verbal communication skills. They should have good judgment about what should be published and what should not by their magazine. They need to have tact and the ability to direct and motivate staff members and freelance writers. They should be creative, have a vigorous sense of curiosity, and be able to meet deadlines and manage budgets. Finally, a thorough knowledge of production and printing processes are extremely important.

Unions and Associations

The American Society of Magazine Editors is the primary professional organization for editors. Other major professional associations include the American Society of Journalists and Authors and the Association for Women in Communications. In addition, Editors often join writer's groups as well as trade and industry groups. The Newspaper Guild represents some employees on major news and feature magazines.

Tips for Entry

1. To aspire to a position as Editor, be prepared to put in three to seven years' experience in lower editorial positions, such as editorial assistant or assistant Editor, and then associate Editor.
2. Gain expertise in a field of your interest to make a transfer to a specialized trade magazine position that much easier.
3. Gain production experience by working in a newspaper environment, as an intern, or on your college newspaper or magazine. Layout and typesetting functions are a necessary part of an Editor's background.
4. Study consumer and trade magazines to understand how magazines are put together and what works for readers and what does not.
5. Attend national conferences, such as those sponsored by the American Society of Magazine Editors, to network with other Editors and publishers.

EXECUTIVE EDITOR

CAREER PROFILE

Duties: Supervise preparation of magazine; manage staff; assign stories/articles; rewrite and edit

Alternate Title(s): Editor; Editorial Director; Managing Editor; Senior Editor

Salary Range: $22,000 to $95,000+

Employment Prospects: Fair

Advancement Prospects: Fair

Prerequisites:

　Education or Training—Undergraduate degree in communications, English, journalism, or liberal arts; advanced or specialized degrees for scientific, technical, or other specialty publications

　Experience—Five to eight years' background preferably as editor, or journalist or writer

　Special Skills and Personality Traits—Thorough knowledge of editing, grammar, and magazine production; good organizational skills and ability to manage and direct people; knowledge of a particular field or specialty

CAREER LADDER

```
┌─────────────────────────────────────────┐
│                 Editor                    │
└─────────────────────────────────────────┘

┌─────────────────────────────────────────┐
│            Executive Editor               │
└─────────────────────────────────────────┘

┌─────────────────────────────────────────┐
│  Assistant Editor, Associate Editor, or   │
│              Senior Editor                 │
└─────────────────────────────────────────┘
```

Position Description

The Executive Editor is a title usually utilized by larger publications, as smaller magazines tend to allocate the Executive Editor's duties to senior editors and/or the top editors. The Executive Editor has the total responsibility for the editorial direction and content, including art, text, and cover, for one or more magazines. The position usually reports to the editor-in-chief in charge of a magazine group under common ownership, or directly to the publisher. The structure of magazine staffs, however, varies greatly from one publication to another.

Similar to a senior editor, Executive Editors oversee the activities of lower-level editors and may be responsible for freelancers, photographers, and illustrators. The assigning of stories/articles and the monitoring of the editorial department and of the entire magazine's workings is the task of the Executive Editor. This person also has the ultimate responsibility for all final editing. In addition, the individual may write features or articles, but the primary responsibility is the editing. Being in charge of the entire magazine production means that the Executive Editor must maintain and meet all deadlines.

Generally next in command to the editor (or editor-in-chief, or editorial director), the Executive Editor delegates authority and story/article assignments, often without prior approval. When the editor is out of town or is ill, the Executive Editor takes over complete control of the magazine.

In addition to these editorial duties, an Executive Editor may also handle production matters, such as page-checking and proofreading, as well as work with the editor on budget and be responsible for editorial expenses. An Executive Editor is also expected to represent the magazine at professional meetings and workshops, as well as attend these meetings, seminars, and trade shows to keep informed on industry trends, practices, and procedures.

Salaries

Executive Editors of consumer magazines are likely to receive higher wages than those of specialty trade magazines. According to *Folio* magazine's 2004 Editorial Salary Survey, the lowest annual salary reported of an Executive Editor was $22,000, and the highest was $220,000. However, the average yearly salaries for Executive Editors ranged from a low of $54,000 to a high of $95,000. These incomes varied according to the Executive Editor's age, experience as an editor, and tenure at the specific publication. Other factors included how many magazines and employees the Executive Editors supervised, how frequently their magazine(s) were published, how many pages they produced annually, and the circulation of their magazine(s).

On the matter of editorial bonuses, *Folio* found that, generally, many magazines are still holding back on them. Only 51.5 percent of the survey respondents indicated they expected a bonus for 2004, of anywhere from $500 to $40,000, with an average of $8,936.

Employment Prospects

The best employment opportunities for Executive Editors lie with large publications, as smaller magazines often have no such positions in their staffing formats. Within large publications, competition is strong for such positions, so much so that it is unusual that an Executive Editor is hired from outside the company, rather than promoting within the organization.

As the overall supply/demand for Executive Editors has not improved dramatically over the last several years, positions that had been eliminated in the downturn period previous to 2004 are not yet being restored, and may not be until publishers feel that the advertising gains are sustainable. *Folio* found that in some categories, such as shelter (housing) and entertainment, publishers are starting to rehire, and advertising is proving to be strong in entertainment-oriented magazines. However, consumer publications are generally still reluctant to start rehiring without assurance that the jobs can be maintained on a long-term basis.

Advancement Prospects

Since the Executive Editor reports directly to the editor or editor in chief, advancement opportunities are not very promising. If an editor has been with a publication for several years and shows no intention of leaving, an Executive Editor may have to join another publication in order to advance to a post as editor or editor in chief. When editors do move, they often do so in order to start their own magazines.

Education and Training

An accomplished Executive Editor will have had an undergraduate degree in communications, English, or journalism, or some other type of liberal arts degree. Most will most likely acquire advanced degrees (or have taken advanced course work) in journalism or in a scientific/technical field

allied with the type of publication they edit. Specialized magazines, such as those dealing with law, medicine, science, or technology, usually require advanced education from their Executive Editors.

Experience, Skills, and Personality Traits

Prior experience as a senior editor or editor of smaller publications are almost a pro forma requirement for most Executive Editor openings. Work as a professor or academic researcher may be sufficient for certain publications, especially if such operations require more writing than editing from their Executive Editors. In these cases, the editor's job title reflects more on that editor's background and expertise than his/her editorial and managerial qualifications.

Vital to an Executive Editor are good writing and editing skills, as well as the capability of managing and directing people effectively. Organizational and budgetary abilities are also paramount. Depending upon the particular levels of responsibility of an Executive Editor, he or she may also have to deal directly with the publisher, the advertising and promotion departments, and the readers.

Unions and Associations

Executive Editors, like other editorial positions in magazine publishing, may belong to the American Society of Magazine Editors, the American Society of Journalists and Authors, or various other writers' trade organizations.

Tips for Entry

1. To get to a position as Executive Editor, be prepared to devote three to seven years to gaining experience in lower editorial positions, such as editorial assistant or assistant editor, and then associate editor.
2. Gain expertise in a field of your interest to make a transfer to a specialized trade magazine position that much easier (though your title may not be Executive Editor, your job functions may be the same as those of such an editor with a consumer magazine).
3. Gain production experience by working in a newspaper environment, as an intern, or on your college newspaper or magazine, as such experience is necessary for an Executive Editor who oversees the entire magazine.
4. Study consumer and trade magazines to understand how magazines are put together and what works for readers and what does not.
5. Interact and network with other editors (and Executive Editors) at conferences sponsored by the associations related to magazine publishing.

FEATURE WRITER

CAREER PROFILE

Duties: Collect and report information for feature stories on specific or a wide variety of topics

Alternate Title(s): Journalist; Magazine Columnist

Salary Range: $19,000 to $90,000+

Employment Prospects: Fair

Advancement Prospects: Fair

Prerequisites:

Education or Training—Undergraduate degree in communications, English, journalism, or liberal arts; graduate degree or advanced courses in area of specialization may be required

Experience—Several years of experience as a magazine reporter or in other journalistic positions

Special Skills and Personality Traits—Ability to research and write in-depth feature stories; inquisitiveness; excellent writing skills; good interviewing and interpersonal skills; persistence; self-discipline

CAREER LADDER

```
┌─────────────────────────────┐
│  Editor or Executive Editor │
└─────────────────────────────┘

┌─────────────────────────────┐
│       Feature Writer        │
└─────────────────────────────┘

┌─────────────────────────────┐
│          Reporter           │
└─────────────────────────────┘
```

Position Description

Consumer newspapers (weeklies) and consumer magazines (monthlies) vary greatly in both style and content. Most weeklies are very news-oriented and tend to hire journalists who have worked for several years in the trenches of daily newspapers. Consumer monthlies (other than news magazines) place a smaller emphasis on news as breaking information cannot be covered effectively on a monthly basis. Instead, monthlies present highly researched feature articles that delve into long-term trends. These in-depth feature stories go into much greater depth and include more sources and background research. Monthlies tend to look for journalists who have experience working as special reporters or columnists. They are seeking seasoned journalists adept at research and skilled in writing "thought" pieces.

Magazine Feature Writers usually are assigned topics by the executive editor (if a large magazine), or the editor (if a smaller operation). A Feature Writer may spend up to six weeks on an article (in comparison to a reporter on a weekly who seldom spends more than two or three days). Editors typically work from editorial calendars that have been set up months in advance. These editorial calendars usually are designed to attract specific groups of advertisers, but the division between editorial and advertising for the magazine is always clearcut and strong.

Magazine Feature Writers report directly to the editor (or executive editor) of the magazine, and must keep that person fully apprised of developments in the writing of the feature article and any problems that may have occurred. Feature Writers need to monitor any news event that may affect their story as well as research all important news sources for information pertaining to the article at hand. Like newspaper beat reporters, they have to maintain a rapport with their sources, even when the final article might displease these individuals. The personal trust of their sources can help immeasurably in a Feature Writer finding the real story behind the account they may have originally intended to write.

Work schedules for magazine Feature Writers need to remain flexible, but they are more likely to work regular hours than other journalists. Their research time (which may include interviews), however, may take extra time and, as the deadline comes closer, overtime is expected. Some Feature Writers may work within their home environment as well as at the magazine's office.

Salaries

The salaries of magazine Feature Writers vary depending upon the size and nature of the magazine and its locale. At smaller magazines and some trade publications, the annual salary may be as low as $19,000, whereas at the glossy New York magazines, the yearly salaries of well-known Feature Writers may well be over $100,000. It is reputed that Dominick Dunne, one of the nation's highest-paid magazine writers, had a 2003 salary of close to $500,000. Usual salaries for most Feature Writers, however, will range between $20,000 and $40,000.

Employment Prospects

Magazine Feature Writer is not an entry-level position. It is a job earned from solid experience as a reporter. Many Feature Writers continue to do regular reporting for their magazine. Freelance writers are often hired as Feature Writers and, sometimes, join the magazine staff as a full-time writer. The competition for this position is always stiff, more so with the large national consumer magazines, and less so with the trade magazines for various industries and associations.

Advancement Prospects

Advancement prospects are only fair. Feature Writers for small trade magazines can move to larger national or industry magazines, or transfer to the consumer magazine world. Some Feature Writers of either type of publication can also move into editorial positions on their magazine, or other publications (both print and, increasingly, online).

Education and Training

The most common undergraduate degree preferred by consumer magazine editors is one in communications, English, or journalism, though a comparable degree in liberal arts may be acceptable. With specialty magazines (industry trade journals), editors would like an additional degree in the subject area of the magazine. For example, publications that rely heavily on financial analysis look for Feature Writers with a master's degree in business administration. Trade magazines that cover biotechnology, pharmaceuticals, or, say, genome development, look for Feature Writers with a life science degree. The closer the degree to the magazine's subject area, the better.

Regardless of this preference of double degrees for feature writing and specialized reporting, an editor will always choose excellent writing ability over technical education. As a former *Wall Street Journal* executive editor, Frederick Taylor, once said, "It's easier to make a reporter into an economist than an economist into a reporter."

Experience, Skills, and Personality Traits

Most Feature Writers are expected to be qualified journalists, though the degree of experience may vary according to both the size and the subject matter of the journal. Good reporter instincts and skills are essential, as well as knowing how to research and organize information and be able to explain potentially complicated topics in a simple but meaningful manner.

Feature Writers have to be detail-oriented, and exhibit good interviewing skills. They need to follow their story through to its logical conclusion, taking the time to check all facts and opinions to be used in the article, and to meet required deadlines.

Unions and Associations

Professional associations for specialized reporters and Feature Writers include the American Society of Journalists and Authors; Investigative Reporters and Editors; and the Society of Professional Journalists. In addition, there are innumerable professional associations related to the subject areas of individual trade magazines. For example, among others, there is the American Management Association, the American Marketing Association, the Associated Business Writers of America, and the Association for Business Communication for business and financial journals. There are also numerous professional associations that represent the magazine industry, as well as reporters and Feature Writers of different racial and ethnic backgrounds.

Tips for Entry

1. Get as much journalistic writing experience as you can during college, on the campus newspaper or other publications.
2. Look for internship programs with local newspapers, magazines, or broadcast stations to add practical journalistic experience to your college course work.
3. Work on perfecting your researching capabilities, as this skill will be absolutely essential to your success as a magazine reporter and, later, as a Feature Writer.
4. Practice your interviewing skills as much as you can during your college years and internship programs, as this will be another key ability you must possess as a magazine reporter, and later as a Feature Writer.
5. In addition, practice developing sources of information during your journalistic efforts in college and in internship programs, as sources will become your livelihood as a Feature Writer developing stories for your magazine.

REPORTER

Duties: Collect information to report in news and feature article on a wide range of topics

Alternate Title(s): Journalist

Salary Range: $17,000 to $70,000+

Employment Prospects: Fair to Good

Advancement Prospects: Fair

Prerequisites:

Education or Training—Undergraduate degree in communications, English, journalism, or liberal arts

Experience—Work within a journalistic environment during college; minimum of one to two years' professional journalistic experience for publications

Special Skills and Personality Traits—Aggressiveness; good interpersonal skills; persistence; self-discipline; solid organizational abilities and meticulous research habits

CAREER LADDER

```
┌─────────────────────────────────────┐
│  Assistant Editor, Section Editor, or│
│            Executive Editor          │
└─────────────────────────────────────┘

┌─────────────────────────────────────┐
│               Reporter               │
└─────────────────────────────────────┘

┌─────────────────────────────────────┐
│   Copy Aide, Desk Assistant, or      │
│            College Student           │
└─────────────────────────────────────┘
```

Position Description

In general, journalists interview sources and research and review data to assemble, sift through, and report information for a story, as well as explore the implications of the facts as reported. Magazine Reporters can cover all kinds of topics and events. They are assigned news stories by an executive editor (if a large magazine) or an editor (if a smaller magazine). Magazine Reporters may work one or more weeks on a story if the magazine is a monthly publication, or longer if it is a quarterly publication, or if the piece is to be a featured cover article.

Even with this expanded completion schedule (and unlike newspaper reporters with their daily or weekly deadlines) magazine Reporters need to work as quickly as possible and then, flexibly, move on to their next assignment, regardless of its subject (or how it may differ from the one they have just finished).

With the usual additional leeway at their disposal, magazine Reporters can devote more time and energy to exploring the background of their stories and accomplish the needed research (and possible interviewing) to flesh out the piece more fully. Throughout this process, they need to keep their editor informed as to developments in the story, as well

as the various steps they are undertaking and whom they are interviewing.

While Reporters at magazines generally keep to regular weekly schedule hours (unless they are freelance workers), they may have to work longer hours and even odd schedules as the publication deadlines come closer. They also have to keep abreast of any news changes that will affect the outcome of their reporting of the piece on which they are currently working.

As Reporters gain experience for a magazine and begin to develop a reputation for their output, they may find opportunities to become a feature writer for the magazine. Their experience at gaining news sources and their skill at researching stories as a Reporter will be extremely useful to them as a feature writer.

Salaries

According to the U.S. Department of Labor's Bureau of Labor Statistics, as outlined in their *Occupational Outlook Handbook* in March of 2004, annual salaries for Reporters during 2002 throughout the United States ranged from a low of $17,600 to a high of $69,500. However, within large urban centers—particularly New York City—the salaries tended to be higher. For New York, the low was an income of $21,600 yearly, and the high was $104,500.

Employment Prospects

According to the Bureau of Labor Statistics, employment of Reporters is expected generally to grow more slowly than the average for most other occupations through the year 2012. However, the magazine industry is an extremely volatile one, with new publications debuting (including online magazines) and folding all the time. Reporters with experience in magazine work should be able to locate full-time work without too much difficulty.

Advancement Prospects

Reporters may be able to progress into feature writing as well as their regular reporting, thus expanding their career options (and their salary). Some Reporters may be able to make a career move into the editorial department of the magazine to any number of specific editorial positions. Other Reporters may decide to make a lateral move (of sorts) to newspaper work at one of the larger national dailies.

Education and Training

Most magazines require their Reporters to have an undergraduate degree in communications, English, journalism, or liberal arts. The traditional educational part is a bachelor's degree in journalism. However, a well-rounded education that a liberal arts degree will give may prove to be a valuable preparation for a Reporter position.

Even more important than the specifics of the degree is the practical experience in writing, whether on a school publication or in an internship program.

Experience, Skills, and Personality Traits

The job of Reporter with a magazine is often an entry-level position for those applicants just getting into journalistic work with such publications. The most valuable background that a new applicant can have is lots of writing experience while in college, or in an internship program with either a magazine or a newspaper.

Reporters need to be very detail-oriented, and be good listeners as they will do a lot of interviewing in their career.

They cannot afford to be intimidated by anyone or any story, and they have to persevere in asking questions incessantly. Their research abilities must be exemplary, and they need to develop the skill to explain complex subjects in a clear, simple, but thorough, manner. A nose for news and knowing how to follow a story through to its logical conclusion, as well as a good memory, persistence, poise, and physical stamina are all requirements of the job.

Unions and Associations

Professional associations for Reporters include the American Society of Journalists and Authors; Investigative Reporters and Editors; and the Society of Professional Journalists. In addition, there are numerous professional associations that represent the magazine industry, as well as reporters in a wide variety of specialties or of different racial and ethnic backgrounds.

Tips for Entry

1. Get as much journalistic experience as you can during college to prepare yourself for the continuous demands of a magazine Reporter. Work on the campus newspaper or other publications.
2. Look for internship programs with local newspapers, magazines, or broadcast stations to add practical journalistic experience to your college course work. Working as part of a news staff in competition with others will provide you with a valuable insight into the news world beyond the campus.
3. Focus on perfecting your researching capabilities, as this skill will be absolutely essential to your success as a magazine Reporter.
4. During your college years and in internship programs, practice improving your proficiency at interviewing as much as you can, as this will also be a requisite key ability to be a successful Reporter for magazines.
5. Practice developing sources of information during your journalistic efforts in college and in internship programs, as sources will be your major advantage in developing stories for your magazine.
6. Offer to write articles for local newspapers or community publications to gain experience.

RESEARCHER

CAREER PROFILE

Duties: Examine all articles/stories and indicate facts needing verification; check with author and sources; keep records of any changes and inform editor of such changes

Alternate Title(s): Editorial Assistant; Fact Checker; Research Editor

Salary Range: $14,000 to $35,000+

Employment Prospects: Poor

Advancement Prospects: Good

Prerequisites:

Education or Training—Undergraduate degree in communications, English, journalism, or liberal arts required; advanced degrees or course work for specialized subject areas

Experience—Entry-level researcher needs no previous experience; background as editor, journalist, or writer helpful

Special Skills and Personality Traits—Excellent editing and writing skills; good telephone skills; organization; scrupulous attention to detail

CAREER LADDER

```
┌─────────────────────────────────────────┐
│  Associate Editor or Assistant Editor    │
└─────────────────────────────────────────┘

┌─────────────────────────────────────────┐
│              Researcher                   │
└─────────────────────────────────────────┘

┌─────────────────────────────────────────┐
│  Editorial Assistant or College Student   │
└─────────────────────────────────────────┘
```

Position Description

The job of Researcher is frequently an entry-level position at a magazine, working directly for the associate or executive editor, and it is generally a stepping-stone to greater editorial responsibility. Researchers have to confirm each piece of information in a reporter's story and ensure that all necessary corrections to such information are made. They need to verify everything that is written in the story, from the quotations to the name and place spellings. Researchers must let both the reporter and the assistant editor know about any changes that are necessary.

Smaller publications seldom hire Researchers, depending upon their own reporters to verify the facts as given in the finished articles/stories. At larger magazines, the Researcher not only checks all the data, but also guides the stories through the entire production process, making certain that everything that has been verified remains correct at each step in the process.

In order to train Researchers for reporting and/or editorial positions, editors may assign small, bylined stories,

columns, or features to Researchers. Also, announcements of personnel changes or new-business columns may become the regular responsibility of a Researcher. In addition, Researchers may also take on the duties of proofreading galleys and even writing headlines and captions (cutlines). In some cases, they may be required to handle other production details as well.

It is usually understood that Researchers should attend seminars, trade shows, and workshops to keep abreast of industry trends and new usages of technology.

Salaries

Some Researchers working for magazines are represented by the Newspaper Guild. Salaries vary widely depending on the magazine, the Researcher's level of experience and command of subject matter, and so forth.

Annual salaries range from a low of about $14,000 to a high of $35,000 or more. Some researchers may even earn less than $14,000 yearly and are seldom represented by a union.

Employment Prospects

As Researcher is usually an entry-level post, there is a lot more turnover in such positions than in higher ones. Employees who have great patience and who are capable of meticulous attention to detail are not that common, but a magazine's public credibility is dependent upon the accuracy of its stories. Thus, the constant need for good Researchers. Beginners with journalism skills and superior organizational skills have a good chance of obtaining work with a newspaper as a Researcher, and from there move onwards into the editorial staff. However, it should be noted that not all magazines employ Researchers.

Advancement Prospects

Most Researchers have a good likelihood of promotion. Frequently, a Researcher is hired with the understanding that, after time in that position, promotion to assistant or associate editor is likely to occur within two or three years. On smaller publications, Researchers may accelerate upward even faster. However, as with all magazine editorial positions, competition is strong.

Education and Training

An undergraduate degree in communications, English, journalism, or some other liberal arts field is essential. Any secretarial training gives a Researcher the organizational skills necessary for this position. Advanced course work, or a degree, may be required for researcher jobs on specialized publications, such as those for business, health, law, medicine, or technology.

Experience, Skills, and Personality Traits

While no formal experience in journalism is really necessary for this entry-level position, Researchers who have taken editing or writing courses, who have been involved in school publications, and who have undertaken summer internship programs with magazines or newspapers, have a distinct advantage in applying for this type of position.

Many editors think a good Researcher needs to have a background in liberal arts (for its breadth of coverage of subjects) and have a strong interest in reading. They also feel that summer seminars or workshops in related subjects are advantageous.

Researchers must show excellent organizational talents, good editing and writing abilities, and an above-average degree of patience and perseverance. It is also helpful to have a working knowledge of magazine production procedures.

Unions and Associations

Researchers are eligible to join the American Society of Journalists and Authors and the American Society of Magazine Editors, as well as other writers' trade groups. Also, the Association for Women in Communications is open to both men and women journalists. The Newspaper Guild represents employees on some of the major news and feature magazines.

Tips for Entry

1. All the journalistic experience that can be gained during college (preferably including editing, writing, and production experience on, say, the college newspaper) or after would be of help in gaining a beginning researching position with a newspaper.
2. Enroll in a summer internship program with a newspaper or a magazine while in college to gain experience in the journalistic production process, and ask to practice researching and fact checking while in the program.
3. Consider working within a library (or even an internship where possible) to become familiar with standard reference and potential research studies.
4. Explore the Internet for useful reference/research portals and Web sites.

SENIOR EDITOR

CAREER PROFILE

Duties: Supervise editorial department/division; manage lower-level editors, freelancers, writers, and photographers; generate ideas for articles; write some articles and/or columns

Alternate Title(s): Associate Editor; Executive Editor

Salary Range: $30,000 to $66,000+

Employment Prospects: Fair to Poor

Advancement Prospects: Poor

Prerequisites:

Education or Training—Undergraduate degree in communications, English, journalism, or liberal arts; advanced degree in journalism or specialized degrees for business, scientific, or technical publications

Experience—Background as editor, journalist, or writer an absolute requirement; academic career sometimes beneficial

Special Skills and Personality Traits—Excellent editing, managerial, and organizational skills; graphics and production expertise; knowledge of a particular field or specialty

CAREER LADDER

```
┌─────────────────────────────────┐
│   Editor or Executive Editor    │
└─────────────────────────────────┘

┌─────────────────────────────────┐
│         Senior Editor           │
└─────────────────────────────────┘

┌─────────────────────────────────┐
│ Associate Editor or Assistant Editor │
└─────────────────────────────────┘
```

Position Description

Senior Editors plan, write, or assign features, other articles, and stories, thus making them responsible for a magazine's content, usually in consultation with the editor. They are sometimes referred to as the middle managers of the magazine world. On small trade magazines, Senior Editors often write the lead or most important articles as well as news features. Their story ideas are usually taken up by the other writers. On larger publications, such as consumer magazines, Senior Editors often manage a single major editorial department. This management position is often reflected in the additional title of the area of responsibility that the Senior Editor holds, such as sports editor, fashion editor, or news editor.

Although associate editors under the supervision of a Senior Editor may handle all the day-to-day editorial tasks—reading unsolicited manuscripts, working with freelancers—it is the Senior Editor who has the final responsibility for all this activity. Senior Editors may deal directly with freelancers and even determine and assign photographs and graphic work on illustrations for individual articles/stories. Any problems with assignments or with writers must be known by and solved by Senior Editors.

Senior Editors partake on a regular basis in editorial meetings, keeping the editor (or editorial director) aware of the department's progress, as well as suggesting ideas for future stories or articles. At a large operation, the Senior Editor may have the leeway of assigning stories or articles without the editor's approval, but this is seldom the case with smaller publications. While these assignments may be the Senior Editor's idea, it is usually the immediate responsibility of the associate editor to either write the article/story, or hire a freelancer for the task.

The Senior Editor may also write, a situation particularly true of small magazines. The Senior Editor may be responsible for an ongoing column or may produce stories or articles upon assignment by the editor. Senior Editors on the larger publications rarely write, as their supervisory and editorial work consume most of their time.

Senior Editors may also take on production tasks, such as editing manuscripts or proofreading galleys. They are usually expected to attend seminars, trade shows, and workshops to keep abreast of industry trends and technologies, as well as represent the magazine at professional meetings and functions. In some instances, they may also handle day-to-day relations with printers.

Salaries

Senior Editors of consumer magazines are frequently, but not always, paid more than those of trade magazines. According to *Folio's* 2004 editorial salary survey, both bonuses and raises are still being held back, as the overall supply and demand picture for magazines has not improved dramatically. Positions that were eliminated during the economic crunch of the last several years are not being restored, at least until advertising revenues gain substantially. With editorial positions being eliminated, Senior Editors note they are bearing the brunt of work reassigned with little or no pay increases, as reported in this salary survey.

According to *Folio,* Senior Editors' average annual salaries varied from the high $40,000s to the high $60,000s according to their age and experience, how many magazines and employees they supervise, how frequently their magazine(s) are published, how many total pages are produced annually, and the circulation of their magazine(s).

Employment Prospects

The better work opportunities for Senior Editors are usually with small and special-interest publications, such as trade magazines. These publications have smaller staffs and often need people who are experienced editors, journalists, or writers. For such special-interest magazines, background data may be learned on the job, but familiarity with the particular field or subject of the magazine optimizes the possibility of employment with them.

Advancement Prospects

The prospect of a Senior Editor moving up the ladder to the position of executive editor or editor depends solely on the publication. Although Senior Editors on smaller operations may have more visibility and perform more tasks (such as editing or writing), advancement may be impossible due to a longtime editor who has no plans of stepping down.

At larger publications, Senior Editors have more of a chance in switching departments (often to positions with more responsibility) or, even, to be promoted to executive editor. There tends to be more job mobility in the editorial departments of larger publications.

Education and Training

Senior Editors must have a degree in communications, English, journalism, or other liberal arts field. An advanced degree can give a Senior Editor an additional edge. For publications covering specialized fields, such as economics, law, medicine, science, or technology, extensive course work or degrees in that specialty may be required of a Senior Editor.

Experience, Skills, and Personality Traits

Prior experience as either a journalist or a lower-level editor is usually a requirement for an aspiring Senior Editor. Academic experience as a teacher or researcher is often acceptable as qualification for a Senior Editor on a specialized publication, such as those dealing with medicine or scientific subjects. This additional scholastic experience is particularly necessary if the Senior Editor is expected to write regular columns for the publication.

Since so much of a Senior Editor's time is spent in supervising, excellent organizational and personal skills are essential. In addition, Senior Editors need to have superb editing competence and should also be equipped to write well.

Unions and Associations

The American Society of Magazine Editors is the primary professional organization for editors. Editors and writers often join writer's groups, such as the American Society of Journalists and Authors. Editors of large news and feature magazines may belong to the Newspaper Guild.

Tips for Entry

1. To aspire to a position as Senior Editor, be prepared to put in two to five years in lower editorial positions, such as editorial assistant or assistant editor.
2. Gain expertise in a field of your interest to make a transfer to a specialized trade magazine position that much easier.
3. Acquire production experience by working in a newspaper environment, as an intern, or on your college newspaper/magazine. Layout and typesetting knowledge are a necessary part of the background of a Senior Editor.
4. Take further computer courses to become proficient in word processing and desktop publishing techniques.
5. Network with other editors at conferences to keep abreast of job opportunities and editorial procedures and practices.

NEWSPAPERS, NEWS SERVICES, AND NEWS SYNDICATES

ASSISTANT EDITOR

CAREER PROFILE

Duties: Assist news editor or department editor in news assembling and editing activities; assign articles to reporters

Alternate Title(s): Assignment Editor; Assistant City Editor; Assistant Metropolitan Editor; Deputy Editor

Salary Range: $24,000 to $60,000+

Employment Prospects: Fair

Advancement Prospects: Fair

Prerequisites:

Education or Training—Undergraduate degree in communications, English, journalism, or liberal arts

Experience—Background as a journalist required

Special Skills and Personality Traits—Directing and motivating others; editing skills; news judgment

CAREER LADDER

```
┌─────────────────────────────┐
│  City Editor, News Editor, or │
│      Section Editor          │
└─────────────────────────────┘

┌─────────────────────────────┐
│      Assistant Editor        │
└─────────────────────────────┘

┌─────────────────────────────┐
│        Journalist            │
└─────────────────────────────┘
```

Position Description

Assistant Editors are the vanguard editors for nearly all copy, relieving editors of many tasks so they can concentrate on administrative and policy-making duties. Most Assistant Editors serve on the general-news desk, while some may report directly to a section editor.

Assistant Editors are in charge of the progression of copy through the editing process. They examine and choose stories and do the preliminary editing. They have the authority to ask reporters to make needed changes to their work. They decide on the importance of the piece and its placement and position in the upcoming issue of the newspaper. Sensitive stories may be referred to the news editor or editor in charge for special attention to decisions and/or editing.

When Assistant Editors complete their editing of stories, they hand over the material to the copy desk for additional editing and headline writing. They apprise the makeup or layout editor on the positions the stories are to occupy on various pages and their approximate lengths.

Assistant Editors help to implement editorial decisions, field questions from reporters, and, generally, assign which reporters will cover any given story. Some Assistant Editors divide their time between being journalists and working on the desk, particularly with smaller local newspapers. At times, this position is a tryout job to test a promising reporter's news judgment, editing, and management skills.

Assistant Editors can expect to be assigned to function on any shift, depending upon the changing needs of the newspaper. In addition to their other duties, Assistant Editors often write news stories themselves, and may write headlines and cutlines as well.

Salaries

Assistant Editors are often excluded from membership in the Newspaper Guild and thus are not covered by the guild's contract negotiations, as they are considered to be in a managerial position. This, however, is not a steadfast rule, and may vary from one newspaper or bargaining unit to the next.

Annual salaries may range from $24,000 to $60,000 or more, depending upon the size of the newspaper. Papers with larger circulations pay the most and have this position on staff in one form or another. The smallest papers will combine this position with that of the editor.

Employment Prospects

The Assistant Editor is typically a training post for higher editorial positions, with candidates chosen from the reporting staff. Small newspapers may offer the best opportunity for beginning Assistant Editors.

Advancement Prospects

The job of Assistant Editor is usually a stepping-stone to middle and upper editorial management positions. Moving from one paper to another as Assistant Editor is unlikely. However, an Assistant Editor on one newspaper may likely qualify for an editor's post on another newspaper based on the experience gained as Assistant Editor.

Education and Training

Most Assistant Editors have undergraduate degrees in either communications, English, journalism, or liberal arts. Print journalism graduates who are looking for entry positions as Assistant Editors should have as much experience as possible in editorial positions on college newspapers and/or journals. As the Assistant Editor is most frequently an entry-level position, most job training occurs during the execution of the editor's duties.

Experience, Skills, and Personality Traits

On small publications, a journalist with one or two years of experience may be promoted to (or hired as) an Assistant Editor. On larger papers, four to six years of reporting experience is usually required.

Assistant Editors must have excellent editing abilities and solid news judgment. They must be especially well organized and fully able to meet deadlines without fail. In addition, they should be equipped to direct, manage, and motivate others at the newspaper.

Unions and Associations

The major professional associations for Assistant Editors include the American Society of Newspaper Editors; the Association of Women in Communications; the International Society of Weekly Newspaper Editors; Investigative Reporters and Editors; the National Association of Black Journalists; the National Federation of Press Women; and the Society of Professional Journalists.

Tips for Entry

1. All the journalistic experience that can be gained during college (preferably including editing experience on, say, the college newspaper, and/or a summer internship on a newspaper) or after college would be of a help in acquiring a beginning editorial position with a newspaper.
2. Deciding on a specialty aligned with your interests (sports, food, health care, and so forth) may give you an edge in applying for a position at large newspapers where the Assistant Editors are often section editors.
3. Some production background would be useful, as Assistant Editors have to decide on page layouts and where stories can best appear on various pages of the publication.
4. Study both large and small newspapers to see how stories are handled (and learn to distinguish between what is considered important news and what is filler).

COLUMNIST

CAREER PROFILE	CAREER LADDER

Duties: Write daily or weekly column

Alternate Title(s): None

Salary Range: $20,000 to $250,000+

Employment Prospects: Poor

Advancement Prospects: Poor

Prerequisites:

Education or Training—Undergraduate degree in communications, English, journalism, or liberal arts; advance degrees required for specialized subjects

Experience—Background as journalist

Special Skills and Personality Traits—Ability to write a good story; creativity and imagination

```
┌─────────────────────────────────────┐
│   Assistant Editor or Section Editor │
└─────────────────────────────────────┘

┌─────────────────────────────────────┐
│              Columnist               │
└─────────────────────────────────────┘

┌─────────────────────────────────────┐
│      Journalist or Copy Editor       │
└─────────────────────────────────────┘
```

Position Description

The Columnist's job may be perceived as prestigious and relatively easy, but the work is a lot harder than it appears. As they are showcased and become well known, such writers are also subject to more criticism than most other journalists. Nonetheless, it is a preferred career move for reporters who choose not to advance to the editorial staff.

The majority of Columnists deal in human interest topics, local happenings, or social events. Their columns may be collections of gossipy or newsy items, usually short in duration, or they may each consist of a single feature piece revolving around a particularly interesting person, or someone's quandary, or topical events that may affect a body of people. Also common to most papers are political Columnists who scrutinize or comment on the activities of politicians, both on the local and national levels. Specialized Columnists, on the other hand, deal with just about any topic that may catch the public's fancy (or that of the newspaper's editor), such as bridge or chess, computers, health, love and romance, medicine, pets, plants, show business, and so forth. A few (that is, the elite) Columnists are nationally syndicated.

Columns may be either daily or weekly. Columnists are expected to generate their own material, which is not always an easy task. The deadline is inflexible: the column goes to press regardless of what material might be on hand.

Mostly, Columnists operate autonomously and have a great deal of freedom in what they write. They frequently become known personalities in their own right and build up a audience/fan base, thus becoming substantial assets to their newspapers. As a consequence, these newspaper personalities often can bargain for higher pay than their fellow journalists. In many instances, a position as Columnist is usually an end goal rather than an expedient means to another newspaper position. Few Columnists are willing to give up their domain and their audience for something else.

Not all Columnists work at their column full time. Many act as reporters for the general news pages of the newspaper as well. Successful Columnists often have a support staff who help in the news gathering for the column.

Salaries

At smaller newspapers, many reporters and/or editors write columns in addition to their regular duties in the hope that such experience and visibility will open the pathway for them to obtain full-time Columnist positions later. Targeted annual salary data, therefore, is too muddled to be available. Salaries for full-time Columnists generally range from starting salaries of about $20,000 to $80,000 or more. A prominent or popular Columnist may command an even higher salary (sometimes much larger depending on the reputation of the Columnist) at a large newspaper or in national or international syndication.

Columnists are sometimes grouped with reporters by the Newspaper Guild for the purposes of labor negotiations, but there may be a differential in the salaries negotiated that gives Columnists a higher salary, especially if they are well known to the public and, thus, have more professional clout.

Employment Prospects

Most newspapers do not hire journalists (beginning or experienced) to be Columnists unless they have an established track record, an audience as such, or some special cachet that gives them access to specialized news, contacts, or information of particular interest to the publication's readers. The best way to obtain a Columnist position is to use a journalist's post to build a local readership and, thus, a reputation that can be the launching point to gain a Columnist job with a larger newspaper.

Advancement Prospects

Once established, few Columnists desire to change their prestige position (which often contains many perks) for that of higher managerial jobs. However, a popular column can help establish a writer's expertise in a particular area, and lead to syndication with many newspapers and an even more public reputation as a book author or radio/television/Internet commentator.

Education and Training

Parallel to their fellow journalists, Columnists usually have undergraduate degrees in communications, English, journalism, or liberal arts. A Columnist who aspires to write about specific subject matter, such as economics, health, law, or medicine, will most likely need to have the appropriate education and credentials to support his or her writing.

Experience, Skills, and Personality Traits

The majority of Columnists are seasoned journalists, though the degree of experience varies according to the market and the medium (e.g., small or large newspapers).

Columnists have to be highly imaginative and, since most columns are short, must be able to write concisely. For human-interest topics, they need to be excellent storytellers. For political Columnists, they are expected to have good analytical skills, as well as solid news instincts. For many Columnists, their ability to make pertinent contacts and to constantly network from this base is essential to the success of their columns.

Unions and Associations

A good many Columnists are members of the Newspaper Guild union. Professional associations for Columnists include the Association of Women in Communications; the National Association of Black Journalists; the National Federation of Press Women; and the Society of Professional Journalists.

Tips for Entry

1. All the journalistic experience that can be gained during college can be helpful, such as joining the staff of the college newspaper or participating in internships.
2. In writing on a college newspaper, try your hand at writing a column and check with its readers to gauge reaction to your writing and the subjects you choose to cover.
3. Read popular newspaper Columnists daily to understand their writing style and to appreciate what the elements of the column are that make them so popular.
4. Deciding on a specialty aligned with your concerns (sports, food, entertainment, health care, or other interests) may give you an edge in your journalistic reporting that may catch the attention of editors when you apply for a Columnist position.
5. Convince your editor to let you try to write a column in addition to your other journalistic duties, in order to see the response to the topics of the column, as well as to determine whether this is a career worth pursuing. If the response to the column is positive, contact available syndicates to see what they need and pitch your ideas to them.

COPY AIDE

CAREER PROFILE	CAREER LADDER

Duties: Assist reporters and editors in low-level newsgathering, background writing, general editing, and other news-related tasks

Alternate Title(s): Copy Assistant; Copy Person; Editorial Assistant; Newsroom Assistant

Salary Range: $9,000 to $35,000+

Employment Prospects: Fair to good

Advancement Prospects: Good

Prerequisites:

Education or Training—Undergraduate degree in communications, English, journalism, or liberal arts

Experience—None

Special Skills and Personality Traits—Excellent writing ability; good interpersonal skills in dealing with the public; solid organizational abilities

```
┌─────────────────────────────────────┐
│ Journalist, Reporter, or Copy Editor │
└─────────────────────────────────────┘

┌─────────────────────────────────────┐
│              Copy Aide               │
└─────────────────────────────────────┘

┌─────────────────────────────────────┐
│           College Student            │
└─────────────────────────────────────┘
```

Position Description

The job of Copy Aides is the lowest step on the newsroom ladder, and is typically an entry-level position. They frequently are communications or journalism students who are working at newspapers while attending college. Some are journalism graduates who have been unable to land positions as reporters.

At one time, many reporters began as Copy Aides who chiefly delivered copy from reporters to editors, ran errands, and distributed material throughout the newsroom at the order of editors. Now, with most copy transmitted electronically, the job of Copy Aide has changed somewhat. Currently, Copy Aides monitor the wire machines of news services and Internet news sites and get the stories from these services into the hands of the appropriate editor. They also deliver press releases, sort mail, answer phones, assist reporters and editors, and perform general news-related tasks. As an example, a Copy Aide may help out reporters with research for their stories by interacting with the news library's collection of material. They may make basic routine calls for reporters, such as those to police stations or to regional weather services, and they may draft obituaries and other small news items. Copy Aides may work directly for either reporters or editors.

Resourceful Copy Aides may be able to transform their temporary posts into full-fledged internships and accompany reporters on assignments. This, in turn, may lead to actually writing their own stories and seeing them published in the newspaper. As a part of their training, Copy Aides also gain basic skills in the general duties of the copy desk, and may do minor editing and headline writing under the direction of an editor.

Salaries

On unionized newspapers, annual minimum wages for Copy Aides range from about $9,000 to about $35,000. While some Copy Aides at the more prestigious papers may earn even higher top minimums, most aides make toward the lower end of this scale.

Employment Prospects

College programs and internships can develop into part- and even full-time jobs as Copy Aides, though these positions also can be obtained without utilizing specific school programs. Most medium to large newspapers have a staff of Copy Aides, and many of the larger newspapers hire Copy

Aides for evening and weekend shifts, which dovetails nicely with student schedules.

Advancement Prospects

Experience as a Copy Aide, particularly if the job involves editing, researching, or writing tasks, can be an important factor in potential promotion to reporter positions or that of copy editor. Even if their particular work does not include these tasks, Copy Aides may find opportunities to utilize spare time to research and write stories. This can open the way to potential promotion either at the newspaper on which they are currently working or at another paper.

Education and Training

A goodly number of Copy Aides are undergraduate students in schools of communication, journalism, or liberal arts. When the college itself does not offer degrees in communication or journalism, it is preferable for potential Copy Aides to take as many journalism and writing courses as possible. A journalism internship is also desirable.

Experience, Skills, and Personality Traits

No particular experience is required to be a Copy Aide, but most Copy Aides are aspiring writers. Journalistic skills can be learned on the job, as the position puts the Copy Aide close to the action of a newsroom, giving the aide a comprehensive view of how a newsroom operates.

Unions and Associations

High school students may join the Quill and Scroll Society. Membership is open to all publication staff members in a chartered high school. College students may join a collegiate chapter of the Society of Professional Journalists. Some other journalist associations have specific programs or memberships for college students as well.

Tips for Entry

1. Get as much journalistic experience (on the college newspaper, or other publications) as you can during college, and look for internship programs that can lead to part- or full-time work with a newspaper.

2. As a Copy Aide, use your spare time to research and write stories, if your goal is to become a full-time reporter.

3. Think of articles that have not been covered by reporters or angles to stories that have not been pursued and pitch them to your editor.

4. Make sure all your writing assignments are well researched, error free, and submitted on time. Your editor may become an important reference for your search for a full-time reporting post.

5. Find a mentor on the staff of the newspaper (a reporter or an editor) to help you edit and polish your stories before submitting them.

COPY EDITOR

CAREER PROFILE

Duties: Edit reporters' copy for clarity, conciseness, grammar, and organization; write headlines and photo cutlines; lay out pages

Alternate Title(s): Copy Reader; Copy Chief

Salary Range: $20,000 to $60,000+

Employment Prospects: Good

Advancement Prospects: Poor

Prerequisites:

Education or Training—Undergraduate degree in communications, English, journalism, or liberal arts

Experience—Often an entry-level position; for large newspapers journalistic and copyediting experience is generally necessary

Special Skills and Personality Traits—Ability to spot weaknesses or inconsistencies in articles; careful attention to detail; creativity; excellent knowledge of grammar; speed with accuracy

CAREER LADDER

```
┌─────────────────────────────┐
│    Copy Chief or Editor     │
└─────────────────────────────┘

┌─────────────────────────────┐
│        Copy Editor          │
└─────────────────────────────┘

┌─────────────────────────────┐
│  Journalist, Copy Aide, or  │
│       College Student       │
└─────────────────────────────┘
```

Position Description

Copy Editors (who are not proofreaders, although proofreading is a part of their duties) are often the hidden heroes of the newspaper world. Reporters may get the bylines, but the quality of their writing often depends on the caliber of the Copy Editor.

The Copy Editor usually is the last person to edit a reporter's story before it is set for publication, after it has been read and edited by a news editor. For nearly every newspaper (except some small operations) there are usually several Copy Editors always available on duty, and their place is usually near the news editor and the copy chief.

Copy Editors verify the copy for correct newspaper style (that is, the publication's guidelines for consistency in how words, phrases, typographical elements, and so forth, are to be used, or not used), punctuation, spelling, and all other points of grammar. They may be allowed to question reporters about unclear sentences or discrepancies in their stories. While substantial editing is the prerogative of the news editors, Copy Editors at some publications are allowed to revise stories. Tightening up wordy prose and smoothing out awkward transitions are usually considered part of a Copy Editor's job. More extensive rewriting, usually the prerogative of assistant or assigning editors, may also be done by Copy Editors in some instances. Usually news editors are under too much deadline stress to spend a great deal of time painstakingly editing each piece, so this chore may become one more duty of the Copy Editor.

A Copy Editor's mandate also includes looking out for potential libel (defamatory untruths or rumors that could lead to lawsuits), questionable facts, and actual errors of fact. In addition, Copy Editors write headlines ("heds") and photo captions (or "cutlines") for the stories they handle (though assistant editors, if there are any on the particular newspaper, may also do this task). Copy Editors may also handle page layouts, that is, designing pages, and they usually have some sort of page-makeup tasks.

At deadline time the work pace is accelerated and Copy Editors must make speedy and correct news judgment decisions. During slow times, enterprising Copy Editors research and write news or feature stories for the paper. Also, Copy Editors may monitor wire service terminals and the Internet for incoming stories.

Copy Editors report to the copy chief, who works in coordination with the news editor in charge. Sometimes, especially on the small newspapers, the copy chief is also the wire editor or page-makeup editor.

Salaries

Experienced Copy Editors usually make more than general reporters. On some newspapers the starting pay for both jobs is approximately the same, but Copy Editors, who are usually in great demand, move up the salary scale more quickly.

On smaller newspapers, median annual salaries for Copy Editors range from the low $20,000s (usually a beginner salary) to the high $20,000s to the mid $30,000s after several years of experience. At the larger newspapers (with circulations of 5,000 or more), beginning Copy Editors make a median yearly salary from the mid $30,000s to the low or mid $40,000s, and the more experienced Copy Editors (three to five years' experience) may expect a median annual salary in the upper $40,000s to the low $60,000s.

Employment Prospects

While taken as a whole the journalism job market is highly competitive, it is often less difficult to get a position as a Copy Editor than as a journalist or reporter. Copy Editors tend to be in high demand. Many would-be reporters take a post as Copy Editor in order to get on the payroll of a desired newspaper, and then work their way into reporting by writing stories on their own time. Some newspapers even require every journalist on staff to spend a stretch of time on the copy desk before joining the reportorial staff.

Advancement Prospects

Copy Editors' goals vary widely. Some of them enjoy working only with copy and have little interest in actual news reporting, while some individuals wish to utilize their experience as soon as possible to move into a reporting position.

The usual career path for Copy Editors is to move upward to copy chief and/or wire editor. Those Copy Editors with experience in news reporting may look for promotion to assistant news editor or assistant city editor jobs, supervising reporters and making decisions about news coverage. Most top-level managerial positions in the newsroom (for example, executive editor or editor-in-chief) require news reporting experience.

Since good Copy Editors are not easy to find and, thus, are in great demand, it may be easier to get a copyediting position than a reporting job. However, if the ultimate goal is to become a reporter, taking a position as Copy Editor may make that switch harder, unless a transfer to a smaller newspaper is made, or even a move out of the main newsroom into a news bureau.

Education and Training

An undergraduate degree in journalism or mass communications is usually required. A degree in English may be especially valuable for a Copy Editor, while a liberal arts degree may be acceptable at some newspapers.

Experience, Skills, and Personality Traits

Copyediting is often an entry-level job, although some of the larger newspapers may require experience before hiring. The Copy Editor must be highly skilled in grammar, punctuation, and spelling, as well as be able to edit quickly and under pressure of deadlines. Knowledge of type point sizes and column pica widths are necessary for the writing of headlines and cutlines. Other typographical knowledge is also a necessity. The ability to write tight and catchy phrases is also valuable in the devising of headlines and cutlines.

Newspaper Copy Editors have to be painstakingly thorough in their labor, be able to function under deadline pressures, and be flexible in their working hours to fit the required deadlines.

Unions and Associations

The Newspaper Guild, affiliated with the AFL-CIO, represents Copy Editors on most newspapers. Professional associations for Copy Editors include the Association for Women in Communications; the National Association of Black Journalists; and the Society of Professional Journalists. In addition, Copy Editors sometimes join a wide range of groups or associations related to the writing or editing fields.

Tips for Entry

1. All the journalistic experience (such as on the campus newspaper) that can be gained during college will be helpful.
2. Summer internships at local or city newspapers may be excellent experience and the best possibility for employment after college.
3. Copyediting jobs can be found at places other than newspapers. Nonprofit organizations and big companies that have publication needs (newsletters, brochures, and so forth) are always in need of Copy Editors, as are Internet-based publications. They might be a good place to begin building a résumé that will get you a job on a newspaper.
4. Once employed at a newspaper, network with other editors, read journalism publications, and attend journalism conferences to further your pursuit of a higher editorial or reporter position.

CRITIC

CAREER PROFILE

Duties: Review artistic performances, exhibits, books, and recordings; write columns

Alternate Title(s): Reviewer

Salary Range: $18,000 to $60,000+

Employment Prospects: Poor

Advancement Prospects: Poor

Prerequisites:

Education or Training—Undergraduate degree in communications, English, journalism, or liberal arts; specialization in particular field may require further course work or degree

Experience—Background as a journalist and expertise in the area being reviewed

Special Skills and Personality Traits—Good writing ability; thorough knowledge of area of subject matter

CAREER LADDER

```
┌─────────────────────────────────┐
│        Section Editor           │
└─────────────────────────────────┘

┌─────────────────────────────────┐
│            Critic               │
└─────────────────────────────────┘

┌─────────────────────────────────┐
│   Journalist or Copy Editor     │
└─────────────────────────────────┘
```

Position Description

A Critic may be defined as one who is professionally engaged in the analysis, evaluation, interpretation, and judgment of literary or artistic works. Critics can exert a great degree of influence on the public and can affect the success, of artists, books, films, musical and/or dance productions, and plays. Good reviews can help to ensure financial success, and bad reviews can lead audiences to stay away from movies or plays. Good or bad reviews can shape the sales of books, recordings, and even artwork.

The Critic can also provoke a public discussion about the subjects being reviewed and aid that discussion by putting the creative works under consideration in their historical, social, or political contexts in their columns. In this way, readers can be stimulated to become involved in critical give and take with other readers or viewers and thus help enrich public perception of art forms.

Critics often work evenings and weekends, attending concerts and operas, dance productions, art galleries and museums, films, nightclub acts, and plays. They may review anything connected with the arts and entertainment fields, including books and recordings, and write their opinions in columns on a regular or irregular basis. They may be very specialized in what they do: music Critics do not often review films or plays, art Critics, in addition to writing about exhibitions, may review books about art only, and so forth. Some small- or medium-size newspapers, however, have only one or two persons on staff to take on all the arts and entertainment reviewing.

Critics are expected to be well informed about their subjects and remain up-to-date with all developments and trends on these subjects. They frequently interview artists, celebrities, and performers, and must do extensive reading in and studying of their areas of expertise. They need to maintain an objectivity toward their subjects and have good artistic judgment. Like columnists, Critics often build a readership who believe in and act upon their views and opinions.

Besides preparing their review columns, Critics often write celebrity interviews, feature articles, and comprehensive articles on new directions or other aspects of the arts and entertainment fields.

Salaries

Critics earn approximately the same amount as, or in some cases, more than their fellow experienced journalists, roughly $18,000 to $60,000 or more per year. High salaries depend much upon the credentials and experience of the

Critic, as well as the size of the newspaper for which they work.

The Newspaper Guild sometimes includes Critics with reporters in its negotiations for salaries with newspapers. Nonetheless, Critics (similar to columnists) may get a differential increase in their salaries, especially if they are well known and are particularly popular with their reading public.

Employment Prospects

Many Critics begin as journalists of one kind or another and work their way into full-time positions as Critics by doing occasional reviews, or filling in for indisposed staff Critics. A position as a staff writer or assistant editor for the lifestyle or arts-and-entertainment sections of a newspaper is one of the best ways to break into the desired field. Once a Critic is established and has become well known, it is possible to change employers, but the competition is stiff as this job market tends to be quite tight. A very few Critics may also make a name for themselves with public appearances on such media as radio, television, or the Internet. (Roger Ebert of the *Chicago Sun-Times* is the outstanding present example of this.)

Advancement Prospects

As with newspaper columnists, most Critics would prefer to remain Critics and not undertake any other kind of news work. The one advancement that might be likely is to become editor of the arts-and-entertainment section or the book review section.

Education and Training

Critics are required to have thorough background in their subject area(s), as well as a basic undergraduate education in communications, English, journalism, or liberal arts. This background may involve specialized or advanced degrees in order to bolster the credentials of the Critic.

Experience, Skills, and Personality Traits

Critics must be extremely knowledgeable of their specialization in order to write balanced, impartial reviews. This requires them to read extensively and study their field(s) often. They should be expert in interviewing artists and celebrities and be able to write quickly and concisely to meet deadlines. As Bob Ross, the *Tampa* (Florida) *Tribune*'s film Critic says, "I see a movie Tuesday night and my review is due Wednesday. Fifteen inches. It has to be fast and I have to fill the space. I don't have time for dissertations, and neither does the reader."

Unions and Associations

Professional associations for Critics include the American Theatre Critics Association, the Association for Women in Communications, the Dance Critics Association, the Music Critics Association of North America, the National Association of Black Journalists, the National Federation of Press Women, and the Society of Professional Journalists. The Newspaper Guild negotiates wages for many journalists, including Critics.

Tips for Entry

1. All the journalistic experience (preferably including writing experience on, say, the campus newspaper) that can be gained during college (or after) would be of great help in gaining a beginning position with a newspaper.
2. Try your hand at reviewing while working on your college newspaper (or when you get a summer Internship with a local newspaper) or for an Internet site.
3. In going after a position with a newspaper to land a job (eventually) as a Critic, identify as your target the newspaper(s) that have a Critic position on staff. Contact a section editor, or an assistant or deputy managing editor as your best contact there, and keep in touch with them.
4. Hone your expertise in your chosen field of interest by further course work and lots of reading, all of which can only enhance your reviewing skills.
5. Practice your interviewing skills on whomever you can, and write up the results to critically appraise your writing abilities.

EDITORIAL WRITER

CAREER PROFILE

Duties: Research and write editorial comments on issues and topics of reader interest to stimulate or mold public opinion, in accordance with viewpoints and policies of a publication; screen columns, letters to the editor, and other editorial articles; help decide newspaper's position on issues

Alternate Title(s): Editorial Page Editor

Salary Range: $25,000 to $125,000+

Employment Prospects: Fair

Advancement Prospects: Fair

Prerequisites:

Education or Training—Undergraduate degree in communications, English, journalism, or liberal arts; advanced degree helpful

Experience—Background as editor and journalist

Special Skills and Personality Traits—Excellent and clear writing; logical thought processes; objectivity; persuasiveness; thoroughness in accuracy and detail

CAREER LADDER

```
┌─────────────────────────────────────┐
│   Senior Editor or Managing Editor   │
└─────────────────────────────────────┘

┌─────────────────────────────────────┐
│           Editorial Writer           │
└─────────────────────────────────────┘

┌─────────────────────────────────────┐
│    News Editor, Section Editor, or   │
│              Journalist              │
└─────────────────────────────────────┘
```

Position Description

Editorial Writers are concerned primarily with the issues generated by, or lying behind, events rather than the news of the events. Thus they usually work away from the daily busywork and commotion of the newsroom. Their primary responsibility is the contents of the editorial page and the page opposite it, termed the "Op-Ed" page. Usually, they report directly to the publisher.

Generally, the opinion section of a newspaper is split into two sections: the editorial page and the Op-Ed page. Editorials are written by Editorial Writers and reflect the opinion of the newspaper, representing both the quality and character of the publication. Editorial pieces are submitted and discussed with senior editorial staff for approval. Op-Ed pieces are sometimes written by newspaper staff (Editorial Writers generally) but more often are written by non-staff persons expressing views that are not necessarily endorsed by the publication. Nonetheless, the Editorial Writer is responsible for the grammar, punctuation, and so forth (if not the style) of such articles.

Editorial Writers make up an editorial board, which also encompasses members of senior management (editor, man-

aging editor, and/or senior editor) and the publisher. A small newspaper may have one or two Editorial Writers to share all the duties, whereas a large publication may allow particular Editorial Writers to focus on subject areas of their expertise (such as fiscal matters, international affairs, or national and local politics). On the largest newspapers junior Editorial Writers may be assigned to do the necessary research for more senior Editorial Writers of the board.

Editorial Writers explore issues that arise and the events that surround them, research those issues, and decide on a position for the newspaper. Some editorials will be timely, in quick response to the latest breaking news. Others, on topics of interest but not necessarily tied to current events, may be researched and written more leisurely for publication at a later date. Editorial Writers undertake their research investigation the same way reporters do theirs, by calling sources and consulting library clips, other published sources, and Internet sites. In addition, Editorial Writers sometimes consult journalists who covered events related to the issue at hand.

In examining a matter, Editorial Writers must be comprehensive and accurate in their appraisal. So that they can be wholly informed about local, national, and international news, most Editorial Writers do extensive reading of other news and commentaries from other publications and media sources. All sides of the issue at hand must be carefully weighted in order to arrive at a measured editorial position for the newspaper. The influence of editorial opinion is widespread. For example, it is well recognized that members of Congress (and of local governing bodies) pay attention to the opinion pages of the local newspapers as another means of staying in touch with their local constituencies.

In addition, Editorial Writers screen letters for the "letters to the editors" section, as well as the opinion columns to be included on the Op-Ed page. These pieces may be written by newspaper staff but, generally, are more likely written by syndicated writers or local opinion makers.

Smaller newspapers may only have an editorial page editor to write the editorials and supervise the letters and opinion sections, or the news editor may write them.

Salaries

The Newspaper Guild often bargains for Editorial Writers along with copy editors, but this may depend upon how the management of the publication views the job of Editorial Writer. In some cases, there may be a differential that gives Editorial Writers a higher salary than copy editors, especially if the Editorial Writer is experienced and well known.

Annual salaries may range from $25,000 to $125,000 or more for long-term, experienced, and well-known Editorial Writers. The larger the circulation of the paper, the higher the salaries tend to be.

Employment Prospects

Several years of experience are required to season a journalist for the position of Editorial Writer. Candidates have to display their reporting and analytical abilities as journalists first. In addition, editorial experience as a newsroom editor may be necessary as well.

According to the U.S. Department of Labor's Bureau of Labor Statistics (in its *2004 Occupational Outlook Handbook*), employment of news analysts is expected to grow more slowly than most other occupations through the year 2012, as a result of mergers, consolidations, and closures of newspapers, decreased circulation, increased expenses, and a decline in advertising profits. Furthermore, according to this study, the best opportunities will be with small-town and suburban newspapers, as competition will remain especially keen in the large metropolitan and national newspapers.

Advancement Prospects

Some opportunities exist for advancement within the editorial board staff structure. However, senior management at most newspapers are selected from editors who run the daily operations of the newsroom. Many Editorial Writers have no desire to leave the editorial department for the newsroom, thus limiting their chances for significant advancement at the publication.

Education and Training

Editorial Writers should have at least an undergraduate degree in communications, English, journalism, or liberal arts. Graduate degrees in business, economics, law, or other similar subjects are likely to help career advancement for an Editorial Writer, due mainly to the specialized nature of many editorial-writing positions.

Experience, Skills, and Personality Traits

Many Editorial Writers will have had several years of experience as journalists, and in some cases even as newsroom editors. Before being promoted into the position of Editorial Writer, they must demonstrate their ability to write balanced, clear, and concise news analyses and accurate news stories. They must display their good news judgment, their objectivity, and their accomplished editorial skills.

As Editorial Writers they will have to do thorough research, as well as extensive reading to be constantly aware of public opinion and public trends. They need to be well-organized and able to work under tight deadlines.

Unions and Associations

Associations include the American Society of Newspaper Editors; the Association for Women in Communications; the International Society of Weekly Newspaper Editors; the National Association of Black Journalists; the National Conference of Editorial Writers; the National Federation of Press Women; and the Society of Professional Journalists.

Tips for Entry

1. All the journalistic experience (preferably including writing and editing experience on, say, the campus newspaper) that can be gained during college (or after) would be of a help in gaining a beginning position with a newspaper.
2. After gaining experience as a journalist with a publication, get acquainted with the editorial style of the newspaper by writing pieces for the Op-Ed page and to gain an entrée with the editorial staff.
3. Study the publication's editorial page over a period of time to familiarize yourself with the editorial stance of the paper.
4. Become familiar with standard reference and potential research studies, and explore the Internet for useful reference/research portals and Web sites.
5. Strive for strong political connections, within the community, which will be invaluable for your work as an Editorial Writer.

FINANCIAL WIRE REPORTER

CAREER PROFILE

Duties: Track the performance of companies and financial markets and report on changes that might affect the economy or the stock market; report economic developments and indicators; provide other financial information of interest to the wire service's customers

Alternate Title(s): Real-time Financial Database Reporter

Salary Range: $23,000 to $80,000+

Employment Prospects: Fair

Advancement Prospects: Fair

Prerequisites:

Education or Training—Undergraduate degree in communications, English, journalism, or liberal arts; course work in business, computers, and economics will be very helpful

Experience—Entry-level positions require none; otherwise, experience at a newspaper, trade publication, or wire service as a journalist is required; some public relations experience a plus

Special Skills and Personality Traits—Must be able to work accurately and quickly to meet deadlines; should be aggressive and determined; able to clarify complicated business and financial information in a direct and clear manner without distorting its meaning

CAREER LADDER

```
┌─────────────────────────────────────────┐
│   Newspaper Business Reporter or         │
│   Trade Magazine Financial Reporter      │
└─────────────────────────────────────────┘

┌─────────────────────────────────────────┐
│        Financial Wire Reporter           │
└─────────────────────────────────────────┘

┌─────────────────────────────────────────┐
│  Entry-Level Position or College Student │
└─────────────────────────────────────────┘
```

Position Description

A wire service is *not* a newspaper. It is a company, or a cooperative news venture, that specializes in the gathering and distributing of news. Before the advent of online computer services, a wire service job involved working for one of several worldwide service companies that supplied both general and specific topical news to newspapers. Now with the widespread use of online computer services, the World Wide Web, and e-mail newsletters, anyone interested in a specific topic can subscribe to news services or databases or e-mail newsletters that are devoted to the specific field on a "real-time" basis. Some of these services also provide copy to newspapers, but others are strictly designed for subscribers.

Some Financial Wire Reporters file stories intended for mainstream newspapers, which take these stories off the wire and print them. Other reporters send their information directly to subscribers of the online service electronically, bypassing the printed word altogether. In the case of business and financial wire reporting, this information helps money managers decide what investments to make, and when.

Because this is such a specialized audience, the pressure for accuracy on the part of the Financial Wire Reporter is even more intense than on those in other wire reporting positions. Investors on Wall Street need information as soon as it becomes available, as any delay may cost them a great deal of money in the missed opportunity to act on the information in a timely fashion. In addition, it could have marked financial repercussions on the wire service subscribers.

Likewise, any information that might affect the stock of a particular company must be put out "on the wire" immediately, even if only in the briefest notational or headline form. Then, further details have to follow as soon as possible as reporters hustle to be the first with the news.

Financial Wire Reporters usually work a regular workhour day, as their work is tied tightly to the business hours of the stock market. However, as hot topics (such as business acquisitions, mergers, or financial repositions) occur, a Financial Wire Reporter can expect to put in as many hours as it takes to follow the story completely.

As many financial wire services also offer general news, reporters may find they have to work weekends preparing news summaries, or even be called upon during off-hours to cover hot, breaking business stories.

In some cases, Financial Wire Reporters may cover a specific industry, following changes within that particular industry and its assorted businesses, as well as tracking fluctuating stock prices within the industry and attempting to discover why a particular stock price has altered dramatically and to speculate upon its effect upon the industry as a whole.

Salaries

Salaries in the wire service field generally are higher than those at newspapers, according to the Newspaper Guild. The guild negotiates wire service reporter's salaries, including those of Financial Wire Reporters, when they begin work at a unionized wire service, and usually during their entire tenure at a wire service. Salaries may diverge widely dependent upon the size of the organization and the experience of the journalist.

Annual salaries of Financial Wire Reporters are usually similar to those of other general wire reporters, ranging from the low $20,000s for beginning reporters to the $80,000s or higher for those Financial Wire Reporters with years of experience. Pay tends to be highest in those cities that have the highest cost of living.

Employment Prospects

With all the mergers, consolidations, and closures of newspapers of the last several years, many news-supplying organizations have suffered severe cutbacks. However, business service databases and financial wire services have tended to blossom along with the huge expansion of the Internet. Competition among wire services has increased, particularly as the more traditional wire service companies have added business-reporting resources to their staffs to stay competitive. Due to the affluence and specificity of its target market, financial wire services have a ready-made audience and a guarantee of income from its marketplace to sustain growth.

Opportunities in the field of business and financial service reporting are better than those in general news, due to both the aforementioned captive audience and the slower growth of employment. The accelerating market for financial news to be made available online from such electronic information services makes the job of a Financial Wire Reporter all the more attractive.

Advancement Prospects

At the newer wire service companies, advancement can be more rapid than elsewhere, as the company's constant growth is continually opening up fresh opportunities. Some financial wire services maintain bureaus in major cities around the globe, particularly in New York and Tokyo to cover the stock markets in those key metropolises. Experience in the financial wire services also can lead to jobs at business and financial magazines, or other business and trade publications, as well as to online services.

Education and Training

As with most other jobs in journalism, Financial Wire Reporters should have an undergraduate degree in communications, journalism, English, or liberal arts. In addition, courses (or even advanced degrees) in business, computers, or economics are highly desirable.

Experience, Skills, and Personality Traits

Most financial and business wire services expect their newly hired reporters to already be conversant with sophisticated financial matters and to fully understand the world's financial markets. Some other services prefer to hire promising young writers or journalists and train/educate them about the business world in-house. Notwithstanding this, previous experience as a business reporter elsewhere, or a background in business or economics with good writing skills are excellent qualifications for the job of a Financial Wire Reporter. Proficiency in one or more foreign languages is a plus.

Financial Wire Reporters need to be aggressive, resolute, and persistent. They must have good news judgment and be able to act quickly on their instincts honed by their knowledge of the world's financial markets and trends.

Unions and Associations

The Newspaper Guild represents employees of some of the financial wire service companies. For these companies now devoting so much of their business to their electronic information services, the Software and Information Industry Association has become a pertinent trade association for them. Financial Wire Reporters may also belong to such other professional associations as the American Press Institute, the International Press Institute, the National Press Club, and the Society of Professional Journalists, as well as appropriate business or financial professional organizations.

Tips for Entry

1. All the journalistic experience (on the campus news-paper, or in internships) that can be gained during college is necessary for the demands of working for a news wire service.

2. Look for internship programs with local newspapers or broadcast stations to add practical journalistic experience to your college course work. Working as part of a news staff in competition with others will provide you with a valuable insight into the news world beyond the campus.

3. Take as many business and economics courses as are available to you to understand today's financial markets both nationally and internationally.

4. Besides your business and financial knowledge-gathering, familiarize yourself thoroughly with the workings of the Internet and the related computer technology.

GENERAL ASSIGNMENT REPORTER

CAREER PROFILE

Duties: Collect and report information for news and feature stories on a broad range of subjects

Alternate Title(s): Bureau Reporter; Journalist

Salary Range: $17,000 to $70,000+

Employment Prospects: Fair to Good

Advancement Prospects: Fair

Prerequisites:

Education or Training—Undergraduate degree in communications, English, journalism, or liberal arts

Experience—Work on a college newspaper or internship for small daily or weekly newspapers; minimum of one to two years' professional journalistic experience for most large dailies.

Special Skills and Personality Traits—Aggressiveness; excellent organizational ability; good interpersonal skills; persistence; self-discipline; solid research habits

CAREER LADDER

```
┌─────────────────────────────────────────┐
│   Assistant Editor, Reporter Specialist, │
│              or Section Editor            │
└─────────────────────────────────────────┘

┌─────────────────────────────────────────┐
│        General Assignment Reporter        │
└─────────────────────────────────────────┘

┌─────────────────────────────────────────┐
│        Copy Aide or College Student       │
└─────────────────────────────────────────┘
```

Position Description

General Assignment Reporters can cover topics and events of all kinds. If they are based at a newsroom, an assignment editor gives them news stories. If the reporter works in an bureau distant from the newsroom covering a particular geographic area or another city, the field assignments are made in conjunction with a bureau chief after the reporter has checked with sources and prepared a brief presentation of the gist of the story.

General Assignment Reporters must operate at a quick pace, meet their deadlines, and then, flexibly, move on quickly to the next project, regardless of its subject (or how different it may be from the one they have just completed). For example, they may cover a local fire, next handle a governmental meeting or press conference, and then turn to interviewing a visiting celebrity. In addition, General Assignment Reporters frequently do follow-up pieces on subjects last covered in their newspaper by someone else. In these cases, they need to quickly find and read through all other relevant stories on the topic and any other related material, as well as follow all major stories currently appearing in their newspaper. Much of this work has to be accomplished on a daily basis—even on the days they are not assigned stories—so that they can fill in at a minute's notice.

On smaller newspapers or in many bureaus, General Assignment Reporters are also the photographers assigned to the piece. They may also give out assignments to freelance reporters (otherwise known as stringers), and edit the resulting stories, or file the breaking story directly from the scene using laptop computers or by dictating the story over the phone.

Because these wide-ranging duties of a General Assignment Reporter help build solid journalistic skills in many areas, a good number of newspapers require inexperienced reporters to labor as General Assignment Reporters before considering them for any type of specialty reporting.

As a rule, General Assignment Reporters work lengthy hours and cope with irregular schedules. Long-range reporting projects may be interrupted by breaking news, making it difficult to plan ahead. Night and weekend shifts are common, and reporters may have to travel to follow stories. Depending on how many editions the newspaper prints, deadlines may occur around the clock (as with some large newspapers) or one or two times a day (for smaller dailies). At morning newspapers, reporters might work from late afternoon to midnight. At evening or afternoon papers, they may toil from early morning until mid afternoon. At all times they need to be flexible in changing their work hours to suit the demands of following particular stories.

Salaries

According to the U.S. Department of Labor's Bureau of Labor Statistics, as reported in their *Occupational Outlook Handbook* in March of 2004, annual salaries for reporters during 2002 throughout the United States ranged from a low of $17,600 to a high of $69,500, but within large urban centers, such as New York City, the yearly salaries tended to be higher. For New York, the low was $21,600, and the high was $104,500.

Newspaper reporters' salaries are negotiated by the Newspaper Guild-CWA when they start a new job at a Newspaper Guild paper, and again after a specified number of years, all of which varies from one paper to another. Pay differs widely as well. According to the Newspaper Guild's salary survey of 2003, the top minimum weekly salary after two years at the *New York Times* was $1,445.17, whereas the top minimum weekly salary after four years at the Rochester (New York) *Democrat & Chronicle* was $419. The survey found that the average reporter top minimum as of January 1, 2003, was $857.42 (or an annual salary of approximately $44,585).

Employment Prospects

Employment of reporters is expected to grow more slowly than the average for most other occupations through the year 2012, according to the U.S. Department of Labor's Bureau of Labor Statistics as reported in their *Occupational Outlook Handbook* in March of 2004. This is mainly a result of closures of newspapers, consolidations, and mergers, as well as decreased circulation with the resultant decline in advertising profits, and an increase in expenses.

The best opportunities will be with small town and suburban newspapers. The number of large daily metropolitan and national newspapers is expected to remain relatively static, with competition for reporter jobs remaining keen. Some job openings may occur as established journalists leave the field altogether or transfer to other media, such as Internet and multimedia reporting.

Advancement Prospects

Advancement prospects remain fair. Reporters based at news bureaus in the field generally move into city pressroom jobs, starting out as General Assignment Reporters and moving their way into more specialized reporting positions or management. The first step into management is often as section editor or assistant editor.

Some General Assignment Reporters make a lateral transfer into Internet reporting. Typically, print reporters are more prepared by their work experience in the print media for Internet journalism than are television reporters, thus making it easier for print news reporters to make the necessary adjustments in a new media.

Education and Training

Most newspapers require from General Assignment Reporters an undergraduate degree in communications, English, journalism, or liberal arts. The traditional educational path is a bachelor's degree in journalism. Some newspaper employers feel, however, that a well-rounded education is just as valuable a preparation for a newspaper person. Others feel that the practical instruction offered by programs within a journalism curriculum is more valuable. In the long run, it is the practical experience in writing, whether on the school paper or in an internship program, that is important.

Experience, Skills, and Personality Traits

The position of General Assignment Reporter is generally considered to be an entry level into reporting as a career. Having writing experience while in college, or in an internship program, can help to distinguish newcomers from the rest of the applicants.

General Assignment Reporters need to be very attentive to detail, good listeners, and versatile. They must not be intimidated by anyone or any story, and they must be willing to ask questions endlessly. They need to be able to research topics thoroughly and be able to explain complex subjects in a clear, simple way to a lay audience. A nose for news, initiative, a good memory, persistence, poise, and physical stamina are important, as is emotional stability in dealing with pressing deadlines. Above all, accuracy, clarity, and speed in writing is critical.

Unions and Associations

The Newspaper Guild is the primary union for print journalists. Other professional associations include the American Society of Journalists and Authors; Investigative Reporters and Editors; and the Society of Professional Journalists. In addition, there are numerous professional associations that represent reporters in a wide variety of specialties or reporters of different racial or ethnic backgrounds.

Tips for Entry

1. Get as much journalistic experience (on the college newspaper, or in internships) as you can during college to prepare you for the constant demands of a General Assignment Reporter.
2. Look for internship programs with local newspapers or broadcast stations to add practical journalistic experience to your college course work. Working as

part of a news staff in competition with others will provide you with a valuable insight into the news world beyond the campus.

3. Extend your skills in computer technology to include a thorough knowledge of word processing, computer graphics, and desktop publishing methodologies.

4. Other valuable courses to take in college include computer science, speech, and as many courses in writing as you can find.

5. Add photography to your list of specialties, as well as at least one foreign language, which is bound to become handy one day in your journalistic career.

6. Offer to write reporting articles for local community publications to gain experience.

NEWS EDITOR

CAREER PROFILE

Duties: Supervise a news-gathering staff; establish the direction and content of the newspaper; make policy decisions

Alternate Title(s): City Editor; Executive Editor; Metropolitan Editor

Salary Range: $38,000 to $90,000+

Employment Prospects: Fair

Advancement Prospects: Good

Prerequisites:

　Education or Training—Undergraduate degree in communications, English, journalism, or liberal arts

　Experience—Extensive background in reporting and copyediting required

　Special Skills and Personality Traits—Ability to supervise and motivate others; editing skills; good news judgment

CAREER LADDER

```
┌─────────────────────────────────────┐
│ Assistant Managing Editor, Managing  │
│    Editor, or Executive Editor       │
└─────────────────────────────────────┘

┌─────────────────────────────────────┐
│             News Editor              │
└─────────────────────────────────────┘

┌─────────────────────────────────────┐
│   Assistant Editor or Section Editor │
└─────────────────────────────────────┘
```

Position Description

The News Editor is the major person who supervises the day-to-day operations of a newsroom. This highly visible position is responsible for the quality of the newspaper and plays a key role in the decision-making process of gathering, evaluating, interpreting, and packaging news. News Editors must keep on top of all major breaking and developing news stories, must determine how the paper will cover these stories, how they will be displayed on the pages, and where in the newspaper the stories will appear. They also must decide who will write the stories. News Editors keep aware of all reporters' activities, and must make instantaneous decisions on how to deal with breaking news.

News Editors generally make story assignments (or direct assignment editors in this task) and select which reporters will handle what beats (i.e., regular assignments, such as police work, society news, and other such topics). Besides editing copy, News Editors watch the progress of stories and the progression of copy through the editing process. They ensure that all the news in which the newspaper is interested is being covered, with suitable photographs and graphics. They get together daily with higher-level editors (such as the managing editor, executive editor, or senior

editor) to settle on the content and direction of the newspaper and to thrash out any current problems.

In addition to their editing and flow supervision duties, News Editors are also staff administrators. They prepare work schedules for reporters and assistant editors, settle problems, write reports and summaries for upper management, and have a substantial say in the hiring, promotion, and firing of subordinates in light of all labor laws pertaining to their employees. Above all, and most crucially, they have to be able to work within a given budget.

Finally, News Editors link directly with the community at large. Often they will speak for, or represent the paper, at civic functions and in classrooms.

On a small or local newspaper, the News Editor may control the operation of the entire newsroom, and have no assistant editors. On the largest papers, typically the News Editor post is divided into geographic (or subject) areas, and individual News Editors are assigned to them, with one or more helpers.

The job of News Editor is extremely challenging, as an average shift can embrace a wide array of news and administrative duties. While News Editors generally work a regular business-hour day, that day may run long dependent upon breaking major stories. The counterpart of the News Editor for the nighttime shift is the night editor, who oversees the operation of the newsroom when the News Editor's day ends.

Salaries

News Editors are generally excluded from Newspaper Guild contracts as they are considered management. However, this may vary from one newspaper or bargaining unit to another.

Annual salaries vary widely from a low of about $38,000 to $90,000 or more, depending upon the circulation of the paper and the length of employment of the News Editor and the extent of the editor's duties. The larger the paper, usually the higher the salary.

Employment Prospects

Experienced and accomplished News Editors are always in demand on papers of all sizes, with opportunities best found with small daily newspapers and weeklies (local and national). While the number of potential competitors for a job is smaller than that for reporters, opportunities for News Editors may be restricted more by the size of the publication and the need for relocation.

Advancement Prospects

Successful and skilled News Editors are in a unique and excellent position for advancement into upper management, particularly as they work closely with this supervisory level on a day-to-day basis.

Education and Training

Most News Editors have an undergraduate degree in communications, English, journalism, or liberal arts. Advanced degrees are not crucial, but may be useful. Additional training or course work in business administration and management is almost a requirement for this position.

Experience, Skills, and Personality Traits

On a small or local newspaper, three to five years of experience as a journalist, a section editor, or an assistant editor can give one the needed credentials for News Editor. On larger papers, the usual requirement is five to 10 years or more of such background.

News Editors must be well skilled in editing and rewriting, as well as in making quick decisions. They should also be proficient at handling personnel matters and practiced in general management techniques. They must be quite detail-oriented and well organized to fulfill their necessary administrative duties. Skill and ease in public speaking is another prerequisite if the job encompasses community liaison activities.

Unions and Associations

Major professional associations include the American Society of Newspaper Editors; the International Society of Weekly Newspaper Editors; the Investigative Reporters and Editors Association; and the Society of Professional Journalists. Others include the Association for Women in Communications; the National Association of Black Journalists; and the National Federation of Press Women.

Tips for Entry

1. All the journalistic experience (preferably including editing experience on, say, the campus newspaper) that can be gained during college (or after) would be a help in gaining a beginning editorial position with a newspaper.
2. Achieve as much on-the-job experience in both the editing and production processes, even to switching employers to acquire the varied background and training needed by a News Editor.
3. Enroll in business management courses to increase your administrative abilities.
4. Take speech courses to brush up your verbal communication skills.
5. Attend journalism conferences and network with other editors to keep informed on journalistic matters other than the news.

NEWS LIBRARIAN/RESEARCHER

CAREER PROFILE

Duties: Gather, catalog, and maintain information for use by journalists; perform research using Internet, telephone, and print resources for journalists under great deadline pressure

Alternate Title(s): News Information Resource Manager; News Library Director; Newspaper Library Manager

Salary Range: $14,000 to $75,000+

Employment Prospects: Fair to good

Advancement Prospects: Fair

Prerequisites:

Education or Training—Undergraduate degree in communications, English, journalism, or liberal arts; graduate degree in library science for jobs on many (especially the larger) newspapers

Experience—Extensive newspaper experience required, particularly if applicant has no library science degree or library experience; computer skills a necessity

Special Skills and Personality Traits—Excellent research skills; expertise in computerized research techniques; good organizational habits; knowledge of newsroom operations; solid oral and written communication skills; talent for working with journalists under deadline stress

CAREER LADDER

```
┌─────────────────────────────────┐
│     News Library Director        │
└─────────────────────────────────┘

┌─────────────────────────────────┐
│   News Librarian/Researcher      │
└─────────────────────────────────┘

┌─────────────────────────────────┐
│ Library Clerk, Library Assistant, or │
│      Assistant Researcher        │
└─────────────────────────────────┘
```

Position Description

Once a job filled by journalists near retirement (hence the traditional name for a news library as a morgue) or newsroom managers looking for something else to do, traditional news libraries changed as new technology opened new vistas from the 1970s onward. By the late 1980s advanced technology, such as computer-output microfiche, optical disks, computerized indexing, automated full-text retrieval systems, digital photo archiving, online database searching, spreadsheets, computer-assisted reporting, and media polling had appeared on the newspaper scene. Papers were now using commercial electronic systems for full-text storage and retrieval of newspaper stories.

Where News Librarians simply used to handle folders of clippings, today's News Librarians and Researchers manage the information resources library that is stored on files, on tape or microfilm, or in computers for use by news and editorial staffs. As Nora Paul, library director of the Poynter Institute of Media Studies in St. Petersburg, Florida, states, News Librarians "are the collectors, managers, and redistributors of the organization's primary product, information. This is critical in all stages of information's flow through the organization—initial information gathering for use in news reporting, in the collection of the news product into databases, in the repackaging of information created by the organization into new products."

News Librarians are responsible for directing the activities of workers engaged in the clipping, scanning, classifying, cataloging, indexing, and coding of news stories, and retrieving information on demand for the newsroom, or performing these tasks themselves as needed. They research, retrieve, and disseminate information from the resource library or from commercial databases in response to requests from news or editorial staff. They maintain records and statistics on the use of the databases and information services provided. They often manage the in-house database of news information, assign classification terms to news articles, input news articles into the database, and research news information for the in-house database. At some papers, being the resident computer technology experts, they are also in charge of the establishment and maintenance of electronic versions of the newspapers made available online. They may even help in the choice of computer systems for use in the newsroom.

News Librarians may also be in charge of hiring, training, scheduling, and evaluating library staff. They may prepare library budgets and coordinate activities of the library with that of other departments on the newspaper. They may manage the graphics and/or photographic library, assign classification terms to items kept in these libraries, and research graphics or photographs upon demand.

A slightly different role at some of the larger news libraries is that of information brokers. The introduction of online full-text news databases opens up other possibilities for new revenue for newspaper publishers. For a fee ranging from $25 to $75 an hour or a given fee per article, news librarians will research their clip and microfilm files, conduct online searches, and produce the actual documents on demand for the public at large. For the larger newspapers, the research staff needed to satisfy customer demands is a part of the news library, but separate from the newsroom functions of the News Librarian and the library. Even for the smallest newspapers (those with circulation under 30,000) have found the need to consolidate their back files into some coherent and retrievable form other than the files maintained by reporters.

For some news libraries, such as the one for Georgia's *Atlanta Journal-Constitution,* the library has become a profit center with revenues of more than $1 million a year, which includes database sales. Their News Research Service (NRS) helps reporters do their job and trains reporters on how to use specialized databases on the Internet. The public can access the newspaper's Web site and find links to the archive and an online store, which includes posters, books and special sections, all of them interlinked, so that, say, a reader of a sports page may find a link promoting purchase of color reprints of any sports front page. The library department has 25 people, six of them part-timers, 11 of whom have library degrees, and the rest specialized skills rather than an M.L.S. degree. Like other profit-making news libraries, the department has to balance its work between its core mission of serving the newsroom and servicing a growing public demand for access.

Salaries

Top minimum annual salaries for News Librarians represented by the Newspaper Guild ranged from a low of $14,000 for a News Librarian at the *Chattanooga* (Tennessee) *Times* to a high of $77,889 for the chief News Librarian at the *New York Times.* Library clerks and assistants can expect minimum yearly salaries ranging from $12,400 to $40,800.

News Librarians at the larger newspapers can anticipate higher salaries; nonunion newspapers will pay less. Obviously, salaries for all library positions are dependent mainly upon the circulation of the newspaper in question.

Employment Prospects

There has been an erosion in the readership of newspapers as other news options for consumers (such as the Internet) have expanded. Added to this trend is a growing (from 2000 onwards) distrust of the media by segments of the public. Market pressures, revenue expectations by management, rising costs and lowered profits have impacted newsrooms with cuts in staff and budgets. On top of this has been the fallout from the *Tasini* case in which the U.S. Supreme Court found, on June 25, 2001, that the *New York Times* and other publishers had committed copyright infringement when they resold freelanced newspaper articles, via their electronic databases (usually managed by News Librarians and their staff), without permission of or making additional payments to the authors of these articles. This outcome led some publishers to withdraw some of their papers' content from availability to the public and, even in one case, to shutting down their Research Library.

Nonetheless, News Librarians and their adjunct staff are still much in demand to help with needed information structures as news organizations merge their newsprint (and even television) and online operations. News Librarians are required to provide information more efficiently for reporters, as well as improve journalists' skills in utilizing research sources. The News Librarian has the advantage of expertise in information architecture and information evaluation, access to available digital technology, control of the archive (which can prove to be a source of revenue), and a useful interaction among all departments of the newspaper.

The best sources for positions within newspaper library departments, as well as that of a News Librarian, is with the larger daily and national journalist organizations.

Advancement Prospects

The right combination of skills and experience can be a tremendous boost upward to a position as News Library Director for News Librarians, though such moves are more dependent upon job attrition and being at the right place at the right time. Assistant Librarians may find that they can use their research skills to move into freelance book research or other research jobs within publishing or business organizations.

Education and Training

Most journalism jobs require an undergraduate degree in communications, English, journalism, or liberal arts. For library management positions a master's degree in library science (M.L.S.) is usually required. Most M.L.S. programs include courses in abstracting, cataloging, computer automation, indexing, and library administration, as well as specialized training in information organization, storage, retrieval, and the legal and ethical considerations of these activities. It is recommended, in addition, that candidates for this degree also take courses in business management, computer use, development of computer databases, and statistics.

Most large newspapers hire library professionals outside the newspaper profession to run their news libraries, but smaller papers still may promote from within, mainly newsroom employees, to learn on the job. Traditional library science programs do not usually offer courses in newspaper librarianship.

Experience, Skills, and Personality Traits

A thorough knowledge of computer systems, a solid familiarity with the operations of the newsroom, the ability to find information efficiently and fast, and excellent organizational skills are all important qualities to possess for the job of a News Librarian. Essentially, people in this job are information seekers and need to be well-rounded in their interests. Previous news experience, preferably in newspapers, but also in other media outlets, will be extremely helpful.

Unions and Associations

The Special Libraries Association has a separate division just for news libraries. News Librarians are also represented by the Newspaper Guild at unionized newspapers. Both the American Library Association and the American Society for Information Science are useful professional societies for News Librarians. Many News Librarians may also belong to the larger umbrella organization of the Society for Professional Journalists.

Tips for Entry

1. During undergraduate work, get employment with the school library (or a local library) to familiarize yourself with library methodology and potential sources.
2. While working within a news library department, it is recommended that you consider seriously the completion of a M.L.S. (Masters in Library Science) degree to further your career and expand your knowledge in the organization, storage, and retrieval of information.
3. Add to your computer knowledge with additional course work (or actual job experience during the college year or in summer internships).
4. Expand your areas of interest and knowledge as it has been frequently suggested that a successful News Librarian is truly a "Renaissance person."

REPORTER SPECIALIST

Duties: Collect and report information about a specific area of expertise or "beat"; keep up-to-date on new developments in this area as the newspaper's expert on the topic

Alternate Title(s): Beat Reporter; Journalist

Salary Range: $18,000 to $70,000+

Employment Prospects: Good

Advancement Prospects: Fair

Prerequisites:

Education or Training—Undergraduate degree in communications, English, journalism, or liberal arts; graduate degree or advanced courses in the area of specialization often required

Experience—Several years as a general assignment reporter for a daily paper with some journalistic work indicating an expertise in the selected specialization

Special Skills and Personality Traits—Capability to prepare longer in-depth "feature" stories; aggressiveness; excellent writing skills; good interpersonal relations; solid organizational capability; persistence; self-discipline; proficient research habits

```
Assistant Editor or Section Editor
```

```
Reporter Specialist
```

```
General Assignment Reporter or
Copy Aide
```

Position Description

In contrast to a general assignment reporter who handles an extensive variety of stories at the discretion of an assignment editor, a Reporter Specialist deals with a single area of expertise. Reporter Specialists (sometimes referred to as beat reporters) have to stay current with developments in their fields by developing sources, by researching and reading trade magazines (and other publications like books), keeping abreast of pertinent Internet news Web sites, and taking additional educational courses. Typically, Reporter Specialists work on several stories at the same time (unlike general assignment reporters who focus on one story at a time), tracking the others while completing one for a deadline.

Regarding some specialties, larger newspapers may demand a graduate degree in the field. For example, a business reporter may need to have a master's degree in business administration, or an education reporter may need a master's degree in education, or a health and medical reporter may be required to get an advanced degree in some form of health sciences.

While traditional "beats" or areas of specialization have included city hall, courts, education, and police, there is a growing need to cover other areas in order to compete with the growing reliance of the younger market on television news or Internet sites to keep informed. These other areas include environmental issues, ethics, family concerns, health and medicine, hobbies and pets, shopping, and transportation. Within these arenas there may also be subdivisions into smaller categories, such as aspects of business, broken down into banking, biotechnology, computer companies, insurance, manufacturing, or other fields of pertinent concern. While some of this fragmentation of general areas into smaller target areas to be covered by individual Reporter Specialists may have changed dramatically with the general cutbacks throughout the journalistic profession, many of the larger newspapers have maintained certain fields to be kept separate from each other in terms of the responsibility of staff reporters.

Beat reporters need to become acquainted with important news sources, to monitor new events, and cover meetings, as well as always to be on the outlook for stories of interest to the public. Beat reporters have to maintain their sources, even when they have written articles that might have displeased those sources. As Chip Scanlan writes in his article on beat reporting for Poynter Online (http://www.poynter.org), "Beat reporting takes courage, discipline and judgment, knowing which story has to be written today and which can be put off . . . [it requires] getting to sources and obtaining information and then writing on deadline stories that give the news and why it matters." Beat reporters must always keep their editors informed of their activities and progress regarding upcoming stories, as much of this activity is really newspaper teamwork.

Beats are generally long-term assignments, in that reporters need to build their sources and their expertise in the area. They work against deadlines on breaking stories, the number of which will vary widely with the size of the newspaper and the number of editions produced (larger papers may have five or six deadlines per day, but smaller newspapers only one or two).

Reporter Specialists are usually required to prepare longer, in-depth articles that require more than the usual research and interviewing. Work schedules need to remain flexible, but the beat reporter is more likely to work more regular hours than a general assignment reporter. However, when news events related to the area of expertise ("beat") occur, Reporter Specialists may find themselves toiling around the clock and on weekends, and even traveling to keep up with the unfolding news. An example of this is a sports beat reporter who often travels with the local teams during the season, working continuously with no days off (and only making up the time in the off-season).

On smaller newspapers beat reporters may also need to fill some of the less popular shifts, such as nights, weekends, or holidays, or fill in generally as general assignment reporters due to the limited size of the newspaper staff.

Salaries

Because Reporter Specialists generally have more experience and training than other reporters, they by and large earn more than general assignment reporters, even when the position is an entry-level one. Indeed, the smallest newspapers almost always have sports reporters (frequently an entry-level reporter), and possibly business reporters as well.

According to the U.S. Department of Labor's Bureau of Labor Statistics, as reported in their *Occupational Outlook Handbook* in March of 2004, annual salaries for reporters in the United States during 2002 ranged from a low of $17,600 to a high of $69,500, but within large urban centers, such as New York City, the salaries tended to be higher. For New York, the yearly low was $21,600, and the high was $104,500.

Newspaper reporters' salaries are negotiated by the Newspaper Guild-CWA when they start a new job at a Guild paper, and again after a specified number of years, which varies from one paper to another. The Newspaper Guild often treats Reporter Specialists and general assignment reporters as one broad group for salary bargaining purposes. Specialists may rate a differential to make their salary higher, especially if they are exclusively Reporter Specialists (such as business reporters or medical reporters) rather than general assignment reporters simply assigned to a beat.

Nonetheless, pay still varies widely. According to the Newspaper Guild's salary survey of 2003 the top minimum weekly salary after two years at the *New York Times* was $1,445.17, whereas the top minimum weekly salary after four years at the Rochester (New York) *Democrat & Chronicle* was $419. The survey found that the average top minimum income for a reporter as of January 1, 2003, was $857.42 (or an annual salary of approximately $44,585).

Employment Prospects

Employment of reporters is expected to grow more slowly than the average for most other occupations through the year 2012, according to the U.S. Department of Labor's Bureau of Labor Statistics as reported in their *Occupational Outlook Handbook* in March of 2004. This is mainly a result of closures of newspapers, consolidations, and mergers, as well as decreased circulation with the resultant decline in advertising profits, and an increase in expenses.

Whatever growth in employment does occur, it will probably be from an increase in small town and suburban daily and weekly newspapers. However, small newspapers typically offer only the lower salary ranges.

Other job openings will come when journalists leave the field altogether, or move up into management. The number of large city daily newspapers is expected to remain static, and the competition for jobs on them is exceptionally competitive. Another area drawing journalists away from traditional print journalism has burgeoned with the tremendous growth of Internet journalism. Print journalists seem more adept at making this transition than, say, television reporters.

Advancement Prospects

Advancement prospects are only fair. Reporter Specialists have more of a chance in moving to the larger newspapers than general assignment reporters, due mostly to the added expertise that they possess. In addition, Reporter Specialists may have fairly good chances at becoming section editors or columnists, depending upon their area of expertise and its importance in today's journalistic world. Those reporters who handle highly specialized scientific or technical subjects successfully are at an advantage in this highly competitive job market.

Education and Training

The job of Reporter Specialist requires, first, an undergraduate degree in communications, English, journalism, or liberal arts. Then, Reporter Specialists often are required to hold advanced degrees in the subjects related to their area of expertise. For example, business reporters may need an M.B.A. degree, as an education reporter may need a master's degree in education.

Experience, Skills, and Personality Traits

Good fundamental reporting skills are essential. Beat reporters must boast intense curiosity and sharp observational skills. They must be comfortable in dealing with and interviewing people in positions of authority and power. They need to know how to research and organize information and be able to explain complicated topics in a simple but meaningful manner to those uninformed on the topic. Speed, clarity, and accuracy are essential to their work being successful. Chip Scanlan, in an article at Poynter Online (http://www.poynter.org) points out, "The best reporters know how the world works, whether it's the world of law enforcement, the laboratory, or the corporate boardroom. That takes time, dedication, discipline, and courage." As Diana Sugg, health reporter for the *Baltimore Sun,* suggests to aspiring Reporter Specialists, "Much of the work of the great beat reporter doesn't show up in the paper. A lot of your work isn't the stories, but everything around those stories: how you handle your time, develop sources, balance long vs. short pieces, deal with your editors, [and] your own perfectionism."

Most specialized reporter positions require several years of general reporting experience, as well as some additional training or work in the particular area of specialization.

Unions and Associations

The Newspaper Guild is the primary union for print journalists. Other general professional associations include the American Society of Journalists and Authors, Investigative Reporters and Editors, the Newspaper Association of America, and the Society of Professional Journalists.

In addition, there are numerous professional associations that represent reporters in a wide variety of specialties or of different ethnic backgrounds, such as the American Medical Writers Association, the Asian-American Journalists Association, the Associated Business Writers of America, the Association of Food Journalists, the Association of Health Care Journalists, the Construction Writers Association, the Education Writers Association, the National Association of Black Journalists, the National Association of Hispanic Journalists, the National Association of Science Writers, the Native American Journalists Association, the National Turf Writers Association, the Outdoor Writers Association of America, the Religion Newswriters Association, the Society of American Travel Writers, the Society of Environmental Journalists, and many more.

Tips for Entry

1. Get as much journalistic experience (on the college newspaper, or in internships) as you can during college to prepare you for the constant demands of a Reporter Specialist.
2. Look for internship programs with local newspapers or broadcast stations to add practical journalistic experience to your college course work. Working as part of a news staff in competition with others will provide you with a valuable insight into the news world beyond the campus.
3. Work on perfecting your research capabilities, as this skill will be essential to your job as a beat reporter.
4. Perfect your interviewing skills as much as you can during your college or internship programs, as this will also be a key talent you must possess as a beat reporter.
5. Practice developing sources of information during your training as a journalist, as this particular ability is paramount for a successful beat reporter.

SECTION EDITOR

CAREER PROFILE

Duties: Supervise content, layout, and production of special-interest section (or page) of newspaper

Alternate Title(s): Arts and Entertainment Editor; Business Editor; Food Editor; Lifestyle Editor; Sports Editor; Sunday Editor; and similar titles

Salary Range: $20,000 to $75,000+

Employment Prospects: Fair

Advancement Prospects: Good

Prerequisites:

Education or Training—Undergraduate degree in communications, English, journalism, or liberal arts; advanced degree preferable for specialized fields

Experience—Background as assistant editor, copy editor, or journalist

Special Skills and Personality Traits—Editing and graphics proficiency; good news judgment; supervisory ability

CAREER LADDER

```
┌─────────────────────────────────┐
│      News Editor or             │
│  Assistant Managing Editor      │
└─────────────────────────────────┘

┌─────────────────────────────────┐
│        Section Editor           │
└─────────────────────────────────┘

┌─────────────────────────────────┐
│  Assistant Editor, Copy Editor, │
│        or Journalist            │
└─────────────────────────────────┘
```

Position Description

Section Editors are in charge of specialized parts or pages of a newspaper. Such parts might cover such subjects as arts and entertainment, business, food and wine, health, lifestyle, real estate, sports, suburban news, or the various sections of the Sunday edition of the newspaper. Section Editors are in charge of assigning reporters and photographers to stories, the content of the section, editing copy, monitoring deadlines for the copy, and executing or overseeing page graphics and layout. Most editors are expected to write for their pages as well.

Section Editors work directly under the news editor in charge, who may be called the city editor, the executive editor, or the metropolitan editor. Depending upon the newspaper, some Section Editors may be more independent from the news editor and may work with other editors on a coordinating or an advisory basis.

Section Editors must be well organized and be equipped to supervise others working for them. They need to scrutinize other sources of news in their chosen area(s), such as magazines, other newspapers, wire stories, or Internet sites to retrieve story ideas. Some of the pieces they assign may be long-term and some due on a far shorter deadline. The

coordination of all this copy is the direct responsibility of the Section Editor.

In general, the Section Editor meets daily with other editors, evaluates copy to determine which stories will be used in the section (or page) and when, assigns future stories, edits copy, and selects photos and other artwork to illustrate the text. Many Section Editors (particularly those on smaller newspapers) do their own page layouts, while others work with the newspaper's art and photo departments on the layout. A Section Editor of a daily page, such as business or suburban news, must have solid news judgment and react rapidly to breaking news that would affect that page.

While hectic, the job can be gratifying for the decision-making freedom inherent in it and for the potential for the Section Editor to instill his viewpoint on part of the newspaper. As they are usually not directly involved in breaking news events, Section Editors usually have regular business hours and are not prone to working different shifts or suddenly being thrust into night work.

Salaries

Section Editors are usually excluded from Newspaper Guild contracts, as they are considered managerial staff. Nonetheless, this exclusion may vary from one newspaper or bargaining unit to another.

Annual salaries differ widely from a low of about $20,000 to $75,000 or more, depending upon the size of the paper and the length of employment of the Section Editor. The larger the paper's circulation, usually, the higher the salary.

Employment Prospects

Most Section Editors are promoted from within the staff of the newspaper. Some publications (particularly large urban dailies), however, may conduct national searches for talent to head their special sections. Journalists and editors with advanced degrees or specialized education in certain fields, such as business, health services, law, science, or sports, have a decided hiring advantage. Section Editor jobs are highly desirable and thus extremely competitive.

Advancement Prospects

Section Editors are well-positioned for promotion to higher editorial positions, particularly to posts as news editor or managing editor. Competition, however, is keen from both within the staff structure of the newspaper and from without.

Education and Training

Section Editors must have an undergraduate degree in communications, English, journalism, or liberal arts. In addition, an advanced degree or course work in their special field(s) of interest is recommended.

Experience, Skills, and Personality Traits

The amount of background experience needed to be hired as a Section Editor will depend much on the size of the newspaper. A journalist with only a few years of work in the field may become a Section Editor for a small or local paper, while larger urban or national papers will require four to six or more years of hands-on journalistic experience. Many Section Editors previously have been copy editors or assistant news editors.

Section Editors must have a comprehensive understanding of their subject area(s) and the newspaper audience their paper serves. They should be excellent editors and writers and have a good background in page layout and production. They also need to have solid people skills to supervise reporters and staff that work for them.

Unions and Associations

Major professional associations for Section Editors include the American Society of Newspaper Editors; the International Society of Weekly Newspaper Editors; the Investigative Reporters and Editors Association; and the Society of Professional Journalists. Others include the Association for Women in Communications; the National Association of Black Journalists; and the National Federation of Press Women.

Tips for Entry

1. All the journalistic experience (preferably including editing and writing experience on, say, the campus newspaper) that you can gain during college (or after) would be a help in gaining a beginning editorial job with a newspaper and would position you well for editorial work.

2. Acquire as much on-the-job experience in both editing and production processes, even to switching employers to gain the varied background and training needed by a Section Editor.

3. Enhance your knowledge of your interest specialty by further study and, above all, the availability of resources about it.

4. Take business management courses to increase your administrative and supervisory skills.

5. Get assigned as a reporter to the area of your interest and begin building a reputation as a knowledgeable journalist in this area, which will make your candidacy for a Section Editor that much more appealing.

WIRE SERVICE REPORTER

CAREER PROFILE

Duties: Report unfolding events to meet publication deadlines; write summaries of stories for news digests; edit stories from local newspapers and local broadcast (radio and TV) stations for wire release

Alternate Title(s): None

Salary Range: $29,000 to $85,000+

Employment Prospects: Good

Advancement Prospects: Fair

Prerequisites:

    Education or Training—Undergraduate degree in communications, English, journalism, or liberal arts

    Experience—None for a temporary position; two years or more experience at a newspaper or other news organization for a permanent post with most wire services

    Special Skills and Personality Traits—Ability to work swiftly and accurately under pressure of deadlines; aggressive in pursuing stories; good news judgment

CAREER LADDER

```
┌─────────────────────────────────────┐
│   Assistant Editor, Assistant Bureau │
│   Chief, or Foreign Correspondent    │
└─────────────────────────────────────┘

┌─────────────────────────────────────┐
│       Wire Service Reporter          │
└─────────────────────────────────────┘

┌─────────────────────────────────────┐
│    Temporary Reporter or Intern      │
└─────────────────────────────────────┘
```

Position Description

A wire service is *not* a newspaper. It is a company, or a cooperative news venture, that specializes in the gathering and distributing of news. Traditionally a wire service job involved working for one of several worldwide services that supplied general news to newspapers. As most newspapers do not have overseas or national bureaus (offices), they tend to rely on wire services for most international and national news.

With the advent of online computer services and the World Wide Web, anyone interested in a specific topic can subscribe to news services, databases, or e-mail newsletters that are devoted to the specific field on a "real-time" basis. Some of these services also provide copy to newspapers, but others are strictly designed for subscribers.

Wire services also contrast with newspapers in that they are *not* bound by printing deadlines, Similarly, they differ from the electronic news media in that they have *no* broadcast deadlines to meet. Thus, their stories can be updated around the clock, from hour to hour.

While a Wire Reporter for a general wire service may cover a broader scope of news that those at most newspapers, they still collect news in the same way, by interviewing, checking sources, and on-site investigation. As news events break, the pressure of getting the story into the bureau is the same as that of regular reporters, with the resultant economic gains and prestige at stake as well.

In the case of wire services, the stories are edited by the service and sent to subscribing newspapers electronically. These newspapers, which pay a subscription fee, choose which stories they want to print, write their own headlines, and are free to edit the stories for length. Upon subscribing to a wire service, each member newspaper is expected to provide news and feature stories to the service from its own circulation local area.

Wire services have their own network of reporters on assignment around the world and maintain news bureaus throughout the world. For general wire news services, such as the Associated Press (American) or Reuters (British), bureau reporters are expected to generate routine news copy (on such matters as commodity market prices, police arrests, weather reports, and other common topics), as well as cover unfolding national or international news events. Hours are almost guaranteed to be erratic, with much nighttime and weekend hours, and holiday work shifts to be expected.

Wire Service Reporters must be able to work both in the field, reporting stories, and at a desk, editing copy submitted by other reporters and subscriber newspapers, broadcast stations, and assorted Internet news sources. They face continuous deadline pressure, but have the satisfaction of seeing their work reach a worldwide audience. Due to the deadline nature of this job, Wire Service Reporters seldom have the time or opportunity to write in-depth pieces or features, except as special follow-up articles.

Salaries

Salaries at wire services generally are higher than those at newspapers, according to the Newspaper Guild. The Guild negotiates salaries for Wire Service Reporters when they begin work at a unionized wire service, and usually during their entire tenure at a wire service. Salaries vary widely with the size of the organization and the experience of the journalist.

Salaries often also depend upon the size of the city in which the Wire Services Reporter works. Most wire services, such as the Associated Press (AP), have differentials in their salary offerings depending upon the local cost of living. In other words, New York City would have a higher cost-of-living differential than those found in, say, Oklahoma, Kansas, or Rochester, New York.

The top minimum annual salaries for unionized Wire Service Reporters range from approximately $30,000 to the low $70,000s, depending on the wire service.

Employment Prospects

Well-established wire services have hundreds of news bureaus around the world. In addition, there are specialized wire services, such as ones focusing on business or finance, that also create jobs in this marketplace. With the abundance of experienced journalists from which wire services can pick for their staff, they seldom maintain any in-house training programs any longer.

News Wire Service Reporters can anticipate that for some time after joining the organization they will work at a desk. They will receive information from reporters in the field and edit these reports and those that are submitted by subscriber member newspapers or broadcast stations. It is also expected that these newcomers will perform assorted clerical tasks.

Advancement Prospects

Working as a Wire Service Reporter is excellent training experience for reporting positions on any of the large national or international daily newspapers. Also, Wire Service Reporters can move up within the wire service to positions as news editors, assistant or senior bureau chiefs, both in foreign news bureaus of the service as well as capital bureaus in Washington, D.C.

Education and Training

Generally, Wire Service Reporters must have a bachelor's degree in communications, English, journalism, or liberal arts. Some wire services also require applicants to pass vocabulary and news writing tests.

Experience, Skills, and Personality Traits

Wire Service Reporters need to be able to function well under extreme deadline pressure. They have to be both precise and quick. They need to be totally conversant with news that has already been reported to be able to evaluate the newsworthiness and value of the events unfolding.

They must be able to think quickly and compose stories on the spot, which they then can detail to an editor over the phone or an Internet connection. They must be aggressive, resolute, and unrelenting, cool-headed, and have a solid news perspective.

Most wire services require at least 18 months to two years or more of journalistic experience on a daily newspaper or broadcast (radio or television) station. Those with less experience may be qualified for temporary posts, which, in time, may lead to full-time employment once they have proven their usefulness.

An additional bonus is proficiency in a foreign language, which may become necessary if one is posted to a bureau overseas (and may help get that posting).

Unions and Associations

Employees at the Associated Press, Reuters, and United Press International are represented by the Newspaper Guild. Other professional associations include the American Press Institute, the Asian-American Journalists Association, the Association of Women in Communications, the International Press Institute, Investigative Reporters and Editors, the National Association of Black Journalists, the National Association of Hispanic Journalists, the National Federation of Press Women, the National Press Club, and the Society of Professional Journalists.

Tips for Entry

1. All the journalistic experience (on the campus newspaper, or in internships) that can be gained during college can be helpful.
2. Seek internship programs with local newspapers or broadcast stations to add practical journalistic experience to your college curriculum. Working as part of a news staff in competition with others will provide you with a valuable insight into the fast-paced news world beyond the campus.
3. Hone your foreign language skills in anticipation of bureau work in foreign countries.
4. Practice your interviewing skills on whomever you can and write up the results to appraise critically your writing and reporting skills.

RADIO

NEWS DIRECTOR

CAREER PROFILE

Duties: Supervise content of newscasts; edit, rewrite, report, and deliver news as needed

Alternate Title(s): News Editor

Salary Range: $20,000 to $60,000+

Employment Prospects: Fair

Advancement Prospects: Fair to good

Prerequisites:

Education or Training—Undergraduate degree in broadcasting, communications, English, journalism, or liberal arts

Experience—Two to five years in broadcast journalism

Special Skills and Personality Traits—Decision-making ability; supervisory and managerial capabilities; sound news judgment

CAREER LADDER

```
┌────────────────────────────────────────┐
│  Program Director or General Manager    │
└────────────────────────────────────────┘

┌────────────────────────────────────────┐
│              News Director              │
└────────────────────────────────────────┘

┌────────────────────────────────────────┐
│      Reporter or College Student        │
└────────────────────────────────────────┘
```

Position Description

The News Director is the person in charge of a radio news operation. This journalist-manager sets policies and makes choices as to news coverage and its presentation, recruits and trains newscaster and news writer personnel, supervises the newsroom finances, and works in tandem with managers of other departments at the radio station. Many News Directors are called upon to make fast decisions on news-breaking stories. In addition, many News Directors have production duties, which include tape editing and overall supervision of individual programs.

At larger stations, radio News Directors may manage staffs of 30 to 40 persons. However, most stations are a lot smaller, and the smallest ones may utilize a News Director to be director, editor, reporter, and newscaster—all in one.

News Directors report to general managers or station managers. Besides their managerial and administrative duties (and any production obligations), News Directors typically have to handle correspondence, reports, and any paperwork relating to the station and its programs.

Besides their administrative and production duties, News Directors may have to be active reporters and gather, edit, and rewrite news stories. On occasion, they may also deliver the news on the air, act as an anchor for the station's programs, or even become involved with sales. In a report on

the state of the news media in 2004, made by Journalism.org, it was found that the major other responsibility of radio News Directors, beyond their administrative and production work, was as announcer for the station.

Salaries

A survey taken in 2003 by AMFMTVOnline.com of radio and television salaries and job satisfaction statistics showed that radio News Directors' annual salaries ranged from approximately $20,000 to $60,000, with a median average being $31,000. This median average represents a $6,000 increase over yearly salaries surveyed in 1998. According to a study made by the Radio-Television News Directors Association, entry-level annual salaries in radio news for the year 2000 averaged about $22,000 as compared to $26,000 for journalism graduates taking jobs with daily newspapers. Obviously, the larger the radio station's market (and its advertising revenues) the higher the salary of its News Director.

Employment Prospects

Small- and medium-size radio stations offer the best job opportunities for persons seeking positions as News Directors. Turnover in radio tends to be high, as established News

Directors with a few years of experience look to move upward to higher management positions with the station, or move on to television posts. Competition for employment is tougher at stations and networks that have large news staffs.

Advancement Prospects

Upward advancement mobility for radio News Directors has been helped greatly by the increasing importance and profitability of news operations. While general managers of stations used to come from the sales and programming departments, more and more of them now are advancing from the news department. Ambitious News Directors should become familiar with all the operations of their radio station, including engineering, production, programming, and sales.

In a study on "Career Goals in Radio News" made by Vernon Stone of the Missouri School of Journalism in 2000, it was found that most News Directors look to either become station general managers or do other on-air radio work, like news anchoring, sports, or talk show hosting. They also would rather join a network, or move on to television jobs, or even look for jobs outside of broadcasting.

Education and Training

An undergraduate degree in communications, journalism, liberal arts, or social studies (government, history, sociology, or other related areas) is preferred. Some broadcast journalists have graduate degrees in communications.

Experience, Skills, and Personality Traits

Most radio News Directors have had several years of experience as radio newscasters or news writers. Some start their careers as News Directors with very small stations and move on from there. In addition to news writing, some have general experience in radio production.

News Directors should have good writing and verbal communication skills and be knowledgeable about the relevant technologies. In addition, their general appearance and business manner is also key. They need the capabilities to successfully supervise others, make quick decisions and assignments, and boast solid news judgment.

Unions and Associations

Many broadcast professionals are represented by such unions as the American Federation of Television and Radio Artists, the National Association of Broadcast Employees and Technicians, or the Writers Guild of America. Other major professional associations relevant to News Directors include the American Women in Radio and Television; the National Association of Broadcasters; and the Radio-Television News Directors Association (or RTNDA).

Tips for Entry

1. During college take as many writing courses as you can, as well as journalism or communication Courses, and work on the campus radio station.
2. Additional study in social studies (government, history, sociology and related areas) would be helpful.
3. Look for internships (summer or otherwise) to get hands-on experience in actual work situations in broadcasting.
4. Hone your skills in analyzing and understanding current events and history as a means of putting breaking news into perspective.
5. Work on your speech skills, and gain some experience in public speaking, debate, or dramatic arts, as your entry-level position may be as a reporter and you need to be able to tell the news effectively into a microphone.
6. Become proficient with your computer, the Internet, and Web page construction.

REPORTER

Duties: News gathering; editing and rewriting; announcing

Alternate Title(s): Newscaster

Salary Range: $16,000 to $40,000+

Employment Prospects: Fair

Advancement Prospects: Good

Prerequisites:

Education or Training—High-school diploma sufficient in some entry-level cases; undergraduate degree in broadcasting, communications, journalism, or liberal arts necessary for most positions

Experience—None (for entry-level positions) to two or more years

Special Skills and Personality Traits—Concise and clear writing; good speech communication abilities; sound news judgment

```
┌─────────────────────────────────────┐
│  News Director, Radio Personality,   │
│            or Anchor                 │
└─────────────────────────────────────┘

┌─────────────────────────────────────┐
│              Reporter                │
└─────────────────────────────────────┘

┌─────────────────────────────────────┐
│  Continuity Writer or High School or │
│           College Student            │
└─────────────────────────────────────┘
```

Position Description

A radio Reporter is one who covers news stories, either on the air (or prerecorded for later broadcast) from the scene or from the station newsroom. Radio Reporters generally have two major responsibilities: to collect and prepare news stories for broadcast, and to read (tell) the story on the air. At large stations, these two responsibilities may be split by two distinct persons: one who collects, writes, and edits; and one who announces the news on the air. Above all, the radio Reporter has the job of making listeners feel as though they are right on the scene as events unfold. This may necessitate looking for sounds that illustrate the news story being recounted, whether in the form of recorded interviews, live audio feeds from news conferences, sound effects, or other means to add color to the news story. When it seems that the radio Reporter is having a conversation with the listener, radio is transformed into a particularly personal medium of communication.

Many radio Reporters do their main work in the station studio, where they monitor incoming wire-service copy and other news sources. They select stories for the newscasts and edit and rewrite the copy to fit the time limitations of the broadcast and to aim at the interests of the station's listeners. Other radio Reporters may do their own news gather-

ing, by taping interviews over the phone or in person and by checking out stories with their network of contacts. Some radio Reporters may actually be dispatched into the field to cover disasters or major breaking news events. Reporting live from the news scene is usually done without a script or even notes. The tapes of these events, called "actualities," usually are edited for quotes to be aired.

Most radio stations have news breaks every hour and give short periodic updates throughout the day as well. Some AM radio stations are almost entirely news or talk shows. This type of program planning allows for longer and more in-depth stories, additional background, related feature stories, or relevant personality interviews to be aired—far more than the newscast itself can undertake.

Radio Reporters work under the direction of the news director who assigns coverage and responsibilities. Working hours can be long (even all day and night), and seven days a week. Beginners usually draw evening, night, and weekend shifts, and overtime is expected.

Most radio stations' facilities are restricted in size and, correspondingly, have limited staffs. At smaller stations, Reporters often are part time or share in other duties, such as ad-writing or programming. In addition, radio Reporters often prepare and read news analyses and/or editorials, as well as research stories for major on-air personalities.

Salaries

A survey by the Radio-Television News Directors Association (RTNDA) found that the annual salaries of radio Reporters generally rose by 15 percent between 1998 and 2003 (excepting sports Reporters). In 2003, the median yearly salary was $23,000 (which is less than $11 an hour), with a range from $16,000 to more than $40,000.

What has affected radio Reporter salaries (and those of most other nonmanagement radio personnel) is the tremendous amount of consolidation that the industry has undergone in the last several years. This has meant fewer people are doing the news, and those who are left frequently have multiple responsibilities. In addition, it is found that the salaries of news Reporters drop as they cover more and more stations (that are now part of the consolidated groupings). In an analysis of the RTNDA salary data, Journalism.org (in its report at http://www.stateofthenewsmedia.org) speculates that either these lower salaries encourage Reporters to work with more than one outlet, or that the necessity of having many Reporters has lessened since the number of radio stations served by a single news outlet has increased.

Obviously, under these circumstances, the larger the radio station's market, the higher the median pay for the Reporter. Alternatively, the more experience that Reporters have, the move the quality of their education and breadth of interest may influence starting salaries, but it does not guarantee any great increases in salary.

Employment Prospects

Most of the nation's AM radio stations and FM stations have at least one full-time newsperson. Many have more than one, with the medium to large stations having news staff of 10 to 30 persons or more, though this may be changing due to consolidation of stations and the use of single news outlets for more than one station.

As an entry point for beginners, there are other broadcast news jobs available at most major networks and news wire services, jobs which will provide them with the experience necessary to move on to news positions as radio Reporters or announcers. Beginners will probably find the best opportunities at small stations, though competition is stiff and consolidation of stations has made employment more unpredictable.

Advancement Prospects

Turnover in radio jobs is generally high. According to industry sources and surveys, openings occur more frequently in news and clerical jobs than in other areas, such as programming, sales, and marketing. A successful radio Reporter has a good chance of advancing to news director, or, alternatively, of building an audience so as to become a personality or announcer.

Education and Training

A high school diploma is the minimum requirement for many entry-level jobs in radio. A college degree in broadcast journalism or mass communications is highly recommended, as radio news directors have indicated that they prefer broadcast news major to others such as newspaper journalism or speech. Most of the better journalism programs at good schools give a broader spectrum of related education subjects, such as courses in the role law plays in the field of mass communications.

It should be noted that, as a result of the Telecommunications Act of 1996, the Federal Communications Commission (FCC) no longer requires anyone who works for a broadcasting station to have a license. Only the station is required to be licensed.

Experience, Skills, and Personality Traits

Beginners who have had experience on school newspaper staffs or radio or television stations (in, say, internship programs) have a significant advantage at getting a radio Reporter job. Most large radio stations, however, hire only experienced newscasters, mainly from smaller stations. Another valuable experience for an applicant is to have had some experience in continuity writing (i.e., writing advertising copy for broadcast).

Radio Reporters need to possess good news judgment and to work quickly under deadline pressure. They need strong script-writing skills and should be able to write for a listening audience (rather than a reading audience). In addition, they should be skilled in handling studio broadcasting, editing, and taping equipment. They need to have strong interviewing abilities, and have a good speaking ability, with clear enunciation and correct grammar.

Unions and Associations

Many broadcast professionals are represented by such unions as the American Federation of Television and Radio Artists, the National Association of Broadcast Employees and Technicians, or the Writers Guild of America. Other major professional associations relevant to radio Reporters include the American Women in Radio and Television; the National Association of Broadcasters; and the Radio-Television News Directors Association (or RTNDA).

Tips for Entry

1. Consider broadcast journalism as a major in order to combine liberal arts education with basic skills training for radio (and even television) work.

2. Try to choose a school whose faculty members are professional instructors who have actually worked in radio or television and understand the real world of present-day radio/television news operations.

3. Look for internship programs with radio or television stations to add practical experience to your college course work. Working as part of a news staff in competition with others for audiences will provide you with a valuable insight into the news world beyond the campus.

4. Another reason for seeking out internship programs is that it will aid you in developing a networking base of professional contacts to help you get a job and advance your career.

5. Experience in public speaking, debate, or dramatic arts will help to prepare you for an on-the-air reporting job, as live reporting requires you to think and talk on your feet without a preset script.

6. Become a knowledgeable listener and viewer of broadcast news.

TELEVISION

ANCHOR

CAREER PROFILE

Duties: Host news or other current events programs; read the news and/or other copy on air; interview guests; go on location for coverage of key happenings when required

Alternate Title(s): Anchorperson; Newscaster

Salary Range: $17,000 to $1,000,000+

Employment Prospects: Poor to fair

Advancement Prospects: Poor

Prerequisites:

Education or Training—Undergraduate degree in communications, English, journalism, or political science with emphasis on liberal arts; graduate degree may, in some cases, be required

Experience—Many years as news correspondent, reporter, or other television news positions

Special Skills and Personality Traits—Ability to work well with people; capacity for working under pressure; competitiveness; good voice and diction; pleasing on-camera appearance; spontaneity

CAREER LADDER

```
┌─────────────────────────────┐
│    Major Market Anchor      │
└─────────────────────────────┘

┌─────────────────────────────┐
│          Anchor             │
└─────────────────────────────┘

┌─────────────────────────────┐
│  Reporter or Correspondent  │
└─────────────────────────────┘
```

Position Description

News Anchors, or newscasters, present news stories and introduce videotaped news or live transmissions from on-the-scene reporters. The Anchor acts as host to a news or entertainment show, reading the news, introducing the stories, and interviewing any guests who appear on the program. Essentially, the entire show really revolves around the all-important Anchor (or Anchors). These individuals can become public personalities and celebrities, and therefore the job of Anchor is a coveted one within the broadcasting business. Understandably, competition for such openings is intense. Anchors earn their jobs by putting in years of hard work as reporters or correspondents, and becoming knowledgeable in politics, social trends, and other issues of great public concern.

Some news Anchors at large stations or networks specialize in a particular type of news, such as sports or weather. In small markets, Anchors may only read accounts of the day's stories and introduce background reports provided by the networks or by a television news service. In other cases,

they may do their own research and writing, and work with production personnel on the edition of videotape for broadcast. In larger markets (and on the networks), these functions are performed by support staff, and the Anchor's primary job is to host the show, read the news copy, and conduct interviews.

Prior to broadcast time, the Anchor reviews the contents of the broadcast with the news director and staff. At large stations (and on the networks) the Anchor has the deciding voice in the content of the broadcast and the time to be devoted to each of the various stories. Most of the network news and entertainment shows (and those of many other stations as well) provide time for Anchors to question reporters and exchange conversation and banter. Some of this is, of course, orchestrated, and some of it is spontaneous.

In addition, Anchors sometimes report on location, usually regarding a major story or news event. They may also do the primary coverage on site for conferences and conventions. Moreover, they may work on documentaries or specials to be broadcast at special times.

Salaries

Similar to other television news posts, salaries for Anchors largely depend on the size of the market in which they are employed. According to a study made in 2002 by the Radio-Television News Directors Association, annual salaries for television news Anchors ranged from $17,000 minimum to $1 million at the top range, with a median salary being $50,000, and an average annual salary for the job being $69,800. Yearly salaries for sports Anchors ranged from $16,000 to a high of $1 million, with a median salary of $35,000, and an average annual salary of $50,600. The range of salaries of weather Anchors (sometimes known as weathercasters) were similar to sports Anchors, but had median yearly salary of $43,800, and an average of $54,000. These salaries represented a 25 percent increase over those of 1996.

Additionally, according to the above survey, starting salaries usually were commensurate with the size of the market. Small market entry-level salaries ranged from an annual income of $17,000 to $25,000, middle markets ranged from $30,000 to $75,000, while major market entry-level yearly salaries ranged from $100,000 upwards.

Employment Prospects

Only a very small percentage of television reporters or correspondents ever become Anchors. The typical small television station hires only one or two Anchors, whereas major stations and networks have numerous Anchors on staff. The success of news Anchors is frequently judged by television ratings in their time slot within their market. This perpetual emphasis on ratings guarantees high turnover in Anchor positions as Anchors fail to meet the ratings standards or are hired away by competing local stations or higher-paying stations in larger markets (or by the networks). The wider proliferation of cable and satellite television systems, with the resultant expansion of cable and Internet news programs, increases the chance of employment as an Anchor. Job openings continue to be somewhat better for minorities and women as stations seek to provide a balance in this highly visible position.

Advancement Prospects

As the Anchor job is the highest position for a reporter or correspondent to gain, the only real opportunity for advancement for an Anchor at a station is to shift up to larger markets or to a national network.

Education and Training

Practically all jobs in broadcast journalism demand an undergraduate degree in communications, journalism, or one of the liberal arts. Course work in English and speech may also be valuable, as good grammar and diction are important elements of the success of an Anchor, as is a general widespread familiarity with most branches of learning. An emphasis on study in political science may also be helpful. Some Anchor posts may also demand a graduate degree.

Experience, Skills, and Personality Traits

Reporters and correspondents typically devote many years to working in the field before becoming eligible for promotion to an Anchor position. Anchors need to possess excellent writing skills and solid news judgment. They must have a pleasing on-camera appearance (good grooming) and personality, as well as a good, clear voice. Their presentation needs to convey authority and they should have knowledge of issues, names, geography, and history, and the ability to put all of these into perspective for the average viewer. Their command of grammar, syntax, diction, storytelling, and tone needs to be dead-on. They need to be able to process new information fast, be skillful in the interviewing process, and be sensitive to the ethical problems of unconfirmed information, as well as words that can convey the wrong message to viewers or thoughtlessly add pain to already traumatized victims being interviewed.

In addition, Anchors must be able to ad-lib convincingly and think spontaneously as news events or other unexpected things often occur live on the air. They must be adroit at multitasking and appreciate all the work and the technology that goes into the execution of a live broadcast.

Unions and Associations

Anchors may belong to the American Federation of Television and Radio Artists, the National Association of Broadcasters, the Radio-Television News Directors Association, the Society of Professional Journalists, or the Writers Guild of America.

Tips for Entry

1. While in college become actively involved your campus radio and television stations.
2. Participate in internship programs at local independent, cable, or network affiliated stations.
3. When applying for a position with a television station be sure that you have a taped audition that well represents the quality of your delivery, appearance, and style and that is appropriate for handling commercials, interviews, and news reporting.
4. Gain needed television experience by being employed in other television newsroom positions.
5. Fluency in another language than English is a plus.

ASSISTANT NEWS DIRECTOR

CAREER PROFILE

Duties: Assign news coverage; assist in supervising news operation

Alternate Title(s): Assistant Editor; Assistant News Editor; Assistant News Producer; City Editor; Managing Editor

Salary Range: $19,000 to $150,000

Employment Prospects: Poor

Advancement Prospects: Good

Prerequisites:

Education or Training—Undergraduate degree in communications, English, history, liberal arts, political science, or the social sciences

Experience—Several years of experience as a reporter

Special Skills and Personality Traits—Good news judgment; organizational skills; solid managerial ability

CAREER LADDER

```
┌─────────────────────────────────┐
│         News Director           │
└─────────────────────────────────┘

┌─────────────────────────────────┐
│     Assistant News Director     │
└─────────────────────────────────┘

┌─────────────────────────────────┐
│     Reporter or Correspondent   │
└─────────────────────────────────┘
```

Position Description

Assistant News Directors are the mid-level managers in charge of supervising the day-to-day operation of newsrooms at television stations. They work under the direction of the news director, and execute the director's decisions. Based upon the size of the staff, they may have a certain degree of independence in assigning reporters and news crews to handle stories. They evaluate suggestions for pieces and monitor the reports made by reporters.

Assistant News Directors handle all the nitty-gritty decisions that keep a newsroom running. They may make up work schedules so that the newsroom has adequate personnel at all times, while seeing that the newsroom complies with any union regulations concerning varying the shifts in any given period of time. Assistant News Directors also monitor assignments and, usually, all work-in-progress. Depending upon the decision of the news director, Assistant News Directors may assume full responsibility for fast-breaking news stories.

Managerial responsibilities include synchronizing the work of assorted departments, resolving any problems, and dealing with complaints (or least monitoring them before passing them on to the news director). In the absence of the news director, it is the Assistant News Director who is in charge of the newsroom.

At smaller stations, Assistant News Directors may even undertake some of the writing, editing, and reporting, in addition to performing their regular duties.

Salaries

In the 2002 Radio and Television Salary Survey it was noted that annual salaries for Assistant News Directors nationally varied from a low of $19,000 to a high of $150,000. The median yearly salary for this range was $57,000, whereas the average salary was $62,300. These salaries represented a 28.1 percent increase from those of 1996. As is true in the broadcast journalism arena, salaries prove to be highest at the stations with the largest markets and at the networks.

Employment Prospects

While job changeover is high for the job of Assistant News Director, the competition for this position is extremely keen. Small stations may not even have this middle-management position on their staff lineups, but large stations may have several Assistant News Director posts. It should be noted that, generally, Assistant News Directors are promoted from within the ranks of correspondents or reporters. Again, the effect of the expanding cable and Internet industries are providing more opportunities.

Advancement Prospects

The obvious next step for an Assistant News Director is the position of news director. These latter positions also undergo high turnover, making promotion that much easier. The best opportunities exist in both commercial and cable television, not public television, where government funding is highly variable and cutbacks in staff are more likely. Assistant News Directors may also choose to advance their careers by making a parallel move to a related communication field, such as newspapers, magazines, government, or journalism wire services.

Education and Training

As a minimum educational requirement, an undergraduate degree in communications, English, history, liberal arts, or the social sciences is considered obligatory. Other acceptable degree fields include business, economics, or political science. A graduate degree might enhance the possibilities of promotion.

Experience, Skills, and Personality Traits

Most Assistant News Directors have worked for several years as news desk assistants or, preferably, as reporters or researchers. They may also have had experience in radio or print journalism. It is recommended that they be thoroughly familiar with video and studio operations.

Solid news judgment coupled with excellent managerial and leadership qualities are extremely important for this job. Decisions have to be made rapidly and, often, under a great deal of pressure. Assistant News Directors need the capacity to edit, write, and even report when needed. In addition, just like their boss, the news director, they must understand the Federal Communications Commission regulations governing fairness and equal-use time, as well as laws concerning copyright and libel.

Unions and Associations

The major professional associations for Assistant News Directors are the Academy of Television Arts and Sciences, the National Academy of Television Arts and Sciences, and the Radio-Television News Directors Association.

Assistant News Directors who write or report on air may also belong to such unions as the American Federation of Television and Radio Artists, the National Association of Broadcast Employees and Technicians, or the Writers Guild of America. In addition, some Assistant News Directors may belong to the umbrella organization, the Society of Professional Journalists.

Tips for Entry

1. While in college, become actively involved with your campus radio and television stations and work on any school publication to gain journalistic experience.
2. Participate in internship programs at local independent, cable, or network affiliated stations.
3. Anticipate your management responsibilities as an Assistant News Director by taking advanced courses in business and management.
4. Be willing to put in your time as a reporter or correspondent in order to gain the needed experience in broadcast journalism.

DESK ASSISTANT

CAREER PROFILE

Duties: Supply clerical and general assistance to television newsroom personnel

Alternate Title(s): News Desk Assistant; News Assistant

Salary Range: $9,000 to $50,000+

Employment Prospects: Good

Advancement Prospects: Good

Prerequisites:

Education or Training—High school diploma required; college degree may be required

Experience—None necessary, but news-related work is helpful

Special Skills and Personality Traits—Clerical and organizational skills; writing ability

CAREER LADDER

```
┌─────────────────────────────────────┐
│   News Writer, Production Assistant, │
│            or Reporter               │
└─────────────────────────────────────┘


┌─────────────────────────────────────┐
│           Desk Assistant             │
└─────────────────────────────────────┘


┌─────────────────────────────────────┐
│   High School or College Student     │
└─────────────────────────────────────┘
```

Position Description

The job of Desk Assistant is an entry-level position in broadcast journalism. The Desk Assistant is a jack-of-all-tasks apprentice who performs routine office and clerical tasks while learning the trade. Generally Desk Assistants will be found only at medium and large stations and networks, where staffs are sufficiently large to warrant a need for such clerical backup. Desk Assistants may work part or full time, any hours of the day or night as needed, or any days of the week, or on holidays.

Desk Assistants help producers assemble news programs for broadcast. Their duties include distributing messages and mail, undertaking research and fact checking, fielding telephone calls, logging tapes, and typing (or computer keying) and filing letters, reports, and scripts. They may be responsible for maintaining newsroom office supplies and being sure that equipment, such as typewriters, copiers, or computers, are serviced and repaired.

Duties associated directly with newsroom operations encompass monitoring copy from wire service printer terminals and distributing the copy to the appropriate reporters and editors, as well as filling requests for information and tapes from newsroom library or storage rooms. Desk Assistants may also take care of the logging in and out of tapes; the handling, sending, and receiving of tapes to and from associate stations and affiliates; and may even be required to act as couriers in this distribution.

Desk Assistants may also help with script preparation (which may also be the province of production assistants in the newsroom). "Breaking script," as it is called, is done for every news broadcast. This process includes typing (or computer keying), updating, and delivering scripts to all the appropriate persons. As major stories occur, multiple updatings may be needed.

Research duties may include collecting background information on stories or people and updating facts, such as sports scores, weather reports, and other constantly changing data. Such individuals may accompany reporters on assignments, thus learning about reporting from the field. They may also be called upon to help in assisting in the control room of the station, thus gaining hands-on experience in production work. Many news producers and managers initiate their careers in this position of Desk Assistant.

Salaries

Entry-level jobs in television pay low salaries. According to the 2002 salary survey made by the Radio-Television News Directors Association, Desk Assistants earned annual salaries ranging from a low of $8,000 (entry-level salary) to a high of $55,000 (much dependent upon number of duties and years of experience in this position). The average yearly salary for Desk Assistants was found to be $22,000. Generally they are paid either a weekly rate if full time, or an hourly wage if part time.

Employment Prospects

Most Desk Assistant posts are found in medium- to large-market cities, including the headquarters of networks and bureaus. The expansion of cable television news has opened more opportunities for Desk Assistants, as has the growing availability of news services on the Internet.

Demand for filling this position is generally steady due to the relatively rapid turnover in the job as individuals are promoted or leave the field altogether.

Advancement Prospects

The Desk Assistant is an outstanding training ground for nearly every work opportunity at a television station, in particular for promotion to production, newswriting, or reporting work. To best achieve that promotion, a Desk Assistant needs to demonstrate a thorough knowledge of broadcast operations, reliable news judgment, and solid writing and speaking skills. The applicant should possess high motivation by seeking assignments beyond the normal range of a Desk Assistant's duties.

Education and Training

While a college degree is not essential for the post of Desk Assistant, such a degree will be needed for higher positions within broadcast journalism. For this reason, some Desk Assistants work part time while completing their college work. Whatever their major may be, aspiring broadcast journalists should include courses in broadcasting (if available), communications, English, history, and the social sciences.

Experience, Skills, and Personality Traits

Experience in any type of news-related job is helpful. These might include working on a community newspaper or a school publication, or an internship at a local radio or television station. Clerical and office skills are principal requirements for a Desk Assistant, who must type (or key) and file reports, correspondence, and scripts. Another key requirement is good organization, as Desk Assistants may have to locate quickly and handle information for a reporter, correspondent, or editor under tight deadline pressure. Those Desk Assistants who aspire to newswriting or reporting jobs must have, or acquire, good quality journalistic research and writing skills, as well as demonstrating ambition and a lot of self-motivation.

Unions and Associations

Desk Assistants may belong to the American Federation of Television and Radio Artists, the National Association of Broadcast Employees and Technicians, the Society of Professional Journalists, or the Writers Guild of America.

Tips for Entry

1. While in school, become actively involved in any campus radio or television station, or work on any school publication to gain journalistic experience.
2. Participate in internship programs at local independent, cable, or network-affiliated radio or television stations.
3. Take any office part-time job during school to gain needed clerical and office skills.
4. Enroll in English and/or speech courses to aid your speech abilities.
5. Hone your researching and computer skills as both will be essential in your career as a broadcast journalist.

NEWS DIRECTOR

CAREER PROFILE

Duties: Assign news coverage; determine station policy; supervise entire news operation of a television station

Alternate Title(s): News Editor; News Producer

Salary Range: $18,000 to $250,000

Employment Prospects: Poor

Advancement Prospects: Poor

Prerequisites:

Education or Training—Undergraduate degree in communications, English, history, liberal arts, political science, or the social sciences

Experience—Several years in television or radio news work

Special Skills and Personality Traits—Excellent news judgment; solid managerial and administrative abilities

CAREER LADDER

```
┌─────────────────────────────────┐
│  General Station Manager or     │
│  News Vice President            │
└─────────────────────────────────┘

┌─────────────────────────────────┐
│  News Director                  │
└─────────────────────────────────┘

┌─────────────────────────────────┐
│  Assistant News Director or Reporter │
└─────────────────────────────────┘
```

Position Description

Television News Directors have the overriding accountability for a television station's news operations. They set the tone for the staff in determining what is news and the final content of news programs. They determine what will be covered, how the stories will be presented, and which reporters will be assigned to handle them. They edit and review all scripts and file reports. In their supervision of every aspect of the news department, from the photographers to the anchors, they have the final responsibility for, and authority over, what appears on the air.

An average station has a news team of 15 to 20 people; larger stations typically have 40 to 50 or more. News Directors are typically the key decision-makers in all newsroom personnel matters. They help develop the budget for the department and handle many administrative responsibilities. At small stations, News Directors may also take part in the gathering and reporting of news, and they may even serve as talk show hosts.

In addition, News Directors typically coordinate the technical operations of the news production (they are even sometimes referred to as news producers). This aspect of their job involves assigning camera crews to stories and camera operatives to work in the studio.

News Directors report directly to station general managers or, in the case of large stations or networks, to the vice president of news. They often are on duty for extremely long hours and work under much pressure, along with having to make many very quick decisions as to what major stories need to be covered right away. The security of their jobs is heavily dependent upon station ratings.

Finally, News Directors frequently supervise the station's public-affairs programs. They may also synchronize news activities with the programming and other departments of the station.

Salaries

The 2002 Salary survey undertaken by the Radio-Television News Directors Association found that annual salaries for News Directors ranged from a minimum of $18,000 to a maximum of $250,000, with a median yearly salary being $64,000, and an average annual salary being $73,800. These salaries represented a 26.7 percent increase over those of 1996.

The same report compared the markets covered by stations to the salaries of station personnel and found that the bigger the market, the bigger the salary. In a related survey within this study, salaries were compared to the number of staff. Again, it was noted that the larger the staff that a News Director supervised, the larger the Director's salary tended to be. At stations with news staff of 10 or fewer, the News Director's median salary was $39,000, whereas at stations with news staff of 51 or more, the median salary jumped to $121,000.

A study of minorities and women in television news made by Vernon Stone of the Missouri School of Journalism made in 1995 and updated in 2000, pointed out that 16 percent of News Directors in 1990 were women, and that jumped up to 24.1 percent by 1996. Minorities, however, lost during that same period, dropping from 10 percent in 1990 to 7.7 percent in 1994. In a 2004 study made by Media Report to Women, it was noted that women at present hold 26.5 percent of television's News Director jobs (as reported in 2003 by the Radio and Television News Directors Association).

Employment Prospects

Although the U.S. Department of Labor's Bureau of Labor Statistics projects slow to moderate growth in television jobs through the year 2012, competition will remain strong for News Director positions, particularly in the highly desirable major cities and the larger markets. While turnover in this position is high, especially at big stations where News Directors frequently move on after two or three years, there are many aggressive job candidates for this opening. The growth of alternative media sources, such as cable television, satellite radio, and Internet journalism, provide more opportunities.

Advancement Prospects

News Directors have limited opportunities for advancement, as at many stations their job is the highest in the news department. Some News Directors may seek promotion to general managers, though most general managers promoted from within come from the sales department rather than the news department. Large stations and networks usually have vice president and assistant vice president positions in news to which News Directors can aspire.

Education and Training

The minimum educational requirement for a newsroom supervisory position such as News Director is an undergraduate degree in communications, English, history, liberal arts, or one or more of the social sciences. Many, if not most, News Directors have degrees in political science. A master's degree might be very beneficial both for employment and for advancement.

Experience, Skills, and Personality Traits

Television News Directors usually must have several years of experience as reporters or assistant News Directors in television or radio before achieving their promotion to the title. Large stations, with all the attendant additional responsibilities and larger staff, require more hands-on experience than small stations. Know-how is what counts in getting this job.

News Directors must possess extremely sound news judgment coupled with the facility to make swift decisions. They must comprehend Federal Communications Commission regulations governing fairness and equal-use time, as well as applicable laws concerning copyright and libel. They need to be high-quality writers and good administrators as well.

Unions and Associations

News Directors usually belong to such major professional associations as the Academy of Television Arts and Sciences, the National Academy of Television Arts and Sciences, and the Radio-Television News Directors Association. Since the position is a management one, News Directors generally do not belong to unions. However, they may be members of such umbrella associations as the Society of Professional Journalists.

Tips for Entry

1. A journalism major in college may be the best scholastic preparation if you intend to become a News Director.
2. While in college become actively involved with your campus radio and television stations and work on any school publication to gain journalistic experience.
3. Participate in internship programs at local independent, cable, or network affiliated stations.
4. Anticipate your management responsibilities as a News Director by taking advanced courses (and possibly getting a degree) in business or business management.
5. Be willing to put in your time as a reporter or correspondent in order to gain the required experience in broadcast journalism.

NEWS WRITER

CAREER PROFILE

Duties: Write scripts (stories) for news programs

Alternate Title(s): Senior Editor

Salary Range: $12,000 to $90,000

Employment Prospects: Fair to good

Advancement Prospects: Fair to good

Prerequisites:

    Education or Training—Undergraduate degree in communications, English, history, liberal arts, or social sciences

    Experience—Ranging from none to several years in similar or related writing position

    Special Skills and Personality Traits—Excellent scriptwriting ability; good news judgment; speed and accuracy

CAREER LADDER

```
┌─────────────────────────────────────┐
│  News Editor, Reporter, or Producer  │
└─────────────────────────────────────┘

┌─────────────────────────────────────┐
│             News Writer              │
└─────────────────────────────────────┘

┌─────────────────────────────────────┐
│   Desk Assistant, Researcher, or     │
│           College Student            │
└─────────────────────────────────────┘
```

Position Description

The job of News Writers in television news departments is a hectic and high-pressure position. It demand swiftness, good reportorial skills, sound news judgment, and the special knack to be able to write for the ear rather than the eye.

News Writers may be consigned to any shift around the clock, any day of the week, any holiday, depending upon the station's immediate needs. They habitually start their workday by reviewing (and later rewriting) press releases and news stories from wire and satellite news services such as CNN and Associated Press. They also review newspapers and stories aired on previous newscasts, and study Internet news sites. They participate at one or more editorial meetings each day in which decisions are made as to what stories will be covered and who will be responsible for tracking and updating breaking stories.

A News Writer may be responsible for writing copy for a major newscast and one or more regularly scheduled news breaks or digests of news stories (which usually last about 30 seconds at a time). News Writers typically undertake their own research, corroborating other news sources and investigating conflicting reports, such as differences in the number of injuries reported in an accident, or the specific number of people involved in social disturbances or events. They interview sources by phone and rewrite the information they have collected, as well as research information in the news sta-

tion's library and on the Internet. In this latter job they are often assisted by desk assistants or researchers. In some cases, they may be assigned to coordinate graphics and tapes to be used during newscasts, even working with artists, producers, or representatives of other television stations.

News Writers must be able to write succinct scripts that are both easy for the newscaster to read and simple for listeners to understand. In addition, it must be kept in mind that these scripts must fit onto a teleprompter screen. They are constricted by time (average news stories seldom run over 90 seconds and may be as short as 10 seconds for a news break or news digest), and their scripts must match what viewers are seeing on the television sets. News Writers either preview tapes of what is going to be shown or are given "shot sheets" in which visuals and time lengths are given. Scripts have to be written down to the very second, a skill that is honed only with a lot of hands-on experience over time.

As many reporters prefer to prepare their own scripts and anchors often write their own scripts for key lead stories, the specific daily workload of a News Writer will vary widely. This workload also depends upon the day's actual news breaks. On any given day, a News Writer may work on a few big stories, or write many small ones.

Other duties of a News Writer include assisting assignment editors, producers, or reporters with various tasks as needed (which, for example, might include monitoring police beat calls). They may also work on the production of news digests, news documentaries, or other special programs. They may be required to supervise tape editing for news reports and even write promotional scripts that publicize upcoming broadcasts.

News Writers usually work under the direct supervision of an assistant news director, a news editor, or a news director (depending very much upon the size of the station staff). Overtime is a constant requirement, with shifts of 10 to 12 hours not uncommon.

Salaries

In its 2002 salary survey, the Radio-Television News Directors Association found that the salaries of News Writers may vary widely from an annual minimum of $12,000 to a high of $90,000, obviously dependent upon the skills and experience of the writer. In addition, it was found that the median yearly salary for a News Writer was $27,500, but the average salary was $32,300. These figures represented an increase of 19.6 percent from similar figures of 1996. The more heavily staffed larger television stations provided the higher salaries.

Employment Prospects

While prospects for News Writers are generally fair to good, beginners will most likely have to start with the smaller stations. Networks and the larger stations in major markets usually hire only seasoned News Writers (three to five years or more of experience), who have worked their way up from the smaller venues. For beginners, local/regional cable and independent stations may be the best place to start.

Advancement Prospects

News Writers have potential opportunities of advancing to such positions as news director or news editor, but only after they have proven their worth to the station. Some experienced News Writers may look to gain experience from production assignments in order to move on to a position as a producer.

Education and Training

As News Editors need to be able to deal with a large array of subjects, they need to have a solid historical perspective of the news events they are covering. A broad education in history, liberal arts, political science, or the social sciences may prove to be far more useful than a degree in broadcast journalism or communications. Nonetheless, courses in broadcasting techniques and production methodologies are extremely helpful in learning the technical side of the business.

Experience, Skills, and Personality Traits

At small outlets News Writers are frequently entry-level employees with or without experience. In contrast, large stations and networks demand extensive experience and proven talents. Many candidates will work as desk assistants or researchers (even at small stations) before becoming News Writers.

News Writers have to be able to compress important data into scripts geared to be heard, *not* seen. They seldom have time to revise, and any revisions must be done on the spot. As researchers, they have to be detail-oriented and thorough, but also speedy. Above all, News Writers need to be exceedingly adaptable and versatile, as they must be able to absorb and understand many different topics and issues, and, in turn, make them understandable to average television viewers.

Unions and Associations

News Writers in the larger markets usually are members of a union, such as the American Federation of Television and Radio Artists, the National Association of Broadcast Employees and Technicians, or the Writers Guild of America. Major professional associations of interest to News Writers include the Academy of Television Arts and Sciences, the National Academy of Television Arts and Sciences, the Radio-Television News Directors Association, and the Society of Professional Journalists.

Tips for Entry

1. While in college become actively involved with your campus radio and television stations to gain hands-on broadcast experience and work on any school publication to gain concrete writing experience.
2. Participate in internship programs at local independent, cable, or network-affiliated stations.
3. As the skills of a News Writer (such as writing tight scripts to be heard, not read) are usually learned on the job, acquire all the writing experience you can. Even writing publicity material for local businesses would be helpful.
4. Broaden your educational background as much as possible to gain the breadth that a good News Writer must possess. Add a foreign language to your skills as it may become helpful on the job.

REPORTER

CAREER PROFILE

Duties: Put together news and feature stories; report on air

Alternate Title(s): Correspondent; Newscaster

Salary Range: $17,000 to $300,000

Employment Prospects: Poor to fair

Advancement Prospects: Fair

Prerequisites:

Education or Training—Undergraduate degree in communications, history, journalism, liberal arts, political science, or the social sciences

Experience—Work as news writer or researcher in newsroom environment helpful

Special Skills and Personality Traits—Excellent speaking, reporting, and writing abilities; comfortable on camera and in the interviewing process; self-motivation; solid news judgment

CAREER LADDER

```
┌─────────────────────────────────────┐
│  Anchor or Assistant News Director   │
└─────────────────────────────────────┘

┌─────────────────────────────────────┐
│              Reporter                │
└─────────────────────────────────────┘

┌─────────────────────────────────────┐
│      Assistant, Researcher,          │
│   News Writer, or College Student    │
└─────────────────────────────────────┘
```

Position Description

Television Reporters' main responsibility is to assemble news items and get stories ready for broadcast. This process includes interviewing sources, researching facts, composing the script of the story, directing a video crew, working with video editors in the studio, and, finally, delivering the news on the air.

Reporters are always working against time, not only against the clock for scheduled news programs for which their story must be ready to be aired, but also limited in the time they have to present the news story on the air. Most major stories typically run about two minutes of airtime, while many stories have 90 seconds or less in which to be presented. Reporters have to abridge the story into highlights, giving the most important information, and, at the same time, making the piece visually interesting.

Reporters are usually assigned stories and provided the estimated time allotments for these pieces by an assignment editor or a news director. Editors often rely on the Reporter's news judgment and instincts to determine the focus or emphasis of a particular story, as well as its length. Some Reporters, particularly those based at large stations or with the networks, specialize in particular fields, such as business, consumer affairs, crime and the police, foreign affairs, health, politics, religion, science, social events, sports, or theater and film. Specialist Reporters usually have more say over the stories they generate than those who cover news events. Some Reporters also serve as anchors, and vice versa, particularly with smaller stations.

Assembling data for stories includes interviewing people either by phone or in person. While some stations have researchers and assistants to handle background fact checking and news writers to prepare the actual stories, most reporters do all these tasks. Thereafter, Reporters go on location with a camera crew and direct the shooting of the story. Their on-air report may include parts of one or more taped interviews, a voiceover for the visual images, and a standup summary. Thanks to the technology of smaller, portable cameras, live reports by Reporters have now become the norm for network news and on many large and small stations

In addition, Reporters need to generate ideas for potential stories. After developing such story ideas, they must dig for extra information to bolster the piece, and, next, deliver those stories with accuracy and a sense of urgency. They require strong conversational writing skills and the ability to ad-lib when required. They need to understand complex issues and information, and generate compelling and informative stories.

Reporters are generally assigned to either a day or evening shift. Stories may range from local political events to major disasters. Covering stories such as wars, political uprisings or turmoil, and natural disasters, here at home or abroad, can be dangerous work, but some Reporters (frequently called correspondents) find such risky work exciting. Reporters may also work on special features or investigative pieces that may take weeks to reach fulfillment before the story is ready to air. In addition, some Reporters may prepare special series of reports on specific subjects to be aired on a succession of programs.

Salaries

In his 2002 study of television and radio news careers, veteran researcher Vernon Stone of the Missouri School of Journalism found that entry-level salaries in television and radio news for 2000 averaged $22,000 a year, compared with $26,000 for journalism graduates taking jobs with daily newspapers. This discrepancy is due primarily to the higher demand for television jobs and the surplus of applicants for each television post, exceeding the number applying for newspaper jobs. In addition, advertising revenues tend to be less when three or more television stations exist in the same area, whereas most daily newspapers enjoy a monopoly. Stone goes on to estimate that the median annual salaries in 2002 would range from $18,000 in smaller stations (servicing the smallest markets) to $72,000 in the largest stations servicing the largest markets.

According to the U.S. Department of Labor's Bureau of Labor Statistics, median annual earnings of reporters and correspondents in 2002 were $33,320. In a study done in 2002 by the Radio and Television News Directors Association, television news Reporter salaries varied from a yearly low of $17,000 to a maximum high of $300,000, with a median annual salary of $26,000 and an average of $32,300. The report indicates that the median salary represents a 18.2 percent upward change from a comparable salary of 1996. This report also indicates that median yearly salaries for news Reporters at the larger stations (51 or more employees) were $52,500, as opposed to $19,500 at the smallest stations (one to 10 employees).

It still remains true that the best salaries are offered in the East, with the lowest in the Midwest (except for larger cities such as Chicago) and the South. Reporters who specialize in areas of news expertise also will have an advantage in the job market.

Employment Prospects

Market size is an important determinant in the size of television salaries, even more so for Reporters than for production personnel. As there tend to be more job applicants for Reporter positions in television than jobs available at most of the larger stations and the networks, the best places to look for employment are the small-town local television sta-

tions (which will have the lower salaries), preceding a move onward to a Reporter job in a larger city.

Advancement Prospects

The Bureau of Labor Statistics projects slower growth in the employment of news analysts, Reporters, and correspondents than the average for all occupations through 2012. In the case of television, this slow growth is due mostly to the consolidation of local television ownerships, as well as the increasing competition for viewers from cable networks and new media opportunities online.

Most job openings will come about from the need to replace Reporters and correspondents who have left the occupation altogether, due mostly to the highly stressful nature of the occupation and its irregular hours.

Many Reporters aspire to become news anchors, a position with a semi-celebrity status, higher salary, and attendant glamour. However, prospects for obtaining such jobs are poor, as there is extreme competition for the limited number of these openings. Some Reporters may turn their ambitions to off-camera jobs, such as assistant news director or, eventually, news director.

Education and Training

Most television station employers prefer applicants with a degree in communications, journalism, or liberal arts, though some may hire graduates with other majors. Some successful applicants may have combined a liberal arts education with a major in broadcast journalism. It should be noted that broadcast journalism programs are often found in the academic curricula as telecommunications or mass communications.

Taped auditions are also extremely important when applying for a Reporter position. Specialized degrees in such areas as business, health, or law, may become advantageous in career advancement. As reporting and photojournalism are so tightly bound together, knowledge of news photography and postproduction editing are skills that are extremely valuable for entry-level positions for combination Reporter/camera operator or Reporter/photographer. To a television station manager, such a new staff member with varied talents can only be cost efficient for the station.

Internships with news organizations (television, radio, or print) provide superb experience for those who aspire to broadcast journalism positions. Many Reporters acquired their first hands-on experience in a real news operation as interns. A bonus in such work (usually unpaid) is that the applicant can begin to develop a networking base of professional contacts.

Experience, Skills, and Personality Traits

Most large television stations (and networks) only hire Reporters with several years of experience. It may be possible to get employment as a Reporter right out of college at small stations or cable operations. In these places, a Reporter may be required to shoot the film, edit it, and then deliver it on the air. However, most Reporters have had some kind of journalistic experience before they get to go on the air as a broadcast Reporter. Entry-level jobs, instead of Reporter, might include copy editor, news writer, production assistant, or researcher. Another avenue of employment might be obtaining a job as a newspaper reporter and then switching to television. In addition, experience on college publications or at radio and television stations is a decided asset.

Needing to deliver the news in a conversational, credible style, Reporters should have a pleasant and well-controlled voice, excellent timing (and the ability to ad-lib when necessary), good pronunciation, a neat and well-groomed appearance, and correct English. They need tact, objectivity, and persistence. They must be able to understand and explain complex issues and information and have knowledge of a wide variety of subjects. Primarily, television Reporters need the same skills as all journalists—ability to work under heavy pressure, accuracy, savvy news judgment, and strong self-motivation.

Unions and Associations

The major unions representing most television Reporters include the American Federation of Television and Radio Artists, the National Association of Broadcast Employees and Technicians, and the Writers Guild of America. While some small stations may not be unionized, most reporting, photography, producing, tape-editing and even writing jobs are off limits except to union members.

Professional associations include the Academy of Television Arts and Sciences, the Association for Women in Communications, the International Radio and Television Society, the National Academy of Television Arts and Sciences, the Radio-Television Correspondents' Gallery (for Congressional Reporters), the Radio-Television News Directors Association, and the Society for Professional Journalists.

Tips for Entry

1. Get as much journalistic experience as possible during college outside your course work (as on the campus newspaper or other publications).
2. Having an internship (preferably with a local radio or television station) gives you working experience in a real news operation and adds a credential that helps get you hired after college.
3. Experience in public speaking, debate, or dramatic arts will help prepare you for on-air reporting.
4. Learn to use a computer effectively, and understand the Internet and Web construction. In other words, become proficient with things digital.
5. Read and observe all you can about all kinds of people and activities, and become a knowledgeable listener and viewer of broadcast news programs.

RESEARCHER

Duties: Support television staff with background research for news and other on-air programs

Alternate Title(s): None

Salary Range: $11,000 to $50,000

Employment Prospects: Fair

Advancement Prospects: Fair to good

Prerequisites:

Education or Training—Undergraduate degree in communications, English, journalism, or liberal arts

Experience—Any kind of background in media is helpful

Special Skills and Personality Traits—Accuracy and careful attention to detail; curiosity; good writing ability; solid organizational skills

```
Reporter, News Writer, or
   Associate Producer
```

```
        Researcher
```

```
Desk Assistant, Production Assistant, or
          College Student
```

Position Description

The majority of Researchers working at television stations are based in the news department. The post is usually an entry-level position, though some of the bigger stations, as well as the networks, may have separate levels of junior and senior Researchers.

Researchers help news directors or editors, news writers, and reporters with assembling background information for pieces to be aired. A 30-minute news broadcast may contain anywhere from 15 to 30 stories, and an individual Researcher may be working on several stories for each broadcast.

A lot of the research work is done by telephone, previewing and checking sources to find the best ones for the reporter to interview. This checking with sources also helps to gather and verify specific data pertaining to stories. The Researcher then prepares summary reports of their findings for reporters or news writers to use. The position is a challenging one filled with constant pressure. Researchers have to be able to soak up a range of information quickly, sifting out the most important material, and then writing this information up in a concise way.

Other work may consist of deeper background searching for data for feature stories to be aired later. Researchers may use television or newspaper archives or such online research

engines as NewsLab (http://www.newslab.org), Nielsen Media Research (http://www.nielsenmedia.com), World News Connection (http://wnc.fedworld.gov), and other such Web sites. Researchers may also generate ideas for stories. They have to sustain contact with news sources, as well as continuously scan magazines, newspapers, and Internet news sites. In some cases, Researchers may be assigned to specific geographic areas of responsibility or to particular topics, such as business, education, or government.

Researchers may also help reporters (or anchors) amass audio and visual materials for pieces, searching library files or contacting other stations to acquire film or videotape footage. Researchers generally are expected to do follow-up work on stories for any further development, as well as focus on other special features, programs, or documentaries. They also may be assigned to the station's marketing department, tracking ratings on various new shows.

Salaries

Researchers are frequently recompensed on a weekly or hourly rate, with extra pay for overtime. Some Researchers may be employed only part time. Beginner Researchers may earn anywhere from $11,000 to $15,000 or more annually, while seasoned Researchers with more than three years of experience can earn up to $40,000 annually or more, including overtime. The best-paid positions tend to be at the larger stations or with the networks.

Employment Prospects

The position of Researcher is generally regarded as entry level in the news department. However, some of the larger stations and the networks may demand a level of experience. Part-time positions are also viable as they often can expand into full-time positions, either as Researchers or desk assistants.

Advancement Prospects

Obtaining a full-time position as a Researcher at a television station may be problematic. However, once established, a Researcher will find advancement opportunities are quite good. They will discover that they have several options available to them. They may end up reporting the news, writing scripts for the news, or assisting in the production of news and other television fare.

Education and Training

As with most jobs in the television news media, an undergraduate degree in communications, English, history, liberal arts, or the social sciences is preferred. Other degrees that usually are acceptable are those in business or political science. Courses in broadcast journalism would be helpful.

Experience, Skills, and Personality Traits

Any experience in the news media is useful in attempting to gain a job as a Researcher for a television station. Such experience could include participating on school or community publications, or working in intern programs with publications or television stations. Researchers may have previous experience as desk or production assistants, reporters, or even as news writers for newspapers or radio stations.

Researchers have to be skillful at gathering information quickly. They need to be comfortable at interviewing over the telephone, extremely detail-oriented, and extremely well-organized. They must be able to cope with a lot of on-the-job pressure (including meeting constant deadlines throughout their day). At the same time they must turn out clearly written and concise reports and summaries of their findings. They must be knowledgeable about resources for information and must have solid news judgment.

Unions and Associations

Researchers may belong to such unions as the American Federation of Television and Radio Artists, the National Association of Broadcast Employees and Technicians, or the Writers Guild of America. Some Researchers may want to join professional associations as well, such as the Academy of Television Arts and Sciences, the National Academy of Television Arts and Sciences, or the Society of Professional Journalists.

Tips for Entry

1. While in college, become actively involved with your campus radio and television stations to gain broadcast experience, and work on any school publication to acquire writing experience.
2. Participate in internship programs at local independent, cable, or network affiliated stations.
3. Volunteer to work on local community newsletters and other publications for the writing and interviewing experience and for the potential sources for future research.
4. A summer job within a research facility, such as a library, would aid you in your understanding the dimensions and demands of the research process.

SCHOLASTIC, ACADEMIC, AND NONPROFIT INSTITUTIONS

ALUMNI COMMUNICATIONS SPECIALIST

CAREER PROFILE

Duties: Prepare circulars, invitations, letters, newsletters, and other materials for distribution to alumni

Alternate Title(s): Alumni Information Officer; Donor Relations Specialist; Gift Recognition Specialist

Salary Range: $23,000 to $40,000

Employment Prospects: Good

Advancement Prospects: Good

Prerequisites:

Education or Training—Undergraduate degree in communications, English, journalism, or liberal arts

Experience—Familiarity with desktop publishing, professional writing experience, and word processing skills all helpful

Special Skills and Personality Traits—Ability to write and edit

CAREER LADDER

```
┌─────────────────────────────────────┐
│        Alumni Office Director        │
└─────────────────────────────────────┘

┌─────────────────────────────────────┐
│   Alumni Communications Specialist   │
└─────────────────────────────────────┘

┌─────────────────────────────────────┐
│           College Student            │
└─────────────────────────────────────┘
```

Position Description

Alumni communications duties are very similar to those involved in public relations work. An Alumni Communications Specialist must publicize the university or college and its activities to its alumni and solicit donations from them to support the institution's assorted programs. Frequently, this job is an entry-level position within the alumni office.

Alumni communications may encompass a variety of activities. Some of these tasks include helping local alumni clubs plan events and contacting alumni members with fliers, invitations to events, and e-mail newsletters. Other alumni communication activities include writing acknowledgment and thank-you notes to alumni for gifts to the university or college, as well as preparing letters soliciting donations.

The alumni office and its Communications Specialist also publicize educational programs for the alumni, frequently spotlighting one or more of the institution's professors, as well as cruises and trips geared for the alumni. Generally, Alumni Communications Specialists do not participate in promoting any continuing education programs as they are usually controlled by a separate department. However, Alumni Communications Specialists frequently serve as a liaison between the faculty and the alumni.

Additionally, the alumni office and its Communications Specialist may also arrange speaking engagements involving the alumni and graduation events that also include alumni. The office is responsible for making contacts with recent graduates and maintaining files on the whereabouts of all graduates.

Salaries

As a newcomer in the alumni office with no experience, an applicant can anticipate an annual salary around $20,000. Salaries for this position can range up to $35,000 or more.

Employment Prospects

Since employment in alumni offices tends to have a strong changeover rate, the potential of getting such a position is good. Also, as most Alumni Communications Specialists are involved in soliciting alumni donations, which generate significant revenue for the institution, their jobs are less susceptible to cutbacks when the economy takes a downturn. It should be noted, however, that most of the institution's fund-raising activities are done by a development director completely separate from the alumni office.

Advancement Prospects

An Alumni Communications Specialist who performs well can expect a good chance at advancement within the alumni office, even though most of these departments tend to be small-staffed. In addition, a person in this position may well be able to transfer into public relations, either with the university or college, performing similar functions at a public relations agency, or working in private industry.

Education and Training

A bachelor's degree is essential for this work. If the institution has a specialized curriculum, such as business, law, medical, or other profession, a degree in that subject may also be required of an Alumni Communications Specialist. It should be noted that anyone working in the alumni office of a particular school does not necessarily have to be a graduate of that school. A degree from a comparable educational institution should be more than sufficient.

A journalism degree and/or work within a journalistic environment may be helpful. Also, it might be helpful to have had some experience in public relations.

Experience, Skills, and Personality Traits

While no specific experience is required for a beginner job as an Alumni Communications Specialist, a familiarity with desktop publishing and word processing systems may be required, particularly for more advanced positions within the alumni office.

Alumni Communications Specialists should be imaginative, have a great deal of tact, and be skilled at communicat-ing easily with people. They should have outgoing personalities and be able to write well.

Unions and Associations

Career information and support for Alumni Communications Specialists is available from the Council for the Advancement and Support of Education—known as CASE (http://www.case.org).

In addition, Alumni Communications Specialists may belong to some of the same groups that serve other public relations professionals, such as the Association for Women in Communications, and, most important, the Public Relations Society of America.

Tips for Entry

1. While in college, take extra writing courses to help refine your abilities to write clearly and informatively.
2. Become knowledgeable about word processing systems and desktop publishing as these will be necessary skills while working in an alumni office.
3. Work on school publications to gain both writing and editing experience.
4. Find ways of talking with alumni during your college years to gain insight on communication with them about college matters.

ALUMNI MAGAZINE EDITOR

CAREER PROFILE

Duties: Oversee alumni magazine preparation and production; supervise staff; edit and rewrite copy for magazine

Alternate Title(s): Alumni Magazine Editor in Chief; Editorial Director

Salary Range: $39,000 to $90,000+

Employment Prospects: Fair

Advancement Prospects: Poor

Prerequisites:

Education or Training—Undergraduate degree in communications, English, journalism, or liberal arts (does not have to be from institution issuing the magazine)

Experience—Background as editor, journalist, or writer essential

Special Skills and Personality Traits—Excellent editing and writing skills; skill at understanding a wide range of alumni readership groups and being sensitive to their concerns; tact in dealing with controversial topics without compromising the editorial integrity of the magazine

CAREER LADDER

```
┌─────────────────────────────────┐
│  Editorial Director of University/ │
│     College Publications          │
└─────────────────────────────────┘

┌─────────────────────────────────┐
│      Alumni Magazine Editor       │
└─────────────────────────────────┘

┌─────────────────────────────────┐
│         Associate Editor          │
└─────────────────────────────────┘
```

Position Description

Alumni Magazine Editors are responsible for the editorial content and the production of the magazine. They assign stories, oversee the magazine's budget, and perform the usual editing and production tasks related to magazine publishing.

At smaller alumni magazines, the Editor may have other responsibilities as well, such as handling assorted public relations functions for the institution. The relationship between the editorial integrity of the magazine and the necessary public relations and fund-raising functions of the institution is often an uneasy one. Many Alumni Magazine Editors view their publications as less a promotional vehicle for the institution (college or university) and more a forum for information about the institution and its noteworthy alumni. Development professionals (public relations and administrative staff involved in fund-raising) tend to view the alumni magazine as a tool for making alumni, nostalgic for their alma mater, open up their checkbooks to help it. In the dialogue over these differing views, some Alumni Magazine Editors cite a 1995 survey conducted by eight univer-

sities asking alumni to rate the stories in their magazine that they found the most interesting. Tom Griffin, editor of *Columns Magazine* at the University of Washington, which participated in this survey, indicated that general-interest stories were the most popular, followed by articles about research, news of the university, class news and notes, and university history, with stories about gifts to the university last. Nonetheless, the debate on the function of the alumni magazine continues.

Generally, the duties required of the Alumni Magazine Editor are similar to those for a commercial publication, with the additional need to remain sensitive to the concerns of the alumni, the administration and faculty, and the students and parents of students. Articles on potentially controversial subjects or faculty members may evoke differing reactions from different groups. The viewpoint of all these factions need to be fairly represented while maintaining the magazine's editorial integrity, sometimes a difficult balance for the Alumni Magazine Editor to maintain.

Along with the production duties of the job, Alumni Magazine Editors assign photographs and articles (frequently to freelancers), edit manuscripts, and plan future issues. It is said that good editorial planning is essential to good content. Alumni Magazine Editors also oversee all personnel matters (hiring and firing), answer letters from readers and alumni, and have the final say on placement of articles and features in the magazine.

In addition, the Alumni Magazine Editor must ensure that the magazine operates within its budgetary boundaries. The publication may rely solely on advertising revenue, or alumni donations, or a combination of both, plus some degree of subsidy allocated by the institution.

Salaries

Alumni Magazine Editors may earn salaries ranging from $39,000 to $90,000, depending upon the size of the magazine and the institution it serves. Prestigious colleges and universities with larger endowments may pay more.

Employment Prospects

While there are definite employment prospects in the academic environment for a practiced professional editor, the field is competitive. Alumni magazines provide work opportunities away from the centers, such as New York City, where many business and consumer magazines are based. Some editors and writers who have toiled in these commercial environments are attracted to alumni magazine positions for their contrasting academic environment.

Advancement Prospects

The position of Alumni Magazine Editor is usually the highest post at many alumni publications. Advancement may come about by moving on to larger organizations, either in the commercial sector or at larger educational institutions.

Education and Training

As a bare minimum, a bachelor's degree in communications, English, journalism, or liberal arts is a must for this position. Most alumni magazines do not require that the degree come from the institution employing the Alumni Magazine Editor. If the institution is a specialized one, such as an engineering, law, or scientific school, some graduate-level education in the field may be necessary background.

Experience, Skills, and Personality Traits

The degree of know-how required of an applicant for the job of Alumni Magazine Editor will depend upon the publication. Three to five years' experience as an editor may be necessary for some positions, while others may demand 10 years or more. Such experience can include, beyond editing, news reporting (for newspapers radio, or television), or magazine reporting, as well as production experience with magazines or newspapers.

Unions and Associations

Alumni Magazine Editors can receive valuable career development information (as well as good practical advice on publication methods, design, advertising, and story ideas) from the Council for the Advancement and Support of Education (or CASE) (http://www.case.org).

The major professional associations that serve the magazine industry are the American Society of Journalists and Authors and the American Society of Magazine Editors. In addition, there are many writer and communications associations, as well as trade and industry groups, which are open to magazine editors.

Tips for Entry

1. Get as much journalistic experience as possible while in college by participating on campus publications.
2. Gain production experience by working in a newspaper or magazine environment as an intern. Layout and typesetting functions are a necessary part of the background of a magazine editor.
3. As an Alumni Magazine Editor it is important to remember that you are primarily a special-audience publisher, not really a journalist. Your publication is aimed at a very particular market, and it is necessary to play up the strengths of the institution that you represent.
4. As your market is the alumni, keep a file of newsworthy alumni and look for human-interest stories about them and about the institution that you represent.
5. Study many types of publications to expand your knowledge of suitable styles for a variety of writing genres and appealing layout formats—all of which could help you invigorate your magazine's content and design.

EDUCATION RESEARCHER

CAREER PROFILE

Duties: By interviewing, observing, and researching, collect data and information on current educational concerns to be included in studies or reports

Alternate Title(s): None

Salary Range: $20,000 to $60,000+

Employment Prospects: Fair

Advancement Prospects: Poor

Prerequisites:

Education or Training—Undergraduate degree in communications, education, English, or journalism; advanced degree(s) might be required for some types of research

Experience—Two or more years of interviewing and research study experience

Special Skills and Personality Traits—Familiarity with data collection, qualitative research, statistical analysis, and survey methodologies; good computer and writing skills

CAREER LADDER

```
┌─────────────────────────────────┐
│  Development Director or        │
│  Senior Research Associate      │
└─────────────────────────────────┘

┌─────────────────────────────────┐
│  Education Researcher           │
└─────────────────────────────────┘

┌─────────────────────────────────┐
│  Research Assistant, Teacher, or│
│  College Student                │
└─────────────────────────────────┘
```

Position Description

Education Researchers investigate academic processes, teaching methods, and educational technology through a wide range of methodologies, from in-depth case studies to randomized field trials. They design research studies, develop data collection instruments, gather and analyze data, and interpret the research findings for educational policymakers and practitioners.

They first have to prepare for the research by examining relevant published material about the area of the research study, and then frame the specific process of data analysis and collection accordingly. In the collecting of data, extensive field notes on what the Education Researcher hears, sees, experiences, and thinks are critical in helping to reconstruct the specifics of setting and interaction with those being interviewed. This interviewing process helps to fine-tune the investigation by clarifying the purpose of the interviews and the process of the overall research. After the interview, the prepared written transcription of what has been discussed allows for detailed analysis and determination of the reliability, relevance, and validity of the material collected. Thus the compiling of detailed,

exhaustive notes is essential to this research process. It is also important to have the focus (a question, or a central problem to be investigated) of the research study always in mind. The collecting of notes systematically and carefully over the full time of the research study will help to point to patterns or themes that can be supported by the data accumulated.

Education Researchers must have experience managing and coordinating a team of people who will be involved in the overall research process. They will need to work closely with relevant school personnel and be sensitive to the needs and perceptions of those being interviewed.

Another means of collecting observational data for a research study is through a shadow study, a systematic observation and recording of events in a student's or teacher's day over a period of time. This shadowing of events as experienced by the participant usually is followed by an interview, which can more fully explore the events and anecdotes that occurred during the shadow study. This methodology is particularly useful for exploring questions about what students or teachers experience in schools as well as to reveal patterns of learning and teaching behavior.

Salaries

Annual salaries for Education Researchers may vary widely depending upon the complexity of the research and the expertise of the Researcher. Generally, yearly salaries may range from $20,000 to $60,000 or more, depending upon the size and prestige of the education institution with whose guidance and support the research is being conducted.

Employment Prospects

As research is the backbone of all policy decision-making, qualified and experienced Education Researchers are always in demand. However, openings for Education Researchers are strongly dependent upon budgetary concerns, and any cutbacks in federal or state funding in education can affect the funding for research studies adversely.

Advancement Prospects

Advancement to a more senior research position, or even development director for the educational institution, is a possibility as openings occur, or a lateral move to another education institution as an alternative way to advancement.

Education and Training

Most research positions require extensive education beyond a bachelor's degree in communications, education, English, or liberal arts. Many Education Research positions will require a master's degree, and, in some cases, a Ph.D. in education or social science. A specialization in data evaluation is an added bonus.

Experience, Skills, and Personality Traits

While a background in communications or journalism is helpful, actual education experience is even more valuable. Experience in dealing with qualitative research and survey methodologies, as well as evaluating data may be crucial.

Managing research studies and coordinating personnel efforts are also important, and teaching or administrative experience in a school is a distinct plus.

Education Researchers need to be careful, well-focused observers of the people being interviewed and the data being compiled. They must be attentive and have excellent writing and presentation skills. They have to be adept at working within deadlines, as well as be sensitive to any issues of partiality in working with school personnel in the collection of data needed for the research.

Unions and Associations

Career information and support for Education Researchers is available from the Council for the Advancement and Support of Education (http://www.case.org). Other professional associations may include the American Educational Research Association, the American Association for Higher Education, the Association for Institutional Research, the Association for the Study of Higher Education, the Higher Education Data Sharing Consortium, the National Council for Research and Planning, or the National Education Association. If the Researcher has been, or still is, a teacher, he or she may belong to the American Federation of Teachers.

Tips for Entry

1. Take writing courses to become familiar with the researching process needed to prepare comprehensive written reports for research projects.
2. Become familiar with reference protocols and research studies in the field of education.
3. Volunteer to work on local community newsletters and other publications for the writing experience and for the potential sources for future research.
4. A summer job within a research facility, such as a library, would aid you in your understanding of the research process.

NEWS DIRECTOR

CAREER PROFILE

Duties: Write and distribute news about the educational institution to newspapers, faculty, and staff members

Alternate Title(s): None

Salary Range: $21,500 to $88,000+

Employment Prospects: Fair

Advancement Prospects: Good

Prerequisites:

Education or Training—Undergraduate degree in communications, English, journalism, or liberal arts

Experience—None for entry-level positions at smaller educational institutions; several years in journalism or public relations at larger schools

Special Skills and Personality Traits—Ability to identify specific groups to which the school circulates information and develop a distinct approach to each; excellent writing and organizational skills

CAREER LADDER

```
┌─────────────────────────────────────┐
│     Public Relations Director        │
└─────────────────────────────────────┘

┌─────────────────────────────────────┐
│          News Director               │
└─────────────────────────────────────┘

┌─────────────────────────────────────┐
│    Assistant News Director,          │
│  Journalist, or College Student      │
└─────────────────────────────────────┘
```

Position Description

News Directors at educational institutions disseminate (and often write) information about the institution to be delivered to the public through news releases. They also provide data about campus events to the school's faculty, staff, and students.

To be sufficiently effective at accomplishing their tasks, News Directors need to describe what the institution is all about and how the school wishes to be perceived by both the public and its faculty, staff, and students. Information distributed to different groups needs to be adjusted to help promote the institution to that target audience. News Directors have to be aware of how these different factions view themselves, their role in the public arena, and their particular relationship with educational institutions. What type of person constitutes each such group and what information they need (or want) will help determine the tenor of the messages that the News Director will communicate to them.

Salaries

Salaries vary widely according the size of the institution and what monies have been allocated to support the news office functions on campus. Some schools prefer to allocate more funds for those involved with admissions or fund-raising, and, thus, downplay the role of a News Director. Others hire experienced public relations professionals to serve as News Director and pay generous salaries.

The annual pay range can be from approximately $21,000, for an entry-level job that requires no experience, to $88,000 or more at prestigious educational institutions that are interested in promoting their interests aggressively.

Employment Prospects

The need for public relations professionals has become readily apparent in recent years. The U.S. Bureau of Labor Statistics estimates that the employment of public relations specialists is anticipated to increase faster than the average of all other occupations through 2012. However, within the educational sector, this expansion of job opportunities in the field might be limited due to the cutback of funding for education from both the state and national governments.

Advancement Prospects

Advancement prospects for a successful News Director are good. This promotion could entail moving up within the specific institution's staff to become director of public relations or director of development. On the other hand, advancement could be effected by moving to a larger school and taking a similar job, but at a higher pay scale.

Education and Training

At a minimum, an undergraduate degree in communications, English, journalism, or liberal arts is required. For entry-level positions, no other educational degrees are usually necessary, but for larger schools, some further education (or courses) in public relations might be requested.

Experience, Skills, and Personality Traits

Experience required will vary with the job market and the particular institution. For some entry-level jobs, no particular experience may be necessary, or, in contrast, several years as a newspaper or magazine journalist or a public relations professional may be required.

Additionally, a News Director must be sensitive to how the educational institution wants to present itself to the public, to its own campus community, and to that of other institutions. Thus, the News Director needs to be able to adapt the information conveyed to suit various audiences.

Unions and Associations

Many educational News Directors belong to many of the same groups that other public relations professionals join, such as the Association for Women in Communications, the Council of Communication Management, and the Public Relations Society of America. In addition, News Directors may belong to the Council for the Advancement and Support of Education, or any other professional associations related to the field of education.

Tips for Entry

1. Gain as much journalism experience as possible, both in college and in intern programs. Also look at intern programs in public relations.
2. Join the Public Relations Student Society of America (http://www.prssa.org) in order to meet with professional public relations practitioners, and to initiate valuable industry contacts.
3. Be active in local community groups to learn to interact effectively with a wide assortment of people and to understand their perceptions of their role in the community.
4. Explore with faculty and the administration the needs and goals of the educational institution for which you work.

APPENDIXES*

*Throughout these appendixes are street addresses, Web site addresses, and other contact information for schools, companies, associations, organizations, and publications. However, since this information may change at any time, neither the publisher nor the authors take any responsibility for the accuracy of the listings. In addition, listing in these appendixes does not imply that the authors are recommending an association, company, product, school, publication, or service, nor does omission from these lists, due to space or other considerations, imply disapproval. The publisher and authors shall have neither liability nor responsibility to any person or entity with respect to any loss or damage caused or alleged to be caused directly or indirectly by the professionals, associations, schools, or companies listed and/or their services rendered to the reader.

APPENDIX I
EDUCATIONAL INSTITUTIONS

Compared with many vocations (for example engineering and nursing), most careers in writing (such as advertising, broadcasting, and publishing) do not necessitate a specific academic degree for the applicant to break into that field. Most individuals who enter the work areas detailed in this book have at least acquired an undergraduate college degree, frequently in communications, film/video arts, journalism, or public relations. As indicated within this guide, a postgraduate degree is often useful in climbing the career ladder and acquiring a higher-level position.

Among the wide spectrum of majors offered by colleges today, many candidates for a degree who pursue careers discussed in this volume have majored in such varied disciplines as American literature, creative writing, foreign languages, and theater arts. In actuality, book editors, copy editors, and proofreaders may well have majored in anything ranging from anthropology to political science, which often leads them to specialize in such fields in their publishing careers. Then too, once an individual is established on one of the career paths discussed herein, the person may well take evening courses or weekend seminars in particular topics to enhance their knowledge in their chosen work.

With the above in mind, an undergraduate degree in communications or journalism is often a good stepping-stone to being eligible for one of the many jobs in the writing fields discussed in this book. (Hands-on experience, of course, is a necessity for successfully obtaining higher-level posts.) Many academic institutions offer specialized programs within these broad majors, such as broadcasting, communications technology, film/video arts, public relations, publishing, and speech/rhetorical studies. Sometimes these specialized majors are termed *sequences*.

The following is a list of many of the U.S. four-year colleges/universities that offer undergraduate degrees in communications and/or journalism. Many of these institutions also offer master's and other higher degrees not detailed here. For these schools, the listings below provide addresses, telephone numbers, fax numbers, and e-mail addresses, as well as Web sites. Also provided (in alphabetical order) are each school's majors/specialties allied to communications and journalism. For further information about courses offered, admission requirements, and such topics as scholarships, campus housing, and academic calendar, contact the institution(s) of choice. Since college admissions e-mail addresses frequently change, it is advised to check the institution's Web site. (Many colleges provide a link/form on their Web sites for directly contacting school departments.)

Those institutions whose programs have satisfied the standards established by the Accrediting Council on Education in Journalism and Mass Communications (ACEJMC) have been flagged with an asterisk (*). Note that the ACEJMC does not always accredit all the listed degree programs for an asterisked school. Thus while the ACEJMC may have accredited only communications and journalism majors at a particular institution, the school may offer—and have listed in this volume—other related majors such as advertising, public relations, or speech/rhetorical studies. The ACEJMC's Web site (http://www.ukans.edu/acejmc) provides information on which programs it has accredited at each institution and the most recent year of accreditation. Typically the ACEJMC makes accreditation evaluations every six years.

Many of the professional associations listed in Appendix III offer scholarships and internships and may be consulted directly about them. The Dow Jones Newspaper Fund prepares an annual *Journalist's Road to Success* manual containing useful information about journalism careers, scholarship, and internships. This is published at their Web site.

The Dow Jones Newspaper Fund, Inc.
U.S. Highway 1 North
Monmouth Junction, NJ 08852
Phone: (609) 452-2820
E-mail: newsfund@wsj.dowjones.com
http://djnewspaperfund.dowjones.com/fund/pubcareerguide.asp

ALABAMA

Alabama State University
915 South Jackson Street
Montgomery, AL 36104
Phone: (334) 229-4291
Fax: (334) 229-4984
E-mail: dlamar@asunet.alasu.edu
http://www.alasu.edu

Broadcasting, communications, journalism, public relations, speech/rhetorical studies

Auburn University*
202 Mary Martin Hall
Auburn, AL 36849
Phone: (334) 844-4080
Fax: (334) 844-6179
E-mail: admissions@auburn.edu

http://www.auburn.edu
Communications, journalism, public relations, speech/rhetorical studies

Jacksonville State University
700 Pelham Road North
Jacksonville, AL 36265
Phone: (256) 782-5268
Fax: (256) 782-5953

E-mail: info@jsucc.jsu.edu
http://www.jsu.edu
Communications

Samford University
800 Lakeshore Drive
Birmingham, AL 35229
Phone: (205) 726-3676
Fax: (205) 726-2171
E-mail: admissions@samford.edu
http://www.samford.edu
Communications, journalism, speech/
rhetorical studies

Spring Hill College
4000 Dauphin Street
Mobile, AL 36608
Phone: (251) 380-3030
Fax: (251) 460-2186
E-mail: admit@shc.edu
http://www.shc.edu
Advertising, broadcasting, journalism,
public relations

Troy State University
111 Adams Administration
Troy, AL 36082
Phone: (334) 670-3179
Fax: (334) 670-3733
E-mail: admit@troy.edu
http://www.troy.edu
Broadcasting, communications, journal-
ism, speech/rhetorical studies

University of Alabama—Birmingham
HUC 260
1530 Third Avenue South
Birmingham, AL 35294
Phone: (205) 934-8221
Fax: (205) 975-7114
E-mail: undergradadmit@uab.edu
http://www.uab.edu
Communications

University of Alabama—Tuscaloosa
P.O. Box 879132
Tuscaloosa, AL 35487
Phone: (205) 348-5666
Fax: (205) 348-9046
E-mail: admissions@ua.edu
http://www.ua.edu
Advertising, film/video arts, journalism,
public relations

University of South Alabama
182 Administration Building
Mobile, AL 36688
Phone: (334) 460-6141
Fax: (334) 460-7023

E-mail: admiss@jaguari.usouthal.edu
http://www.usouthal.edu
Communications

ALASKA

University of Alaska—Anchorage*
3211 Providence Drive
Anchorage, AK 99508
Phone: (907) 786-1480
Fax: (907) 786-4888
E-mail: enroll@uaa.alaska.edu
http://www.uaa.alaska.edu
Communications, journalism

University of Alaska—Fairbanks*
P.O. Box 757480
Fairbanks, AK 99775
Phone: (907) 474-7500
Fax: (907) 474-5379
E-mail: fyapply@uaf.edu
http://www.uaf.edu
Journalism, speech/rhetorical studies

ARIZONA

Arizona State University East*
P.O. Box 870112
Tempe, AZ 85387
Phone: (480) 965-7788
Fax: (480) 727-1008
E-mail: Stacie.dana@asu.edu
http://www.east.asu.edu
Broadcasting, communications, journal-
ism, media studies

Arizona State University West
4701 West Thunderbird Road
Phoenix, AZ 85306-4908
Phone: (602) 543-813
Fax: (602) 543-8312
E-mail: west-admissions@asu.edu
http://www.west.asu.edu
Media studies

Northern Arizona University
P.O. Box 4080
Flagstaff, AZ 86011
Phone: (926) 523-5511
Fax: (928) 523-0226
E-mail: undergraduate.admissions@nau.
edu
http://www.nau.edu
Advertising, broadcasting, communica-
tions, journalism, public relations, speech/
rhetorical studies

University of Arizona*
P.O. Box 210040
Tucson, AZ 85721

Phone: (520) 621-3237
Fax: (520) 621-9799
E-mail: appinfo@arizona.edu
http://www.arizona.edu
Communications, creative writing, jour-
nalism, media studies

ARKANSAS

Arkansas State University*
P.O. Box 1630
State University, AR 72467
Phone: (870) 972-3024
Fax: (870) 910-8094
E-mail: admissions@astate.edu
http://www.astate.edu
Communications technology, journalism,
speech/rhetorical studies

Arkansas Tech University
Doc Bryan #414
Arkansas Tech University
Russellville, AR 7280
Phone: (479) 968-0343
Fax: (479) 964-0522
E-mail: tech.enroll@mail.atu.edu
http://www.atu.edu
Journalism, speech/rhetorical studies

Harding University
P.O. Box 12255
Searcy, AR 72149
Phone: (501) 279-4407
Fax: (501) 279-4865
E-mail: admissions@harding.edu
http://www.harding.edu
Advertising, broadcasting, communica-
tions, journalism

Henderson State University
1100 Henderson Street
HSU P.O. Box 7560
Arkadelphia, AR 71999
Phone: (870) 230-5028
Fax: (870) 230-5066
E-mail: hardwrv@hsu.edu
http://www.hsu.edu
Communications, speech/rhetorical studies

John Brown University
2000 West University Street
Siloam Springs, AR 72761
Phone: (800) 634-6969
Fax: (501) 524-4196
E-mail: jbuinfo@jbu.edu
http://www.jbu.edu
Broadcasting, journalism, public relations

University of Arkansas—Fayetteville*
232 Silas Hunt Hall
Fayetteville, AR 72701
Phone: (479) 575-5346
Fax: (479) 575-7515
E-mail: uofa@uark.edu
http://www.uark.edu
Communications, journalism

University of Arkansas—Little Rock
2801 South University Avenue
Little Rock, AR 72204
Phone: (501) 569-3127
Fax: (501) 569-8915
E-mail: admissions@ualr.edu
http://www.ualr.edu
Advertising, communications, communications technology, journalism, technical and business writing

University of Central Arkansas
201 Donaghey Avenue
Conway, AR 72035
Phone: (501) 450-3128
Fax: (501) 450-5228
E-mail: admissions@mail.uca.edu
http://www.uca.edu
Communications, journalism, speech/rhetorical studies

CALIFORNIA

California Polytechnic State University—San Luis Obispo
1 Grand Avenue
San Luis Obispo, CA 93407
Phone: (805) 756-2311
Fax: (805) 756-5400
E-mail: admissions@calpoly.edu
http://www.calpoly.edu
Journalism, speech/rhetorical studies

California State Polytechnic University—Pomona
3801 West Temple Avenue
Pomona, CA 91768
Phone: (909) 468-5020
Fax: (909) 869-5020
E-mail: cppadmit@csupomona.edu
http://www.csupomona.edu
Communications

California State University—Chico*
400 West First Street
Chico, CA 95929
Phone: (530) 898-4428
Fax: (530) 898-6456
E-mail: info@csuchico.edu
http://www.csuchico.edu
Communications, journalism, public relations

California State University— Dominguez Hills
100 East Victoria Street
Carson, CA 90747
Phone: (310) 243-3600
Fax: (310) 516-3609
E-mail: lwise@csudh.edu
http://www.csudh.edu
Communications, public relations

California State University—Fresno
5150 North Maple Avenue M/S JA 57
Fresno, CA 93740
Phone: (559) 278-2261
Fax: (559) 278-4812
E-mail: vivian_franco@csufresno.edu
http://www.csufresno.edu
Communication, public relations, speech/rhetorical studies

California State University— Fullerton*
800 North State College Boulevard
Fullerton, CA 92834
Phone: (714) 773-2370
Fax: (714) 278-2356
E-mail: admissions@fullerton.edu
http://www.fullerton.edu
Advertising, broadcasting, communications, journalism, public relations, speech/rhetorical studies

California State University—Hayward
25800 Carlos Bee Boulevard
Hayward, CA 94542
Phone: (510) 885-2624
Fax: (510) 885-4059
E-mail: adminfo@csuhayward.edu
http://www.csuhayward.edu
Communications, speech/rhetorical studies

California State University—Long Beach
1250 Bellflower Boulevard
Long Beach, CA 90840
Phone: (562) 985-5471
Fax: (562) 985-4973
E-mail: eslb@csulb.edu
http://www.csulb.edu
Broadcasting, creative writing, film/video arts, journalism, public relations, speech/rhetorical studies

California State University—Los Angeles
5151 State University Drive
Los Angeles, CA 90032
Phone: (323) 343-3901
Fax: (323) 343-6306

E-mail: admission@calstatela.edu
http://www.calstatela.edu
Broadcasting, communications, communications technology, journalism, speech/rhetorical studies

California State University— Northridge*
P.O. Box 1286
Northridge, CA 91328
Phone: (818) 677-3773
Fax: (818) 677-4665
E-mail: lorraine.newlon@csun.edu
http://www.csun.edu
Broadcasting, communications, communications technology, creative writing, journalism, speech/rhetorical studies

California State University— Sacramento
6000 J Street
Lassen Hall
Sacramento, CA 95819
Phone: (916) 278-3901
Fax: (916) 279-5603
E-mail: admissions@csus.edu
http://www.admissions@csus.edu
Communications, journalism

California State University—San Bernardino
5500 University Parkway
San Bernardino, CA 92407
Phone: (909) 880-5188
Fax: (909) 880-7034
E-mail: moreinfo@mail.csusb.edu
http://www.csusb.edu
Communications, creative writing

Humboldt State University
1 Harpst Street
Arcata, CA 95521
Phone: (707) 826-4402
Fax: (707) 826-6194
E-mail: hsuinfo@humboldt.edu
http://www.humboldt.edu
Communications, journalism, speech/rhetorical studies

Menlo College
1000 El Camino Real
Atherton, CA 94027
Phone: (650) 543-3753
Fax: (650) 543-4496
E-mail: admissions@menlo.edu
http://www.menlo.edu
Advertising, broadcasting, communications, journalism, media studies

Pacific Union College
Enrollment Services
One Angwin Avenue
Angwin, CA 94508
Phone: (800) 862-7080
Fax: (707) 965-6432
E-mail: enroll@puc.edu
http://www.puc.edu
Communications, journalism, public relations

Pepperdine University
24255 Pacific Coast Highway
Malibu, CA 90263
Phone: (310) 456-4861
Fax: (310) 506-4861
E-mail: admission-seaver@pepperdine.edu
http://www.pepperdine.edu
Advertising, communications, journalism, public relations, speech/rhetorical studies

Point Loma Nazarene University
3900 Lomaland Drive
San Diego, CA 92106
Phone: (619) 849-2273
Fax: (619) 849-2601
E-mail: admissions@ptloma.edu
http://www.ptloma.edu
Communications, journalism, speech/rhetorical studies

Saint Mary's College of California
P.O. Box 4800
Moraga, CA 94575-4800
Phone: (925) 631-4224
Fax: (925) 376-7193
E-mail: smcadmit@stmarys-ca.edu
http://www.stmarys-ca.edu
Communications

San Diego State University
5500 Campanile Drive
San Diego, CA 92182
Phone: (619) 594-7800
Fax: (619) 594-1250
E-mail: admission@sdsu.edu
http://www.sdsu.edu
Broadcasting, journalism, public relations, speech/rhetorical studies

San Francisco State University*
1600 Holloway Avenue
San Francisco, CA 94132
Phone: (415) 338-6486
Fax: (415) 338-7196
E-mail: ugadmit@sfsu.edu
http://www.sfsu.edu
Broadcasting, film/video arts, journalism, speech/rhetorical studies

San Jose State University
One Washington Square
San Jose, CA 95112
Phone: (408) 283-7500
Fax: (408) 924-2050
E-mail: contact@sjsu.edu
http://www.sjsu.edu
Advertising, broadcasting, film/video arts, journalism, speech/rhetorical studies

Santa Clara University
500 El Camino Real
Santa Clara, CA 95053
Phone: (408) 554-4700
Fax: (408) 554-5255
E-mail: none@scu.edu
http://www.scu.edu
Communications

Stanford University
Undergraduate Admission
Old Union 232
Stanford, CA 94305
Phone: (650) 723-2091
Fax: (650) 723-6050
E-mail: admissions@stanford.edu
http://www.stanford.edu
Communications

University of California—Berkeley*
110 Sproul Hall #5800
Berkeley, CA 94720
Phone: (510) 642-3175
Fax: (510) 642-7333
E-mail: ouars@uclink.berkeley.edu
http://www.berkeley.edu
Communications, film/video arts, speech/rhetorical studies

University of California—Los Angeles
405 Hilgard Avenue
P.O. Box 951436
Los Angeles, CA 90095
Phone: (310) 825-3101
Fax: (310) 206-1206
E-mail: ugadm@saonet.ucla.edu
http://www.ucla.edu
Film/video arts

University of California—Santa Barbara
Office of Admissions
1210 Cheadle Hall
Santa Barbara, CA 93106
Phone: (805) 893-2881
Fax: (805) 893-2676
E-mail: appinfo@sa.ucsb.edu
http://www.ucsb.edu
Film/video arts

University of La Verne
1950 Third Street
La Verne, CA 91750
Phone: (909) 392-2800
Fax: (909) 392-2714
E-mail: admissions@ulv.edu
http://www.ulv.edu
Broadcasting, communications, journalism

University of San Francisco
2130 Fulton Street
San Francisco, CA 94117
Phone: (415) 422-6563
Fax: (415) 422-2217
E-mail: admission@usfca.edu
http://www.usfca.edu
Communications, media studies

University of Southern California*
700 Childs Way
Los Angeles, CA 9008
Phone: (213) 740-1111
Fax: (213) 740-6364
E-mail: admitusc@usc.edu
http://www.usc.edu
Broadcasting, communications, creative writing, film/video arts, journalism, public relations

University of the Pacific
3601 Pacific Avenue
Stockton, CA 95211
Phone: (209) 946-2211
Fax: (209) 946-2413
E-mail: admissions@pacific.edu
http://www.pacific.edu
Communications

COLORADO

Adams State College
Office of Admissions
One Adams State College
Alamosa, CO 81102
Phone: (719) 587-7712
Fax: (719) 587-7522
E-mail: ascadmit@adams.edu
http://www.adams.edu
Advertising, journalism

Colorado State University*
Spence Hall
Fort Collins, CO 80523
Phone: (970) 491-6909
Fax: (970) 491-7799
E-mail: admissions@colostate.edu
http://www.colostate.edu
Creative writing, journalism, public relations, speech/rhetorical studies, technical and business writing

Colorado State University—Pueblo
Admissions
2200 Bonforte Boulevard
Pueblo, CO 81001
Phone: (719) 549-2461
Fax: (719) 549-2419
E-mail: info@colostate-pueblo.edu
http://www.colostate-pueblo.edu
Broadcasting, communications, journalism, speech/rhetorical studies

Mesa State University
P.O. Box 2647
Grand Junction, CO 81502
Phone: (970) 248-1875
Fax: (970) 248-1973
E-mail: admissions@mesastate.edu
http://www.mesastate.edu
Communications

Metropolitan State College of Denver
Campus P.O. Box 16
P.O. Box 173362
Denver, CO 80217
Phone: (303) 556-3058
Fax: (303) 556-6345
E-mail: askmetro@mscd.edu
http://www.mscd.edu
Communications, journalism, speech/rhetorical studies

University of Colorado—Boulder*
Campus P.O. Box 30
Boulder, CO 90309
Phone: (303) 492-6301
Fax: (303) 492-7115
E-mail: apply@colorado.edu
http://www.colorado.edu
Communications, film/video arts, journalism

University of Denver
University Hall, Room 110
2197 South University Boulevard
Denver, CO 80208
Phone: (303) 871-2036
Fax: (303) 871-3301
E-mail: admission@du.edu
http://www.du.edu
Communications, journalism, public relations

University of Northern Colorado
UNC Admissions Office
Greeley, CO 80639
Phone: (970) 351-2881
Fax: (970) 351-2984
E-mail: unc@mail.unco.edu
http://www.unco.edu

Advertising, communications, journalism, public relations

CONNECTICUT

Southern Connecticut State University
131 Farnham Avenue
New Haven, CT 06515
Phone: (203) 392-5656
Fax: (203) 392-5727
E-mail: adminfo@scsu.ctstateu.edu
http://www.southernct.edu
Communications, journalism

University of Bridgeport
380 University Avenue
Bridgeport, CT 06601
Phone: (203) 576-4552
Fax: (203) 576-4941
E-mail: admit@bridgeport.edu
http://www.bridgeport.edu
Communications, creative writing, journalism, media studies, public relations

University of Connecticut*
2131 Hillside Road, Unit 3088
Storrs, CT 06286
Phone: (860) 486-3137
Fax: (860) 486-1476
E-mail: beahusky@uconn.edu
http://www.uconn.edu
Communications, journalism

University of Hartford
200 Bloomfield Avenue
West Hartford, CT 06117
Phone: (860) 768-4296
Fax: (860) 768-4961
E-mail: admissions@mail.hartford.edu
http://www.hartford.edu
Communications, film/video arts, technical and business writing

University of New Haven
300 Orange Avenue
West Haven, CT 06516
Phone: (203) 932-7319
Fax: (203) 931-6093
E-mail: adminfo@newhaven.edu
http://www.newhaven.edu
Communications

Yale University
P.O. Box 208234
New Haven, CT 06520
Phone: (203) 432-9316
Fax: (203) 432-9392
E-mail: undergraduate_admissions@yale.edu

http://www.yale.edu
Film/video arts

DELAWARE

Delaware State University
1200 DuPont Highway
Dover, DE 19901
Phone: (302) 857-6361
Fax: (302) 857-6362
E-mail: admissions@desu.edu
http://www.desu.edu
Communications, public relations, speech/rhetorical studies

University of Delaware
Admissions Office
116 Hullihen Hall
Newark, DE 19716
Phone: (302) 831-8123
Fax: (302) 931-6095
E-mail: admissions@udel.edu
http://www.udel.edu
Communication, journalisum

DISTRICT OF COLUMBIA

American University*
4400 Massachusetts Avenue, NW
Washington, DC 20016
Phone: (202) 885-6000
Fax: (202) 885-1025
E-mail: afa@american.edu
http://www.american.edu
Communications, creative writing, film/video arts, journalism, media studies, public relations

George Washington University
2121 I Street, NW, Suite 201
Washington, DC 20052
Phone: (202) 994-6040
Fax: (202) 994-0325
E-mail: gwadm@gwu.edu
http://www.gwu.edu
Broadcasting, communications, journalism

Howard University*
2400 Sixth Street, NW
Washington, DC 20059
Phone: (202) 806-2700
Fax: (202) 806-4462
E-mail: admission@howard.edu
http://www.howard.edu
Broadcasting, communications, film/video arts, journalism

FLORIDA

Florida A&M University*
Suite G-9, Foote-Hilyer Administration
    Center
Tallahassee, FL 32307
Phone: (850) 599-3796
Fax: (950) 599-3069
E-mail: adm@famu.edu
http://www.famu.edu
Journalism

Florida International University*
University Park, PC 140
Miami, FL 33119
Phone: (305) 348-2363
Fax: (305) 348-3648
E-mail: admiss@flu.edu
http://www.flu.edu
Journalism

Florida Southern College
111 Lake Hollingsworth Drive
Lakeland, FL 33801
Phone: (863) 680-4131
Fax: (863) 680-4120
E-mail: fscadm@flsouthern.edu
http://www.flsouthern.edu
Advertising, communications, journalism,
public relations

Florida State University
2500 University Center
Tallahassee, FL 32306
Phone: (850) 644-6200
Fax: (850) 644-0197
E-mail: admissions@admin.fsu.edu
http://www.fsu.edu
Broadcasting, creative writing, media
studies, public relations

Jacksonville University
2800 University Boulevard North
Jacksonville, FL 32211
Phone: (904) 256-7000
Fax: (904) 256-7012
E-mail: admissions@ju.edu
http://www.jacksonville.edu
Communications, speech/rhetorical studies

University of Central Florida
P.O. Box 160111
Orlando, FL 32816
Phone: (407) 823-3000
Fax: (407) 823-5625
E-mail: admission@mail.ucf.edu
http://www.ucf.edu
Advertising, journalism, public relations,
speech/rhetorical studies

University of Florida*
201 Criser Hall, P.O. Box 11400
Gainesville, FL 32611-4000
Phone: (352) 392-1365
Fax: (352) 392-3987
E-mail: At Web site
http://www.ufl.edu
Advertising, journalism, public relations,
speech/rhetorical studies

University of Miami*
P.O. Box 248025
Coral Gables, FL 33124
Phone: (305) 284-4323
Fax: (305) 284-2507
E-mail: admission@miami.edu
http://www.miami.edu
Advertising, broadcasting, communica-
tions, film/video arts, journalism, public
relations, speech/rhetorical studies, tech-
nical and business writing

University of North Florida
4567 St. Johns Bluff Road, South
Jacksonville, FL 32224
Phone: (904) 620-2624
Fax: (904) 620-2414
E-mail: osprey@unf.edu
http://www.unf.edu
Communications

**University of South Florida—
    St. Petersburg***
140 Seventh Avenue South
St. Petersburg, FL 33701
Phone: (727) 553-4USF
Fax: (727) 553-974-2592
E-mail: admissions@stpt.usf.edu
http://www.stpt.usf.edu
Communications, journalism

University of South Florida—Tampa*
4202 East Fowler Avenue SVC-1036
Tampa, FL 33620-9951
Phone: (813) 874-3350
Fax: (813) 974-9689
E-mail: jglassma@admin.usf.edu
http://www.usf.edu
Communications, speech/rhetorical studies

University of West Florida
11000 University Parkway
Pensacola, FL 32514
Phone: (850) 474-2230
Fax: (850) 474-3360
E-mail: admissions@uwf.edu
http://uwf.edu
Communications, public relations

GEORGIA

Berry College
P.O. Box 490159
Mount Berry, GA 30149
Phone: (706) 236-2215
Fax: (706) 236-2248
E-mail: admissions@berry.edu
http://www.berry.edu
Communications

Brenau University Women's College
One Centennial Circle
Gainesville, GA 30501
Phone: (770) 534-6100
Fax: (770) 538-4306
E-mail: wcadmissions@lib.brenau.edu
http://www.brenau.edu
Corporate communications, mass commu-
nications

Clark Atlanta University
223 James P. Brawley Drive
Atlanta, GA 30314
Phone: (404) 880-8000
Fax: (404) 880-6174
E-mail: admissions@panthernet.cau.edu
http://www.cau.edu
Communications speech/rhetorical studies

Emory University
Boisfeuillet Jones Center
201 Dowman Drive NE
Atlanta, GA 30322
Phone: (404) 727-6036
Fax: (404) 727-4303
E-mail: admiss@emory.edu
http://www.emory.edu
Creative writing, film/video arts, journalism

Georgia Southern University
P.O. Box 8024
Statesboro, GA 30460
Phone: (912) 681-5391
Fax: (912) 486-7240
E-mail: admissions@georgiasouthern.edu
http://www.georgiasouthern.edu
Communications, journalism, public rela-
tions, speech/rhetorical studies

Georgia State University
P.O. Box 4009
Atlanta, GA 30302
Phone: (404) 651-2365
Fax: (404) 651-4811
E-mail: admissions@gsu.edu
http://www.gsu.edu

Creative writing, film/video arts, journalism, media studies, speech/rhetorical studies

University of Georgia*
Terrell Hall
Athens, GA 30602
Phone: (706) 542-8776
Fax: (706) 542-1466
E-mail: undergrad@admissions.uga.edu
http://www.uga.edu
Advertising, broadcasting, communications, communications technology, film/video arts, journalism, public relations, speech/rhetorical studies

HAWAII

University of Hawaii—Hilo
200 West Kawili Street
Hilo, HI 96720
Phone: (808) 974-7414
Fax: (808) 933-0861
E-mail: uhhadm@hawaii.edu
http://www.hawaii.edu
Communications, speech/rhetorical studies

University of Hawaii—Manoa
2600 Campus Road, QLCSS Room 001
Honolulu, HI 96822
Phone: (808) 956-8975
Fax: (808) 956-4148
E-mail: ar-info@hawaii.edu
http://www.uhm.hawaii.edu
Communications, journalism, speech/rhetorical studies

IDAHO

Boise State University
1910 University Drive
Boise, ID 83725
Phone: (208) 426-1156
Fax: (208) 426-3765
E-mail: bsuinfo@boisestate.edu
http://www.boisestate.edu
Communications, creative writing, journalism

Idaho State University
Admissions Office
Campus P.O. Box 8270
Pocatello, ID 93208
Phone: (208) 282-2475
Fax: (208) 282-4231
E-mail: info@isu.edu
http://www.isu.edu
Communications, media studies, speech/rhetorical studies

University of Idaho
UI Admissions Office
P.O. Box 44264
Moscow, ID 83844
Phone: (308) 885-6326
Fax: (308) 885-9119
E-mail: admappl@uidaho.edu
http://www.uidaho.edu
Communications, journalism

ILLINOIS

Bradley University
1501 West Bradley Avenue
Peoria, IL 61625
Phone: (309) 677-1000
Fax: (309) 677-2797
E-mail: admissions@bradley.edu
http://www.bradley.edu
Communications, public relations

Columbia College—Chicago
600 South Michigan Avenue
Chicago, IL 60605
Phone: (312) 344-7130
Fax: (312) 344-8024
E-mail: admissions@colum.edu
http://www.colum.edu
Advertising, communications technology, film/video arts, journalism, public relations

DePaul University
One East Jackson Boulevard
Chicago, IL 60604
Phone: (312) 362-8300
Fax: (312) 362-5749
E-mail: admitdpu@depaul.edu
http://www.depaul.edu
Communications

Eastern Illinois University*
600 Lincoln Avenue
Charleston, IL 61920
Phone: (217) 581-2223
Fax: (217) 581-7060
E-mail: cdadmit@www.eiu.edu
http://www.eiu.edu
Communications, journalism

Illinois State University
Admissions Office
Campus P.O. Box 2200
Normal, IL 61790
Phone: (309) 438-2181
Fax: (309) 438-3932
E-mail: ugradadm@ilstu.edu
http://www.ilstu.edu
Communications, public relations, speech/rhetorical studies

Loyola University of Chicago
Admissions Office
820 North Michigan Avenue
Chicago, IL 60611
Phone: (312) 915-6500
Fax: (312) 915-7216
E-mail: admission@luc.edu
http://www.luc.edu
Communications

Northern Illinois University
Office of Admissions
Williston Hall 101, NIU
DeKalb, IL 60115
Phone: (815) 753-0446
Fax: (815) 753-1783
E-mail: admissions-info@niu.edu
http://www.niu.edu
Communications, journalism

Northwestern University*
P.O. Box 3060
1801 Hinman Avenue
Evanston, IL 60208
Phone: (847) 491-7271
Fax: (847) 491-5565
E-mail: ug-admission@northwestern.edu
http://www.northwestern.edu
Broadcasting, communications, communications technology, creative writing, journalism, public relations, speech/rhetorical studies

Roosevelt University
430 South Michigan Avenue
Chicago, IL 60605
Phone: (312) 341-3515
Fax: (312) 341-3523
E-mail: applyRU@roosevelt.edu
http://www.roosevelt.edu
Broadcasting, journalism, public relations, speech/rhetorical studies

**Southern Illinois University—
    Carbondale***
Admissions & Records, MC 4710
Carbondale, IL 62901
Phone: (618) 453-4405
Fax: (618) 453-3250
E-mail: joinsiuc@siuc.edu
http://www.siuc.edu
Advertising, broadcasting, journalism, media studies, speech/rhetorical studies

**Southern Illinois University—
    Edwardsville**
P.O. Box 1600
Edwardsville, IL 62026
Phone: (618) 650-3705

Fax: (618) 650-5013
E-mail: admis@siue.edu
http://www.siue.edu
Communications, speech/rhetorical studies

**University of Illinois—Urbana-
    Champaign***
901 West Illinois Street
Urbana, IL 61801
Phone: (217) 333-0302
Fax: (217) 333-9758
E-mail: admissions@oar.uiuc.edu
http://www.uiuc.edu
Broadcasting, communications, journalism,
media studies, speech/rhetorical studies

University of Saint Francis
500 Wilcox Street
Joliet, IL 60435
Phone: (815) 740-5037
Fax: (815) 740-5032
E-mail: admissions@stfrancis.edu
http://www.stfrancis.edu
Communications journalism

Western Illinois University
One University Circle
115 Sherman Hall
Macomb, IL 61455
Phone: (309) 298-3157
Fax: (309) 298-3111
E-mail: wiuadm@wiu.edu
http://www.wiu.edu
Communications, journalism

INDIANA

Anderson University
1100 East Fifth Street
Anderson, IN 46012
Phone: (765) 641-4080
Fax: (765) 641-4091
E-mail: info@anderson.edu
http://www.anderson.edu
Communications

Ball State University*
Office of Admissions
2000 West University Avenue
Muncie, IN 47306
Phone: (765) 285-8300
Fax: (765) 285-1632
E-mail: askus@bsu.edu
http://www.bsu.edu
Advertising, broadcasting, communica-
tions, film/video arts, journalism, speech/
rhetorical studies

Butler University
4600 Sunset Avenue
Indianapolis, IN 46208
Phone: (317) 940-8100
Fax: (317) 940-8150
E-mail: admission@butler.edu
http://www.butler.edu
Broadcasting, communications, journal-
ism, speech/rhetorical studies

Calumet College of Saint Joseph
2400 New York Avenue
Whiting, IN 46394
Phone: (219) 473-4215
Fax: (219) 473-4259
E-mail: admissions@ccsj.edu
http://www.ccsj.edu
Communications

DePauw University
101 East Seminary
Greencastle, IN 46135
Phone: (765) 658-4006
Fax: (765) 658-4007
E-mail: admission@depauw.edu
http://www.depauw.edu
Communications, media studies

Franklin College
501 East Monroe Street
Franklin, IN 46142
Phone: (317) 738-8062
Fax: (317) 738-8274
E-mail: admissions@franklincollege.edu
http://www.franklincollege.edu
Journalism

Goshen College
1700 South Main Street
Goshen, IN 46526
Phone: (574) 535-7535
Fax: (574) 535-7609
E-mail: admissions@goshen.edu
http://www.goshen.edu
Communications, journalism

Indiana State University
Office of Admissions
Trey Hall 134
Terre Haute, IN 47809
Phone: (812) 237-2121
Fax: (812) 237-8023
E-mail: admissions@indstate.edu
http://www.indstate.edu
Broadcasting, communications, film/video
arts, journalism

Indiana University—Bloomington*
300 North Jordan Avenue
Bloomington, IN 47405

Phone: (812) 855-0661
Fax: (812) 855-5102
E-mail: iuadmit@indiana.edu
http://www.indiana.edu
Communications, journalism, media stud-
ies, speech/rhetorical studies

**Indiana University–Purdue University
    Indianapolis**
425 North University Boulevard
Cavanaugh Hall, Room 129
Indianapolis, IN 46202
Phone: (317) 274-4591
Fax: (317) 278-1862
E-mail: apply@iupui.edu
http://www.iupui.edu
Communications, journalism, public
relations

Purdue University—West Lafayette
1080 Schleman Hall
West Lafayette, IN 47907
Phone: (765) 494-1776
Fax: (765) 494-0544
E-mail: admissions@purdue.edu
http://www.purdue.edu
Advertising, communications, film/video
arts, journalism, public relations

Saint Mary-of-the-Woods College
Office of Admissions
Guerin Hall
Saint Mary-of-the-Woods, IN 47876
Phone: (812) 535-5106
Fax: (812) 535-4900
E-mail: smwcadms@smwc.edu
http://www.smwc.edu
Communications technology, creative
writing, journalism, public relations

University of Evansville
1800 Lincoln Avenue
Evansville, IN 47722
Phone: (812) 479-2468
Fax: (812) 474-4076
E-mail: admission@evansville.edu
http://www.evansville.edu
Advertising, communications, journalism,
public relations

University of Southern Indiana*
8600 University Boulevard
Evansville, IN 47712
Phone: (812) 464-1765
Fax: (812) 465-7154
E-mail: enroll@usi.edu
http://www.usi.edu
Advertising, communications technology,
journalism, media studies, public relations

Valparaiso University
Office of Admissions, Kretzman Hall
1700 Chapel Drive
Valparaiso, IN 46383-4520
Phone: (219) 464-5011
Fax: (219) 464-6898
E-mail: undergrad.admissions@valpo.edu
http://www.valpo.edu
Broadcasting, communications, journalism, media studies, public relations

IOWA

Drake University*
2507 University Avenue
Des Moines, IA 50311
Phone: (515) 271-3181
Fax: (515) 271-2831
E-mail: admission@drake.edu
http://www.choose.drake.edu
Advertising, broadcasting, communications, journalism, public relations, publishing, speech/rhetorical studies

Grand View College
1200 Grandview Avenue
Des Moines, IA 50316
Phone: (515) 263-2810
Fax: (515) 263-2974
E-mail: admiss@gvc.edu
http://www.gvc.edu
Broadcasting, communications, journalism

Iowa State University*
100 Alumni Hall
Ames, IA 50011
Phone: (515) 294-5836
Fax: (515) 294-2592
E-mail: admissions@iastate.edu
http://www.iastate.edu
Advertising, communications, journalism, speech/rhetorical studies

University of Iowa*
107 Calvin Hall
Iowa City, IA 52242
Phone: (319) 335-3847
Fax: (319) 335-1535
E-mail: admissions@uiowa.edu
http://www.uiowa.edu
Broadcasting, communications, film/video arts, journalism, media studies, speech/rhetorical studies

KANSAS

Fort Hays State University
600 Park Street
Hays, KS 67601
Phone: (785) 628-5666
Fax: (785) 628-4187
E-mail: tigers@fhsu.edu
http://www.fhsu.edu
Communications

Kansas State University*
119 Anderson Hall
Manhattan, KS 66506
Phone: (785) 532-6250
Fax: (785) 532-6393
E-mail: kstate@ksu.edu
http://www.consider.k-state.edu
Communications, journalism, speech/rhetorical studies

Pittsburg State University
1701 South Broadway
Pittsburg, KS 66762
Phone: (620) 235-4251
Fax: (620) 235-6003
E-mail: psuadmit@pittstate.edu
http://www.pittstate.edu
Broadcasting, communications, creative writing

University of Kansas*
Office of Admissions and Scholarships
1502 Iowa Street
Lawrence, KS 66045-7575
Phone: (785) 864-3911
Fax: (785) 864-5017
E-mail: adm@ku.edu
http://www.ku.edu
Advertising, broadcasting, journalism, speech/rhetorical studies

Washburn University
1700 SW College Avenue
Topeka, KS 66621
Phone: (785) 231-1030
Fax: (785) 296-7933
E-mail: zzdpadm@washburn.edu
http://www.washburn.edu
Speech/rhetorical studies

Wichita State University
1845 Fairmount Street
Wichita, KS 67260
Phone: (316) 978-3085
Fax: (316) 978-3174
E-mail: admissions@wichita.edu
http://www.wichita.edu
Communications, creative writing

KENTUCKY

Eastern Kentucky University
Coates, P.O. Box 2A
Richmond, KY 40475
Phone: (859) 622-2106
Fax: (606) 622-8024
E-mail: stephen.byn@eku.edu
http://www.eku.edu
Broadcasting, journalism, public relations, speech/rhetorical studies

Morehead State University
100 Admission Center
Morehead, KY 40351
Phone: (606) 783-2000
Fax: (606) 783-5038
E-mail: admissions@morehead-st.edu
http://www.moreheadstate.edu
Advertising, communications, journalism, speech/rhetorical studies

Murray State University*
P.O. Box 9
Murray, KY 42071
Phone: (270) 762-3741
Fax: (270) 762-3780
E-mail: admissions@murraystate.edu
http://www.murraystate.edu
Advertising, broadcasting, communications, journalism, speech/rhetorical studies

Northern Kentucky University
Administrative Center 400
Nunn Drive
Highland Heights, KY 41099
Phone: (859) 572-5220
Fax: (859) 572-6665
E-mail: admitnku@nku.edu
http://www.nku.edu
Communications technology, journalism, speech/rhetorical studies

University of Kentucky*
100 Funkhuser Building
Lexington, KY 40506
Phone: (859) 257-2000
Fax: (859) 257-2000
E-mail: admission@uky.edu
http://www.uky.edu
Advertising, communications, journalism

Western Kentucky University
Potter Hall 117
One Big Red Way
Bowling Green, KY 42101
Phone: (270) 745-2551
Fax: (270) 745-6133
E-mail: admission@wku.edu
http://www.wku.edu
Advertising, broadcasting, communications, journalism, public relations, speech/rhetorical studies

LOUISIANA

Grambling State University*
P.O. Box 864
Grambling, LA 71245
Phone: (318) 274-6423
Fax: (318) 274-3292
E-mail: taylorn@gram.edu
http://www.gram.edu
Communications, journalism, speech/rhetorical studies

**Louisiana State University—
    Baton Rouge***
110 Thomas Boyd Hall
Baton Rouge, LA 70803
Phone: (225) 578-1175
Fax: (225) 578-4433
E-mail: admissions@lsu.edu
http://www.lsu.edu
Communications, speech/rhetorical studies

Louisiana Tech University
P.O. Box 3178
Ruston, LA 71272
Phone: (318) 257-3036
Fax: (318) 257-2499
E-mail: bulldog@latech.edu
http://www.latech.edu
Journalism, speech/rhetorical studies

Loyola University—New Orleans
6363 St. Charles Avenue, P.O. Box 18
New Orleans, LA 70811
Phone: (504) 865-3240
Fax: (504) 865-3383
E-mail: admit@loyno.edu
http://www.loyno.edu
Communications, communications technology, creative writing

McNeese State University
P.O. Box 92495
Lake Charles, LA 90609
Phone: (318) 475-5146
Fax: (318) 475-5189
E-mail: info@mail.mcneese.edu
http://www.mcneese.edu
Broadcasting, communications, speech/rhetorical studies

Nicholls State University*
P.O. Box 2004
Thibodaux, LA 70310
Phone: (985) 448-4507
Fax: (985) 448-4929
E-mail: nicholls@nicholls.edu
http://www.nicholls.edu
Communications, journalism

Northwestern State University*
209 Roy Hall
Natchitoches, LA 71497
Phone: (318) 357-4503
Fax: (318) 357-4257
E-mail: admissions@nsula.edu
http://www.nsula.edu
Advertising, journalism

Southeastern Louisiana University
SLU 10752
Hammond, LA 70402
Phone: (985) 549-2066
Fax: (985) 549-5632
E-mail: admissions@selu.edu
http://www.selu.edu
Communications

Southern University and A&M College*
P.O. Box 9901
Baton Rouge, LA 70813
Phone: (225) 771-2430
Fax: (225) 771-2500
E-mail: admit@subr.edu
http://www.subr.edu
Broadcasting, communications, journalism, speech/rhetorical studies

Tulane University
6823 St. Charles Avenue
New Orleans, LA 70118
Phone: (504) 865-5731
Fax: (504) 862-8715
E-mail: undergrad.admission@tulane.edu
http://www.tulane.edu
Media studies

University of Louisiana—Lafayette*
P.O. Drawer 41210
Lafayette, LA 70504
Phone: (337) 482-6457
Fax: (337) 482-6195
E-mail: admissions@louisiana.edu
http://www.louisiana.edu
Advertising, broadcasting, communications, journalism, public relations

University of Louisiana—Monroe*
700 University Avenue
Monroe, LA 71209
Phone: (318) 342-5252
Fax: (318) 342-5274
E-mail: rehood@ulm.edu
http://www.ulm.edu
Communications technology, journalism, film/video arts, journalism, speech/rhetorical studies

MAINE

University of Maine—Augusta
46 University Drive
Augusta, ME 04330
Phone: (207) 621-3185
Fax: (207) 621-3116
E-mail: umaar@maine.edu
http://www.uma.maine.edu
Communications, journalism

University of Maine—Orono
5713 Chadbourne Hall
Orono, ME 04469
Phone: (207) 581-1561
Fax: (207) 581-1213
E-mail: um-admit@maine.edu
http://www.maine.edu
Communications, journalism, speech/rhetorical studies

MARYLAND

Bowie, State University
14000 Jericho Park Road
Henry Administration Building
Bowie, MD 20715
Phone: (301) 860-3415
Fax: (301) 860-3438
E-mail: schanaiwa@bowiestate.edu
http://www.bowiestate.edu
Broadcasting, journalism, public relations

University of Maryland—College Park*
Mitchell Building
College Park, MD 20742
Phone: (301) 314-8385
Fax: (301) 314-9693
E-mail: um-admit@uga.umd.edu
http://www.maryland.edu
Broadcasting, communications, journalism

**University of Maryland—University
    College**
3501 University Boulevard, East
Adelphi, MD 20783
Phone: (301) 985-7000
Fax: (301) 985-7364
E-mail: umucinfo@nova.umuc.edu
http://www.umuc.edu
Communications

MASSACHUSETTS

Babson College
Mustard Hall
Babson Park, MA 02457
Phone: (781) 239-5522
Fax: (781) 239-4315

E-mail: ugradadmission@babson.edu
http://www.babson.edu
Advertising

Boston College
140 Commonwealth Avenue
Devlin Hall 208
Chestnut Hill, MA 02467
Phone: (617) 552-3100
Fax: (617) 552-0798
E-mail: ugadmis@bc.edu
http://www.bc.edu
Communications

Boston University
121 Bay State Road
Boston, MA 02215
Phone: (617) 353-2300
Fax: (617) 353-9695
E-mail: admissions@bu.edu
http://www.bu.edu
Advertising, broadcasting, communications, film/video arts, journalism, public relations

Emerson College
120 Boylston Street
Boston, MA 02116
Phone: (617) 824-8600
Fax: (617) 824-8609
E-mail: admission@emerson.edu
http://www.emerson.edu
Advertising, broadcasting, communications, communications technology, creative writing, film/video arts, journalism, media studies, public relations, publishing, speech/rhetorical studies

Harvard College
Byerly Hall
8 Garden Street
Cambridge, MA 02138
Phone: (617) 495-1551
Fax: (617) 495-8821
E-mail: college@fas.harvard.edu
http://www.fas.harvard.edu
Creative writing, film/video arts

Simmons College
300 The Fenway
Boston, MA 02115
Phone: (617) 521-2051
Fax: (617) 521-3190
E-mail: ugadm@simmons.edu
http://www.simmons.edu
Advertising, communications, public relations

Suffolk University
8 Ashburton Place
Boston, MA 02108
Phone: (617) 573-8460
Fax: (617) 742-4291
E-mail: admission@suffolk.edu
http://www.suffolk.edu
Advertising, broadcasting, communications, journalism, media studies, public relations, speech/rhetorical studies

University of Massachusetts—Amherst
University Admissions Center
Amherst, MA 01003
Phone: (413) 545-0222
Fax: (413) 545-4312
E-mail: mail@admissions.umass.edu
http://www.umass.edu
Communications, journalism

MICHIGAN

Central Michigan University*
205 Warriner Hall
Mount Pleasant, MI 48859
Phone: (989) 774-3076
Fax: (989) 774-7267
E-mail: cmuadmit@cmich.edu
http://www.cmich.edu
Broadcasting, communications, creative writing, journalism, public relations, speech/rhetorical studies

Eastern Michigan University
400 Pierce Hall
Ypsilanti, MI 48197
Phone: (734) 487-3060
Fax: (734) 487-1484
E-mail: admissions@emich.edu
http://www.emich.edu
Advertising, broadcasting, communications, communications technology, film/video arts, journalism, public relations, speech/rhetorical studies

Ferris State University
1201 South State Street
Center for Student Services
Big Rapids, MI 49307
Phone: (231) 591-2100
Fax: (231) 591-3944
E-mail: admissions@ferris.edu
http://www.ferris.edu
Advertising, public relations

Madonna University
36600 Schoolcraft Road
Livonia, MI 48150
Phone: (734)-432-5339

Fax: (734) 432-5393
E-mail: muinfo@smtp.munet.edu
http://www.munet.edu
Communications, journalism, public relations, technical and business writing

Michigan State University*
250 Administration Building
East Lansing, MI 48824-1046
Phone: (517) 355-8332
Fax: (517) 353-1647
E-mail: adis@msu.edu
http://www.msu.edu
Advertising, communications, journalism, media studies, public relations

Oakland University
Office of Admissions
101 North Foundation Hall
Rochester, MI 48309
Phone: (248) 370-3360
Fax: (248) 370-4462
E-mail: ouinfo@oakland.edu
http://www.oakland.edu
Communications, journalism

**University of Michigan—
   Ann Arbor**
1220 Student Activities Building
Ann Arbor, MI 48109
Phone: (734) 764-7433
Fax: (734) 936-0740
E-mail: ugadmiss@umich.edu
http://www.umich.edu
Communications, journalism, media studies, speech/rhetorical studies

Wayne State University
656 West Kirby Street
Detroit, MI 48202
Phone: (313) 577-3577
Fax: (313) 577-7536
E-mail: admissions@wayne.edu
http://www.wayne.edu
Broadcasting, communications, film/video arts, journalism, public relations, speech/rhetorical studies

Western Michigan University
1903 West Michigan Avenue
Kalamazoo, MI 49008
Phone: (269) 387-2000
Fax: (269) 387-2096
E-mail: ask-wmu@wmich.edu
http://www.wmich.edu
Creative writing, journalism

MINNESOTA

Bemidji State University
1500 Birchmont Drive, NE
Deputy Hall
Bemidji, MN 56601
Phone: (218) 755-2040
Fax: (218) 755-2074
E-mail: admissions@bemidjistate.edu
http://www.bemidjistate.edu
Broadcasting, communications, journalism

Minnesota State University—Mankato
122 Taylor Center
Mankato, MN 56001
Phone: (570) 389-1822
Fax: (507) 389-1511
E-mail: admissions@mnsu.edu
http://www.mnsu.edu
Creative writing, journalism, public relations, speech/rhetorical studies

Minnesota State University—Moorhead
Owens Hall
Moorhead, MN 56563
Phone: (218) 236-2161
Fax: (218) 291-4374
http://www.mnstate.edu
Advertising, broadcasting, communications, journalism, public relations, speech/rhetorical studies

Saint Cloud State University*
720 South Fourth Avenue
Saint Cloud, MN 56301
Phone: (320) 308-2244
Fax: (320) 308-2243
E-mail: scsu4u@stcloudstate.edu
http://www.stcloudstate.edu
Advertising, broadcasting, communications, journalism, public relations, speech/rhetorical studies

Saint Mary's University of Minnesota
700 Terrace Heights #2
Winona, MN 55987
Phone: (507) 457-1600
Fax: (507) 457-1722
E-mail: admissions@smumn.edu
http://www.smumn.edu
Public relations, publishing, speech/rhetorical studies

University of Minnesota—Twin Cities*
240 Williamson Hall
231 Pillsbury Drive SE
Minneapolis, MN 55455
Phone: (612) 625-2008
Fax: (612) 626-1693

E-mail: admissions@tc.umn.edu
http://www1.umn.edu/twincities
Film/video arts, speech/rhetorical studies

Winona State University
Office of Admissions
P.O. Box 5838
Winona, MN 55987
Phone: (507) 457-5100
Fax: (507) 457-5620
E-mail: admissions@winona.edu
http://www.winona.edu
Advertising, broadcasting, communications, communications technology, journalism, public relations, speech/rhetorical studies

MISSISSIPPI

Jackson State University*
1400 Lynch Street
P.O. Box 17330
Jackson, MS 39217
Phone: (601) 979-2100
Fax: (601) 979-3445
E-mail: schatman@ccaix.jsums.edu
http://www.jsums.edu
Communications, communications technology, journalism, public relations, speech/rhetorical studies

Mississippi State University
P.O. Box 6305
Mississippi State, MS 39762
Phone: (662) 325-2224
Fax: (662) 325-7360
E-mail: admit@admissions.msstate.edu
http://www.msstate.edu
Communications

Mississippi University for Women
West Box 1613
Columbus, MS 39701
Phone: (662) 329-7106
Fax: (662) 241-7481
E-mail: admissions@muw.edu
http://www.muw.edu
Communications, journalism, public relations

Rust College
150 Rust Avenue
Holly Springs, MS 38635
Phone: (662) 252-8000
Fax: (662) 252-8895
E-mail: jbmcdonald@rustcollege.edu
http://www.rustcollege.edu
Communications, journalism

University of Mississippi*
145 Martindale
Oxford, MS 38677
Phone: (662) 915-7226
Fax: (662) 915-5869
E-mail: admissions@olemiss.edu
http://www.olemiss.edu
Advertising, broadcasting, communications technology, journalism

University of Southern Mississippi*
P.O. Box 5166
Southern Station
Hattiesburg, MS 38406
Phone: (601) 266-5000
Fax: (601) 266-5148
E-mail: admissions@usm.edu
http://www.usm.edu
Advertising, broadcasting, communications, journalism, public relations, speech/rhetorical studies

MISSOURI

Central Missouri State University
Office of Admissions
WDE 1401
Warrensburg, MO 64093
Phone: (660) 543-4290
Fax: (660) 543-8517
E-mail: admit@cmsuvmb.cmsu.edu
http://www.cmsu.edu
Broadcasting, communications, film/video arts, journalism, public relations, speech/rhetorical studies

Culver-Stockton College
One College Hillanton
Canton, MO 63435
Phone: (217) 231-6331
Fax: (217) 231-6618
E-mail: enrollment@culver.edu
http://www.culver.edu
Communications, journalism

Evangel University
1111 North Glenstone Avenue
Springfield, MO 65802
Phone: (417) 865-2811
Fax: (417) 520-0545
E-mail: admissions@evangel.edu
http://www.evangel.edu
Broadcasting, communications, journalism, speech/rhetorical studies

Lincoln University
Admissions Office
P.O. Box, 29
Jefferson City, MO 65102

Phone: (573) 681-5599
Fax: (573) 681-5889
E-mail: enroll@lincolnu.edu
http://www.lincolnu.edu
Journalism

Lindenwood University
309 South Kingshighway
St. Charles, MO 63301
Phone: (314) 949-4949
Fax: (314) 949-4989
E-mail: admissions@lindenwood.edu
http://www.lindenwood.edu
Communications

Northwest Missouri State University
800 University Drive
Maryville, MO 64468
Phone: (800) 633-1175
Fax: (660) 562-1121
E-mail: admissions@mail.nwmissouri.
    edu
http://www.nwmissouri.edu
Broadcasting, communications, journalism, public relations, speech/rhetorical studies

Southeast Missouri State University
One University Plaza
Mail Stop 3550
Cape Giradeau, MO 63701
Phone: (573) 651-2590
Fax: (573) 651-5936
E-mail: admissions@semo.edu
http://www.semo.edu
Advertising, communications, communications technology, journalism, public relations, speech/rhetorical studies

Stephens College
1200 East Broadway
P.O. Box 2121
Columbia, MO 65215
Phone: (573) 876-7207
Fax: (573) 876-7237
E-mail: apply@wc.stephens.edu
http://www.stephens.edu
Communications, creative writing, journalism, public relations

University of Missouri—Columbia*
230 Jesse Hall
Columbia, MO 65211
Phone: (573) 882-786
Fax: (573) 882-7887
E-mail: admissions@missouri.edu
http://www.missouri.edu
Advertising, broadcasting, communications, journalism, public relations

Webster University
470 East Lockwood Avenue
Saint Louis, MO 63119
Phone: (314) 968-6991
Fax: (314) 968-7115
E-mail: admit@webster.edu
http://www.webster.edu
Advertising, broadcasting, communications, film/video arts, journalism, media studies,public relations

MONTANA

University of Montana—Missoula*
103 Lodge Building
Missoula, MT 59812
Phone: (406) 243-62667
Fax: (406) 243-5711
E-mail: admiss@selway.umt.edu
http://www.umt.edu
Broadcasting, communications, journalism, speech/rhetorical studies

NEBRASKA

Creighton University
2500 California Plaza
Omaha, NE 68178
Phone: (402) 280-2703
Fax: (402) 280-2685
E-mail: admissions@creighton.edu
http://www.creighton.edu
Communications, journalism, speech/rhetorical studies

Hastings College
800 Turner Avenue
Hastings, NE 68901
Phone: (402) 461-07403
Fax: (402) 461-7490
E-mail: mmollicon@hastings.edu
http://www.hastings.edu
Broadcasting, communications, communications technology, creative writing, journalism, media studies, public relations, speech/rhetorical studies

Midland Lutheran College
900 North Clarkson Street
Fremont, NE 68025
Phone: (402) 721-5487
Fax: (402) 721-0250
E-mail: admissions@admin.mlc.edu
http://www.mlc.edu
Advertising, communications, journalism, public relations

University of Nebraska—Kearney
905 West 25th Street
Kearney, NE 68849

Phone: (800) 532-7639
Fax: (308) 865-8987
E-mail: admissionsug@unk.edu
http://www.unk.edu
Advertising, broadcasting, communications, journalism, speech/rhetorical studies

University of Nebraska—Lincoln*
313 North 13th Street
Van Brunt Visitors Center
Lincoln, NE 68588
Phone: (402) 472-2023
Fax: (402) 472-0670
E-mail: nuhusker@unl.edu
http://www.unl.edu
Advertising, broadcasting, communications, journalism, speech/rhetorical studies

University of Nebraska—Omaha
Office of Admissions
6001 Dodge Street, EAB Room 103
Omaha, NE 68182
Phone: (402) 554-2393
Fax: (402) 554-3472
E-mail: unoadm@unomaha.edu
http://www.unomaha.edu
Broadcasting, communications, creative writing, journalism, speech/rhetorical studies

NEVADA

University of Nevada—Las Vegas
4505 Maryland Parkway
P.O. Box 451021
Las Vegas, NV 89154
Phone: (702) 774-8658
Fax: (702) 774-8008
E-mail: undergraduate.recruitment@
    ccmail.nevada.edu
http://www.unlv.edu
Communications

University of Nevada—Reno*
1664 North Virginia Street
Reno, NV 89557
Phone: (775) 784-4700
Fax: (775) 784-4283
E-mail: asknevada@unr.edu
http://www.unr.edu
Journalism, speech/rhetorical studies

NEW HAMPSHIRE

Keene State College
229 Main Street
Keene, NH 03435
Phone: (603) 358-2276
Fax: (603) 358-2767

E-mail: admissions@keene.edu
http://www.keene.edu
Communications, journalism

**University of New Hampshire—
   Durham**
Four Garrison Avenue
Durham, NH 03024
Phone: (603) 862-1360
Fax: (603) 862-0077
E-mail: admissions@unh.edu
http://www.unh.edu
Communications, creative writing, jour-
nalism, media studies

NEW JERSEY

Rider University
2083 Lawrenceville Road
Lawrenceville, NJ 08648
Phone: (609) 896-5042
Fax: (609) 895-6645
E-mail: admissions@rider.edu
http://www.rider.edu
Advertising, communications, journalism,
speech/rhetorical studies

Rowan University
201 Mullica Hill Road
Glassboro, NJ 08028
Phone: (856) 256-4200
Fax: (856) 256-4430
E-mail: admissions@rowan.edu
http://www.rowan.edu
Broadcasting, communications, journal-
ism, public relations, speech/rhetorical
studies

**Rutgers, the State University of New
   Jersey—University College at New
   Brunswick**
65 Davidson Road
Piscataway, NJ 08854
Phone: (732) 932-4636
Fax: (732) 445-0237
E-mail: admissions@ugadm.rutgers.edu
http://www.rutgers.edu
Communications, journalism, speech/
rhetorical studies

Seton Hall University
Enrollment Services
400 South Orange Avenue
South Orange, NJ 07079
Phone: (973) 761-9332
Fax: (973) 275-2040
E-mail: thehall@shu.edu
http://www.shu.edu
Communications

NEW MEXICO

Eastern New Mexico University
Station #7, ENMU
1500 South Avenue K
Portales, NM 88130
Phone: (505) 562-2178
Fax: (505) 562-2118
E-mail: admissions@enmu.edu
http://www.enmu.edu
Communications, journalism, speech/
rhetorical studies

New Mexico Highlands University
NMHU Office of Student Recruitment
P.O. Box 900
Las Vegas, NM 87701
Phone: (505) 454-3593
Fax: (505) 454-3511
E-mail: recruitment@nmhu.edu
http://www.nmhu.edu
Communications

New Mexico State University*
P.O. Box 30001, MSC 3A
Las Cruces, NM 88003
Phone: (505) 646-3121
Fax: (505) 646-6330
E-mail: admissions@nmsu.edu
http://www.nmsu.edu
Communications, journalism

University of New Mexico
Office of Admissions
Student Services Center 150
Albuquerque, NM 87131
Phone: (505) 277-2446
Fax: (505) 277-6686
E-mail: apply@unm.edu
http://www.unm.edu
Communications, journalism, media stud-
ies, speech/rhetorical studies, technical
and business writing

NEW YORK

Buffalo State College, SUNY
1300 Elmwood Avenue
Buffalo, NY 14222
Phone: (716) 878-4017
Fax: (716) 878-6100
E-mail: admissions@buffalostate.edu
http://www.buffalostate.edu
Communications, journalism, media
studies

Canisius College
2001 Main Street
Buffalo, NY 14208
Phone: (716) 888-2200

Fax: (716) 888-3230
E-mail: inquiry@canisius.edu
http://www.canisius.edu
Communications

**City University of New York—
   Baruch College**
Undergraduate Admissions
One Bernard Baruch Way
P.O. Box H-0720
New York, NY 10010
Phone: (646) 312-1400
Fax: (646) 312-1361
E-mail: admissions@baruch.cuny.edu
http://www.baruch.cuny.edu
Advertising, communications, creative
writing, journalism

Columbia University*
Office of Undergraduate Admissions
1130 Amsterdam Avenue, MC 2807
New York, NY 10027
Phone: (212) 854-2521
Fax: (212) 894-1209
E-mail: At Web site
http://www.columbia.edu
Creative writing, film studies, journalism
(graduate program only)

Cornell University
Undergraduate Admissions
410 Thurston Avenue
Ithaca, NY 14850
Phone: (607) 255-5241
Fax: (607) 255-0659
E-mail: admissions@cornell.edu
http://www.cornell.edu
Communications

Fordham University
441 East Fordham Road
Thebaud Hall
Bronx, NY 10458
Phone: (718) 817-4000
Fax: (718) 367-9404
E-mail: enroll@fordham.edu
http://www.fordham.edu
Broadcasting, communications, journalism

Hofstra University*
Admission Center
Bernon Hall
1000 Fulton Avenue
Hempstead, NY 11549
Phone: (516) 463-6700
Fax: (516) 463-5100
E-mail: admitme@hofstra.edu
http://www.hofstra.edu
Broadcasting, communications, creative
writing, film/video arts, journalism, media

studies, public relations, speech/rhetorical studies

Iona College*
715 North Avenue
New Rochelle, NY 10801
Phone: (914) 633-2502
Fax: (914) 633-2642
E-mail: icad@iona.edu
http://www.iona.edu
Advertising, communications, film/video arts, journalism, public relations

Ithaca College
100 Job Hall
Ithaca, NY 14850
Phone: (607) 274-3124
Fax: (607) 274-1900
E-mail: admission@ithaca.edu
http://www.ithaca.edu
Advertising, broadcasting, communications, creative writing, film/video arts, journalism, media studies, public relations, speech/rhetorical studies, technical and business writing

Long Island University—Brooklyn
One University Plaza
Brooklyn, NY 11201
Phone: (800) 548-7526
Fax: (718) 797-2399
E-mail: admissions@brooklyn.liu.edu
http://www.brooklyn.liu.edu
Broadcasting, communications, journalism, speech/rhetorical studies

Marist College
3399 North Road
Poughkeepsie, NY 12601
Phone: (845) 575-3226
Fax: (845) 575-3215
E-mail: admissions@marist.edu
http://www.marist.edu
Communications, film/video arts, journalism

New York University
22 Washington Square North
New York, NY 10011
Phone: (212) 998-4500
Fax: (212) 995-4902
E-mail: admissions@nyu.edu
http://www.nyu.edu
Communications, communications technology, film/video arts, journalism, media studies, speech/rhetorical studies

Niagara University
Bailo Hall
P.O. Box 2011
Niagara Falls, NY 14109

Phone: (716) 286-8700
Fax: (716) 286-8710
E-mail: admissions@niagara.edu
http://www.niagara.edu
Communications

Pace University
One Pace Plaza
New York, NY 10038
Phone: (212) 346-1323
Fax: (212) 346-1040
E-mail: infoctr@pace.edu
http://www.pace.edu
Communications, speech/rhetorical studies

Saint Bonaventure University
P.O. Box D
Bonaventure, NY 14778
Phone: (716) 375-2400
Fax: (716) 375-4005
E-mail: admissions@sbu.edu
http://www.sbu.edu
Journalism

Saint John Fisher College
3690 East Avenue
Rochester, NY 14618
Phone: (585) 385-8064
Fax: (585) 385-8386
E-mail: admissions@sjfc.edu
http://www.sjfc.edu
Communications, journalism

State University of New York at New Paltz
75 South Manheim Boulevard, Suite 1
New Paltz, NY 12561
Phone: (845) 257-3200
Fax: (914) 257-3209
E-mail: admissions@newpaltz.edu
http://www.newpaltz.edu
Broadcasting, communications, journalism, speech/rhetorical studies

Syracuse University*
201 Tolley Administration Building
Syracuse, NY 13244
Phone: (315) 443-3611
Fax: (315) 443-4226
E-mail: orange@syr.edu
http://www.syracuse.edu
Advertising, broadcasting, communications, film/video arts, journalism, media studies, public relations, publishing, speech/rhetorical studies

Utica College of Syracuse University
1600 Burnstone Road
Utica, NY 13502

Phone: (315) 792-3006
Fax: (315) 792-3003
E-mail: admiss@utica.ucsu.edu
http://www.utica.edu
Communications, journalism, public relations, speech/rhetorical studies

NORTH CAROLINA

Johnson C. Smith University
100 Beatties Ford Road
Charlotte, NC 28216
Phone: (704) 378-1011
Fax: (704) 378-01242
E-mail: admissions@jcsu.edu
http://www.jcsu.edu
Communications

North Carolina State University
P.O. Box 7103
Raleigh, NC 27695
Phone: (919) 515-2434
Fax: (919) 515-5039
E-mail: undergrad_admissions@ncsu.edu
http://www.ncsu.edu
Journalism, media studies, public relations, speech/rhetorical studies

University of North Carolina— Asheville
CPO #2210
117 Lipinsky Hall
Asheville, NC 28804
Phone: (828) 251-6481
Fax: (828) 251-6482
E-mail: admissions@unca.edu
http://www.unca.edu
Communications, journalism

University of North Carolina— Chapel Hill*
Office of Undergraduate Admissions
Jackson Hall 153A
Campus P.O. Box 2220
Chapel Hill, NC 27599
Phone: (919) 966-3621
Fax: (919) 962-3045
E-mail: uadm@email.unc.edu
http://www.unc.edu
Journalism, media studies, speech/rhetorical studies

University of North Carolina— Wilmington
601 South College Road
Wilmington, NC 28403
Phone: (910) 962-3243
Fax: (910) 962-3038
E-mail: admissions@uncwil.edu

http://www.uncwil.edu
Creative writing, film/video arts, speech/
rhetorical studies

NORTH DAKOTA

North Dakota State University
P.O. Box 5454
Fargo, ND 58105
Phone: (701) 231-8643
Fax: (701) 231-8802
E-mail: ndsu.admission@ndsu.nodak.edu
http://www.ndsu.edu
Communications, media studies, speech/
rhetorical studies

University of North Dakota
Enrollment Services
Twamley Hall, Room 312
P.O. Box 8135
Grand Forks, ND 58202
Phone: (701) 777-4463
Fax: (701) 777-2696
E-mail: enrolser@sase.und.nodak.edu
http://www.und.edu
Advertising, communications

OHIO

Bowling Green State University*
110 McFall Center
Bowling Green, OH 43403
Phone: (419) 372-2478
Fax: (419) 372-6955
E-mail: admissions@bgnet.bgsu.edu
http://www.bgsu.edu
Broadcasting, communications, creative
writing, film/video arts, journalism, pub-
lic relations, speech/rhetorical studies

Kent State University*
161 Michael Schwartz Center
Kent, OH 44242
Phone: (330) 672-2444
Fax: (330) 672-2499
E-mail: kentadm@admissions.kent.edu
http://www.kent.edu
Advertising, broadcasting, communica-
tions, film/video arts, journalism, public
relations, speech/rhetorical studies

Ohio State University—Columbus
Enarson Hall
154 West 12th Avenue
Columbus, OH 43210
Phone: (614) 292-3980
Fax: (614) 292-4818
E-mail: askabuckeye@osu.edu
http://www.osu.edu

Communications, journalism, public relations

Ohio University—Athens*
120 Chubb Hall
Athens, OH 45701
Phone: (740) 593-4100
Fax: (740) 593-0560
E-mail: admissions.freshmen@ohiou.edu
http://www.ohiou.edu
Advertising, broadcasting, communications, creative writing, film/video arts,
journalism, media studies, public relations, speech/rhetorical studies

University of Toledo
2801 West Bancroft Street
Toledo, OH 43606
Phone: (419) 530-8700
Fax: (419) 530-5713
E-mail: enroll@utnet.utoledo.edu
http://www.utoledo.edu
Communications

OKLAHOMA

East Central University
Office of Admissions & Records
1100 E 14 PMB J8
Ada, OK 74820
Phone: (580) 332-8000
Fax: (580) 436-5495
E-mail: pdenny@mailclerk.ecok.edu
http://www.ecok.edu
Advertising, communications, journalism,
media studies, public relations, speech/
rhetorical studies

Northeastern State University
Office of Admissions and Records
600 North Grand Avenue
Tahlequah, OK 74464
Phone: (918) 456-5511
Fax: (918) 458-2342
E-mail: nsuadmis@cherokee.nsuok.edu
http://www.nsuok.edu
Advertising, broadcasting, communica-
tions, journalism, speech/rhetorical studies

Oklahoma Baptist University
2501 North Blackwelder Avenue
Oklahoma City, OK 73106
Phone: (405) 521-5050
Fax: (405) 521-5264
E-mail: uadmission@okcu.edu
http://www.okcu.edu
Advertising, broadcasting, communica-
tions, journalism, public relations, speech/
rhetorical studies

Oklahoma State University*
323 Student Union
Stillwater, OK 74078
Phone: (405) 744-6858
Fax: (405) 744-5285
E-mail: admit@okstate.edu
http://www.okstate.edu
Broadcasting, communications, journalism,
media studies, speech/rhetorical studies

University of Central Oklahoma
100 North University Drive
Edmond, OK 73034
Phone: (405) 974-2338
Fax: (405) 341-4964
E-mail: admituco@ucok.edu
http://www.ucok.edu
Advertising, broadcasting, communica-
tions, journalism, public relations, speech/
rhetorical studies

University of Oklahoma*
1000 Asp Avenue
Norman, OK 73019
Phone: (405) 325-2252
Fax: (405) 325-7124
E-mail: admrec@ou.edu
http://www.ou.edu
Advertising, broadcasting, communica-
tions, film/video arts, journalism, public
relations

OREGON

Southern Oregon University
Office of Admissions
1250 Siskiyou Boulevard
Ashland, OR 97520
Phone: (541) 552-6411
Fax: (541) 552-6614
E-mail: admissions@sou.edu
http://www.sou.edu
Broadcasting, communications, journal-
ism, public relations

University of Oregon*
1217 University of Oregon
Eugene, OR 97403
Phone: (541) 346-3201
Fax: (541) 346-5815
E-mail: uoadmit@oregon.uoregon.edu
http://www.uoregon.edu
Journalism, public relations

PENNSYLVANIA

Bloomsburg University of Pennsylvania
104 Student Services Center
400 East Second Street
Bloomsburg, PA 17815

Phone: (570) 389-4316
Fax: (570) 389-4741
E-mail: buadmiss@bloomu.edu
http://www.bloomu.edu
Communications, speech/rhetorical studies

Duquesne University
600 Forbes Avenue
Pittsburgh, PA 15282
Phone: (412) 396-5000
Fax: (412) 396-5644
E-mail: admissions@duq.edu
http://www.duq.edu
Advertising, broadcasting, communications, journalism, media studies, public relations, speech/rhetorical studies

Indiana University of Pennsylvania
216 Pratt Hall
Indiana, PA 15075
Phone: (724) 357-2230
Fax: (724) 357-6281
E-mail: admissions-inquiry@iup.edu
http://www.iup.edu
Communications, journalism, media studies

Lehigh University
27 Memorial Drive West
Bethlehem, PA 18015
Phone: (610) 758-3000
Fax: (610) 758-4361
E-mail: admissions@lehigh.edu
http://www.lehigh.edu
Journalism

Pennsylvania State University–University Park*
201 Shields Building
P.O. Box 3000
University Park, PA 16802
Phone: (814) 865-5471
Fax: (814) 863-7590
E-mail: admissions@psu.edu
http://www.psu.edu
Advertising, broadcasting, communications, film/video arts, journalism, media studies, speech/rhetorical studies

Point Park College
201 Wood Street
Pittsburgh, PA 15222
Phone: (412) 392-3430
Fax: (412) 391-1980
E-mail: enroll@ppc.edu
http://www.ppc.edu
Communications, film/video arts, journalism

Shippensburg University of Pennsylvania
Old Main 105
1871 Old Main Drive
Shippensburg, PA 17257
Phone: (717) 477-1231
Fax: (717) 477-4016
E-mail: admiss@ship.edu
http://www.ship.edu
Journalism, media studies, speech/rhetorical studies

Temple University*
1801 North Broad Street
Philadelphia, PA 19122
Phone: (215) 204-7200
Fax: (215) 204-5694
E-mail: tuadm@mail.temple.edu
http://www.temple.edu
Broadcasting, communications, film/video arts, journalism, media studies, speech/rhetorical studies

University of Pennsylvania
One College Hall
Philadelphia, PA 19104
Phone: (215) 898-7507
Fax: (215) 898-9670
E-mail: info@admissions.ugao.upenn.edu
http://www.upenn.edu
Communications

RHODE ISLAND

University of Rhode Island
Undergraduate Admissions Office
14 Upper College Road
Kingston, RI 02881
Phone: (401) 874-7100
Fax: (401) 874-5523
E-mail: uriadmit@etal.uri.edu
http://www.uri.edu
Communications, journalism, public relations, speech/rhetorical studies

SOUTH CAROLINA

Benedict College
1600 Harden Street
Columbia, SC 29204
Phone: (803) 253-5143
Fax: (803) 253-5167
E-mail: admission@benedict.edu
http://www.benedict.edu
Journalism

University of South Carolina—Columbia*
Office of Undergraduate Admissions
Columbia, SC 29208

Phone: (803) 777-7000
Fax: (803) 777-0101
E-mail: admissions-ugrad@sc.edu
http://www.sc.edu
Advertising, broadcasting, journalism, media studies, public relations, speech/rhetorical studies

Winthrop University*
Office of Admissions Joynes Hall
Rock Hill, SC 29733
Phone: (803) 323-2395
Fax: (803) 323-2137
E-mail: admissions@winthrop.edu
http://www.winthrop.edu
Communications, public relations, speech/rhetorical studies

SOUTH DAKOTA

Black Hills State University
1200 University Avenue, USB 9502
Spearfish, SD 57799
Phone: (605) 642-6343
Fax: (605) 642-6022
E-mail: admissions@bhsu.edu
http://www.bhsu.edu
Broadcasting, communications, journalism, speech/rhetorical studies

South Dakota State University*
P.O. Box 2201
Brookings, SD 57007
Phone: (605) 688-4121
Fax: (605) 688-6891
E-mail: admissions@sdstate.edu
http://www.sdstate.edu
Communications, journalism

University of South Dakota*
414 East Clark Street
Vermillion, SD 57069
Phone: (605) 677-5434
Fax: (605) 677-6753
E-mail: admiss@usd.edu
http://www.usd.edu
Communications, media studies, speech/rhetorical studies

TENNESSEE

East Tennessee State University*
ETSU P.O. Box 70731
Johnson City, TN 37614
Phone: (423) 439-4213
Fax: (423) 439-4630
E-mail: go2etsu@etsu.edu
http://www.etsu.edu

Broadcasting, communications, journalism, media studies, speech/rhetorical studies

Middle Tennessee State University*
Office of Admissions
1301 East Main Street
Murfreesboro, TN 37132
Phone: (800) 433-6878
Fax: (615) 898-5478
E-mail: admissions@mtsu.edu
http://www.mtsu.edu
Advertising, broadcasting, communications, journalism, media studies, speech/rhetorical studies

Tennessee Technological University
P.O. Box 5006
Cookeville, TN 38505
Phone: (931) 372-3888
Fax: (931) 372-6250
E-mail: admissions@tntech.edu
http://www.tntech.edu
Journalism, technical and business writing

University of Memphis*
229 Administration Building
Memphis, TN 38152
Phone: (901) 678-2111
Fax: (901) 678-3053
E-mail: recruitment@memphis.edu
http://www.memphis.edu
Journalism, media studies

University of Tennessee—Chattanooga
615 McCallie Avenue
131 Hooper Hall
Chattanooga, TN 37403
Phone: (423) 425-4662
Fax: (423) 425-4157
E-mail: yancy-freeman@utc.edu
http://www.utc.edu
Advertising, broadcasting, film/video arts, journalism, speech/rhetorical studies

University of Tennessee—Knoxville*
320 Science Building
Circle Park Drive
Knoxville, TN 37996
Phone: (865) 974-2184
Fax: (865) 974-6341
E-mail: admissions@tennessee.edu
http://www.utk.edu
Advertising, broadcasting, film/video arts, journalism, speech/rhetorical studies

University of Tennessee—Martin*
200 Hall-Moody
Administrative Building
Martin, TN 38238

Phone: (731) 587-7020
Fax: (731) 587-7029
E-mail: admitme@utm.edu
http://www.utm.edu
Communications

TEXAS

Abilene Christian University*
ACU P.O. Box 29000
Abilene, TX 79699
Phone: (325) 674-2650
Fax: (325) 674-2130
E-mail: info@admissions.acu.edu
http://www.acu.edu
Advertising, journalism, communications, journalism, speech/rhetorical studies

Angelo State University
2601 West Avenue North
San Angelo, TX 76909
Phone: (325) 942-2041
Fax: (325) 942-2078
E-mail: admissions@angelo.edu
http://www.angelo.edu
Communications, journalism

Baylor University*
P.O. Box 97056
Waco, TX 76798
Phone: (254) 710-3435
Fax: (254) 710-3436
E-mail: admissions_serv_office@baylor.
    edu
http://www.baylor.edu
Broadcasting, communications, journalism, public relations, speech/rhetorical studies

Hardin-Simmons University
2200 Hickory Street
Abilene, TX 79698
Phone: (915) 670-1206
Fax: (915) 670-1527
E-mail: enroll@hsutx.edu
http://www.hsutx.edu
Communications

Midwestern State University
3410 Taft Building
Wichita Falls, TX 76308
Phone: (940) 397-4334
Fax: (940) 397-4672
E-mail: admissions@mwsu.edu
http://www.mwsu.edu
Communications

Prairie View A&M University
P.O. Box 3089
University Drive
Prairie View, TX 77446
Phone: (936) 857-2626
Fax: (936) 857-2699
E-mail: admissions@pvamu.edu
http://www.pvamu.edu
Broadcasting, communications journalism, speech/rhetorical studies

Sam Houston State University
P.O. Box 2418
SHSU
Huntsville, TX 77341
Phone: (936) 294-1828
Fax: (936) 294-3758
E-mail: admissions@shsu.edu
http://www.shsu.edu
Journalism, speech/rhetorical studies

Southern Methodist University
P.O. Box 750296
Dallas, TX 75275
Phone: (214) 768-2058
Fax: (214) 768-2507
E-mail: enroll_serv@mail.smu.edu
http://www.smu.edu
Advertising, broadcasting, film/video arts, journalism, media studies, public relations

Stephen F. Austin State University
P.O. Box 13051, SFA Station
Nacogdoches, TX 75962
Phone: (936) 468-2504
Fax: (936) 468-3849
E-mail: admissions@sfasu.edu
http://www.sfasu.edu
Broadcasting, communications, journalism, speech/rhetorical studies

Texas A&M University—College Station
Admission Counseling
College Station, TX 77843
Phone: (979) 845-3741
Fax: (979) 845-8737
E-mail: admissions@tamu.edu
http://www.tamu.edu
Journalism, speech/rhetorical studies

Texas A&M University—Corpus Christi
6300 Ocean Drive
Corpus Christi, TX 78412
Phone: (361) 825-2624
Fax: (361) 825-5887
E-mail: judith.perales@mail.tamucc.edu
http://www.tamucc.edu
Communications, speech/rhetorical studies

Texas A&M University—Kingsville
700 University Boulevard, MSC 128
Kingsville, TX 78363
Phone: (361) 593-2315
Fax: (361) 593-2195
E-mail: ksossrx@tamuk.edu
http://www.tamuk.edu
Communications

Texas Christian University*
Office of Admissions
TCU, P.O. Box 297013
Fort Worth, TX 76129
Phone: (817) 257-7490
Fax: (817) 257-7268
E-mail: frogmail@tcu.edu
http://www.tcu.edu
Advertising, broadcasting, communications, film/video arts, journalism, media studies, public relations

Texas Southern University
3100 Cleburne Street
Houston, TX 77004
Phone: (713) 313-7420
Fax: (713) 313-4317
E-mail: admissions@tsu.edu
http://www.tsu.edu
Communications, journalism, speech/rhetorical studies

Texas State University—San Marcos
429 North Guadalupe Street
San Marcos, TX 78666
Phone: (512) 245-2364
Fax: (512) 245-9020
E-mail: admissions@txstate.edu
http://www.txstate.edu
Advertising, broadcasting, communications, journalism, speech/rhetorical studies

Texas Tech University*
P.O. Box 45005
Lubbock, TX 79409
Phone: (806) 742-1480
Fax: (806) 742-0062
E-mail: admissions@ttu.edu
http://www.ttu.edu
Advertising, broadcasting, journalism, public relations, speech/rhetorical studies

Texas Wesleyan University
1201 Wesleyan Street
Fort Worth, TX 76105
Phone: (817) 531-4422
Fax: (817) 531-7515
E-mail: info@txwesleyan.edu
http://www.txwesleyan.edu
Communications, public relations

Texas Woman's University
P.O. Box 425589
Denton, TX 76204
Phone: (940) 898-3188
Fax: (940) 898-3081
E-mail: admissions@twu.edu
http://www.twu.edu
Advertising, communications, media studies

Trinity University
One Trinity Place
San Antonio, TX 78212
Phone: (210) 999-7207
Fax: (210) 999-8164
E-mail: admissions@trinity.edu
http://www.trinity.edu
Communications, journalism, speech/rhetorical studies

University of Houston—Houston
Office of Admissions
122 East Cullen Building
Houston, TX 77204
Phone: (713) 743-1010
Fax: (713) 743-9633
E-mail: admissions@uh.edu
http://www.uh.edu
Communications, communications technology, journalism, media studies, public relations, speech/rhetorical studies

University of North Texas*
P.O. Box 311277
Denton, TX 76203
Phone: (940) 565-2681
Fax: (940) 565-2408
E-mail: undergrad@unt.edu
http://www.unt.edu
Communications, communications technology, film/video arts, journalism, public relations, speech/rhetorical studies

University of Texas—Arlington
Office of Admissions
P.O. Box 19111
Arlington, TX 76019
Phone: (817) 272-6287
Fax: (817) 272-3435
E-mail: admissions@uta.edu
http://www.uta.edu
Advertising, broadcasting, communications, journalism, public relations, speech/rhetorical studies

University of Texas—Austin*
P.O. Box 8058
Austin, TX 78713
Phone: (512) 475-7440

Fax: (512) 475-7475
E-mail: frmn@uts.cc.utexas.edu
http://www.utexas.edu
Advertising, film/video arts, journalism, public relations, speech/rhetorical studies

University of Texas—El Paso
500 West University Avenue
El Paso, TX 79968
Phone: (915) 747-5576
Fax: (915) 747-8893
E-mail: admission@utep.edu
http://www.utep.edu
Communications, journalism, media studies, public relations, speech/rhetorical studies

University of Texas—Pan American
Office of Admissions and Records
1201 West University Drive
Edinburg, TX 78541
Phone: (956) 381-8872
Fax: (956) 381-2212
E-mail: admissions@panam.edu
http://www.panam.edu
Communications, journalism, speech/rhetorical studies

West Texas A&M University
P.O. Box 60907
Canyon, TX 79016
Phone: (806) 651-2020
Fax: (806) 651-5268
E-mail: admissions@mail.wtamu.edu
http://www.wtamu.edu
Communications, journalism, speech/rhetorical studies

UTAH

Brigham Young University*
A-153 ASB
Provo, UT 84602
Phone: (801) 422-2507
Fax: (801) 422-0005
E-mail: admissions@byu.edu
http://www.byu.edu
Advertising, broadcasting, communications, film/video arts, journalism, media studies, speech/rhetorical studies, public relations

University of Utah*
210 South 1460 East, Room 250 South
Salt Lake City, UT 84112
Phone: (801) 581-7281
Fax: (801) 585-7864
E-mail: admiss@sa.utah.edu
http://www.utah.edu
Communications, film/video arts, media studies, speech/rhetorical studies

Utah State University
0160 Old Main Hill
Logan, UT 84322
Phone: (435) 797-1079
Fax: (435) 797-3708
E-mail: admit@cc.usu.edu
http://www.usu.edu
Journalism

Weber State University
1137 University Circle
Ogden, UT 84408
Phone: (801) 626-6744
Fax: (801) 626-6747
E-mail: admissions@weber.edu
http://www.weber.edu
Communications, journalism, speech/
rhetorical studies

VERMONT

Middlebury College
Emma Willard House
Middlebury, VT 05763
Phone: (802) 443-3000
Fax: (802) 443-2056
E-mail: admissions@middlebury.edu
http://www.middlebury.edu
Film/video arts

Saint Michael's College
One Winooski Park
Colchester, VT 05439
Phone: (802) 654-3000
Fax: (802) 654-2906
E-mail: admission@smcvt.edu
http://www.smcvt.edu
Journalism

VIRGINIA

Emory & Henry College
P.O. Box 947
Emory, VA 24327
Phone: (800) 848-5493
Fax: (276) 944-6935
E-mail: ehadmiss@ehc.edu
http://www.ehc.edu
Communications, journalism

Hampton University*
Office of Admissions
Hampton, VA 23668
Phone: (757) 727-5328
Fax: (757) 727-5095
E-mail: admissions@hamptonu.edu
http://www.hamptonu.edu
Communications, journalism, media stud-
ies, public relations, speech/rhetorical
studies

James Madison University
Sonner Hall, MSC 0101
Harrisonburg, VA 22807
Phone: (540) 568-5681
Fax: (540) 568-3332
E-mail: gotojmu@jmu.edu
http://www.jmu.edu
Communications, media studies, speech/
rhetorical studies

Liberty University
1971 University Boulevard
Lynchburg, VA 24502
Phone: (434) 582-5985
Fax: (800) 542-2311
E-mail: admissions@liberty.edu
http://www.liberty.edu
Communications, journalism, public
relations

Norfolk State University*
700 Park Avenue
Norfolk, VA 23504
Phone: (757) 823-8396
Fax: (757) 823-2078
E-mail: admissions@nsu.edu
http://www.nsu.edu
Communications, journalism, media
studies

Radford University
P.O. Box 6903
RU Station
Radford, VA 24142
Phone: (540) 831-5371
Fax: (540) 831-5038
E-mail: ruadmiss@radford.edu
http://www.radford.edu
Broadcasting, journalism, speech/rhetori-
cal studies

University of Richmond
28 Westhampton Way
Richmond, VA 23173
Phone: (804) 289-8640
Fax: (804) 289-6003
E-mail: admissions@richmond.edu
http://www.richmond.edu
Journalism, speech/rhetorical studies

Virginia Commonwealth University
821 West Franklin Street
P.O. Box 842526
Richmond, VA 23284
Phone: (804) 828-01222
Fax: (804) 828-1899
E-mail: vcuinfo@vcu.edu
http://www.vcu.edu
Communications

**Virginia Polytechnic Institute and
    State University**
7054 Haycock Road
Blacksburg, VA 24061
Phone: (540) 231-6267
Fax: (540) 231-3242
E-mail: admissions@vt.edu
http://www.vt.edu
Communications

Virginia Union University
1500 North Lombardy Street
Richmond, VA 23220
Phone: (804) 257-5600
Fax: (804) 257-5808
E-mail: admissions@vuu.edu
http://www.vuu.edu
Journalism

Washington and Lee University*
Letcher Avenue
Lexington, VA 24450
Phone: (540) 458-8710
Fax: (540) 458-8062
E-mail: admissions@wlu.edu
http://www.wlu.edu
Journalism

WASHINGTON

Central Washington University
Admissions Office
400 East Eighth Avenue
Ellensburg, WA 98926
Phone: (509) 963-1211
Fax: (509) 963-3022
E-mail: cwuadmis@cwu.edu
http://www.cwu.edu
Broadcasting, communications, journal-
ism, public relations, speech/rhetorical
studies

Gonzaga University
502 East Boone Avenue
Spokane, WA 99258
Phone: (509) 323-6572
Fax: (509) 324-5780
E-mail: admissions@gonzaga.edu
http://www.gonzaga.edu
Broadcasting, journalism, public rela-
tions, speech/rhetorical studies

Pacific Lutheran University
Office of Admissions
12180 Park Street South
Tacoma, WA 98447
Phone: (253) 535-7151
Fax: (253) 536-5136
E-mail: admissions@plu.edu

http://www.plu.edu
Communications

Seattle University
Admissions Office
900 Broadway
Seattle, WA 98122
Phone: (206) 296-2000
Fax: (206) 296-5656
E-mail: admiss@seattleu.edu
http://www.seattleu.edu
Communications, journalism, public relations

University of Washington*
1410 NE Campus Parkway
320 Schmitz, P.O. Box 355840
Seattle, WA 98195
Phone: (206) 543-9686
Fax: (206) 685-3655
E-mail: askuwadm@u.washington.edu
http://www.washington.edu
Communications, speech/rhetorical studies, technical and business writing

Walla Walla College
Office of Admissions
204 South College Avenue
College Place, WA 99324
Phone: (509) 527-2327
Fax: (509) 527-2397
E-mail: info@wwc.edu
http://www.wwc.edu
Communications, journalism, media studies, speech/rhetorical studies

Washington State University
370 Lighty Student Services
Pullman, WA 99164
Phone: (509) 335-5586
Fax: (509) 335-4902
E-mail: admiss2@wsu.edu
http://www.wsu.edu
Advertising, broadcasting, communications, journalism, public relations, speech/rhetorical studies

WEST VIRGINIA

Bethany College
Office of Admissions
Bethany, WV 26032
Phone: (304) 829-7611
Fax: (304) 829-7142
E-mail: admission@bethanywv.edu
http://www.bethanywv.edu
Communications, journalism, public relations

Marshall University*
One John Marshall Drive
Huntington, WV 25755
Phone: (304) 696-3160
Fax: (304) 696-3135
E-mail: admissions@marshall.edu
http://www.marshall.edu
Advertising, broadcasting, communications, journalism

West Virginia University*
Admissions Office
P.O. Box 6009
Morgantown, WV 26506
Phone: (304) 293-2121
Fax: (304) 293-3080
E-mail: wvuadmissions@arc.wvu.edu
http://www.wvu.edu
Advertising, broadcasting, communications, journalism, public relations, speech/rhetorical studies

WISCONSIN

Marquette University*
P.O. Box 1881
Milwaukee, WI 53201
Phone: (414) 288-7302
Fax: (414) 288-3764
E-mail: admissions@marquette.edu
http://www.marquette.edu
Advertising, broadcasting, communications, creative writing, journalism, media studies, public relations

University of Wisconsin—Eau Claire*
105 Garfield Avenue
Eau Claire, WI 54701
Phone: (715) 836-5415
Fax: (715) 836-2409
E-mail: admissions@uwec.edu
http://www.uwec.edu
Advertising, broadcasting, communications, journalism, media studies

University of Wisconsin—LaCrosse
1725 State Street
LaCrosse, WI 54601
Phone: (608) 785-8939
Fax: (608) 785-8940
E-mail: admissions@uwlax.edu
http://www.uwlax.edu
Communications, public relations, speech/rhetorical studies

University of Wisconsin—Madison
716 Langdon Street
Madison, WI 53706
Phone: (608) 262-3961
Fax: (608) 262-3961

E-mail: onwisconsin@admissions.wisc.edu
http://www.wisc.edu
Communications, film/video arts, journalism

University of Wisconsin—Milwaukee
P.O. Box 749
Milwaukee, WI 53201
Phone: (414) 229-3800
Fax: (414) 229-6940
E-mail: uwmlook@uwm.edu
http://www.uwm.edu
Communications, film/video arts, journalism

University of Wisconsin—Oshkosh*
Dempsey Hall 135
800 Algoma Boulevard
Oshkosh, WI 54901
Phone: (920) 424-0202
Fax: (920) 424-1098
E-mail: oshadmuw@uwosh.edu
http://www.uwosh.edu
Broadcasting, film/video arts, journalism, speech/rhetorical studies

University of Wisconsin—River Falls*
410 South Third Street
112 South Hall
River Falls, WI 54022
Phone: (715) 425-3500
Fax: (715) 425-0676
E-mail: admit@uwrf.edu
http://www.uwrf.edu
Communications, journalism, speech/rhetorical studies

University of Wisconsin—Whitewater
800 West Main Street
Baker Hall
Whitewater, WI 53190
Phone: (414) 472-1234
Fax: (414) 472-1515
E-mail: uwwadmit@uww.edu
http://www.uww.edu
Communications, journalism, public relations

WYOMING

University of Wyoming
Admissions Office
P.O. Box 3435
Laramie, WY 82071
Phone: (307) 766-5160
Fax: (307) 766-4042
E-mail: why-wyo@uwyo.edu
http://www.uwyo.edu
Broadcasting, communications, journalism

APPENDIX II
FURTHER READING

The following is a listing of some of the principal trade publications targeted to writers in various fields. For information on additional publications, consult these reference books at your public library: *Directory of Publications and* *Broadcast Media, Literary Marketplace, Magazine Marketplace, Subject Guide to Books in Print,* and *Writer's Market.* In addition, most trade and professional associations and unions publish periodicals for their membership.

A. MAJOR TRADE PERIODICALS, NEWSLETTERS, AND OTHER PUBLICATIONS

ADVERTISING AND MARKETING

Advertising Age
Crain Communications, Inc.
711 Third Avenue
New York, NY 10017
Phone: (212) 210-0100
Fax: (212) 210-0200
E-mail: editor@adage.com
http://www.adage.com

Adweek
BPI Communications, Inc.
770 Broadway
New York, NY 10003
Phone: (646) 654-5421
Fax: (646) 654-5365
E-mail: editor@adweek.com
http://www.adweek.com

Big Idea
2145 Crooks Road, Suite 28
Troy, MI 48084
Phone: (248) 458-5500
Fax: (248) 458-7099
E-mail: info@bigideaweb.com
http://www.bigideaweb.com

Brand Packaging
Stagnito Communications
210 South Fifth Street
St. Charles, IL 60174
Phone: (630) 377-0100
Fax: (630) 377-1688
E-mail: bswientek@stagnito.com
http://www.brandpackaging.com

Catalog Age
Primedia Business Magazines and Media
11 Riverbend Drive South
P.O. Box 4242
Stamford, CT 06907
Phone: (203) 358-9900
Fax: (203) 358-5823

E-mail: schiger@primediabusiness.com
http://catalogagemag.com

Catalog Success
401 North Broad Street
Philadelphia, PA 19108
Phone: (215) 238-5300
Fax: (215) 238-5270
E-mail: phatch@napco.com
http://www.catalogsuccess.com

Deca Dimensions
1908 Association Drive
Reston, VA 20191
Phone: (703) 860-5000
Fax: (703) 860-4013
E-mail: deca-dimensions@deca.org
http://www.deca.org

Direct
Primedia Business Magazines and Media
11 River Bend Drive South
P.O. Box 4949
Stamford, CT 06907
Phone: (203) 358-9900
Fax: (203) 358-5812
E-mail: rschultz@primediabusiness.com
http://www.directmag.com

DM News/Marketing News
100 Avenue of the Americas
New York, NY 10013
Phone: (212) 925-7300
Fax: (212) 925-8752
E-mail: info@dmnews.com
http://www.dmnews.com

Fundraising Success
401 North Broad Street
Philadelphia, PA 19108
Fax: (215) 238-5270
E-mail: mbattistelli@napco.com
http://www.fundraisingsuccessmag.com

Inside Direct Mail
401 North Broad Street
Philadelphia, PA 19108
Phone: (800) 777-8074
E-mail: hmummert@napco.com
http://www.insidedirectmail.com

Journal of Advertising Research
The ARF
641 Lexington Avenue
New York, NY 10022
Phone: (212) 751-5656
Fax: (212) 319-5265
E-mail: info@thearf.org
http://www.arfsite.org

Media, Inc.
P.O. Box 24365
Seattle, WA 98124
Phone: (206) 382-9220
Fax: (206) 382-9437
E-mail: media@media-inc.com
http://www.media-inc.com

MIN
Access Intelligence, LLC
110 William Street, 11th floor
New York, NY 10038
Phone: (212) 621-4880
Fax: (212) 621-4879
E-mail: acooper@accessintel.com
http://www.accessintel.com

The National Business Wire Newsletter
Business Wire
44 Montgomery Street
San Francisco, CA 94104
Phone: (415) 986-4422
Fax: (415) 956-2803
E-mail: info@bizwire.com
http://www.businesswire.com

Promo
Primedia Business Magazines and Media
11 Riverbend Drive
Stamford, CT 06907

Phone: (203) 358-9900
Fax: (203) 358-9900
E-mail: kyoyce@primediabusiness.com
http://www.promomagazine.com

Target Marketing
401 North Broad Street
Philadelphia, PA 19108
Phone: (215) 238-5410
Fax: (215) 238-5378
E-mail: jdipasquale@napco.com
http://www.targetmarketingmag.com

BOOK PUBLISHING

Children's Book Insider
901 Columbia Road
Fort Collins, CO 80525
Phone: (970) 495-0056
Fax: (970) 493-1810
E-mail: mail@write4kids.com
http://www.write4kids.com

Independent Publisher
Jenkins Group, Inc.
121 East Front Street, Fourth Floor
Traverse City, MI 49684
Phone: (231) 933-0445
Fax: (231) 933-0448
E-mail: jpmag@bookpublishing.com
http://www.bookpublishing.com

Library Journal
Reed Business Information
360 Park Avenue South
New York, NY 10010
Phone: (646) 746-6819
Fax: (646) 746-6734
E-mail: tbarnes@reedbusiness.com
http://www.libraryjournal.com

PMA Newsletter
Publishers Marketing Association
627 Aviation Way
Manhattan Beach, CA 90266
Phone: (310) 372-2732
Fax: (310) 374-3342
E-mail: PMAOnline@aol.com
http://www.pma-online.org

Publishers Weekly
Reed Business Information
360 Park Avenue South
New York, NY 10010
Phone: (646) 746-6758
Fax: (646) 746-6631
E-mail: itaylor@reedbusiness.com
http://www.publishersweekly.com

BUSINESS COMMUNICATIONS AND PUBLIC RELATIONS

Business Communication Quarterly
Sage Publications
2455 Teller Road
Thousand Oaks, CA 91320
Phone: (805) 499-0721
E-mail: At Web site
http://bcq.sagepub.com

CIO
CXO Media, Inc.
492 Old Connecticut Path
P.O. Box 9208
Framingham, MA 01701
Phone: (508) 872-0080
Fax: (508) 879-7784
E-mail: jhanson@cio.com
http://www.cio.com

Journal of Business and Technical Communications
Sage Publications
2455 Teller Road
Thousand Oaks, CA 91320
Phone: (805) 499-0721
E-mail: At Web site
http://jbt.sagepub.com

The Public Relations Strategist
Public Relations Society of America
33 Maiden Lane, 11th Floor
New York, NY 10038
Phone: (212) 460-1400
Fax: (212) 995-0757
E-mail: info@www.prsa.org
http://www.prsa.org

Public Relations Tactics
Public Relations Society of America
33 Maiden Lane, 11th Floor
New York, NY 10038
Phone: (212) 460-1400
Fax: (212) 995-0757
E-mail: info@www.prsa.org
http://www.prsa.org

ENTERTAINMENT
Film, music, television, and theater

American Drama
Department of English, ML 69
University of Cincinnati
Cincinnati, OH 45221
E-mail: norma.jenckes@uc.edu
http://www.americandrama.org

American Songwriter
50 Music Square West, Suite 604
Nashville, TN 37203
Phone: (615) 321-6096
Fax: (615) 321-6097
E-mail: info@americansongwriter.com
http://www.americansongwriter.com

American Theater Magazine
520 Eighth Avenue, 24th Floor
New York, NY 10018
Phone: (212) 609-5900
Fax: (212) 609-5901
E-mail: tcg@tcg.org
http://www.tcg.org

Backstage
VNU eMedia, Inc.
770 Broadway, Sixth Floor
New York, NY 10003
Phone: (646) 654-5500
Fax: (646) 654-5743
E-mail: info@backstage.com
http://www.backstage.com

B&C (Broadcasting & Cable)
Broadcaster Publications, Inc.
1705 DeSales Street, NW
Washington, DC 20036
Phone: (202) 659-2340
E-mail: info@broadcastingcable.com
http://www.broadcastingcable.com

Billboard
VNU eMedia, Inc.
1515 Broadway, 14th Floor
New York, NY 10036
Phone: (212) 536-5230
Fax: (212) 536-5358
E-mail: info@billboard.com
http://www.billboard.com

Creative Screenwriting
404 Hollywood Boulevard, Suite 415
Los Angeles, CA 90028
Phone: (323) 957-1405
Fax: (323) 957-1406
E-mail: info@creativescreenwriting.com
http://www.creativescreenwriting.com

Daily Variety
Reed Business Information
5700 Wilshire Boulevard, Suite 120
Los Angeles, CA 90036
Phone: (323) 857-6600
Fax: (323) 857-0494
E-mail: news@reedbusiness.com
http://www.variety.com

Dramatics
2343 Auburn Avenue
Cincinnati, OH 45219
Phone: (513) 421-3900
Fax: (513) 421-7077
E-mail: dcorathers@edta.org
http://www.edta.org

Fade In
2289 South Robertson Boulevard,
   Suite 465
Beverly Hills, CA 90211
Phone: (800) 646-3896
E-mail: inquiries@fadeinonline.com
http://www.fadeinmag.com

Film Quarterly
University of California Press
Journals Division
2000 Center Street, Suite 303
Berkeley, CA 94704
Phone: (510) 643-7154
Fax: (510) 642-9917
E-mail: journals@ucpress.edu
http://www.ucpress.edu/journals/fq

The Hollywood Reporter
VNU Business Publications
5055 Wilshire Boulevard, 6th Floor
Los Angeles, CA 90036-4396
Phone: (323) 525-2000
Fax: (323) 525-2377
E-mail: At Web site
http://www.hollywoodreporter.com

Hollywood Scriptwriter
P.O. Box 10277
Burbank, CA 91510
Phone: (818) 845-5525
E-mail: info@hollywoodscriptwriter.com
http://www.hollywoodscriptwriter.com

**Journal of Broadcasting and Electronic
   Media**
Broadcast Education Association
1771 N Street, NW
Washington, DC 20036
Phone: (888) 380-7222
E-mail: Don.Godfrey@asu.edu
http://www.beaweb.org/publications.html

Lyricist Review
305 Marquardt Avenue NW
North Canton, OH 44720
Phone: (330) 305-9130
E-mail: lyricistreview@aol.com
http://www.lyricistreview.com

Performing Songwriter
P.O. Box 40931
Nashville, TN 37204

Phone: 615-385-7796
Fax: 615385-5637
E-mail: jen@performingsongwriter.com
http://www.performingsongwriter.com

Screenwriter
655 Fulton Street, Suite 276
Brooklyn, NY 11217
Phone: (800) 418-5637
Fax: (323) 372-3898
E-mail: info@screenwritermag.com
http://www.screenwritermag.com

Scr(i)pt
5638 Sweet Air Road
Baldwin, MD 21013
Phone: (888) 245-2228
Fax: (410) 592-8062
E-mail: editor@scriptmag.com
http://www.scriptmag.com

The Sondheim Review
P.O. Box 11213
Chicago, IL 60611
Phone: (773) 275-4254
Fax: (773) 275-4254
E-mail: info@sondheimreview.com
http://www.sondheimreview.com

SongwriterUniverse
11684 Ventura Boulevard, Suite 975
Studio City, CA 91604
E-mail: info@songwriteruniverse.com
http://www.songwriteruniverse.com

TV Today
National Association of Broadcasters
1771 N Street, NW
Washington, DC 20036
Phone: (202) 429-5300
Fax: (202) 429-4199
E-mail: info@www.nab.org
http://www.nab.org

Written By
7000 West Third Street
Los Angeles, CA 90048-4329
Phone: (323) 782-4522
Fax: (323) 782-4802
E-mail: info@wga.org
http://www.wga.org

FUND-RAISING

Grassroots Fundraising
3781 Broadway
Oakland, CA 94611
Phone: (888) 458-8588
Fax: (510) 596-8822

E-mail: info@grassrootsfundraising.org
http://www.grassrootsfundraising.org

GREETING CARDS

Gifts and Decorative Accessories
Reed Business Information
360 Park Avenue South
New York, NY 10010
Phone: (646) 746-6400
Fax: (646) 746-7431
E-mail: qhalford@reedbusiness.com
http://www.giftsanddec.com

Party and Paper Retailer
P.O. Box 128
Sparta, MI 49345
Phone: (616) 887-9008
Fax: (616) 887-2666
E-mail: At Web site
http://www.partypaper.com

MEDIA

The American Reporter
812 North Ivar Avenue, Suite 5
Hollywood, CA 90028
Phone: (213) 467-0616
E-mail: joeshea@netcom.com
http://www.american-reporter.com

Media
MediaPost Communications
16 West 19th Street, Ninth Floor
New York, NY 10011
Phone: (212) 204-2000
Fax: (212) 204-2038
E-mail: info@mediapost.com
http://www.mediapost.com

MediaFile
814 Mission Street, Suite 205
San Francisco, CA 94103
Phone: (415) 546-6334
Fax: (415) 546-6218
E-mail: info@media-alliance.org
http://www.media-alliance.org

MEDIA—INTERNET AND
E-ZINES

There are thousands of e-zines on the Internet and the number is growing every day. To obtain a good up-to-date list to determine which ones would be useful for you, do a search engine query for "writing e-zines."

Many e-zines feature the work of new writers. Here is a sampling to get you started. Some are databases that allow you to search for other e-zines.

AJR (American Journalism Review)
http://ajr.org

Ezine Directory
http://www.ezine-dir.com

e.zine movement
http://www.asphyzia.com/ezm

eZINESearch
http://www.homeincome.com/search-it/ezine

EzineSeek
http://ezinearticles.com

forwriters.com
http://www.forwriters.com

Inkpot's Zine Scene
http://inkpot.com/zines

Lifted
http://www.lifted.com

Literary Arts WebRing
http://www.lit-arts.com/WebRing/RingIndex.html

Literary E-zines
http://www.suite101.com/welcome.cfm/literary_ezines

Literature Buzz
http://www.literaturebuzz.com

Low Bandwidth
http://www.disobey.com/low

Nerd World Media
http://www.nerdworld.com/nw8633.html

Newslink
http://newslink.org

Published.com
http://www.published.com

Suite 101.com
http://www.suite101.com

Web Del Sol
http://www.webdelsol.com

Web-Source
http://www.web-source.net/web/Ezines

Xenith
http://www.xenith.net

Zinos
http://zinos.com

MEDIA—MAGAZINES

Folio: The Magazine for Magazine Management
Primedia Business Magazines and Media
11 Riverbend Drive South
P.O. Box 4272
Stamford, CT 06907
Phone: (203) 358-9900
Fax: (203) 854-6735
E-mail: info@red7media.com
http://www.foliomag.com

MEDIA—NEWSPAPERS, NEWS SERVICES, AND NEWS SYNDICATES

American Journalism Review
University of Maryland
1117 Journalism Building
College Park, MD 20742
Phone: (301) 405-8803
Fax: (301) 405-8323
E-mail: editor@ajr.umd.edu
http://www.ajr.org

Columbia Journalism Review
Columbia University
704 Journalism Building
New York, NY 10027
Phone: (212) 854-1881
Fax: (212) 854-8580
E-mail: cjr@columbia.edu
http://www.cjr.org

Editor & Publisher
Adweek Magazines
770 Broadway
New York, NY 10003
Phone: (800) 562-2706
Fax: (646) 654-5370
E-mail: info@editorandpublisher.com
http://www.editorandpublisher.com

Presstime
Newspaper Association of America
1921 Gallows Road, Suite 600
Vienna, VA 22182
Phone: (703) 902-1600
Fax: (703) 917-0636

E-mail: alber@naa.org
http://www.naa.org

Quill & Scroll
School of Journalism
University of Iowa
Iowa City, IA 52242
Phone: (319) 355-5795
Fax: (319) 335-5210
E-mail: quill-scroll@uiowa.edu
http://www.uiowa.edu/~quill-sc

World Press Review
700 Broadway
New York, NY 10003
Phone: (212) 982-8880
Fax: (212) 982-6968
E-mail: info@worldpress.com
http://www.worldpress.com

SCHOLASTIC, ACADEMIC, AND NONPROFIT INSTITUTIONS

The American Historical Review
American Historical Association
Indiana University
914 Atwater Avenue
Bloomington, IN 47401
Phone: (812) 855-7609
Fax: (812) 855-5827
E-mail: ahr@indiana.edu
http://www.indiana.edu/~ahr

TECHNICAL WRITING

American Medical Writers Association Journal
American Medical Writers Association
9650 Rockville Pike
Bethesda, MD 20814
Phone: (301) 294-5303
Fax: (301) 294-9006
E-mail: amwa@amwa.org
http://www.amwa.org

Journal of Technical Writing & Communication
Baywood Publishing Company
26 Austin Avenue
P.O. Box 337
Amityville, NY 11701
Phone: (631) 691-1270
Fax: (631) 691-1770
E-mail: info@baywood.com
http://www.baywood.com

The Newsletter of the National Association of Science Writers
National Association of Science Writers, Inc.
P.O. Box 890
Hedgesville, WV 25427
Phone: (304) 754-5077
Fax: (304) 754-5076
E-mail: lfriedmann@nasw.org
http://www.nasw.org

Technical Communication
Society for Technical Communication
901 North Stuart Street, Suite 904
Arlington, VA 22203-1854
Phone: (703) 522-4114
Fax: (703) 522-2075
E-mail: stc@stc-va.org
http://www.stc-va.org

Technical Communication Quarterly
Department of English
Utah State University
3200 Old Main Hill
Logan, UT 84322
E-mail: TCQ@english.usu.edu
http://www.attw.org

WRITING AND POETRY

Authorship
National Writers Association
3140 South Peoria
PMB #295
Aurora, CO 80014
Phone: (303) 841-0246
Fax: (303) 841-2607
E-mail: authorship@nationalwriters.com
http://www.nationalwriters.com

Byline
P.O. Box 52140
Edmond, OK 730083
Phone: (405) 348-5991
E-mail: mpreston@bylinemag.com
http://www.bylinemag.com

Children's Writer
Institute of Children's Literature
93 Long Ridge Road
West Redding, CT 06896
Phone: (800) 443-6078
Fax: (203) 792-8406
E-mail: cwtierney@childrenswriter.com
http://www.childrenswriter.com

Freelance Writer's Report
CNW Publishing, Inc.
Main Street
P.O. Box A
North Stratford, NH 03590
Phone: (603) 922-8338
Fax: (603) 922-8339
E-mail: fwrwm@writers-editors.com
http://www.writers-editors.com

Horn Book Magazine
Horn Book, Inc.
56 Roland Street, Suite 200
Boston, MA 01219
Phone: (617) 628-0225
Fax: (617) 628-0882
E-mail: info@hbook.com
http://www.hbook.com

The Lion and the Unicorn: A Critical Journal of Children's Literature
Johns Hopkins University Press
P.O. Box 19966
Baltimore, MD 21211
Phone: (410) 516-6987
Fax: (410) 516-6968
E-mail: jlorder@jhu.edu
http://www.press.jhu.edu/press/journals/uni/uni.html

Poetry
Poetry Foundation
1030 North Clark Street, Suite 420
Chicago, IL 60610
Phone: (312) 787-7070
Fax: (312) 787-6650
E-mail: info@poetrymagazine.org
http://www.poetrymagazine.org

Poets & Writers Magazine
Poets & Writers, Inc.
72 Spring Street
New York, NY 10012
Phone: (212) 226-3586
Fax: (212) 226-3963
E-mail: editor@pw.org
http://www.pw.org

Travelwriter Marketletter
P.O. Box 1782
Springfield, VA 22151
Phone: (253) 399-6270
E-mail: At Web site
http://www.travelwriterml.com

The Writer
Kalmbach Publishing Company
21027 Crossroads Circle
P.O. Box 1612
Waukesha, WI 53187
Phone: (262) 796-8776
Fax: (262) 796-1615
E-mail: editor@writermag.com
http://www.writermag.com

Writer's Apprentice
Prairie River Publishing
607 North Cleveland Street
Merrill, WI 54452
Phone: (715) 536-3167
Fax: (715) 536-3167
E-mail: tina@writersapprentice.com
http://writersapprentice.com

Writer's Chronicle
Mailstop 1E3
George Mason University
Fairfax, VA 22030
Phone: (703) 993-4301
E-mail: awp@gmu.edu
http://www.awp.com

Writer's Digest
4700 East Galbraith Road
Cincinnati, OH 45236
Phone: (800) 333-0133
E-mail: wdsubmission@fwpubs.com
http://www.writersdigest.com

Writer's Guidelines & News
P.O. Box 18566
Sarasota, FL 34276
Phone: (941) 924-3201
Fax: (941) 925-4468
E-mail: WritersGN@aol.com
http://www.fiber-net.com

Writers' Journal
P.O. Box 394
Perham, MN 56573
Phone: (218) 346-7921
Fax: (218) 346-7924
E-mail: writersjournal@lakesplus.com
http://www.writersjournal.com

Writing That Works
7481 Huntsman Boulevard, Suite 720
Springfield, VA 22153
Phone: (703) 643-2200
Fax: (703) 643-2329
E-mail: inq@writingthatworks.com
http://www.apexawards.com

B. SELECTED BOOKS AND DIRECTORIES

AGENTS AND MARKETING

Agents Directory
by Rachel Vater
Emmis Books, 2004

Agents, Editors, and You: The Insider's Guide to Getting Your Book Published
edited by Michelle Howry
Writer's Digest Books, 2004

The American Directory of Writer's Guidelines: What Editors Want, What Editors Buy
edited by John C. Mutchler
Quill River Books, 1997

Be Your Own Literary Agent: The Ultimate Insider's Guide to Getting Published (3rd edition)
by Martin P. Levin
Ten Speed Press, 2002

Beyond the Bookstore: How to Sell More Books Profitably to Non Bookstore Markets
by Brian Jud
Reed Press, 2003

Book Promotion Made Easy: Event Planning, Presentation Skills & Product Marketing
by Eric Gelb
Career Advancement Center, 2000

The Career Novelist: A Literary Agent Offers Strategies for Success
by Donald Maass
Heinemann, 1996

The Frugal Book Promoter: How to Do What Your Publisher Won't
by Carolyn Howard-Johnson
Star Publishing, 2004

Guerrilla Marketing for Writers
by Jay Conrad Levinson, Rick Frishman, and Michael Larsen
Writer's Digest Books, 2001

Guide to Literary Agents 2005
by Kathryn S. Brogan
Writer's Digest Books, 2005

How to Be Your Own Literary Agent: The Business of Getting a Book Published (revised edition)
by Richard Curtis
Mariner Books, 1996

The Insider's Guide to Getting an Agent
by Lori Perkins
Writer's Digest Books, 1999

Jump Start Your Book Sales: A Money-Making Guide for Authors, Independent Publishers and Small Presses
by Marilyn and Tom Ross
Writer's Digest Books, 2001

Literary Agents: What They Do, How They Do It, and How to Find and Work with the Right One for You
(revised and expanded edition)
by Michael Larsen
John Wiley & Sons, 1996

Marketing Strategies for Writers
by Michael Sedge
Allworth Press, 1999

Networking Magic
by Rick Frishman and Jill Lublin
Adams Media, 2004

Nonfiction Book Proposals Anybody Can Write
by Elizabeth Lyon and Natasha Kern
Perigree Books, 2002

1001 Advertising Tips
by Luc Dupont
White Rock Publishing, 1999

1001 Ways to Market Your Books
(5th edition)
by John Kremer
Open Horizons, 2004

Poor Richard's Internet Marketing and Promotions: How to Promote Yourself, Your Business, Your Ideas Online
by Peter Kent and Tara Calishain
Top Floor Publishing, 1999

Publicize Your Book: An Insider's Guide to Getting Your Book the Attention It Deserves
by Jacqueline Deval
Berkley Publishing, 2003

The Publishing Game: Find an Agent in 30 Days
by Fern Reiss
Peanut Butter & Jelly Press, 2002

The Savvy Author's Guide to Book Publicity
by Lissa Warren
Carroll & Graf, 2004

The Writer's Guide to Queries, Pitches and Proposals
by Moira Anderson Allen
Allworth Press, 2001

Writing.com: Creative Internet Strategies to Advance Your Writing Career
by Moira Allen
Allworth Press, 1999

Your Novel Proposal: From Creation to Contract: The Complete Guide to Writing Query Letters, Synopses and Proposals for Agents and Editors
by Blythe Camenson and Marshall I. Cook
Writer's Digest Books, 1999

AUTOBIOGRAPHIES AND MEMOIRS

Another Life: A Memoir of Other People
by Michael Korda
Random House, 2000

At Random: The Reminiscences of Bennett Cerf
by Bennett Cerf
Random House, 1977

Education of a Wondering Man
by Louis L'Amour
Bantam Books, 1990

Edward R. Murrow and the Birth of Broadcast Journalism
by Bob Edwards
John Wiley & Sons, 2004

In the Company of Writers: A Life in Publishing
by Charles Scribner
Scribner, 1991

On Writing: A Memoir of the Craft
by Stephen King
Scribner, 2002

The Way the Future Was
by Frederick Pohl
Del Rey Books, 1978

BUSINESS GUIDES FOR WRITERS AND EDITORS

The Art and Science of Book Publishing
by Herbert S. Bailey, Jr.
Ohio University Press, 1990

Book Business: Publishing: Past, Present, and Future
by Jason Epstein
W.W. Norton, 2002

The Book Publishing Industry
by Albert N. Greco
Allyn & Bacon, 1996

Business and Legal Forms for Authors and Self-Publishers (3rd edition)
by Tad Crawford
Allworth Press, 2004

The Business of Writing for Children: An Award-winning Author's Tips on Writing and Publishing Children's Books
by Aaron Shepard
Shepard Publications, 2000

The Case of Peter Rabbit: Changing Conditions of Literature for Children
by Margaret MacKey
Garland Publishing, 1999

The Complete Guide to Book Marketing (revised edition)
by David Cole
Allworth Press, 2004

The Complete Guide to Book Publicity
by Jodee Blanco
Allworth Press, 2004

The Complete Guide to Writer's Groups, Conferences, and Workshops
by Eileen Malone
John Wiley & Sons, 1996

The Copyright Permission and Libel Handbook : A Step-by-Step Guide for Writers, Editors, and Publishers
by Lloyd J. Jassin and Steve C. Schecter
John Wiley & Sons, 1998

The Craft and Business of Songwriting (2nd edition)
by John Braheny
Writer's Digest Books, 2001

The Effective Editor: How to Lead Your Staff to Better Writing and Better Teamwork
by Foster Davis and Karen F. Dunlap
Poynter Institute, 2000

How to Publish Your Articles: Complete Guide to Making the Right Publication Say Yes
by Shirley Kawa-Jump
Square One Publishing, 2001

How to Sell, Then Write Your Nonfiction Book
by Blythe Camenson
McGraw-Hill, 2002

How to Sell Your Screenplay: A Realistic Guide to Getting a Television or Film Deal
by Lydia Wilen and Joan Wilen
Square One, 1999

Job Hunting on the Internet
by Richard Nelson Bolles
Ten Speed Press, 2005

The Joy of Publishing
by Nat Bodian
Oryx Press, 1996

Kirsch's Guide to the Book Contract: For Authors, Publishers, Editors, and Agents
by Jonathan Kirsch
Acrobat Books, 1998

Kirsch's Handbook of Publishing Law: For Authors, Publishers, Editors and Agents (2nd expanded edition)
by Jonathan Kirsch
Silma-Jones Press, 2005

Literary Law Guide for Authors: Copyrights, Trademarks and Contracts in Plain Language
by Tonya Marie Evans
Writersandpoets.com, 2003

The Magazine Publishing Industry
by Charles P. Daly, Patrick Henry, and Ellen Ryder
Allyn & Bacon, 1996

Negotiating a Book Contract: A Guide for Authors, Agents and Lawyers
by Mark L. Levine
Moyer Bell, 1999

Publishing Confidential: The Inside Guide to What It Really Takes to Land a Nonfiction Book Deal
by Paul Brown
AMACOM, 2004

Publishing for Profit (2nd edition)
by Thomas Woll
Fisher Books, 1998

The Radio Broadcasting Industry
by Alan B. Albarran and Gregory G. Pitts
Allyn & Bacon, 2001

Selling Subsidiary Rights: An Insider's Guide
by Thomas Woll
Fisher Books, 1999

Starting and Running a Successful Newsletter or Magazine (3rd edition)
by Cheryl Woodard
Nolo.com, 2002

Successful Syndication: A Guide for Writers and Cartoonists
by Michael Sledge
Allworth Press, 2000

This Business of Books: A Complete Overview of the Industry from Concept through Sales (4th edition)
by Claudia Suzanne
WC Publishing, 2003

This Business of Publishing: An Insider's View of Current Trends and Tactics
by Richard Curtis
Alworth Press, 1998

Vault Career Guide to Media and Entertainment (2nd edition)
by Sucharita Mulpuru
Vault.com, 2003

The Writer Got Screwed (But Didn't Have To): Guide to the Legal and Business Practices for the Entertainment Industry
by Brooke A. Wharton
HarperResource, 1997

The Writer's Legal Companion: The Complete Handbook for the Working Writer
by Brad Bunnin and Peter Bevin
HarperCollins, 1998

The Writer's Legal Guide: An Authors
    Guild Desk Reference (13th edition)
by Tad Crawford and Kay Murray
Allworth Press, 2002

DESKTOP PUBLISHING AND SELF-PUBLISHING

The African-American Writer's Guide
    to Successful Self-Publishing
by Takesha Powell
Amber Books, 2004

All-By-Yourself Self-Publishing
by David H. Li
Premier Publishers, 1996

Alleviating Prepress Anxiety: How to
    Manage Your Print Projects for
    Savings, Schedule and Quality
by Ann Goodheart
Leaping Antelope Productions, 2002

The Art of Self-Publishing: A
    Successful Solution to Your Book
    Publishing Needs
by Bonnie Shahlman Speer
Reliance Press, 1997

Before You Self-Publish
by Dick Lutz
Dimi Press, 2002

Book Production: Composition,
    Layout, Editing & Design
by Dan Poynter
Para Publishing, 1988

The Complete Guide to Self-Publishing:
    Everything You Need to Know to
    Write, Publish, Promote and Sell
    Your Own Book (4th edition)
by Tom and Marilyn J. Ross
Writer's Digest Books, 2002

A Complete Guide to Selling Books for
    the Self-Published Author
by Linda Coleman-Willis
Coleman-Willis, 2004

The Complete Guide to Successful
    Publishing (3rd edition)
by Avery Cardoza
Cardoza Publishing, 2003

The Complete Self-Publishing
    Handbook (revised edition)
by David M. Brownstone and Irene M.
    Frank
Plume Books, 1999

Creative Self-Publishing in the World
    Marketplace
by Marshall Chamberlain
Grace Books, 2004

How to Make Money Publishing from
    Home: Everything You Need to
    Know to Successfully Publish
    Books, Newsletters, Greeting Cards,
    Zines, and Software (2nd edition)
by Lisa Shaw
Prima, 2000

How to Start a Home-Based Desktop
    Publishing Business (3rd edition)
Globe Pequot, 2002

How to Start and Run a Small Book
    Publishing Company: A Small
    Business Guide to Self-Publishing
    and Independent Publishing
by Peter I. Hupalo
HCM, 2002

Make Money Self-Publishing: Learn
    How from Fourteen Successful
    Small Publishers
by Suzanne P. Thomas
Gemstone House, 2000

Poor Richard's Web Site: Geek-Free,
    Commonsense Advice on Building a
    Low-Cost Web Site
by Peter Kent
Top Floor Publishing, 2000

The Publishing Game: Publish a Book
    in 30 Days
by Fern Reiss
Peanut Butter and Jelly Press, 2003

The Self-Publishing Manual: How to
    Write, Print, and Sell Your Own
    Book (14th edition)
by Dan Poynter
Para Press, 2004

A Simple Guide to Self-Publishing: A
    Time and Money Saving Handbook
    to Printing, Distributing and
    Promoting Your Own Book
    (3rd revised edition)
by Mark Ortman
Wise Owl Books, 2003

Smart Self-Publishing: An Author's
    Guide to Producing a Marketable
    Book (3rd edition)
by Linda G. Salisbury
Tabby House, 2002

So You Want to Self-Publish
by Steve Meyer
Meyer Publishing, 1997

Start & Run a Desktop Publishing
    Business
by Barbra A. Fanson
Self-Counsel Press, 2003

Successfully Marketing Print-on-
    Demand Fiction
by Austin Camacho
Infinity Publishing, 2003

Teach Yourself Desktop Publishing
by Christopher Lumgair
NTC Pub. Group, 2001

REFERENCE BOOKS

Advice to Writers: A Compendium of
    Quotes, Anecdotes, and Writerly
    Wisdom from a Dazzling Array of
    Literary Lights
edited by Jon Winokur
Vintage, 2000

The American Directory of Writer's
    Guidelines: A Compilation of
    Information for Freelancers (3rd
    edition)
compiled by Brigitte M. Phillips, Susan
    D. Klasson, and Doris Hill
Quill Driver Books, 2003

Anchoring America: The Changing
    Face of Network News
by Jeff Alan and James Martin Lane
Bonus Books, 2003

The Art of Indexing
by Larry S. Bonura
John Wiley & Sons, 1994

The Associated Press Reporting
    Handbook
McGraw-Hill, 2002

The Associated Press Sports Writing
    Handbook
by Steve Wilstein
McGraw-Hill, 2002

The Associated Press Stylebook and
    Brief on Media Law (revised and
    updated edition)
edited by Norm Goldstein
Perseus Books Group, 2002

Bacon's Internet Media Directory: Media Web Sites with News Content and Editorial Contacts (5th edition)
Bacon's Information, Inc., 2004

Bartlett's Familiar Quotations
by John Bartlett
Little, Brown, 1992

Broadcast News Handbook
by Forrest Carr, Suzanne Huffman, and C. A. Tuggle
McGraw-Hill, 2001

Broadcast News Writing Stylebook
by Robert A. Papper
Allyn & Bacon, 2002

The Chicago Manual of Style: The Essential Guide For Writers, Editors, and Publishers (15th edition)
University of Chicago Press, 2003

Children's Writer's Word Book
by Alijandra and Alihandra Mogilner
F & W Publishers, 1992

The Complete Guide to Literary Contests
compiled by Literary Fountain
Prometheus Books, 2000

The Copy Editing and Headline Handbook
by Barbara G. Ellis
Perseus Books Group, 2001

The Copyeditor's Handbook: A Guide for Book Publishing and Corporate Communications
by Amy Einsohn
University of California Press, 2000

Copy Editor's Handbook for Newspapers (2nd edition)
by Anthony R. Fellow and Thomas N. Clanin
Morton Publishing, 2002

The Copyright Permission and Libel Handbook: A Step-by-Step Guide for Writers, Editors, and Publishers
by Lloyd L. Jassin and Steve C. Schecter
John Wiley & Sons, 1998

Dos, Don'ts & Maybes of English Usage
by Theodore M. Bernstein
Random House, 1999

The Elements of Grammar
by Margaret Shertzer
Longman, 1996

The Elements of Style (4th edition)
by William Strunk, Jr., E. B. White, and Roger Angell
Longman, 2000

English through the Ages
by William Brohaugh
Writer's Digest Books, 1998

The Fact Checker's Bible: A Guide to Getting It Right
by Sarah Harrison Smith
Anchor, 2004

Grammatically Correct: The Writer's Essential Guide to Punctuation, Spelling, Style, Usage and Grammar
by Anne Stillman
Writer's Digest Books, 1997

Grants and Awards Available to American Writers 2002–2003 (22nd edition)
by John Morrone
PEN American Center, 2002

Handbook for Writers: Grammar, Punctuation, Diction, Rhetoric, Research
by Celia M. Millward
Holt, Rinehart & Winston, 1980

The Handbook of Good English
by Edward D. Johnson
Washington Square Press, 1991

Handbook of Technical Writing (7th edition)
by Gerald J. Alred, Charles T. Brusaw, and Walter E. Oliu
Bedford/St. Martin's Press, 2003

How a Book Is Made: An Insider's Look at the Publishing Process, from Manuscript to Reader
by Dominique Raccah and Jon Malysiak
Sourcebooks, 2003

The H. W. Fowler Book and Bio Set: Consisting of the New Fowler's Modern English Usage and the Warden of English
by H. W. Fowler and Jenny McMorris
Oxford University Press, 2002

Indexing: A Nuts-and-Bolts Guide for Technical Writers
by Kurt Ament
Noyes Publications, 2001

Indexing Books
by Nancy C. Mulvany
University of Chicago Press, 1994

The International Directory of Little Magazines & Small Presses (38th edition)
edited by Len Fulton
Dustbooks, 2002

The Investigative Reporter's Handbook (4th edition)
by Brant Houston, Len Bruzzese, and Steve Weinberg
Bedford/St. Martin's Press, 2002

Literary Law Guide for Authors
by Tonya and Susan Bordan Evans
FYOS Entertainment, 2003

Literary Market Place 2005: The Directory of the American Book Publishing Industry
Information Today, 2004

Living the Questions: A Guide for Teacher-Researchers
by Ruth Shagoury Hubbard and Brenda Miller Power
Stenhouse Publishers, 1999

The Longman Handbook for Writers and Readers (2nd edition)
by Christ M. Anson and Robert A. Schwegler
Addison Wesley Longman, 2000

Media Relations Handbook, for Agencies, Associations, Nonprofits, and Congress
by Brad Fitch
TheCapitol.Net, 1999

Media Writer's Handbook
by George T. Arnold
McGraw-Hill, 2003

Merriam-Webster's Manual for Writers and Editors
Merriam-Webster, 1998

The Microsoft Manual of Style for Technical Publications
Microsoft Press, 2003

Modern American Usage: A Guide
(revised edition)
by Wilson Follett and Erik Wensberg
Hill and Wang, 1998

My Big Sourcebook: For People Who Work with Words or Pictures
EEI Communications, 1998

New Media Libraries: A Management Handbook
edited by Barbara O. Semonche
Greenwood Press, 1993

News Is People: The Rise of Local TV News and the Fall of News from New York
by Craig M. Allen
Iowa State University Press, 2001

The Newspapers Handbook (3rd edition)
by Richard Keeble
Routledge, 2001

Newton's Telecom Dictionary, 20th edition: Covering Telecommunications, Networking, Information Technology, Computer, and the Internet
by Harry Newton
CMP Books, 2004

The New York Times Almanac
edited by John W. Wright
Penguin, 2004

Only Connect: A Cultural History of Broadcasting in the United States
by Michele Hilmes
Wadsworth, 2002

The Oxford Desk Dictionary of People and Places
edited by Frank Abate
Oxford University Press, 1999

The Oxford Dictionary for Writers & Editors (2nd edition)
Oxford University Press, 2000

Qualitative Research and Case Study Applications in Education (revised edition)
by Sharan B. Merriam
Jossey-Bass, 1997

The Radio Handbook
by Carol Fleming
Routledge, 2002

Read Me First! A Style Guide for the Computer Industry (2nd edition)
by Sun Technical Publications
Prentice-Hall, 2003

Roget's Thesaurus (indexed 6th edition)
edited by Barbara Ann Kipfer
HarperCollins, 2001

Roget's Thesaurus of Phrases
edited by Barbara Ann Kipfer
Writer's Digest Books, 2002

Roget's 21st Century Thesaurus in Dictionary Form (2nd edition)
edited by Barbara Ann Kipfer
Delacorte Press, 2001

Stay Tuned: A Concise History of American Broadcasting
by Christopher H. Sterling and John Michael Kittross
Lawrence Erlbaum Associates, 2002

Style Meister: The Quick-Reference Custom Style Guide
by Lana R. Castle
Independent Publishers Group, 1999

Synonym Finder (revised edition)
edited by J. I. Rodale, Nancy Laroche, and Faye C. Allen
Warner Books, 1986

Teachers Doing Research: The Power of Action through Inquiry (2nd edition)
by Gail E. Burnaford, Joseph Fischer, and David Hobson
Lea, 2001

The Wall Street Journal Guide to Business Style and Usage
edited by Paul R. Martin
Simon & Schuster, 2002

Web Site Source Book: A Guide to Major U.S. Businesses, Organizations, Agencies, Institutions, and Other Information Resources on the World Wide Web
edited by Pam Ganlin
Omnigraphics, 2001

The White House Press Secretary
by Joanne Mattern
Blackbirch Press, 2003

Woe Is I: The Grammarphobe's Guide to Better English in Plain English
(2nd edition)
by Patricia T. O'Conner
Riverhead Books, 2003

Words into Type (3rd edition)
by Marjorie E. Skillin and Robert Malcolm Gay
Prentice Hall, 1974

The Writers Complete Fantasy Reference: An Indispensable Compendium of Myth and Magic
Writer's Digest Books, 2000

Writer's Digest Flip Dictionary
by Barbara Ann Kipfer
Writer's Digest Books, 2000

Writer's Encyclopedia (3rd edition)
Writer's Digest Books, 2003

A Writer's Guide to Magazine Articles for Book Promotion and Profit
by Patricia Fry
Matilija Press, 2000

The Writer's Guide to Research: An Invaluable Guide to Gathering Material for Articles, Novels and Non-Fiction Books (2nd edition)
by Marion Field
Trans-Atlantic Publications, 2000

The Writer's Quotation Book (4th edition)
edited by James Charlton
Faber & Faber, 1997

A Writer's Reference: 2003 MLA Update (5th edition)
by Diana Hacker
Bedford/St. Martin's Press, 2003

WRITER'S MARKET DIRECTORIES

Children's Writer's & Illustrator's Market 2005
edited by Alice Pope and Rebecca Chrysler
Writer's Digest Books, 2003

Christian Writer's Market Guide 2005
by Sally Stuart
Shaw, 2005

**The Directory of Poetry Publishers
    2004–2005**
edited by Len Fulton
Dustbooks, 2004

**Jeff Herman's Guide to Book
    Publishers, Editors, and Literary
    Agents 2005**
by Jeff Herman
Writer Inc, 2004

**Novel & Short Story Writer's Market
    2005**
edited by Anne Bowling and Michael
    Schweer
Writer's Digest Books, 2004

**Online Market for Writers: How to
    Make Money by Selling Your
    Writing on the Internet**
by Anthony and Paul Tedesco
Owl Books, 2000

Poet's Market 2005
edited by Nancy Breen and Erika Kruse
Writer's Digest Books, 2004

The Writer's Handbook 2005
edited by Elfrieda Abbe
Writer, Inc, 2004

The Writer's Market Companion
by Joe Feiertag, Mary Carmen Cupito &
    The Editors of *Writer's Market*
Writer's Digest Books, 2000

Writer's Market 2005
edited by Kathryn Struckel Brogan
Writer's Digest Books, 2004

**Writer's Online Marketplace: How and
    Where to Get Published Online**
by Debbie Ridpath Ohi
Writer's Digest Books, 2001

WRITING AND EDITING

**The ABC's of Writing for Children:
    114 Children's Authors and
    Illustrators Talk about the Art,
    Business, the Craft, and the Life of
    Writing Children's Literature**
by Elizabeth Koehler-Pentacoff
Quill Driver Books, 2002

Advanced Writing: Fiction and Film
by Wells Earl Draughon
iUniverse, 2003

**Alone in a Room: Secrets of Successful
    Screenwriters**
by Jon Scott Lewinski
Michael Wiese Productions, 2004

The Art of Editing (7th edition)
by Floyd K. Baskette, Jack Z. Sissors,
    and Brian S. Brooks
Allyn & Bacon, 2001

The Art of the Interview (2nd edition)
by Martin Perlich
Empty Press, 2003

The Art of Writing Great Lyrics
by Pamela Phillips Oland
Allworth Press, 2001

**Ask the Pros: Screenwriting: 101
    Questions Answered by Industry
    Professionals**
by Paul Duran and Howard Meibach
Lone Eagle, 2004

**Beginnings, Middles & Ends (Elements
    of Fiction Writing)**
by Nancy Kress
Writer's Digest Books, 1999

**Bestseller: A Must-Read Author's
    Guide to Selling More of Your
    Books**
by George Arnold
Eakin Press, 2003

Book Editors Talk to Writers
by Judy Mandell
John Wiley & Sons, 1995

**The Book on Writing: The Ultimate
    Guide to Writing Well**
by Paula LaRocque
Marion Street Press, 2003

**Book Report: Publishing Strategies,
    Writing Tips, and 101 Literary
    Ideas for Aspiring Authors and
    Poets**
by Mark Shaw
Books for Life Foundation, 2003

**Breakfast with Sharks: A
    Screenwriter's Guide to Getting the
    Meeting, Nailing the Pitch, Signing
    the Deal, and Navigating the Murky
    Waters of Hollywood**
by Michael Lent
Three Rivers Press, 2004

**Broadcast Journalism: Techniques of
    Radio and TV News** (5th edition)
by Andrew Boyd
Focal Press, 2001

**Broadcast News Writing, Reporting,
    and Producing** (3rd edition)
by Ted White
Focal Press, 2001

**BUGS in Writing: A Guide to
    Debugging Your Prose** (2nd edition)
by Lyn Dupre
Addison Wesley Longman, 1995

**The Careful Writer: A Modern Guide
    to English Usage**
by Theodore M. Bernstein
Free Press, 1995

**Characters and Viewpoint (Elements of
    Fiction Writing)**
by Orson Scott Card
Writer's Digest Books, 1999

**Coaching Writers: The Essential Guide
    for Editors and Reporters**
    (2nd edition)
by Roy Peter Clark and Don Fry
Bedford/St. Martin's Press, 2001

**A Complete Guide to Writing for
    Publication**
edited by Susan Titus Osborn
ACW Press, 1999

**The Complete Idiot's Guide to
    Technical Writing**
by Krista Van Laan, Catherine Julian, and
    JoAnn Hackos
Alpha Books, 2001

Concise Guide to Copy Editing
by Paul LaRocque
Marion Street Press, 2003

Copyediting: A Practical Guide
    (2nd edition)
by Karen Judd
Crisp Publications, 2001

Copy Editing for Professionals
by Edmund J. Rooney and Oliver R.
    Witte
Stipes Pub, 2000

The Craft of Revision (5th edition)
by Donald M. Murray
Thomson/Heinle, 2003

Creating Catalogs That Sell
by Carol Ann Waugh
Xcellent Marketing, 2003

Creating Character Emotions
by Ann Hood
Story Press Books, 1998

Creative Editing (3rd edition)
by Dorothy A. Bowles and Diane L.
    Borden
Wadsworth, 2000

**Creative Interviewing: The Writer's
    Guide to Gathering Information by
    Asking Questions** (3rd edition)
by Ken Metzler
Allyn & Bacon, 1996

**Damn! Why Didn't I Write That? How
    Ordinary People Are Raking in
    $100,000.00 . . . or More Writing
    Nonfiction Books & How You Can
    Too!**
by Marc McCutcheon
Quill Driver Books, 2001

**Description (Elements of Fiction
    Writing)**
by Monica Wood
Writer's Digest Books, 1999

Designing Technical Reports (2nd
    edition)
by John Mathes and Dwight W.
    Stevenson
Pearson/Allyn & Bacon, 1991

**Developing Proofreading and Editing
    Skills** (4th edition)
by Sue C. Camp
McGraw-Hill, 2000

**Dynamics in Document Design:
    Creating Text for Readers**
by Karen A. Schriver
John Wiley & Sons, 1996

**Editing by Design: For Designers, Art
    Directors, and Editors: The Classic
    Guide to Winning Readers** (revised
    edition)
by Jan V. White
Allworth Press, 2003

**Editing Fact and Fiction: A Concise
    Guide to Book Editing**
by Richard Marek, Leslie T. Sharpe, and
    Irene Gunther
Cambridge University Press, 1994

The Editorial Eye (2nd edition)
by Jane T. Harrigan and Karen Brown
    Dunlap
Bedford/St. Martin's Press, 2003

**Editors on Editing: What Writers Need
    to Know about What Editors Do**
    (3rd revised edition)
edited by Gerald Gross
Grove Press, 1993

**Edit Yourself: A Manual for Everyone
    Who Works with Words**
by Bruce Ross-Larson
Norton, 1982

**Effective Reports for Managerial
    Communication** (3rd revised edition)
by Malra Treece and Larry Harman
Allyn & Bacon, 1991

**The Elements of Authorship:
    Unabashed Advice, Undiluted
    Experience, and Unadulterated
    Inspiration for Writers and
    Writers-to-be**
by Arthur Plotnik
toExcel Press/iUniverse, 2000

The Elements of Technical Writing
by Gary Blake and Robert W. Bly
Longman, 2000

**Feature Writing for Newspapers and
    Magazines: The Pursuit of
    Excellence** (5th edition)
by Edward Jay Friedlander and John Lee
Allyn & Bacon, 2003

The Fine Art of Copyediting
    (2nd edition)
by Elsie Myers Stainton
Columbia University Press, 2002

**The Forest for the Trees: An Editor's
    Advice to Writers**
by Betsy Lerner
Riverhead Books, 2001

**The Freelance Success Book: Insider
    Secrets for Selling Every Word You
    Write**
by David Taylor
Peakwriter.com, 2003

**Freelance Writing for Magazines and
    Newspapers**
by Marcia Yudkin
Perennial (HarperCollins), 1988

Grassroots Journalism
by Eesha Williams
Apex Press, 2000

**GUI Bloopers: Don'ts and Do's for
    Software Developers and Web
    Designers**
by Jeff Johnson
Morgan Kaufman, 2000

**Heads You Win: An Easy Guide to
    Better Headline and Caption
    Writing**
by Paul LaRoque
Marion Street Press, 2003

**Hollywood 101: The Film Industry:
    How to Succeed in Hollywood
    Without Connections**
by Frederick Levy
Renaissance Books, 2000

**How to Become a Fulltime Freelance
    Writer: A Practical Guide to Setting
    up a Writing Business at Home**
by Michael A. Banks
Watson-Guptill Publications, 2003

**How to Build a Great Screenplay: A
    Master Class in Storytelling for
    Film**
by David Howard
St. Martin's Press, 2004

**How to Communicate Technical
    Information: A Handbook of
    Software and Hardware
    Documentation**
by Jonathan Price and Henry Korman
Addison-Wesley, 1993

**How to Grow a Novel: The Most
    Common Mistakes Writers Make
    and How to Overcome Them**
by Sol Stein
St. Martin's Press, 1999

**How to Publish Your Newsletter: A
    Complete Guide to Print and
    Electronic Newsletter Publishing**
by Carol Luers Eyman
Square One, 2005

**How to Publish Your Poetry: A
    Complete Guide to Finding the
    Right Publishers for Your Work**
by Helene Ciaravino
Square One, 2001

How to Write a Book Proposal
by Michael Larsen
Writer's Digest Books, 2004

How to Write a Damn Good Novel II: Advance Techniques for Dramatic Storytelling
by James N. Frey
St. Martin's Press, 1994

How to Write & Publish Papers in the Medical Sciences (3rd edition)
by Edward J. Huth
Lippincott Williams & Wilkins, 19990

How to Write and Sell Your First Nonfiction Book
by Oscar Collier and Frances Spatz Leighton
St. Martin's Press, 1994

How to Write and Sell Your First Novel
by Oscar Collier and Frances Spatz Leighton
St. Martin's Press, 1997

How to Write Articles for Newspapers and Magazines (2nd revised edition)
by Dawn B. Sova
ARCO, 2002

How to Write Fast (While Writing Well)
by David Fryxell
Writer's Digest Books, 1995

How to Write for Magazines: Consumers, Trade and Web
by Charles H. Harrison
Allyn & Bacon, 2001

How to Write for the New Age Market
by Richard Webster
Llewellyn, 2003

How to Write It: A Complete Guide to Everything You'll Ever Write
by Sandra E. Lamb
Ten Speed Press, 2001

How to Write Science Fiction & Fantasy
by Orson Scott Card
Writer's Digest Books, 2001

Inside the Writer's Mind: Writing Narrative Journalism
by Stephen G. Bloom
Iowa State University Press, 2002

Interviewing for Journalists
by Sally Adams
Routledge, 2001

In the Palm of Your Hand: The Poet's Portable Workshop
by Steve Kowit
Tilbury House, 1995

A Journalistic Approach to Good Writing: The Craft of Clarity
by Robert M. Knight
Iowa State University Press, 2003

The Journalistic Interview (revised edition)
by Hugh C. Sherwood
Harper/Collins, 1972

The Journalist's Craft: A Guide to Writing Better Stories
edited by Dennis Jackson and Douglas A. Anderson
Allworth Press, 2002

Lapsing into a Comma: A Curmudgeon's Guide to the Many Things That Can Go Wrong in Print—and How to Avoid Them
by Bill Walsh
McGraw-Hill, 2000

Local Radio Journalism
by Paul Chantler and Peter Steward
Focal Press, 2003

The Magazine Article: How to Think It, Plan It, Write It
by Peter P. Jacobi
Indiana University Press, 1997

Magazine Editing: How to Develop and Manage a Successful Publication (2nd edition)
by Joan Morrish
Routledge, 2003

Managing Your Documentation Projects
by JoAnn T. Hackos
John Wiley & Sons, 1994

Mediawriting: Print, Broadcast and Public Relations
by Wayne R. Whitaker, Janet E. Ramsey and Ronald D. Smith
Longman, 2000

Medical Writing: A Prescription for Clarity (2nd edition)
by Neville W. Goodman and Martin B. Edwards
Cambridge University Press, 1997

Modern Media Writing
by Rick Wilber and Randy Miller
Thomson/Wadsworth, 2002

Music Publishing: A Songwriter's Guide (2nd edition)
by Randy Poe
Writer's Digest Books, 1997

News Reporting and Writing (7th edition)
by Brian S. Brooks, George Kennedy, Daryl R. Moen, and Don Ranly
Bedford/St. Martin's Press, 2002

Newsthinking: The Secret of Making Your Facts Fall into Place
By Bob Baker
Allyn & Bacon, 2001

News Writing and Reporting for Today's Media (6th edition)
by Bruce D. Itule and Douglas A. Anderson
McGraw-Hill, 2003

Nonfiction Book Proposals Anybody Can Write: How to Get a Contract and Advance Before Writing Your Book
by Elizabeth Lyon
Perigee/Penguin, 2002

On Writing Well: The Classic Guide to Writing Nonfiction (25th anniversary edition)
by William Zinsser
HarperResource, 2001

Opportunities in Technical Writing Careers
by Jay R. Gould and Wayne A. Losano
revised edition by Blythe Camenson
NTC/Contemporary, 2000

Plot (Elements of Fiction Writing)
by Ansen Dibell
Writer's Digest Books, 1999

A Poet's Guide to Poetry
by Mary Kinzie
University of Chicago Press, 1999

Precision Journalism (4th edition)
by Philip Meyer
Rowman & Littlefield, 2002

The Publishing Game: Bestseller in 30 Days
by Fern Reiss
Peanut Butter & Jelly Press, 2002

Ready, Aim, Specialize!: Create Your Own Writing Specialty and Make More Money
by Kelly James-Enger
Writer, Inc., 2003

The Renegade Writer: A Totally Unconventional Guide to Freelance Writing Success
by Linda Formichelli and Diana Burrell
Marion Street Press, 2003

Reporting and Writing: Basics for the 21st Century
by Christopher Scanlan
Oxford University Press, 2000

Revising Business Prose (4th edition)
by Richard Lanham
Longman, 1999

The Right to Write: An Invitation and Initiation into the Writing Life
by Julia Cameron
Putnam Publishing Group, 2000

Scene and Structure (Elements of Fiction Writing)
by Jack M. Bickham
Writer's Digest Books, 1999

The Science of Science Fiction Writing
by James E. Gunn
Scarecrow Press, 2000

Self-Editing for Fiction Writers (2nd edition)
by Renni Browne and Dave King
HarperResource, 2004

Starting Your Career as a Freelance Writer
by Moira Allen
Allworth Press, 2003

Story: Substance, Structure, Style and the Principles of Screenwriting
by Robert McKee
Regan Books, 1997

Style: Toward Clarity and Grace
by Joseph M. Williams
University of Chicago Press, 1995

Take Joy: A Book for Writers
by Jane Yolen
Writer, Inc., 2003

Technical Communication
by Rebecca E. Burnett
Wadsworth, 1990

Technical Editing: The Practical Guide for Editors and Writers
by Judith Tarutz
Addison Wesley, 1993

Technical Writer's Freelancing Guide
by Peter Kent
Sterling Publications, 1992

Technical Writing in the Corporate World
by Hermann Estrin and Norbert Elliot
Crisp Publications, 1990

Technical Writing 101: A Real-World Guide to Planning and Writing Technical Documentation (2nd edition)
by Alan S. Pringle and Sarah S. O'Keefe
Scriptorium Press, 2003

The Tech Writer's Survival Guide: A Comprehensive Handbook for Aspiring Technical Writers (revised edition)
by Janet Van Wicklen
Facts on File, 2001

Telling the Story: Writing for Print, Broadcast and Online Media
by Brian S. Brooks, George Kennedy, Daryl R. Moen, and Don Ranly
Bedford/St. Martin's Press, 2001

Untechnical Writing: How to Write about Technical Subjects and Products So Anyone Can Understand
by Michael Bremer
UnTechnical Press, 1999

User Manual: How to Research, Write, Test, Edit & Produce Software
by Michael Bremer
UnTechnical Press, 1999

The Well-Fed Writer: Back for Seconds A Second Helping of "How-To" for Any Writer Dreaming of Great Bucks and Exceptional Quality of Life
by Peter Bowerman
Fanove Publishing, 2004

When Words Collide: A Media Writer's Guide to Grammar and Style
by Lauren Kessler and Duncan McDonald
Wadsworth, 2001

Working with Words (5th edition)
by Brian S. Brooks, James Pinson, and Jean Gaddy Wilson
Bedford/St. Martin's Press, 2003

Write a Book without Lifting a Finger
by Mahesh Grossman
10 Finger Press, 2004

The Write Book: An Illustrated Treasure of Tips, Tactics, and Tirades
by Bob Perlongo
Art Direction Book Company, 2004

Writer Tells All: Insider Secrets to Getting Your Book Published
by Robert Masello
Owl Books, 2001

The Writer's Idea Workshop: How to Make Your Good Ideas Great
by Jack Heffron
Writer's Digest Books, 2003

The Writer's Little Instruction Book: 385 Secrets for Writing Well and Getting Published
by Paul Raymond Martin and Polly Keener
Writer's World Press, 1998

The Writer's Workbook
by Judith Appelbaum and Florence Janovic
Pushcart Press, 1991

Write the Perfect Book Proposal: 10 Proposals That Sold and Why (2nd edition)
by Jeff Herman and Deborah M. Adams
John Wiley & Sons, 2001

**Writing & Designing Manuals:
    Operator and Service Manuals,
    Manuals for International Markets**
by Gretchen H. Schoff and Patricia A.
    Robinson
Lewis Publications, 1991

**Writing and Reporting News: A
    Coaching Method** (4th edition)
by Carole Rich
Belmont/Wadsworth, 2003

Writing & Revising Your Fiction
by Mark Wisniewski
Writer, Inc., 1995

**Writing Better Computer User
    Documentation: From Paper to
    Hypertext**
by R. John Brockmann
John Wiley & Sons, 1990

Writing Better Lyrics
by Pat Pattison
Writer's Digest Books, 2001

Writing Dialogue
by Tom Chiarella
Story Press Books, 1998

**Writing Feature Stories: How to
    Research and Write Newspaper and
    Magazine Articles**
by Matthew Ricketson
Allen & Unwin, 2004

**Writing for Story: Craft Secrets of
    Dramatic Nonfiction**
by Jon Franklin
Plume Books, 1994

Writing News for TV and Radio
by Mervin Block and Joe Durso Jr.
Bonus Books, 1999

**Writing Nonfiction: Turning Thoughts
    into Books**
by Dan Poynter
Para Publishing, 2000

**Writing Right for Broadcast and
    Internet News**
by Sharyl Attkisson and Don Rodney
    Vaughan
Allyn & Bacon, 2003

**Writing Short Stories and Articles:
    How to Write Successfully for
    Magazines and Newspapers**
by Adele Ramet
How To Books, 1998

**Writing Spiritual Books: A Best-Selling
    Writer's Guide to Successful
    Publication**
by Hal Zina Bennett
Ocean Publishing, 2004

**Writing Successful Self-Help and
    How-to Books**
by Jean Marie Stine
John Wiley & Sons, 1997

**Writing the News: A Guide for Print
    Journalists** (3rd edition)
by Walter Fox
Iowa State University Press, 2001

**Writing the Nonfiction Book: A
    Successful Writer's Guide**
by Eva Shaw
Loveland Press, 1999

**Writing to Inform and Engage: The
    Essential Guide to Beginning News
    and Magazine Writing**
by Conrad C. Fink
Westview Press, 2003

**Your Novel Proposal: From Creation to
    Contract: The Complete Guide to
    Writing Query Letters, Synopses and
    Proposals for Agents and Editors**
by Blythe Camenson and Marshall J. Cook
Writer's Digest Books, 1999

WRITING ON-LINE AND E-PUBLISHING

**The Associated Press Guide to Internet
    Research and Reporting**
by Frank Bass
Perseus Books Group, 2002

**A Cheap and Easy Guide to Self-
    Publishing E-Books**
by Wayne F. Perkins
1st Books Library, 2000

**Collaborative Writing in Industry:
    Investigations in Theory & Practice**
edited by Mary M. Lay and William Karis
Baywood Publishing, 1991

**The Craft of Writing Technical
    Manuals**
by Robert W. McQuaid
R. W. McQuaid, 1990

**Designing and Writing Online
    Documentation: Help Files to
    Hypertext**
by William K. Horton
John Wiley & Sons, 1990

**Designing Web Usability: The Practice
    of Simplicity**
by Jakob Nielsen
New Riders Press, 1999

**Drastically Increase Web Traffic and
    Sales**
by Judy Cullins
Skills Unlimited, 2004

Ebook Marketing Made Easy
by Rusty Fischer
Bookbooter.com, 2002

**Electronic Publishing: The Definitive
    Guide**
by Karen S. Wiesner
Avid Press, 2003

**Fabjob Guide to Become a Movie
    Reviewer**
by Mark Juddery
Fabjob.com (e-book), 2004

**The Freelance Writer's E-Publishing
    Guidebook: 25 + E-Publishing
    Home-Based Online Writing
    Businesses to Start for Freelancers**
by Anne Hart
iUniverse.com, 2001

**How to Be a Syndicated Newspaper
    Columnist**
by Angela Adair-Hoy
writingcareer.com (e-book), 2004

**How to Break in as a Syndicated
    Columnist**
by Marcia Yudkin
Intellectua.com (e-book), 2001

**How to Get Started as a Technical
    Writer**
by Kim LaPolla
Inellectua.com (e-book), 2001

**How to Get Your E-Book Published:
    An Insider's Guide to the World of
    Electronic Publishing**
by Richard Curtis and W. T. Quick
Writer's Digest Books, 2002

How to Publish and Promote Online
by M. J. Rose and Angela Adair-Hoy
Griffin/St. Martin's Press, 2001

**How to Submit Articles to Top Web
    Sites: Step by Step**
by Judy Cullins
Skills Unlimited, 2004

**How to Write & Publish Papers in the
    Medical Sciences** (2nd edition)
by Edward J. Huth
Williams & Wilkins, 1990

Hypertext and Hypermedia
by Jakob Nielsen
Academic Press, 1993

**Online Markets for Writers: How to
    Make Money by Selling Your
    Writing on the Internet**
by Anthony and Paul Tedesco
Owl Books, 2000

**Poor Richard's E-Mail Publishing:
    Creating Newsletters, Bulletins,
    Discussion Groups, and Other
    Powerful Communication Tools**
by Chris Pirillo
Top Floor Publishing, 1999

**Standards for Online
    Communication**
by JoAnn T. Hackos
John Wiley & Sons, 1997

**10 Non-Techie Ways to Market Your
    Book Online**
by Judy Cullins
Skills Unlimited, 2003

**21st Century Publishing: An Author's
    Introduction to Print on Demand
    Book Publishing**
by Julie Duffy
http://www.julieduffy.com/ebook, 2002
    (an e-book)

**U-Publish.Com: How 'U' Can
    Effectively Compete with the
    Giants of Publishing** (2nd revised
    edition)
by Dan Poynter and Danny O. Snow
Unlimited Publishing, 2002

**Weave Your Web: The Promotional
    Companion to Electronic Publishing**
    (revised edition)
by Karen S. Wiesner
Hard Shell Word Factory, 2003

**Writer's Online Marketplace:
    How & Where to Get Published
    Online**
by Debbie Ridpath Ohi
Writer's Digest Books, 2001

**Writing.Com: Creative Internet
    Strategies to Advance Your Writing
    Career**
by Moira Anderson Allen
Allworth Press, 2003

**Your Guide to Ebook Publishing
    Success: How to Create and
    Profitably Sell Your Writing on the
    Internet**
by James Dillehay
Warm Snow Publishers, 2001

APPENDIX III
UNIONS AND ASSOCIATIONS

Since many of these organizations operate on limited funds, be sure to enclose a self-addressed, stamped envelope when querying any of them for information not available online. Not all of these organizations maintain full-time offices, so some cannot be reached via phone, fax, or e-mail. In addition, contact information for some of these organizations may change when a new president or director is selected.

Several other useful lists of writing and/or publishing associations may be found online. For example, try http://

pma-online.org, compiled by the Publishers Marketing Association and listed on the Web site http://www.business.com or the listings of magazines by subjects at Gebbie Press at http://www.gebbieinc.com.

For the section below on unions, annotations have been provided for each entry to point out the connection between the organization and the writing profession.

A. UNIONS

American Federation of Government Employees (AFGE)
80 F Street, NW
Washington, DC 20001
Phone: (202) 737-8700
Fax: NA
E-mail: comments@afge.com
http://www.afge.org
An affiliate of the AFL-CIO, the American Federation of Government Employees is the largest federal employee union, representing 600,000 federal (and District Colombia) government workers nationwide and overseas.

American Federation of State, County and Municipal Employees (ADSCEME)
1625 L Street, NW
Washington, DC 20036
Phone: (202) 429-1000
Fax: (202) 429-1293
E-mail: NA
http://www.afscme.org
An affiliate of the AFL-CIO, the American Federation of State, County and Municipal Employees is the largest and fastest-growing public service employees union in the United States, with more than 1.4 million members.

American Federation of Teachers (AFT)
555 New Jersey Avenue, NW
Washington, DC 20001
Phone: (202) 879-7481
Fax: (202) 393-7481
E-mail: NA
http://www.aft.org

American Federation of Teachers is a labor union that represents teachers as well as faculty and staff in higher education, school-related personnel, health care professionals, and public employees. The labor union is an affiliate of AFL-CIO.

Local 2110, United Auto Workers
113 University Place, 5th Floor
New York, NY 10003
Phone: (212) 387-0220
Fax: (212) 228-0198
E-mail: ocal2110@2110uaw.com
http://www.2110uaw.org
At most major large and small publishers editors, senior editors, copy editors, book publicists, and administrative assistants may belong to Local 2110 of the United Auto Workers labor union.

National Association of Broadcast Employees and Technicians (NABT)
501 Third Street, NW, 8th Floor
Washington, DC 20001
Phone: (202) 434-1254
Fax: NA
E-mail: NA
http://www.nabetcwa.org
A part of the Communications Workers of America and affiliated with the AFL-CIO, the NABT is a Union devoted to aiding workers who are employed in the broadcasting, distributing, telecasting, recording, cable, video, sound recording and related industries in North America.

National Writers Union (NWU)
113 University Place, 6th Floor
New York, NY 10003
Phone: (212) 254-0279
Fax: (212) 254-0673
E-mail: nwu@nwu.org
http://www.nwu.org
Affiliated with the AFL-CIO, the NWU represents its union members, who are mostly freelance writers working for magazines, newspapers, or the World Wide Web, or who wrote books. Throughout, the United States there are local affiliate chapters, which provide their members with contract advice, grievance resolution, health insurance, networking, and press passes.

Newspaper Guild International
501 Third Street, Suite 250
Washington, DC 20001
Phone: (202) 434-7177
Fax: (202) 434-1472
E-mail: guild@cwa-union.org
http://www.newsguild.org
The Newspaper Guild is a part of the AFL-CIO and its members are also part of the Communication Workers of America. Begun in 1933, the guild sets minimum wages for reporters. It also maintains a list of magazines, news services, weekly and semiweekly newspapers, and wire services that have union contracts.

Writers Guild of America, East (WGAE)
555 West 57th Street
New York, NY 10019

Phone: (212) 767-7800
Fax: (212) 582-1909
E-mail: info@wgaeast.org
http://www.wgaeast.org
See listing below for Writers Guild of America, West. Both branches offer similar services, but membership in each one is determined by geographic location of the member.

ADVERTISING

Advertising Club of Kansas City
79229 Ward Parkway, Suite 260
Kansas City, MO 64144
Phone: (816) 822-0300
Fax: (816) 822-1840
E-mail: kcadclub@sprintmail.com
http://www.kcadclub.com

Advertising Club of Los Angeles
4223 Glencoe Avenue, Suite C100
Marina del Rey, CA 90292
Phone: (310) 823-7320
Fax: (310) 823-7325
E-mail: info@laadclub.com
http://www.laadclub.com

Advertising Club of Metro Washington
717 Princess Street
Alexandria, VA 22314
Phone: (703) 683-5954
Fax: (703) 683-5480
E-mail: unfo@dcadclub.com
http://www.dcadclub.com

Advertising Club of New York
235 Park Avenue South, Sixth Floor
New York, NY 10003
Phone: (212) 533-8080
Fax: (212) 533-1929
http://www.theadvertisingclub.org

Advertising Mail Marketing Association
1333 F Street, NW, Suite 710
Washington, DC 20004
Phone: (202) 347-0055
Fax: (412) 963-8753
E-mail: info@amma.org
http://www.amma.org

Advertising Research Foundation
641 Lexington Avenue
New York, NY 10022
Phone: (212) 751-5656
Fax: (212) 319-5265

Writers Guild of America, West (WGA)
7000 West Third Street
Los Angeles, CA 90048
Phone: (323) 951-4000
Fax: (323) 782-4800
E-mail: website@wga.org
http://www.wga.org
The WGA is a labor union for writers working in film, radio, and television.

B. ASSOCIATIONS

E-mail: info@thearf.org
http://www.arfsite.org

Advertising Women of New York
25 West 45th Street, Suite 1001
New York, NY 10036
Phone: (212) 221-7969
Fax: (212) 221-8296
E-mail: awny@awny.org
http://www.awny.org

American Advertising Federation (AAF)
1101 Vermont Avenue, Suite 500
Washington, DC 2005
Phone: (202) 898-0089
Fax: (202) 898-0159
E-mail: aaf@aaf.org
http://www.aaf.org

American Association of Advertising Agencies
405 Lexington Avenue, 18th Floor
New York, NY 10174
Phone: (212) 682-2500
Fax: (212) 953-5665
E-mail: abd@aaaa.org
http://www.aaaa.org

American Marketing Association
250 South Wacker Drive, Suite 200
Chicago, IL 60606
Phone: (312) 542-9000
Fax: (312) 542-9001
E-mail: info@ama.org
http://www.marketingpower.com

Association of Hispanic Advertising Agencies
8201 Greensboro Drive, Third Floor
McLean, VA 22102
Phone: (703) 610-9014
Fax: (703) 610-9005
E-mail: info@abaa.org
http://www.abaa.org

For requirements for membership, visit their Web site. Whether membership will be in WGAE or WGA is determined by where the writer member is based in the United States. Almost three times as many members belong to WGA as to WGAE.

Business Marketing Association
400 North Michigan Avenue, 15th Floor
Chicago, IL 60611
Phone: (800) 644-4262
Fax: (312) 822-0054
E-mail: bma@marketing.org
http://www.marketing.org/bma

Chicago Association of Direct Marketing
435 North Michigan Avenue, Suite 1717
Chicago, IL 60611
Phone: (312) 644-0828
Fax: (312) 849-2239
E-mail: At Web site
https://www.cadm.org

Copywriter's Council of America
CCA Building
Seven Putter Lane
P.O Box 102
Middle Island, NY 11953
Phone: (631) 924-8555
Fax: (631) 924-3888
E-mail: cca4dmcopy@att.net
http://www.lgroup.addr.com/CCA.htm

Direct Marketing Association
1120 Avenue of the Americas
New York, NY 10036
Phone: (212) 768-7277
Fax: (212) 302-6714
E-mail: membership@the-dma.org
http://www.the-dma.org

Direct Marketing Association of Detroit
32425 Grand River Avenue
Farmington, MI 48336
Phone: (248) 478-4888
Fax: ((248) 478-6437
E-mail: kimberly@ameritech.net
http://www.dmad.org

Entertainment Marketing Association
5155 Rosecrans Avenue, Suite 217
Los Angeles, CA 90750

E-mail: info@emainc.org
http://emainc.org

ARTS AND ENTERTAINMENT

Including books; commercial arts; and film, music, television, and theater writers

Academy of American Poets
588 Broadway, Suite 1203
New York, NY 10012
Phone: (212) 274-0343
Fax: (212) 274-9727
E-mail: academy@poets.org
http://www.poets.org

Academy of Motion Picture Arts and Sciences
8949 Wilshire Boulevard
Beverly Hills, CA 90211
Phone: (310) 247-3000
Fax: (310) 859-9351
E-mail: ampas@oscars.org
http://www.oscars.org

All Songwriters Network
Department A95
P.O. Box 15711
Boston, MA 02215
http://www.writesongs.com/links.htm

American Academy of Arts & Letters
633 West 155th Street
New York, NY 10032
Phone: (212) 368-5900

American Association of Language Specialists
P.O. Box 39339
Washington, DC 20016
Phone: (301) 986-1542
E-mail: admin@taals.net
http://www.taals.net

American Film Institute
John F. Kennedy Center for the Performing Arts
Washington, DC 20566
Phone: (202) 828-4000
Fax: (202) 296-5149
E-mail: At Web site
http://www.afi.com

American Historical Association
400 A Street, SE
Washington, DC 20003
Phone: (202) 544-2422

Fax: (202) 544-8307
E-mail: info@historians.org
http://www.theaha.org

American Literary Translators Association
University of Texas–Dallas
Box 830588
Richardson, TX 75083
Phone: (214) 690-2093
Fax: (214) 705-6303
E-mail: jdickey@utdallas.edu
http://www.literarytranslators.org

American Medical Writers Association
40 West Guide Drive, Suite 101
Rockville, MD 20850
Phone: (301) 294-5303
Fax: (301) 294-9006
E-mail: amwa@amwa.org
http://www.amwa.org

American Society of Composers, Authors, and Publishers (ASCAP)
One Lincoln Plaza
New York, NY 10023
Phone: (212) 621-6000
Fax: (212) 724-9064
E-mail: info@ascap.com
http://www.ascap.com

American Society of Journalists and Authors
1501 Broadway, Suite 302
New York, NY 10036
Phone: (212) 997-0947
Fax: (212) 768-7414
E-mail: staff@asja.org
http://www.asja.org

American Translators Association
1735 Jefferson Davis Highway, Suite 903
Arlington, VA 22202
Phone: (703) 412-1500
Fax: (703) 412-1501
E-mail: ata@atanet.org
http://www.atanet.org

Arizona Authors' Association
P.O. Box 87857
Phoenix, AZ 85080
Phone: (602) 769-2066
Fax: (623) 780-0468
E-mail: info@azauthors.com
http://www.azauthors.com

Asian American Writers' Workshop
16 West 32nd Street, Suite 10A
New York, NY 10001

Phone: (212) 494-0061
Fax: (212) 494-0062
E-mail: desk@aaww.org
http://www.aaww.org

Associated Business Writers of America, Inc.
1450 Havana Street, Suite 424
Aurora, CO 80012
Phone: (303) 751-7844
Fax: (303) 751-8593
http://www.newswriting.net

Associated Writing Programs
George Mason University
Carty House, Mail Stop 1E3
Fairfax, VA 22030
Phone: (804) 683-3839
Fax: (804) 683-5901
E-mail: awp@gum.edu
http://www.awpwriter.org

Association of Authors and Publishers
6124 Highway 6 N, PMB 107
Houston, TX 77064
E-mail: info@authorsandpublishers.org
http://www.authorsandpublishers.org

Association of Authors' Representatives, Inc.
P.O. Box 237201
Ansonia Station
New York, NY 10003
Phone: (212) 353-3709
E-mail: info@aar-online.org
http://www.aar-online.org

Association of Book Travelers
100 Fifth Avenue
New York, NY 10011
Phone: (212) 229-7102
Fax: (212) 645-8437

Association of Professional Translators
2623 Mellon Bank Center
Pittsburgh, PA 15259
Phone: (412) 234-5751
Fax: (412) 234-0214

Association of Writers & Writing Programs
10808 Kelley Drive
Fairfax, VA 22030
Phone: (703) 993-4301
E-mail: awp@awpwriter.org
http://www.awpwriter.org

Austin Writers League
1501 West Fifth Street, Suite E2
Austin, TX 78703

Phone: (512) 499-8714
Fax: (512) 499-044
E-mail: wlt@writersleague.org
http://www.writersleague.org

Authors Guild
31 East 28th Street
New York, NY 10016
Phone: (212) 563-5904
Fax: (212) 564-5363
E-mail: staff@authorsguild.com
http://www.authorsguild.org

Authors League Fund
234 West 44th Street
New York, NY 10036
Phone: (212) 398-0842
Fax: (212) 944-0420

Authors League of America
31 East 28th Street, 10th Floor
New York, NY 10016
Phone: (212) 564-8350
Fax: (212) 564-8363
E-mail: staff@authorguild.org
http://www.authorsguild.org

Authors Resource Center
P.O. Box 64785
Tucson, AZ 85728
Phone: (602) 325-4733

Bibliographical Society of America
P. O. Box 397
Grand Central Station
New York, NY 10163
Phone: (212) 647-9171
Fax: (212) 647-9171
E-mail: bsa@bibsocamer.org
http://www.bibsocamer.org

Black Writer's Alliance
c/o Tia Shabazz
P.O. Box 700065
Dallas, TX 75370
E-mail: tiashabazz@blackwriters.org
http://www.blackwriters.org

Bread Loaf Writers Conference
Middlebury College
Middlebury, VT 05753
Phone: (802) 443-5286
Fax: (802) 443-2087
E-mail: blwc@middlebury.edu
http://www.middlebury.edu/~blwc

Brooklyn Writers Club
P.O. Box 184
Bath Beach Station

Brooklyn, NY 11214
Phone: (718) 837-3484

Brooklyn Writers Network
2509 Avenue K
Brooklyn, NY 11210
Phone: (718) 377-4945

California Writers' Club
2214 Derby Street
Berkeley, CA 94705
E-mail: membership@calwriters.org
http://www.calwriters.org

Cat Writers' Association, Inc.
256 Timbertop Road
New Ipswich, NH 03071
E-mail: CWA-Admin@catwriters.org
http://www.catwriters.org

Chicago Book Clinic
5443 North Broadway, Suite 101
Chicago, IL 60640
Phone: (773) 561-4150
Fax: (773) 561-1343
E-mail: kgboyer@ix.netcom.com
http://www.chicagobookclinic.org

Christian Writers Guild
P.O. Box 88196
Black Forest, CO 80908
Phone: (866) 495-5177
Fax: (719) 495-5181
E-mail: contactus@christianwritersguild.com
http://www.christianwritersguild.com

Council for the Advancement of Science Writing
P.O. Box 910
Hedgesville, WV 25427
Phone: (304) 754-5077
Fax: (304) 754-5076
E-mail: diane@nasw.org
http://www.casw.org

Council of Authors & Journalists, Inc.
P.O. Box 830184
Stone Mountain, GA 30083

Council of Writers Organizations
12724 Sagamore Road
Leawood, KS 66209
Phone: (913) 451-9023
Fax: (913) 451-4866
E-mail: hurleypr@sound.net
http://www.councilofwriters.com

Dramatists Guild of America, Inc.
1501 Broadway, Suite 701
New York, NY 10036-9366
Phone: (212) 398-9366
Fax: (212) 944-0420
E-mail: info@dramatistsguild.com
http://www.dramaguild.com

Electronic Literature Organization
c/o UCLA Department of English
2225 Rolfe Hall, P. O. Box 951530
Los Angeles, CA 90095
Phone: (310) 206-1863
Fax: (310) 206-5093
E-mail: jesspres@ucla.edu
http://www.eliterature.org

Football Writers Association of America
P.O. Box 1022
Edmond, OK 73083
Phone: (405) 341-4731
E-mail: webmaster@sportswriters.net
http://www.sportswriters.net/fwaa

Garden Writers Association
10210 Leatherleaf Court
Manassas, VA 20111
Phone: (703) 257-1032
Fax: (703) 257-0213
E-mail: info@gwaa.org
http://www.gwaa.org

Georgia Writers Association and Young Georgia Writers
1266 West Paces Ferry Road, Suite 217
Atlanta, GA 30327
Phone: (678) 407-0703
Fax: (678) 407-9917
E-mail: gawriter@mindspring.com
http://www.georgiawriters.org

Greeting Card Association
1156 15th Street, NW, Suite 900
Washington, DC 20005
Phone: (202) 393-1778
Fax: (202) 331-2714
E-mail: info@greetingcard.org
http://www.greetingcard.org

Haiku Society of America
1710 Interlachen, Suite 40C
Seal Beach, CA 90740
E-mail: jersan.haiku@verizon.net
http://www.hsa-haiku.org

Horror Writers Association
P.O. Box 50577
Palo Alto, CA 94303

Phone: (650) 322-4610
E-mail: hwa@horror.org
http://www.horror.org

Illinois Writers, Inc.
c/o Jim Elledge
Illinois State University, English
    Department
Normal, IL 61790
Phone: (309) 438-7705
E-mail: At Web site
http://www.ilstu.edu

Independent Writers of Chicago
PMB 119 5465 West Grand Avenue,
    Suite 100
Gurnee, IL 60031
Phone: (847) 855-6670
Fax: (847) 855-4502
E-mail: At Web site
http://www.iwoc.org

**International Association of Crime
    Writers, Inc., North American
    Branch**
JAF Box 1500
New York, NY 10116
Phone: (212) 757-3915

International Black Writers
P.O. Box 437134
Chicago, IL 60643
http://www.members.tripod.com/~ibwa/
    home.htm

**International Travel Writers and
    Editors Association**
1244 North Nolcomis NE
Alexandria, MN 56308
Phone: (320) 763-7626
Fax: (320) 763-9290
E-mail: ifec@aol.com
http://www.iami.org/assoc

**International Science Writers'
    Association**
Smithsonian Institute Astrophysical
    Observatory
60 Garden Street
Cambridge, MA 02138
Phone: (617) 495-7461
Fax: (617) 495-7468
E-mail: jcornell@cfa.harvard.edu
http://www.eurekalert.org/static

International Women's Writing Guild
P.O. Box 810, Gracie Station
New York, NY 10028
Phone: (212) 737-7536

Fax: (212) 737-9469
E-mail: iwwg@iwwg.com
http://www.iwwg.com

Jokewriters Guild
c/o Robert B. Makinson
P.O. Box 605, Times Plaza Station
542 Atlantic Avenue
Brooklyn, NY 11217
Phone: (718) 855-3351

Maine Publishers & Writers Alliance
1326 Washington Street
Bath, ME 04530
Phone: (207) 386-1400
Fax: (207) 386-1401
E-mail: info@mainewriters.org
http://www.mainewriters.org

Midwest Travel Writers Association
P.O. Box 83542
Lincoln, NE 68501
Phone: (402) 438-2253
Fax: (402) 438-2253
E-mail: glhinz@alltel.net
http://www.mtwa.org

Mirage Group
P.O. Box 803282
Santa Clarita, CA 91380
Phone: (661) 799-0694
Fax: (213) 383-3447
E-mail: ieromembrooke@aol.com
http://hometown.aol.com/mrg291/
    myhomepage/business.html

**Modern Language Association of
    America, Inc.**
26 Broadway, Third Floor
New York, NY 10004
Phone: (646) 576-5000
Fax: (646) 458-0030
E-mail: info@mla.org
http://www.mla.org.

Mystery Writers of America
17 East 47th Street, Sixth Floor
New York, NY 10017
Phone: (212) 888-8171
Fax: (212) 888-8107
E-mail: mwa@mysterywriters.org
http://www.mysterywriters.org

**Nashville Songwriters Association
    International**
1701 West End Avenue, Third Floor
Nashville, TN 37203
Phone: (615) 256-3354
Fax: (615) 256-0034

E-mail: nsai@nashvillesongwriters.com
http://www.nashvillesongwriters.com

National Academy of Popular Music
330 West 58th Street, Suite 411
New York, NY 10019
Phone: (212) 957-9230
Fax: (212) 957-9227
E-mail: 73751.1142@compuserve.com
http://www.songwritershalloffame.org

National Academy of Songwriters
6255 Sunset Boulevard, Suite 1023
Hollywood, CA 90028
Phone: (323) 462-5430
Fax: (323) 462-5430
E-mail: la@songwritersguild.com
http://www.songwriters.org

National Alliance of Short Story Authors
P.O. Box 440735
Miami, FL 33144
Phone: (904) 705-6806

**National Association of Home and
    Workshop Writers**
P.O. Box 12
Baker, NV 89311
Phone: (702) 234-7167
Fax: (702) 234-7361
E-mail: dondly@aol.com

National Association of Science Writers
P.O. Box 890
Hedgesville, WV 25427
Phone: (304) 754-5077
Fax: (304) 754-5076
E-mail: diane@nasw.org
http://www.nasw.org

National Catalog Managers Association
4600 East-West Highway, Suite 300
Bethesda, MD 20814
Phone: (240) 333-1087
Fax: (301) 654-3299
E-mail: info@ncmacat.org
http://www.ncmacat.org

**National Federation of State Poetry
    Societies**
c/o Sy Swann
2736 Creekwood Lane
Fort Worth, TX 76123
E-mail: johnfisher@sbcglobal.net
http://www.nfsps.com

**National League of American PEN
    Women**
1300 17th Street, NW
Washington, DC 20036

Phone: (202) 785-1997
Fax: (202) 452-6868
E-mail: nlapw1@juno.com
http://www.americanpenwomen.org

National Society of Arts and Letters
4227 46th Street, NW
Washington, DC 20016
Phone: (202) 363-5443
E-mail: sums@ix.netcom.com
http://www.arts-nsal.org

National Women Bowling Writers
Association
3001 21st Street
Lubbock, TX 79410
Phone: (806) 795-3830
E-mail: jsbwrite@aol.com

National Writers Association
3140 South Peoria Street, Suite 295
Aurora, CO 80014
Phone: (303) 841-0246
Fax: (303) 841-2607
E-mail: ExecDirSandyWhelchel@
    nationalwriters.com
http://www.nationalwriters.com

Nebraska Writers Guild, Inc.
941 O Street
Lincoln, NE 68508
Phone: (402) 475-1123
E-mail: At Web site
http://www.nebraskawriters.org

New Dramatists
424 West 44th Street
New York, NY 10036
Phone: (212) 757-6960
Fax: (212) 265-4738
E-mail: newdramatists@newdramatists.
    org
http://www.newdramatists.org

New England Poetry Club
137 West Newton Street
Boston, MA 02118
Phone: (617) 423-9585
E-mail: info@nepoetryclub.org
http://www.nepoetryclub.org

New Mexico Book League
8632 Horacio Place NE
Albuquerque, NM 87111
Phone: (505) 299-8940
Fax: (505) 294-8032

North American Snowsports
Journalists Association
11728 Southeast Madison
Washington, DC 20439

Phone: (503) 255-3771
Fax: (503) 255-3771
E-mail: skicat1@comcast.net
http://www.nasja.org

Novelists, Inc.
P.O. Box 1166
Mission, KS 66222
Phone: (913) 262-6435
E-mail: At Web site
http://www.ninc.org

Oregon Christian Writers Association
17768 SW Pointe, Forest Court
Aloha, OR 97006
Phone: (503) 642-9844
E-mail: membership@
    oregonchristianwriters.org
http://www.oregonchristianwriters.org

Organization of American Historians
Indiana University
112 North Bryan Street
P.O. Box 5457
Bloomington, IN 47408
Phone: (812) 855 7311
Fax: (812) 855 0696
E-mail: oah@oah.org
http://www.oah.org

PEN American Center
568 Broadway
New York, NY 10012
Phone: (212) 334-1660
Fax: (212) 334-2181
E-mail: pen@pen.org
http://www.pen.org

PEN Center U.S.A. West
672 South Lafayette Park Place,
    Suite 42
Los Angeles, CA 90057
Phone: (213) 365-8500
Fax: (213) 365-9616
E-mail: pen@penusa.org
http://www.pen-usa-west.org

Philadelphia Book Clinic
c/o Thomas J. Colaiezzi
136 Chester Avenue
Yeadon, PA 19050
Phone: (610) 259-7022

Playwrights Conference
534 West 42nd Street
New York, NY 10036
Phone: (212) 244-7008
Fax: (212) 921-5538

Poetry Project
St. Mark's Church
131 East 10th Street at Second Avenue
New York, NY 10003
Phone: (212) 674-0910
Fax: (212) 529-2318
E-mail: poproj@thron.net
http://www.poetryproject.com

Poetry Society of America
16 Gramercy Park
New York, NY 10003
Phone: (212) 254-9628
Fax: (212) 673-2352
E-mail: brett@poetrysociety.org
http://www.poetrysociety.org

Poets and Writers
72 Spring Street
New York, NY 10012
Phone: (212) 226-3586
Fax: (212) 226-3963
E-mail: denise@pw.org
http://www.pw.org

Professional Association of Résumé
Writers and Career Coaches
1388 Brightwaters Boulevard, NE
St. Petersburg, FL 33704
Phone: (727) 821-2274
Fax: (727) 894-1277
E-mail: parwhq@aol.com
http://www.parw.com

Romance Writers of America
16000 Stuebner Airline Road, Suite 140
Spring, TX 77379
Phone: (281) 440-6885
Fax: (281) 440-7510
E-mail: info@rwanational.com
http://www.rwanational.com

San Francisco Bay Area Book Council
555 DeHaro Street, Suite 220
San Francisco, CA 94107
Phone: (415) 861-2665
Fax: (415) 861-2670
E-mail: At Web site
http://www.greatbooks-sf.com.

Science Fiction and Fantasy Workshop
1193 South 1900 East
Salt Lake City, UT 84108
Phone: NA
Fax: (801) 650-2168
E-mail: workshop@burgoyne.com
http://www.burgoyne.com/pages/workshop

Science Fiction and Fantasy Writers of America
P.O. Box 877
Chestertown, MD 21620
Phone: (410) 778-3052
E-mail: execdir@sfwa.org
http://www.sfwa.org

Science Fiction Research Association Inc.
6021 Grassmere
Corpus Christi, TX 78145
Phone: (512) 855-9304
E-mail: At Web site
http://www.sfra.org

Small Publishers, Artists and Writers Network
PMB 123
323 East Matilija Street, Suite 110
Ojai, CA 93023
Phone: (818) 886-3320
Fax: (818) 886-3320
E-mail: execdir@spawn.org
http://www.spawn.org

Society for the History of Authorship, Reading & Publishing Inc.
Drew University, Department of History
Madison, NJ 07940
Phone: (201) 408-3545
Fax: (201) 408-3768
E-mail: At Web site
http://www.drew.edu

Society of American Archivists
527 South Wells, Fifth Floor
Chicago, IL 60607
Phone: (312) 922-0140
Fax: (312) 347-1452
E-mail: info@archivists.org
http://www.archivists.org

Society of American Travel Writers
1500 Sunday Drive, No. 102
Raleigh, NC 27607
Phone: (919) 787-5181
Fax: (919) 787-4916
E-mail: satw@satw.org
http://www.satw.org

Society of Architectural Historians
1365 North Astor Street
Chicago, IL 60610
Phone: (312) 573-1365
Fax: (312) 573-1141
E-mail: info@sah.org
http://www.sah.org

Society of Children's Book Writers and Illustrators
8271 Beverly Boulevard
Los Angeles, CA 90048
Phone: (323) 782-1010
Fax: (323) 782-1892
E-mail: scbwi@scbwi.org
http://www.scbwi.org

Society of Midland Authors
P.O. Box 10419
Chicago, IL 60610
Phone: (312) 337-1482
E-mail: At Web site
http://www.midlandauthors.com

Society of Southwestern Authors
P.O. Box 30355
Tucson, AZ 85751
Phone: (601) 296-599
E-mail: wporter202@aol.com
http://www.azstarnet.com/nonprofit/ssa

Songwriters & Lyricists Club
P.O. Box 605, Times Plaza Station
432 Atlantic Avenue
Brooklyn, NY 11217
Phone: (718) 855-3351

Songwriters Guild of America
1500 Harbor Boulevard
Weehawken, NJ 070806
Phone: (201) 867-7603
Fax: (201) 867-7535
E-mail: songwritersnj@aol.com
http://www.songwriters.org

Space Coast Writers Guild
P.O. Box 362143
Melbourne, FL 32936
Phone: (321) 723-7345
E-mail: david@dreamnetstudios.com
http://www.members.tripod.com/~scwg

Tall Grass Writers Guild
c/o Outrider Press
937 Patricia
Crete, IL 60417
Phone: (708) 672-6630
Fax: (708) 672-5820
E-mail: outrider@aol.com
http://www.outriderpress.com

Teachers and Writers Collaborative
Five Union Square West
New York, NY 10003
Phone: (212) 691-6590
Fax: (212) 675-0171
E-mail: info@twc.org
http://www.twc.org

Text and Academic Authors Association
University of South Florida
140 Seventh Avenue, South
St. Petersburg, FL 33701
Phone: (727) 553-1195
Fax: (727) 553-3122
E-mail: taa@bayflash.stpt.usf.edu
http://www.taaonline.net

Washington Independent Writers
220 Woodward Building
733 15th Street, NW
Washington, DC 20005
Phone: (202) 347-4973
Fax: (202) 628-0298
E-mail: info@washwriter.org
http://www.washwriter.org

West Coast Book People Association
27 McNear Drive
San Rafael, CA 94901
Phone: (415) 459-1227
Fax: (415) 459-1227

Western Writers of America Inc.
c/o Larry K. Brown
209 East Iowa
Cheyenne, WY 82009
E-mail: hogranch@email.msn.com
http://www.westernwriters.org

Women's National Book Association
c/o Susannah Greenberg
26 West 17th Street, Suite 504
New York, NY 10011
Phone: (212) 727-7271
Fax: (212) 208-4629
E-mail: publicity@bookbuzz.com
http://bookbuzz.com

World Bowling Writers
122 South Michigan Avenue, Suite 1506
Chicago, IL 60603
Phone: (312) 341-1110
Fax: (312) 341-1480
E-mail: bobj@bowlersjournal.com
http://www.bowlersjournal.com

Writers Alliance
12 Skylark Lane
Stony Brook, NY 11790
Phone: (516) 751-7080

Writers Connection
P.O. Box 24770
San Jose, CA 95154
Phone: (408) 445-3600
Fax: (408) 445-3609

Writers Workshop
175 Huntington Avenue, Suite C-42
Boston, MA 02115

Writing Academy
H010 Singleton Road
Rockford, IL 6114
Phone: (815) 877-9675
E-mail: pattyk@wams.org
http://www.wams.org

BOOK PUBLISHING

American Book Producers Association
156 Fifth Avenue, Suite 302
New York, NY 10010
Phone: (212) 645-2365
Fax: (212) 645-8769
E-mail: office@abpaonline.org
http://www.abpaonline.org

American Booksellers Association
828 South Broadway
Tarrytown, NY 10591
Phone: (914) 591-2665
Fax: (914) 591-2720
E-mail: info@bookweb.org
http://www.bookweb.org

American Library Association
50 East Huron Street
Chicago, IL 60611
Phone: (800) 545-2433
Fax: (312) 944-3897
E-mail: library@ala.org
http://www.ala.org

**American Medical Publishers
    Association**
Box 944
14 Fort Hill Road
Huntington, NY 11743
Phone: (516) 423-0075
Fax: (516) 423-0075
E-mail: info@ampaonline.org
http://www.ampaonline.org

**American Society for Information
    Science**
8720 Georgia Avenue, Suite 501
Silver Spring, MD 20910
Phone: (301) 495-0900
Fax: (301) 495-0810
E-mail: asis@asis.org
http://www.asis.org

Arizona Book Publishing Association
6340 South Rural Road #118-152
Tempe, AZ 85283
http://www.azbookpub.com

Association of American Publishers
71 Fifth Avenue
New York, NY 10003
Phone: (212) 255-0200
Fax: (212) 255-7007
E-mail: amyg@publishers.org
http://www.publishers.org

**Association of American University
    Presses, Inc.**
71 West 23rd Street
New York, NY 10010
Phone: (212) 989-1010
Fax: (212) 989-0275
E-mail: info@aaupnet.org
http://www.aaupnet.org

Association of Authors and Publishers
6124 Highway 6 North, PMB 107
Houston, TX 77064
Phone: (281) 340-0185
E-mail: info@authorsandpublishers.org
http://www.authorsandpublishers.com

Association of Earth Science Editors
554 Chess Street
Pittsburgh, PA 15205
E-mail: info@aese.org
http://www.aese.org

Association of Educational Publishers
510 Heron Drive, Suite 309
Logan Township, NJ 08085
Phone: (856) 241-7722
Fax: (856) 241-0709
E-mail: mail@edpress.org
http://www.edpress.org

Audio Publishers Association
627 Aviation Way
Manhattan Beach, CA 90266
Phone: (310) 372-0546
Fax: (310) 374-3342
E-mail: apaonline@aol.com
http://www.apaonline.com

**Bay Area Independent Publishers
    Association**
P.O. Box E
Corte Madera, CA 94976
E-mail: baipa@onebox.com
http://www.baipa.org

Bookbuilders of Boston
44 Highland Circle
Halifax, MA 02338
Phone: (781) 293-8600
Fax: (866) 820-0469
E-mail: office@bboston.org
http://www.bboston.org

Bookbuilders of Washington
P.O. Box 23805
Washington, DC 20025
Phone: (202) 287-3738

Bookbuilders West
P.O. Box 7046
San Francisco, CA 94120
Phone: (510) 934-1440
Fax: (510) 934-7020
E-mail: webmaster@bookbuilders.org
http://www.bookbuilders.org

Book Industry Study Group, Inc.
9 West 21st Street, Suite 905
New York, NY 10010
Phone: (646) 336-7141
Fax: (646) 336-6214
Phone: (212) 929-1393
Fax: (212) 989-7542
E-mail: info@bisg.org
http://www.bisg.org

Book Publicists of Southern California
6464 Sunset Boulevard, Room 755
Hollywood, CA 90028
Phone: (213) 461-3921
Fax: (213) 461-0917
E-mail: info@bookpublicists.org
http://www.bookpublicists.org

Book Publishers Northwest
350 North 74th Street
Seattle, WA 98103
Phone: (206) 941-6514
E-mail: bpnwnews@aol.com

Book Publishers of Texas Association
3404 South Ravina Drive
Dallas, TX 75233
Phone: (214) 330-8759
Fax: (214) 330-9795

**Catholic Book Publishers Association,
    Inc.**
8404 Jamesport Drive
Rockford, IL 61108
Old Brookville, NY 11545
Phone: (815) 332-3245
E-mail: info@cbpa.org
http://www.cbpa.org

Chicago Publishers Association
c/o Follett Corporation
2233 West Street
River Grove, IL 60171
Phone: (708) 583-2000

Chicago Women in Publishing
P.O. Box 268107
Chicago, IL 60626
Phone: (312) 641-6311
E-mail: mail@cwip.org
http://www.cwip.org

Children's Book Council, Inc.
12 West 37th Street, Second Floor
New York, NY 10018
Phone: (212) 966-1990
Fax: (212) 966-2073
E-mail: At Web site
http://www.cbcbooks.org

Classroom Publishers Association
107 Park Washington Court
Falls Church, VA 22046
Phone: (703) 532-9255
Fax: (703) 532-0086

Colorado Independent Publishers Association
9249 South Broadway, Suite 506
Littleton, CO 80126
Phone: (303) 365-2472
E-mail: info@cipabooks.com
http://www.cipabooks.com

Copywriter's Council of America
CCA Building
7 Putter Lane
P.O. Box 102
Middle Island, NY 11953
Phone: (516) 924-8555
Fax: (516) 924-3890
http://www.lgroup.addr.com

COSMEP: The International Association of Independent Publishers
P.O. Box 420703
San Francisco, CA 94142
Phone: (415) 922-9490

Council of Biology Editors
60 Revere Drive, Suite 500
Northbrook, IL 60062

Council of Literary Magazines & Presses
154 Christopher Street, Suite 3C
New York, NY 10014
Phone: (212) 741-9110
Fax: (212) 741-9112
E-mail: info@clmp.org
http://www.clmp.org

Educational Paperback Association
P.O. Box 1399
East Hampton, NY 11937
Phone: (212) 879-6850
E-mail: info@edupaperback.org
http://www.edupaperback.org

Evangelical Christian Publishers Association
1969 East Broadway Road, Suite 2
Tempe, AZ 85282
Phone: (480) 966-3998
Fax: (480) 966-1944
E-mail: jmeegan@ecpa.org
http://www.ecpa.org

Florida Publishers Association, Inc.
P.O. Box 430
Highland City, FL 33846
Phone: (813) 648-4420
Fax: (813) 648-4420
E-mail: FPABooks@aol.com
http://www.flbookpub.org

Gotham Publishing Society
P.O. Box 61, Village Station
New York, NY 10014
Phone: (212) 645-3913

Independent Mystery Publishers
c/o Deadly Serious Press
868 Arlington Avenue
Berkeley, CA 94707
Phone: (510) 527-1821
Fax: (510) 527-0600
E-mail: info@deadlyserious.com
http://www.deadlyserious.com

Independent Travel Publishers Association
96 Ingham Hill
Essex, CT 06426
Phone: (203) 767-7622
Fax: (203) 767-7622

Indianapolis Publishers Association
3842 Wolf Creek Circle
Carmel, IN 46033
Phone: (317) 844-6070
Fax: (317) 844-8935

Information Industry Association
1625 Massachusetts Avenue, NW, Suite 700
Washington, DC 20036
Phone: (202) 319-0154
Fax: (202) 638-4403
E-mail: info@infoindustry.org
http://www.infoindustry.org

International Association of Scholarly Publishers
109 Church Street
New Brunswick, NJ 08901
Phone: (908) 932-1039
Fax: (908) 932-7039
E-mail: info@ipa-uie.org
http://www.ipa-uie.org

Jewish Book Council
15 East 26th Street
New York, NY 10010
Phone: (212) 532-4949
Fax: (212) 481-4174
E-mail: info@jewishbookcouncil.org
http://www.jewishbookcouncil.org

Kansas City Publishers Association
5822 Reinhardt Drive
Fairway, KS 66205
Phone: (913) 236-5595
Fax: (816) 531-6113

Maine Publishers & Writers Alliance
1326 Washington Street
Bath, ME 04530
Phone: (207) 386-1400
Fax: (207) 386-1401
E-mail: info@mainewriters.org
http://www.mainewriters.org

MidAtlantic Publishers Association
c/o Bookwise Associates
P.O. Box 50277
Baltimore, MD 21211

Minnesota Book Publishers Roundtable
430 First Avenue North, Suite 400
Minneapolis, MN 55401
Phone: (612) 332-3192
Fax: (612) 215-2550
E-mail: market@milkweed.org
http://www.milkweed.org

Multicultural Publishing & Educational Council
2280 Grass Valley Highway, Suite 181
Auburn, CA 96503
Phone: (916) 888-0696
Fax: (916) 888-0696

National Association of Independent Publishers
P.O. Box 430
Highland City, FL 33846
Phone: (813) 648-4420
Fax: (818) 648-4420
E-mail: NAIP@aol.com

National Directory Publishing Association
4201 Connecticut Avenue, NW, Suite 610
Washington, DC 20008
Phone: (202) 342-0250
Fax: (202) 686-9822
E-mail: info@idpa.org
http://www.idpa.org

National Federation of Abstracting & Information Services
1518 Walnut Street, Suite 1004
Philadelphia, PA 19102
Phone: (215) 893-1561
Fax: (215) 893-1564
E-mail: NFAIS@nfais.org
http://www.nfais.org

Networking Alternatives for Publishers, Retailers and Artists
109 North Beach Road
P.O. Box 9
Eastsound, WA 98245
Phone: (360) 376-2702
Fax: (360) 376-2704
E-mail: napraexec@napra.com
http://www.napra.com

New England Publishers Association
P.O. Box 2061
Natick, MA 01760
Phone: (508) 628-1891
E-mail: nepublishers@hotmail.com

New Mexico Book Association
P.O. Box 1285
Santa Fe, NM 87504
Phone: (505) 983-1412
Fax: (505) 983-0894
E-mail: oceantree@earthlink.net
http://www.nmbook.org

Newsletter and Electronic Publishers Association
1501 Wilson Boulevard, Suite 509
Arlington, VA 22209
Phone: (703) 527-2333
Fax: (703) 841-0629
E-mail: neap@newsletters.org
http://www.newsletters.org

Northern California Book Publicity & Marketing Association
P.O. Box 192803
San Francisco, CA 94119
Phone: (415) 777-7240
E-mail: info@ncbpma.org
http://www.ncbpma.com

Northwest Association of Book Publishers
P.O. Box 3786
Wilsonville, OR 97070
Phone: (503) 223-9055
E-mail: ncukell50@hotmail.com

Orange County Publishers Network
818 North Via Alhambra
Laguna Hills, CA 92653
Phone: (714) 855-0640
Fax: (714) 855-4860

Periodical & Book Association of America
481 8th Avenue, Suite 826
New York, NY 10001
Phone: (212) 563-6502
Fax: (212) 563-4098
E-mail: lscott@pbaa.net
http://www.pbaa.net

Philadelphia Publishers Group
P.O. Box 42681
Philadelphia, PA 19101
Phone: (215) 732-1863
Fax: (215) 735-5399

Protestant Church-Owned Publishers Association
1100 Country Club Road
St. Charles, MO 63303
Phone: (314) 949-3156
Fax: (314) 949-9978

Publishers Association of the South
P.O. Box 43533
Birmingham, AL 35243
Phone: (205) 967-4387
Fax: (205) 967-0580
E-mail: executive@pubsouth.org
http://www.pubsouth.org

Publishers Association of the West
501 South Cherry Street, Suite 320
Denver, CO 80246
Phone: (303) 447-2320
Fax: (303) 447-9710
E-mail: executivedirector@pubwest.org
http://www.pubwest.org

Publishers Marketing Association
627 Aviation Way
Manhattan Beach, CA 90266
Phone: (310) 372-2732
Fax: (310) 374-3342
E-mail: info@pma-online.org
http://www.pma-online.org

Regional Publishers Association
2503 Davidsonville Road
Gambrills, MD 21054
Phone: (410) 721-7987
Fax: (410) 721-7987

Rocky Mountain Book Publishers Association
P.O. Box 19013
Boulder, CO 80308
Phone: (303) 499-9540
Fax: (303) 499-9584

Rocky Mountain Publishing Professionals Guild
P.O. Box 17721
Boulder, CO 80308
Phone: (303) 282-9294
E-mail: info@rmppg.org
http://www.rmppg.org

Saint Louis Publishers Association
244 Mid Rivers Center, Suite 198
Saint Peters, MO 63376
Phone: (314) 278-1462
E-mail: editor@stlouispublishers.org

San Diego Publishers Alliance
4679 Vista Street
San Diego, CA 92116
Phone: (619) 280-8711
Fax: (619) 280-8713
E-mail: sdpa@ellipsys.com

Small Press Center for Independent Publishing
20 West 44th Street
New York, NY 10036
Phone: (212) 764-7021
Fax: (212) 354-5365
E-mail: info@smallpress.org
http://www.smallpress.org

Small Publishers, Artists and Writers Network
PMB 123
323 East Matilija Street, Suite 110
Ojai, CA 93023
Phone: (818) 886-3320
Fax: (818) 886-3320
E-mail: execdir@spawn.org
http://www.spawn.org

Small Publishers Association of North America
P.O. Box 1306
Buena Vista, CA 81211
Phone: (719) 395-5761
Fax: (719) 395-8374

E-mail: SPAN@spannet.org
http://www.spannet.org

Society for Scholarly Publishing
10200 West 44th Avenue, Suite 304
Wheat Ridge, CO 80033
Phone: (303) 422-3914
Fax: (303) 422-8894
E-mail: info@sspnet.org
http://www.sspnet.org

Society of National Association
Publications
8405 Greensboro Drive, Suite 800
McLean, VA 22102
Phone: (703) 506-3285
Fax: (703) 506-3266
E-mail: snapinfo@snaponline.org
http://www.snaponline.org

Software and Information Industry
Association
1090 Vermont Avenue NW, Sixth Floor
Washington, DC 20005
Phone: (202) 289-7442
Fax: (202) 289-7097
E-mail: At Web site
http://www.siia.net

Software Publishers Association
1730 M Street, NW, Suite 700
Washington, DC 20036
Phone: (202) 452-1600
Fax: (202) 223-8756
E-mail: At Web site
http://www. spa.org

Special Libraries Association
331 South Patrick Street
Alexandria, VA 22314
Phone: 703-647-4900
Fax: 703-647-4901
E-mail: sla@sla.org
http://www.sla.org

West Coast Book People Association
27 Mc Near Drive
San Rafael, CA 94901
Phone: (415) 459-1227
Fax: (415) 459-1227

Women in Scholarly Publishing
c/o Trudy McMurrin
University of Nevada Press
W2D Executive Offices
6375 West Charleston Boulevard
Las Vegas, NV 89146
Phone: (702) 895-2937
Fax: (702) 651-5938
E-mail: membership@wispnet.org
http://www.wispnet.org

Women's National Book Association
160 Fifth Avenue, Room 604
New York, NY 10010
Phone: (212) 675-7804
Fax: (212) 989-7542
http://www.wnba.books.org

BUSINESS COMMUNICATIONS AND PUBLIC RELATIONS

American Business Women's
Association
P.O. Box 8728
9100 Ward Parkway
Kansas City, MO 64114
Phone: (800) 228-0007
Fax: (816) 361-4991
E-mail: abwa@abwa.org
http://www.abwa.org

American Management Association
1601 Broadway
New York, NY 10019
Phone: (212) 586-8100
Fax: (212) 903-8168
E-mail: customerservice@amanet.org
http://www.amanet.org

American Marketing Association
311 South Wacker Drive, Suite 5800
Chicago, IL 60606
Phone: (800) AMA-1150
Fax: (312) 542-9001
E-mail: info@ama.org
http://www.marketingpower.com

American Society of Business
Publication Editors
710 East Ogden Avenue, Suite 600
Naperville, IL 60563
Phone: (630) 579-3288
Fax: (630) 369-2488
E-mail: info@asbpe.org
http://www.asbpe.org

Associated Business Writers of
America
1450 Havana Street, Suite 424
Aurora, CO 80012
Phone: (303) 751-7844
Fax: (303) 751-8593

Association for Business
Communication
P.O. Box B8-240, Baruch College
One Bernard Baruch Way
New York, NY 10010
Phone: (646) 312-3727

Fax: (646) 349-5297
E-mail: myers@businesscommunication.
org
http://www.businesscommunication.org

Association for Women in
Communications
780 Ritchie Highway, Suite 28-S
Severna Park, MD 21146
Phone: (410) 544-7442
Fax: (410) 544-4640
E-mail: info@womcom.org
http://www.womcom.org

Association of Area Business
Publications
5820 Wilshire Boulevard, Suite 500
Los Angeles, CA 90036
Phone: (212) 353-3709
Fax: (323) 937-0959
E-mail: info@bizpubs.org
http://www.bizpubs.org

Business Marketing Association
400 North Michigan Avenue, 15th Floor
Chicago, IL 60611
Phone: (312) 822-0005
Fax: (312) 822-0054
E-mail: bma@marketing.org
http://www.marketing.org

Communications Managers Association
1201 Mount Kemble Avenue
Morristown, NJ 07960
Phone: (973) 425-1700
Fax: (973) 425-0777
E-mail: info@cma.org
http://www.cma.org

Council of Communication
Management
65 Enterprise
Aliso Viejo, CA 92656
Phone: (866) 463-6226
Fax: (949) 715-6931
E-mail: membership@ccmconnection.com
http://www.ccmconnection.com

Direct Marketing Association
1120 Avenue of the Americas
New York, NY 10036
Phone: (212) 768-7277
Fax: (212) 302-6714
E-mail: membership@the-dma.org
http://www.the-dma.org

Information Technology Association of
America
1401 Wilson Boulevard, Suite 1100
Arlington, VA 22209

Phone: (703) 522-5055
Fax: (703) 525-2279
E-mail: hmiller@itaa.org
http://www.itaa.org

International Association of Business Communicators
One Hallidie Plaza, Suite 600
San Francisco, CA 94102
Phone: (415) 544-4700
Fax: (415) 544-4747
E-mail: service_centre@iabc.com
http://www.iabc.com

International Publishing Management Association
1205 West College Street
Liberty, MO 64068
Phone: (816) 781-1111
Fax: (816) 781-2790
E-mail: ipmainfo@ipma.org
http://www.ipma.org

National Black Public Relations Society
6565 Sunset Boulevard, Suite 301
Hollywood, CA 90028
Phone: (323) 466-8221
Fax: (323) 856-9510
E-mail: nbprs@aol.com
http://www.nbprs.com

North American Case Research Association
c/o Bob Crowner
3719 Meadow Lane
Saline, MI 48176
Phone: (734) 429-5032
E-mail: rpcnacra@worldnet.att.net
http://nacra.net

Public Relations Society of America
33 Irving Place, Third Floor
New York, NY 10003
Phone: (212) 995-2230
Fax: 212-995-0757
E-mail: hq@prsa.org
http://www.prsa.org

Society for Technical Communication
901 North Stuart Street, Suite 904
Wheat Ridge, CO 80033
Phone: (703) 522-4114
Fax: (703) 522-2075
E-mail: stc@stc.org
http://www.stc.org

Society of American Business Editors and Writers
c/o University of Missouri, School of Journalism

76 Gannet Hall
Columbia, MO 65211
Phone: (573) 882-7862
Fax: (573) 884-1372
E-mail: sabew@missouri.edu
http://www.sabew.org

U.S. Chamber of Commerce
1615 H Street, NW
Washington, DC 20062
Phone: (710) 822-9382
Fax: (202) 463-5836
E-mail: info@uschamber.org
http://www.uschamber.org

FEDERAL, STATE, AND MUNICIPAL GOVERNMENTS

American Academy of Political & Social Science
3814 Walnut Street
Philadelphia, PA 19104
Phone: (215) 746-6500
Fax: (215) 898-1202
E-mail: At Web site
http://www.aapss.org

American Political Science Association
1527 New Hampshire Avenue, NW
Washington, DC 20036
Phone: (202) 483-2512
Fax: (202) 483-2657
E-mail: apsa@apsanet.org
http://www.apsanet.org

Association of House Democratic Press Assistants
House of Representatives
P.O. Box 007
Washington, DC 20515
Fax: (202) 226-8843

Capitol Press Club
P.O. Box 19403
Washington, DC 20036
Phone: (202) 628-1122
Fax: (301) 588-7739
E-mail: cappress44@aol.com

Federally Employed Women
1666 K Street, NW, Suite 400
Washington, DC 20006
Phone: (202) 898-0994
E-mail: few@few.org
http://www.few.org

National Association of Government Communicators
526 King Street, Suite 423

Alexandria, VA 22314
Phone: (703) 691-0377
E-mail: info@nagc.com
http://www.nagc.com

National Association of Government Employees
159 Burgin Parkway
Quincy, MA 02169
Phone: (617) 376-0220
Fax: (617) 376-0285
http://www.nage.org

National Communication Association
1765 N Street, NW
Washington, DC 20036
Phone: (202) 464-4622
Fax: (202) 464-4600
E-mail: info@natcom.org
http://www.natcom.org

National Federation of Federal Employees
1016 16th Street, NW, Suite 300
Washington, DC 20036
Phone: (202) 862-4471
Fax: (202) 862-4432
E-mail: info@nffe.org
http://www.nffe.org

Society for Technical Communication
901 North Stuart Street, Suite 904
Arlington, VA 22203
Phone: (703) 522-4114
Fax: (703) 522-2075
E-mail: stc@stc.org
http://www.stc.org

Speech Communication Association
5105 Backlick Road, Building E
Annandale, VA 22003
Phone: (703) 750-0533
Fax: (703) 914-9471

FREELANCE SERVICES AND SELF-PUBLISHING
Including desktop publishing, graphic communication, and technical writing

About Books
425 Cedar Street
P.O. Box 1500, Department EA
Buena Vista, CO 81211
Phone: (719) 395-2459
Fax: (719) 395-8374
E-mail: deb@about-books.com
http://www.about-books.com

American Association for the Advancement of Science
1200 New York Avenue, NW
Washington, DC 20005
Phone: (202) 326-6400
Fax: (202) 371-9526
E-mail: info@aaas.org
http://www.aaas.org

American Institute of Graphic Arts
164 Fifth Avenue
New York, NY 10010
Phone: (212) 807-1990
Fax: (212) 807-1799
E-mail: comments@aiga.org
http://www.aiga.org

American Self-Publisher Association
P.O. Box 232233
Sacramento, CA 95823
Phone: (916) 422-8435
Fax: (916) 422-1918
E-mail: aspublish@aol.com
http://www.aspublish.com

American Society of Indexers
10200 West 44th Avenue, Suite 304
Wheat Ridge, CO 80033
Phone: (303) 463-2887
Fax: (303) 422-8894
E-mail: info@asindexing.org
http://www.asindexing.org

Association of Computer Professionals
Nine Forest Drive
Plainview, NY 11803
Phone: (516) 938-8223
Fax: (516) 938-3073
E-mail: sybosworth@aol.com

Association of Desk-Top Publishers
4677-30th Street, Suite 800
San Diego, CA 92116
Phone: (619) 563-9714
Fax: (619) 280-3778

Association of Graphic Communications
330 Seventh Avenue, Ninth Floor
New York, NY 10001
Phone: (212) 279-2100
Fax: (212) 279-5381

Editorial Freelancers Association
71 West 23rd Street, Suite 1910
New York, NY 10010
Phone: (212) 929-5400
Fax: (212) 929-5439
E-mail: info@the-efa.org
http://www.the-efa.org

Florida Freelance Writers Association
CNW Publishing/FFWA
P.O. Box A
North Stratford, NH 03590
Phone: (603) 922-8338
Fax: NA
E-mail: FFWA@writers-editors.com
http://www.ffwamembers.com

Graphic Communications Association
100 Dangerfield Road
Alexandria, VA 22314
Phone: (703) 519-8160
Fax: (703) 548-2867
E-mail: info@gca.org
http://www.gca.org

Information Technology Association of America
1401 Wilson Boulevard, Suite 1100
Arlington, VA 22209
Phone: (703) 522-5055
Fax: (703) 525-2279
E-mail: hmiller@itaa.org
http://www.itaa.org

National Association of Desktop Publishers
462 Old Boston Street
Topsfield, MA 01983
Phone: (508) 887-7900
Fax: (508) 887-6117

Small Publishers Association of North America
P.O. Box 1306
Buena Vista, CA 81211
Phone: (719) 395-5761
Fax: (719) 395-8374
E-mail: span@spannet.org
http://www.spannet.org

Society for Software Quality
P.O. Box 86958
San Diego, CA 92138
E-mail: At Web site
http://www.ssq.org

Society for Technical Communication
901 North Stuart Street, Suite 904
Arlington, VA 22203
Phone: (703) 522-4114
Fax: (703) 522-2075
E-mail: stc@stc.org
http://www.stc.org

Software and Information Industry Association
1090 Vermont Ave, NW, Sixth Floor
Washington, DC 20005

Phone: (202) 289-7442
Fax: (202) 289-7097
E-mail: At Web site
http://www.siia.net

Special Interest Group on Software Engineering
c/o Association for Computing Machinery
1515 Broadway
New York, NY 10036
Phone: (212) 626-0613
Fax: (212) 302-5826
E-mail: ignatoff@acm.org
http://www.acm.org/sigsoft

Working Today
55 Washington Street, Suite 557
Brooklyn, NY 11201
Phone: (718) 222-1099
Fax: (718) 222-4440
E-mail: info@workingtoday.org
http://www.workingtoday.org

MEDIA

Including Internet, magazines, newspapers and news services, radio, and television

Academy of Television Arts and Sciences
5220 Lankershim Boulevard
North Hollywood, CA 91601
Phone: (818) 754-2800
Fax: (818) 761-2827
E-mail: bryce@emmys.org
http://www.emmys.org

Alliance of Area Business Publications
4929 Wilshire Boulevard, Suite 428
Los Angeles, CA 90010
Phone: (323) 937-5514
Fax: ((323) 937-0959
E-mail: jdowden@prodigy.net
http://www.bizpubs.org

American Agricultural Editor's Association
120 West Main Street
P.O. Box 156
New Prague, MN 56071
Phone: (952) 758-6502
Fax: (952) 758-5813
E-mail: ageditors@aol.com
http://www.ageditors.com

American Amateur Press Association
535 Kickerillo Drive
Houston, TX 77079

Phone: (281) 497-8493
E-mail: leswboyer@prodigy.net
http://www.members.aol.com/aapa96

American Association of Dental Editors
735 North Water Street, Suite 617
Milwaukee, WI 53202
Phone: (414) 272-2759
Fax: (414) 272-2754
E-mail: aade@dentaleditors.com
http://www.dentaleditors.com

**American Association of Sunday and
Feature Editors**
Merrill College of Journalism
University of Maryland
1117 Journalism Building
College Park, MD 20742
Phone: (301) 314-2631
Fax: (301) 314-9166
E-mail: aasfe@jmail.umd.edu
http://www.aasfe.org

**American Auto Racing Writers and
Broadcasters Association, Inc.**
922 North Pass Avenue
Burbank, CA 91505
Phone: (818) 842-7005
Fax: (818) 842-7020
E-mail: aarwba@compuserve.com
http://beta.motorsportsforum.com/ris01/
aarwbaap.htm

American Copy Editors Society
38309 Genesee Lake Road
Oconomowoc, WI 53066
Phone: (800) 393-7681
E-mail: carolafj@execpc.com
http://www.copydesk.org

**American Federation of Television and
Radio Artists**
260 Madison Avenue
New York, NY 10016
Phone: (212) 532-0800
Fax: (212) 532-2242
E-mail: info@aftra.com
http://www.aftra.org

American Jewish Press Association
1828 L Street, NW, Suite 720
Washington, DC 20036
Phone: (202) 785-2282
Fax: (202) 785-2307
E-mail: info@ajpa.org
http://www.ajpa.org

American News Women's Club
1607 22nd Street, NW
Washington, DC 20008

Phone: (202) 332-6770
Fax: (202) 265-6477
E-mail: anwc@sprynet.org
http://www.anwc.org

American Press Institute
11690 Sunrise Valley Drive
Reston, VA 20191
Phone: (703) 620-3611
Fax: (703) 620-5814
E-mail: info@americanpressinstitute.org
http://www.americanpressinstitute.org

**American Society of Business
Publication Editors**
710 East Ogden Avenue, Suite 600
Naperville, IL 60563
Phone: (630) 579-3288
Fax: (630) 369-2488
E-mail: info@asbpe.org
http://www.asbpe.org

**American Society of Journalists and
Authors**
1501 Broadway, Suite 302
New York, NY 10036
Phone: (212) 997-0947
Fax: (212) 768-7414
E-mail: staff@asja.org
http://www.asja.org

American Society of Magazine Editors
919 Third Avenue
New York, NY 10022
Phone: (212) 872-3737
Fax: (212) 906-0128
E-mail: asme@magazine.org
http://asme.magazine.org

**American Society of Media
Photographers**
14 Washington Road, Suite 502
Princeton Junction, NJ 08550
Phone: (609) 799-8300
Fax: (609) 799-2232
E-mail: info@asmp.org
http://www.asmp.org

American Society of Newspaper Editors
1190B Sunrise Valley Drive
Reston, VA 20191
Phone: (703) 453-1122
Fax: (703) 453-1133
E-mail: asne@asne.org
http://www.asne.org

American Theatre Critics Association
c/o Theatre Service
P.O. Box 15282
Evansville, IN 47716

Phone: (812) 474-0549
Fax: (812) 476-4168
E-mail: ts@evansville.edu
http://www.americantheatrecritics.org

**American Women in Radio and
Television**
8405 Greensboro Drive, Suite 800
McLean, VA 22102
Phone: (703) 506-3290
Fax: (703) 506-3266
E-mail: info@awrt.org
http://www.awrt.org

Arab-American Press Guild
13313 Debell Street
Arieta, CA 91331
Phone: (818) 896-5860
Fax: (818) 896-5860
E-mail: aman29@msn.com

Asian American Journalists Association
1182 Market Street, Suite 320
San Francisco, CA 94102
Phone: (415) 346-2051
Fax: (415) 346-6343
E-mail: national@aaja.org
http://www.aaja.org

Associated Press
50 Rockefeller Plaza
New York, NY 10020
Phone: (212) 621-1500
Fax: (212) 621-1723
E-mail: info@ap.org
http://www.ap.org

Associated Press Broadcast Services
1825 K Street, NW, Suite 8000
Washington, DC 20006
Phone: (202) 736-1100
E-mail: info@apbroadcast.com
http://www.apbroadcast.com

Associated Press Managing Editors
50 Rockefeller Plaza
New York, NY 10020
Phone: (212) 621-1838
Fax: (212) 506-6102
E-mail: apme@ap.org
http://www.apme.org

**Association for Education in
Journalism and Mass
Communication**
234 Outlet Pointe Boulevard, Suite A
Columbia, SC 29210
Phone: (803) 798-0271
Fax: (803) 772-3509

E-mail: aejmc@aol.com
http://www.aejmc.org

Association for Women in
  Communications
1255 Ritchie Highway, Suite 6
Arnold, MD 21012
Phone: (410) 544-7442
Fax: (410) 544-4640
E-mail: pat@womcom.org
http://www.womcom.org

Association for Women in Sports
  Media
P.O. Box 726
Farmington, CT 06034
E-mail: info@awsmonline.org
http://www.awsmonline.org

Association for Women Journalists
P.O. Box 2199
Fort Worth, TX 76113
Phone: (214) 740-9251
E-mail: ssprague@kera.org
http://www.awjdfw.org

Association of Alternative
  Newsweeklies
1020 16th Street, NW, Fourth Floor
Washington, DC 20036
Phone: (202) 822-1955
Fax: (202) 822-0929
E-mail: aan@aan.org
http://www.aan.org

Association of Earth Science
  Editors
c/o Nancy Gilson Secretary/Treasurer
101 Fire Academy Road
Socorro, NM 87801
E-mail: nancy@gis.nmt.edu
http://www.aese.org

Association of Food Journalists
38309 Genesee Lake Road
Oconomowoc, WI 53066
Phone: (262) 965-3521
E-mail: carolafj@execpc.com
http://www.afjonline.com

Association of Free Community
  Papers
1630 Miner Street, Suite 204
P.O. Box 1989
Idaho Springs, CO 80452
Phone: (877) 203-2327
Fax: (781) 459-7770
E-mail: info@afcp.org
http://www.afcp.org

Association of Paid Circulation
  Publications
P.O. Box 15289
Washington, DC 20003
Phone: (202) 296-8487
Fax: (202) 296-0343

Association of Professional
  Communication Consultants
3924 South Troost
Tulsa, OK 74105
Phone: (918) 743-4793
Fax: (615) 269-5442
http://www.consultingsuccess.org

Association of Railway Communicators
c/o Ron Shumate
327 East Mason Avenue
Alexandria, VA 22301
Phone: (703) 548-3451
E-mail: capnron@erols.com

Baseball Writers Association of America
78 Olive Street
Lake Grove, NY 11755
Phone: (631) 981-7938
Fax: (631) 585-4669
E-mail: bbwaa@aol.com

Bay Area Book Reviewers Association
11-A Commercial Boulevard
Novato, CA 94949
Phone: (415) 883-2353
Fax: (415) 883-4280

Boating Writers International
108 Ninth Street
Wilmette, IL 60091
Phone: (847) 736-4142
E-mail: info@bwi.org
http://www.bwi.org

Bowling Writers Association of America
128 Preston Drive
Braddock, PA 15104
Phone: (412) 824-7183
http://www.bowlingwriters.com

Catholic News Service
3211 Fourth Street, NE
Washington, DC 20017
Phone: (202) 541-3250
Fax: (202) 541-3255
E-mail: cns@catholicnews.com
http://www.catholicnews.com

Catholic Press Association of the U.S.
  and Canada
3555 Veterans Memorial Highway, Unit O
Ronkonkoma, NY 11779

Phone: (631) 471-4730
Fax: (631) 471-4804
E-mail: rosep@catholicpress.org
http://www.catholicpress.org

Caucus for Television Producers,
  Writers and Directors
P.O. Box 11236
Burbank, CA 91510
Phone: (818) 843-7572
Fax: (818) 846-2159
E-mail: caucuspwd@aol.com
http://caucus.org

Center for Investigative Reporting
131 Stuart Street, Suite 600
San Francisco, CA 94105
Phone: (415) 543-1200
Fax: (415) 543-8311
E-mail: center@cironline.org
http://www.muckraker.org

Chess Journalists of America
Two Budd Street
Morristown, NJ 07960
Phone: (973) 984-3832
E-mail: ptamburro@aol.com
http://www.correspondencechess.com/cja

City & Regional Magazine
  Association
4929 Wilshire Boulevard, Suite 428
Los Angeles, CA 90010
Phone: (323) 937-5514
Fax: (323) 937-0959
E-mail: info@citymag.org
http://www.citymag.org

College Press Service
435 North Michigan Avenue, Suite 1500
Chicago, IL 60611
Fax: (312) 222-3459
http://www.tms.tribune.com

Columbia Scholastic Press Association
Mail Code 5711
Columbia University
New York, NY 10027
Phone: (212) 854-9400
Fax: (212) 854-9401
E-mail: cspa@columbia.edu
http://www.columbia.edu/cu/cspa

Comics Magazine Association of
  America, Inc.
355 Lexington Avenue, 17th Floor
New York, NY 10017
Phone: (212) 661-4261
Fax: (212) 370-9047

Construction Writers Association
P.O. Box 5586
Buffalo Grove, IL 60089
Phone: (847) 398-7756
Fax: (847) 590-5241
E-mail: office@constructionwriters.org
http://www.constructionwriters.org

Corporation for Public Broadcasting
901 E Street, NW
Washington, DC 20004
Phone: (202) 879-9600
Fax: (202) 783-1019
E-mail: At Web site
http://www.cpb.org

**Council for the Advancement of
  Science Writing**
P.O. Box 910
Hedgesville, WV 25427
Phone: (304) 754-5077
Fax: (304) 754-5076
E-mail: diane@nasw.org
http://www.casw.org

Council of Authors & Journalists, Inc.
P.O. Box 830184
Stone Mountain, GA 30083

**Council of Literary Magazines &
  Presses**
154 Christopher Street, Suite 3C
New York, NY 10014
Phone: (212) 741-9110
Fax: (212) 741-9112
E-mail: info@clmp.org
http://www.clmp.org

Council of Science Editors
c/o Drohan Management Group
11250 Roger Bacon Drive, Suite 8
Reston, VA 20190
Phone: (703) 437-4377
Fax: (703) 435-4390
E-mail: cse@councilscienceeditors.org

Dance Critics Association
P.O. Box 1882, Old Chelsea Station
New York, NY 10011
E-mail: contactus@dancecritics.org
http://www.dancecritics.org

Dog Writers' Association of America
173 Union Road
Coatesville, PA 19320
Phone: (610) 384-2436
Fax: (610) 384-2471
E-mail: dwaa@dwaa.org
http://www.dwaa.org

Dow Jones Newspaper Fund
4300 Route One North
South Brunswick, NJ 08852
Phone: (609) 452-2820
Fax: (609) 520-5804
E-mail: newsfund@wsj.dowjones.com
http://www.djnewspaperfund.dowjones.
  com

East-West News Bureau
531 Main Street, Suite 902
El Segundo, CA 90245
Phone: (310) 836-8712
Fax: (310) 836-8769
E-mail: membership@eastwestnews.org
http://www.eastwestnews.org

**Educational Press Association of
  America**
c/o Rowan College of New Jersey
Glassboro, NJ 08028
Phone: (609) 863-7349
Fax: (609) 863-5012

Education Writers Association
1331 H Street, NW, Suite 307
Washington, DC 20005
Phone: (202) 452-8830
Fax: (202) 452-9837
E-mail: ewa@ewa.org
http://www.ewa.org

**Engineering College Magazines
  Associated**
c/o Paul Sorenson and Sharon Kurtt,
  co-chairs
University of Minnesota
Institute of Technology
105 Walter Library
117 Pleasant Street SE
Minneapolis, MN 55414
Phone: (612) 626-7959
E-mail: ecma@it.umn.edu
http://www.ecmaweb.org

Essential Information
P.O. Box 19405
Washington, DC 20036
Phone: (202) 387-8030
Fax: (202) 234-5176
E-mail: info@essential.org
http://www.essential.org

Evangelical Press Association
P.O. Box 28129
Crystal, MN 55428
Phone: (763) 535-4793
Fax: (763) 535-4794

E-mail: director@epassoc.org
http://www.gospelcom.net/epa

Florida Magazine Association
900 Fox Valley Drive, Suite 204
Longwood, FL 32779
Phone: (407) 774-9587
Fax: (407) 774-6751
E-mail: tom@camco.biz
http://www.floridamagazine.org

**Foundation for American
  Communications**
85 South Grand Avenue
Pasadena, CA 91105
Phone: (626) 584-0010
Fax: (626) 584-0627
http://www.facsnet.org

Fund for Investigative Journalism
P.O. Box 60184
Washington, DC 20039
Phone: (202) 362-0260
Fax: (301) 576-0804
E-mail: fundfij@aol.com
http://www.fij.org

Gridiron Club of Washington, DC
16th and K Streets, NW, Suite 402
Washington, DC 20036
Phone: (202) 639-5480

Independent Press Association
2729 Mission Street, Suite 201
San Francisco, CA 94110
Phone: (415) 643-4401
Fax: (415) 643-4402
E-mail: indypress@indypress.com
http://www.indypress.org

Inter American Press Association
1801 Southwest Third Avenue
Miami, FL 33129
Phone: (305) 634-2465
Fax: (305) 635-2272
E-mail: info@sipiapa.org
http://www.sipiapa.org

International Center for Journalists
1616 H Street, NW, Third Floor
Washington, DC 20006
Phone: (202) 737-3700
Fax: (202) 737-0530
E-mail: editor@icfj.org
http://www.icfj.org

**International Communications
  Association**
1730 Rhode Island Avenue, NW, Suite 300
Washington, DC 20036

Phone: (202) 530-9855
Fax: (202) 530-9851
E-mail: icahdq@icahdq.org
http://www.icahdq.org

International Foodservice Editorial
Council
P.O. Box 491
Hyde Park, NY 12538
Phone: (845) 229-6973
Fax: (845) 229-6993
E-mail: ifec@aol.com
http://www.ifec-is-us.com

International Food, Wine and Travel
Writers Association
P.O. Box 8249
Calabasas, CA 91372
Phone: (818) 999-9959
Fax: (818) 347-7545
E-mail: ifwtwa@aol.com
http://www.ifwtwa.org

International Game Developers
Association
600 Harrison Street
San Francisco, CA 94107
Phone: (415) 947-6215
Fax: (415) 947-6090
E-mail: info@igda.org
http://www.igda.org

International Motor Press
Association
Four Park Street
Harrington Park, NY 07640
Phone: (201) 750-3533
Fax: (201) 750-2010
E-mail: tab@kgpr.com
http://www.impa.org

International Newspaper Group
c/o Marty Donner
4335 Northwest 36th Terrace
Gainesville, FL 32605
Fax: (602) 256-7334
E-mail: hite@scripps.com
http://www.azcentral.com/advert/ing

International Newspaper Marketing
Association
10300 North Central Expressway,
Suite 467
Dallas, TX 75231
Phone: (214) 373-9111
Fax: (214) 373-9112
E-mail: info@inma.org
http://www.inma.org

International Pentecostal Press
Association
c/o ICFG
1910 West Sunset Boulevard, Suite 200
Los Angeles, CA 90026
Phone: (423) 478-7005
Fax: (423) 478-7012
E-mail: hgrhea@usa.net

International Press Institute, American
Committee
819 North Kiowa Street
Allentown, PA 18103
Phone: (610) 432-6700

International Radio and Television
Society–Alpha Epsilon Rho
Millersville University
Department of Communications and
Theatre
Millersville, PA 17551
Phone: (717) 871-03233
Fax: (717) 871-2051
E-mail: At Web site
http://muweb.millersville.edu/~theatre

International Radio and Television
Society Foundation
420 Lexington Avenue, Suite 1601
New York, NY 10170
Phone: (212) 867-6650
Fax: (212) 867-6653
E-mail: membership@irts.org
http://www.irts.org

International Regional Magazine
Association
P.O. Box 124
Annapolis, MD 21404
Phone: (410) 451-2892
E-mail: info@regionalmagazines.org
http://www.regionalmagazines.org

International Science Writers'
Association
Smithsonian Institute Astrophysical
Observatory
60 Garden Street
Cambridge, MA 02138
Phone: (617) 495-7461
Fax: (617) 495-7468
E-mail: jcornell@cfa.harvard.edu
http://www.eurekalert.org/static

International Society of Weekly
Newspaper Editors
Missouri Southern State College
3950 South Newman Road
Joplin, MO 64801

Phone: (417) 625-9736
Fax: (417) 659-4445
E-mail: stebbins-c@mail.mssc.edu
http://www.mssc.edu/iswne

International Women's Media
Foundation
1726 M Street, NW, Suite 1002
Washington, DC 20036
Phone: (202) 496-1992
Fax: (202) 496-1977
E-mail: info@iwmf.org
http://www.iwmf.org

Investigative Reporters and
Editors
School of Journalism
138 Neff Annex
Columbia, MO 65211
Phone: (573) 882-2042
Fax: (573) 882-5431
E-mail: info@ire.org
http://www.mww.ire.org

Journalism Education
Association
Kansas State University
103 Kedzie Hall
Manhattan, KS 66506
Phone: (785) 532-5332
Fax: (785) 532-5563
E-mail: jea@spub.ksu.edu
http://www.jea.org

Kappa Tau Alpha
University of Missouri
School of Journalism
100 Neff Hall
Columbia, MO 65211
Phone: (573) 882-7685
Fax: (573) 884-1720
E-mail: umcjourtta@missouri.edu
http://www.missouri.edu/~ktahq

Livestock Publications Council
910 Currie Street
Fort Worth, TX 76107
Phone: (817) 336-1130
Fax: (817) 232-4820
E-mail: dianej@flash.net
http://www.livestockpublications.com

Magazine Publishers of America
919 Third Avenue, 22nd Floor
New York, NY 10022
Phone: (212) 872-3700
Fax: (212) 888-4217
E-mail: infocenter@magazine.org
http://www.magazine.org

Media Alliance
814 Mission Street, Suite 205
San Francisco, CA 94103
Phone: (415) 546-6491
Fax: (415) 546-6218
E-mail: info@media-alliance.org
http://www.media-alliance.org

Media Coalition
139 Fulton Street, Suite 302
New York, NY 10038
Phone: (212) 587-4025
Fax: (212) 587-2436
E-mail: info@mediacoalition.org
http://www.mediacoalition.org

**Media Communications Association
    International**
1000 Executive Parkway, Suite 220
St. Louis, MO 63141
Phone: (314) 514-9995
Fax: (314) 576-7960
E-mail: info@mca-i.org
http://www.mca-i.org

Media Networks
P.O. Box 10096
One Station Place
Stamford, CT 06904
Phone: (203) 967-3100
Fax: (203) 967-6472
E-mail: info@mni.com
http://www.mni.com

Minorities in Media
P.O. Box 9198
Petersburg, VA 23806
Phone: (804) 524-5935
Fax: (804) 524-5757
E-mail: vthota@vsu.edu

Motion Picture Association of America
15503 Ventura Boulevard
Encino, CA 91436
Phone: (818) 995-6600
http://www.mpaa.org

**Music Critics Association of North
    America**
Seven Pine Court
Westfield, NJ 07090
Fax: (908) 233-8468
E-mail: beethoven2@prodigy.net

**National Academy of Television Arts
    and Sciences**
111 West 57th Street, Suite 1050
New York, NY 10019
Phone: (212) 586-8424

Fax: (212) 246-8129
E-mail: natashq@aol.com
http://www.emmyonline.com

**National Academy of Television
    Journalists**
P.O. Box 31
Salisbury, MD 21803
Phone: (410) 548-5343
Fax: (410) 543-0658
E-mail: nbayne@shore.intercom.net
http://www.GoldenViddyAwards.com

National Amateur Press Association
12311 Winding Lane
Bowie, MD 20715
http://www.amateurpress.org

**National Association of African-
    American Sportswriters and
    Broadcasters**
308 Deer Park Avenue
Dix Hills, NY 11746
Phone: (631) 462-3933
E-mail: cldavis@suffolk.library.us

National Association of Black Journalists
8701-A Adelphi Road
Adelphi, MD 20783
Phone: (301) 445-7100
Fax: (301) 445-7101
E-mail: nabj@nabj.org
http://www.nabj.org

National Association of Broadcasters
1771 N Street, NW
Washington, DC 20036
Phone: (202) 429-5300
Fax: (202) 429-5410
E-mail: sdelanghe@nab.org
http://www.nab.org

**National Association of Farm
    Broadcasters**
P.O. Box 500
Platte City, MO 64079
Phone: (816) 431-4032
Fax: (816) 431-4087
E-mail: info@nafb.com
http://www.nafb.com

**National Association of Hispanic
    Journalists**
1000 National Press Building
Washington, DC 20045
Phone: (202) 662-7145
Fax: (202) 662-7144
E-mail: nah@nahj.org
http://www.nahj.org

**National Association of Hispanic
    Publications**
941 National Press Building
Washington, DC 20045
Phone: (202) 662-7250
Fax: (202) 662-7251
E-mail: communication@nahponponline.
    org
http://www.nahp.org

**National Association of Minority Media
    Executives**
1921 Gallows Road, Suite 600
Vienna, VA 22182
Phone: (703) 893-2410
Fax: (703) 893-2414
E-mail: nammeexecutivedirector@att.net
http://www.namme.org

**National Association of Real Estate
    Editors**
1003 Northwest, Sixth Terrace
Boca Raton, FL 33486
Phone: (561) 391-3599
Fax: (561) 391-0099
E-mail: madkimba@aol.com
http://www.naree.org

National Association of Science Writers
P.O. Box 890
Hedgesville, WV 25427
Phone: (304) 754-5077
Fax: (304) 754-5076
E-mail: diane@nasw.org
http://www.nasw.org

National Book Critics Circle
c/o Rebecca Skloot
444 West 35th Street #5B
New York, NY 10001
E-mail: bookcritics@earthlink.net
http://www.bookcritics.org

National Communications Association
1765 N Street, NW
Washington, DC 20036
Phone: (202) 464-4622
Fax: (202) 464 4600
E-mail: dwallick@natcom.org
http://www.natcom.org

**National Conference of Editorial
    Writers**
3999 North Front Street
Harrisburg, PA 17110
Phone: (717) 703-3015
Fax: (717) 703-3014
E-mail: ncew@pa-news.org
http://www.ncew.org

**National Elementary School Press
    Association**
P.O. Box 5556
Arlington, VA 22205
Phone: (828) 274-0758
Fax: (828) 277-8832
E-mail: mlevin@cdschool.org
http://www.nespa.org

National Federation of Press Women
P.O. Box 5556
Arlington, VA 22205
Phone: (703) 534-2500
Fax: (703) 534-5750
E-mail: presswomen@aol.com
http://www.nfpw.org

**National Lesbian and Gay Journalists
    Association**
1420 K Street, NW, Suite 910
Washington, DC 20005
Phone: (202) 588-9888
Fax: (202) 588-1818
E-mail: info@nlgja.org
http://www.nlgja.org

National News Bureau
P.O. Box 43039
Philadelphia, PA 19129
Phone: (215) 849-9016
Fax: (215) 893-5394
E-mail: nnbfeature@aol.com
http://www.NationalNewsBureau.com

National Newspaper Association
University of Missouri-Columbia
129 Neff Annex
P.O. Box 7540
Columbia, MO 65205
Phone: (573) 882-5800
Fax: (573) 884-5490
E-mail: info@nna.org
http://www.nna.org

**National Newspaper Publishers
    Association**
3200 13th Street, NW
Washington, DC 20010
Phone: (202) 588-8764
http://www.nnpa.org

National Press Club
National Press Building
529 14th Street, NW, 13th Floor
Washington, DC 20045
Phone: (202) 662-7500
Fax: (202) 662-7512
E-mail: info@npcpress.org
http://www.press.org

National Press Foundation
1211 Connecticut Avenue, NW, Suite 310
Washington, DC 20036
Phone: (202) 663-7280
Fax: (202) 530-2855
E-mail: donna@nationalpress.org
http://www.nationalpress.org

**National Press Photographers
    Association, Inc.**
3200 Croasdaile Drive, Suite 306
Durham, NC 27705
Phone: (919) 383-7246
Fax: (919) 383-7261
E-mail: info@nppa.org
http://www.nppa.org

National Scholastic Press Association
University of Minnesota
2221 University Avenue SE, Suite 121
Minneapolis, MN 55414
Phone: (612) 625-8335
Fax: (612) 626-0720
E-mail: info@studentpress.org
http://www.studentpress.org

**National Society of Newspaper
    Columnists**
1410 Steiner Street, Apartment 709
San Francisco, CA 94115
Phone: (415) 563-5403
Fax: NA
E-mail: director@columnists.com
http://www.columnists.com

**National Sportscasters and
    Sportswriters Association**
322 East Innes Street
Salisbury, NC 28144
Phone: (704) 633-4275
Fax: (704) 633-2027
http://www.nssahalloffame.com

National Turf Writers Association
1244 Meadow Lane
Frankfort, KY 40601
Phone: (502) 875-4864
Fax: (606) 276-4450
E-mail: dliebman@bloodhorse.com
http://www.ntra.com

**National Verbatim Reporters
    Association**
2729 Drake Street, PMB 130
Fayetteville, AR 72703
Phone: (479) 582-2200
Fax: (479) 521-7459
E-mail: nvra@aol.com
http://www.nvra.org

**Native American Journalists
    Association**
414 East Clark Street
Vermillion, SD 57069
Phone: (605) 677.5282
Fax: (866) 694.4264
E-mail: info@naja.com
http://www.naja.com

Newspaper Association Managers
70 Washington Street, Suite 214
Salem, MA 01970
Phone: (978) 744-8940
Fax: (978) 744-0333
E-mail: NENA@nenews.org
http://www.nenews.org

Newspaper Association of America
1921 Gallows Road, Suite 600
Vienna, VA 22182
Phone: (703) 902-1600
Fax: (703) 917-0636
E-mail: syska@naa.org
http://www.naa.org

Newspaper Features Council
P.O. Box 7421
Greenwich, CT 06830
Phone: (203) 661-3386
Fax: (203) 661-7337
http://www.nfccouncil.com

Newswomen's Club of New York
15 Gramercy Park South
New York, NY 10003
Phone: (212) 777-1610
Fax: (212) 353-9569
E-mail: staff@
    newswomensclubnewyork.com
http://www.newswomensclubnewyork.com

**New York Financial Writers'
    Association**
P.O. Box 338
Ridgewood, NJ 07451
Phone: (201) 612-0100
Fax: (201) 612-9915
E-mail: nyfwa@aol.com
http://www.nyfwa.org

**North American Agricultural
    Journalists**
Texas A&M University
2604 Cumberland Court
College Station, TX 77845
Phone: (979) 845-2872
Fax: (979) 845-2414
E-mail: ka-phillips@tamu.edu
http://naaj.tamu.edu/naajMay01.htm

Online News Association
P.O. Box 30702
Bethesda, MD 20824
Phone: (617) 450-7023
Fax: (617) 450-2974
E-mail: tom@csmonitor.com
http://www.journalist.org

Organization of News Ombudsmen
c/o Gina Lubrano
P.O. Box 120191
San Diego, CA 92112
Phone: (619) 293-1525
E-mail: ono@uniontrib.com
http://www.newsombudsmen.org

**Outdoor Writers Association of
    America**
121 Hickory Street, Suite 1
Missoula, MT 59801
Phone: (406) 728-7434
Fax: (406) 728-7445
E-mail: owaa@montana.com
http://www.owaa.org

Outer Critics Circle
101 West 57th Street
New York, NY 10019
Phone: (212) 765-8557
Fax: (212) 765-7979

Overseas Press Club of America
40 West 45th Street
New York, NY 10036
Phone: (212) 626-9220
Fax: (212) 626-9210
E-mail: Sonya@opcofamerica.org
http://www.opcofamerica.org

People's News Agency
c/o Proutist Universal New York Sector
P.O. Box 56533
Washington, DC 20040
Phone: (202) 829-2278
E-mail: nysector@prout.org
http://www.prout.org/pna

**Periodical & Book Association of
    America Inc.**
481 Eighth Avenue, Suite 826
New York, NY 10001
Phone: (212) 563-6502
Fax: (212) 545-8328
E-mail: lscott@pbaa.net
http://www.pbaa.net

Pew Center for Civic Journalism
7100 Baltimore Avenue, Suite 101
College Park, MD 20740

Phone: (301) 985-4020
Fax: (301) 985-4021
E-mail: news@j-lab.org
http://www.j-lab.org

**Professional Hockey Writers'
    Association**
1480 Pleasant Valley Way, No. 44
West Orange, NJ 07052
Phone: (973) 669-8607
Fax: (973) 669-8607

Public Media Foundation
North Western University
337 Ryder Hall
Phone: (617) 373-4698
E-mail: Publicmedia@neu.edu.
http://www.scribblingwomen.org

Quill and Scroll Society
University of Iowa
School of Journalism
Iowa City, IA 52242
Phone: (319) 335-5795
Fax: (319) 335-5210
E-mail: quill-scroll@uiowa.edu
http://www.uiowa.edu/~quill-sc

**Radio-Television News Directors
    Association**
1600 K Street, NW, Suite 700
Washington, DC 20006
Phone: (202) 659-6510
Fax: (202) 223-4007
E-mail: rtnda@rtnda.org
http://www.rtnda.org

Red Tag News Publications Association
P.O. Box 429
Flossmoor, IL 60422
Phone: (708) 957-5525
E-mail: jim@redtag.org
http://www.redtag.org

Regional Reporters Association
1255 National Press Building
Washington, DC 20045
Phone: (202) 662-8731
Fax: (202) 662-8996
E-mail: lisafriedman@angnewspapers.
    net

Religion News Service
1101 Connecticut Avenue, NW, Suite 350
Washington, DC 20036
Phone: (202) 463-8777
Fax: (202) 463-0033
E-mail: info@religionnews.com
http://www.religionnews.com

Religion Newswriters Association
P.O. Box 2037
Westerville, OH 43086
Phone: (614) 891-9001
Fax: (614) 891-9774
E-mail: info@religionwriters.com
http://www.religionwriters.com

**Reporters Committee for Freedom of
    the Press**
1100 Wilson Boulevard, Suite 1100
Arlington, VA 22209
Phone: (800) 336-4243
E-mail: info@rcfp.org
http://www.rcfp.org

Reuters Information Services
1700 Broadway
New York, NY 10019
Phone: (212) 603-3300
Fax: (212) 603-3446
E-mail: info@reuters.com
http://www.reuters.com

Society for News Design
1130 Ten Rod Road, F 104
North Kingstown, RI 02852
Phone: (401) 294-5233
Fax: (401) 294-5238
E-mail: snd@snd.org
http://www.snd.org

**Society of American Business Editors
    and Writers**
c/o University of Missouri, School of
    Journalism
76 Gannet Hall
Columbia, MO 65211
Phone: (573) 882-7862
Fax: (573) 884-1372
E-mail: padenc@missouri.edu
http://www.sabew.org

Society of American Travel Writers
1500 Sunday Drive, No. 102
Raleigh, NC 27607
Phone: (919) 787-5181
Fax: (919) 787-4916
E-mail: satw@satw.org
http://www.satw.org

**Society of Environmental
    Journalists**
P.O. Box 2492
Jenkintown, PA 19046
Phone: (215) 884-8174
Fax: (215) 884-8175
E-mail: sej@sej.org
http://www.sej.org

Society of Professional Journalists
3909 North Meridan Street
Indianapolis, IN 46208
Phone: (317) 927-8000
Fax: (317) 920-4789
E-mail: questions@spj.org
http://www.spj.org

South Asian Journalists Association
c/o Sreenath Sreenivasan
Columbia Graduate School of
    Journalism
2950 Broadway
New York, NY 10027
Phone: (212) 854-5979
Fax: (212) 854-4837
E-mail: saja@columbia.edu
http://www.saja.com

Travel Journalists Guild
P.O. Box 10643
Chicago, IL 60610
Phone: (312) 664-9279
Fax: (312) 664-0701
http://www.tjgonline.com

United Press International
1510 H Street, NW
Washington, DC 20005
Phone: (202) 898-8000
Fax: (202) 898-8057
E-mail: support@upi.com
http://www.upi.com

United States Harness Writers'
    Association
11 Woodstock Gardens
Batavia, NY 14020
Phone: (716) 343-5900
Fax: (716) 344-1187
E-mail: ushwa@eznet.net

U.S. Marine Corps Combat
    Correspondents Association
238 Cornwall Circle
Chalfont, PA 18914
Phone: (215) 822-6723
Fax: (215) 822-0163
E-mail: usmccca@aol.com
http://www.usmccca.org

Western Publications Association
823 Rim Crest Drive
Westlake Village, CA 91361
Phone: (805) 495-1863
Fax: (805) 497-1849
E-mail: wpa@wpa-online.org
http://www.wpa-online.org

White House Correspondents'
    Association
1067 National Press Building
Washington, DC 20045
Phone: (202) 737-2934
Fax: (202) 783-0841
http://www.whca.net

Women in Cable and
    Telecommunications
14555 Avion Parkway, Suite 250
Chantilly, VA 20151
Phone: (703) 234-9810
Fax: (703) 817-1595
E-mail: aiverson@wict.org
http://www.wict.org

Women in Film and Video
1400 K Street, NW, 10th Floor
Washington, DC 20005
Phone: (202) 408-1476
Fax: (202) 408-1479
E-mail: wifv@hers.com
http://www.wifv.org

World Communication
    Association
University of Wisconsin-Whitewater
Department of Communication
800 West Main Street
Whitewater, WI 53190
Phone: (262) 472-1034
Fax: (262) 472-1419
E-mail: monfilsb@uww.edu
http://ilc2.doshisha.ac.jp/users/kkitao/
    organi/wca

SCHOLASTIC, ACADEMIC, AND NONPROFIT INSTITUTIONS

American Association of University
    Professors
1012 14th Street, NW, Suite 500
Washington, DC 20005
Phone: (202) 737-5900
Fax: (202) 737-5526
E-mail: info@aaup.org
http://www.aaup.org

American Council on Education
One Dupont Circle, NW
Washington, DC 20036
Phone: (202) 939-9300
Fax: (202) 833-4760
E-mail: info@acenet.edu
http://www.acenet.edu

Association of American
    Universities
1200 New York Avenue, NW, Suite 550
Washington, DC 20005
Phone: (202) 408-7500
http://www.aau.edu

Association of Teachers of Technical
    Writing
University of North Texas
P.O. Box 311307
Denton, TX 76203
Phone: (940) 565-2115
E-mail: sims@unt.edu
http://www.attw.org

Council for the Advancement and
    Support of Education
1307 New York Avenue, NW, Suite 1000
Washington, DC 20005
Phone: (202) 329-2273
Fax: (202) 387-4973
E-mail: info@case.org
http://www.case.org

Education Writers Association
2122 P Street, NW, Suite 201
Washington, DC 20037
Phone: (202) 452-9830
Fax: (202) 452-9837
E-mail: ewa@ewa.org
http://www.ewa.org

National Association of Black
    Professors
P.O. Box 526
Crisfield, MD 21817
Phone: (410) 968-2393

National Center for Education
    Statistics
1990 K Street, NW
Washington, DC 20006
Phone: (202) 502-7300
Fax: (202) 502-7466
E-mail: nceswebmaster@ed.gov
http://nces.ed.gov

National Education Association
1201 16th Street, NW
Washington, DC 20036
Phone: (202) 833-4000
Fax: (202) 822-7974
E-mail: At Web site
http://www.nea.org

National School Public Relations Association
15948 Derwood Road
Rockville, MD 20855
Phone: (301) 519-0496
Fax: (301) 519-0494
E-mail: nspra@nspra.org
http://www.nspra.org

National Writing Project
University of California
2105 Bancroft
Berkeley, CA 94720
Phone: (510) 642-0963
Fax: (510) 642-4545
E-mail: nwp@writingproject.org
http://www.writingproject.org

Teachers and Writers Collaborative
Five Union Square West
New York, NY 10003
Phone: (212) 691-6590
Fax: (212) 675-0171
E-mail: info@twc.org
http://www.twc.org

APPENDIX IV
USEFUL WEB SITES FOR WRITERS

INTRODUCTION

For anyone involved in any aspect of writing as a vocation the Internet has become an increasingly valuable resource in today's high-tech electronic age.

The following are a selection of useful Web sites for writers to help in researching, fact checking, and networking. (Web sites that do *not* have self-explanatory names are annotated with an explanation in italics situated between the site name and its URL.)

These listed URLS may well be ones you wish to bookmark and/or list in your Favorites folder. In addition, by utilizing one or more of the search engines listed below—or using one of your own preferred search engines—you can fairly easily lay the foundation for researching most any organization or individual, or check with applicable Web sites to verify use of grammar and spelling in your current project.

Naturally the information offered on any Web site is only as good as the source itself and needs to constantly reevalu-

ated by you for its track record of providing consistently reliable data. As has always been true, the Internet is in a constant state of flux. Even well-established Web sites often change their URLs. Typically, if you click on a link that has recently changed its URL, you will be switched automatically to its new Web address (which you can then bookmark and/or list in your Favorites). If your link proves to be cold/dead, use a search engine to provide hits for the Web site in question. Most times this step will lead you to the new home page of the desired site. (As always, when using a search engine, if your query is more than one word, place the name/term in quotes to narrow and target the search.)

While the Internet and e-mail are great tools to employ in your writing career, do not ignore traditional person-to-person contact with colleagues, mentors, family, friends, and others within your support network. They are equally vital in keeping you on track in your work and life.

A. SEARCH ENGINES

Alltheweb
http://alltheweb.com

Alta Vista
http://www.altavista.com

A9
http://a9.com

AOL
http://www.aol.com

Ask Jeeves
http://www.ask.com

AT1
http://www.at1.com

Clusty
http://clusty.com

Copernic
Free and paid versions of special
  download software available at site;
  generally does not work with
  Macintosh system
http://www.copernic.com

Dogpile
http://www.dogpile.com

Excite
http://www.excite.com

Findspot
http://www.findspot.com

Galaxy
http://www.galaxy.com

Gigablast
http://www.gigablast.com

GoFish
http://www.gofish.com

Gimpsy
http://www.gimpsy.com

Google
http://www.google.com

Google Scholar
http://scholar.google.com

HotBot
http://www.hotbot.com

HotSheet
http://www.hotsheet.com

Itool
http://www.itools.com

Kartoo
http://www.kartoo.com

LookSmart
http://search.looksmart.com

Lycos
http://www.lycos.com

MSN
http://www.msn.com

Singingfish
http://www.singingfish.com

Soople
http://www.soople.com

Starting Page
http://www.startingpage.com

Starting Point
http://www.stpt.com

Teoma
http://www.directhit.com

WebCrawler
http://webcrawler.com

WiseNut
http://www.wisenut.com

Yahoo!
http://www.yahoo.com

How to Use Search Engines

   Bare Bones 101
   http://www.sc.edu/beaufort/library/
     pages/bones/bones.shtml

   Search.com
   http://www.search.com

   SearchEngineWatch
   http://searchenginewatch.com

Spider's Apprentice
http://www.monash.com/spidap4.html

WebRef
http://webreference.com/content/search

B. DICTIONARIES AND ENCYCLOPEDIAS

Bartlett's Familiar Quotations
http://www.bartleby.com/100

**Biographical Dictionary of the United
   States Congress**
http://bioguide.congress.gov/biosearch/
   biosearch.asp

Brainy Quote
http://www.brainyquote.com

Britannica Concise
http://concise.britannica.com

**The Cambridge History of English and
   American Literature**
http://www.bartleby.com/cambridge

Computer User High-Tech Dictionary
http://www.computeruser.com/resources/
   dictionary

Creative Quotations
http://www.creativequotations.com

Dictionary.com: Writing Resources
A free online English dictionary and
   reference guide
http://dictionary.reference.com/writing

Dictionary Definitions
Definitions from the *American Heritage
   Dictionary* and *Webster's Revised
   Unabridged Dictionary*
http://www.dictionary.com

Dictionary of the History of Ideas
http://etext.lib.virginia.edu/DicHist/dict.
   html

Eh.Net Encyclopedia
http://www.eh.net/encyclopedia

Encyclopaedia Britannica
http://www.britannica.com

Encyclopedia.Com
http://www.encyclopedia.com

Merriam-Webster Online Dictionary
http://www.m-w.com

NetLingo
http://www.netlingo.com

OneLook Dictionary
http://www.onelook.com

Oxford Online Dictionaries
http://www.askoxford.com/dictionaries

RhymeZone
http://www.rhymezone.com

Simpson's Contemporary Quotations
http://www.bartleby.com/63

Slang City
http://www.slangcity.com

Slanguage
http://www.slanguage.com

TravLang Translating Dictionaries
http://dictionaries.travlang.com

Wikipedia
http://en.wikipedia.org

Writers Market Encyclopedia
http://www.writersmarket.com/encyc

C. GENERAL REFERENCE

AMFMTVOnline.com
A comprehensive directory of radio and
   television stations in the United States
http://www.amfmtvonline.com

Acronym and Abbreviations Server
http://www.ucc.ie/cgi-bin/acronym/acro.
   html

Area Codes Lookup

   Anywho
   http://www.anywho.com

   MelissaData
   http://www.melissadata.com/lookups/
     phonelocation.asp

Verizon
http://www22.verizon.com/areacodes

Biography.com
Profiles of celebrities, historical figures,
   and personalities
http://www.biography.com

Blogs

Search engines to check out blogs by topics

Blogdigger
http://www.blogdigger.com

Bloggernity
http://www.bloggernity.com

Blogging Network
http://www.bloggingnetwork.com

LSBlogs.com
http://www.lsblogs.com

QuackTrack
http://quacktrack.com

Yahoo! Search Blog
http://ysearchblog.com

Books Online
Catalogs all known books available for downloading and includes a newsletter on forthcoming new titles and when they will be available
http://www.books-on-line.com

Business.com
Multiple listings of Web sites, publications, and associations for media, publishing, and writers
http://www.business.com/directory/media_and_entertainment

CardinalBook
Offers online books, mini-reviews, recommended bookstores and sites
http://www.cardinalbook.com

CEOExpress.com
Portal to media news outlets including Internet sources, magazines, newsfeeds, and newspapers
http://www.ceoexpress.com

City-Data.com
Statistics of larger U.S. cities
http://www.city-data.com

Consumer Price Index Calculator
http://woodrow.mpls.frb.fed.us/Research/data/us/calc

Copyright
Guidelines regarding terms of copyright and what materials fall into the public domain

http://www.copyright.cornell.edu/training/Hirtle_Public_Domain.htm

The Currency Site
Global currency converters; historical and present-day currency news
http://www.oanda.com

CountryReports.org
Information on more than 260 countries around the world
http://www.countryreports.org

DeadlineOnline.com
News items, information links, and public records
http://www.deadlineonline.com

Digital Librarian
A portal and links to a wide assortment of topics
http://www.digital-librarian.com

Encyberpedia
Links to assorted encyclopedias and researching sites
http://www.encyberpedia.com/ency.htm

50 States
A portal to a mass of information for all 50 states
http://www.50states.com

Find a Grave
A locator for celebrities' death dates and burial sites
http://www.findagrave.com

Fodors.com
A major source regarding travel destinations, restaurants, hotels, articles and information
http://www.fodors.com

Front Page
The Internet's largest news site
http://www.topix.net

Genealogy

Major sites providing both free and paid access to researching family trees

Ancestry.com
http://www.ancestry.com

RootsWeb.com
http://www.rootsweb.com

GlobalEdge
History, political structure, economic climate, statistics, and current news for 196 countries
http://globaledge.msu.edu/ibrd/ibrd.asp

The Great Idea Finder
A portal to sites involving unchampioned great inventors and ideamakers
http://www.ideafinder.com/resource/rpo.htm

GuideStar
A national database of nonprofit organizations
http://www.guidestar.org

Guinness World Records
http://www.guinnessworldrecords.com

Highbeam Research
A subscription service to access full text of articles and photos from a wide variety of publications archived back two decades
http://www.highbeam.com

Information Please Almanac
http://www.infoplease.com

The Internet Archive
A digital library of Internet sites and other cultural artifacts in digital form
http://www.archive.org

The Internet Public Library
A portal to online libraries and archives grouped by subject; has free online query system
http://www.ipl.org/ref/AON

International Trademark Association
Information on various aspects of trademarks, including a glossary
http://www.inta.org

ITools
Links to an assortments of reference sources
http://itools.com

Journalists' Resources

American Press Institute—The Journalist's Toolbox
http://www.americanpressinstitute.org/toolbox

Journalism.org
http://www.journalism.org

Journalist's Guide to the Internet
http://reporter.umd.edu

PowerReporting.com
http://www.powerreporting.com

Poynter Online
http://www.poynter.org

Legends
A scholarly guided tour of legends down
    through the ages
http://www.legends.dm.net

Librarians' Index to the Internet
http://lii.org

LibWeb
A portal to libraries throughout the world
http://sunsite.berkeley.edu/Libweb

Looksmart's Find Articles
Online access to articles from over 900
    publications
http://www.findarticles.com

Maps

City-Data.com
Maps and statistics about U.S. cities
http://www.city-data.com

Maporama
http://maporama.com/share

MapQuest
http://www.mapquest.com

Maps in the News
http://www.maptech.com

MSN Maps and Directories
http://www.mapblast.com

**U.S. Census Bureau Maps and
    Cartographic Resources**
http://www.census.gov/geo/www/maps

National Obituary Archive
A search engine to locate obituaries of
    notables
http://www.arrangeonline.com/Obituary/
    obituary.asp?ObituaryID=69626128

Network World, Inc.
Provider of Internet news services and
    Internet community services
    pertaining to network information
http://www.networkworld.com

NIST: Time and Frequency Division
Aspects of time and frequency in assorted
    disciplines
http://www.boulder.nist.gov/timefreq

The Old Farmer's Almanac
http://www.almanac.com

OnlineConversion.com
Converts just about anything to anything
    else
http://www.onlineconversion.com

Portico
Wide variety of resources for researching
    many topics
http://indorgs.virginia.edu/portico/home.
    html

PollingReport.com
A resource for trends in American public
    opinion
http://www.pollingreport.com

PopMatters
An online magazine of global culture
http://www.popmatters.com

Quotations.About.com
Data and links to famous quotations
    through the centuries
http://quotations.about.com/?once=true&

RefDesk.com
A portal and links to a wide assortment of
    topics
http://www.refdesk.com

Roget's Thesaurus
http://www.bartleby.com/62

Rulers
Information on heads of state/
    governments around the world since
    the 1700s
http://rulers.org

SearchSystems
Links to free public records databases on
    the Internet
http://www.searchsystems.net

The Smoking Gun
Documents involving celebrity
    wrongdoings
http://www.thesmokinggun.com

Social Security Death Index
A search engine to locate deceased
    individuals who had a social security
    number; links to track birth and death
    certificates
http://ssdi.genealogy.rootsweb.com

Stateline.org
News and facts on all 50 states, written by
    journalists for journalists, policy
    makers, and general public
http://www.stateline.org

Telephone Lookup Directories

AnyWho
http://www.anywho.com

BigBook
http://www.bigbook.com

BigYellow
http://www.bigyellow.com

International White and Yellow Pages
http://www.wayp.com

NumberWay
http://numberway.com

Switchboard
http://www.switchboard.com

WorldPages.com
http://www.worldpages.com

Time Zone Converter
http://www.timezoneconverter.com

Today's Date and Time
A wide number of links to calendars/time
    related to geography, history, and
    religion, as well as this-day-in-history
    sites
http://www.ecben.net/calendar.shtml

Trade Associations Directory from
    Yahoo
http://dir.yahoo.com/business_and_econo
    my/organizations/trade_associations

UM-Weather
The world of weather
http://cirrus.sprl.umich.edu/wxnet

Urban Legends Reference Pages
http://www.snopes.com/snopes.asp

Words Without Borders
A site devoted to translating foreign
    writing into English
http://www.wordswithoutborders.org

The World Factbook
http://www.cia.gov/cia/publications/
    factbook

**The Yearbook of Experts, Authorities
    & Spokespersons**
A directory of sources used by journalists
    and writers
http://www.yearbooknews.com

Zip Code Lookup Search Engines

International
World Postal Codes
http://www.execulink.com/~~louisew/
    postal-links.htm

United States
**National Address and ZIP+4
    Browser**
http://www.semaphorecorp.com/cgi/
    form.html

**U.S. Postal Service Zip Code
    Lookup**
http://zip4.usps.com/zip4/welcome.jsp

D. SPECIALIZED REFERENCE

Advertising and Marketing

Advertising Age
A leading advertising industry journal
http://www.adage.com

Advertising Media Internet Center
http://www.amic.com

Advertising Media Resource Center
http://www.admedia.com

DM News
A leading direct marketing industry
    journal
http://www.dmnews.com

E Marketer Newsletter
Includes tables and charts covering
    Internet, e-business and online
    marketing research
http://www.emarketer.com

Folio Magazine
Online version of the primary
    publication of the advertising,
    marketing, and promotion industries
http://www.foliomag.com

**Occupational Outlook Handbook
    2004-2005: Advertising, Market,
    Promotions, and Public
    Relations**
National government database from
    the U.S. Department of Commerce,
    Bureau of Labor Statistics
http://www.bls.gove/oco/ocos020.htm

Business

**American Express Small Business
    Resources**
http://www133.americanexpress.com/
    osbn/tool/biz_plan/index.asp

Bloomberg.com
Web portal for financial news,
    information, and tools
http://www.bloomberg.com

**Business Publications Audit
    International**
Global supplier of consumer and
    business media audits, providing
    audited data of marketing and
    media information to business
    organizations
http://bpai.com

Business Wire
International press release distribution
    service that delivers news, photos,
    and other multimedia content to
    the business, financial, and media
    communities
http://www.businesswire.com

CNN Money
A glossary of financial terms
http://money.cnn.com/services/glossary/
    a.html

Economist.com
An encyclopedia of economic
    terminology
http://www.economist.com/
    encyclopedia

Education Index
Business news and information made
    available in the form of a daily
    business newspaper
http://www.educationindex.com/bus

Eh.Net. Encyclopedia
An encyclopedia of reference articles
    on economic and business history
http://www.eh.net/encyclopedia

ERI Online
Business definations glossary
http://www.eridlc.com/resources/index
    .cfm?fuseaction=resource.glossary

Glossarist
Topical dictionary of business terms
http://www.glossarist.com

Inc.com
Small business resources for the
    entrepreneur, home-based business,
    advice and ideas for starting a
    business, writing a business plan,
    and other business matters
http://www.inc.com

Nabobs.net
Provider of business news, humor, and
    analysis
http://www.nabobs.net

NewsAlert.com
Provides customized business and
    financial news by industry, U.S.
    market reports, research reports,
    and other related business
    information
http://www.newsalert.com

SBC Yahoo Directory
http://dir.yahoo.com/business

Small Business Resources
http://www.smallbusinessresources.com

**Trade Associations Directory from
    Yahoo**
http://dir.yahoo.com/business_and_
    economy/organizations/trade_
    associations

Education

Choice
Online monthly magazine that reviews significant books and electronic media of interest to those in higher education
http://www.ala.org

Educator's Reference Desk
http://www.edref.org

EduFind
A multitude of educational resources
http://www.edufind.com

Eric: Education Resource Information Center
http://www.eric.ed.gov

Gateway to Educational Material
http://www.thegateway.org

Glossarist
Topical dictionary of education terms
http://www.glossarist.com/glossaries/education

NACEWeb
Web site of the National Association of Colleges and Employers, serves at the major source of information for career service practitioners on college campuses who advise students and alumni in career development
http://www.naceweb.org

NOAA Education Resources
http://www.education.noaa.gov

OnlineDegrees.com
Provides information about online degrees, online schools, distance learning courses, and student loans
http://www.onlinedegrees.com

SBC Yahoo Directory
http://dir.yahoo.com/Education

Entertainment

Including film, radio, stage, and television

Academy of Motion Pictures Arts and Sciences
Academy Awards database
http://www.oscars.org

Academy of Television Arts and Sciences
Emmy Awards database
http://www.emmys.tv

Alliance of Los Angeles Playwrights
http://www.laplaywrights.org

American Film Marketing Association
http://www.afma.com

Broadway.com
Broadway news and information
http://www.broadway.com

Catalog of Movie Images
A catalog of movie images from various collections managed by Georgia Tech University
http://mjc.imtc.gatech.edu

Current Online
A Web service that reports on public TV and public radio
http://www.current.org

Directory of International Film & Video Festivals
http://www.britfilms.com/festivals

E! Entertainment Online
An archive of biographies, interviews, and news of celebrities
http://www.eonline.com

Entertainment Publicists Professional Society
Supplies publicity and marketing education, sponsoring media workshops on publicity trends and protocols in pitching weekly and daily entertainment, and provides seminars highlighting industry resources and networking opportunities
http://www.eppsonline.org

FilmFestivals.com
http://www.filmfestivals.com

Film Industry Network
A networking organization for the film industry providing a means for members of the film and television industries to communicate in meetings, with a network of topical e-mails
http://www.filmindustrynetwork.com

Film-Makers.com
A huge portal to many aspects of filmmaking and films
http://www.film-makers.com

Hollywood Radio and Television Society
An organization of executives from the networks, stations, studios, production companies, advertisers, ad agencies, cable companies, media companies, legal firms, publicity agencies, talent and management agencies, performers, services, suppliers and allied fields.
http://www.hrts-iba.org

The Hollywood Reporter
A major entertainment industry trade publication
http://www.hollywoodreporter.com

Internet Movie Database [free version]
A film and television database
http://www.imdb.com

Internet Movie Database [paid subscription version]
Subscription database of film and television with additional statistics, news, and searches available
http://www.pro.imdb.com

Internet Theatre Database
American theatre database
http://www.theatredb.com

I Want Media
Media news and resources
http://www.iwantmedia.com

Library of American Broadcasting
The library is located on the campus of the University of Maryland
http://www.lib.umd.edu/UMCP/LAB

Lortel Archives
An Off-Broadway theater database
http://www.lortel.org/lla_archive/index.cfm

Mandy.com
International film and TV resources
http://www.mandy.com

Motion Picture Association of America
http://www.mpaa.org

Movie Review Query Engine
http://www.mrqe.com

Musicals101.com
An encyclopedia of musical theater, TV and film
http://www.musicals101.com

National Association of Broadcasters
http://www.nab.org

National Cable Television Association
http://www.ncta.com

NewsLab
A nonprofit television news laboratory affiliated with the Columbia University Graduate School of Journalism and the Project for Excellence in Journalism
http://www.newslab.org

Nielsen Media Research
http://www.nielsenmedia.com

Playbill
A wide range of theater information
http://www.playbill.com

Radio & Television News Association of Southern California
http://www.rtna.org

Romanesko
Media industry news, commentary, and memos
http://www.poynter.org/column. asp?id=45

ShowBiz Data
A subscription source for show business information
http://www.showbizdata.com

Singingfish
A search engine for a variety of audio and video topics
http://www.singingfish.com

Television Episode Guides Search Engines

AllYourTV.com
http://www.allyourtv.com/showguides. html

CGS Success Systems TV Database
http://www.cgstv.com

Epguides.com
http://epguides.com

Jam! Show Business Television Database
http://www.canoe.ca/TelevisionShows/ home.html

Tim's TV Showcase
http://timstvshowcase.com

TV Tome
http://www.tvtome.com

Television Week
Online version of the weekly newspaper of broadcast, cable, and interactive media
http://www.emonline.com

TheaterMania.com
Current and archival information, reviews, and interviews on Broadway/regional theater
http://www.theatermania.com

Tony Awards
The American Theatre Wing's Tony awards database
http://www.tonyawards.com

TVnewz.com
A webzine for TV news professionals
http://www.tvnewz.com

TV-Now
Much data, trivia, and links on television genres, personalities, trends
http://www.tv-now.com

TVTattle
A weblog of TV news/criticism
http://www.tvtattle.com

Variety
A major entertainment industry trade publication
http://www.variety.com

Women in Animation
http://www.womeninanimation.org

Women in Film
http://www.wif.org

Zap2It.com
A wide variety of entertainment data/links
http://www.zap2it.com

Government

Federal Agencies Statistics
http://www.fedstats.gov

Federal Bureau of Investigation
http://www.fbi.gov

FirstGov.com
A portal to U.S. government Web sites
http://www.firstgov.gov

Governing.com
Links to home pages of U.S. states, counties, and major cities
http://www.governing.com/source.htm

GovSpot
A portal to local/state/federal/world governments
http://www.govspot.com

National Archives and Records Administration
http://www.archives.gov

Peace Corps
http://www.peacecorps.com

United Nations Organization
An alphabetic index of Web sites of the United Nations System of Organizations
http://www.unsystem.org

U.S. Blue Pages
An online guide to U.S. government
http://www.usbluepages.gov/ gsabluepages

U.S. Census Bureau
http://www.census.gov

U.S. Department of State International Information Programs
http://usinfo.state.gov

U.S. Government Printing Office
http://www.gpoaccess.gov

Votenet
Provider of Internet solutions for public policy and politics
http://www.votenet.com

The White House
http://www.whitehouse.gov

History

Best of History Web Sites
http://www.besthistorysites.net

Digital History
Links to key events and topics in U.S. history
http://www.digitalhistory.uh.edu/historyonline/annot_links_list.cfm

HyperHistory
Links to key events and topics in world history
http://www.hyperhistory.com/online_n2/History_n2/a.html

Links to the Past
Links to key events and topics in U.S. history
http://www.cr.nps.gov/colherit.htm

PBS History
Links to key events and topics in world history
http://www.pbs.org/history

Today in History
http://lcweb2.loc.gov/ammem/today/today.html

Journalism and Publishing

Including books, magazines, newsletters, and newspapers

About.com
Information on literary publishing
http://publishing.about.com/cs/literarypublisher

AltWeeklies.com
News and arts reporting from more than 100 alternative newsweeklies
http://www.altweeklies.com/gyrobase/AltWeeklies

American Journalism Review
http://www.ajr.org

Archive.org
Listings of books whose full text is available online in PDF files
http://www.archive.org/texts

Arts & Letters Daily
Links to magazines, newspapers, weblogs, columnists, and much more
http://www.aldaily.com

Assignment Editor
A portal to magazines, newspapers, TV news services, and wire services
http://assignmenteditor.com

Association of Alternative Newsweeklies
http://aan.org

AuthorLink.com
News, information, and marketing services for editors, literary agents, writers, and readers
http://authorlink.com

Books AtoZ: Publishing Organizations in North America
Listings of publishing organizations in North America
http://www.booksatoz.com/puborgls.htm

Blue Moon Review
A literary review providing an online forum for writers to present their works
http://www.thebluemoon.com

Booklist
Digital counterpart to the American Library Association Booklist magazine, providing reviews of all book material including reference books
http://www.ala.org

Booklist Magazine
Provides reviews of the latest books and electronic media
http://ala8.ala.org

Book Magazine
Online magazine aimed at readers and the book publishing industry, providing book news and reviews
http://www.bookmagazine.com

Book Searching

Among the most useful Web sites to track information about a book's title, publisher, author, ISBN, and publication date

Alibris.com
http://www.alibris.com

Amazon.com
http://www.amazon.com

BarnesandNoble.com
http://www.barnesandnoble.com

Borders.com
http://www.borders.com

Bookstores.com
http://www.bookweb.org.bookstores.com

Broadcasting and Cable
Online version of the Broadcasting journal
http://www.broadcastingcable.com

Childrens Writing Resource Center
An online newsletter for children's writers
http://www.write4kids.com

Columbia Journalism Review
http://www.cjr.org

Cyberjournalist.net
The media center of the American Press Institute
http://www.cyberjournalist.net

Directories of Literary Publishers
http://www.bsu.edu/english/cwp/links

Directory of Technical Magazines
http://www.techexpo.com

Editor & Publisher
A leading trade journal of the newspaper industry
http://www.editorandpublisher.com

Education Writer's Association
A national professional organization of education reporters, writers, and editors
http://www.ewa.org

Electronic and Print Resources
A guide to electronic and print resources for journalists and writers
http://www.cio.com

The Electronic Journalist
Resource includes Freedom of Information Act contacts and information, professional development, awards, fellowships, and journalism ethics information
http://spj.org

Entertainment Weekly: Books
Online book reviews from the magazine, Entertainment Weekly
http://www.ew.com

Finding Data on the Internet: A Journalist's Guide
http://www.robertniles.com

Gebbie Press, Inc.
An all-in-one media directory, listing all U.S. print and broadcast media, including TV and radio stations, daily and weekly newspapers, trade and consumer magazines, news syndicates, AP and UPI bureaus, and more
http://www.gebbieinc.com

Investigative Reporters
http://www.ire.org

I Want Media
Media news and resources
http://www.iwantmedia.com

January Magazine
Online magazine of interviews with authors from around the world, as well as book reviews
http://www.januarymagazine.com

Journal of Electronic Publishing
http://www.press.umich.edu

Journalism Collections
Columbia University Library offering of a vast array of links to previously written journals
http://www.columbia.edu/cu/web

Journalism.Net
http://www.journalismnet.com

Library Journal: Books
Independent national library publication reviewing everything from books, audio and video, CD-ROMs, Web sites, and magazines
http://www.ljdigital.com

LiteraryMarketPlace.com
Online version of Information Today's "Literary Market Place" or "LMP," a book industry resource and news source containing thousands of annotated links to book-related sites
http://www.literarymarketplace.com

Magazine Publishers of America
http://www.mpa.org

Media Resource Service
Links journalists with scientists to locate information on science and technology
http://www.mediaresource.org

Media Watch
Reporting and analysis of news, trends, issues, and controversies involving the information industries
http://www.pbs.org/newshour/media

MediaWeek
Online news magazine of the media
http://www.mediaweek.com

The Narrative Newspaper
A collection of links to literary journalism being published in newspapers
http://www.inkstain.net/narrative

National Arts Journalism Program
Resource for journalists who specialize in arts and culture
http://www.najp.org

NewsCom.com
Media Web resource for news materials for text, photos, and graphics
http://www.newscom.com

Newsletter and Electronic Publishers Association
http://www.newsletters.org

NewspaperArchive.com
Archival services at this site are fee-based
http://www.newspaperarchive.com

Newspaper Association of America
http://www.naa.org

NewsVoyager.com
Links to newspapers around the globe searchable by title, location, and type
http://www.newsvoyager.com

Newswise
A database of current/archival news from research institutions, laboratories, organizations, and campuses in the fields of business, humanities, medicine, and science
http://www.newswise.com

New York Review of Books
Online version of weekly book review publication
http://www.nyrev.com

Occupational Outlook Handbook 2004-2005: Writers & Editors
National government database from the U.S. Department of Commerce, Bureau of Labor Statistics
http://www.bls.gov/oco/ocos089.htm

Online Journalism Review
http://www.ojr.org

Opinion-Pages
Access to editorials, opinions, commentaries, and columnists
http://www.opinion-pages.org

Power Reporting: Resources for Journalists
http://powerreporting.com

Poynter Online's "Ask Dr. Ink"
Tackles tough and weird questions about journalism
http://poynteronline.org/column.asp?id=1

Poynter Online's "Chip on Your Shoulder"
Chip Scanlan's Web site column
http://poynteronline.org/column.asp?id=52

Poynter Online's "Newsroom Newsletters"
Internal publications shared by print & broadcast newsrooms nationally
http://poynteronline.org/column.asp?id=38

Poynter Online's Writing and Editing Tip Sheets
Journalism tips
http://pointeronline.org/content/content_view.asp?id=31907&sid=2

Promote Your e-Book
Offering advice on how to enter the e-book trade
http://publishing.about.com

Public Journalism
Information on and links to other sites dealing with civic/public journalism
http://www.ncew.org

Publishers Weekly
Online version of a leading trade journal of the publishing world
http://publishersweekly.com

Publishing Trends
A monthly subscription newsletter featuring news and opinion on the changing world of publishing.
http://www.publishingtrends.com

PubList
An Internet directory of publications containing bibliographic

information on more than 150,000 serials and periodicals.
http://www.publist.com

Pulitzer Prizes
http://www.pulitzer.org

Quality Solutions, Inc.
Developer of software specifically for the book publishing industry
http://www.qsolution.com

Salon Books
Web publication reporting on the book industry news and book reviews
http://www.salon.com

TabloidBaby.com
Links to tabloid articles and columns
http://www.tabloidbaby.com

Tapestry
E-zine of Women Online Worldwide, offering fiction, nonfiction, poetry, interviews, and articles, as well as film and book reviews by female authors or related to women's issues
http://www.wowwomen.com

Travelwriter Marketletter
http://www.travelwriterml.com

Travelwriters.com
Online resources for travel writers, photographers, and members of the travel industry
http://www.travelwriters.com

USUS
Internet guide for journalists, containing suggested research techniques and links
http://www.usus.org

Watch: Writers, Artists, and Their Copyright Holders
A database of copyright holders/contact persons for authors and artists whose archives are housed in libraries and archives in North America and the United Kingdom
http://tyler.hrc.utexas.edu

Web Resources for Newsrooms
http://www.gannett.com

World Press Review
http://www.worldpress.org

Writer Beware
A collection of information regarding literary agents, book doctors, copyright, electronic rights, print on demand, vanity publishers, and writers' alerts
http://www.aldaily.com

The Writer Magazine
Covers the art and business of writing
http://www.writermag.com

Writers on Writing
An archive of The New York Times "Writers on Writing" column
http://www.nytimes.com/books/specials/writers.html

Writer's Write: The Write Resource
Information about books, writing, and publishing
http://www.writerswrite.com

Writing for Radio
Provides creative suggestions and ideas to radio news reporters, writers, and anchors
http://www.newscript.com

Legal

Federal Law
http://www.thecre.com/fedlaw

Publishing Law Center
Links and articles regarding intellectual property and allied legal issues
http://www.publaw.com

The Virtual Chase
Legal researching links
http://www.virtualchase.com

Medical

American Medical Association
http://www.ama-assn.org

Directory of Health Organizations
Contain a directory of Health Hotlines, organization with 1-800 numbers to answer health-related questions
http://dirline.nlm.nih.gov

MedicineNet
A medical dictionary
http://www.medterms.com

MedlinePlus
Data provided by U.S. National Library of Medicine and the National Institutes of Health
http://www.nlm.nih.gov/medlineplus

MedWatch
Data and alerts provided by U.S. Food and Drug Administration
http://www.fda.gov/medwatch

National Association of Health Data Organizations
http://www.nahdo.org

National Center for Health Statistics
http://www.cdc.gov/nchs

National Institute of Health
http://www.nih.gov

National Library of Medicine
http://www.nlm.nih.gov

U.S. Food and Drug Administration
http://www.fda.gov

Museums and Archives

Artcyclopedia
Links to art museums of the world
http://www.artcyclopedia.com/museums.html

Museum of Broadcast Communications
Using the sights and sounds of television and radio, the museum examines popular culture and contemporary American history
http://www.museum.tv

Museum of Television and Radio
A collection of preserved television and radio programs made available to the public
http://www.mtr.org

Museums in the United States
http://www.museumca.org/usa

Naval and Maritime Museums in the United States
http://www.bb62museum.org/usnavmus.html

SIBMAS International Directory of Performing Arts Collections and Institutions
http://www.theatrelibrary.org/sibmas/idpac/idpac.html

Smithsonian Institution
http://www.si.edu

Music and Recording

Academy of Country Music
http://www.acmcountry.com

AllMusic
Musicians and recorded music
  database
http://www.allmusic.com

American Music Awards
http://www.seeing-stars.com/Awards/
  AmericanMusicAwards.shtml

American Society of Composers, Authors, and Publishers
A large organization for
  music/recording industry
http://www.ascap.com

Billboard
A leading music trade publication
http://www.billboard.com

BMI
A leading performing rights
  organization for the
  music/recording industry
http://www.bmi.com

Golden Pages
A portal for music-related links on the
  Internet
http://www.sun.rhbnc.ac.uk/Music/
  Links

Grammy Awards
National Academy of Recording Arts
  and Sciences' awards database
http://www.grammy.com/awards

Latin Grammy Awards
National Academy of Recording Arts
  and Sciences' awards database for
  Latin Grammys
http://www.grammy.com/awards/
  latin_grammy

Metacritic
Music reviews and
  musicians/recordings information
http://www.metacritic.com/music

Musesmuse
Songwriting tips, tools, interactivities
  and opportunities to connect with
  other songwriters
http://www.musesmuse.com

Music-Critic
An online source for music reviews
http://www.music-critic.com

Musicfans
A portal to topics regarding music and
  musicians
http://www.musicfans.com

Musicfolio
An Internet music critic site focusing
  on darkwave, darksynth, goth rock,
  gothic metal, ethereal, synthpop,
  new-wave, post-punk, EBM and
  industrial music, with reviews, site
  posts news updates, yearly album
  charts, and archives
http://www.musicfolio.com

Music Publishers' Association
http://www.mpa.org

Recording Industry Association of America
http://www.riaa.org

Rock and Roll Hall of Fame and Museum
http://www.rockhall.com

Rolling Stone
A leading music trade publication
http://www.rollingstone.com

SESAC
A leading performing rights
  organization for the music/
  recording industry
http://www.sesac.com

Soul Train Music Awards
http://www.soultraintv.com/stma/stma.
  html

Politics

FactCheck.org
A project of the Annenberg Public
  Policy Center
http://factcheck.org

Political Advocacy Groups
http://www.csuchico.edu/~~kcfount

Political Database of the Americas
http://www.georgetown.edu/pdba

Politics.com
http://www.politics.com

Public Opinion

Gallup Organization
http://www.pollingreport.com

Pew Research Center for the People and the Press
http://people-press.org

PollingReport.com
http://www.pollingreport.com

Public Agenda Online
http://www.publicagenda.org

Public Relations

PR Newswire
Breaking news from thousands or
  organization around the globe
http://www.prnewswire.com

ProfNet
A collaborative of news/information
  officers at colleges and facilities
  in the U.S. and abroad offering
  information
http://www2.profnet.com

Shareware Software

5 Star Shareware.com
http://www.5star-shareware.com

Jumbo!
http://www.jumbo.com

Nonags Freeware
http://www.nonags.com

Shareware.com
http://www.shareware.com

Tucows
http://www.tucows.com

ZDNet
http://downloads-
  zdnet.com.com/?tag=hdr

Science and Technology

AllRefer.com
An encyclopedia of scientific and
  technological terminology
http://reference.allrefer.com/encyclo
  dia/Science_and_Technology

BioTech Science Resources
http://biotech.icmb.utexas.edu/pages/
  scitools.html

Education Index
Education news and information made available in the form of a daily education newspaper
http://www.educationindex.com/tech

Eric Weisstein's World of Physics
Online encyclopedia of physics terms and formulas. Full searchable, and also browsable alphabetically and by topic
http://scienceworld.wolfram.com/physics

EverythingBio.com
A free resource of biology-related information
http://www.everythingbio.com

Frank Potter's Science Gems
Links to various scientific resources
http://www.sciencegems.com

Glossarist: Science
http://www.glossarist.com/glossaries/science

Glossarist: Technology
http://www.glossarist.com/glossaries/technology

Media Resource Service
Links journalists with scientists to locate information on science and technology
http://www.mediaresource.org

NASA: Aerospace Science and Technology Dictionary
http://www.hq.nasa.gov/office/hqlibrary/aerospacedictionary

National Science Foundation
http://www.nsf.gov/sbe/srs/stats.htm

SBC Yahoo Directory
http://dir.yahoo.com/Science

ScienceMaster
Links to various scientific dictionaries
http://www.sciencemaster.com/tech/item/dictionaries.php

TECHtionary
Animated dictionary of technical terms
http://www.techtionary.com

USGS Water Science Glossary
A list of water-related scientific terminology
http://ga.water.usgs.gov/edu/dictionary.html

Webopedia
An online computer dictionary and Internet search engine for internet terms and technical support
http://www.webopedia.com

E. WRITERS' RESOURCES

Absolute Write
How-to articles and interviews with agents, producers, publishers and writers, concentrating on screenwriting, freelance writing, novels, playwriting, non-fiction and technical writing
http://www.absolutewrite.com

Acronyms, Emoticons, & Similes Page
Definitions of acronyms, emoticons, and similes
http://www.muller-godschalk.com/acronyms.html

Archiver Unbound
A site to purchase archival data from assorted journals, magazines, newspapers, and the BBC
http://pqasb.pqarchiver.com/archiverunbound/newspaper.html

Article Announce
Designed to get writers published and assist e-zine publishers in finding articles
http://www.web-source.net/article-announce.htm

The American Heritage Book of English Usage
http://www.bartleby.com/64

ArtForge's WordForge Project
Site for online collaborative writing projects
http://www.artsforge.com/wordforge.html

Aspiring Writers
Links to publishers, self-publishing software and information
http://www.aspiringwriters.net

Authorlink
Geared for agents, editors, readers, and writers
http://www.authorlink.com

Author Network
Provides resources for writers, including links, columns, articles, monthly E-zine, competitions, and advice on getting published
http://www.author-network.com

Bisoncreek.com
Writing resources directory with free content articles
http://bisoncreek.com

Bookannouncements.com
Helping authors, publishers, and speakers gain more publicity/promotion
http://www.bookannouncements.com

Bookreporter.com
Features, profiles, and reviews dealing with new books/authors
http://www.bookreporter.com

Bookslut
Articles, features, and interviews about publishing
http://www.bookslut.com

Caelin-day.com
A search engine for online magazines, and a directory of writers' resources
http://www.caelin-day.com

Carrotwriter.com
Articles, e-zines and links for writers of several genres, both nonfiction and fiction
http://users.bluecarrots.com/writer

The Chicago Manual of Style
http://www.chicagomanualofstyle.org

Chat Groups Search Engines

Google Group
http://groups.google.com

Usenet Groups
http://www.ibiblio.org/usenet-i/search.html

Yahoo Groups
http://groups.yahoo.com

The Children's Writing Supersite
http://www.write4kids.com

The Complete Review
Links to literary review sites and an
online literary salon
http://www.complete-review.com

The Critters Writers' Workshop
An online workshop/critique group for
writers of science fiction, fantasy,
and horror
http://www.critters.org

Cybergraphica
Listings of writing organizations, Web
sites, and writers resources
http://www.cybergraphica.net/prose.
html

The Dramatic Exchange
A site for playwrights, producers, and
others involved in the theater
http://www.dramex.org

Drew's Script-o-Rama
A resource to access drafts and/or
completed scripts for feature films
and TV shows, with links
regarding the particular property
http://www.script-o-rama.com/table.
shtml

**Everyone Who's Anyone in Adult
Trade Publishing**
A listing of U.S. and U.K. literary
agents, and publishers
http://www.everyonewhosanyone.com

e-Writers.net
Contains writing-related links, an
online bookstore, book reviews,
messageboards, research links, and
writing tips
http://e-writers.net

FictionAddiction.net
Links to publishers, types of writing,
and writing organizations
http://www.fictionaddiction.net

Fiction Writers' Connection
Geared for membership use, but
provides free tips, newsletter
http://www.fictionwriters.com

*Financial and Business Terms
Glossaries*

**New York Times Glossary of
Financial and Business Terms**
http://www.nytimes.com/library/finan
cial/glossary/bfglosa.htm

Yahoo Glossary of Financial Terms
http://biz.yahoo.com/f/g

Focusing on Words Newsletter
English-language vocabulary newsletter
available free of charge
http://www.wordexplorations.com

4Writers
Support for professional and aspiring
writers, covering conferences, artists'
colonies, and creative writing programs
http://www.4writers.com

FreelanceWriting.com
Aimed at working writers, including job
board, genre magazines submission
guidelines, and newsletter
http://www.freelancewriting.com

Good Grammar, Good Style
Articles and frequently asked question on
grammar
http://www.protrainco.com

The Greenlight Zone
Resource for writers, screenwriters,
agents, directors, and other
professionals in the entertainment and
publishing industries
http://www.angelfire.com/film/
thegreenlightzone

Groups and Associations for Writers
A listing of writers' organizations
http://www.poewar.com/articles/
associations.htm

Guide to Grammar and Style
http://andromeda.rutgers.edu/~jlynch/
Writing

IdiomSite
http://www.idiomsite.com

Indispensable Writing Resources
Links to reference material, writing labs,
Web search engines, and writing-
related Web sites
http://www.quintcareers.com/writing

InkSlingers
A writer's site for query and cover letters,
submissions, how to be published,
agents, and editors, with a message
board and a chat room
http://inkslingers.8m.com

Internet for Writers
Contains links for writers and editors
http://home.teleport.com/~cdeemer

LitDoc
Workshop articles, writing tips, Christian
writing links, research links, writing
software books and booklets
http://www.litdoc.com

LiteraryAgent.com
http://nt9.nyic.com/literaryagent/sch-page.
html

Literary Agents
Guidelines to selecting a good literary
agent
http://www.sfwa.org/beware/agents.html

**Louis E. Catron's Links for
Playwrights**
http://lecatr.people.wm.edu/
playwritinglinks.html

Master Freelancer
Products and services for freelance
writers
http://masterfreelancer.com

MaximsNet
A site devoted to origin and use of
maxims and proverbs
http://www.maximsnet.org

NetLingo
A dictionary of Internet terms
http://www.netlingo.com

No Train, No Gain
Newspaper training editors present their
favorite exercises and ideas to improve
and expand newsroom training
http://www.notrain-nogain.org

One Woman's Writing Retreat
Online magazine with links and
discussions
http://www.prairieden.com

The Online Communicator
Site of useful files, links and other
communication resources
http://www.communicator.com

Online Reality Check for Nonfiction Writers
A class for aspiring nonfiction writers that is taught online by successful writers and professionals
http://www.youcanwrite.com

Owl Online Writing Lab
http://owl.english.purdue.edu

Page One
A literary newsletter
http://www.pageonelit.com

People Finders Sites (*most are fee-based in all or part of their services*)

Findability.org
http://findability.org

Harris Digital Publishing
http://www.privateinvestigatorsoftware.com

The Information Center
http://www.theinformationcenter.net

Joseph Culligan
http://www.josephculligan.com

Knowx
http://www.knowx.com

US Search.com
http://www.ussearch.com/consumer

The Phrase Finder
http://www.phrases.org.uk

Pilot-Search.com
Literary search engine and directory to sites for writing markets, tips, and articles
http://www.pilot-search.com

Preditors and Editors
Portal for variety of services for writers, composers, and other artists
http://www.anotherealm.com/prededitors/pubjob.htm

ProsToGo.com
A freelance worker directory and project locator
http://www.prostogo.com

Publishers Lunch
An e-mail newsletter about the publishing industry

http://www.publishersmarketplace.com

Questia
A tiered subscription service to online reference research sources
http://www.questia.com

The Readers and Writers' Cookie Jar
Offers articles, tips, links, and information for writers, who can add their own URL to the site
http://www.cookiecreation.com

reporter.org
Provides a variety of resources to journalists, journalism educators, and the public
http://www.reporter.org

Reporter's Resources
A site for Web-assisted reporting with carefully chosen links for journalists
http://www.henrichs.net

Representative Poetry Online
http://eir.library.utoronto.ca/rpo/display/indexpoet.html

Research Haven
Online dictionaries and thesauri, term papers, journals, style guides, tips, and writing tutorials
http://www.researchhaven.com

Resources for Writers
Categories include publishers, agents, writers organizations, marketing, job opportunities, and writing for specific genres
http://www.manuscriptediting.com/resourcesforwriters.htm

RhymeZone
Dictionaries of definitions, quotations, rhyming, synonyms; reverse dictionary
http://www.rhymezone.com

Salary Surveys

Careers: Wall Street Journal
http://www.careers.wsj/com

Center for Mobility Resources
http://www.homefair.com/homefair/cmr/salcalc.html

Hot Jobs
http://www.hotjobs.com

Jobsearchtech.about
http://jobsearchtech.about.com/od/salary6

JobSmart Salary Info
http://jobsmart.org/tools/salary/sal-prof.htm

JobStar Central
http://www.jobstar.org/tools/salary/sal-prof.cfm#PR

The Real Rate Survey
http://www.realrates.com/survey.htm

Salary.com
http://www.salary.com

Salary Wizard
http://swz-hoovers.salary.com

STC (Society for Technical Communications) Salary Surveys
http://www.stcsig.org/usability/topics/salary.html

Wageweb Salary Survey Data Online
http://www.wageweb.com

Yahoo!
http://careers.yahoo.com/employment/carrer_resources/salaries_and_benefits

SharpWriter.com
Writers' resources with links to copyright information, dictionaries, grammar, jobs, and quotations
http://www.sharpwriter.com

The Slot
Writing and editing tips by Bill Walsh, copy editor at the Washington Post
http://www.theslot.com

SPAWN
Resources for writers, artists, publishers, and researchers
http://www.spawn.org/resource.htm

SpellWeb
http://www.spellweb.com

Storyform
Writers' resources, reference and Web searches, research tools, and links
http://www.storyform.com

Submissions Junction
Guide to sites for submitting original
 articles, essays, documents, and e-books
http://submissionjunction.com

Symbols.com
An encyclopedia of graphic symbols
http://www.symbols.com

The Tale Wins Author Showcase
Directory with links for newsletter
 publishers and writers, and articles
 about writing in print and on the Web
http://www.talewins.com

Thesaurus.Com
http://thesaurus.reference.com

Useful Books for Writers
Directory of recommended books for
 writers, along with other resources and
 a messageboard
http://www.diane.com/readers/useful.html

Visual Thesaurus
Provides meanings and relationships
 between words
http://www.visualthesaurus.com

Web del Sol
A portal to literary magazines
http://www.webdelsol.com

The Well-Fed Writer
Stresses self-sufficiency as a freelance
 writer and includes links
http://www.wellfedwriter.com

What's?Com
A glossary of Internet word usage
http://whatis.techtarget.com

Word Museum
Spotlights authors and books
http://www.wordmuseum.com

Wordplay
Geared for the screenwriter
http://www.wordplayer.com

World Wide Words
The etymology and evolution of words
http://www.worldwidewords.org

WriteLinks
A directory of articles for writers
http://www.writelinks.com

WriteMovies.com
Information and links for screenwriters,
 novelists, playwrights, short story
 writers, and journalists
http://www.writemovies.com

The Write Page
A resource for genre writers
http://www.writepage.com

Writer.Net
Directory of published writers and
 literary agents
http://www.writer.net

Writer Network.com
Online writers' community (including
 weekly job list, store, and lounge) and
 publishing resources
http://www.writernetwork.com

WriterPage.com
Links to news, media, movies, TV,
 publishing, and research
http://writerpage.com

Writers.com
Online classes in all genres and formats
 of writing
http://www.writers.com

Writer's Digest
A broad base of helpful tips for the writer
http://www.writersdigest.com

Writer's Help Desk
Self-publishing and writing resources,
 including contests
http://www.writershelpdesk.com

Writer's Loft
A community of international
 independent authors
http://home.att.net/~Writer_loft/Writerloft/
 INDEX2.html

The WritersMind.com
Online resource for agents, authors, and
 publishers
http://thewritersmind.com

WritersNet
Links to URLs of editors, literary agents,
 publishers, and published authors
http://www.writers.net

The Writers' Portal
Directory of writers' groups and
 freelancers that includes events and
 announcements of interest to writers
http://www.smotu.org

Writers Retreat
Directory of writing listings for jobs,
 career information, organizations, and
 research

http://www.angelfire.com/va/dmsforever/
 main.html

Writers Store
http://www.writersstore.com

Writers Web Resource
Information on books, authors,
 magazines, chat, competition, news,
 letters, words, poems, and paying Web
 markets
http://www.leizure.com.uk/writers

Writers Write
Resource for writers of all genres with
 job listings, writer's guidelines, chat,
 message boards, book reviews,
 classifieds, and an online magazine
http://www.writerswrite.com

Writing and Markets
Articles on writing; links to markets for
 writers of articles, fiction, and poetry;
 tips for writers; a free writer's
 newsletter
http://members.tripod.com/~Beawriter/
 write.html

Writing.Com
An online writing and reading community
http://www.writing.com

The Writing on the Wall
Gateway to e-texts, archives, literary
 reference, interactive writing, and
 online poetry, with fiction resources
http://www.angelfire.com/id2/stetct

Writing-World.com
Writing tips for all aspects of the craft
http://www.writing-world.com

Zoetrope
A cooperative for short stories and one-act
plays; with both the magazine's staff and
other writers reading posted submissions
and allowing for feedback
http://www.all-story.com

Zuzu's Petals
Literary resources with a huge number of
 categorized, pertinent links
http://www.zuzu.com

F. JOB POSTINGS

About Freelance Writers
http://freelancewrite.about.com/od/
freelancejobs

After College
http://www.jobresource.com

American Copy Editors Society Job Bank
http://groups.yahoo.com/group/ACESjobs

American Society of Business Publications Editors
http://www.asbpe.org/jobs/joblist.htm

America's Career InfoNet
http://www.acinet.org/acinet/links1.asp

America's Job Bank
http://www.ajb.dni.us

Artists Resource
http://www.artistresource.org/jobs.
htm#Writers

Association of Alternative Newsweeklies
http://aan.org/gyrobase/Aan/
helpWanted

CareerBuilder
http://www.careerbuilder.com

Career Magazine
http://www.careermag.com

College Central Network
http://www.collegecentral.com

College Grad Job Hunter
http://www.collegegrad.com

CollegeJobBoard.com
http://www.collegejobboard.com

College Jobs
http://www.collegejobs.com

College Journal
http://collegejournal.com

College Recruiter
http://www.collegerecruiter.com

EditorandPublisher.com Job Links
http://www.editorandpublisher.com/
eandp/classifieds

Freelance Marketplace
http//www.mediabistro.com/fm

Freelance Work Exchange
http://www.freelanceworkexchange.com

Freelance Success
Resources and links include online
reference guides, job listings, as well
as lists of experts, sources, and links
to government databases
http://writersdatabase.com

Freelance Writing & Editors
http://freelancewrite.about.com/od/
freelancejobs

Investigative Reporter Job Postings
http://www.ire.org/jobs/look.html

JobHuntersBible.com
http://www.jobhuntersbible.com/jobs/
regions.shtml

Job-Hunt.org
http://www.job-hunt.org/general.shtml

Job Link for Journalists
http://newslink.org/joblink

JobScene
http://www.jobscene.allardice.com.au

Jobs in Journalism
http://www.writejobs.com/jobs

JobStar Central
http://www.jobstar.org

Journalism Job Bank
http://www.journalism/berkeley.edu/jobs

Journalism Job Opening
http://eb.journ.latech.edu/jobs.html

JournalismNet.com
http://www.journalismnet.com/jobs

JournalismNext.com
http://www.journalismnext.com

JustTechWriterJobs.com
http://www.justtechwriterjobs.com/
JSSearchJobs.asp

MediaBistro.com
http://www.mediabistro.com/joblistings

MonsterTrak
http://www.monstertrak.com

National Association of Broadcasters
http://www.nab.org/bcc

National Diversity News Job Bank
http://www.newsjobs.com

Nation's Job Network
http://www.nationjob.com

NewsJobs.net
http://www.newsjobs.net/usa

Newspaper Job Bank
http://newsjobs.com

Power Reporting
http://powerreporting.com/category/
Journalism_shoptalk/Jobs

Publishers Marketplace
http://www.publishersmarketplace.com/
jobs

Publishing Companies
http://www.vault.com

Sunoasis
http://www.sunoasis.com

Telecommuting Jobs for Writers
http://www.tjobs.com/new/writers.shtml

TVJobs.com
http://www.tvjobs.com/jbcenter.htm

The Write Jobs
http://www.writejobs.com/jobs

WriteMovies.com
http://www.writemovies.com/jobs

WriterFind
http://www.writerfind.com/freelance_jobs

Writer Gazette
http://www.writergazette.com/jobf4m.
shtml

Writers Job Market
http://www.sharpwriter.com/jobmarket.
htm

Writers Resource Center
http://www.poewar.com/jobs

WritersWeekly.com
http://www.writersweekly.com/markets_
and_jobs.php

Yahoo Careers
http://careers.yahoo.com

GLOSSARY OF TERMS FOR WRITERS

AA   See AUTHOR'S ALTERATIONS.

AAP   See ASSOCIATION OF AMERICAN PUBLISHERS.

AAR   Association of Authors' Representatives.

ABA   See AMERICAN BOOKSELLERS ASSOCIATION.

ABC   Association of Booksellers for Children.

abstract   A precise summary of a paper or article, sometimes used as on overview or preface at the beginning of the paper or article itself.

abstract poem   A poem that conveys emotion through sound, textures, and rhythm rather than through any specific meaning of its words.

account representative (account rep)   A member of an advertising firm's sales force who is in constant touch with the firm's clients about that client's advertising and promotion campaign(s).

acid-free paper   Paper that has a low or no acid content. This type of paper resists deterioration from exposure to the elements. More expensive than many other types of paper, publications done on acid-free paper can last a long time.

acknowledgment   Typically a list of individuals and entities who provided assistance and/or encouragement to the author in the creation of the work; usually found in the front of a book following the title and copyright pages.

acronym   An abbreviation whose letters begin some or all of the words in the full name, such as NASA for National Aeronautics and Space Administration.

acrostic   When the initial letters of each line of a poem or other composition when read downward, form a word, phrase, or complete sentence.

ad   Advertisement.

adage   A saying that presents a general truth that has gained credibility through long usage.

adaptation   A rewriting or reworking of a written piece for another medium, such as the adaptation of a novel for the screen or TV.

add   Copy to be added to a news story already written for a newspaper or a magazine.

addendum   A brief document that contains information that was omitted from the text of a published work, or information that clarifies information within that work.

ad flow   Refers to the computer system that shuffles classified ads in newspapers and magazines within their categories so that they fit best on a page.

ad send   A computer system for newspapers and magazines that receives camera-ready advertisements from businesses using a MODEM.

advance   The sum of money a publisher pays a writer prior to the publication of his/her book. It is typically paid in installments, one-half upon signing the contract and the other half upon delivery of a complete and acceptable manuscript, or some other arrangement (such as a third on signing, a third on delivery of manuscript, and a third on actual publication of the work). The advance is paid against the royalty money earned from the sales of the published book. In some cases, the advance may be the entire sum a writer receives for the book, which makes it a work for hire.

advance orders   Orders placed by booksellers and others in advance of a book's publication date. Generated by the publisher's beginning sales efforts, the quantity of advance orders can help to determine the number of copies to print, the price of the book, and even the extent of the promotion desired.

affiliated relationship   A contractual agreement between a small publisher (the affiliate) and a larger publisher who agrees to handle all details of billing, shipping, and warehousing, for an agreed-upon percentage of the net billing.

afterword   Closing remarks on the topic of the book or the process of writing the book. Sometimes the material in the afterword is written by someone other than the author.

agate   Small type often used in newspapers and magazines for statistical data.

agent   An intermediary between a writer and an editor or a publisher, acting on behalf of the writer. An agent shops a manuscript (or a book proposal) around to publishers and receives a commission when the manuscript is accepted. Agents usually take a fee of between 10 and 15 percent from the advance and royalties. In the case of dramatic rights and if a co-agent is involved, the fee is between 10 and 20 percent. In addition, most agents handle for the writer client the subsequent subsidiary rights not acquired by the publisher. Some agents act on behalf of publishers to find special types of material or authors to develop such material. Also known as author's agent or representative, or literary agent.

agented material   Submissions from literary or dramatic agents to a publisher on behalf of writers. Many of the larger publishing companies only accept agented material, never unsolicited manuscripts.

air   The white space on a printed page in a newspaper or a magazine.

ALA   See AMERICAN LIBRARY ASSOCIATION.

all rights   Some magazines purchase all rights to the material they publish, which means they can use the material in any way they see fit, and as often as they wish. In complying, an author signs away all rights to all the work he does for them and is unable to ever use or submit such material to another publisher of any sort. Such rights must be given by the writer in a written permission.

alphabet poem   A poem that arranges its lines alphabetically according to an initial letter.

American Booksellers Association (ABA)   The national trade association of retail chain and independent bookstores, founded in 1900.

American Library Association (ALA)   The national professional association for librarians and others interested in the educational and cultural responsibilities of libraries. It was founded in 1876.

American Society of Journalists and Authors (ASJA)   A membership organization for professional writers.

analogy   A comparison between two things, often on the basis of shared characteristics.

anapest   In poetry, a FOOT consisting of two unstressed syllables followed by a stress.

anecdote   A brief story or account of a personal experience, often used to get a reader's (or listener's) attention.

anthology   A collection of selected writings by various writers or a compilation of a single writer's works. Anthologies are compiled rather than written, and their editors (rather than authors) are responsible for securing the necessary reprint rights for the material collected, as well as writing (or contracting authors to write) introductory or supplemental material and/or commentary.

antonym   A word opposite in meaning to another word, such as "hot" and "cold."

aphorism   A concise expression of a truth or of a principle, which implies both depth of understanding and distinction in style of expression.

appendix   Supplementary material appearing at the end of a book's text, usually as a separate section of the BACK MATTER.

approval copy   A book sent to teachers/professors, accompanied by an invoice seeking payment or return of the book within a specified time period, for consideration for purchase by, or recommendation to, students.

approval plan   An agreement between a library and a publisher or WHOLESALER under which the latter takes on the responsibility of selecting and supplying all current books published in specific subject areas or languages as specified by the library. Most approval plans permit returns for credit.

artwork   Any material, such as drawings, paintings, or photographs, prepared as illustrations for printed matter and publication.

ASAP   As soon as possible.

ascender   In printing, the part of a lowercase letter that extends above the body of the letter.

ASJA   See AMERICAN SOCIETY OF JOURNALISTS AND AUTHORS.

assignment   A contract (or agreement), written or oral, between an editor and a writer, confirming the commission and completion of a specific writing project in a given time frame (or by a certain date), for a determined fee, and within a specified word count range; also any news-gathering task given to a reporter.

Association of American Publishers (AAP)   The national trade association of publishers of educational, general, medical, reference, religious, scientific, and technical books.

Association of Authors' Representatives (AAR)   An organization for literary agents committed to maintaining excellence in literary representation.

attribution   Determining a particular person, place, or time as the creator, source, or era of a literary work or a work of art.

auction   Publishers sometime bid for the acquisition of a specific manuscript that has excellent sales potential. The bids are usually for the amount of the writer's advance, advertising and promotional expenses, royalties, and other such items. The auction is handled by the writer's agent.

audio books   Works produced for distribution in an audio medium, typically audiotape cassette or audio compact disc (CD). Audio books are usually spoken-work adaptations of already printed works and frequently feature the author's own voice. Some may be given a dramatic reading with one or more actors and sound effects.

authorized biography   A written history of a person's life that has been written with the authorization, cooperation, and, at times, participation of either the subject or the heirs.

author's agent   See AGENT.

author's alterations (AA)   Changes made on a typeset copy of the manuscript by the author of the forthcoming publication. Contracts usually detail that the cost of author's alterations above a certain percentage of the full typeset work (as specified) are to be charged to the author. This penalty does not apply to errors generated by the publisher and/or typesetter.

author's discount   The percentage less than list price, as stipulated in the contract, at which an author can buy copies of his or her book directly from the publisher. In some cases, the author may be allowed to resell them at readings, lectures, or other public engagements. As set by contract, the discount may range from 20 to 40 percent, and may apply to books other than the author's own.

author's earn-out   The point at which an author's earned royalties equal the author's contractual advance.

author's proofs (master proofs)   See PROOFS.

author's questionnaire   A form that authors are usually requested to complete and return to the publisher to provide guidance (or advice) on marketing and promotion plans for the author's work, (Such needed information includes the names of personal contacts to solicit blurbs for jacket copy, as well as persons to receive free copies for potential reviews).

author's representative   See AGENT.

author tour   A planned series of promotional appearances and travel by an author on behalf of the author's book (and usually arranged by the publisher).

autobiography   A history of a person's life written by that same person or, typically, in collaboration with a professional writer (with an "as told to" or "with" attribution sometimes being made), or a GHOSTWRITER. See also COAUTHOR, and COLLABORATION. By definition, autobiographies imply the authorization, cooperation, participation, and ultimate approval of its subject.

automatic distribution   A procedure in which a publisher (or WHOLESALER) supplies books to a bookstore according to predetermined appropriate quantities. In trade publishing, quantities are usually subject to the dealer's approval.

avant-garde   Writing that is innovative, experimental, and cutting edge in form, subject, or style, often thought of as difficult or challenging.

axiom   A self-evident or universally recognized truth.

backgrounder   A story assigned without a deadline or publication schedule, that is needed for internal informational purposes. Also, a published story that details the background or profile of a subject. Also, a meeting with the press in which a source gives information not for publication; or an informative, factual story that relates the history or background of a current news event in order to aid audience understanding.

backlist   A publisher's list of books not published in the current season, but still in print. Such backlist titles frequently represent the publisher's cash flow mainstays and may continue to sell either briskly or slowly over the years. While many bookstores will not stock backlist titles, they can be ordered through a local bookseller, or directly from the publisher, or online from any number of INTERNET outlets.

back matter (backmatter)   Parts of a book that follow the main text. Back matter may include an appendix or appendixes, notes, bibliography and other references, glossary, lists of resources, index, and author's biography. In some cases, it may also offer listings of the author's and/or publisher's additional books, as well as related merchandise.

backstory   The characters' lives before the story, play, novel, or film began.

ballad   A narrative poem.

B&W (B/W)   Abbreviation for black and white photographs.

bank   In newspaper parlance, the lower portion of a headline; or a computer file in which stories are kept before they are placed in their designated page form.

banner   A headline, sometimes called a "streamer" or "banner line," stretching across the top of a page of a newspaper or magazine.

baseline   In type, an imaginary line connecting the bottoms of letters.

beat   The area of subject matter or geographical territory than an editor or a reporter covers on a regular basis. Also, a word used to identify a pause during a character's speech in a screenplay.

beat poetry   Fast-paced free verse resembling jazz. It is an antiacademic school of poetry started in 1950s San Francisco.

bed   In LETTERPRESS PRINTING, the surface of a printing press, against which type or plates are clamped and over which ink rollers and an impression cylinder pass.

belles lettres   A form of literary writing, presently referring to stories focused on the internal lives of its characters and/or writing that especially focus on elegance and aesthetic qualities. Each generation has tended to redefine what is and is not belles lettres.

best seller   On the basis of sales or orders from bookstores, wholesalers, distributors, and other bookselling outlets, best sellers are those titles that generate the largest quantities of sold copies. Lists of best-selling books can be local (as in metropolitan newspapers), regional (as in geographically oriented trade or consumer publications), or national (as in the large national newspapers or trade magazines), as well as international and on the INTERNET (as generated by bookselling outlets). Fiction and nonfiction are usually listed separately, as are hardcover and paperback classifications. Some bestseller lists are geared to specific industry sectors, particular genre or specialty fields, or particular social groups.

bibliography   A list of books, articles, and other sources that have been used in the writing of the text in which the bibliography appears. Bibliographies may be A–Z listings, or broken down into discrete subject areas.

biennially   Occurring once every two years

bimonthly   Occurring once every two months (or twice each month)

binary digit   See BIT.

binding   The materials that keep a book together (including the cover). Bindings are generally hardcover (a heavy cardboard covered with durable cloth and/or paper, or other material) or paperback (a pliable, resilient grade of paper, sometimes infused or laminated with other substances, usually plastic). Types of binding include CASE BINDING, COMB BINDING, PERFECT BINDING, SADDLE STITCHING, SPIRAL BINDING, and VELO BINDING. In olden times, hardcover bindings sometimes had tooled leather, silk, precious stones, or gold and silver leaf ornamentation added lavishly.

bio   A sentence or group of sentences about the writer. It usually appears at the bottom of the first or last page of a writer's article or short story, or appears in the listings on a contributor's page, or at the back of the writer's book (and is frequently repeated on one of the flaps of the dusk jacket if the book utilizes one). In a query letter, the bio section comes usually at the end of the communication and establishes the writer's credentials and abilities in preparing the work proposed in the letter. Note: the bios at the ends of articles and on a contributor's page are frequently written by the editors.

biography   A history of a person's life. (See also AUTHORIZED BIOGRAPHY, AUTOBIOGRAPHY, and UNAUTHORIZED BIOGRAPHY.)

BISG   Book Industry Study Group, an organization of publishers, booksellers, librarians, book manufacturers, and suppliers, formed in 1976 for the purpose of promoting and supporting RESEARCH that will enable the various sectors of the book industry to realize their professional and business plans. BISG collects and compiles statistics, as well as issuing research reports on the book industry.

bit (binary digit)   The smallest component of electronic data—a 1 or 0 in the binary number system.

bits per second   See BPS.

biweekly   Occurring once every two weeks (or twice each week).

blank verse   Unrhymed IAMBIC PENTAMETER.

bleed   An illustration filling one or more margins and running off the edge of the page or border, partially trimmed off when the page is cut for binding; used frequently in magazines and advertisements.

blind ad   A classified ad that does not reveal the identity of the advertiser; responses are generally sent to a P.O. box.

blind-blocking (blind-stamping or **blind-tooling)**   Impressing a design on a book cover by hot tools only, using no ink or gold leaf.

blind folio   A page number that is counted during PAGE MAKEUP but not printed on the page.

blind interview   An interview story for a newspaper or magazine in which the interviewed person is not disclosed; for example, a "highly placed official," or "a source close to the mayor."

block quotations   Extended excerpts, usually in reduced type and separated from the body of a text. Also called "extract."

blog   Essentially a journal that is available on the Web. The action of updating a blog is "blogging" and someone who maintains an online blog is a "blogger." In general, blogs are updated daily using software that permits individuals with little or no technical background to update and maintain their blogs. Postings on a blog are almost always arranged in chronological order with the most recent additions featured most prominently (at the top of the file).

blow up   To play a story beyond its actual news value; or to enlarge something, such as a photo, art illustration, or copy.

bluelines (blues)   See PROOFS.

blueprints   See PROOFS.

blurb   Written copy or an extracted quotation used for publicity and promotional purposes on a flyer, in a catalog, or in an advertisement. See also COVER BLURBS.

board books   Small, often square-shaped books intended for infants and toddlers and consisting of a small number of thick pages.

boards   Stiff cardboard used for the sides of books, which may be covered with paper, cloth, leather, or other material.

body type   In newspapers, the type used in the text of stories, not in headlines, and generally less than 12-point size, as opposed to DISPLAY TYPE, which can be any point size. See also TYPE SIZE.

boilerplate   A standardized contract. When editors or publishers refers to "our standard contract," they mean a generic boilerplate contract with no changes to the basic terms (which are always most favorable to the publisher). Most editors consider the standard contract as a beginning point for negotiation. Writers should be aware that most authors and/or agents frequently make many changes to such contracts.

boldface type (boldface)   Type that is heavier and thicker than the rest of text type with which it appears.

bond paper   This kind of paper is often used for stationery and is more transparent than TEXT PAPER. It can be made of either sulphite (wood) or cotton fiber. Some bonds have a mixture of both wood and cotton (such as "25 percent cotton" paper). This is the type of paper most often used in photocopying or as standard typing paper.

book club   A book-marketing business that ships selected titles to subscribing members on a regular basis, sometimes at a somewhat or greatly reduced price.

book club rights   The rights purchased by a BOOK CLUB allowing it to offer a book to its membership. The negotiations for these rights are made through the publisher's subsidiary rights department. Terms vary, but the usual split of royalties between author and publisher is often 50-50. The club may get permission to print its own edition, or acquire copies of the book printed by the original publisher to sell at discount pricing.

book contract   A legally binding document between author and publisher that spells out the terms for the monetary ADVANCE, ROYALTIES, SUBSIDIARY RIGHTS, advertising, promotion, publicity, and a number of other contingencies and responsibilities. It is important for writers to be thoroughly familiar with the concepts and terminology of the standard book-publishing contract.

book developer   See book PACKAGER.

book distribution   The method of getting books from the publisher's warehouse to its buying public. Distribution is traditionally through bookstores (including INTERNET outlets), but frequently also includes such means as telemarketing, mail-order sales, and sales through a wide variety of special-interest outlets, such as health-food stores, or sports and fitness businesses. Publishers use their own sales force personnel as well as independent salespeople, wholesalers, and distributors. Many large and some smaller publishers distribute for other publishers as well.

book doctor   A person who provides a freelance editorial service to writers, for a fee, in critiquing manuscripts and shorter material. Some book doctors provide detailed suggestions and line-editing of manuscripts. They usually charge by the hour, or by the nature of the assignment. Others, who provide a much more extensive rewriting—or even development of the manuscript, are called GHOSTWRITERS.

book fair   An exhibition (local, regional, national, and international) of books and related material by publishers, WHOLESALERS, and other book outlets, along with talks by authors and illustrators, as well as other events. There may also be a trading center for the sale of books and rights, in addition to the making of publishing and copublishing arrangements.

book jacket   See DUST JACKET.

book leasing plan   A WHOLESALER's merchandising program in which, for a set fee, libraries can lease current books and return to the wholesaler those books when user demand drops, to be replaced with other current titles.

bookmark   An electronic feature in many desktop computer programs that allows users to create a list of topics to revisit. An analogy would be using markers or post-it notes to tag pages in a book to be able to revisit those pages easily.

book number   See ISBN.

book outline   A chapter-by-chapter summary of a book allowing an editor to evaluate the book's content, style, and pacing as a means to judge whether the entire manuscript would be worth looking at for possible publication. The summaries are usually in paragraph format. Sometimes the outline is accompanied by one or more sample chapters.

book packager   An individual or company that puts together all the elements of a book, from the initial concept to the writing and publishing of it, as well as marketing strategies to be used by a publisher that will release and market the book as its own or as an acknowledged copublishing project. The book packager may negotiate separate contracts with the publisher and with the writers, editors, and illustrators who contribute to the book. Also called BOOK PRODUCER or BOOK DEVELOPER.

book producer   See BOOK PACKAGER.

book proposal   See PROPOSAL.

book review   A critical appraisal of a book (usually reflecting the reviewer's personal opinion or recommendation) that evaluates the book's organization and writing style, and its market appeal, as well as its cultural, literary, or political significance. Before any reviews ever appear in local or national print media, important reviews usually have been published in such respected booktrade journals and services as *Booklist, Kirkus Reviews, Library Journal, and Publishers Weekly.* Good or rave reviews from one or more of these journals will encourage booksellers to stock the book, and copies of these reviews will be used for promotion and publicity purposes by the publisher to encourage more reviews and more extensive sales.

book signing   A publicized event, often held at bookstores or book fairs, featuring an author reading from and discussing the author's book (usually recently published) and autographing the book for customers.

Books in Print   Published by R. R. Bowker, a listing of books currently in print as confirmed by publishers. These yearly volumes (also available online), along with periodic supplements (such as *Forthcoming Books in Print*) provide ordering information, including titles, authors, ISBN numbers, prices, type of binding (hardcover or paperback), and publisher names. While mainly intended for use by the book trade, these volumes are also of tremendous value for writers or readers who are conducting RESEARCH of any kind. Listings are alphabetically by author, title, and subject area.

border   In newspapers or magazines, this is a box or frame around a picture, a story, or an advertisement. Borders are computer generated and are available in many different styles.

bound galleys   Copies of uncorrected typesetter's page PROOFS or printouts of electronically produced mechanicals that are bound together as advance copies of the book. They are sent to trade journals (see BOOK REVIEW) as well as to a selected number of national reviewers.

box   In journalistic parlance, a SIDEBAR or extra information in a framed BORDER to give it prominence. The space within the box is sometimes shaded.

bps (bits per second)   A measurement of how fast a computer modem can send and receive data.

break   That part of a newspaper or magazine story that is continued on another page. Sometimes, several breaks are gathered together and printed on a "break page." Also called a jump.

breakline   A mid-sentence or paragraph that continues the news story onto the following page. Sometimes confused with a TURNLINE.

breakout (highlighted text box)   The synopsis of a news story in a newspaper or magazine, usually containing the key highlights of that story.

broadsheet   Refers to the size of most daily newspapers, such as the *Wall Street Journal,* the *New York Times,* the *Los Angeles Times, USA Today,* and the *Free Press.* Folded in half, it becomes a TABLOID.

broadside   A large sheet of paper printed on one side only, such as a poster, or printed on both sides and folded in a special way. A broadside table or illustration is one printed with the top at the left side of the page, requiring a quarter turn of the book to the right to be in position for reading it.

browser   Software that translates HTML files, converts them into Web pages, and displays them on the computer screen. Some browsers can access e-mail and news-groups and play sound and video files.

budget   In newspaper jargon, this refers to the various news departments' proposals for what they want to put in the newspaper. It has to do with space and news, not dollars.

bug   A software glitch that prevents computer software from operating properly.

bulk   The thickness of a book, not including the cover; the thickness of paper as measured by number of sheets per inch.

bulk sales   The sale at a set discount of numerous copies of a single book title.

bulldog   The earliest edition of a newspaper, usually scheduled to come out in the early evening; or one printed outside its regular schedule, as a Sunday paper printed days ahead of its publication date.

bullet   Within a newspaper or a magazine, a large dot, arrow, square, or other shape used to attract attention and to point out key topics of a news story.

bump   To move a story ahead or behind its original publication date. Sometimes it can apply to a pay rate as well.

bumped heads   In a newspaper, similar headlines running side by side that create monotony and take the reader's eye across the page too quickly.

business-size envelope   Usually known as a #10 envelope, this is the standard-size envelope used for business correspondence.

byline   Name of the author as it appears on the published piece. Ghostwriters, by definition, do not receive byline credit. In newspapers (and some magazines) the name of the writer appears at the top of the article, and artists and photographers generally get credit. When the reporter's name appears at the end of the story or article, it often is preceded by a dash and is called a "signer."

byte   A group of eight BITS that the computer processes as one unit.

©   A copyright notice symbol used for books, maps, works of art, models or designs for works of art, reproductions of a work of art, drawings or plastic works of a scientific or technical character, photographs, prints, and pictorial illustrations. It must be accompanied by the name, initials, monogram, mark, or symbol of the copyright owner.

calender   To make paper smooth and glossy by passing it through rollers.

camera-ready   Refers to anything that is in its finished form, with no further changes needed before being printed and published; art that is completely prepared for copy camera platemaking.

cancel   To cut out blank pages from a SIGNATURE at the end of a book, or to cut out printed pages. Also, a leaf reprinted to correct an error in a printed book and inserted by the binder in place of the incorrect page or pages.

caps   short for *capital letters.*

caption   A description of the subject matter of a graph, illustration, or photograph; photo captions usually include attribution of the source of the photo where appropriate. Also called "cutline." See also LEGEND.

carding   Increasing the vertical spaces between lines by less than a POINT (done to lengthen a type page). In photocomposition, the film is advanced to increase the space between lines, and, thus, lengthen the page. In the old cold type process of printing, cardboard strips had to be inserted between the sluglines of type.

caret   The proofreading symbol ∧, which is used to indicate that an insertion is to be made in a line.

case   The cover of a hardcover book.

case binding   In case binding, SIGNATURES (groups of pages) are stitched together with thread rather than glued together. The stitched pages are then trimmed on three sides and glued into a hardcover or board "case" or cover. Most hardcover books and thicker magazines are bound this way.

cash discounts   Discounts (for instance, 5 percent off the total of a bill if it is paid in 30 days or less) offered by dealers, publishers, or WHOLESALERS for prompt payment of an invoice. See also DISCOUNT (PUBLISHING).

cast off   To estimate the number of pages a given manuscript will make; also, to estimate the number of pages of text from a set of GALLEYS.

catchline   See SLUGLINE.

catch phrase   A motto in wide or popular use, especially one that serves as a slogan for a group or a social or political movement.

CD (computer CD or CD-ROM)   High-capacity compact discs for use by readers via computer technology. Many commercial CDs are issued with a variety of audiovisual as well as textual components. When produced by publishers, these are sometimes referred to as books in electronic format.

CD-R   A compact disc onto which data (or music) can be written but not erased or modified.

CD-RW   A compact disc onto which data (or music) can be written multiple times.

center point (centered dot)   A period cast higher than the baseline of the type line. Used to show syllabication, to indicate multiplication, to separate words set in roman caps composed in the classic style of tablet inscriptions. Sometimes, it is called a "space dot."

chant A poem in which one or more lines are repeated over and over.

chapbook A small book, or booklet, usually paperback, of ballads, poetry, or tales.

character A letter of the alphabet, numeral, punctuation mark, or other symbol in a font of type. also any person, usually fictional, in a literary work.

character count A count of each letter, numeral, punctuation mark, space, or other symbols in a piece of copy.

characters per pica The number of characters of a particular font that will fit into a one-PICA space.

chaser A late edition of a newspaper for which the presses are not stopped before the printing plates are ready. These pages, then, are said to be "chasing" a running press.

chat room An INTERNET location where people can "chat" with other people around the world by typing messages and receiving responses in real time. Chat groups are often identified by their special interests.

children's books Books for children. As defined by the book-publishing industry, children are generally readers age 17 and younger. Some distinction is made between titles intended for younger readers (12 and below) and young adults (12 to 17). Children's books (also called juveniles) fall into a number of categories (usually by age ranges), each with particular requirements as to readability ratings, length, and inclusion of graphic elements. Picture books usually are for very young readers, for toddlers (who do not themselves yet read) and preschoolers (who may have some reading ability). Other classifications include easy storybooks (for younger school children), middle-grade books (for elementary and junior high school students), and young adults (frequently abbreviated to YA, for readers through age 17).

chromatic press See PRINTING PRESS.

chunks (chunking) A method of dividing information into digestible blocks based on theories of human short-term memory capacities and applied to magazine and newspaper writing (where it is often referred to as "multiple-entry journalism," wherein readers are provided with many entry points on a single page instead of one large unit of print. Thus, many articles are divided into sidebars, lists, charts, NUTGRAPHS, and illustrations with captions, all of which are tied together (if at all) by a shortened main story. Many consumer magazines now divide text on the average of every 100 words, or less.

Chunking allows readers to scan an article and read only the parts most interesting and relevant to them. It is a type of customizing of sometimes complex information that is being driven by the design demands of the web and the INTERNET.

Chunking is regularly achieved by three different methods: visual separation (the use of white space to frame chunks of text), visual progression (giving a sequence to the chunks by using letters, numbers, colors, or horizontal and vertical arrangements), and visual differentiation (by the use of various type styles, sizes, and colors to make each chunk visually different).

circulation The number of subscribers to a magazine or newspaper; also the total number of copies of a publication distributed to subscribers and vendors in one day. Frequently also used to measure INTERNET usage.

circulation-builder Books given as a reward to subscribers or for renewing a newspaper or magazine subscription.

citation A quoting of an authoritative source for substantiation.

classified advertising In newspapers and magazines, advertising arranged according to the product or service advertised, and usually restricted in size and format. The ads are "classified" into various categories such as help wanted, autos for sale, apartments for rent, and other such categories.

clause A string of words containing a noun (subject) and a finite verb. It may be a complete sentence, or part of a longer sentence, either in a dependent position or independent of that longer sentence.

clean copy A manuscript free of errors, indicated corrections, wrinkles, or smudges. Also refers to a submitted manuscript that is characterized by writing that fits the assignment and audience, has strong sentences and structure that needs no editorial work, has no spelling or grammar errors, contains usable heads and subheads, and, above all, is totally accurate in its reporting.

cliché A trite or overused expression or idea.

cliffhanger A fictional event in which the reader (or viewer in the case of film or television) is left in suspense at the end of a chapter or episode, so that interest in the outcome of the written or visual story will be sustained.

clip In newspaper jargon, an abbreviation for a clipping from a newspaper or from the files of the newspaper's library.

clips Samples of a writer's published work, usually articles (and sometimes known as TEAR SHEETS), most often used by editors in their evaluation of a writer's talent. Today this function (of convincing editors about an author's writing skill) is often replaced by author WEB SITES and LINKS.

cloak-and-dagger This melodramatic, romantic type of fiction writing deals primarily with espionage and intrigue.

coated/uncoated stock (paper) Coated and uncoated are terms usually used when referring to book or TEXT PAPER. More opaque than bond, coated paper is most used for offset printing. As the name implies, uncoated paper has no coating. Coated paper is covered with a layer of clay, varnish or other chemicals. It comes in various sheens and surfaces depending on the type of coating, but the most common are dull, matte, and gloss.

coauthor   A writer who shares authorship of a work. Coauthors have bylines and share royalties based on their contribution to the book as set out in their contract with their coauthor.

COBOL   See COMMON BUSINESS ORIENTED LANGUAGE.

codex   Any book made of bound pages.

coffee-table book   An oversize book, usually heavily illustrated.

collaboration   Writers sometimes collaborate with professionals in any number of fields to produce books extending the author's formally credentialed expertise (for example, an author with an interest in exercise or nutrition might collaborate with a doctor to write a book on health or healing). The writer may be accredited as a COAUTHOR (with a BYLINE), or act as a GHOSTWRITER (without a BYLINE). In any case, ROYALTIES are usually shared, based on the type and extent of their respective contributions to the book, which might include both expertise and promotional abilities beyond the actual writing.

collate   To arrange the folded sheets or SIGNATURES of a book or other printed matter in correct order.

collating marks   A short rule (or letter, figure, or shortened book title) inserted in the form to print midway between the first and last pages of a SIGNATURE. The mark on the first signature is placed near the top, that on the second somewhat lower, the third lower still, and so on. When the signatures are assembled, the marks show in a regular series, which would be broken if a signature were missing or duplicated.

colloquialism   A word or expression that is used informally (often in specific regions or among specific groups of people) but is not usually considered appropriate in formal or academic prose.

colophon   Generally, a publisher's LOGO, but it also may refer to a listing of materials used in the production of the book, as well as typeface details, information related to any artwork, and credits for its design and composition. Such credits are to be found either on a separate page in the BACK MATTER or as part of the COPYRIGHT PAGE.

color   In newspaper parlance, "coloring a story" implies introducing an element of bias or an editorial point of view. "Giving a story color" means brightening the story with human interest material.

color separation   The separation of the color of a full-color transparency or print by photographing it with separate color filters.

column   The area on a news page usually 10 to 14 PICAS wide or 8 picas wide on a classified page; also an article appearing regularly, written by a writer or "columnist."

column inch   The amount of text contained in one inch of a typeset column. It measures both ads and articles, and often serves as a basis for payment.

.com   INTERNET extension for commercial sites.

comb binding   A comb is a plastic spine used to hold pages together with bent tabs that are fed through punched holes in the edge of the paper.

commercial novels   Genre of fiction designed to appeal to a broad audience. They are often broken down into categories such as mystery, romance, science fiction, and western. See also GENRE.

commissioned representative   See PUBLISHER'S REPRESENTATIVE/SALES REPRESENTATIVE.

commissioned work   See ASSIGNMENT.

Common Business Oriented Language (COBOL)   A programming language for business applications.

compound heading   An indexing heading of two or more elements (with or without any connecting hyphen), each of which could stand alone as an index term with its own meaning. For example, settlement house, lowest common denominator, ill-favored, or mass-produced.

concept   A summarizing of a screenplay or teleplay, usually done before an outline or treatment is written. Also the term for a general statement of the idea behind a proposed book.

concept books   Books that deal with ideas, theories, abstractions, and large-scale problems. With children's books, they promote an understanding of what's happening within a child's world. Examples are alphabet and counting books, but also entries that deal with various concerns facing young readers.

condensed type   Type with characters that are narrower than those of standard width, permitting more characters per line.

confessional   Genre of fiction in which the author, or first-person narrator, owns up to something embarrassing or shocking. When real-life identities are only vaguely disguised by the writer, the resultant work is called a "roman à clef."

confessional poetry   Work that uses personal and private details from the poet's own life.

consumer magazines   Refers to magazines that appeal to both general and special interests of the public. They are usually the magazines to be found on newsstands. Trade magazines, on the other hand, tend to focus on the members of professions or trades, athletes, or other special areas, and are usually distributed mainly via membership lists.

contemporary   Written or visual material dealing with popular current trends, themes, or topics.

content editing   Editing a manuscript for flow, logic, and its overall message, as opposed to COPYEDITING.

context-sensitive help   Help on the computer that is available in online documents with the click of the computer mouse. It provides a quick means of accessing information.

contract   A written agreement concerning the rights to be purchased by a publisher and the amount of payment (and how the payment will be made) to the writer for the sale of his/her work to that firm. Contracts usually also detail services rendered by both parties, deadlines and delivery dates, rights purchased, and whether the author's original work is to be returned

contributor's copies   Copies of a publication sent to a writer whose work is included in it.

cooperative advertising   Familiarly known as coop (pronounced and alternatively spelled co-op) advertising, it is when the publisher pays partial or total cost of an advertisement placed by a retailer to promote the publisher's book or books. Usually requiring a contractual agreement between retailer and publisher, such advertising can appear either in print or on the broadcast media.

co-publication   A book published jointly by two or more publishers, this venture may involve companies of more than one nation, although the work may be produced in one or more languages in a single country. There is almost always a sharing of developmental costs and/or production costs, which otherwise might be economically unfeasible for a single publisher to undertake.

copublishing   An arrangement where the writer and the publisher share both publication costs and profits. Also known as "cooperative publishing." See also SUBSIDIARY PUBLISHER.

copy   Manuscript pages (containing the manuscript and any pictures or artwork) before they are set into type or, if existing in electronic form, before the final computer file version is saved; also referring to all written material for a newspaper or magazine.

copy desk   The desk at a newspaper where articles and other copy are edited, headlines and captions written. It is here that newspaper style is enforced and deadlines either made or missed

copyediting   Editing line-by-line of a manuscript for appropriate word and grammar usage, punctuation, printing style, and spelling, not content.

copyright   Legal protection, granted by the federal government, of creative works from unauthorized usage. Legally a U.S. copyright is secured by the writer automatically when the creative work is set down for the first time in written or recorded form. Nonetheless, for protection against potential plagiarism or other infringement, it is wise for the author or publisher to register the work formally with the U.S. Copyright Office, and all copies of the work must bear the copyright notice for that protection. U.S. copyright protection extends for the lifetime of the writer/creator plus 70 years. However, copyright law does not extend protection to titles, ideas, or facts.

copyright page   A page toward the front of the book, which indicates that the book is protected by COPYRIGHT, and that permission must be obtained to reproduce all or part of the book. Typically, this page also includes cataloging data for libraries. Also included sometimes is production information about the book, known as the **colophon.**

copywriting   Usually refers to copy written for advertising or marketing purposes.

correspondent   A reporter assigned to cover stories away from the home office in another city, state, or country.

couplet   A stanza of two lines; a pair of rhymed lines.

courtesy discounts   See PROFESSIONAL OR COURTESY DISCOUNTS.

cover   To RESEARCH and put together a story; also the foremost portion of a publication.

cover letter   A brief letter accompanying a manuscript or a book proposal. It is not a QUERY LETTER.

cover price   The retail price of a book (or other publication) suggested by its publisher and printed on the dust jacket or cover.

cover stock (paper)   Cover stock is heavier book or TEXT PAPER used to cover publications such as booklets, brochures, catalogs, and similar pieces. It comes in a variety of colors and textures and can be coated on one or both sides.

cq   Stands for "correct as is." This symbol lets copy editors know that something has been checked and needs no further checking. Usually, these letters are put just after the copy to which they refer.

crash   Coarse gauze fabric used in bookbinding to strengthen the spine and joints of a book. See also SUPER.

creative nonfiction   A style of nonfiction writing that uses an unconventional approach to its subject and the language employed. It is a blend of a reporter's objectivity and accuracy with a fiction writer's emotive impact and techniques in such elements as plot, narrative, character development, conflict, and resolution.

credit   To acknowledge the source for a given fact or opinion, or an ACKNOWLEDGMENT of a person's contribution to the writer's work.

credit line   A photographer's byline. The name of the person or organization responsible for making or distributing a photograph usually appears in small type under the reproduced picture.

critical notes   RESEARCH notes that include comments, interpretations, or evaluations of a source of information.

CRM (customer relationship management)   Computer software that gives sales, marketing, customer service, and help desk personnel access to the same database so they can serve customers more efficiently.

crop/cropping   Changing the composition of a picture by cutting part of it out. A picture may be cropped to remove undesired background, to create more impact, or to adjust the photograph to fit the available space on the printed page.

cross-reference   A reference made from one part of a book, article, or other printed matter to another part of the text containing related information; also, a reference from one entry, as in an INDEX, to another for additional information.

cub   A beginning reporter.

cumulative index   An index containing entries from multiple volumes in a set of books. Also called a "master index." Often the index to the final volume will not appear separately but will be merged into the cumulative index.

curriculum vitae (CV)   A brief listing of a writer's qualifications and/or career accomplishments. Also known as a RÉSUMÉ.

cursive   meaning running or flowing; applied to certain faces of type similar to ITALIC but more decorative.

customer relationship management   See CRM.

cut   A printer's term for a halftone engraving or a zinc etching. Commonly used to refer to any printed illustration.

cutline   See CAPTION.

cyberpunk   A type of science fiction writing that is usually concerned with computer networks and human-computer combinations. Their protagonists are usually young and sophisticated.

dactyl   In poetry, a FOOT consisting of a stress followed by two unstressed syllables.

daily   Refers to newspapers that print a new newspaper each day.

dangler   A PHRASE, usually at the beginning of a sentence, that is grammatically attached to the subject of the sentence but, in fact, refers to something other than that subject. It is sometimes called a dangling participle.

dateline   A line at the beginning of a news story from out of town that indicates both the place and the date of origin of the story. Some newspapers strictly enforce the rule that the dateline must say where the reporter was when the story was gathered. A foreign story gathered by phone, fax, or computer at home, however, might run with no dateline.

deadline   Per agreement between author and editor, this is the date on which a written work is due at the editor's office; for newspapers it is the last moment (either the time for the last type to be set, or the time when the presses are scheduled to start) to get copy in for an edition. Other types of deadlines occur throughout the production process of a publication.

dead matter   Material, such as blues, page PROOFS, or proof copies returned by the printer after a book has been printed.

deck   Usually a single sentence or phrase printed below the title of an article and before the text begins. It is used to summarize and suggest the slant of the article and what the reader might get from it. They may be humorous or serious, short or long. Sometimes called "teaser" or "bank."

deckle edge   The untrimmed, rough edge of a sheet of paper, formed where the liquid pulp flowed under the frame (the deckle). The rough edges are often left untrimmed on handmade paper and can be artificially produced on machine-made paper.

dedication   An author's statement of appreciation or compliments to a specific person or group of people to whom the book is dedicated. Often appears as a separate page in the FRONT MATTER.

delete   To mark for elimination a letter, word, or portion of a manuscript.

demographics   Data about the size and characteristics of a population or an audience (for example, gender, age group, income group, and personal preferences).

derivative work   A written work that has been abridged, adapted, condensed, translated, or otherwise produced by amending an already existing work. Before producing a derivative work, written permission must be obtained from the copyright owner.

descender   The part of a LOWERCASE letter that extends below the baseline of the letter.

designated service line   See DSL.

desktop publishing   A personal computer publishing system that is capable of typesetting, and has some capacity for handling illustrations, LAYOUT, design, and printing so that the final product can be distributed and/or sold.

Dial-a-Writer   A service provided by the AMERICAN SOCIETY OF JOURNALISTS AND AUTHORS in which members can be listed in the organization's project-referral service providing accomplished writers in most specialty fields and subjects.

diction   Choice of words, probably the best identifier of quality in writing.

dictum   An authoritative statement, or a dogmatic saying.

didactic poetry   Poetry written with the intension of instructing its reader.

dies   Brass, copper, magnesium, or other alloy stamps used for impressing letters or designs on covers of books. Also called "brasses" or "binder's dies."

digraph   A combination of two letters to express a sound. Vowel digraphs, such as "ae," are called diphthongs.

dingbat   A typographic decorative device, such as a star, arrow, or heart.

diphthong   See DIGRAPH.

direct marketing   Generally, advertising that involves a "direct response" from a consumer (for example, an order form or coupon in the back of a book, or mailings to groups that are presumed to be interested in the subject area of the book).

Direct Marketing Association (DMA)   Oldest and largest international trade association representing creators, suppliers, and users of direct-mail advertising and other direct marketing techniques (including e-mail and tele-marketing).

direct quotation   A quotation of a speaker's or writer's own words expressing ideas and feelings, and set off by quotations marks from the rest of the text.

discount (publishing)   A percentage deducted from the list (retail) price of a book or other publication, thereby determining the unit cost to the dealer purchasing it from the publisher or WHOLESALER. Thus, a $20 book sold to a dealer at a 40 percent discount would cost $12, and from this 40 percent difference the store's operating costs and profit must be derived. See also CASH DISCOUNTS, LIBRARY DISCOUNTS, PROFESSIONAL OR COURTESY DISCOUNTS, SHORT DISCOUNTS, and TRADE DISCOUNTS.

display ad   This refers to advertising matter (in newspapers and magazines) other than in-column classified ads. Display ads usually have a BORDER.

display type   Type, usually 18-point or larger and often in BOLDFACE and of a distinctive design, used for headings, in advertisements, or in text of a smaller size, to attract a reader's attention.

distributor   An agent or business that buys books from a publisher to resell, usually at a higher cost, to wholesalers, retailers, or individuals. Distribution houses, with their own sales force, publicity and promotion personnel, and published in-house catalogs, usually have excellent marketing expertise.

.dll   Computer filename extension for dynamic-link library files.

DMA   See DIRECT MARKETING ASSOCIATION.

.doc   Computer filename extension for documents.

docudrama   A fictional feature film or made-for-TV movie that recounts recent actual events involving real-life people.

dog watch   The late shift on a morning newspaper, or the earliest shift on an afternoon newspaper.

domain name   A unique Web address. See also URL.

.dot   Computer filename extension for document templates.

double spread   Two facing printed pages.

double truck   An ad or editorial project in a newspaper (or magazine) that covers two facing pages. If it prints across the GUTTER between the two pages, and if the pages are on the same print sheet, rather than two adjacent print sheets, it might be called a "true" double truck. This name comes from the days when the heavy forms for newspaper pages, largely filled with lead type, were rolled around the composing room floor on heavy carts called trucks. Two pages for one project meant a double truck.

download   The action of copying a file electronically onto a computer.

draft   A finished version of an article, story, book, and other writing formats. First drafts are usually referred to as ROUGH DRAFTS.

dramatic, TV, and motion picture rights   These concern the rights for the use of material on the stage, in TV, or in the movies. Usually a one-year option to buy such rights is offered to the author (usually for 10 percent of the total price). The party making the offer then tries to sell the work to other people—actors, directors, film studios, or TV networks. Some works may be optioned many times over and, even then, still fail to come to full production. In these instances, the author can sell such rights over and over again.

drop   For newspapers, drop is short for "drop head," which is a headline accompanying a streamer and based on the same story; also a story that was planned to run and then didn't.

drop folio   A page number (FOLIO) placed at the bottom of the page.

DSL (Designated Service Line)   A high-speed telephone service for computer systems.

dummy   A preliminary LAYOUT mock-up of a book showing the positioning of illustrations and text as they will appear in the final production. For magazines, a dummy is usually a large piece of paper, or its electronic equivalent, that contains thumbnail sketches of all pages so that editorial and advertising elements can be positioned together, providing a schematic of the magazine. For newspapers, it is usually a diagram or layout of a newspaper page showing the position each story, picture, headline, and advertisement is to have. Also a set of blank pages made up in advance to demonstrate the form, general style, shape, and size of a piece of printing.

Duotone   A reproduction of a black-and-white photograph for which two closely related color inks, or even two black inks, are used in the printing process in order to capture both the highlights and the shadows of the picture.

dust jacket (dustcover or **book jacket)**   Refers to the wrapper that covers the binding of hardcover books, designed especially for the book by either the art department of the publisher or a freelance artist under contract. Dust jackets were originally conceived as protective devices for the book during shipment, but now are generally considered to be promotional devices to influence a book browser to buy the book because of its attractive graphics and enticing promotional copy.

dust-jacket copy   A description of the book printed on the dust-jacket flaps. While it may be written by the book's editor, it is often recast or written outright by in-house copywriters or freelance specialists. Books may be sent as advance copies to other writers, experts, or celebrities, in order to solicit quotable praise that will appear on the jacket.

earn out   Before a book author receives any ROYALTY payment, the book has to generate in sales the amount of money given to that author by the publisher as an ADVANCE, at which point it is said that the book has "earned out."

ears   The white space at the top of the front page on each side of the newspaper's name. Some newspapers put weather news, the index to pages, lottery information, or announcement of special features in these spaces.

edge color (edge stain)   Colored stain or gold leaf that is added to the edges of a book's pages.

edition   For newspapers, this indicates the press run. A daily newspaper generally has more than one edition a day—for example, "City Edition," "Early Edition," or "Late Edition." Also refers to the first printing of a book (and all subsequent printings that are done without any revision to the text). When the book is revised, it becomes a revised edition or a second edition.

editorial cartoon   A cartoon that expresses an opinion about a news personality, issue, or event. In newspapers, they generally appear on the OP-ED page.

.edu   Computer INTERNET extension for educational sites.

EFA   Editorial Freelancers Association.

electronic rights   Concerns the use of a written work in electronic form, rather than printed hard copy format. There is some ambiguity about the preciseness of the term, as publishers may define it differently. For writers, it would be wise to get a precise definition from the publisher, in order to consider what rights are reasonable depending upon the fee, advance, or royalties offered by the publisher. Also known as e-rights.

electronic submission   A submission of a written work to a publisher by modem or on a computer disk or CD-ROM or forwarded to the publisher by e-mail attachment.

electrotype (electro)   A metal replica of a page of type or engravings. An impression is taken in a thin layer of softened wax, lead, or plastic. By an electrolytic process the impression so obtained is cast to form a copper, nickel, or steel shell, which is the electrotype. The shell is reinforced with a lead backing. Electros are used today only where very high quality of printing is required.

elegy   A lament in verse for someone who has died, or a reflection on the tragic nature of life.

ellipsis, points of   Three points (periods or dots) are used to indicate an omission in the text.

em   A unit of measuring column widths in publications (generally newspapers and magazines). An em (for the letter *M*) is a square of any given size of type, and is most frequently used as the unit in measuring a PICA (the width of an em in 12-point type).

e-mail   Electronic mail. This is mail generated on a computer and delivered via the INTERNET through service providers to one or more individuals. To send or receive such mail, a user must have an account with an online service, which provides the e-mail address and electronic mailbox for such mail.

embargo   In journalistic parlance, this is the appointed time when a news announcement can be released. News may be released early so that news outlets can be ready to publish or air it, but there may be a restriction (depending upon sources' concerns) on when it can be released to the public. Breaking an embargo—reporting information early—may cause news sources to be less willing to release news.

emblematic poem   Words or letters arranged to imitate a shape, often the subject of the poem.

embossing   Printing or stamping in relief to produce a raised image.

en   One-half the size of an EM.

end matter   See BACK MATTER.

endnotes   Explanatory notes or specific source citations that appear either at the end of individual chapters or at the end of the book's text (sometimes as an APPENDIX); used primarily in scholarly, technical, or academically oriented works.

end paper   A folded sheet of paper different from the text paper, one-half of which is pasted to the inside of the front cover of a book; one-half of a similar sheet is pasted to the inside of the back cover.

engraver's proof   Proof of a line-cut or halftone engraving made by the photoengraver and sent to the editor for approval.

enjambment   In poetry, a continuation of sense and rhythmic movement from one line to the next; also called a "run-on" line.

epic poetry   A long narrative poem telling a story central to a society, culture, or nation.

epigram   An incisive, witty expression, often paradoxical or satirical and neatly or brilliantly phrased.

epilogue   A final segment of a book, which comes after "the end" of the story or the text. In both fiction and non-fiction, an epilogue usually offers commentary or further information about the subject without bearing directly upon the central design of the text.

episodic fiction   A story told in parts in which one event happens after another without seeming to be integrated into the whole.

epitaph   A summary statement of commemoration for a dead person.

e-rights   See ELECTRONIC RIGHTS.

erotica   Fiction or art that is of a sexual nature.

errata   A loose sheet of paper detailing errors found in a printed book. Frequently bound into the book in its subsequent printings.

escalation clause   Clause in an author's contract that entitles the writer to additional or increased payments from the publisher if the book in question achieves certain measures of success. These may include one or more appearances on a best-seller list, a movie/TV sale, or a book club sale. Another type of escalation clause enables the author to earn a higher royalty rate as the number of copies sold reaches specified levels.

estimate   A calculation of the length of copy and the amount of space it will fill, accomplished by a word or character count, in order to determine the cost of the printing work.

ethnographic research   Research that interprets the attitudes, behaviors, language, and practices of particular groups that are tied together by their interests and ways of understanding and acting in the world.

etymology   The study of the history of words, the tracing of their origins, primitive significance, and changes in their form and meaning.

even pages   The left-hand pages of a book, numbered 2, 4, 6, and so on. Often these pages are called "verso pages."

examination copy   A free or on-approval sample copy of a book given to a prospective buyer (usually educators) who will, the publisher hopes, study the work, approve of it, and then adopt the book, resulting in multiple orders for institutional use.

exchanges   Copies of newspapers received by a paper when it exchanges subscriptions with other papers. Some large newspapers have an exchange editor to scan these papers.

exclusive   A story printed by only one newspaper (or aired by only one television news station); a SCOOP.

.exe   Computer filename extension for executable program files.

experimental poetry   Work that challenges conventional ideas of poetry by exploring new techniques, form, language, and visual presentation.

exposition   The portion of a storyline, frequently at the beginning, where background information about the main character (and other characters as well) and setting is related.

extended type   Type with characters that are wider or have more space between them than those of standard width, resulting in fewer characters fitting in a line.

extra   A newspaper edition other than a regular one, and usually only published when an event of transcending news importance warrants it.

e-zine   A magazine that is published electronically and available on the INTERNET.

face   The style of type.

fact checking   The process of verifying the accuracy within a manuscript (or article) of all statements and claims of fact, dates, quotations, spellings, and more. For some publications, writers have to cite their sources within the manuscript (through the use of ENDNOTES or FOOTNOTES), as well as list the RESEARCH materials used in a BIBLIOGRAPHY. Fact checking not only helps to maintain the credibility of the publication but also is useful as a legal safeguard in any potential libel cases. In many cases, the fact-checking materials must be stored at least until the statute of limitations for potential libel have been exceeded.

fair use   A provision within copyright law that allows for short passages from copyrighted material to be used— usually in reviews, reference works, and textbooks— without infringing on the rights of the owner of the copyrighted material.

F&G's   Folded and gathered sheets. An early, not-yet-bound copy of a picture book.

fanzine   A noncommercial, small-circulation magazine usually dealing with fantasy, horror, or science-fiction literature and art.

FAQ (frequently asked questions)   A document (or part of a software program) that lists commonly asked questions and their answers.

feature   An article (in magazines or newspaper) giving the reader information of interest (such as trends, human interest items, or issues) other than news. Magazines often use the term to refer to lead articles or specific departments at the magazine.

field resources   Original documents, interviews, surveys, questionnaires, and personal observations gathered during the process of RESEARCH.

file   To send news by wire; also used to designate one day's output by a press association.

filename extension   Used to distinguish between computer file types, such as .DOC or .EXE.

File Transfer Protocol   See FTP.

filler   A brief item used to fill out a newspaper or magazine column. It could be a well-known news item, a joke, an anecdote, a puzzle, or a poem. Some writers specialize in writing fillers for selected publications.

film proofs   See PROOFS.

final draft   The last version of a completed and polished manuscript ready for submission to an editor.

First Amendment   The first article of the American Bill of Rights, guaranteeing Americans freedom of religion, speech, press, assembly and petition.

first-day story   A story published for the first time and dealing with something that has just happened, as distinguished from a FOLLOW-UP story.

First North American Serial Rights (FNASR)   The specific right to use an author's work in a serial PERIODICAL in North America for its initial public appearance. Thereafter, all rights revert back to the author.

first-person point of view   For nonfiction works, the author writes or reports from his own perspective; in fiction the author (as narrator) tells the story from his/her point of view.

first proofs   See PROOFS.

first reference   The first time someone is mentioned in an article or news story, which generally requires full name identification.

first serial   See SERIALIZATION.

first serial rights   The right of a magazine or newspaper to publish a portion or the entirety of a book for the first time in any PERIODICAL, in one or more parts before the book's official publication date. After this initial publication, the rights revert back to the writer.

flab   In writing, extraneous words, phrases, and sometimes lengthier matter, the elimination of which will strengthen the prose.

flag   The printed title (that is name and logo) of a newspaper at the top of the front page. Also called the nameplate and, sometimes, the MASTHEAD.

flash   The first brief bulletin from a press association with information about an important news event.

flashback   In fiction, a scene that precedes the time of the present story.

flat   A sheet on which NEGATIVES, or positives, are assembled in correct order, for STRIPPING in, and from which an OFFSET plate is made.

flat fee   A one-time payment.

floor   In bidding for paperback reprint or other subsidiary rights to a manuscript or book, the first serious offer, generally a sum of significant size, represents the minimum amount for which rights to the book will be sold, even though the seller will most likely try to better it by interesting other potential buyers in the property. A floor may also be established by a seller as the absolute minimum price for which a manuscript or book will be sold.

flop   In newspaper jargon, to reverse artwork laterally on the newspaper page.

flush   To make all typeset lines even with the column margin. Text that is set flush will not have the opening lines of paragraphs indented.

flyleaf   A blank leaf, or page, at the front or back of a book, not to be confused with END PAPERS.

folded and gathered   Describes the organization of paper for binding. The sheets are fold into signatures and collected (gathered) into the correct order.

foldout (folding plate)   An oversize leaf, often an illustration, that must be folded to fit within the TRIM size of a book or a magazine.

folio   A page number or a paper/parchment page that is numbered on the front but not on the back side. With newspapers, a folio may include the newspaper name and date, as well as the page number, and appears at the top of each page. It also can refer to the total number of pages in a newspaper or magazine, not counting covers. In addition, it can mean a manuscript or book in the largest size (for example, 12 inches × 15 inches) typical for books.

follow-up   A published piece that details developments about a subject of a previously published story or article.

font   The designation of type (to be used for a manuscript or a publication) of one size, style, and design.

foot   The unit of measure in a metrical line of poetry.

footbands   See HEADBANDS.

footline   Name of the publication and date of issue, placed as a small line of type somewhere at the bottom of a page (usually in a lower corner) and coordinated with the folio.

footnotes   Explanatory notes and/or source citations that appear at the bottom of a page. Footnotes are rarely to be found in general interest books, where such information is usually either worked into the text or made available in a backend bibliography.

foreign rights   The right to publish a book, whether in its own language or in translation, outside its country of origin. Foreign rights belong to the author but can be sold by individual country or en masse as world rights. Usually, the U.S. publisher will own the world rights, and the author will be entitled to somewhere between 50 percent and 80 percent of their revenues.

foreword   An introductory section written either by the author or by an expert (or celebrity) in the given field, which provides a strong selling point for the book. (See also INTRODUCTION.)

form   All the pages of a book, either in REPROS or NEGATIVES, that are to be printed on one side of a sheet at one time, arranged in the correct order.

format   Anything relating to the outward appearance, as the typeface, arrangement, makeup, and binding, of a book or other printed piece.

formula story   A familiar, or overused theme treated in an expected plot manner, such as "boy meets girl, boy loses girl, boy regains girl."

foul galley (foul proof)   A GALLEY or PROOF after the corrections indicated on it have been made and new PROOFS pulled.

found poem   Text lifted from a nonpoetic source, such as an advertisement, and presented as a poem.

four-color process   A printing process that reproduces a full range of colors by overprinting red, yellow, blue and black (The true names are magenta, yellow, cyan, and black.)

fourth estate   The traditional term for "the press" which originated in the 18th-century English Parliament.

Frankfurt Book Fair   The largest international publishing exhibition, dating back more than 500 years. The fair takes place every October in Frankfurt, Germany, where thousands of publishers, agents, and writers from all over the world negotiate, network, and buy and sell rights. Similar activities occur in other book fairs held in individual countries throughout the year.

Freedom of Information Act (FOIA)   A U.S. statute that protects the public's right to access public records, except in cases violating the right to privacy, national security, or certain other instances. A related law, the Government in the Sunshine Act, ensures that certain government agencies announce and open their meetings to the public.

free verse   Unmetrical verse (lines not counted for accents, syllables, or other measurements).

freewriting   A technique involving writing as quickly as possible without concern for style or grammar. Freewriting is often used to avoid writer's block, to "warm up" for more formal writing, or to generate ideas for an article, paper, or book.

freight passthrough   A bookseller's freight cost of getting a book from the publisher to the bookseller. It is added to the basic price charged to the bookseller by the publisher.

frequently asked questions   See FAQ.

frontispiece   An illustration appearing before the first pages of a book.

frontlist   A publisher's list of new books for the current or upcoming publishing season. Some publishers include the immediate prior season's books as a part of their frontlist.

front matter   In a book, all the opening text, which can include (in this order): blanks or advertisements, half-title page, list of other works by the author, TITLE PAGE, COPYRIGHT PAGE, list of contributors, DEDICATION PAGE, TABLE OF CONTENTS, TABLE OF ILLUSTRATIONS, FOREWORD, PREFACE, ACKNOWLEDGMENTS or CREDITS, EXPLANATORY NOTES, half-title. Page numbers are usually not printed on front matter pages, but sometimes lowercase Roman numerals or lowercase alphabetic letters are used for some of the front matter pages.

FTP (File Transfer Protocol)   The INTERNET service that transfers files from one computer to another.

fulfillment   The procedures utilized in warehousing, shipping, and collection during which a publisher processes the orders it receives, sends out books, and supplies invoices to its customers.

fulfillment house   A business commissioned to fulfill orders for a publisher. Such services may include warehousing, shipping, and receiving returns, as well as mail-order and DIRECT-MARKETING functions. Used extensively by magazine publishers, such houses may also service book publishers.

full bleed   A photograph or some other art element that runs from edge to edge of the page on which it appears.

full measure   Extending across the entire width of the typeset page, without indention.

galleys   The initial typeset version of a written work before the manuscript is divided into pages for publication. They are sometimes called "galley proofs."

genre   Refers generally to a specific classification of writing, such as the novel, or poem, or play. It also can refer to different categories within these classifications, such as the problem novel or the sonnet.

genre fiction   Refers to types of commercial novels, such as action-adventure (which is further broken down into military, paramilitary, law enforcement, and martial arts), crime novels, horror and supernatural, mysteries and detective fiction, romances (including both historical and contemporary), science fiction and fantasy, thrillers (tales of espionage, and national or international crisis), and westerns. Sometimes called "category fiction."

ghostwriter   A writer who puts into a literary format any written material based on another person's ideas, experiences, or knowledge, for which the latter gets the credit.

Ghostwriters usually get flat fees for their work. Also called "ghosting."

GIF (Graphics Interchange Format)   The programming format for graphic files that are compressed to minimize the time it takes to transfer them over standard phone lines.

gift book   A book designed as a special gift item. Usually small in size with limited illustrations, such an item is frequently displayed for "impulse" buying and is aimed at specific reader markets.

glossary   An alphabetical listing of words or terms used in a particular subject, often with more in-depth explanations than definitions found in most dictionaries.

good night   A newspaper reporter is released from duty for the day when he or she gets a "good night" from the news editor.

Gothic novel   A category or genre of fiction which has as its main character a beautiful young woman, its setting an old mansion or ruined castle, and a handsome hero, as well as a real menace, either natural or supernatural and usually grotesque. Such writing is characterized by gloom and darkness.

.gov   Computer INTERNET extension for government sites.

graf (graph)   Shortened version of the word "paragraph."

graphic novel   Adaptation of a novel into a comic strip, a graphic form, or a heavily illustrated story, usually of 40 pages or more and produced in a soft-cover form.

Graphics Interchange Format   See GIF.

graveyard shift   The same shift as the DOG WATCH: the late shift on a morning newspaper, or the earliest shift on an afternoon newspaper.

greeting card poetry   Poetry that resembles verses found in greeting cards with their sing-song meter and rhyme.

gross margin   In accounting, the difference between revenue from sales and the costs of the goods sold. It is sometimes called gross margin from sales. In publishing, it is the amount of total sales revenue less plant and running (also called unit) costs, expressed as a percentage. In retail bookselling it is the difference between the retailer's cost of product, with discounts, and the retail sales price.

guidelines   Lines drawn or printed in order to orient placement on DUMMIES, or LAYOUTS.

gutter   The area where the left and right pages of an open publication meet in the middle and are bound; also the space between two columns in newspapers or magazines.

haiku   Japanese verse whose essential elements include brevity, immediacy, spontaneity, and imagery, and which often illuminates nature and the changing seasons.

hairline   A .5-point rule line.

hair space   Very narrow space used to separate words, for justifying lines, and letterspacing.

half-title   The title of the book, standing alone on the page. When used in a book it immediately precedes the text or the front matter, and may be in both places. (Sometimes called "bastard title.")

halftone Reproduction of a continuous tone illustration (such as a photograph) with the image formed by dots produced by a camera lens crossline or contact screen.

handle A short description of a book designed to evoke interest in it.

handout A press release; prepared material given to news people in the hope that it will be printed without change or that it will be helpful in preparing news stories; also hard news (important news) as straight news reporting without interpretation or background material.

hanging indentation Type set with the first line of the paragraph flush left, and the lines following it indented.

hard-boiled detective novel A type of mystery novel that features a private detective ("private eye") or police detective as the protagonist usually becoming involved in a murder. The emphasis is on the details of the crime.

hard copy The printed copy of material written with a computer.

hardcover Books bound in thick, sturdy, relatively stiff binding boards and a cover composed (usually) of a cloth spine and finished binding paper. Hardcover books are usually, but not always, wrapped in a DUST JACKET. (See also BINDING.)

hard science fiction Science fiction writing that emphasizes science and technology over fantasy.

hardware The mechanically integrated parts of a computer that are not software, such as circuit boards, transistors, and all other machine parts that are the actual computer.

head (hed) See HEADLINE.

headbands Thin strips of cloth (frequently colored or patterned) that decorate the top of a book's spine where the SIGNATURES are held together. The headbands cover the glue or other binding materials and help to offer some protection against accumulation of dust and constant handling. Such bands, placed at the bottom of the spine, are known as footbands.

header See RUNNING HEAD.

heading (head) A word or words identifying specific divisions, paragraphs, or sections within the text, and differentiated in some way (type face, type size or style) from the rest of the text.

headline Display type placed over a news story, acting as the main title of the story and summarizing it for the reader; commonly thought of as the largest line of type across the top of the newspaper, calling attention to the most important story of that edition. Sometimes called the "head" or "hed."

head margin The blank area from the top edge of the page to the topmost printed element of the type page.

head shot A photograph of someone that includes the head and shoulders only. Frequently used to publicize an author. Sometimes called a MUG SHOT.

high fantasy A type of fantasy writing, with a medieval setting, that emphasizes the chivalry of its protagonists and their quest.

high-lo Material written for inexperienced readers, generally adults, who have a high level of interest, but a low ability to read.

historical fiction Works in which all or some of the characters are fictional, but the setting and other details are rooted in actual history.

hold A "hold for release" instruction to hold a news story until the news editor (on a newspaper or a magazine) releases it for publication.

home page The first page of an INTERNET-based document or Web site.

homophones Words that sound like each other but are spelled differently, such as principal" and "principle," or "stationary" and "stationery."

honorarium A modest, token payment, sometimes money and sometimes a byline in the publication, paid to an author by a publication in gratitude for the written submission.

hook A technique used at the beginning of a written work (usually a magazine or newspaper article) to grab the reader's interest. A hook can be an author's special point of view as expressed in his work, and often summarized in a catchy or provocative phrase intended to attract interest. Hooks have become more prevalent because of the tremendous competition for a reader's attention today.

horror A genre of writing that stresses fear, death, and other aspects of the macabre and fantastic.

how-to Books or magazine articles that offer a blend of information and advice in describing how something is done or made. Subjects range broadly from hobbies to psychology and science. See also SELF-HELP.

HTK Stands for Head(line) to come. This means that the news story has been edited and the headline for it will come later.

HTML (Hypertext Markup Language) The standard computer language for documents on the Web.

HTTP (Hypertext Transfer Protocol) A computer protocol to prepare Web pages for display when the user clicks on a hyperlink.

human interest Indicates an emotional appeal in a news story. A "human interest" story, as compared with a "straight news" story, bases its appeal more on the unusual than on consequence.

hyperbole An extreme exaggeration, usually intentional.

hypertext Words, or a group of words, in an electronic document, that are linked to other related material (including text, images, and sounds) in other electronic documents. Also called "hyperlink."

hypertext books Productions (available on computer diskettes or CDs) are books that incorporate documents, graphics, sounds, and even blank slates upon which readers can compose their own variations on the authored components in the rest of the book. They are conceived to take advantage of the computer's capacities and the readers' and writers' desires to seek out new twists in the usual narrative elements of fiction. They incorporate tradition elements of story telling with a nonlinear plot line, which allows the reader to determine the direction of the story by opting for one of many author-supplied plot links.

hypertext jump   See JUMP.

Hypertext Markup Language   See HTML.

Hypertext Transfer Protocol   See HTTP.

iamb   In poetry, a FOOT consisting of an unstressed syllable followed by a stress.

iambic pentameter   Consists of five iambic feet per line of poetry.

IBBY   International Board on Books for Young People.

idiom   A common expression that usually means something different than its literal interpretation, such as "kick the bucket."

ids   See INDEPENDENT DISTRIBUTOR.

illustrations   Photographs, engravings, or artwork usually paid for separately from the manuscript advance (and royalties). Illustrations may also include charts or graphs, usually considered to be part of the manuscript text.

imagist poetry   Short, free-verse lines that present images without comment or explanation.

imposition   The arrangement of pages of type and/or illustrations in a form that organizes the page in proper order when the sheet is folded after printing.

imprint   Publisher's name for a specific line (or type) of books. An imprint may be composed of one or two series of books, or a full-fledged, diversified list. Imprints may enjoy certain types of autonomy from the parent publisher, in that they may have their own editorial departments and their own procedures for acquisition of titles. An imprint may publish only a certain type of book (such as travel books), or have its own personal touch (such as a literary tone exemplified by its editor). Some imprints may overlap with other imprints or with the publisher's core booklist, but an imprint can offer a distinctive personalized editorial approach, while taking advantage of the larger company's production, marketing, sales, and advertising resources.

indention   The amount by which a line of the text is less than the full measure of other lines. Paragraph indention is space left blank at the left in the first line of the paragraph.

independent distributor   A WHOLESALER who specializes in the distribution of magazines and paperback publications to newsstands, supermarkets, and outlets other than traditional bookstores. Frequently know as Ids, these wholesalers are generally local or regional in their coverage of markets.

index   An alphabetical directory of systematic entries at the end of the book that references names, subjects, and, in some cases, concepts, discussed in the book along with the pages on which such mentions can be found. The searchable order of the index (whether it be alphabetical, chronological, or numerical) is usually different from that of the items mentioned, or concepts developed, in the book itself. Also, for newspapers, the term "index" refers to the table of contents of the newspaper, usually found on page one.

index entry   A unit of the index consisting of a heading (and qualifying expression, if any) with at least one reference to the location of the item in the text (or else with a *see* reference), together with any subheadings and their relevant references. The presence of subheadings, when references are numerous enough for a systematic grouping of them, constitutes a COMPLEX ENTRY.

indirect quotation   A quotation in which a writer reports the substance of someone's words but not the exact words the person used. In this case, quotation marks are not used.

inferior letters or NUMERALS   Letters or numerals smaller than the body type, printed below the alignment of normal letters. Also called "subscripts."

informational notes   RESEARCH notes that record facts, concepts, details, interpretations, and quotations from sources.

.ini   Computer filename extension for initial settings files.

insert   A flyer (usually advertising) or magazine that is inserted into the folded newspaper after it has been printed.

inset   A sheet or folded section of printed page or pages set within another in binding; a small illustration, such as a map, set in the text.

inside   A newspaper term referring to the placement of a news story not on the front page, as in "we'll run this story inside."

inside margin   The blank area between the text and the binding edge of a page.

interactive fiction   Fiction in book or computer software format in which the reader decides the path the story will take, choosing from various alternatives at the end of each chapter or section within a chapter. The choice determines the structure of the tale. Such fiction always has multiple plots and conclusions.

international copyright   Rights secured for countries that are members of the INTERNATIONAL COPYRIGHT CONVENTION and that respect the authority of the international copyright symbol, ©.

International Copyright Convention   Refers to countries that are signatories to the various international copyright treaties. As some treaties are contingent upon certain conditions being met at the time of publication of written work, authors should inquire into the particular country's copyright laws before publication of their work.

international reply coupon (IRC)   This is sold at the post office to enclose with text or artwork sent to a recipient outside of the writer's (or artist's) own country to cover postage costs when replying or returning work. It should be included with any correspondence or submissions to foreign publications or publishers. It allows the editor to reply by mail without postal costs.

Internet   A worldwide network of computer networks that allows for access electronically to a wide assortment of resources (including E-MAIL, CHAT ROOMS, NEWS GROUPS, and the WORLD WIDE WEB).

Internet rights   Concerns the rights to post an author's work on a Web site. In some cases, these rights may also contain permission to distribute or allow the distribution of the author's work further via the INTERNET. See also ELECTRONIC RIGHTS.

Internet Service Provider   See ISP.

interpolation   The introduction of the author's words, marked by brackets, into direct quotations from someone else.

introduction   Refers to the preliminary remarks pertaining to a written piece. Like a FOREWORD, an introduction can be written by the author or by an appropriate authority (or celebrity) on the subject. If a book has both a FORE-WORD and an introduction, the FOREWORD usually is written by someone other than the author, and the introduction will be closely tied to the subject of the text and will be written by the text's author.

invasion of privacy   A legal term that describes photographing or writing about a nonpublic figure without their permission.

inverted pyramid   This is the standard news story structure for newspapers and magazines, in which facts are arranged in descending order of importance.

IRA   International Reading Association.

IRC   See INTERNATIONAL REPLY COUPON.

ISBN (International Standard Book Number)   An international standard for exclusive identification of books. The ISBN identifies one title, or edition of a title, from one specific publisher, and is unique to that title or edition. It is frequently used for ordering and cataloging books and appears on all DUST JACKETS, on the back cover of the book, and on the COPYRIGHT page.

ISP (Internet Service Provider)   A business that provide connectivity to e-mail and the INTERNET, such as AOL, AT&T, or SBC.

ISSN (International Standard Serial Number)   An eight-digit cataloging and order number that identifies all U.S. and foreign-published PERIODICALS.

issue   In newspaper parlance this refers to all the copies that a newspaper publishes in one day.

italic   The style of letters that slope to the right, in distinction to upright, or roman, letters. Used to give words emphasis and also for some title citations.

jargon   Words or expressions developed for use by one group determined not to let people outside the group

readily understand what is being said. One purpose of jargon is to confuse and hide the true meaning of what is being said, and another purpose is to provide a shorthand expression for ease of use by the group.

jobbers   Large-volume buyers of hardcover and softcover trade titles for resale to retail bookstores and libraries. Jobbers are distinct from WHOLESALERS in the inventory they carry and the services they offer, but this distinction has become increasingly blurred.

job lot   Often a combination of published book titles forming a singular group, which are offered by a publisher or WHOLESALER at special low prices to close out or cut down stock.

joint   The hinge where the sides of a CASEBOUND book are attached to the back.

JPEG (Joint Photographic Experts Group)   A graphics file format for displaying graphics on the Web. It has a higher level of compression than GIF but results in a lower quality.

jump   A cross-reference that lets computer users navigate from one topic to another. It should appear as a dotted line underneath the text. Also known as "Hypertext Jump" or "Link"; also, in journalistic jargon, that part of a news story that is continued onto another page, usually referred to as a BREAK. The reader gets directions to the page where the story continues in a JUMPLINE.

jumpline   The continuation instructions for a story in a newspaper or magazine that is jumped to another page, for example, "Continued on page 5," or "Continued from page 1."

justification   The adjustment of the spacing within lines of type to fit the lines to a specific measure on the type page.

justify   Type that is aligned evenly on the left and the right. Computers generally automatically add spaces between words or individual letters of type so that lines of a column are flush left and flush right

juveniles   See CHILDREN'S BOOKS.

kerning   In typesetting, adjusting the space between two characters to avoid excessive separation between them due to the particular shape of one of them (such as *T* in *To*).

keyboarding   The term for typing in the computer age.

keyline   Identification of the positions of illustrations and copy for printing company personnel.

keyword in a computer program   Describes a search topic. For example: if the search topics are named *Coke* and *Pepsi*, the topic as keyed by a searcher on the computer may not include the word *soda*. Using a keyword prescription, users will be able to retrieve any hits on the words *Coke* and *Pepsi* when they type the keyword *soda*.

kicker   The first sentence or first few words of a (newspaper's or magazine's) lead into a story, often set in a font size larger than the body text.

kill   In journalistic parlance this term means to eliminate all or part of a news story.

kill fee   Fee paid for a completed article that was subsequently not published, usually a percentage of the original fee agreed upon if the article had been published.

LAN (local area network)   A computer network that covers local distances and uses specialized computers to link smaller networks together.

language poetry   Attempts to detach words from their traditional meanings to produce something new and unprecedented.

launch meeting   The first presentation by an editor of forthcoming titles to the marketing and sales staff of the publishing company. This first step in defining the publisher's seasonal list, these meetings allow editorial, marketing, production, and sales staffs to discuss the marketing and production requirements of each upcoming title. Based on this discussion, the marketing director will project a first printing and, later, will develop the marketing plan through discussion with individual departments.

layout   The overall design of a book's pages, including the arrangement of charts, diagrams, illustrations or photographs, other graphic material, page numbers and font/typeface usage, text and headlines for printed material. For newspapers and magazines, the layout is a sketch or drawing that indicates the arrangements of pictures and copy on a printed page, and is used synonymously with the term DUMMY. It also can mean a combination of stories, pictures, and other graphic elements about a single subject.

lc   See LOWERCASE.

lead (pronounced "led")   The space between lines of type. In newspapers and magazines this space is often altered so that stories form perfect boxes. Also called "leading."

lead (pronounced "leed")   The opening section, or first few sentences, of a written work—whether an advertisement, book proposal, news or publicity release, novel or nonfiction work, query letter, or sales tip sheet. The lead is designed to immediately attract the attention of the agent, consumer, editor, or reader. Sometimes lead (meaning the start of a story) is spelled *lede* to avoid confusion with its other meanings in journalism. In journalistic terms, *lead* can also mean a tip that may lead to a news story.

leaders   Periods or dashes used in tables of contents, programs, tables, and other graphics to lead the reader's eye across what would otherwise be open space.

lead time   The time between the receipt of a manuscript and its actual publication.

lead title(s)   The one (or more) major book(s) on a publisher's seasonal list, and usually given the publisher's maximum promotional push.

leg   A column of type. A two-column headline (in newspapers or magazines) will likely have two legs of type under it.

legend   The explanatory or descriptive material accompanying an illustration, chart, table, or other graphic element, sometimes used interchangeably with the term *caption;* also, a key to the symbols on a chart or map. See also CAPTION.

leg man   A reporter who gathers news that he or she telephones to a REWRITE person, instead of coming to the office to write the story.

letter-by-letter alphabetizing   An alphabetizing method (in indexes and other listings) that treats the group (phrase) of two or more words up to the first parenthesis or comma (ignoring all other punctuation marks or word spaces between them) as single entities.

letterhead   Business stationery and envelopes imprinted with the company's (or author's) name, address, and LOGO.

letterpress   A form of printing that uses a raised surface, such as type. The preset type is inked, and then impressed directly onto the paper surface by the printing device. Unlike OFFSET printing, only a limited number of impressions can be made, as the surface of the type can wear down. Such printing is now used primarily for limited-run books generally and for those which need careful attention, such as fine art limited print runs.

letter to the editor   A letter in which a reader expresses his or her views in the newspaper (or magazine); usually printed on the editorial page or the page opposite the editorial page.

libel   A false and malicious accusation or any published statement or representation that causes a person public embarrassment, ridicule, loss of income, or damage to the individual's reputation. Under litigation, the falseness of the statements or representations, as well as their malicious intent, has to be proved for there to be libel. In addition, financial damages to the parties involved must have occurred as a result of the release of the material in question. This is in contrast to slander, which is defamation through the spoken word only.

library   In journalism this term refers to the newspaper's collection of clippings, files, books, and other archived material.

library discounts   Special discounts offered by publishers to library purchasers. See also DISCOUNT (PUBLISHING).

Library of Congress (LOC)   The largest library in the world is in Washington, D.C. It will provide to a writer, as a part of its many services, a list of up-to-date sources and bibliographies in all fields. For details, write to the Library of Congress, Central Services Division, Washington, DC 20540.

Library of Congress Catalog Card Number   An identifying number issued by the LIBRARY OF CONGRESS to books it has accepted into its collection. These books, when published and submitted by the publisher, are announced by the library to the library industry, which often uses the Library of Congress numbers for their own ordering and cataloging purposes.

limerick A five-line stanza rhyme, often bawdy or scatological.

linage The amount of advertising printed in a newspaper or magazine over a specified period of time.

line Basic compositional unit of a poem, measured in feet if metrical.

line-by-line format An indexing format where all subheadings are arranged in columnar form under the heading.

line copy Copy that can be reproduced without using a screen, such as a pen-and-ink drawing.

line cut A drawing or artwork that is in black and white without shadows or shades of gray, the opposite of a HALFTONE.

line drawing Illustration done with pencil or ink, using no wash or other shading.

line space Four blank lines in a double-spaced manuscript, sometimes containing repetitive special characters (that is, DINGBATS), for lines of space on a printed page, used within chapters to indicate a break of time, or a shift in emphasis or location, or to separate elements for clarity.

line wrap In indexing this is an index line that continues beyond one typeset line onto a second or third. Also called a "turnover line."

link An online document that "jumps" a computer user from one piece of information to another. Also, a picture, icon, or piece of text on the computer screen, usually shown in blue, that, when clicked on, takes the user to another part of the Web page being viewed, or to another Web site altogether. See also JUMP.

linked poetry Poetry written through the collaboration of two or more poets creating a single poetic work.

list All the titles a publisher has available for sale, including the entire BACKLIST, the new books for the current season (the FRONTLIST), and forthcoming books. A publisher's spring list usually is the roster of books scheduled for release during the spring season. Other seasonal lists are usually utilized by hardcover and trade paperback publishers (or departments of publishers), and may be issued twice a year (spring and fall) or three times a year (spring, fall, and winter).

list price The price of a publication to the retail consumer as suggested by the publisher; it is sometimes printed on the jacket or cover. Also known as retail price.

list royalty A royalty payment based on a percentage of a book's list (or retail) price.

list segmentation A means of targeting a mailing list to a selected segment of a larger mailing list, from which one or more common characteristics can be isolated, such as buyers of books in a certain subject area or above a certain price, or buyers from a given geographic region or from a certain year or from a particular income level. (Sometimes called LIST SELECTION.)

list selection A selected part of a mailing list that may be rented separately from the whole list. See LIST SEGMENTATION.

literals Alphabetic characters. In proofreading, to "read for literals" is to read for wrong fonts, defective letters, transpositions, spelling, and the like.

literary agent See AGENT.

literary fiction A general category of fiction that uses a more than usually sophisticated technique in its writing and is driven as much, or more, by the evolution of character than action in the plot.

Literary Market Place (LMP) An annual directory of the publishing industry that contains a comprehensive list of publishers in both alphabetical and category formats, along with their addresses, phone numbers, appropriate personnel, and the types of books they publish. Also included are various listings allied to the publishing industry, such as editorial and distribution services, literary agencies, and writers' conferences and competitions. *LMP* is published by Information Today, Inc., and is available in most public libraries and online, by subscription, at http://www.literarymarketplace.com.

little magazine Publications with limited circulation, usually dealing with literary or political matters.

local area network See LAN.

localize In newspaper jargon, this means to emphasize the local angle in an out-of-town news story.

locator In an index, this is the number of the page, folio, section, or paragraph (or other specific indication) where the item or subject being indexed occurs within the text. It is also called a "reference."

logo Shortened form of "logotype," this is an identifier of a company or a product.

long poem A poem that exceeds the length and scope of the short LYRIC or NARRATIVE poem. It is usually defined as more than two pages or 100 lines.

loose blues Blueprints of separate elements of the text, such as illustrations, before makeup.

lowercase (lc) An editorial copy mark to put one or more characters into lowercase, a smaller letter in contrast to UPPERCASE capital letters.

lyric poetry Poetry that expresses personal emotion, with feelings predominating over narrative or drama.

mailing-list broker An independent agent who represents either the buyer or the seller in supplying mailing lists (or e-mail lists or telemarketing lists) to direct-marketing advertisers (such as marketing departments of publishing firms).

mailing-list cleaning Removing from a mailing list those names and addresses that have ceased to be of value.

mainbar The term *mainbar* simply means the main news story (for newspapers and magazines), distinguished from secondary sidebar stories. It's somewhat like calling a city's main library the main branch to differentiate it from its various secondary (local) branches.

main heading   In indexing, this is a descriptor sometimes used for a heading to distinguish it from a subheading.

mainstream fiction   Fiction that goes beyond popular genres, such as mystery, romance, and science fiction but that still appeals to a general readership. Using conventional means, this kind of fiction concerns people and their conflicts and conveys a greater depth (and breadth) of characterization, background, and theme than other popular, but more narrowly focused, types of novels.

makeover   The rearrangement of news stories on a newspaper page to provide for new copy, or to change the position (and importance) of stories.

makeup   The arrangement of composed type into pages, and the insertion of FOLIOS, RUNNING HEADS, CUTS, and all the other elements.

manuscript (MS)   An author's unpublished copy of a work, usually typewritten (now more likely produced by word processing on a computer) or in electronic form. The manuscript becomes the basis for typesetting of the published book. The abbreviation for manuscripts (pl.) is "MSS."

margins   The blank areas that border the printed type page.

marketing plan   Prepared for each title on a publisher's seasonal list, this plan itemizes the projected advertising, promotion, publicity, and sales activities and their associated costs for each entry. Included in the individual marketing plan are subsidiary rights and special sales transactions. Marketing plans are generally prepared after LAUNCH (concept) MEETINGS for forthcoming titles and are subject to constant revision before and after sales conferences.

mark up   A general publishing term that means to put composition or editing instructions on copy or layouts.

mask   In color separation photography, an intermediate photographic negative or positive used in color correction. In OFFSET-LITHOGRAPHY, opaque material used to protect open or selected areas of a printing plate during exposure.

mass market   Nonspecialized books of wide appeal directed toward a large audience and often sold in many outlets other than bookstores, such as drugstores and supermarkets.

mass market paperback   A paperbound book distributed primarily through traditional magazine channels, including newsstands, supermarkets, variety and drugstores, and other mass markets. They are often also marketed to general bookstores, college stores, and department stores and may be either an original publication that has never appeared in any other format or a reprint of a previously published hardcover or trade paperback edition now marketed at a significantly lower price.

master   A plate for a duplicating machine.

master proof   See PROOFS.

masthead   A listing of the names and titles of members of a publication in hierarchical order. This order is impor-tant in that the same job title may denote widely different duties and status at different publications. For newspapers, it is the statement of ownership, place of publication, executive personnel and other information about the newspaper, generally placed on the editorial page. It can also mean the name of the newspaper that appears on page one, and the box of names, phone numbers, and addresses relevant to the publications that may appear in the first few pages of the newspaper.

maxim   A succinct formulation of a fundamental principle, general truth, or rule of conduct.

measure   The width of a full line of type on a type page.

mechanical binding   A mechanical device, usually plastic or metal, such as a comb or a ring, that holds pages together. See also BINDING.

mechanicals   Paste-ups (sheets of stiff paper) on which artwork and type proofs have been pasted to make a printing plate.

memoir   Narrative recounting the writer's personal or family history. In works of fiction, the work may be in the form of a memoir chronicled by the fictional narrator.

metaphor   A figure of speech that occurs when words or phrases are brought together that do not ordinarily belong together, yet by their very proximity convey a fresh meaning. In other words, one thing is spoken of as if it were another. It is a comparison with the use of "as" or "like," unlike a SIMILE. See also MIXED METAPHOR.

meter   The rhythmic measure of a line of poetry.

middle reader   The general classification of books written for readers of approximately ages nine to 11. Also called "middle grade" or "mid-grade."

midlist books   Titles on a publisher's list that are thought not to be big sellers, and are expected to have middling sales. These books are mainstream items, not genre, literary, or scholarly books, and are usually written by unknown authors. Such books generally generate only low-end advances to their authors and tend to be harder to find in bookstores due to their short shelf life.

mixed metaphor   A combination of two METAPHORS that do not match up or that present contradictory images.

modem   An electronic device allowing data to be transmitted from one computer to another via telephone lines.

modernist poetry   Work of the early 20th-century literary movement that attempted to break with the past, rejecting literary traditions, diction, and form in order to encourage innovation and reinvention.

monograph   A detailed and well-documented scholarly study (an article, paper, or book) devoted to a single subject.

montage   A photograph in which several pieces of copy (or photographs) have been placed together to form a single unit.

more   In journalism this word placed at the bottom of a page of copy is meant to indicate that the story does not end there and more pages are coming.

morgue Former name for the newspaper library; and sometimes still used to indicate a separate archive of the older newspapers clippings, cuts, and pictures.

motto A maxim that expresses the aims, character, or guiding principles of a person, a group, or an institution.

movie tie-in See NOVELIZATION.

MS See MANUSCRIPT.

mug shot A small photo of someone. Also called a HEAD SHOT.

multimedia Computer software that integrates such features as text, sound, photographic images, animation, and video. While the CD computer disc is the usual medium for these works, technological innovation is the byword of the electronic publishing industry with new formats always expanding the creative and market potential of this medium.

multiple contract A book contract that includes a provisional agreement by the publisher to produce for the author any future book or books. (See also OPTION CLAUSE/RIGHT OF FIRST REFUSAL.)

multiple-entry journalism See CHUNKS.

multiple submissions The sending of a manuscript, article, poem, story, or other finished written product simultaneously to several publications or publishers at the same time. Once frowned upon, this practice is becoming more frequent. Nonetheless, some publishers refuse even to consider such submissions. Also known as simultaneous submissions and parallel submissions.

NA (North American) The right to publish a piece of work in the North American marketplace, leaving the author free to market the work elsewhere in the world. Term sometimes appears as "1st NA."

NACS See NATIONAL ASSOCIATION of COLLEGE STORES.

nameplate See FLAG.

NANA The North American Newspaper Alliance, a news syndicate.

narration The account of events in the plot of a story as related by the speaker or the voice of the author.

narrative nonfiction A narrative exposition of actual events.

narrative poetry Poetry that tells a story.

narrator The person who tells the story, either someone involved in the action or the voice of the writer.

National Association of College Stores (NACS) This professional organization began in 1922 under the name College Bookstore Association but adopted its present name to indicate the breadth of the merchandise carried by stores catering to college communities.

NCTE National Council of Teachers of English.

negative An image that is opposite the way it will appear in the newspaper or magazine. Dark areas appear light and light areas appear dark.

neologism A word, which may have been invented, that has entered into general use very recently, sometimes not yet having been put into any dictionaries.

.net An INTERNET extension for general sites.

net price What a WHOLESALER or bookseller pays for a product after all discounts and allowances have been made.

net pricing A methodology of determining a wholesale price of a book without referring to its suggested RETAIL PRICE. Under net pricing in the book industry, the publisher sets the price of a book to the bookseller or wholesaler, and each bookselling and wholesaling operation establishes its own resale price to the consumer, thereby determining its own profit margin. In these instances no cover price is preprinted on the book or jacket, and the retail price can fluctuate from dealer to dealer.

net receipts The amount of money a publisher actually receives for sales of a book, which is the retail price minus any bookseller's discount (or any other kind of discount). The number of copies returned is factored in, lowering further the net amount received per book. Many ROYALTIES to the author are figured on these lower amounts rather than on the retail price of the book.

net royalty ROYALTY payment on the sale of the book based on the amount of money the book publisher receives after booksellers' discounts, any special sales, and returns.

net sales The number of books sold minus those returned by DISTRIBUTORS.

network Computers linked electronically to each other to share information and resources.

New Age A "fringe" subject that has become more widely accepted. Examples are UFOs and occult phenomena. While the term may include such subjects as health, psychology, or religion, the emphasis is on the mystical, other-worldly, or spiritual, and may be presented from an alternative or multicultural perspective.

newbie In the world of computers, this term designates someone who is new to using the INTERNET.

newsbreak A late-breaking story, usually brief, added to the front page of a newspaper at press time, or a new item in a magazine of special importance for its readership.

news hole For newspapers and magazines, the amount of space left for news after advertisements have been arranged on the page.

news peg Any topical news item that gives immediacy and relevance to the written story.

newsprint (paper) Inexpensive absorbent pulp wood paper (sometimes also made from recycled paper) often used in newspapers and tabloids.

news services News-gathering agencies, such as Associated Press, or United Press International, that distribute news to subscribing newspapers.

niche marketing Marketing and promoting a book to a specific group of buyers, such as people in a certain geographical region, or people with a specific hobby or interest. Books published for a niche market sometimes are sold nationally, but usually are sold through specialized retail outlets.

noir   A style of mystery fiction that involves hard-boiled detectives and bleak settings.

nom de plume   A French term (literally, "pen name") for a pseudonym.

non sequitur   An inference or conclusion that seems disconnected from the information preceding it.

nostalgia   A literary genre of recollection, recalling fondly past events, or people, products, or subjects of the past. The style of writing will be more or less sentimental, depending upon the requirements of the publication.

novelization   A novel created from the script of a TV show or movie, or a screenplay of a popular film. Often the novel is called a movie "tie-in" and published in paperback.

novella   A short novel, or a long short story, of typically 7,000 to 15,000 words. Also known as a "novelette."

#10 envelope   A 4 × 9¹/₂-inch envelope, used by writers for queries and other business letters.

nutgraph   A paragraph in a story that contains key details of the entire story. Some newspapers have rules about how close this paragraph should be to the top of the story. Also, a list of information in paragraph form using some graphical device (such as bullets or flags) to separate their elements from each other and the section visually from the rest of the text. See also CHUNKING.

obit (obituary)   The biography of a dead person appearing in newspapers and some magazines. Sometimes "canned obits" are kept on file in the newspaper's LIBRARY to be used at the time of a prominent person's death.

oblique dialog   In fiction, an indirect reply not in line with the preceding speech; also not directly responsive.

odd pages   The right-hand pages of a book, numbered 1, 3, 5, and so on. They are often called "recto" pages.

ode   A songlike, or lyric, poem, which can be passionate, rhapsodic, and mystical all at the same time; also a formal address to a person on a public or state occasion.

offcut   A portion of the printed sheet cut off and folded separately; a part cut off a sheet of paper to scale it to press size.

offprint   Copy of a story taken from a magazine before it is bound in the issue of that magazine.

offset (offset lithography)   A printing process that involves the transfer of wet ink from a (usually photosensitized) printing plate onto an intermediate surface (usually a rubber-coated cylinder called a "blanket") and then from the "blanket" onto the paper. In most commercial printing enterprises, this method of printing has replaced the LETTERPRESS methodology, where printing is done by direct impression of inked type onto paper.

off the record   In journalism, this is information not for publication, or at least not to be attributed to a source if used as background for a news story.

omniscient   Describes the point of view in which the author roams everywhere, including into the minds of all the characters.

on-demand book/on-demand printing   A book manufactured as a single copy at the time a customer wants to buy it. With the widespread expansion of the World Wide Web and the INTERNET, the technology for on-demand printing has come of age, as both companies and individuals may now sell books one at a time easily, as well as produce them relatively inexpensively using a computer and laser imaging technology.

one-time rights   These are nonexclusive rights, that is, rights that can be licensed to more than one market, purchased by a PERIODICAL to publish the work once. The author has a right to sell the work to other publications simultaneously (that is why these are also known as SIMULTANEOUS RIGHTS). See also MULTIPLE SUBMISSIONS.

online   Being connected to the INTERNET.

online document   A document is an organized body of information with words and, sometimes, graphics. Online is simply the delivery medium for the document: a computer, instead of paper.

on spec(ulation)   An editor indicates an interest in a proposed idea (for an article or a book) and agrees to consider the finished piece for publication, but with no guarantees that the finished work will be accepted for publication.

Op-Ed (oped)   The page opposite the editorial page of a newspaper. It may contain columns and guest pieces that articulate a personal viewpoint or opinion on current newsworthy items, and EDITORIAL CARTOONS.

opener   In magazine layouts, editors and art directors attempt to design compelling opening pages that clearly identify the piece's topic and emotional content and simultaneously draw the reader in. As the opening paragraph of a manuscript or article, the opener is frequently considered the story's most important 100 to 200 words. It should display zing and flair that mark the writing as fresh and strong and, at the same time, adequately set up what is to follow in the piece.

optical center   About one-eighth of the page length above the actual center of the page. A line that is to appear to be in the center of a page should be in this position.

option clause/right of first refusal   The clause in a book contract that stipulates that the publisher will have the exclusive right to consider and make an offer on the author's next book. However, the publisher is not obligated to publish the book, and in most variations of the clause the author may, under certain circumstances, decide to publish this next work elsewhere. (See also MULTIPLE CONTRACT.)

.org   INTERNET extension for nonprofit sites.

outline   A summary of a book's contents in five to 15 double-spaced pages. It may have chapter headings with descriptive sentences to show the scope of the book. An article summary will contain its subheads with one or two sentences for each entry. For a SCREENPLAY or a TELEPLAY, the outline is a scene-by-scene narrative of the story (10–15 pages for a half-hour teleplay; 15–25 pages for a one-hour teleplay; 25–40 pages for a 90-minute teleplay; 40–60 pages for a two-hour feature film or teleplay), and is called a TREATMENT.

out-of-print books   Refers to books no longer available from their original publisher; rights for such books usually revert to the author.

overline   In journalism this is a caption printed above a photograph.

overrun   In printing, copies printed in excess of the specified quantity required. Printing agreements with publishers usually specify allowable overruns.

over-the-transom   The submission for potential publication of unsolicited material by a freelance writer. (The term derives from when mail was commonly delivered through the open window above an office door.)

oxymoron   A combination of words that contradict each other. For example, "The lively corpse fell out of the closet."

package sale   When an editor buys in one payment a manuscript and photos as a "package." Sometimes known as a "package deal."

pad   To make a written piece longer, usually with nonessential filler, or more words than really are necessary.

page makeup   In STRIPPING, the assembly of all elements to make up a page. In PHOTOTYPESETTING, the electronic assembly of a page on a video display terminal and on the phototypesetter.

page one   In journalism this refers to either the first page of the newspaper or, as an adjective, to important news, as in "page one news."

page proof   See PASTE-UP and PROOFS.

page rate   When magazines pay for publishable material at a fixed rate per published page, rather than per word.

paginate   The act of making a page on a computer screen.

paperback original   A work of either fiction or nonfiction published in paperback format without having been available previously as a hardback publication, or being published simultaneously with a hardcover edition. It may be a mass market paperback or a trade/quality paperback.

paperback rights   The rights to publish a book in a MASS MARKET or TRADE paperback format, as opposed to hardcover format. Such a book may be a PAPERBACK ORIGINAL or a paperback reprint. Rights to mass market and trade paperback editions are usually negotiated separately, but they can be combined together in one deal as arranged for a writer by an AGENT with a publisher.

paper master   A paper printing plate used on an offset-duplicator. The image is made by hand drawing, typewriter, computer input, or electrophotography.

paper weight and thickness   Paper thickness is often described in terms of pounds, such as 80 lb. or 60 lb. paper. The weight is determined by figuring how many pounds in a ream of a particular paper (a ream is 500 sheets). However, this figure is based on a standard sheet size, and standard sheet sizes can vary depending on the type of paper used. This information is helpful when comparing papers of the same type—for example, 80 lb. versus 60 lb. book paper. Since the size of the paper is the same it would follow that 80 lb. paper is the thicker, heavier paper. Some paper, especially COVER STOCK, is described by the actual thickness of the paper. This is expressed in a system of points. Typical paper thicknesses range from 8 points to 14 points thick.

parallel submission   See MULTIPLE SUBMISSIONS.

paraphrase   A rewording for the purpose of clarification; to express the same message in a different way with different words. Note that paraphrases never used quotation marks.

parody   The conscious imitation of a work or a style of writing or a musical style/type, usually intended to ridicule or make fun of that work or style.

partial remaindering   Selling off at sale or remainder prices an excess portion of a publisher's unsold stock of a book, rather than the entire stock. Thus, some part of the stock remains in print to be sold at the publisher's list price. See also REMAINDERS.

part title   The number or title of a division of a book, more important than a chapter title, and often printed alone on a separate page preceding the division to which it refers.

paste-up   A page's textual elements assembled along with its graphical elements. Also known as a PAGE PROOF.

patent insides   In journalism the name given to "ready-print" inside pages bought from syndicates by smaller papers. Also called BOILERPLATE.

payment on acceptance   Payment to the author when the manuscript has been submitted and accepted for publication.

payment on publication   Payment to the author when the manuscript is actually published.

PDAs (Personal Digital Assistants or Personal Device Applications)   Handheld, wireless computers such as palm units.

PE   See PRINTER'S ERRORS.

penalty copy   Copy that is difficult to compose because it is faint, foreign, heavily corrected, or otherwise difficult to read, and for which the typesetter charges an additional percentage above the regular typesetting rate.

pen name   The use of a name other than the writer's legal name for written work that the writer wishes to remain anonymous or wishes to attach to a different genre of work that he or she publishes. Also called a "pseudonym."

perfect binding   Used for paperback books and heavier magazines, perfect binding involves gathering the

SIGNATURES (groups of pages) into a stack, trimming off the folds so the edge lies flat and gluing the cover to that edge (a central spine).

perfector press   A press that prints on both sides of a sheet of paper in one pass through the press.

periodical   A magazine or journal published at regular intervals.

permissions   The right to use part of another individual's copyrighted material in a forthcoming work. The job of obtaining permissions is usually the author's, including any copyright fees that must be paid. Usually the publisher supplies the author with guidelines for obtaining permission and blank permission request forms.

Personal Device Applications   See PDAS.

Personal Digital Assistants   See PDAS.

photo-composing   In phototypesetting, the assembly of separate elements into an integrated page layout. In platemaking, exposure of multiple images on a plate. Sometimes called "step-and-repeat."

photoengraving   A metal relief plate prepared by etching a photographically produced image on the metal with acid.

photo feature   Feature (such as a magazine article) where the emphasis is on the photographs, not the accompanying written text.

photomechanical   Referring to any platemaking process using photographic negatives or positives exposed onto plates or cylinders covered with photosensitive coatings.

Photoshop   A computer program for photographs. Photos are scanned into the computer, and the image appears on the monitor. The image can then be cropped and the size altered to fit a desired space.

phototext   Text composed or set onto film or paper by means of keyboard input or computer-tape-driven phototypesetting machines.

phrase   A string of words that expresses a thought but does not contain all the elements of a CLAUSE. Phrases tend to be brief, apt, and cogent.

pi   A journalistic word for disarranged type that is hopelessly jumbled.

pica   Printer's unit of measurement used principally in measuring lines of type. One pica equals 12 POINTS, approximately $1/6$ inch (or 0.422 cm). Used especially in measuring the length of print lines.

picture book   A type of book aimed at children from preschool age to eight-year-olds that tells a story using a combination of text and artwork. In some cases, it may contain artwork only.

pigeonhole   See RIVER.

pitch   An idea for a book, movie, story, or other project. Also used as a verb.

pix   An abbreviation for "pictures."

plagiarism   Using without permission the words and expression of ideas of another writer and passing them off as one's own original work.

plant costs   Although the components will vary according to the accounting procedures used from publisher to publisher, these generally are the one-time costs in manufacturing a book, such as those involved in composition of the text, preparation of artwork and illustrations, and the production of plates.

plate   In printing, a plate contains the image of one page and is installed onto the press.

plate proof   A proof of the finished plates, pulled on smooth stock so that imperfections in the type can be detected.

platitude   A trite or banal remark or statement, especially if expressed as if it were original or significant.

play   In journalism, play means the emphasis given a piece of news. A story may be "played down" or "played up."

plot   In a work of fiction, this is the carefully devised series of events through which the characters progress.

POD   See PRINT ON DEMAND.

point   A unit of measurement in which typographical element sizes are designated; approximately $1/72$ of an inch.

police procedural   A type of mystery fiction in which a police detective or a police officer uses standard professional police practices and procedures to solve a crime.

pool   In journalism, it is a certain number of reporters, or one reporter, who represents everyone else. For example, a high-interest court case or a presidential appearance at a public event such as a concert may not have room for all the journalists who want to cover it. So the organizers may restrict coverage to a press pool. Pool coverage is usually shared with other media outlets, such as radio and television.

pork   Material held for later use.

porkchop   For newspapers and magazines, this is a half-column picture. Also called THUMBNAIL.

precede   In journalistic jargon this refers to material to be printed ahead of COPY already set.

pre-date   Refers to a newspaper (or magazine) edition issued before its announced date of publication.

preface   A section in the book's front matter in which the author may discuss the purpose behind the writing or format of the book, the type of RESEARCH upon which it is based, or its genesis and underlying philosophy.

premium   Refers to books sold at a reduced price as part of some special promotion. These cost savings are passed on to the bookseller who, in turn, sells them at a reduced price to the book buyer (as in the case of a series of moderately priced art books or travel books). On the other hand, such books may be produced as part of a broader marketing package. The best example of this is when a business organization acquires a number of books (such as those detailing its own corporate history or a biography of its founder) to use in personnel training and as giveaways to clients. (See also SPECIAL SALES.)

prepress   The process of creating color PROOFS and film that will be used by a print shop to set the publication on paper and bind the pages together. This is when original artwork is scanned digitally and the four-color process is applied. Also includes "ad stripping," or preparing the ad materials on the magazine page along with the text copy.

preprint   A copy of a book or a section of a book or PERIODICAL usually issued in a limited paperbound quantity for some special purpose before publication date (frequently used as a promotion for the book in limited markets).

press agent   See PUBLICIST.

press conference   A meeting called to give information to the news media.

press junket   Usually a "free" trip offered to writers by travel-related companies and their marketing agents. Such businesses likely will expect positive coverage in some publication in return for their largesse.

press kit   An information package, usually a folder with flaps or pockets, containing a press release about the publication to be released, a glossy photo of the author, information about the book, advance quotes or reviews for the book, and other pertinent data such as the author's book tour schedule. It is used as a publicity or sales promotion tool. Increasingly such material is provided through e-mail attachments as electronic press kits.

press proofs   In color reproduction, a proof of a color subject on a printing press, in advance of the production run.

press release   An information sheet about a forthcoming book and its author, used as a publicity tool, or a specially prepared statement for the news media. Also called a HANDOUT.

press run   The number of copies that are to be printed. The run usually allows extra copies to be printed to allow for spoilage.

presswork   The part of the printing process that involves the running of paper through the press, the actual printing of the work. The major steps in the printing of a book are COMPOSITION, MAKEUP, presswork, and BINDING.

price   There are several prices pertaining to any one book. The invoice price is the amount the publisher charges the bookseller, whereas the retail, cover, or list price refers to what the consumer pays for the book.

print   An impression pulled from an original photographic plate, stone, block, screen, or negative; also a positive made from a photographic negative.

printer's error (PE)   A typographical error made by the printer or typesetter, not by the publisher's staff or the author. PEs are corrected at the printer's expense.

printing plate   A surface that holds a reproduction of the set type and artwork of a book, from which the pages are printed.

printing press   A machine in which the printing impression is transferred from inked plates or type onto the paper, either by direct impression or by offset. There are basically three kind of presses—platen, flat-bed cylinder, and rotary. *Platen,* in which the paper is pressed by a flat surface onto a flat printing surface, and *flat-bed cylinder,* in which the paper is pressed by a cylinder onto a flat printing surface, are both used only in LETTERPRESS. *Rotary* presses, with various modifications, are used for LETTERPRESS, OFFSET LITHOGRAPHY, and gravure. In a rotary press, the inked plates, attached to a cylinder, transfer the impression either directly onto the paper on a second cylinder or onto a rubber blanket cylinder that offsets the impression onto the paper on a third cylinder. A web *perfecting* press prints both sides of a roll of paper, cuts the fold, and delivers in folded signatures. See PERFECTOR PRESS and WEB-FED PRESS. A *multicolor* press prints several colors before the paper leaves the press. Also called a "chromatic" press. See also FOUR-COLOR PRESS.

print on demand (POD)   This term refers to novels that are produced digitally (electronically) one at a time, as ordered by customers. SELF-PUBLISHING through print on demand technology usually involves some fees for the writer. Some authors utilize POD to create a manuscript in book form to send to prospective traditional publishers.

process printing   A printing process in which a full color original is reproduced through the use of several (between two and four) halftone plates.

professional or courtesy discounts   Discounts on book price offered to individuals (usually professionals in the publishing or media businesses or friends) by publishers. See also DISCOUNT (PUBLISHING).

progressive proofs   A series of PROOFS, consisting of one plate in each of three or four colors (yellow, magenta, cyan, and sometimes black), and of combinations of two, three, and four colors. They are used to check color quality and as a printing guide.

proof   Shortened version of PROOFREADING. Also for newspapers it refers to any printed copy before it goes to press, and is usually made on a printer or a photocopying machine.

proofreaders' marks   Internationally known and understood symbols used (with some variations) to mark errors and changes on PROOFS.

proofreading   Close reading and correction of text for any typographical errors. Sometimes also includes checking for any punctuation or spelling errors.

proofs   Text send to a typesetter is returned to the publisher as "first proofs" or "galley proofs" (originally named after the long sheets of paper on which they used to be printed). Galley proofs from magazines usually omit artwork and captions or other graphical elements. However, galley proofs from book publishers today closely resemble the finished product. Proofs are provided to the author as they are completed so that proofreading can begin.

"Second proofs" or "page proofs" are a second set of pages that contain the revisions requested from the author as well as the art elements. These proofs are what the published page will look like. "Printer's proofs" are proofs sent by the typesetter or prepress house to the printer. "Film proofs" or "bluelines" or simply "blues" (because they are usually printed in blue ink) are sent by the printer to the publisher for one last look. Any error or problem not caught here will appear in the final published form.

proposal   A detailed summary (or outline) of a proposed book submitted to an editor for consideration, particularly used for nonfiction manuscripts. A proposal often contains an individualized cover letter, a one-page overview of the book, marketing information, potentially competitive books, information about the author, a chapter-by-chapter outline, and, sometimes, two to three sample chapters. It may also contain listings of magazine articles about the topic and articles or past books that the author has written on the subject.

proscenium   The area of a theater's stage in front of the curtain.

prose poem   Brief prose work usually filled with intensity, condensed language, and poetic devices and elements.

prospectus   A prefatory written description of a book or article, usually one page in length. Sometimes known as an abstract.

protagonist   The principal or leading character in a work of fiction.

proverb   A short, pithy saying in frequent and widespread use that expresses a basic truth or practical precept.

pseudonym   See PEN NAME.

PTLA   *Publisher's Trade List Annual.*

publication date (pub date)   A book's official date of publication, usually set by the publisher to occur six weeks after complete bound books are delivered to the publisher's warehouse. The publication date becomes the focus of promotional activities on behalf of the title, so that there will be enough time for the books to be ordered, shipped, and made available in stores to coincide with the appearance of advertising and publicity for them, let alone appearances of book reviews. This date may also coincide with an author tour. This date also is known as the "release date."

public domain   Published material that is available for use without permission of the author or the author's estate, either because it was never copyrighted or because its copyright term has expired.

publicist (press agent)   The publicity professional who handles the press releases for new books and arranges the author's publicity tours and other professional venues in which the book can be promoted (such as interviews in all forms of the media, speaking engagements, and BOOK SIGNINGS.)

publisher's catalog   A seasonal sales catalog detailing a publisher's new titles. Customarily, it is sent to all potential buyers, including any individual who may request one, and is frequently given out at book promotions, such as book fairs. Catalogs may range from basic listings (with or without descriptions) to glitzy, elaborate promotional pieces. They often include information on the authors, on the quantity of printed books, and the amount of money the publisher anticipates spending on the books' publicity and promotion.

publisher's discount   The percentage by which a publisher discounts the retail price of a book to a bookseller. It is often based partly on the number of copies purchased by the bookseller.

publisher's representative/sales representative   A salesperson who visits prospective customers of a publisher (such as booksellers, librarians, department heads and other authorized personnel in educational institutions, and wholesalers) to show book samples or other literature about the firm's forthcoming titles, as well as backlist titles, and take orders from them. This salesperson often also transmits any complaints and assists in promotional activities with customers.

Publishers' Trade List Annual (*PTLA*)   A collection (in multi-volumes) of current and backlist catalogs arranged alphabetically by publisher. These volumes are published by the R.R. Bowker Company and are available in most libraries.

Publishers Weekly (*PW*)   The publishing industry's primary trade journal. *PW* carries announcements of upcoming books, much-respected book reviews, interviews with authors and professionals within the publishing industry, special reports on various book categories, and trade news (such as mergers, personnel changes, and rights sales).

puff piece   Also known simply as "puff," it is a written work that contains editorialized complimentary statements about a person, place, or business.

pull quote   A quotation from an article, sometimes shortened by an editor, and displayed in larger type as a sort of illustration to the article or to be utilized in promotional materials to generate reader interest.

pulp magazine   A magazine printed on inexpensive paper, usually containing lurid and sensational stories or articles.

put to bed   A printer's term meaning all the pages of an EDITION are completed and the presses are ready to roll.

PW   See *PUBLISHERS WEEKLY*

Q-and-A format   One type of presentation of an interview article, in which questions are printed followed by the responder's answers. Another example is a verbatim report of a court proceeding.

quality   In publishing parlance the word "quality" (whether referring to a book category, such as quality fiction, or to format, such a quality paperback) denotes a special or outstanding product.

query letter   A letter in which a writer proposes to an editor an idea for a potential work. It is usually no longer than a page and uses attention-getting phraseology to describe the suggested piece in a way that fits the current needs of the editor's publication.

quotes   Quotation marks. In journalism, a quote is a portion of a news story that consists of direct quotations.

rag right, rag left   Indication that the line is not to be justified, in other words, uneven on the right or the left ends of the line.

railroad   To rush news copy through to the newspaper without any careful editing.

RAM (Random Access Memory)   A temporary storage system in a computer for creating, loading, manipulating data, and running computer programs.

reader   A person (usually freelance) hired by a publisher to read unsolicited manuscripts.

readertorial   In a newspaper, a long letter to the editor that is written and produced as an editorial.

reading fee   Money charged by some agents and publishers to read a submitted manuscript.

Read Only Memory   See ROM.

ream   500 sheets of paper.

recto pages   See ODD PAGES.

refer   Pronounced "reefer," but spelled this way, this referral device refers readers to pages inside a newspaper for related stories. At some newspapers, these have been called "whips."

reference mark   A mark in the text used to refer the reader to a note pertaining to the material. A corresponding mark appears at the beginning of the notes, which may appear at the end of the chapter or the end of the book as a part of the BACK MATTER. Reference marks may be asterisks, daggers, or, more often, superior figures or letters.

refrain   A repeated line within a poem, similar to the chorus of a song.

regency romance   A genre of romance fiction, usually set in England between 1811 and 1820.

regional poetry   Work set in a particular locale, imbued with the look, feel, and culture of that place.

register   In printing, this is the placement of an impression on a sheet in correct relation to other impressions already printed on the same sheet. In color printing, *register* means the correct placement of each plate so the colors are laid down properly, without running "off-register."

rejection slip   A printed note sent to a writer indicating that a publication (or publisher) is not interested in the writer's current submission.

release   A written statement that the writer signs indicating his/her idea is original, has never been sold to anyone else, and that the writer is now selling the negotiated rights to the idea upon payment. For newspapers and magazines, this can be a common term for a PRESS RELEASE or publicity HANDOUT, or permission to publish a news story or article at a specified time. In news photography, *release* is a form signed by the person photographed to authorize use of the picture.

release date   See PUBLICATION DATE.

remainders   Copies of a published book that have not been sold and can be purchased from the publisher at a reduced price. Depending upon the author's contract, a reduced royalty (or no royalty) may be paid on remainder copies. There are some bookstores (and bookstore chains) that deal only in remainders.

replate   In journalism, to make a new plate for a page in order to correct a major error or to insert an urgent story received after deadline. Also known as a MAKEOVER.

reporting time   See RESPONSE TIME.

reprint   A subsequent edition of material already in print. It frequently denotes a publication of this printed material in a different format, such as a paperback reprint of a hardcover edition.

reprint rights   The nonexclusive right given to a magazine or newspaper to publish a manuscript (article, novel excerpt, poem, story) after it has already appeared in another magazine or newspaper. Also known as SECOND SERIAL RIGHTS.

reproduction proof   In printing composition, the proof of a type form for purposes of photographic reproduction. These final proofs intended for use as CAMERA-READY copy are sometimes known as REPROS.

repros   See REPRODUCTION PROOFS.

research   The process of investigating a topic, either through "primary sources" such as interviews or observations or through "secondary sources" such as other writers' books and articles on the same topic. Library research is conducted primarily using the print and electronic materials in libraries; field research is conducted in settings where the subject of the research can be found in primary form.

response time   The average length of time it takes an editor to accept or reject a submission (or a query) and inform the writer of the decision. The usual time span is four to six weeks.

résumé   A summary of an individual's career experience and education. When it is a writer's résumé being sent to prospective agents or publishers, it should contain the author's publishing credits, any special credentials and personal experience that may be pertinent to the author's writings. Also referred to as "curriculum vitae," or "CV."

retail price   See LIST PRICE.

returns   Unsold books returned to a publisher by a bookstore or other bookseller, for which the bookstore (or bookseller) may receive full or partial credit (depending upon the publisher's policy, the age and condition of the book, and other such factors).

reverse   Copy is said to be "reversed" when the colors are reversed, as when the white is printed as black, and the black as white.

reversion-of-rights clause   In a book contract, this is a clause that states if a book goes out of print or the publisher fails to reprint the book within a stipulated time frame, all rights revert to the author.

review   A writer's critical evaluation of an artistic event, such as an art show, concert, movie, or play.

review copy   A free copy of a new book (or, in some cases, older book) sent to electronic and print media that review books for their audiences.

rewrite   Literally, to write again. On large newspapers, rewrite persons are assigned to such tasks as taking facts over the telephone from a LEG MAN and writing the story, boiling down information received from news and publicity agencies, and revising a story to improve it before publication.

rhyme   Words that sound alike, especially words that end in the same sound.

right-angle fold   In binding, a term used for two or more folds that are at 90-degree angles to each other.

rights   The bundle of permissions negotiated between an author and a publication or a book publisher in exchange for the printing of the author's literary property (of whatever kind). They include the following: prepublication serial (first serial rights); book reprint; dramatization; musical comedy; amateur leasing; motion picture (commercial and noncommercial); radio and television; mechanical, electronic, or xerographic reproduction of other kinds covered in the inclusive term *reprographic* reproduction; condensing of text and abridgement; anthology; translation; quoting from text; merchandising and other commercial exploitation rights. Most of these are also commonly referred to as SUBSIDIARY RIGHTS and are governed by the appropriate and prevailing copyright law.

rim   Refers collectively to the copy editors on a newspaper.

river   A streak of white space in printed matter caused by the spaces between words in several lines happening to fall one almost below another. Also called "river of white," "pigeonhole," and "staircase."

ROM (Read Only Memory)   Internal storage inside the computer that holds instructions to the system.

roman à clef   A French phrase, literally "novel with a key." This type of novel depicts actual living or historical characters and events in a fictionalized (as opposed to biographical) form.

romance   This genre of fiction deals with accounts of passionate love and fictional heroic achievements.

rondeau   A French form of verse, with usually 15 lines in three parts.

ROP   In journalism this refers to run-of-paper news and advertising that can appear in any part of the paper and, thus, is convenient to be shifted anywhere in the makeup of the paper.

ROP color   A term used in advertising referring to color printing from an ordinary newspaper press.

rough   Refers to a preliminary layout of a magazine or newspaper page not yet in finished form.

rough draft   A manuscript that has not yet been checked for errors in content, grammar, punctuation, or spelling.

roughs   Preliminary sketches or drawings.

round-up article   An article containing comments from, or interviews with, a number of celebrities or well-known professionals on a single theme.

routing   Cutting away unnecessary parts of a printing plate with an engraver's tool in order to prevent accidental printing.

royalty   A percentage of the amount received from retail sales of a book that is paid to the author by the publisher. For standard hardcover books, the royalty is generally 10 percent of the retail price on the first 5,000 copies sold; $12\frac{1}{2}$ percent on the next 5,000; 15 percent thereafter. For standard TRADE/QUALITY PAPERBACK books, the royalty is no less than 6 percent of the list price on the first 20,000 copies sold; $7\frac{1}{2}$ percent thereafter. For standard MASS MARKET PAPERBACK books, the royalty is 4 to 8 percent of the retail price on the first 50,000 copies sold, with an ESCALATION CLAUSE often in effect thereafter. Usually no royalty is paid on review copies or on copies sold as REMAINDERS, and a lower rate is paid on book club editions, copies sold by mail order or exported, reprints, and for many scholarly works.

rule   A straight line printed on the page, usually described by its width, as in "a one-point rule."

run   Refers to the territory assigned regularly to a reporter, otherwise known as a BEAT. In addition, It can refer to a press run, or EDITION of the newspaper. Also, when a story is "run," it means that it is printed.

run-around   The body of type that surrounds an odd-shaped picture, as in a feature story of a newspaper or in a magazine.

running costs   The variable costs, such as paper, printing, and binding, in manufacturing a book. These costs are determined by the size of the print run and whatever arrangements are made in the manufacturing contracts.

running head   The title of the book, article, or other publication that is repeated at the top of each page in the "header."

running story   Refers to a news story that develops over a period of several days or more and is reported on from day to day.

run-on format   An indexing format where all subheadings are arranged to follow one another in an ordinary paragraph form, spreading over the entire column.

runover   The part of a news story that continues onto a second page or more. Also known as "turnover."

saddle stitch binding   The binding of a publication in which the pages are attached by metal staples placed through the fold at the spine. Pages lie flat, but there is a limit to the thickness of a publication that can be bound in this manner. This fairly inexpensive type of binding is usually used with books or magazines that are under 80 pages.

saddle wire   In binding, to fasten a booklet by wiring it through the middle fold of the sheets.

sales conference   Usually convened two or three times a year (depending upon the number of selling seasons a publishing house may have), this meeting brings together the editorial, marketing, and sales staffs to introduce new titles for the forthcoming season. Marketing plans for each title will have been prepared in advance, and may be adjusted according to the sales force's response to the title-by-title presentations by the editorial staff at the conference.

sales representative (sales rep)   A member of the publisher's sales force (or an independent contractor) who, equipped with the publisher's catalog and order forms, visits bookstores in specific territories to sell books to retailers.

sample pages   Printed examples of selected pages made by the compositor according to the specifications of the production departments and used to show the solutions to typographical problems, such as tables, unusual symbols, and equations.

SAN   See STANDARD ADDRESS NUMBER.

SASE   The self-addressed, stamped envelope required with all submissions that the author wishes to be returned, either for the return of the material or (if the author does not need the material returned) for the editor's reply to the submission.

satisfactory clause   In book contracts, this clause represents the publisher's right to refuse publication of a manuscript that is deemed unsatisfactory. As the author may be required to pay back all (or some) of the publisher's ADVANCE if the completed work is found not to be satisfactory, the specific criteria for publisher satisfaction should be detailed in the contract to protect both publisher and the author.

saying   A statement, such as an ADAGE or a MAXIM, that is an often repeated and familiar expression.

sc   See SMALL CAPITALS.

scanning   When letter-quality printed text or artwork is read by a computer scanner and converted into workable data to be processed by the computer.

scansion   The metrical analysis of verse.

SCBWI   The Society of Children's Book Writers and Illustrators.

scene   In writing, this is an integral incident with a beginning and an end that in itself is not isolatable as a story. It is visible to the reader or audience as an onstage event, almost always involving dialogue and other action.

schedule   For newspapers this is a news editor's record of news assignments. Can also refer to the copy editor's record of news stories that have been handled.

science fiction   The genre of fiction in which scientific facts and hypotheses form the basis of actions and events. The genre encompasses both the hard-core, imaginatively embellished technological/scientific novel and that fiction that is strictly futuristic in its imaginings.

scoop   An exclusive story or a photograph that no one else has. As a verb, it means to get ahead of the competition with a story they have not covered.

screenplay   Script for a film—either original or one based on written material published previously in another form—intended to be shown in theaters. Called TELEPLAY when used for TV projects.

script   See SCREENPLAY.

seasonal catalog   Publishers produce an announcement catalog describing each book to be published within a season (that is, spring, fall, and winter).

second-day story   A "follow-up" news story giving new developments on one that has already appeared in the newspaper (or magazine). The same definition applies to follow-up stories in the broadcast media.

second front page   The front page of a second section (sometimes containing local news as opposed to the first section covering national and international stories). This sometimes is called the "split page."

second proofs   See PROOFS.

second serial   See SERIALIZATION.

second serial rights   See REPRINT RIGHTS.

sectional story   A major news story with various aspects, featured under two or more HEADLINES.

secure sockets layer   See SSL.

see also **reference**   In indexing, this is a cross-reference from one heading (or subheading), with its relevant page reference to the item in the text, to any additional heading(s), or subheading(s), under which further relevant references to the item that is being indexed in the text are to be found.

see **reference**   In indexing, this is a cross-reference from one heading (or subheading), after which there are no page or other indications, to an alternative heading (or subheading), under which all the relevant page references to the indexed item in the text are collected.

segue   Derived from music, it means to glide as unobtrusively as possible into something new.

self-publishing   A publishing arrangement where the author keeps all income derived from the sale of the book, but pays for its production, manufacturing, and marketing.

self-syndication   The management by writers or journalists of functions in the publishing process that are otherwise performed by syndicates specializing in such services. In self-syndication, it is the author or journalist who handles sales, billing and other such tasks, manages copyright matters, and negotiates fees.

sell through   Percentage of NET SALES for a book or other publication. If 16,000 copies are printed and 8,000 are sold, the book has a 50 percent sell through.

semiannual   Occurring every six months, or twice a year.

semimonthly   Occurring twice a month, usually at equal intervals.

semiweekly   Occurring twice a week.

sequel   A literary work that continues the narrative and plot of a previous related story or novel (either by the same author or another author).

sequence   A group or progression of poems, often numbered as in a series.

serial   A publication appearing periodically, such as a magazine or a newspaper.

serial fiction   Fiction published in parts—typically at regular intervals—in a magazine or newspaper, each of which may be broken off at a suspenseful moment.

serialization   The reprinting of a book, or part of a book, in a newspaper or magazine. Serialization before (or sometimes simultaneously with) the publication of the book is called first serial. The first serialization reprint after publication (either as a book or by another PERIODICAL) is called second serial.

serialized novel   A book-length work of fiction that is published in sequential issues of a PERIODICAL.

serial rights   See REPRINT RIGHTS.

series   Books published as a group either due to their related subject matter (such as a biographical series) and/or their single authorship (say a group of books about science and society by a single author). For newspapers and magazines, it is a group of related stories generally run on successive days or in successive issues.

series fiction   A sequence of novels featuring the same main character or characters. Frequently used in the historical novel, mystery, and science fiction/fantasy genres.

set   To compose or arrange type to be printed.

setting   The environment and time period during which the action of the story takes place.

sheet-fed offset printing   OFFSET printing in which paper is fed one piece at a time into the printing device.

shelf life   The time that an unsold book remains on a bookstore's shelf before being pulled off to make room for newer incoming books with greater (or at least possible) sales potential

shirt tail   In journalism, a short, related story that is added at the end of a longer one.

shoot   To take photographs, or go searching for a photographic opportunity.

short   In newspaper parlance, this is a minor and brief story.

short discounts   Lower discounts offered by publishers (or WHOLESALERS) on the usually few retail sales of books ordinarily sold directly to professional persons or institutions. See also DISCOUNT (PUBLISHING).

short short story   A complete short story ranging from 250 words minimum to a maximum of 1,500 words.

short story   A form of fiction that is brief, more pointed and more economically detailed as to character, situation, and plot than a novel. Published collections of short stories, by one or more authors, may revolve around a single theme, or express related viewpoints, or encompass variations within a particular genre.

showing   Making fiction visible to readers as if it were happening before their eyes, moment by moment.

shrink-wrap   Cellophane put over a book, pad, or other printed material, in a heat process that seals the edges. It is done to protect the book from warping, dust, damage in shipping, or other possible forms of injury.

sidebar   A feature presented as a companion to a straight news story (or a magazine article, or a chapter in a nonfiction book) giving sidelights on human-interest aspects or sometimes clarifying or expanding on a single aspect of the story (or chapter).

side head   A heading placed at the side of a page or column, set either as a separate line flush with the type page margin, or run in with the paragraph with which it belongs.

signature   In printing and binding, the name given to a group of pages printed together in four-, eight-, 16-, or 32-page increments. In the latter case, 32 pages would be printed on the front side of a large piece of paper, and then 32 pages printed on the backside of the piece of paper. Thereafter this large piece of paper is folded and cut to produce the individual pages that are bound together. The term "signature" refers to each completed sheet after it has been folded and cut into a specific size page unit (four, eight, 16 or 32) to be bound with others into the completed book.

signer   See BYLINE.

silhouette halftone   An illustration in which the background has been entirely cut away or masked.

simile   A figure of speech in which two unlike things are compared, linked by "as" or "like." As comparison, see METAPHOR.

simple heading   In indexing, this is a heading consisting of a single word, or a word with a hyphenated prefix (or a suffix), which alone would either have no meaning in itself, or have a completely different meaning.

simultaneous publication   The issuing at the same time of more than one edition of a work, such as both a hardcover edition and a trade paperback edition of the same work. Simultaneous releases can include (yet not often) deluxe gift editions of a book as well as a mass-market paper version. Audio versions of books are most often timed to coincide with the release of the first print edition.

simultaneous submissions   See MULTIPLE SUBMISSIONS.

single-copy sales   Refers to newsstand and store sales of newspapers and magazines, everything not home delivered.

single-title order play (STOP)   A system devised and promoted by the AMERICAN BOOKSELLERS ASSOCIATION (ABA) to maximize discount and minimize handling on special orders of one or more copies of a single published book. Cooperating publishers are supposed to grant full TRADE DISCOUNT, although some offer less, to dealers using the prescribed single-title order form available from ABA.

sinkage   White space, in addition to the top margin, left at the top of a page, as at the beginning of a new chapter. Sinkage throughout a book should be uniform.

skybox   A term for promotional boxes that are usually placed above the nameplate of the newspaper. Also known as a "teaser."

skyline   The area at the top of a magazine cover, above the logo. The skyline usually contains one or more cover lines and secondary images.

slant   The approach, angle, or style of a story or article that is aimed to please readers of a specific magazine or newspaper readership, for example, stories that always end well, or articles dealing supportively with the problems of childhood.

slice-of-life vignette   A short piece of fiction designed to realistically depict an interesting moment of everyday life and usually offers a flash of illumination about the characters or their situation.

slides   See TRANSPARENCIES.

slot   One of the people on the newspaper copy desk who checks over the copy editors' work before committing the story to type. The term can also be used as a verb, as in "Hey, Joey, slot me on this one, will you." See also RIM.

slug   An internal newspaper name for a story, usually just one word. For example, elex might be the slug for a story on school elections.

slugline   A short phrase or title (or other feature) of the story that is used to indicate the story content in the newspaper or magazine, and is repeated on subsequent pages so that the reader can better find the parts of the story in their continuation from page to page in the publication. Also known as a CATCHLINE.

slush pile   The stack of unsolicited (or misdirected) manuscripts in an editor's office (or in the office of a literary agency) for later consideration. Some publishers (and agencies) do not maintain slush piles, preferring to return the work without review (only if an SASE is included), or simply discard the work altogether.

small capitals (sc)   Capital letters smaller than the usual capitals of the given font, equal to the x-height of that font. Also known as "small caps."

small press   A publishing business that operates on a considerably reduced financial model compared with large publishers and usually prints smaller first print runs of a book. As a result, a small press can specialize in a type of books and often will take more risks in its publishing ventures that do most larger publishers, as it does not require huge market successes to keep afloat financially. Small presses publish the majority of nonfiction in America.

Smythe-sewn binding   Binding in which the pages are sewn together with thread. Smythe is the name of the most common machine used for this purpose.

social fiction   Fiction written with the ulterior motive of bringing about positive changes in society.

soft copy   Newspaper or magazine copy seen on a computer screen.

soft/sociological science fiction   Science fiction writing that emphasizes society and culture as opposed to a depiction of scientific endeavors and accuracy.

software   The computer programs that control computer hardware. Word-processing software includes programs that enable writers to compose, edit, print, and store their material. Other professional quality software can allow a writer to feed the results of RESEARCH electronically into the final manuscript, alphabetize and index material, or construct tables, charts, and other graphics into the body of the manuscript.

solicited manuscript   Material that an editor has asked for, or agreed to consider, before it is sent by a writer.

sonnet   A 14-line poem, rhymed in IAMBIC PENTAMETER; often presents an argument, but may also present a description, meditation, or story.

source   An individual whose statements are used for material in an article, news story, or other publication. The source can also be a document.

spacebreaks   Spaces inserted in the text to indicate a change of subject, time, or other break in the train of thought in the text. They are usually one or two lines deep. They may also contain some special character or characters spaced evenly in a line, such as a DINGBAT

space dots   See CENTERPOINT.

space opera   Science fiction writing of the epical kind with an emphasis on the theme of good guys versus bad guys, usually in elaborately imagined settings.

spec   See ON SPEC(ULATION).

special-interest publishing   Publishing of books that address a specific, and sometimes rather limited, topic that will appeal only to those people who share a common interest in the subject matter.

special order   To a bookseller, an order for a single copy of a book not in stock, made at the request of a customer. Because it requires special handling, and sometimes involves a short discount or no discount at all, the bookseller frequently adds a nominal service charge to the transaction to cover these costs.

special release   Any mass market title that receives listing, attention, and promotional effort apart from the monthly publication list. A mass market publishing house that believes a title has exceptional merit or commercial potential, or is particularly timely or newsworthy, may promote that title individually with a special brochure, or sell sheet and other order forms.

special sales   The book sales a publisher makes to nontraditional customers via nontraditional distribution (such as wine guides to liquor stores). In addition to distribution through customary bookstores, a publisher may attempt to increase income derived from the title by bulk sales at a special rate to a company that will distribute the book to its employees or to clients for its own purpose.

speculation (spec)   Creating a piece of writing with no assurance from an editor that it will be purchased or any reimbursements made for the material or labor.

speculative fiction   An all-inclusive term for science fiction, fantasy, and horror.

speech signature   Within dialog, this is a tag identifier that is characteristic of the speaker, such as Sherlock Holmes's "Elementary, my dear Watson."

spike   To kill a news story, feature, or article. At one time, when editors were finished with a piece of paper, such as a story, HEADLINE, or page PROOF, they would slam it down on an upright nail on their desk. At that point, they would know they were done with it, but could go back to it later if they needed to. Today, many newsroom computers have a "spike" key for killing a story or a computer file.

spine   The backbone or bound edge of a publication that has a square back. The square back is the result of perfect binding or side-wire binding. This back connects the front and back covers. Type set lengthwise on the spine commonly reads from top to bottom. Also called "backbone" or "shelfback."

spiral binding   Binding in which a wire spiral is wound through holes punched in the pages. This is the binding process used for spiral notebooks.

splatterpunk   A type of horror fiction known for its extremely violent and graphic content.

split page   See SECOND FRONT PAGE.

spoilage   Planned paper waste. Printers estimate 10 percent spoilage on any printing job.

spondee   In poetry, a FOOT consisting of two stressed syllables.

sponsored book   See SUBSIDY PUBLISHER.

spot news   News obtained on the scene of the event, sometimes unexpectedly.

spot story   A small news story that is usually more specific to its subject, as opposed to a bigger story like a feature story.

spread   In a magazine, two facing pages devoted entirely to the artwork, graphics, and text of a magazine feature. In a newspaper, this refers to the display given to an important story, and if the story spreads across facing pages it is known as a double spread.

squib   A short news item, usually used as a FILLER.

SSL (Secure Sockets Layer)   Encryption on the computer that protects e-mail messages from prying eyes.

staircase   See RIVER.

stamping   In book publishing, the stamp is the impression of ornamental type and images (such as a LOGO or monogram) on the book's binding. The stamping process requires using a die with a raised or intaglioed surface to apply ink stamping or metallic-leaf stamping.

Standard Address Number (SAN)   A unique identification code for each address of each organization in, or served by, the book industry. This includes book distributors, book publishers, book retailers, book wholesalers, college bookstores, libraries, library binders, and serial vendors. The SAN serves to facilitate such activities as billing, crediting, paying, purchasing, receiving, refunding, and shipping. Assignment of code numbers is centrally administered by the R. R. Bowker Company.

standard contract   See BOILERPLATE CONTRACT.

standing heads   HEADLINES that do not change and are usually kept in a newspaper (or magazine) library file on a computer so that they are ready for instant use.

standing order   An order to a publisher, dealer, or WHOLESALER to supply each succeeding issue of a publication, particularly of an annual or SERIAL, as it is published, until notified otherwise.

stanza   A group of lines making up a single unit, like a paragraph in prose.

static   This adjective describes a scene lacking visible action or any dialogue that moves the story forward.

stet   A proofreading symbol that means leave the copy or text the way it is, even to ignoring a change that has been marked on a proof. Comes from the Latin "stetundum."

story   The general term applied to any newspaper (or magazine) article written by a reporter.

straight news   A plain account of news facts written in standard style and structure, without coloring or embellishments.

streamer   See BANNER.

strip   A news story that goes all the way across the top of the page, or nearly so.

stripping   Positioning of all of the layout components on a SIGNATURE (large sheets of paper that are printed in multiples of four that, when folded and trimmed, become the pages in the book) to construct the templates for the platemaking process. In phototypography, the assembly of film positive or negative elements for film mechanicals. Also, insertion of corrections in PHOTOTEXT or display.

strophe   Often cited to mean "STANZA"; also a stanza of irregular line lengths.

style   The way in which a piece of writing is actually written, such as short punchy sentences, or flowing narrative.

stylebook   The newspaper's book of rules and policies for handling copy. It is devised to make uniform the newspaper's treatment of abbreviations, capitalization, punctuation, spelling, typography, and other grammatical concepts, as well as establish the newspaper's procedures on a wide variety of topics. It can include everything from the spelling of local streets to the policy on handling profanities in the reporting of stories, and how juvenile crime victims are handled in print.

style manuals   There is a wide variety of style guides, including *The ACS Style Guide, The Associated Press Stylebook, Words Into Type,* and *The Chicago Manual of Style* (the generalized style guide for the entire writing industry). This multitude of style manuals suggests the wide abundance of writing markets and their contrasting requirements. In addition, many publishing houses generate their own style sheets that serve as in-house style manuals—their own way of doing things—whose requirements can change the copy submitted by an author.

subhead   In newspapers and magazines, this is a small, one-line HEADLINE inserted in the body of a story to break up the monotony of a solid column of small type.

subheading   In indexing, this is the word (or words) or symbol (or symbols) under which references in a COMPLEX ENTRY are specifically located.

subscription agent   An organization that handles the entering and renewal of subscriptions (primarily journals) for a library.

subscripts   See INFERIOR LETTERS.

subsidiary   Refers to an incorporated branch of a company or a conglomerate. An example is the publisher Alfred Knopf, Inc., which is a subsidiary of Random House, Inc.

subsidiary rights   All rights, other than book publishing rights, included in a book contract, such as paperback, book club, and movie/television rights. The division of profits between the publisher and the author from the sales of these rights is usually determined by negotiation at the time of drawing up the initial contract for the publication of the work. In more elaborate commercial projects, further details such as syndication of related articles and licensing of characters or products, may ultimately be involved.

subsidy publisher   A book publisher who charges an author for the cost of the production of the author's book, as opposed to a royalty publisher who pays the author for the manuscript. Usually, the works are of a specialized interest to a small group (for example, a corporation or a local historical society) or are scholarly works generally not expected to be commercial successes, for which a grant or fund is provided by the author (or by a foundation or other institution) to cover production costs either in part or wholly. Such books may be called sponsored books, especially if the sponsoring organization or person has agreed to purchase a significant quantity of the edition. A second type of subsidy publishing is vanity publishing in which a book is produced at the author's expense regardless of any or no merit of the work and at no risk to the publisher. Also called "vanity publisher."

super   A strip of strong, thin cloth pasted over the back of the sections of a book and extending about an inch beyond the back at each side, added for reinforcement. Also called *crash.*

superior numeral   A small numeral used as a reference mark, printed above the x-height of the font. Also called "superior figure."

superscript   A small numeral, fraction, or other symbol that prints above the x-height of the font and is used in mathematical and scientific notation.

surrealistic poetry   Poetry of the artistic movement stressing the importance of dreams and the subconscious, nonrational thought, free associations, and startling imagery and juxtapositions.

suspense   A fiction genre in which the plot's primary function is to build a feeling of anticipation and fear in the reader over the possible outcome of the story.

swash letters   Ornamental ITALIC letters used for headings and initials.

syndicate   In journalism, this is an organization that buys and sells feature material of all kinds, such as comic strips, crossword puzzles, gossip columns, and other such regular features.

syndication   The sale of all or of a portion of an original work to a number of publications (usually newspapers) that will print the material more or less simultaneously.

synonym   A word that is identical or nearly identical in meaning to another word, such as "ill" and "sick."

synopsis   A brief summary of a written work. As part of a book proposal, it is a comprehensive summary condensed onto no more than two pages, single-spaced.

table of contents   A listing of a book's chapters and other sections, such as front matter (introduction, foreword, preface, and acknowledgments) or back matter (appendices, glossary, bibliography, and index), or of a magazine's articles, columns, and special features, in the order in which they appear. In published books, the table of contents always indicates the respective beginning page numbers of each chapter or section.

tabloid (tab)   A newspaper formatted publication, such as *The Star,* about half the size of a regular newspaper page. A tabloid's usual size is 11 inches wide and 16 to 18 inches deep. Tabloids frequently cover news that is more exploitive than regular newspapers will handle. Can also refer to any newspaper or section folded to this size.

tagline   A caption for a photo or a comment to be added to a filler; also an often repeated phrase or slogan associated with an individual, an organization, or a commercial product.

tags   In fiction, the means by which a speaker is identified, most commonly by "he said" or "she said."

tailpiece   A small ornament or illustration at the end of a chapter.

take   A portion of the news copy in a running story that is sent down to the composing room in sections.

takeout   A longer news story that takes a step back from the daily breaking news stories to put a running story with frequent developments into context and perspective.

tanka   A Japanese poetic form of five lines with 31 syllables, less concentrated and mysterious, more emotional and conversational than HAIKU.

tear sheets   The pages of a magazine or newspaper on which an author's work is printed, usually full articles, which is used to showcase the author's ability to write. The term comes from journalism when newspapers used to provide authors with copies of the actual page, or authors tore out copies for themselves. Today this function (of convincing editors about an author's writing skill) is often replaced by author WEB SITES and LINKS.

teleplay   Originally a play or script written for, or adapted for, performance on television. Presently, the term applies frequently to made-for-TV movies.

television rights   The right to adapt a book or other published (or nonpublished) property into a television program, miniseries, or series.

tension   In fiction, these are moments of anxious uncertainty. The word is derived from the Latin *tendere,* meaning "to stretch"

terms   The financial conditions agreed upon in a book or other writing contract.

text   In indexing, this refers to all the reading matter in a book (including its illustrations) other than its index (and, in some cases, all or part of the book's FRONT MATTER and BACK MATTER). In journalism it refers to the verbatim report of a speech or a public statement.

text paper   Text paper is similar to book paper (a smooth paper used in offset printing), but it has been given some texture by using rollers or other methods to apply a pattern to the paper.

text type   The size of type customarily used for setting books or other large print quantities. It is seldom larger than 14-point.

theme   A general term for the underlying concept of a book or an article. (See also HOOK).

thesaurus   A dictionary of SYNONYMS and ANTONYMS—words similar or opposite in meaning to each other.

thesis (thesis statement)   A sentence, often at the conclusion of the first paragraph of an essay or article, that establishes the point, main argument, or direction of a paper, giving the reader a sense of purpose and understanding of the contents of the essay (or paper).

think piece   In journalism, a background or opinion article.

third-party distribution   A book that the sponsor (in educational, public service, or public relations programs) distributes to consumers, dealers, employees, stockholders, visitors, or other interested parties, usually at no cost and for no fee for the product involved.

thumbnail   A rough layout in miniature. Also a half-column picture. See PORKCHOP.

tie-in   The part of a story that reiterates past events in order to make recent developments in the plot clear to the reader. A tie-in is used in journalism to connect a story with some other, perhaps more important, story. Also known as "tie-back." For marketing purposes, a promotional tie-in is a work that helps market another work, such as the novelization of a film.

.tif   Computer filename extension for default pictures files.

tight   With a general meaning of too full, in journalism it applies to crowded lines of type, pages, sections, even entire editions. A tight newspaper is one without much room for additional news and advertising.

tip   Information that may LEAD to a story.

tip in   To paste a leaf, or leaves, into printed sheets or bound books.

tip sheet   An information sheet on a single book that presents general publication information (PUBLICATION DATE, editor, ISBN, and other pertinent material), a brief synopsis of the book, information on relevant other books (sometime in competition with the present one), and other relevant market data, such as an author profile and advance blurbs or quotes about the book. The tip sheet is given to the sales and publicity departments, and a version of it is included in any press kit for the book.

title page   The page at the front of a book that lists the title, any subtitle, author (and possibly any other contributor, such as editor, illustrator, or translator), as well as the publishing house and, sometimes, its LOGO.

TK   Proofreader's insertion mark indicating that there is material or data "to come."

toast   A proposal to drink to someone or something, or a speech given before the taking of such action.

tombstone   In journalism to place two or more HEADLINES of similar size side by side. Reader's eyes will tend to read across the first head into the next, losing the impact of the message of the first.

trade   Either a hardcover or paperback book sold in bookstores and through online retailers and directed toward the layperson rather than the professional. Its subject matter usually deals with a special interest (for example, gardening or health). These books are typically printed in smaller quantities by publishers

trade discounts   A method set up for selling general books to retailers on a scale from 30 to 45 percent and upward (depending on the individual publisher and quantities purchased). A trade discount schedule is printed by a publisher to detail the variations in discounts dictated by the number of books ordered. Legally, a publisher must offer the same trade discount schedule to all booksellers. Also called LONG DISCOUNTS. See also DISCOUNT (PUBLISHING).

trade edition An edition of a book intended for sale through bookstores (and on INTERNET sites) to the general public or for general circulation in libraries, as distinct from an edition of the same book intended for some other use, such as in a classroom.

trade list A catalog of all of a publisher's books in print, with their ISBN's and order information. The trade list may include short descriptions of the current season's new books.

trade magazines See CONSUMER MAGAZINES.

trade publishers Publishers of books for the general readership, that is, nonprofessional, nonacademic books that are distributed primarily through bookstores and electronic book outlets.

trade/quality paperback A higher-priced paperbound book marketed through normal book trade channels. It can be an original title or a reprint published by either a hardcover publishing house or a mass market publisher. Found in highly varied sizes or shapes, trade paperbacks are generally made of more expensive materials that those used for mass market paperbacks. Frequently, a hardcover publisher will produce a title simultaneously as a hardcover book and as a less expensive trade paperback (but still more expensive than most MASS MARKET PAPERBACKS.)

traditional fantasy Fantasy that places on emphasis on magic, and utilizing characters with the ability to do magic, such as wizards, witches, unicorns, elves, and dragons.

transparencies Photographs or images appearing on transparent material (such as slides) rather than on opaque material (such as paper).

treatment A catchy synopsis of a potential film or TV script, sometime including sample dialogue.

trial balloon A project or an idea tentatively announced in the news media to test public opinion.

trim To reduce the length of a written piece. Also refers to the outer dimensions (horizontal and vertical) of a publication, as in "trim size."

trim size The final size of the whole page, including all margins, after trimming.

trochee In poetry, FOOT consisting of a stress followed by an unstressed syllable.

truism An undoubted or self-evident truth; a statement that is palpably true; a proposition needing no proof or argument.

turnover See RUNOVER.

turnover line (turnline) See LINE WRAP.

.txt Computer filename extension for text files.

type (text) page That area of the page that contains all the printed matter, including footnotes, running heads, and folios. It is usually measured in picas.

type size The size of type, based on a unit of measurement called a point, in which one point equals $1/72$ of an inch, and 12 points equal one pica. All sizes of type and materials cast according to this system are exact multiples of this unit. Sizes are designated by points measured by the body (size) of the type.

typo Short for typographical error, usually a mechanical error in typing (or typesetting) a story. Also known as PRINTER'S ERROR.

uc See UPPERCASE.

unauthorized biography A history of a person's life written without the consent or contribution of the subject or the subject's heirs.

unearned revenue A revenue received in advance for which the goods will not be delivered (or the service performed) during the current accounting period.

Uniform Resource Locator See URL.

unit cost The amount of manufacturing expenses incurred in the completion or production of one unit of a product; usually computed by dividing total production costs for a publication, or the period of time needed for the production of the respective number of units.

Universal Product Code (UPC) A preprinted product and price code consisting of vertical bars that appears on the backs of mass market paperbacks, most musical recordings, and innumerable other consumer goods. Now found on most products for sale, UPCs are electronically scanned for sale prices.

university press A publishing house affiliated with a sponsoring educational institution (usually a university). The university press is generally nonprofit and subsidized to a certain extent by the respective university. Generally, university presses publish noncommercial scholarly nonfiction books written by academics or specialists, and their BOOK LISTS may include literary fiction, criticism, and poetry. Some university presses specialize in titles of regional interest, and many acquire projects intended and designed for commercial book-trade distribution.

unsolicited submission A manuscript (article, book, poem, or story) that an editor did not specifically ask to see.

upload To send a file to another computer. (To receive a file is DOWNLOADING.)

uppercase (uc) An indicator to put one or more characters into upper case, a larger letter in contrast to LOWERCASE letters.

urban fantasy A type of fantasy writing that takes magical creatures, such as elves, fairies, vampires, or wizards, out of their usual context and place them in modern-day settings.

URL (Uniform Resource Locator)   A string of information that makes up the address that enables a computer user to get to a Web site. The most common URL starts with "http://."

vanity publisher   See SUBSIDY PUBLISHER.

vellum (paper)   Vellum is a TEXT PAPER that is fairly porous and soft.

verso pages   see EVEN PAGES.

vignette   See SLICE-OF-LIFE VIGNETTE.

villanelle   A French form of poetry of 19 lines.

virus   A computer virus is a self-replicating code designed to damage or destroy computer systems. A virus can be DOWNLOADed from the INTERNET or from an e-mail file, or transferred by an infected CD disc. Software programs, such as the Norton or McAfee virus checkers, can provide an early warning so that the infected file does not get downloaded inadvertently.

vita   See RÉSUMÉ.

voice   The author's "voice" is an amalgam of the many factors that distinguish a writer from all other writers. Many authors first find their voice when they have learned to examine each word for its necessity, precision, and clarity, and have become expert in eliminating the extraneous and imprecise from their work.

WAN (wide area network)   A computer network that covers a wide distance and uses specialized computers to link smaller networks together.

want ads   classified advertisements.

web-fed press   A press whose paper is fed from a continuous roll.

web offset printing   This type of OFFSET printing prints pages on a whole roll of paper, and then cuts them apart to make the individual sheets (pages) of the book.

Web rights   See INTERNET RIGHTS.

well   Sometimes referred to as the "feature well," it is the center or heart of the magazine where the most important stories appear, usually without commercial interruption.

western   A fiction genre with a setting in the American West (usually), typically between 1860 and 1890. It usually contains a formulistic plot about cowboys (and sometimes Indians) or other aspects of frontier life.

whodunit   A type of mystery fiction that deals with murder, suspense, and the detection of crime and its criminals.

wholesale price   See NET PRICING.

wholesaler   In trade book distribution, a large-volume buyer of primarily MASS MARKET PAPERBACK titles for distribution to book racks in bookstores, commercial businesses (such as drugstores and supermarkets), newspaper and magazine stands, and similar outlets. Traditionally, WHOLESALERS differed significantly from jobbers in the services they provided, which included title selection, delivery, rack stocking, and removing slow-moving inventory. Presently, this distinction has blurred as wholesalers carry non-mass market titles and jobbers carry mass market titles.

wide area network   See WAN.

widow   In composition, a single line (or, worse, a single word) at the end of a paragraph that appears at the top of a page (or a column) by itself; considered to be bad typography generally.

wire copy   Editorial matter supplied to newspapers by outside sources, especially that material transmitted by telegraphy or teletype from news services.

wire photo   The Associated Press service that transmits photographs, maps or other illustrations. The illustration is then reproduced electronically in the newsrooms of subscribing newspapers.

wire service   A news collection and transmission service. Such news services include:

AFP (Agence France-Presse)—world news service based in France

AP (Associated Press)—world news service based in the U.S.

CNT-CPT (Canadian National and Canadian Pacific Telegraph)—service for transmission of correspondents' stories

CP (Canadian Press)—news service based in Canada

Reuters—world news service based in the United Kingdom, first of its kind, founded in Great Britain in 1849

Tass—news service based in Russia (the former Soviet Union, now known as the Russian Federation)

UPI (United Press International)—world news service based in the U.S.

word-by-word alphabetization   In indexing, an alphabetizing methodology in which the compound headings and compound subheadings are treated as separate words, each of which are alphabetized in turn.

word count   The number of words in any given document. When noted on a manuscript, the word count is usually rounded off to the nearest 100 words.

work for hire   When a work is written on a "for hire" basis, all rights to and in it become the property of the publisher. Under such an agreement the author does not hold the copyright and is unable to resell the work on his own.

world rights   Publication rights to a particular work throughout the world, frequently restricted to a particular format. A publisher that has acquired world hardcover rights to a specific book will usually have only hardcover publication rights to sell to publishing houses in other countries, which may publish the work either in its original language or, more usually, in translation. (See also FOREIGN RIGHTS.)

worldwide   Pertains to the right to publish written material anywhere in the world. Frequently, this right may be limited by other wording in the contract to, say, publication in English only, or in print form only, or in electronic form only.

World Wide Web (WWW) An INTERNET resource that utilizes hypertext to access information. This resource can support formatted text variants, illustrations, and even sounds, depending upon the user's computer capabilities.

wraparound plates Thin metal plates that are flexible enough to be wrapped around cylinders, such as offset plates, used for ROTARY or OFFSET printing.

writer's commentary A writer's direct address to the reader, or reference to himself or herself in prose that is not intended to convey personal feelings.

writers guidelines A formal statement of a publication's (or publisher's) editorial needs, payment schedules, publishing deadlines, and other essential information.

WWW See World Wide Web.

x-height In type, a vertical dimension equal to the height of lowercase letters (such as *e*) without ascenders or descenders (such as *b* or *p*).

YA See YOUNG ADULT.

yellow journalism A term for sensational journalism.

young adult (YA) The general classification of books written for readers approximately ages 12 to 18.

young reader The general classification of books written for readers approximately ages five to eight.

zine An individualistic, small-circulation magazine production, often a one- or two-person operation, run from the home of the nonprofessional enthusiast publisher/editor. These publications often contain specialized themes that are personal, experimental and, usually, controversial.

zone Refers to a part of a newspaper's circulation area. If the newspaper divides its circulation area into zones, advertisers may buy ads in just their local areas. Often, news coverage is zoned to complement such zoned advertising.

BIBLIOGRAPHY

Abbe, Elfrieda, ed. *The Writer's Handbook 2004.* Waukesha, Wisc.: The Writer Books, 2003.

Abbott, Langer & Associates. "Salary Survey Summaries" and "Salary & Benefits Surveys," 2004. Available online at http://www.abbott-langer.com.

Abdallah, Abdallah Khamis. "How to Build a Career in Freelance Writing" (2004). Available online from Worldwide Freelance Writer at http://www.worldwidefreelance.com/articles/buildcareer.htm.

The Accrediting Council on Education in Journalism and Mass Communications (ACEJMC). *ACEJMC Accredited Programs, 2003–2004.* Available online at http://www.ukans.edu/~acejmc.

Adams, Sally. *Interviewing for Journalists.* New York: Routledge, 2001.

Advertising Age. "The 2003 Advertising Industry Salary Survey, December 8, 2003." Available online at http://www.adage.com

Advertising Educational Foundation. "Career Guide." Available online at http://www.aef.com

Albers, Michael J. "The Technical Editor and Document Databases: What the Future May Hold." *Technical Communication Quarterly,* Spring 2000 (Vol. 9, No. 2).

Alred, Gerald J., Charles T. Brusaw and Walter E. Oliu. *The Business Writer's Handbook* (7th ed.). New York: St. Martin's Press, 2003.

———. *Handbook of Technical Writing* (7th ed.). New York: Bedford/St. Martin's Press, 2003.

American Book Producers Association. "What Is a Book Producer?" Available online at http://www.abpaonlin.org/what.html.

American Society of Composers and Publishers (ASCAP). "Music, Money, Success & the Movies." Available online at http://www.ascap.com/filmtv/movies.

American Society of Indexers. "Working with Freelance Indexers" (2002). Available online at http://www.asindexing.org/site/editorsguide.shtml.

America's Career InfoNet. "Occupation Reports 2002." Available online at http://www.acinet.org.

Anson, Chris M. and Robert A. Schwegler. *The Longman Handbook for Writers and Readers.* New York: Addison Wesley Longman, 2000.

Arrieta, Shery Ma Bell. "Breaking into the Greeting Card Market." Available online at http://www.writing-world.com/poetyr/arriet.shtml.

Arnold, George T. *Media Writer's Handbook.* Boston: McGraw-Hill, 2003.

Association of American Publishers (AAP). "About Publishing: Major/Department Guide" (2004) Available online from Bookjobs.com at http://www.bookjobs.com/page.php?prmID=12.

———. "Industry Statistics, June 4, 2004." Available online at http://www.publishers.org/industry/index.cfm.

Association of Writers & Writing Programs. *AWP Job List: Employment News & Opportunities for Writers and Teachers* (journal). Fairfax, Va.: Association of Writers & Writing Programs.

Atkinson, Claire. "Lee Garfinkel Decries Ad Industry Hypocrisy." Available online at *Advertising Age* Web site: http://adage.com.

Auman, Ann. "On Copy Editing." *The American Editor,* January 2000. Available online at http://www.copydesk.org/words/ASNEJanuary.htm.

Backes, Laura. "Editing Secrets." Available online from Worldwide Freelance Writer at http://www.worldwidefreelance.com/articles/editsecret.htm.

Banks, Michael A. *How to Become a Fulltime Freelance Writer: A Practical Guide to Setting Up a Writing Business at Home.* Waukesha, Wisc.: The Writer Books, 2003.

———. "Newspaper Stringing" (1992). Available online at http://www.empowermentzone.com/stringer.txt.

Bass, Frank. *The Associated Press Guide to Internet Research and Reporting.* New York: Perseus Book Group, 2001.

Bear, Jacci Howard. "Find a DTP Job: The Many Faces of Desktop Publishing and How to Find Where the Jobs Are Hiding" (2004). Available online from About.com at http://desktoppub.about.com/library/weekly/aa980319.htm.

———. "How Much Money Desktop Publishing Makes" (2004). Available online from About.com at http://desktoppub.about.com/library/weekly/aa021402a.htm.

Bernheimer, Martin. "Crrr-itic!" *Andante* magazine, 2004. Available online at http://www.andante.com/article/article.cfm?id=13951.

Bilheimer, Susan. *Fabjob Presents How to Become a Technical Writer* (an e-book). Available online at http://www.fabjob.com/technicalwriter.asp.

Black, Jill. "Become a Freelance Article Writer" (2005). Available online at http://www.publishingcentral.com/articles/200302720-150-46cf.html.

Bloom, Stephen G. *Inside the Writer's Mind: Writing Narrative Journalism.* Ames: Iowa State University Press, 2002.

Blume, Jason. *6 Steps to Songwriting Success: The Comprehensive Guide to Writing and Marketing Hit Songs* (rev. ed.). New York: Billboard Books, 2004.

———. "Writing for Specialty Markets." Available online from TAXI.com at http://www.taxi.com/faq/songwriting/specialty-markets.html.

Borod, Liz. "Folio Magazine Salary Survey 2004: Finally, a Little More in the Paycheck." Available online at http://foliomag.com/careers/salary_survey_04/index.html.

Bowerman, Peter. "Tighter Market, Tighter Message" (2002). Available online at http://www.worldwidefreelance.com/articles/tightermsg.htm.

Bowling, Anne and Michael Schweer. *2005 Novel & Short Story Writer's Market.* Cincinnati, Ohio: Writer's Digest Books, 2004.

Brabec, Jeffrey and Todd Brabec. "Advertising Jingles." Available online from TAXI.com at http://www.musiciansfriend.com.

Braheny, John. *The Craft and Business of Songwriting.* New York: Omnibus Press, 1988.

Brain, Jim. "Riding the Technology Fence in Online Publishing." *CMC Magazine,* May 1, 1996. Available online at http://www.december.com/cmc/mag/1966/may/brain.html

Brandon, Jodi L. *Fabjob Guide to Become a Book Editor* (an e-book). Available online at http://www.fabjob.com/BookEditor.asp

Breen, Nancy (editor). *2004 Poet's Market.* Cincinnati, Ohio: Writer's Digest Books, 2003.

Brogan, Kathryn S. and Robert Lee Brewer. *2005 Writer's Market.* Cincinnati, Ohio: Writer's Digest Books, 2004.

Brogan, Kathryn S. *2004 Writer's Market Online.* Cincinnati, Ohio: Writer's Digest Books, 2003.

Brooks, Brian S., George Kennedy, Daryl R. Moen, and Don Ranly. *Telling the Story: Writing for Print, Broadcast and Online Media.* New York: Bedford/St. Martin's, 2003.

Bruback Enterprises Inc. "Opportunities in Public Affairs—Career Overview: Public Relations Specialists." Available online at http://www.brubach.com/publicrelationsspecialists.htm.

Bureau of Labor Statistics, U.S. Department of Labor. *Federal Government General Schedule Pay Rates, 2003,* compiled by the U.S. Office of Personnel Management. Available online at http://www.bls.gov.

———. *Occupational Outlook Handbook and Career Guide to Industries, 2004–05 Edition.* Advertising and Public Relations Services Report. Available online at http://www/bis/gov/oco/cg/cgs030.htm.

———. "Advertising, Marketing, Promotions, Public Relations, and Sales Mangers Report." Available online at http://stats.bls.gov/oco/ocos929.htm.

———. "Announcers Report." Available online at http://stats.bls.gov/oco/ocos087.htm.

———. "Broadcasters Report." Available online at http://www.bls.gov/oco/cg/cgs017.htm

———. "Desktop Publishers Report." Available online at http://www.gls.gov/oco/ocos276.htm.

———. "Education Administrators Report." Available online at http://www.bls.gov/oco/ocos007.htm.

———. "Federal Government, Excluding the Postal Service Report." Available online at http://stats.bls.gov/oco/cg/cgs041.htm.

———. "Management, Scientific, and Technical Consulting Services Report." Available online at http://bls.gov/oco/cgs037.htm.

———. "Market and Survey Researchers Report." Available online at http://bls.gov/oco/ocos013.htm.

———. "May 2003 National Occupational Employment and Wage Estimates: Management Occupations." Available online at http://stats.abls.gov/oes/2003/may/oes_11Ma.htm.

———. "May 2003 National Occupational Employment and Wage Estimates: Office and Administrative Support Occupations." Available online at http://www.bls.gov/oes/2003/may/oes_43Of.htm.

———. "Network Systems and Data Communications Analysts." Available online at http://www.bls.gov/oes/current/oes151081.htm.

———. "News Analysts, Reporters, and Correspondents Report." Available online at http://www.bls.gov/oco/ocos088.htm.

———. "Public Relations Specialists Report." Available online at http://www.bls.gov/oco/ocos086.htm.

———. "Publishing Industry, except Software, Report." Available online at http://www.gls.gov/oco/cg/cg013.htm.

———. "State and Local Government, Excluding Education and Hospitals, Report." Available online at http://www.bls.gov/oco/cg/cgs042.htm.

———. "Survey Researchers Report." Available at http://stats.bls.gov/oes/2003/may/oes193022.htm.

———. "Writers and Editors Report." Available online at http://www.bls.gov/oco/ocos089.htm.

Burnaford, Gail E., Joseph Fischer, and David Hobson. *Teachers Doing Research: The Power of Action through Inquiry* (2nd ed.). Philadelphia: Lea, 2001.

California Employment Development Department. "California Occupational Guide Number 86: Desktop Publishing Specialists" (2002). Available online at http://www.calmis.cahwnet.gov/file/occguide/Desktop.htm.

———. "California Occupational Guide Number 138: Technical Writers" (2002). Available online at http://www.calmis.cahwnet.gov/file/occguide/Techwrtr.htm.

"Careers in Marketing: Advertising & Public Relations Reports." Available online at http://www.careers-in-marketing.com/adfacts.htm.

Cebik, L. B. "What the Heck Is a Technical Editor?" (2002). Available online at http://www.antennex.com/shack/Jul02/teched.htm.

The College Board Book of Majors. Plano, Tex.: College Board Publications, 2004.

Connect2jobs.org. "Job Descriptions and Information." Available online at http://www./connect2jobs.org.

Conte, Christopher. "Imagemaker." *Governing Magazine,* July 2001. Available online at http://www.governing.com/archive/2001/jul/reeves.txt.

Cornell University. "Careers after Cornell Survey: Careers in Publishing." Available online at http://www.arts.cornell.edu/career/careersafter.asp.

Council for Advancement and Support of Education (CASE). "Editing and Writing Resources." Available online at http://www.case.org/IndexBrowser.cfm?indexEntryID=619.

Daly, Charles P., Patrick Henry and Ellen Ryder. *The Magazine Publishing Industry.* New York: Allyn & Bacon, 1996.

Dunham, Paul. "Newbie Tech Writer Tools" (articles, 1999). Available online at http://www.cloudnet.com/~pdunham.

Edrich, Alyice. "Become a Book Reviewer" (2002). Available online at http://www.thedabblingmum.com/writing.book_reviews.htm.

Eds. *Barron's Profiles of American Colleges* (27th ed.). Hauppauge, N.Y.: Barron's Educational Series, 2004.

eHow.com. "How to Become an Online Reporter" (2004). Available online at http://www.ehow.com/how_246_become-online-reporter.htm.

Endicott, R. Craig. "The 2003 Advertising Industry Salary Survey, December 9, 2003." Available from AdAge.com Online Edition at https://www.adage.com.

FastWeb. "Broadcast Journalism: Career Overview" (2004). Available online at http://fastweb.monster.com/fastweb/content/career_db/broadcast_journalism.

Feiertag, Joe, Mary Carmen Cupito and the Editors of Writer's Market. *The Writer's Market Companion.* Cincinnati, Ohio: Writer's Digest Books, 2000.

Feldman, Barbara J. "Getting Syndicated for Fame and Profit." Available online at http://barbarafeldman.com/getting-syndicated.htm,

Fellow, Anthony R. and Thomas N. Clanin. *Copy Editor's Handbook for Newspapers* (2nd ed.). Englewood. Colo.: Morton Publishing, 2002.

Fetters, Linda K. *Handbook of Indexing Techniques: A Guide for Beginning Indexers* (3rd ed.). Corpus Christi, Tex.: FimCo Books, 2001.

FictionAddiction.net. "A Network and Links for Fiction Writers." Available online at http://www.fictionaddiction.net.

Fischer, Rusty. "Writing for a Book Packager: How to Cash In on an Often Under-Exploited Market." Available online at http://www.author-network.com/fischer.html.

Folio Magazine Editors. "B-to-B Publishing: Where's the Fun Gone? Publishing in the 21st Century." *Folio,* September 21, 2003. Available online at http://www.foliomag.com/This_Issues.this– issue+M5012d6ead72.0.html.

———. "Magazines on the Move: The Road Ahead." *Folio,* August 7, 2004. Available online at http://www.foliomag.com/July__August_2004.486+M5325a8130ed.0.html.

———. "Online Content: Paid and Free, Not Paid or Free." *Folio,* September 22, 2003. Available online at http://www.foliomag.com/This_Issue.this_issue+M575501568ac.0.html.

———. "Where the M&A Action Is: Database Information Services." *Folio,* May 17, 2004. Available online at http://www.foliomag.com/This_Issue.this_issue+M5323ffdf74f.0.htm.

Formichelli, Linda. "Waiting for Dollars." (Originally appeared in *Writer's Digest* magazine, 1998.) Available online at http://www.absolutewrite.com.

Fosdick, Scott. "Newspaper Critic Shapes Chicago Style of Theater." *Newspaper Research Journal,* March 22, 2002. Available online at http://www.highbeam.com/library/doc3.asp?docid=1G1:90115543.

Fox, Walter. *Writing the News: A Guide for Print Journalists* (3rd ed.). Ames: Iowa State University Press, 2001.

Galen, Richard A. "Press Secretary 101." Available online for CNSNews.com Commentary at http://www.cnsnews.com/ViewCommentary.asp

Gallagher, Linda G. "Getting Started as an Independent Technical Communicator." Paper given at 2002 Society for Technical Communication Annual Conference. Available online at http://www.techcomplus.com.

Geisler, Jill. "Skills without Script: The Best News Anchors Are Journalistic Leaders, Not Prompter-Bound Performers." The Poynter Institute, 2002. Available online at http://legacy.poynter.org/centerpiece/01902_anchors.htm.

Gibbons, Sheila. "Top Jobs Elude Women in Broadcast News." *Women's eNews,* November 16, 2004. Available online at http://www./womensenews.org/article.cfm/dyn/aid/1051/context/uncoveringgender.

Glatzer, Jenna. "The Beginner's Guide to Freelance Writing." Available online from Absolute Write at http://www.absolutewrite.com/freelance_writing/guide.htm.

Glover, Anne. "In Search of the Perfect Copy Editor: 10 Copy Editor Traits That Guarantee You Success." (1966). Available online from Poynteronline, http://www.poynter.org/content.

Gold, John. "Working with a Desktop Publisher." Available online at http://internetbrothers.com/johngold.htm.

Gould, Jay R. and Wayne A. Losano. Revised by Blythe Camenson. *Opportunities in Technical Writing Careers.* Chicago: NTC/Contemporary Publishing, 2000.

Greeting Card Association. "Greeting Card Facts: State of the Industry." Available online at http://www.greetingcard.org/gca/facts.htm.

Grimm, Joe. "How Can I Get Started in Newspapers?" (2004). Available online from *Detroit Free Press* at http://www.freep.com/jobspage/interns/break.htm.

Guide to Career Prospects. "Advertising Copywriters Report." Available online at http://www3.ccps.virginia/edu.

Hassan, Adeel. "Annals of the Anal Fact-checkers at the The New Yorker and Elsewhere." *New York Review of Maga-*

zines, Spring, 2002. Available online at http://www.jrn. columbia.edu/studentwork/nymagreviewofmagazines.

Herman, Jeff. *Jeff Herman's Guide to Book Publishers, Editors, & Literary Agents.* Waukesha, Wisc.: The Writer Books, 2003.

Heyman, Bill. "Speechwriters Should Increase Strategic Role" (Presented at the 2003 Speechwriter's Conference, March 14, 2003.) Available online at http://www.heyman associates.com/Spotlight/WCH_Ragan_Speechwriter.

Hill, Mimi. "Finding Technical Writing Jobs Fast." Available online at http://www.altogether.com/technicalwriting/ jobs.htm.

———. "The First Day on Your New Technical Writing Job." Available online at http://www.altogether.com/ technicalwriting/firstdayonjob.htm.

———. "How Much Should You Charge for Technical Writing?" Available online at http://www.altogether.com/ technical writing/charge.htm.

———. "Reading Like a Technical Writer." Available online at http://www.altogether.com/technicalwriting/ qualified.htm.

———. "Technical Writing Is Exciting Work." Available online at http://www.altogether.com/technicalwriting/ notboring.htm.

———. "Technical Writing Is Not Too Hard for You." Available online at http://www.altogether.com/technical writing/nottoohard.htm.

Holt, Karen Jenkins. "As a Matter of Fact." *Folio Magazine,* July 1, 2003. Available online at http://www.circman. com/magazinearticle.asp?magazinearticle.

Hupalo, Peter. "So You'd Like to Learn About Careers in the Publishing Industry, 2 Parts." Available online at http:// www.amazon.com/exec/obidos/tg/guides/guilde-display.

———. "So You'd Like to Understand the Publishing Business?" Available online at http://www.amazon.com/exec/ obidos/tg/guides/guilde-display.

Hynes, Angela. *Fabjob Guide to Become a Screenwriter* (an e-book). Available online at http://www.fabjob.com/ Screenwriter.asp.

Jason, Debra. "Putting a Price on Your Capabilities: How to Set Your Fees As a Freelance Writer" (2003). Available online at http://www.writedirection.com/rprt300e.htm.

Job Report. "Radio and Television Announcers and News-casters." Available online at http://shelomi.com/job_ report_radio_and_television.htm.

Jobprofiles.com. "Career Exploration: Business Support—Technical Writer Job Profile." Available online at http://www.jobprofiles.org/bustechnicalwriter.htm.

———. "Career Exploration: Federal Government—Speechwriter Job Profile." Available online at http:// www.jobprofiles.org/govfspeechwriter.htm.

JobStar: Profession Specific Salary Surveys. *The Wall Street Journal: CareerJournal.com.* Available online at http:// www.jobstar.org/tools/salary/sal-prof.cfm#PR.

JobStar: Salary Information Index. *The Wall Street Journal: CareerJournal.com.* Available online at http://jobstar.org/ tools/salary/index.cfm.

Jones, Patricia Ann. "How to Become a Book Critic" (1999). Available online from Business Know-How at http://www.businessknowhow.com/Writers/Perceptions/ pbecomecritic.htm.

Journalism.org. "Annual Report on American Journalism," made for the Project for Excellence in Journalism, 2003. Available online at http://www.stateofthenewsmedia.org.

Kelly, Melissa. "Putting All the Pieces Together: Effective Speech Writing," (from *Secondary School Educators Newsletter*). Available online at http://712educators.about. com/cs/speeches/a/speechwriting.

Kocian, Lisa. "Veteran Newsman Turns to Internet Columnist." *The Boston Globe,* August 29, 2004. Available online at http://www.knowledgeplex.org/news/42248.html?p=1.

Kremer, John. *1001 Ways to Market Your Books: For Authors and Publishers.* Fairfield, Iowa: Open Horizons Books, 2004.

Khullar, Mridu. "Becoming a Columnist." Available online at http://www.customline.com/wordware/default.html.

Labbé, Theola S. "Interns Confidential: How to *Really* Make the Most of Your Internship" (2004). Available online from *Detroit Free Press* at http://www.freep.com/ jbospage/interns/labbe.htm.

Landbaum, Mark. "Dream Jobs to Go! Desktop Publisher." Available online from Intellectua.com at www.dreamjobs togo.com/titles/djtgoo73.htm.

Levy, Frederick. *Hollywood 101: The Film Industry.* Los Angeles: Renaissance Books, 2000.

Lindsell-Roberts, Sheryl. *Technical Writing for Dummies.* New York: Hungry Minds, 2001.

Magazine Industry survey, May 2004. *Folio Magazine.* Available online at http://foliomag.com/careers/salary_ survey_04

Marketing Research Association. "Careers in Marketing Report, 2004." Available online at www.careers-in-marketing.com/adsal.htm.

Markiewicz, David A. "Voices in the Wilderness" *American Journalism Review,* May 2001. Available online at http:// www.ajr.org/Article.asp?id=272.

Meil, Joanne. "The Joys of Being a News Librarian." Special Libraries Association (SLA) Web site: http://www. ibiblio.org.

Merriam, Sharan B. *Qualitative Research and Case Study Applications in Education* (rev. ed.). Chicago: Jossey-Bass, 1997.

Miller, Keith. "Journalistic Criticism: Popular Entertainment or Populist Critique?" *Art Criticism* 15, no. 2 (2000). Available online at http://www.keith-miller.com/ writing/journalism.htm.

Milliot, Jim. "2002 Publishing Industry Salary Survey." *Publisher's Weekly,* July 8, 2002. Available online at http://www.publishersweekly.com.

————. "2003 Publishing Industry Salary Survey." *Publisher's Weekly,* July 7, 2003. Available online at http://www.publishersweekly.com.

————. "2004 Publishing Industry Salary Survey." *Publisher's Weekly,* July 5, 2004 Available online at http://www.publishersweekly.com.

Milwaukee School of Engineering. "What Is Technical Communication?" Available online at http://www.msoe.edu/gen_st/tc/what.shtml.

Minnesota Internet System for Education and Employment (iseek). "Career and Salaries by Job Titles: Public Relations Specialists." Available online at http://www.iseek.org/sv/13000jsp?id=100170.

Morris, Douglas E. *Fabjob Guide to Become a Travel Writer* (an e-book). Available online at http://www.fabjob.com/TravelWriter.asp.

Morrish, John. *Magazine Editing: How to Develop and Manage a Successful Publication* (2nd ed.). New York: Routledge, 2003.

Mulpuru, Sucharita. *Vault Career Guide to Media & Entertainment* (2nd ed.). New York: Vault.com, 2003.

Mulvany, Nancy J. *Indexing Books.* Chicago: University of Chicago Press, 1994.

National Communication Association (NCA). "Pathways to Careers in Communication, 5th ed." Available online at http://www.natcom.org/Instruction/Pathways/5thed.htm.

Needleman, Sarah E. "Job Market Perks Up for Public-Relations Pros." *The Wall Street Journal,* May 21, 2004. Available online at http://www.careerjournal.com.

Nelms, Rosemary. "News Libraries as Profit Centers—Survey Results." Available online from SLA News Division at http://www.ibiblio.org/slanews/surveys/profit.html

The Newspaper Guild. "Salary Information—2003." Available online at http://www.newsguild.org/salary.

North Carolina State University. "Job Possibilities for Communication Majors." Available online at http://www.ncsu.edu.

Occupational Information Network. "Summary Report for Desktop Publisher (2003)." Available online at http://online.onetcenter.org/report?r=0&id=893.

Papper, Bob. "Women and Minorities in Radio and Television News, 2004 Data: Recovering Lost Ground." The Radio-Television News Directors Association & Foundation: *Communicator,* July/August, 2004. Available online at http://www.rtnda.org/research/research.shtml.

————. "Radio and Television News Salaries, 2004 Data: Salaries Sore." The Radio-Television News Directors Association & Foundation: *Communicator,* June 2004. Available online on subscription basis at http://www.rtnda.org/communicator/showarticle.asp?id=102.

Papper, Bob, and Michael Gerhard. "2002 Radio and Television Salary Survey." The Radio-Television News Directors Association & Foundation. Available online at http://www.rtnda.org/research/salaries02.shtml.

Paul, Nora, and Kathleen A. Hansen. "Reclaiming News Libraries." *Library Journal,* April 1, 2002 (found on *Library Journal*'s Web site at http://www.libraryjournal.com).

Perlman, Alan M. "A Communicator's Guide to Buzzwords." Available online at http://www.alanperlman.com/notes.html.

The Playwriting seminars. Available online at http://www.pubinfo.vcu.edu/artweb.

Pope, Alice, and Rebecca Chrysler, eds. *2005 Children's Writer's & Illustrator's Market.* Cincinnati, Ohio: Writer's Digest Books, 2004.

The Princeton Review Complete Book of Colleges. New York: Princeton Review, 2004.

Public Relations Society of America. "The Public Relations Profession: About Public Relations." Available online at http://www.prsa.org/_Resources/Profession/index.asp.

Public Relations Student Society of America: Puget Sound Chapter. "What Is Public Relations?" Available online at http://www.prsapugetsound.org/students.html.

The Publishing Business Group. "Links to Resources for Magazines and Newsletter Publishers." Available online at http://www.publishingbiz.com/html/links.html.

Pulley, John L. "Alumni Editors Fail to Win Support in Bid for Greater Independence." *The Chronicle of Higher Education: Colloquy.* Available online at http://chronicle.com/colloquy/99/alumni/background.htm.

Ramachandra, Jyoti. "Becoming a 'Complete' Technical Communicator." Available online at http://www.twin-india.org/html/Communicator.html.

Rath, Tiare. "Tips for Getting On-Line" (1997). Available online from *Detroit Free Press* at http://www.freep.com/jobspage/interns/rathtips.htm.

Red River College. "Graduate Satisfaction and Employment Report: A Survey of 2001–2002 RRC Graduates." Available online at http://www.rrc.mb.ca/researchplan/ger2004/occupations.

Reiss, Fern. *The Publishing Game: Publish a Book in 30 Days.* Boston: Peanut Butter and Jelly Press, 2003.

Robinson, William C. "Online Teaching Course on Book Publishing (IS561), September 2004: Author Lecture Notes." Available online at http://web.utk.edu/~wrobinso/561_lec_auth.html.

Rohn, Dan. "Copy Aide—A Great Way to Break In with a Large Newspaper." Available online from Journalism Jobs.com at http://www.journalismjobs.com/career_advice.cfm.

Ross, Tom and Marilyn Ross. Articles on Self-Publishing. Available online at http://www.about-books.com.

Rudman, Jack. *Public Information Officer.* New York: National Learning Corporation, 1985.

Salary Wizard. "Salary data from Salary.Com, Inc." Available online at http://swz.salary.com/salarywizard or http://salary.monster.com/salarywizard.

Scanlan, Chip. "Beat Reporting: What Does It Take to Be the Best?" Poynter Online at http://www.poynter.org.

Scanlan, Christopher. *Reporting and Writing: Basics for the 21st Century.* New York: Oxford University Press, 2000.

Scheer, Ron. "So You'd Like to Be a Copyeditor/Proofreader: A Guide." Available online at http://www.amazon.com/exec/obidos/tg/guides/guide-display.

Schindler, David E. "How Anyone Can Write Better Lyrics." Available online from SongU.com at http://www.musesmuse.com/schind2.html.

Schwartzman, Paul. "Local Officials' Salaries Vault Past $200,000." *Washington Post,* December 16, 2004. Available online at http://www.washingtonpost.com/wp-dyn/articles/A2352-2004Dec15.html.

Self-Pub.net. "Guide to Self-Publishing." Available online at http://www.self-pub.net/guide/html.

Semonche, Barbara P. "History of News Libraries" (excerpt from *News Media Libraries: A Management Handbook,* Greenwood Press, 1993.) Available online from The Park Library at http://parklibrary.jomc.unc.edu/newslibhist.html.

Shelley, Dan. "Trade Secrets: They Keep Moving That Little Sucker." The Radio-Television News Directors Association & Foundation: *Communicator,* November 2001. Available online at http://www.rtnda.org/trades/32.shtml.

Silverman, Jason. "Invasion of the Web Film Critics." Available from *Wired News* at http://www.wired.com/news/digiwood/0,141,62453,00.html.

Smiley, Sarah. "How I Became a Syndicated Columnist—And You Can Too!" (2004). Available online at http://www.SarahSmiley.com.

Smith, Austin. "Confessions of a Songwriter: Making a Living As a Lyricist." Available online at http://www.cleverjoe.com/articles.

Society for Technical Communication. "2003 Technical Communicator Salary Survey." Available online at http://www.stc.org.

Society for Technical Communication, Willamette Valley Chapter. "What Is a 'Technical Communicator'?" Available online at http://www.stcwvc.org/membership/tech_comm.htm.

SongU.com.: Songwriting Courses Online. "Top Ten Songwriting Questions." Available online at http://www.songu.com/topten.asp.

Stone, Vernon. "Career Goals in Radio News" (2000). Available online at http://www.missouri.edu/~jourvs/ragoals.html.

———. "Internships in TV and Radio News: Paid and Unpaid" (1995). Available online at http://www.missouri.edu~jourvs/ginterns.html.

———. "Minorities and Women in Television News, 2001." Available online at http://www.missouri.edu/~jourvs/gtvminw.html.

———. "Television and Radio News Careers, 2002." Available online at http://www.missouri.edu/~jourvs/careers8.html.

Strom, David. "Lessons Learned from Becoming a Self-Publisher on the Web." *CMC Magazine,* May 1, 1996. Available online at http://www.december.com/cmc/mag/1966/may/strom.html.

The Student Club. "Career Success without Stress: Public Relations Account Executive." Available online at http://www.thestudentclub.net/careersuccess/careercentre.

Sugg, Diana K. "Turn the Beat Around: A Special Report, October 5, 2001." Poynter Online at http://legacy.poynter.org/centerpiece/100801.htm.

Sullivan, Michelle. "Ditty Up" (March 6, 2000). Available online from *1099, the Magazine for Independent Professionals* at http://www.1099.com/c/ar/di/jinglewriter_d023.html.

Taylor, David. *The Freelance Success Book: Insider Secrets for Selling Every Word You Write.* Savannah, Ga.: Peak Writing Press, 2003.

Technical Communicators Salary Survey, 2003. Available online at http://jobstar.org/tools/salary/sal-prof.htm.

Toscan, Richard. "The Playwriting Seminars (2002)." Available online at http://www.vcu.edu/artweb/playwriting.

The Trammell Group. "Government Affairs." Available online at http://www.trammel.org/governme.htm.

U.S. Office of Personnel Management (OPM). "Federal Job Classification System Information and Pay Systems Governing the Salary Rates of Federal Civilian Employees." Available online at http://www.opm.giv/fedclass/index.htm.

———. "General Information" (about employment with the federal government). Available at http://www.opm.gov/index.htm.

———. "Obtaining a Position with the Federal Government." Available online at http://www.usajobs.opm.gov.

University of Texas at Austin. "Communication Career Services Reports." Available online at http://communication.utexas.edu/ccs.

Van Wicklen, Janet. *The Tech Writer's Survival Guide: A Comprehensive Handbook for Aspiring Technical Writers.* New York: Checkmark Books, 2001.

Vanguard, Rox. "Video Scriptwriting: Technical Communicating as a Video Scriptwriter." Society for Technical Communications, Pittsburgh Chapter, *Blue Pencil,* 33, no. 8 (February 1997). Available online at http://www.city-net.com/~roxman/script.html.

Vault, Inc. "Advertising Agencies—Freelance and In-house Work," (Sept. 1, 2000). Available online at http://www.vault.com.

———. "Getting Started in Ad Careers," (Nov. 28, 2000). Available online at http://www.vault.com.

Walker, Leslie. "Hot Off Your News Clicking Service," *Washington Post,* March 6, 2003. Available online at http://www.washingtonpost.com/ac2/wp-dyn/A45855-2003Mar5?la.

———. "Where the Game Is the Medium," *Washington Post,* December 2, 2004. Available online at http://www.

washingtonpost.com/wp-dyn/articles/A25512-2004Dec1. html.

Walsh, Bill. "The Slot: A Spot for Copy Editors—What Exactly Is a Copy Editor?" Available online at http://www.theslot.com.

Walters, Jonathan. "Conference Report on Management's Challenge: Leadership for Changing Times." *Governing Magazine,* January 2001. Available online at heep://www.governing.com/archive/2001/jan/conf.txt.

Weber, Jean Hollis. "Gender-Neutral Technical Writing." Available online from TECHWR-L at http://www.techwr-l.com/techwhirl/magazine/writing/genderneutral. html.

———. "Who Needs a Technical Editor?" *Journal of the Australian Society for Technical Communication,* May, 1990. Available online at http://www.jeanweber.com/about/whoneeds.htm.

———. "Working with a Technical Editor." Available online from TECHWR-L at http://www.raycomm.com/techwhirl/magazine/writing/technicaleditor.html.

WetFeet.com. "Career Profiles, 2004." Available online at http://wetfeet.com/asp/careerprofiles.

———. "Industry Profiles, 2004." Available online at http://www.wetfeet.com/asp/industryprofiles.

WetFeet Staff. *Careers in Advertising & Public Relations: The WetFeet Insider Guide* (2005 edition). San Francisco: WetFeet, 2004.

While, Pamela. *Fabjob Guide to Become a Food Writer* (an e-book). Available online at http://www.fabjob.com/foodwriterssample.html.

Widner, Tracy. "Statistically Increase Your Income." Available online from Absolute Write at http://www.absolutewrite.com.

Wilbur, Rick, and Randy Miller. *Modern Media Writing.* Belmont, Calif.: Thomson/Wadsworth, 2002.

Woudstra, Wendy J. "What Is a Self-Publisher?" (2004). Available online from Publishing Central at http://www.publishingcentral.com/articles/20030214-21.

Writer's Encyclopedia. Available online at http://www.writersmarket.com/encyc.

Writers Guild of America. "Schedule of Minimum Salaries, revised May 2, 2003." Available online at http://www.wga.org/minimums/index.html.

Yudkin, Marcia. "The Freelance Writing FAQ: Frequently Asked Questions about Freelance Writing (2001)." Available online at http://www.worldwidefreelance.com/articles.

———. "Publishing on Demand Changes the Equation of Self-Publishing (1999)." Available online at http://www.yudkin/com/demand.htm.

INDEX

ABOUT THE AUTHORS

ALLAN TAYLOR, a freelance copy editor, indexer, and researcher, comes from a family long involved in the publishing and newspaper fields. He is the coauthor of *The Encyclopedia of Ethnic Groups in Hollywood* (Facts On File) and has created special bibliographic indexes for such volumes as *The Great Spy Pictures, Hollywood Songsters, 101 Things I Don't Know about Art, Questions and Answers about Community Associations,* and *Women Doctors Guide to Health and Healing.*

Mr. Taylor's publishing industry posts include tenures at the R. R. Bowker Company (Bibliographic Services), Engineering Information, Inc. (Production Manager), and Graphic Typesetting Services (Proofreading/Technical Specifications Department Manager). He resides in Los Angeles, California. His Web site is at http://www.tataylor.net.

JAMES ROBERT PARISH, a former entertainment reporter, publicist, and book series editor, is the author of many published biographies and reference books about the entertainment industry including *The American Movies Reference Book, The Complete Actors TV Credits, The Hollywood Songsters, The Hollywood Book of Scandals, The Hollywood Book of Death, The RKO Gals, Katharine Hepburn: The Untold Story, Whitney Houston, Gus Van Sant,* and *Whoopi Goldberg.* With Allan Taylor he coauthored *The Encyclopedia of Ethnic Groups in Hollywood* (Facts On File) and has written several entries in the Ferguson Career Biographies series (including Twyla Tharp, Denzel Washington, Katie Couric, Stan Lee, Halle Berry, Steven Spielberg, Tom Hanks, and Stephen King).

Mr. Parish is a frequent on-camera interviewee on cable and network television for documentaries on the performing arts both in the United States and in the United Kingdom. He resides in Studio City, California. His Web site is at http://www.jamesrobertparish.com.